Corrections to pages 7-9

Index

Introduction 11

1. Leonora Christina's *Jammers Minde* 31
    1.1. Theory of Autobiography 31
        1.1.1. Terminological Considerations 31
        1.1.2. A Very Brief History of Autobiography 41
        1.1.3. Classic and Current Theories on Autobiography 51
    1.2. *Jammers Minde*: Confessions Dedicated to the Beloved Ones
    or Political Apologia? 65
        1.2.1. Research on *Jammers Minde* since its Discovery in 1868 ... 76
        1.2.2. *Jammers Minde* as an Autobiographical Enterprise 125

**2. The Literary Reception of Leonora Christina and the
Interdiscursivity of *Jammers Minde*** 145
    2.1. Contemporary Literary Portrayals 145
        2.1.1. Anonymous: 'Fru Kirsten Munks Ballet' (ca. 1650)
        – The Infernal Egocentric 146
        2.1.2. Otto Sperling the Elder: *Selbstbiographie* (1673)
        – Marital Appendage 152
    2.2. Leonora Christina as Subject of Patriotic Debate 157
        2.2.1. Hans Christian Andersen: 'Holger Danske' (1845)
        – Defender of the Author's Fame 160
        2.2.2. Mathilde Fibiger: *En Skizze efter det virkelige Liv* (1852)
        – Impulse for Nationalistic Debate 166
        2.2.3. Hans Christian Andersen: 'Gudfaders Billedbog' (1868)
        – By Order of an Optimistic Town History 176
    2.3. *Kvinde er kvinde værst*: Leonora Christina and Dina 183
        2.3.1. Louise Hegermann Lindencrone:
        Eleonora Christina Uhlfeldt (1817) – The Mother 185
        2.3.2. Adam Oehlenschläger: *Dina* (1842)
        – A Haven of Domestic Tranquility 202

2.3.3. Rolf Gjedsted: *Fordærvede kvinder* (1991)
– The Wise Witch 215
2.4. Leonora Christina's Via Dolorosa:
Stages of a *Christi Kaarßdragerske*'s Life 224
2.4.1. Louise Hegermann Lindencrone: 'Billedet' (1825)
– The Role Model 226
2.4.2. H. F. Ewald: *Leonora Kristina: Billeder af en
Kongedatters Liv* (1895) – The *Liidende Christinne* 243
2.4.3. Ebbe Kløvedal Reich: *Rejsen til Messias* (1974)
– The Covetable Companion..................................... 254
2.5. By Order of Education: Leonora Christina's Admittance
into Denmark's Literary Canon................................ 268
2.5.1. Herta J. Enevoldsen: *Kongedatteren Leonora Christina* and
Leonora Christina i Blåtårn (1979) – Ignorance is Bliss............. 274
2.5.2. Eva Hemmer Hansen: The Leonora Christina Fragment
(1982-1983) – The Feminist Case Study 286
2.5.3. Birgithe Kosovic: *Leonora Christina* (2012)
– The Ambitious Manipulator................................... 298
2.6. A Chip off the Old Block: Denmark's Century of *Femmes Fatales*. 305
2.6.1. Sven Holm: *Leonora Christina. Tre scener for en heltinde*
(1982) – The Writer or How to Craft the Story of Your Life.......... 313
2.6.2. Helle Stangerup: *Spardame* (1989) – Baroque Fatalities 328
2.6.3. Maria Helleberg: *Kongens kvinder* (2013) and
Leonora Christine (2014) – Fine Feathers Make Fine Birds:
The Construction and Deconstruction of a *Femme Fatale* 339
2.7. International Leonora Christina-Literature..................... 356
2.7.1. Leopold Schefer: *Die Gräfin Ulfeld oder die
vierundzwanzig Königskinder* (1834) – Boys Will Be Boys
or Mathilde Fibiger's Nightmare 358
2.7.2. Rainer Maria Rilke: *Die Aufzeichnungen des Malte
Laurids Brigge* (1910) – A Figurehead of Northern Stoicism......... 375
2.7.3. Karin Johnsson: *Kungligt blod* (1919)
– A Woman Making History?................................... 390

3. Leonora Christina in Danish Historiography 401
   3.1. Historiography on Leonora Christina in a Nutshell. 401
   3.2. Leonora Christina in Canonical Historiography 426
      3.2.1. Ludvig Holberg: *Dannemarks Riges Historie* (1732-1735)
      – The Tragic Heroine 431
      3.2.2. Ove Malling: *Store og gode handlinger af Danske, Norske
      og Holstenere* (1777) – The Romance of the Faithful Wife. 442
      3.2.3. J. A. Fridericia: *Danmarks Riges Historie 4* (1896-1902)
      – A Tragedy of Vengeance 450
      3.2.4. Benito Scocozza: *Ved afgrundens rand* (1989)
      – A Comedy of Historical Materialism 466

Résumé 479

Bibliography 495
   Supporting Sources 495
   Primary Literary and Historiographical Sources 496
   Critical Studies. 502
   Contemporary Records. 516
   Internet Sources. 517

The Princess in the Tower Revisited

Helene Peterbauer

The Princess in the Tower Revisited

Four Centuries of Constructing Leonora Christina
through Fact and Fiction

Universitets-Jubilæets danske Samfund 2020

© Universites-Jubilæets danske Samfund and the author

Printed in Denmark by
Tarm Bogtryk a/s

ISBN 978-87-408-3291-4.

Issued as no. 601 in the series of Universitets-Jubilæets danske Samfund.
Supervised by Marita Akhøj Nielsen.

Omslagsdesign: Ann Britt Smedegaard Nilsson med foto af side fra Leonora Christinas manuskript, »Jammers Minde«.

Foto: Det Nationalhistoriske Museum på Frederiksborg Slot. Manuskriptet tilhører Det Nationalhistoriske Museum på Frederiksborg Slot.

The publication of this book was made possible by a grant from Den Hielmstierne-Rosencroneske Stiftelse.

Universitets-Jubilæets danske Samfund
c/o Society for Danish Language and Literature
Christians Brygge 1
DK-1219 Copenhagen K
ujds.dk

Commission agent: Syddansk Universitetsforlag, universitypress.dk

Acknowledgements

The present text is a slightly revised version of a doctoral thesis, which I defended at the University of Vienna in 2018. Throughout the past years, a number of people have supported me in various ways, most of all of course my adviser Sven Hakon Rossel, whom I thank for his rigorous, supportive and encouraging guidance throughout my studies. I am also particularly grateful to Antje Wischmann and Marita Akhøj Nielsen, whose directions and indications have been a valuable source of support to me, and to UJDS and Den Hielmstierne-Rosencroneske Stiftelse for having made this publication possible.

My gratitude also concerns my English proofreader Kyle DeFreitas, as well as Sandrine Picot for advising me on French-related issues.

My colleagues Hannah Tischmann and Philipp Wagner have supported me through many stimulating discussions. Furthermore, my thanks go to all others – including Lise Busk-Jensen, Eva Hættner Aurelius, Toril Moi and Marc Auchet – for valuable tips that have helped me continue my research.

Finally, I thank my husband Miguel for his continuous support and encouragement.

Index

Introduction 11

1. Leonora Christina's *Jammers Minde* 31
    1.1. Theory of Autobiography 31
        1.1.1. Terminological Considerations 31
        1.1.2. A Very Brief History of Autobiography 41
        1.1.3. Classic and Current Theories on Autobiography 51
    1.2. *Jammers Minde*: Confessions Dedicated to the Beloved Ones
        or Political Apologia? 65
        1.2.1. Research on *Jammers Minde* since its Discovery in 1868 76
        1.2.2. *Jammers Minde* as an Autobiographical Enterprise 125

**2. The Literary Reception of Leonora Christina and the
Interdiscursivity of *Jammers Minde*** 145
    2.1. Contemporary Literary Portrayals 145
        2.1.1. Anonymous: 'Fru Kirsten Munks Ballet' (ca. 1650)
        – The Infernal Egocentric 146
        2.1.2. Otto Sperling the Elder: *Selbstbiographie* (1673)
        – Marital Appendage 152
    2.2. Leonora Christina as Subject of Patriotic Debate 157
        2.2.1. Hans Christian Andersen: 'Holger Danske' (1845)
        – Defender of the Author's Fame 160
        2.2.2. Mathilde Fibiger: *En Skizze efter det virkelige Liv* (1852)
        – Impulse for Nationalistic Debate 166
        2.2.3. Hans Christian Andersen: 'Gudfaders Billedbog' (1868)
        – By Order of an Optimistic Town History 176
    2.3. Kvinde er kvinde værst: Leonora Christina and Dina 183
        2.3.1. Louise Hegermann Lindencrone:
        Eleonora Christina Uhlfeldt (1817) – The Mother 185
        2.3.2. Adam Oehlenschläger: *Dina* (1842)
        – A Haven of Domestic Tranquility 202
        2.3.3. Rolf Gjedsted: *Fordærvede kvinder* (1991)
        – The Wise Witch 216
    2.4. Leonora Christina's Via Dolorosa:
        Stages of a *Christi Kaarßdragerske*'s Life 225

2.4.1. Louise Hegermann Lindencrone: 'Billedet' (1825)
– The Role Model 227
2.4.2. H. F. Ewald: *Leonora Kristina: Billeder af en
Kongedatters Liv* (1895) – The *Liidende Christinne* 244
2.4.3. Ebbe Kløvedal Reich: *Rejsen til Messias* (1974)
– The Covetable Companion...................... 255
2.5. By Order of Education: Leonora Christina's Admittance
into Denmark's Literary Canon..................... 269
2.5.1. Herta J. Enevoldsen: *Kongedatteren Leonora Christina* and
Leonora Christina i Blåtårn (1979) – Ignorance is Bliss............. 275
2.5.2. Eva Hemmer Hansen: The Leonora Christina Fragment
(1982-1983) – The Feminist Case Study 287
2.5.3. Birgithe Kosovic: *Leonora Christina* (2012)
– The Ambitious Manipulator...................... 299
2.6. A Chip off the Old Block: Denmark's Century of *Femmes Fatales* .. 306
2.6.1. Sven Holm: *Leonora Christina. Tre scener for en heltinde*
(1982) – The Writer or How to Craft the Story of Your Life.......... 314
2.6.2. Helle Stangerup: *Spardame* (1989) – Baroque Fatalities 329
2.6.3. Maria Helleberg: *Kongens kvinder* (2013) and
Leonora Christine (2014) – Fine Feathers Make Fine Birds:
The Construction and Deconstruction of a *Femme Fatale* 340
2.7. International Leonora Christina-Literature..................... 357
2.7.1. Leopold Schefer: *Die Gräfin Ulfeld oder die
vierundzwanzig Königskinder* (1834) – Boys Will Be Boys
or Mathilde Fibiger's Nightmare 359
2.7.2. Rainer Maria Rilke: *Die Aufzeichnungen des Malte
Laurids Brigge* (1910) – A Figurehead of Northern Stoicism.......... 376
2.7.3. Karin Johnsson: *Kungligt blod* (1919)
– A Woman Making History? 391

3. Leonora Christina in Danish Historiography 403
3.1. Historiography on Leonora Christina in a Nutshell................ 403
3.2. Leonora Christina in Canonical Historiography 428
3.2.1. Ludvig Holberg: *Dannemarks Riges Historie* (1732-1735)
– The Tragic Heroine 433
3.2.2. Ove Malling: *Store og gode handlinger af Danske, Norske
og Holstenere* (1777) – The Romance of the Faithful Wife........... 444

3.2.3. J. A. Fridericia: *Danmarks Riges Historie 4* (1896-1902)
– A Tragedy of Vengeance...................................... 452
3.2.4. Benito Scocozza: *Ved afgrundens rand* (1989)
– A Comedy of Historical Materialism 468

Résumé 481

Bibliography... 497
   Supporting Sources.. 497
   Primary Literary and Historiographical Sources 498
   Critical Studies... 504
   Contemporary Records... 518
   Internet Sources.. 519

Introduction

Der kan digtes så forskelligt om denne verdens store.[1]

The history of research on Leonora Christina (1621-1698) is littered with paradoxes. The most prominent of these is the circumstance that the foremost researcher on Leonora Christina's husband Corfitz Ulfeldt (1606-1664), the Danish historian Steffen Heiberg, initiated his Ulfeldt-biography, *Enhjørningen Corfitz Ulfeldt*, published in 1993, with a lamentation of the comparative lack of research on Corfitz Ulfeldt as opposed to his wife, about whom a substantial amount of biographical research has been conducted.[2] While this observation is accurate, its subtext, which contends that Corfitz Ulfeldt's fame has long been overshadowed by that of his wife and that interest in Leonora Christina has been stronger than in Corfitz Ulfeldt, somewhat contradicts the image presented by literature and historical studies on Leonora Christina up until the late 20th century, when Heiberg's work was published. Although the publication of Leonora Christina's masterpiece *Jammers Minde* in 1869 fuelled academic as well as lay interest in her life and work, the majority of extensive writings concerning Leonora Christina that have been published so far exhibit a hidden, yet striking focus on Corfitz Ulfeldt. Leonora Christina-literature, i.e. literary works depicting Leonora Christina either as a minor, main or title character, predating 1993, often depicts Leonora Christina as a static, predominantly symbolic figure; as a token of her husband's good qualities; as an annex of Corfitz; or as a mere 'pretence-heroine', whose name serves as a pretext for an extensive presentation of her husband. Moreover, even the most prolific and influential Leonora Christina-scholar, Sophus Birket Smith[3] (1838-1919), dedicated a large portion of his two-volume study *Leonora Christina Grevinde Ulfeldts Historie* to the biography of his subject's husband, since »[d]et er Ægteskabet, som gjør Leonora Christina til en historisk Person«.[4]

The few historians that have engaged in studying the life of Leonora Christina's archenemy and sister-in-law, Queen Sophie Amalie (1628-1685), have a similar view on their subject's rival and prisoner: »Det er Sofie Amalies Forbandelse, at

---

1 Hemmer Hansen, Eva. *Den lykkelige hustru: Leonora Christine I*. Copenhagen: Hernov, 1982, p. 132.
2 Heiberg, Steffen. *Enhjørningen Corfitz Ulfeldt*. Copenhagen: Gyldendal, 1993, p. 7.
3 Birket Smith's name can be found both with and without a hyphen. I decided to omit the hyphen since his most relevant works also exhibit the spelling without hyphen.
4 Birket Smith, Sophus. *Leonora Christina Grevinde Ulfeldts Historie: Med Bidrag til hendes Ægtefælles og hendes nærmeste Slægts Historie 1*. Copenhagen: Gyldendal, 1879, p. 82.

hendes Navn næppe kan nævnes, uden at Leonora Kristines samtidig kommer paa Læben«.[5] However, it is important to note that their complaints about Leonora Christina's influence on Sophie Amalie's fame – which is dominated by keywords such as »Ærgerrighed og Herskelyst«[6] – is rather justified since the name of Leonora Christina has mostly served to decry that of Sophie Amalie, while, for example, much of 19th-century scholarship and literature on Corfitz Ulfeldt has utilised the fate of Leonora Christina to exonerate him, as will be demonstrated below. Nevertheless, without Leonora Christina, Sophie Amalie would probably never have attained any kind of fame.

In both cases, the main reason for this stronger focus in literature and scholarship on Leonora Christina may lie in history's relatively unanimous verdict regarding Corfitz Ulfeldt and Sophie Amalie. The latter is widely regarded as an 'evil Queen', and even concerning Ulfeldt, who has also had supporters and fans among contemporaries as well as among later generations, there has been and still is the consensus that regardless of the question, whether he had once been an honourable and competent man, he spent the last years of his life as a – possibly insane – wretch. While the public opinion of these two figures is thus rather uniform, the term 'controversial' applies to Leonora Christina, since the denominations employed to narrate her life's story constitute a list of paradoxes.

If we were to summarise the most common characteristics ascribed to Leonora Christina since the mid-17th century, she would emerge as a loyal traitor; a criminal saint; a national heroine involved in treason against her home country; a strong and independent woman known for her obedience to and sacrifice for her husband; a loving and caring mother mostly known as the daughter of Christian IV and the wife of Corfitz Ulfeldt; and as a highly educated and respectable woman who represented an utterly primitive and impulsive age.

None of these contradictory characteristics assigned to Leonora Christina have emerged by mere chance, but they are all in some way present in her writings, particularly in her autobiographical works – her so-called French autobiography and *Jammers Minde*. This study argues that the productivity and the heterogeneous transmission throughout history of Leonora Christina-subject matter are deeply rooted in Leonora Christina's utilisation and functionalisation of the above-mentioned characteristics, and that their contrapositions have not hindered, but rather fomented their reproduction in subsequent ages. Through the production of

---

5 Jørgensen, Ellen and Johanne Skovgaard. *Danske Dronninger: Fortællinger og Karakteristikker.* Copenhagen: Hagerup, 1910, p. 160.

6 Ibid., p. 156.

her autobiographical works – mostly, though, through her most famous and most critically acclaimed work *Jammers Minde*, whose disclosure in 1869 resulted in the publication of her other works – Leonora Christina averted the one-dimensional fame that Sophie Amalie and Corfitz Ulfeldt, whom produced no such remarkable text, fell victim to.

However, particularly after the publication of *Jammers Minde*, which occurred almost two centuries after Leonora Christina's death, her fame and the characteristics associated with it took on a life of their own as an increasing number of (mostly Danish) authors and historians processed selected traits of Leonora Christina in their works about this woman and her time. In these writings, Leonora Christina fulfills a function dependent on a multitude of factors such as literary conventions, the author's sex, and time of publication.

Through a comparative-chronological analysis of the self-portrayal provided by Leonora Christina's autobiographical writings, and particularly by *Jammers Minde*, as well as of the portrayal of Leonora Christina in selected works of literature and historiography, this study illustrates what the elements of Leonora Christina's self-portrayal are and how these elements have been segregated, isolated, recombined and reproduced in a functional way in literature and historiography published before and after 1869. The objective of the present study is thus to provide a deeper insight into Leonora Christina's self-portrayal in her autobiographical works and to illustrate to what extent and how this self-portrayal is reflected in literature and historiography depicting Leonora Christina.

Thus, this study is guided and determined by the following questions:
1) Which are the topics and elements that constitute Leonora Christina's self-portrayal in her French autobiography and *Jammers Minde*?
2) Which of these topics and elements are present in literature and historiography depicting Leonora Christina?
3) What implications do these topics and elements have for the function of Leonora Christina in the respective texts examined in this study?
4) Do the portrayal and the function of Leonora Christina in these texts exhibit distinguishable trends and/or connections to extratextual factors, such as the publication of *Jammers Minde* in 1869, great historical events such as Denmark's abolition of absolutism in 1848, new literary currents, or new findings in research concerning Leonora Christina?

Within this context, the present study is divided into three main chapters. Chapter 1 is concerned with Leonora Christina's autobiographical enterprises and their position within the context of autobiographical research, particularly in the fields of early modern autobiography and women's autobiography. While this study identifies the elements of Leonora Christina's self-portrayal in both of her autobiographical works, *Jammers Minde* constitutes a more central primary source than the French autobiography, since its impact on the ensuing literary, historiographical and scholarly writings concerned with Leonora Christina outweighs that of the French autobiography and because, as argued in this study, both autobiographical works share the same elements of self-portrayal employed by Leonora Christina. Research into autobiography has a tradition of concern with the tools employed by autobiography in order to create an intentional, stylised self-portrayal, but also with the question of truth in autobiography. This latter issue is of particular relevance to the Leonora Christina-subject matter, since the same question has dominated research on Leonora Christina and *Jammers Minde* until the end of the 20th century. Hence, Chapters 1.1.1.-1.1.3. provide a historical perspective on autobiography as well as an overview of the theories of autobiography most relevant to an analysis of Leonora Christina's autobiographical writings. Specialised research into early modern and women's autobiography is based on the assumption that these subcategories of autobiography depict a different kind of self than the autobiographies of modern and postmodern and/or male autobiographers. Thus, an analysis of *Jammers Minde* in the context of early modern and women's autobiography is undertaken in Chapter 1.2., in order to determine whether Leonora Christina's self-portrayal matches the characteristics established for these two subcategories. Based on the topics and the narrative provided in *Jammers Minde*, this chapter also engages in the question whether *Jammers Minde* matches the characteristics of other subcategories of the autobiographical genre, such as the spiritual or the prison autobiography. These classification reviews are complemented by the equally central question of whether *Jammers Minde* constitutes a rather classic autobiography – an inquiry justified by the fact that the work was written at a time predating the official advent of the autobiographical genre. Lastly, Chapter 1.2. provides a comprehensive review of research on Leonora Christina's writings, as well as an identification of the central elements of Leonora Christina's self-portrayal throughout her auto/biographical writings, i.e. the French autobiography, *Jammers Minde* and the gynæceum *Hæltinners Pryd*.

Subsequently, Chapter 2 examines which elements of Leonora Christina's self-portrayal have been adopted in literature and what function the fictive Leonora Christina, as an ideological manifestation of one or more of these elements, fulfills in the respective work. It is not the objective of this study to provide a complete inventory of writings concerned with Leonora Christina, but Chapter 2 includes the majority of literary works that, to the present author's knowledge, depict her as a main or secondary character. The chapter is divided into seven subchapters, whose respective focal points will be explicated in introductory sections at the beginning of each chapter. Five of these subchapters (Chapters 2.2.-2.6.) represent one narrative strain each of the Leonora Christina-subject matter based on one or more of the elements of Leonora Christina's self-portrayal: Leonora Christina as subject of Danish patriotic debate in relation to her husband (Chapter 2.2.); Leonora Christina's involvement in the Dina affair and her relation to this 'other woman' (Chapter 2.3.); the ordeal of Leonora Christina and the religious/spiritual elements in *Jammers Minde* (Chapter 2.4.); Leonora Christina as a role model for women and writers (Chapter 2.5.); and the 'dark' yet creative and productive side of Leonora Christina (Chapter 2.6.). Chapters 2.1. and 2.7. do not exhibit a common thematic focal point predetermined by Leonora Christina's writings, as they are respectively concerned with the portrayal of Leonora Christina in literary works predating her death in 1698 and in works written by non-Danish authors. The objective of these two chapters is to provide a comparative background for the other texts, whose authors had not met Leonora Christina[7] and whose Danish citizenship arguably affected their outlook on a potential traitor to varying degrees. Furthermore, the astoundingly low number of literary works depicting Leonora Christina and written by non-Danish authors facilitated a subsumption of these works in one group. These seven chapters are further divided into subchapters,[8] each dedicated to one author depicting Leonora Christina as a main or secondary character. The subchapters follow a chronological order based on the works' respective year of publication. The topics of the five chapters exhibiting a thematic focal point and the corpus of texts chosen for this part of the study were established based on the recurrence of topics connected to the Leonora Christina-subject matter[9] and the respective texts' thematic accordance with the established topics.

---

[7] One of the authors presented in Chapter 2.1. was a friend of the Ulfeldt house and the other one is assumed to have been a member of the Danish court at a time when the Ulfeldts were still frequenting it on a regular basis.

[8] Chapters 2.2.-2.7. contain three subchapters each. Chapter 2.1. contains only two subchapters, since I am not aware of more than two (semi-)literary works portraying Leonora Christina and written during her lifetime.

[9] Novels whose eponymous hero is Corfitz Ulfeldt (such as *Korfitz Ulfeldt* by Aage Heinberg (1922)), on the other hand, were deliberately excluded from this study, since a large portion of the novels examined in Chapter 2 do already exhibit an excessive focus on Leonora Christina's husband.

Following, Chapter 3 is concerned with the portrayal of Leonora Christina in historiographic texts, i.e. biographies, biographical writings,[10] and historical-scholarly works making reference to her and, in most of the texts, her husband as well (Chapter 3.1.), while the last subchapters present selected canonical histories, i.e. four national histories, two of which were written before the publication of *Jammers Minde*, and two of which precede it (Chapter 3.2.). The purpose of this last main chapter is to provide an overview of the diverse historical discourses involving Leonora Christina and to determine whether they coincide with or resemble those exhibited in Chapter 2. Despite their modest academic value, the older texts presented in this chapter, i.e. those written before the 20th century, are of particular interest, since they reflect the centrality of the fact vs. fiction discussion that has pervaded the discourse revolving around Leonora Christina since its beginning. Furthermore, these texts provide a critical source for an early history of the French autobiography, since they are based on the different transcripts and translations of the text scholars had to resort to before the rediscovery of the original manuscript in 1952.

Out of the plethora of historiographical texts concerned with the history of Denmark, the texts presented in Chapter 3.2. were selected based on their representativeness and relevance of the respective period (within the corpus of historiography depicting Leonora Christina to an enhanced degree) and/or the frequency of references to these texts in other scholarly works on Leonora Christina. These works are analysed using the narratological terminology developed in Hayden White's influential study *Metahistory: The Historical Imagination in Nineteenth-Century Europe* (1973), for a reading of historiographic texts. This study constitutes a useful tool for a treatment of historiography as archetypes of literature and thus facilitates a comparison with the literary texts analysed in Chapter 2.[11] White's objection against the previously uncontested fundamental distinction between historiography

---

10 As emphasised by Elisabeth Wåghäll Nivre and Maren Eckart, biographical texts written before the 19th century – which constitute a large portion of the texts presented in Chapter 3.1. – can often not accurately be termed 'biography' since this kind of text is largely exclusive to the post-Enlightenment era (Wåghäll Nivre, Elisabeth and Maren Eckart. 'Narrating Life: Early Modern Accounts of the Life of Queen Christina of Sweden (1626-1689)'. In *Cultural Ways of Worldmaking: Media and Narratives*, ed. Vera Nünning et al. Berlin and New York: De Gruyter, 2010 (Concepts for the Study of Culture 1), p. 311).

11 Cf. White, Hayden. *The Content of the Form: Narrative Discourse and Historical Representation*. Baltimore and London: Johns Hopkins University Press, 1987, p. ix: »Many modern historians hold that narrative discourse, far from being a neutral medium for the representation of historical events and processes, is the very stuff of a mythical view of reality, a conceptual or pseudoconceptual 'content' which, when used to represent real events, endows them with an illusory coherence and charges them with the kinds of meanings more characteristic of oneiric than of waking thought«.

and literature[12] has not remained entirely undisputed. Nevertheless, his work, which will be presented in further detail in Chapter 3.2., has contributed to »the more recent debate among philosophers of history on the epistemological status of historical knowledge and the central role of 'narrativization' in the process of human comprehension«.[13]

In merging an analysis of the diverse aspects and elements of Leonora Christina's auto/biographical self-portrayal[14] with a broad review and examination of literary and historiographical depictions of her, this study aims at providing new insights into the field of research on (early modern women's) autobiography and on Leonora Christina's autobiographical writings in particular, as well as their impact on their author's image as portrayed in subsequent literature and historiography. Research on Leonora Christina as a writer has been tentative, yet increasingly prolific in the immediate past (see Chapter 1.2.). However, an extensive study on the literary reception of Leonora Christina has not been conducted so far; there has neither been a review or analysis of Leonora Christina's depiction in historiographic texts. Many of the texts included in Chapter 2 have, in fact, been largely overlooked by literary scholarship. Hence, the objective of this study is also to provide principal insights into a range of texts that have – in some instances unrightfully – eluded the interest of literary scholars altogether. Finally, Leonora Christina's position within Denmark's historical consciousness has been discussed by and large on multiple occasions; lastly in 2010/2011, when a Bornholm ferry named *Leonora Christina* provoked heated debates and a nationwide voting on the ferry's final name (see Chapter 2.2.). However, to date, historiographical and biographical texts concerned with Leonora Christina have not yet been studied as a primary source. Chapter 3 provides thus a broad review of Leonora Christina's portrayal in these texts, as well

---

12 See, for example, the British historian Alun Munslow's summary of this formerly widespread conviction: »[History] is quite unlike literature, which is plainly inferior to history as a form of knowledge« (Munslow, Alun. 'Rethinking *Metahistory: The Historical imagination in nineteenth century Europe*', Rethinking History 19/3 (2015), p. 325).

13 Engler, Bernd. 'The Dismemberment of Clio: Fictionality, Narrativity, and the Construction of Historical Reality in Historiographic Metafiction'. In *Historiographic Metafiction in Modern American and Canadian Literature*, eds. Bernd Engler and Kurt Müller. Paderborn: Ferdinand Schöningh, 1994 (Beiträge zur englischen und amerikanischen Literatur 13), p. 13. Accordingly, Hayden White, too, contends that »the conventional distinction between 'history' and 'historicism'« or between »historiography« and »philosophy of history« is »virtually worthless« (White, Hayden. 'Historicism, History, and the Figurative Imagination'. In White, Hayden. *Tropics of Discourse: Essays in Cultural Criticism*. Baltimore and London: Johns Hopkins University Press, 1978, all quotations p. 101).

14 This refers to Leonora Christina's self-portrayal in her two autobiographies and in the gynæceum *Hæltinners Pryd*, which is widely considered a collection of hidden self-portrayals (see Chapters 1.1.3. and 1.2.1.).

as a selective analysis of national histories depicting Leonora Christina, which have received little to no consideration within previous studies on Leonora Christina.

Lastly, the concluding chapter provides a consolidated recapitulation of the preceding chapters. Topics discussed here include the effect of *Jammers Minde* on the emergence of Leonora Christina as a dominant and independent character in – mostly Danish – literature and historiography; the increasingly variegated depiction of Leonora Christina and the productivity of her reception history as an implication of its eclectic tendencies;[15] and the gradual inclusion, extraction and reallocation of the Leonora Christina-subject matter to more specialised discourses in Danish historiography as a consequence of Leonora Christina's emergence as a literary writer, cultural figure and female role model. Preliminary conclusions and junctions are provided throughout the following chapters in the form of short revisions of previously covered subject matters and cross references to preceding or subsequent chapters.

Finally, one practical remark: the literary texts discussed in Chapter 2 contain a variety of variations of the names of Leonora Christina and her contemporaries, sometimes even within the same text. In order to avoid confusion regarding the spelling of these character names, a remark including the naming variations used in the respective text in question is provided at the beginning of each chapter concerned with a literary text, whose use of a naming or spelling variation, length, degree of fictionality and frequency of Leonora Christina's appearance require such an initial remark. Such explanatory notes seem necessary since Chapter 2 contains a high number of interdependent references to the literary Leonora Christina (as portrayed by the authors presented in Chapter 2) as well as to the historical Leonora Christina (i.e. the author and protagonist of *Jammers Minde*), who will then be distinguished by their naming variations. No such remark, however, is included in chapters presenting texts, which refer to the historical Leonora Christina instead of depicting a (more) literary, fictionalised Leonora Christina, which contain only sparse references to Leonora Christina, or which use the current spelling applied to Leonora Christina and her contemporaries. This concerns the texts presented in Chapters 2.1.1, 2.1.2., 2.2.1., 2.2.2., 2.5.1. and 2.7.2. In these chapters, the differentiation between the depicted and the historical Leonora Christina will be clarified by referring to them as such.

---

15 Hence the plural – Memor*ies* – in the present study's title, a reference to a commonly used English translation of the title of *Jammers Minde* – 'A Memory of Lament'.

For the reader unfamiliar with the details of Leonora Christina's life, the following section offers a comprehensive résumé. Additional and more specific biographical details will be provided in the course of the ensuing chapters.

Leonora Christina was the daughter of King Christian IV (1577-1648) of Denmark and Norway, born on 8 July 1621 as his third child with his second wife Kirsten Munk (1598-1658).[16] The young noblewoman Kirsten Munk, daughter of the rich and widowed estate owner Ellen Marsvin (1572-1649), married Christian IV in a private ceremony and since she was not of royal stock, she never became the Queen of Denmark. Their marriage was thus a morganatic one and its legitimacy was contested altogether at times, due to the lack of witnesses at their wedding ceremony.[17] Kirsten was of lower rank than her husband and hence her children were no princes or princesses.[18] The status of Leonora Christina and her brothers and sisters was thus situated between that of the King's royal children and the diverse illegitimate children he had fostered with his mistresses, i.e. below the children of his first wife, the late Queen Anna Catharina (1575-1612), but above the so-called *Gyldenløver*.[19] Leonora Christina was born in Frederiksborg Castle, but – as was the custom at this time – she spent the first years of her life at her grandmother Ellen Marsvin's fiefdom Dalum Kloster on the island of Funen. Due to Denmark's hapless involvement in the Thirty Years' War (1618-1648), which resulted in an occupation of Jutland by troops of the Habsburg Empire, Leonora Christina was first transferred back to the court in Copenhagen in 1626 and sent to the Netherlands in 1627 to stay with her aunt, the Countess of Nassau-Dietz. These years of war were fateful for Leonora Christina, since she met and lost her first love, her cousin Maurits (see Chapter 1.2.1.), while her mother Kirsten Munk began an affair with the Swedish general Otto Ludvig of Salm (1597-1634), who served under Christian

---

16 The biographical details related in the following are present in much of the primary and secondary literature quoted in this study. However, for a comprehensive and reliable biography of Leonora Christina (and Corfitz Ulfeldt), the reader is referred to Sophus Birket Smith's two-volume work *Leonora Christina Grevinde Ulfeldts Historie* and Steffen Heiberg's biography *Enhjørningen Corfitz Ulfeldt*, which are highly recommendable.

17 These occasional doubts concerning Kirsten Munk's, and hence Leonora Christina's, status, have occasioned Sophus Birket Smith to assure his readers that the subject of his most prolific work was of legitimate birth (see Birket Smith, Sophus. *Leonora Christina Grevinde Ulfeldts Historie 1*, p. 3).

18 However, in order to compensate for this inclined position, Kirsten Munk and her children received the title of Count/Countess of Schleswig-Holstein. Kirsten Munk's daughters furthermore received the denomination *frøken*, indicating that they were of princely descent. When Leonora Christina's half-brother Frederik ascended the throne after their father's death in 1648, he highlighted the lower birth of the Munk clan by withdrawing their titles of Counts and Countesses (officially in 1657 after Leonora Christina's journey to Korsør (see below), but inofficially already years before) and by calling his own daughters *prinsesser* instead of *frøkener* (Heiberg, Steffen. *Enhjørningen Corfitz Ulfeldt*, p. 105).

19 The illegitimate children of the 17th century's Danish kings received the last name *Gyldenløve* in order to compensate for their lack of a patronym.

IV until 1628. This short-lived liaison led to the couple's divorce in early 1630 and furthermore to the above-mentioned doubts regarding the marriage's legitimacy. Yet already since late 1628 the couple had stopped living as husband and wife, after Kirsten Munk had denied her husband access to her bed-chamber. In mid-1629, Vibeke Kruse (1605-1648), a former maid of Kirsten Munk, became the mistress of Christian IV and stayed by his side until his death in 1648. Kirsten Munk and Christian IV, on the other hand, remained enemies, much to the dismay of their children and their spouses, whose position at court depended on Kirsten Munk's reputation. The ensuing divorce battle has become a popular topic in literary representations of Leonora Christina from the second half of the 20th century onwards, which preferably depict her as an insecure child of divorce.

By signing the Treaty of Lübeck in 1629, Christian IV ended his involvement in the Thirty Years' War and the same year Leonora Christina returned to Copenhagen. The King's wilful conduct during the war had created an opposition between him and the Council of the Realm (*rigsråd*), which Christian IV intended to solve by securing the loyalty of prospective members of the Council through marriage with his plentiful daughters. The King's matrimonial policy created a powerful party of privileged, ambitious and corrupt noblemen, often simply referred to as 'the sons-in-law' (*svigersønnerne*), who soon overpowered the rest of the nobility, the other members of the Council, and eventually the King himself. In 1630, Leonora Christina became engaged to Corfitz Ulfeldt, a poor but promising young nobleman, whose education abroad had turned him into an ideal candidate for the position of the King's right hand. On 9 October 1636, after Ulfeldt had become a member of the Council, Leonora Christina and her groom celebrated their wedding at Copenhagen Castle (i.e. at the site of today's Christiansborg Palace). They spent the first months of their marital life on Ulfeldt's fiefdom, the island of Møn, but already in early 1637, the couple moved back to Copenhagen, of which Ulfeldt was appointed Governor. There, Ulfeldt and his wife inhabited a luxuriously furnished mansion on Gråbrødretorv in central Copenhagen, where they would stay until their departure from Denmark in 1651.

In the following years, Ulfeldt enjoyed a stellar career and was thus able to gather a fortune, the likes of which were hardly to be found among Europe's noblemen at that time.[20] In 1643, he was appointed *Rigshofmester*, i.e. Steward of the Realm, which means that he had become almost as powerful as the King himself. This, in turn, elevated Ulfeldt's avarice and self-esteem, which eventually led to disputes

---

20 According to Danish historian Ole Feldbæk, Ulfeldt collected a wealth corresponding to the annual public revenue of Denmark and Norway within ten years (Feldbæk, Ole. *Danmarks historie*. Copenhagen: Gyldendal, 2010 (2004), p. 102).

with Christian IV. However, the aged King had become too dependent on his son-in-law and his support within the Council to accept the pretence-notices Ulfeldt handed in whenever faced with disagreement. The contentions between Ulfeldt and his father-in-law continued until Christian IV's death in 1648.

In the meantime, Kirsten Munk was exiled in Jutland and Vibeke Kruse was not deemed presentable, which is why Leonora Christina enjoyed the status of the country's foremost lady. She accompanied her husband on his diplomatic – and very expensive – journeys to the Netherlands (mid-1646 until early 1647, and then again in 1649) and France (1647), during the first of which she also made a detour to England (1647) together with her and her husband's faithful friend and physician Otto Sperling the Elder (1602-1681). When the Ulfeldt couple returned to Copenhagen in mid-1647, they were received with the unfortunate news of the death of Leonora Christina's halfbrother Christian, *den udvalgte prins*, the implications of which were that Christian IV depended on the support of Ulfeldt and the Council in establishing his son Frederik – the later Frederik III (1609-1670) – as the new heir to the throne, since Denmark was at that time an elective monarchy. Yet a few months later, in early 1648, Christian IV died at Rosenborg Castle, where Leonora Christina is said to have closed her deceased father's remaining eye.[21]

Despite a general averseness to Frederik, who had spent most of his previous life on German soil and was thus regarded with mistrust, he was elected King of Denmark and Norway in 1648, due to a lack of other unanimously approved candidates. Tensions between the royal and the Ulfeldt couple arose already before the coronation, when Ulfeldt, perhaps willingly, failed to inform Frederik of his father's imminent death. There are rumours according to which Ulfeldt, and perhaps Leonora Christina as well, ransacked the King's documents, and even forged his signature, immediately after his death. The situation did not defuse when Frederik was forced to sign an unusually austere *håndfæstning*, i.e. a 'handbinding' document which surrendered a significant portion of the monarch's authority to the Council and to Ulfeldt in particular, before ascending to the throne. To make matters worse, Leonora Christina refused to give way to Frederik's wife, Queen Sophie Amalie of Brunswick-Lüneburg. At the same time, there was a striking difference between the financial situation of the rich Ulfeldt house and that of the King, who had inherited an impoverished country and court, and who was often forced to ask his brother-in-law for monetary support.

In response to these humiliations Frederik III began to dismantle the Council and the party of sons-in-law after his coronation in late 1648. Christian von

---

21 He had lost an eye at the naval battle of Kolberger Heide in 1644 against a Swedish fleet.

Pentz (1600-1651), the husband of Leonora Christina's elder sister Sophie Elisabeth (1619-1657), lost his position as Governor of Glückstadt while Ebbe Ulfeldt (1616-1682), husband of Leonora Christina's younger sister Hedevig (1626-1678), was found guilty of having mismanaged his fiefdom of Bornholm, which, as a result, he lost in the following year. In early 1649, Frederik III saw his chance to rid himself of his most accursed brother-in-law, when Ulfeldt was sent on a second diplomatic journey to the Netherlands. In The Hague, where the Ulfeldt couple arrived in March 1649, they also met a distant relative of Leonora Christina, the later King Charles II of England, Scotland and Ireland, who was living abroad due to the English Civil War (1642-1651). Ulfeldt lent him weapons and money, partially paid for by the King of Denmark, but partially out of his own pocket as well. When Ulfeldt returned to Copenhagen in December 1649, he was met with general disappointment concerning the results of his expensive journey, and he learned that in the meantime his office had been stripped of a few areas of responsibility. Still convinced of his indispensability, Ulfeldt relied on his usual tactics of calling in sick. However, unlike his father, Frederik III would not bow to Ulfeldt's silent show of force. When Ulfeldt continued his practice by threatening to resign, Frederik III is said to have only answered with laughter. Soon afterwards the King ordered an investigation into Ulfeldt's administration since there had long been rumours of corruption and embezzlement pertaining to Ulfeldt and his extraordinary wealth. At approximately the same time, Hannibal Sehested (1609-1666), husband of Leonora Christina's younger sister Christiane (1626-1670), Governor of Norway and the second-most powerful son-in-law of Christian IV (and hence the foremost rival of Ulfeldt at that time), was audited and found guilty of having abused his office.

The majority of the sons-in-law were thus already rendered innocuous in 1650, when the so-called Dina affair (*Dinasagen*) irrevocably brought Ulfeldt's prospects in Denmark to an end. In late 1650, Dina Vinhofvers (1620-1651), a widowed woman of German origin and questionable reputation, claimed to be expecting a child of Corfitz Ulfeldt. She further asserted to have overheard a conversation between him and his wife while covering under bed sheets in Ulfeldt's bedroom, the topic of which was an intended poisoning of Frederik III with a concoction brewed by Otto Sperling. During the secret investigation against Ulfeldt, Dina also contacted Leonora Christina to warn her about a planned attack on her house coordinated by her accomplice, Lieutenant Colonel Jørgen Walter (1610-1670), a commoner who had rendered outstanding services in the previous years of war and who had recently become a protégé of Queen Sophie Amalie. Over the course of several months, Dina thus fed pieces of largely false information to both parties. In April 1651, when Ulfeldt contacted Frederik III to inform him about Dina's warning and to ask for his protection, the entire affair became public and only then both parties learned about Dina's double game.

In the course of the following interrogations, Dina changed her statements several times. Eventually, all accusations against the Ulfeldt couple turned out to be false, leading to Dina's beheading in July 1651. Her accomplice and the actual father of her child, Jørgen Walter, was banned from Denmark, since he had brought his mistress' accusations and subsequent tidings to the attention of the royal couple, yet without being honest about what kind of woman Dina was. Sophus Birket Smith states that it is impossible to determine whether Dina or Walter had been the original instigator of this failed conspiracy, but he also highlights the instrumental role Walter played in figuring as the link between Dina and the court and in chivvying Dina into insisting on her previous accusations, even when her claims were disproven.[22] At any rate, literary interpretations of the Dina affair, which will be the topic of Chapter 2.3., rarely depict their eponymous heroine as a calculating schemer, but rather as the victim of a power struggle that did not even concern her.

Even though the trial against Dina exonerated Ulfeldt, he felt that his enemies were outnumbering his allies,[23] not least since he was still being audited and expected to face new charges rather soon. Hence, Ulfeldt and Leonora Christina secretly left Copenhagen with a small portion of their children and servants a few days after the execution of Dina and headed for the Netherlands. The rest of their children followed them shortly afterwards. When Ulfeldt's house on Gråbrødretorv was searched after their departure it was almost entirely empty, indicating that he had been evacuating his property for quite a while.

While their children remained in Utrecht, Ulfeldt and Leonora Christina travelled to Stockholm to ask for Queen Christina's protection and the permission to settle down in Sweden. Their plea was granted and after an adventurous stopover in Gdańsk, which Leonora Christina refers to in her French autobiography,[24] Ulfeldt and his family took up residence in Stralsund in late 1651, which at that time was

---

22 See Birket Smith, Sophus. *Leonora Christina Grevinde Ulfeldts Historie 1*, p. 201.

23 One justified objection to the outcome of the trial is that the course of events, the motivation for Dina's double game and the true instigator were never elucidated, as stated in a defence written and published abroad by Ulfeldt called *Høytrengende Æris Forsuar* (1652). Birket Smith, too, finds fault with the rather hasty and inconclusive investigation of this affair (Birket Smith, Sophus. *Leonora Christina Grevinde Ulfeldts Historie 1*, p. 216; see also ibid., p. 220).

24 Since the Danish name for Leonora Christina's first attempt at an autobiography – *den franske selvbiografi* (or *levnedsskildring*) – is not the, originally rather long and French, title of the work but rather a denomination (since it was written in French), I will refer to this work as 'the French autobiography', i.e. the common denomination's English translation. The correct title of the French autobiography is *La Vie d'Eleonore Christine comtesse d'Ulfeldt* ('The Life of Leonora Christina, Countess Ulfeldt'; unless indicated otherwise, translations into English are my own). However, no subsequent scholar or editor cared to maintain this title.

Introduction

under Swedish dominion. The following year, the Ulfeldt couple moved to Stockholm, where Ulfeldt spent the following months as one of Christina's minions, particularly since he lent immense sums of money to this ever fortuneless queen. In the meantime, Leonora Christina spent most of her time at home in dedication to her literary and language studies, sometimes in the company of Otto Sperling, who after the Ulfeldts' departure from Denmark lived temporarily in Sweden but returned to his former home in Hamburg in 1654.[25] Occasionally, she was also visited by one of her sisters, but family relations within the Munk clan had never been particularly affectionate. When Ulfeldt asked his wife to travel to Denmark in order to effect a settlement between him and Frederik III in 1656, she followed his request and used the journey to Denmark for a short visit at her mother's domicile in Boller. She documented the course and results of her adventurous yet unfruitful journey to Korsør both in her French autobiography and in a separate account (see Chapters 1.2.1. and 1.2.2.).

Despite his generosity, Ulfeldt did not receive the reward he had hoped for, i.e. a Swedish attack on Denmark. However, when the Queen resigned in 1654 and left the throne to her cousin, Karl X Gustav (1622-1660), Ulfeldt's dream of a Dano-Swedish war was fulfilled. In 1657, he left his temporary home in Barth (Swedish Pomerania), where he had lived with his family since 1655, to join and advise the King of Sweden on his military campaign against Denmark. Leonora Christina followed her husband to the battlefield in Denmark, and even their friend Otto Sperling and eldest son Christian joined them temporarily. After Sperling's departure, Leonora Christina spent her time nursing those in her company who were befallen by a type of typhus, while Ulfeldt and Karl X Gustav continued forward until Denmark was forced to sign the Treaty of Roskilde in 1658, which also included an article aimed at restoring some of the Ulfeldt couple's privileges in Denmark, such as Leonora Christina's peerage.

After this treaty, the relationship between Sweden's King and Ulfeldt turned aloof since the latter was not satisfied with the position and the rewards he had retrieved after the war. When Karl X Gustav resumed his warfare against Denmark in 1658, Ulfeldt did not join him but stayed in his new residence in Malmö, together

---

25 In general, Leonora Christina is said to have avoided the Swedish court, since she did not receive the esteem to which she felt entitled as a King's daughter (see Birket Smith, Sophus. *Leonora Christina Grevinde Ulfeldts Historie 1*, p. 256 and Heiberg, Steffen. *Enhjørningen Corfitz Ulfeldt*, p. 140). Queen Christina's preference for male company did not contribute to drawing Leonora Christina to the court either. Accordingly, Swedish historiographies mention Leonora Christina only scarcely, despite her husband's temporarily central position at the Swedish court and in Swedish foreign politics. Volume 6 of the multi-volume Swedish history book *Den svenska historien*, for example, only briefly mentions her (see Rosén, Jerker. 'Kristinas hovliv'. In *Den svenska historien 6: Drottning Kristina. Vetenskap och kultur blomstrar*, ed. Jan Cornell et al. Stockholm: Bonnier, 1983 (1967), p. 144).

with his family. In the same city, a planned revolt against the Swedish occupation[26] was discovered in 1659 and in the course of the interrogations, Ulfeldt was reported to have been involved with the insurrectionists. As a result, he and Leonora Christina were kept under arrest in their house in Malmö for more than a year.

When the trial against Ulfeldt[27] commenced, he was unable to defend himself due to a severe stroke that left him paralysed and incapable of speaking. Leonora Christina assumed her husband's advocacy, but despite her best efforts he was found guilty of treason, for which the sentence was death. Leonora Christina was also found guilty of having stood in secret contact with the main conspirator Bartholomæus Mikkelsen, who was executed in December 1659, but the punishment was left for the King to choose. However, it was also decided to not inform Ulfeldt and Leonora Christina about the verdict before he had recovered from his stroke, and in the meantime, Karl X Gustav died. The new Swedish government was hard-pressed for money and decided to make Ulfeldt pay a ransom for himself and his wife, but, while they were still waiting for the verdict's pronouncement, Leonora Christina and Ulfeldt received from an unknown friend the misinformation that they would be deported to Finland. Therefore, Leonora Christina decided to venture an escape to Copenhagen. According to her plan, Ulfeldt was supposed to go to Lübeck and wait for his wife's signal to follow her to Copenhagen. Both of them, but particularly Ulfeldt, thought that the Treaty of Roskilde, that had granted them amnesty in Denmark, was still valid.[28] But when Leonora Christina arrived in Copenhagen and, unexpectedly, found her husband there, the couple was arrested and shipped to the island of Bornholm.

From July 1660 until December 1661, the couple was detained[29] in the former fortress of Hammershus on the northwest coast of the island; all the while Frederik III established absolutism in Denmark. The Governor of Bornholm, Major

---

26 In 1658, the formerly Danish province of Scania became Swedish territory.

27 Since she was a married woman, the accusations against Ulfeldt initially did not concern Leonora Christina. Thus, Karl X Gustav offered her the choice to either abandon her husband or to share his arrest, and she chose the latter. Later, however, when new evidence was unearthed, the indictment concerned her as well.

28 The article of the Treaty of Roskilde which had granted Ulfeldt amnesty was not included in the Treaty of Copenhagen, a follow-up document to the Treaty of Roskilde signed in 1660 after Denmark's victory over Sweden. This led Frederik III to the – not indisputable (see Birket Smith, Sophus. *Leonora Christina Grevinde Ulfeldts Historie: Med Bidrag til hendes Ægtefælles og hendes nærmeste Slægts Historie 2*. Copenhagen: Gyldendal, 1881, pp. 60-63) – deduction that this article was null and void.

29 Neither before nor during the months during which the Ulfeldt couple was arrested on Bornholm was there a formal prosecution or trial against them. Ulfeldt's status, both in relation to Denmark and to Sweden, had become uncertain since his secret flight from Sweden. Theoretically, Sweden could still have claimed a voice in a verdict concerning Ulfeldt. Hence, Frederik III was hesitant in taking a final decision in the Ulfeldt case.

General Adolph Fuchs (†1662), was an exceedingly cruel attendant[30] and particularly Ulfeldt, who was still not fully recovered from his stroke, suffered under his superintendence. This time, Ulfeldt's illness seems to have affected his mind as well, perhaps even irrevocably, as his behaviour in the ensuing years suggests. Leonora Christina sought to free her husband and herself by all means necessary and, after failed attempts at bribing the prison warder's wife and Fuchs into letting them escape, the Ulfeldt couple, together with their faithful servant Peter Pflügge, who had been sharing their cell, hazarded an escape from their prison. Their plan was to climb down the tower through their window, escape down the cliffs in front of Hammershus to the beach and take a fishing boat from there, perhaps to German territory. After an arduous night, the escapees did indeed reach the coast, but they were discovered at dawn when Leonora Christina tried to convince a few fishermen she encountered to sell a boat to them, and so were returned to Hammershus. The prisoners were transferred to three separate rooms and remained apart until their release in December 1661, which the Ulfeldt couple effected by agreeing to sign a particularly submissive petition addressed to the King. This document relinquished all debt claims to Frederik III and all claims to any properties outside of Funen, in addition to containing a pledge of loyalty to the King of Denmark, as well as an agreement to remain on Funen and to stay away from Zealand. Leonora Christina furthermore was forced to renounce the peerage her father had awarded to her and her siblings. The document also included the promise to not in any way hold Fuchs accountable for his actions in Hammershus.

From December 1661 onwards, Ulfeldt and his family lived in Ellensborg (Holckenhavn Castle, as it is called today) on Funen, named after Leonora Christina's grandmother Ellen Marsvin and passed down to Leonora Christina after her mother's death in 1658. However, soon after his arrival in Ellensborg, Ulfeldt grew restless and asked for permission to take the waters abroad. His request was eventually granted and in mid-1662, he and his family departed to Amsterdam. There, he is reported to have approached a man working for the son of the Elector of Brandenburg by the name of Daniel Stephani, partially in the presence of Leonora Christina. These initial meetings, about whose actual purpose not even Stephani was informed at that time, seem to have had no other aim than directing the Elector's attention to Ulfeldt.

After having spent a short period of time in Amsterdam, Leonora Christina remained there with her daughter Ellen Christina (1643-1677), who had been taken

---

30 The population of Bornholm, too, complained about Fuchs' despotic demeanour, which is why he was transferred to Funen in 1662. In the same year, he was murdered by Leonora Christina's son Christian in Bruges.

ill, while the rest of her family continued to Bruges. Since his meeting with Stephani had seemingly not yielded any results, Ulfeldt tried to effect a reconciliation with the Swedish government, yet to no avail. In September 1662, Leonora Christina reunited with her husband in Bruges and together they continued to Paris, where he – unavailingly – offered his services to Louis XIV (1638-1715). At this time, Hannibal Sehested, who had managed to regain the favour of Frederik III and had been sent on a diplomatic journey to Paris, informed his King of Ulfeldt's suspicious contact with a foreign regent, which was a breach of the document he and Leonora Christina had signed in 1661. After a few weeks, the Ulfeldt couple returned to Bruges, where their eldest son Christian murdered Adolph Fuchs, who, coincidentally, was visiting Bruges at that time together with his Flemish wife, with the help of Peter Pflügge[31] in November 1662. Christian declared subsequently, that he had assassinated Fuchs on his own will and that his parents had been unaware of his intent.[32] Nevertheless, this was another violation of the document signed in 1661.

In the meantime, the Elector of Brandenburg, Friedrich Wilhelm, had become curious about Ulfeldt's motivation to contact Stephani and sent Major General Alexander von Spaen to Bruges to get further information from Ulfeldt. To this man, Ulfeldt suggested a coup against Frederik III and a subsequent coronation of Friedrich Wilhelm as the new King of Denmark and Norway. Since Friedrich Wilhelm was allied with Frederik III, the latter was eventually informed about Ulfeldt's scheme. In mid-1663, Frederik III announced an arrest order for Ulfeldt and Leonora Christina.

When this arrest order was proclaimed, Ulfeldt and Leonora Christina were already separated. In the past years, the couple had lost a considerable share of their formerly immense fortune and since at this point, they had been travelling for months, they were particularly hard-pressed for money. Hence, Ulfeldt sent his wife to England to collect an old debt. As explained above, the Ulfeldts' had met King Charles II of England, back then exiled and relatively impoverished, in 1649 in The Hague and lent him money as well as valuable goods. In May 1663, Leonora Christina took an – unbeknownst to both of them – final leave of her husband to meet

---

31 When Fuchs' carriage stopped in front of the mayor's house, Christian opened the door, stabbed Fuchs and ran away. After this, Peter Pflügge threw grenades into the carriage. Fuchs' wife, who was with her husband, survived the attack despite the grenades. Christian subsequently fled to Rome, where he enjoyed the protection of the former Queen of Sweden, Christina, who had retired to Italy's capital after her abdication in 1654.

32 'Greve Christian (Corfiz Søn) Ulfelds Missive dateret Calais d. 3die Fbr. 1662, til En i Bryssel i Flandern angaaende det Mord, han giorde paa General-Major Fuchs, hvorudi han opregner Aarsagerne, som tildrev ham, sligt at bedrive', Journal for Politik, Natur- og Menneske-Kundskab 1816/2, p. 96).

Charles II in London. Despite his promises of doing so without delay, Charles did not pay his debt and Leonora Christina prepared to return to her husband. In Dover, she was apprehended and brought to Dover Castle, where she was informed about the arrest order issued by Frederik III, yet not about its cause. Charles II intended to evade public reprimand for extraditing his relative to her enemies. Hence, he staged a false escape of Leonora Christina. Under the pretext of having received the order to help her flee from England, a subordinate of Charles II called Braten[33] lured Leonora Christina into fleeing from Dover. Under the direction of Braten, Leonora Christina thus escaped from her third prison, only to run into the arms of Simon Petkum, Denmark's envoy in England. She was apprehended and shipped directly to Copenhagen, where she arrived on 8 August 1663.

Ulfeldt, on the other hand, had already in July been sentenced to death. When he learned what had happened to his wife in England, he went into hiding and reappeared in late 1663 in the Swiss town of Basel, together with his eldest sons and, for a while, Anna Catharina. Since Ulfeldt could not be captured, he was executed in effigy on 13 November 1663 in front of the Blue Tower (*Blåtårn*) in Copenhagen, where Leonora Christina was already incarcerated at that time. The real Ulfeldt eventually succumbed to his long-term illness and died on a boat on the Rhine in February 1664. He was buried at the final destination of his boat voyage, in the German town of Neuburg am Rhein. His children did not accompany him on his last journey, but when Ulfeldt's sons heard of their father's passing, they claimed his body out of fear that it would be returned to Denmark and buried it at an unknown location.

Despite never being formally convicted, Leonora Christina spent almost twenty-two years in the Blue Tower, since she did not, or could not, provide the Danish authorities with any valuable information about her husband, to whom she was considered a potential accomplice.[34] Since the assassination of Adolph Fuchs, it also seemed safer to keep Leonora Christina as a sort of pawn to ensure that no such

---

33 Cf. Leonora Christina. *Jammers Minde: Diplomatarisk udgave ved Poul Lindegård Hjorth og Marita Akhøj Nielsen under medvirkning af Ingelise Nielsen,* ed. Det Danske Sprog- og Litteraturselskab. Copenhagen: Reitzel, 1998, p. 4 (all following quotations from *Jammers Minde* are taken from the same edition; the page reference is henceforth rendered directly in the text due to the frequent occurrence of quotations from *Jammers Minde* in this study). As suggested by Birket Smith, the man was probably called Broughton (Birket Smith, Sophus. *Leonora Christina Grevinde Ulfeldts Historie 2*, p. 138).

34 Leonora Christina was not the only collateral damage of her husband's aspirations. Throughout the years of their friendship, Otto Sperling the Elder followed Ulfeldt into exile, he took care of his children, he translated and spread his dissident writings and he was the middleman in much of his correspondence, for example with Sweden. Hence, Sperling was also brought to the Blue Tower (where he died in 1681) and convicted in 1664 for lèse-majesté, due to his continued support for Ulfeldt even after the latter's conviction in 1663 (cf. Birket Smith, Sophus. *Leonora Christina Grevinde Ulfeldts Historie 2*, pp. 217-223).

act of revenge would occur again – all of her children were exiled after their father's conviction, but nevertheless free.

During the first couple of days in the Blue Tower, Leonora Christina was interrogated in a dungeon called *Mørke Kirke*. She was subsequently relocated to a different cell, which became her home until 1685. In 1670, Frederik III died and his son and successor, Christian V, granted his imprisoned aunt more space, comfort and recreation. Yet only in 1685, after Sophie Amalie's death, Leonora Christina was released from the Blue Tower and – after two short stays respectively at a niece's house in central Copenhagen and at an in-law's home in Husum (today a suburb of Copenhagen; cf. *Jammers Minde*, p. 248) – transferred to the abandoned Maribo Abbey, where she passed away in 1698. She was buried in Maribo Cathedral.

In the Blue Tower and in Maribo, Leonora Christina passed the time with the composition of two autobiographical works – the so-called French autobiography (exclusively written in the Blue Tower and mostly narrating her life before her imprisonment in the Blue Tower) and *Jammers Minde* (written in the Blue Tower and in Maribo and narrating her life from her extradition to Copenhagen until her release in 1685) – and *Hæltinners Pryd,* a list of creditable historical women comparable to Ludvig Holberg's *Adskillige Heltinders og navnkundige Damers sammenlignede Historier* (see Chapter 3.1.), written in the Blue Tower (and probably revised and rewritten in Maribo), but unfortunately preserved incompletely.[35] While Leonora Christina's auto/biographical writings are indubitably those of her writings that are best known and most deserving of commendation, they are by far not the only literary activities she engaged in throughout her life. When the Ulfeldts' lived in Sweden, Leonora Christina occupied herself with proto-autobiographical writing: *Kong Karl X Gustavs Bryllup 1654*, *Rejsen til Korsør 1656* and *Confrontationen i Malmø 1659*. These are all short accounts of single events, which Leonora Christina penned down for documentary reasons. While Leonora Christina was in Barth, she translated a book written by the Spanish author Matías de los Reyes (1581-1640). She also translated the first part of a French book titled *Cléopatre*, which Birket Smith assumes to have been written by Gautier de Costes de La Calprenède (1609-1663).[36] In Maribo, Leonora Christina is further reported to have written a play subsequently staged by her staff. However, these works are lost and

---

35 According to Leonora Christina's own account, she completed *Hæltinners Pryd* in 1684 (*Jammers Minde*, p. 226), i.e. when she was still in the Blue Tower. Due to her imprecise statements, however, Birket Smith suspects that she rather finished a draft of *Hæltinners Pryd* in 1684 and continued to work on it for many years after her release (Birket Smith, Sophus. *Leonora Christina Grevinde Ulfeldts Historie 2*, p. 264).

36 Birket Smith, Sophus. *Leonora Christina Grevinde Ulfeldts Historie 1*, p. 279.

only known from references.[37] Throughout the second half of her life, Leonora Christina furthermore wrote several poems and church hymns, most of which are preserved in *Jammers Minde*.

Before engaging in one of the core topics of this study, i.e. Leonora Christina's status as a literary writer and the emergence of her auto/biographical works (Chapter 1.2.), the following chapter (1.1.) provides basic theories on, as well as definitions and a short history of the autobiographical genre. As will be demonstrated below, such preliminary considerations are necessary since Leonora Christina's works originate from a time before the advent of the term 'autobiography' and from writing conditions which defy our most common understanding of the work of a professional writer. The implications of these considerations for the reception of Leonora Christina and her work will be the topic of Chapter 1.2.

---

37 On the translations, see *Leonora Christina Grevinde Ulfeldts Franske Levnedsskildring 1673. Trykt i Faksimile*, ed. C. O. Bøggild-Andersen, Copenhagen: Forening for Boghaandværk, 1958, p. 6b (Translation p. 25). On the play, see Birket Smith, Sophus. *Leonora Christina (Ulfeldt) på Maribo Kloster: Et Bidrag til Oplysning om hendes sidste Leveår*. Copenhagen: Gyldendal, 1872, p. 54. Birket Smith's work is largely based on the information provided by Leonora Christina's housekeeper Dorthea Sophie Urne. On the search for Leonora Christina's play, see Rostrup, Egill. *Leonora Christina's Skuespil*. Copenhagen: Krohn, 1918. About the edition of the French autobiography used in this study: even though Bøggild-Andersen's edition of the French autobiography contains no transcription, but only a facsimile of the manuscript, the present study quotes from this edition because as of now, there is no complete, unnormalised edition of the text yet. The transcription of parts of the French autobiography provided in the following are thus my own. However, for the conduct of this enterprise I relied heavily and frequently on Birket Smith's transcribed publication of a French copy of the text (*Leonora Christina (Ulfeldt)s Selvbiografi. Udgivet efter et Håndskrift i det store Kgl. Bibliothek*, ed. Sophus Birket Smith, Danske Samlinger for Historie, Topografi, Personal- og Litteraturhistorie 1/2 (1871-72), pp. 129-231) and on quotations of the original manuscript transcribed by Marita Akhøj Nielsen and published on the website of the *Arkiv for Dansk Litteratur*: Akhøj Nielsen, Marita. 'Leonora Christina Ulfeldt: Forfatterportræt': http://adl.dk/adl_pub/fportraet/cv/ShowFpItem.xsql?nnoc=adl_pub&ff_id=36&p_fpkat_id=fskab.

1. Leonora Christina's *Jammers Minde*

1.1. Theory of Autobiography

1.1.1. Terminological Considerations

In a literal sense, an autobiography is somebody's life story written down by him- or herself. However, this does not quite answer the question in its full extent, especially since autobiographies of persons of different professions are often lumped together and placed in sections dedicated to other literary genres. For example, imagine a customer in a bookshop looking for Jean-Jacques Rousseau's *Confessions*. Although it is an autobiography, the book might be found in the sections for philosophy or discourse alongside his other internationally renowned works, or even amongst biographies or novels. Furthermore, what about autobiographies or memoirs written by people from different professions, such as Arnold Schwarzenegger? Since he is a popular contemporary figure, a customer may simply have to search in the bestseller section at first, but after a few years his autobiography could end up in a number of sections including entertainment, politics, non-fiction, biography, or, if the bookshop is big enough, autobiography. For both bookshop and customer, grouping autobiographies into one section, regardless of the author's profession or the time period, is a pragmatic solution. Nevertheless, it raises the following question about the nature of autobiography: if different autobiographies of persons from different genres are considered one and the same, what legitimises placing the autobiographies of Rousseau and Schwarzenegger in two different sections, or in the same section amongst a different genre?

Questions of this kind have puzzled literary scholars for decades. Autobiographies exhibiting techniques and features of novelistic literature have led some scholars, such as Patricia Meyer Spacks,[38] to question any differences between autobiography and fiction. One of the most evident arguments for abandoning this notion was delivered by Barrett J. Mandel in his influential essay 'Full of Life Now':

> Regardless of the rootedness of both novels and autobiographies in a process that binds them together, the very simple point that critics have been missing in their zeal to deal

---

38 Meyer Spacks, Patricia. 'The Soul's Imaginings: Daniel Defoe, William Cowper', Publications of the Modern Language Association 91 (1976), p. 425.

with the »knotty philosophic and literary question« is that autobiographies and novels are finally totally distinct – and this simple fact every reader knows.[39]

However, let us for a moment put aside any scholarly perspective on autobiography, in order to clarify what we, as *readers* of autobiography, usually deem to be representative of the genre which is autobiography. To begin with, we would expect a literary account of a non-fictional person's life, or at least of large parts of it.[40] Also expected would be a retrospective point of view on one's life narrated in chronological order, thereby underlining the development of the protagonist's character.[41] The main task of this temporal approach to autobiographical narrating is to distinctly highlight the difference between descriptions referring to the »now« versus those referring to the »then«. In order to achieve this marked difference, the mode of narrative must not only be a proceeding, but also a contrasting one.[42] Another typical trait of the autobiographical genre is the use of a first-person narrator. As demonstrated by Leonora Christina's first attempt at an autobiography, however, i.e. her so-called French autobiography (1673) which is written in the third person, this characteristic is fairly optional. Equally important for an essential definition of the term autobiography is what Philippe Lejeune calls *le pacte autobiographique*[43] ('the autobiographical pact'), i.e. a pact agreed to by both author and reader, based on the (implied or, rather, supposed) identity between author, narrator and protagonist,[44] which is then, on the reader's part, translated into authenticity, hence creating the category of autobiography. Lejeune's theory sees autobiography thus essentially as a communicative act between author and reader, instead of basing it on formal criteria. Of course, a formal criterion such as prose form is something an ordinary reader of autobiography would expect to find as well; however, not least thanks to William Wordsworth's much acclaimed autobiographical poem *The Prelude* (posthumously published in 1850), formal criteria do indeed not provide a satisfying and comprehensive basis for defining autobiography, which Jean Starobinski also notes in his essay on autobiographical style.[45] Instead, Philippe Lejeune delivered this compact

---

39 Mandel, Barrett J. 'Full of Life Now'. In *Autobiography: Essays Theoretical and Critical*, ed. James Olney. Princeton University Press, 1980, p. 53.
40 Delany, Paul. *British Autobiography in the Seventeenth Century*. London: Routledge, 1969, p. 1.
41 Smyth, Adam. *Autobiography in Early Modern England*. Cambridge University Press, 2010, p. 13.
42 Heitmann, Annegret. *Selbst schreiben: Eine Untersuchung der dänischen Frauenautobiographik*. Frankfurt: Lang, 1994 (Beiträge zur Skandinavistik 12), p. 51.
43 Lejeune, Philippe. *Le Pacte Autobiographique*. Paris: Éditions du Seuil, 1975, p. 8.
44 Ibid., p. 15.
45 Starobinski, Jean. 'The Style of Autobiography'. In *Autobiography: Essays Theoretical and Critical*, ed. James Olney. Princeton University Press, 1980, pp. 73-83.

and ever since highly praised definition. However, Lejeune's much appraised definition is not without flaws either. It excludes, for example, the possibility of an anonymous autobiography; and although this theoretical deduction is utterly logical, praxis proves Lejeune wrong. Authors like Camilla Collett published their life narratives anonymously and even though one could not prove Collett's authorship, nobody doubted the status of her autobiography as such. In addition, Lejeune even contends that »la vocation autobiographique«[46], i.e. the autobiographical call, and a drive to remain anonymous could not possibly exist within the same person. However, this claim ignores specific cases such as American slave narratives, some of which were published anonymously to protect those left behind.[47]

The abovementioned features can certainly be considered as the most essential characteristics of the autobiographical genre. However, these features serve mostly to distinguish autobiography from its side-genres: the diary, the letter-collection, memoirs, the autobiographical novel, the (literary) self-portrait, and biography, all of which can be subsumed under the umbrella term 'life-writings'.

Experience is the key word distinguishing autobiography from a diary. Of course, one could focus on the highly limited retrospective point of view, which lends the diary its spontaneous flair (which again many readers appreciate as something more 'authentic' than the overly interpretive and selective accounts one finds in a typical autobiography), as the main feature to distinguish it from an autobiography. Yet, this means nothing more and nothing less than making the distinction between memory and experience. From the author's point of view, the person portrayed in a diary does not change, for it is a static personality captured in the moment. Writing an autobiography, on the other hand, requires its author to look back further in time than just a few hours or days to remember and to interpret his or her past environments and behaviour. The acts of analysis and interpretation serve as the main distinctive elements between experience and memory.[48] Meaning, increased distance in time allows one to find an explanation for their own past, enabling them to make out certain behavioural patterns which help place particular incidents into a larger context.

Furthermore, most scholars cannot help mentioning the frequent use of diaries and letters for the composition of an autobiography as a means of aid to memory and,

---

46 Ibid., p. 33.
47 Smith, Sidonie and Julia Watson. *Reading Autobiography: A Guide for Interpreting Life Narratives*. Minneapolis and London: University of Minnesota Press, 2003 (2001), p. 29.
48 Pascal, Roy. *Design and Truth in Autobiography*. London: Routledge & Kegan Paul, 1960, p. 16.

in the case of letters, evidence.[49] To a certain degree, a kind of organisation into a hierarchy is inherent in these statements for they clearly distinguish the 'functional texts' from the literary final product. Another reason for this valuation in favour of autobiography might lie in the historically predetermined association of private writings such as diaries or letters with mostly female authors. Ever since antiquity, women did write, but up until the 20th century professional writing was a predominantly male domain. Women on the other hand had to content themselves with occasional, anonymous or posthumous publications of their personal written records, most of which could hardly compete with counterparts written by men, both on an aesthetic (due to lack in education) and content (due to the limited life options for women in earlier centuries) level. Some of the earliest autobiographies written by women were in fact biographies of their husbands, which barely included a chapter on themselves: an autobiography in the biography.[50] However, over the last three decades notions about letters and diaries, and their importance for female autobiographers, have changed tremendously in two ways: 1) from women favouring life writings in the form of diaries and letters, especially since these forms fit their »fragmentary«[51] lives better than the comprehensive autobiography, to complete negation of any such relations;[52] and 2) from pejorative definitions of the diary such as those mentioned above to objections against any negative conceptions of personal life writings that declare, at least in Europe, the diary a »very respected« genre and a »cultural contribution«.[53]

Significantly less clear to the ordinary reader might be the disparity between autobiography and memoir, even though Kondrup makes it appear almost trivial: »Thi hvor den autobiograferendes motiv er ham selv, er memoireforfatterens alt andet«.[54] To distinguish between introspection and account of the evolution of one's personality (autobiography) on the one hand, and a mere narration of one's life focussing on events and acquaintances (memoir) on the other hand,[55] is anything but an easy

---

49 For example, Kondrup, Johnny. *Levned og tolkninger: Studier i nordisk selvbiografi*. Odense: Odense Universitetsforlag, 1982 (Odense University Studies in Scandinavian Languages and Literatures 10), p. 23.
50 Smith, Sidonie and Julia Watson. *Reading Autobiography*, p. 7.
51 Jelinek, Estelle C. 'Introduction: Women's Autobiography and the Male Tradition'. In *Women's Autobiography: Essays in Criticism*, ed. Estelle C. Jelinek. Bloomington: Indiana University Press, 1980, p. 17 and 19.
52 Cadman Seelig, Sharon. *Autobiography and Gender in Early Modern Literature: Reading Women's Lives, 1600-1800*. Cambridge University Press, 2006, p. 6.
53 Nin, Anaïs. 'The Personal Life Deeply Lived'. In *The American Autobiography: A Collection of Critical Essays*, ed. Albert E. Stone. Englewood Cliffs, NJ: Prentice Hall, 1981 (A Spectrum Book: Twentieth Century Views), p. 157.
54 Kondrup, Johnny. *Levned og tolkninger*, p. 26.
55 Pascal, Roy. *Design and Truth in Autobiography*, p. 5.

assignment, especially in the case of early modern life writings, whose historical and cultural background often excludes the possibility of a clear demarcation between public and private life.[56] Paul Delany presented us with quite an elegant resolution to this problem by simply labelling early modern life writings overly focussed on external happenings, e.g. political affairs, as *res gestae*.[57] Difficulties in distinguishing between autobiography and memoirs presumably constitute one of the main reasons for the commonly negative perceptions of the autobiographical genre among scholars up until the second half of the last century. Since, particularly in the case of life writings, it is practically impossible to judge the book without judging its author first, memoirs have never been granted the status of literary writing, for most memoirs were simply not written by professional writers. Memoirs are usually written by public figures, like politicians. Once a person enters the domain of the broad public, with all its complex hierarchies and connections, the private life must appear comparably insignificant. And if it did not, that would only expose the author's vanity. Exceptions to this 'rule' are rare, yet not impossible. Pascal names Mahatma Gandhi as the most prominent example. His life narrative (English title: *The Story of My Experiments with Truth*, published 1925-1929) acquired the status of an autobiography given that his political activities were based on personal beliefs.[58] On the other hand, that is not to say that professional writers only produce high-quality autobiographies. They too can be over-involved with their public and work life. In addition, writers may seduce themselves into over-poeticising, thus losing track of the essential topic.[59]

As opposed to the memoir, the autobiographical novel is easily distinguishable from an actual autobiography – a brief look at the front cover should suffice. Emergence in the form of a fictive autobiography, a derivation of both autobiography and autobiographical novel, can occur as well. The fictive autobiography exhibits all the features of an autobiography while the autobiographical novel in a stylistic sense usually remains more novel than autobiography. Its only »deficit« is its exclusion from Lejeunes afore mentioned *pacte autobiographique*. Unlike autobiography, the autobiographical novel, especially in the form of the *Bildungsroman*, has enjoyed great popularity ever since its emergence. This »autobiographical archetype«[60] al-

---

56 Condren, Conal. 'Specifying the Subject in Early Modern Autobiography'. In *Early Modern Autobiography: Theories, Genres, Practices*, ed. Ronald Bedford et al. Ann Arbor, Michigan: University of Michigan Press, 2006, p. 37.
57 Delany, Paul. *British Autobiography in the Seventeenth Century*, p. 2.
58 Pascal, Roy. *Design and Truth in Autobiography*, p. 6.
59 Ibid., p. 133.
60 Stanley, Liz. *The Auto/biographical I: The Theory and Practice of Feminist Auto/biography*. Manchester and New York: Manchester University Press, 1995, p. 11.

lowed some of the greatest writers in history not only to integrate parts of their own biography, but also to portray the progress of the protagonist's character, thus coming to terms with their own past without revealing too much about themselves. Thus, for the writer of an autobiographical novel this type of life writing was a safe option. For most readers this compromise between novel and autobiography, which still allowed readers to look for traces of autobiography in fictional writings yet without expecting them to take the author's word at face value, may have also been a great deal more satisfying than dealing with an actual autobiography. That fiction does not automatically equal untruthfulness is a fact universally acknowledged at least half a century ago, for example by Philippe Lejeune, who called it *pacte fantasmatique*[61] ('phantasmatic pact'). Scholars and readers alike never seemed to be bothered by the presence of autobiography in fiction, quite the contrary. However, the presence of fiction in autobiography remained undesirable until the second half of the last century, and still it continues to affront many readers.

Finally, another genre related to autobiography, as readily identifiable by its name, is the common biography. There is no identity between author and narrator on one side, and protagonist on the other side.[62] Usually this departure from the autobiographical pact is overtly signalled by using a third-person narrative. Up until the 20th century, scholars continued to argue over whether to declare autobiography and biography as being distinctly different from each other, or significantly alike. The core of this discussion was to determine whether or not it should be necessary for research on autobiography to include biography as well, as suggested by Liz Stanley.[63] Depending on whether they would focus either on *bios* or *autos* in autobiography, scholars would, respectively, either dispute that the autobiographer's life was representative for the entire humankind (thus rendering autobiography just another type of biography), or that the autobiographer's life was unique in a 'rousseauesque' sense (consequently elevating autobiography from biography). However, there are also intermediate forms, such as the case of an autobiography written with the help of an associate author (usually a journalist or professional writer of another kind) which complicate the distinction between autobiography and biography, especially in terms of determining the true author or even the narrator.[64]

As will be demonstrated in the following chapter, autobiographical writings have a millennia-long tradition, although impartial research on life writings did not

---

61 Lejeune, Philippe. *Le Pacte Autobiographique*, p. 42.
62 Kondrup, Johnny. *Levned og tolkninger*, p. 22.
63 Stanley, Liz. *The Auto/biographical I*, p. 99. The opposite position is taken by Smith, Sidonie and Julia Watson. *Reading Autobiography*, p. 4.
64 Kondrup, Johnny. *Levned og tolkninger*, p. 22.

start before the second half of the 20th century. The main reason for this neglectful treatment of life writings by scholars and authors alike is perhaps a generally confused notion about their correct positioning in either the literary or the historical canon, or in other words, fiction or non-fiction.[65] As in the case of *Tendenzliteratur* or *littérature engageé* ('engaged literature'), scholars were very reluctant to grant autobiography a place in the literary canon due to its reduced degree of fictionality. This holds also true for the aesthetic aspect of life writings. Since the first (secular) autobiographies were hardly meant for publication, sincerity was deemed a virtue of higher rank than literary style. Furthermore, the authors of early modern autobiographies had to face a complete lack of written and acknowledged norms of autobiographical writing to follow (as opposed to the plentiful didactic poetry books which started to flourish in the times of Humanism).[66] Even at the beginning of the 20th century, when autobiography had already become a widely used form of literary expression for writers and non-writers alike, some would still deny autobiography any literary quality whatsoever. Presumably fully in line with this notion, Gertrude Stein would start her autobiography with a clear declaration of her contempt towards this genre: »Anyway autobiography is easy like it or not autobiography is easy for any one and so this is to be Everybody's Autobiography«.[67] To strengthen her view on this »easy« genre, she indeed called her autobiography *Everybody's Autobiography*. Paul de Man, in his now classical essay on autobiography from 1979, even surpassed Stein in her scepticism by challenging whether autobiography could or should be called a genre at all:

> By making autobiography into a genre, one elevates it above the literary status of mere reportage, chronicle, or memoir and gives it a place, albeit a modest one, among the canonical hierarchies of the major literary genres. This does not go without some embarrassment, since compared to tragedy, or epic, or lyric poetry, autobiography always looks slightly disreputable and self-indulgent in a way that may be symptomatic of its incompatibility with the monumental dignity of aesthetic values.[68]

---

65 Barrett J. Mandel was amongst the first to explicitly address and reject this »false dichotomy« (Mandel, Barrett J. 'Full of Life Now', p. 54).
66 Delany, Paul. *British Autobiography in the Seventeenth Century*, p. 173.
67 Stein, Gertrude. *Everybody's Autobiography*. New York: Cooper Square Publishers, Inc., 1971, p. 6.
68 De Man, Paul. 'Autobiography as De-facement', MLN 94/5 (Dec. 1979), p. 919. See also ibid., p. 921: »Autobiography, then, is not a genre or a mode, but a figure of reading or of understanding that occurs, to some degree, in all texts«.

Today, it has been decided to place autobiography in between fiction and non-fiction. For Johnny Kondrup autobiography is »et stykke sagprosa eller, som det tidligere hed, en faglitterær genre [...] et arbejdsområde for historievidenskaben«.[69] Simultaneously, Kondrup has to admit that historians would hardly use autobiography as a source of serious historical value, due to its bad reputation as far as objective commentatorship is concerned.[70] Furthermore, this all too rigorous dichotomy of fiction and non-fiction has led to bewildered notions about the true degree of fiction in 'fiction'. The term 'fiction', especially used in an autobiographical context, must not be confused with perceptions about authors of autobiography obscuring the truth by omitting certain events in their lives, or inventing others, in order to create a more flattering image of themselves. However, autobiographers are required to do more than merely presenting their readers with a list of anecdotes from their life; that would be the task of memoir writers. In order to write an autobiography, one ought to select significant episodes of one's life based on their supposed relevance for the ensuing development, and arrange them in a coherent narrative expressive enough for the reader to understand their meaning for the entity of the account. But is it the work of a poet or a psychologist to select and arrange work in such a way? Is the autobiographer a philosophically ambitious poet seeking for a greater wholeness in life and eventually confronting us with its higher meaning, a truth sugar-coated in fiction?[71] Or is the autobiographer an empirically trained psychologist in need of an explanation for the final outcome of this lifelong development of a personality? As Lejeune points out felicitously, the autobiographical act involves psychological issues such as memory and self-analysis.[72] Accordingly, what is widely referred to as the autobiography of the psychoanalyst par excellence, Sigmund Freud's *Die Medizin der Gegenwart in Selbstdarstellungen* ('Contemporary Medicine in Self-Portrayals', 1925), is in fact the story of psychoanalysis; a collection of patient biographies rather than an intimate account of childhood and private life of the analyst himself. The 19th and early 20th centuries' obsession with psychology and genius (and not least its interest in the role of environment and genetics for the development of the individual) sparked debates about whether autobiographies constituted a form of expression for the ingenious individual. Life writing, now being placed in

---

69 Kondrup, Johnny. *Levned og tolkninger*, p. 68.
70 Ibid.
71 See for example Adam Oehlenschläger in his preface to *Nordiske Digte*: »Kunstens Væsen er at sammentrænge, hvad i Livet findes spredt og adskilt« (Oehlenschläger, Adam. *Poetiske Skrifter 3: Nordiske Digte*, ed. H. Topsøe-Jensen. Copenhagen: Jørgensen & Co, 1928 (Danmarks Nationallitteratur), p. 27.
72 Lejeune, Philippe. *Le Pacte Autobiographique*, p. 7.

between fiction and non-fiction, was considered yet another way of expressing the unconscious and depicting the formation of a character.[73]

But where is autobiography's place today? Since autobiographies very often exhibit features of a novel, they have been granted the status of fictional writing. Yet on the other hand, historical biographies, especially popular editions, require the same kind of selecting and arranging mentioned above. This sometimes renders a reduced degree of subjectivity which is the only attribute of certain kinds of historical or non-fictional writing. Furthermore, both fictional and non-fictional writings can exhibit the stylistic features of fictional writing. However, writings are generally assigned to either the fictional, or the non-fictional side, based upon the extent to which they are deemed to remain faithful to 'the truth'. This raises the anything but recent question regarding the positioning of autobiography on either the historical and psychological, or literary side, as a problem resulting from a presence of fiction in life narratives. As Paul John Eakin contends, »autobiographical truth is not a fixed but an evolving content in an intricate process of self-discovery and self-creation«.[74] An identity between author, narrator and protagonist may well exist, but for long parts of the narrative author and protagonist are not one and the same person. The author remains the same, but the protagonist starts as a child and has to go through adolescence with all its obstacles, until finally reaching the same state of consciousness as the author.[75] Memory, too, is neither fixed nor entirely objective. We remember selectively, often linking events and people based on emotions.[76] Another often over-looked feature of autobiography usually ascribed to fiction is the frequent incorporation of rhetorical acts, e.g. in order to justify one's actions.[77] The reasons why autobiography never portrays life itself, but merely one personal notion of it, are plentiful. However, they all constitute what is called »autobiographical truth« (see above): »det er mindre væsentligt, hvad en autobiografi fortæller, end hvor vidt det fortalte er udtryk for de samlede energier i den fortællendes personlighed«.[78]

---

73 Marcus, Laura. *Auto/biographical Discourses: Theory, Criticism, Practice.* Manchester University Press, 1994, p. 56 and 62.
74 Eakin, Paul John. *Fictions in Autobiography: Studies in the Art of Self-invention.* Princeton University Press, 1985, p. 3.
75 On the diverse 'I's' in autobiography, see Smith, Sidonie and Julia Watson. *Reading Autobiography,* p. 58.
76 Stanley, Liz. *The Auto/biographical I,* p. 62.
77 Smith, Sidonie and Julia Watson. *Reading Autobiography,* p. 10. Thomas Seiler provides one example by referring to the frequent mention of Robin Hood as noble bandit in 18th-century prison life writings, clearly an attempt to justify one's misdeeds (Seiler, Thomas. *Im Leben verschollen: Zur Rekontextualisierung skandinavischer Gefängnis- und Holocaustliteratur.* Heidelberg: Winter, 2006 (Skandinavische Arbeiten 21), p. 19).
78 Kondrup, Johnny. *Levned og tolkninger,* p. 26.

Ever since autobiographical writings were acknowledged as literature (about half a century ago) the authors of those life writings forfeited a bit of their formerly unquestioned credibility. This revalidation turned out to be a rather positive one from the scholarly point of view.[79] However, for readers of autobiography this shift was not an easy one to accept. From the reader's point of view, an autobiographical author taking liberties with the truth was violating Lejeune's *pacte référentiel*,[80] i.e. the referential pact, which completes Lejeune's trinity of pacts: in Lejeune's view, biographical and autobiogaphical texts refer (or claim to refer) to an external reality, much like scientific and historical writings.

Breaching such a pact must inevitably leave the reader feeling betrayed. One example is the discovery and disclosure of Leonora Christina's *Jammers Minde*. Ever since her imprisonment in the Blue Tower in Copenhagen in 1663, Leonora Christina has been a constant object of public debate. She had her enemies, no doubt. With her husband Corfitz Ulfeldt leading the Swedish armies towards victory against his homeland in the war of 1657, she could no longer expect to be commonly perceived as the *grande dame* the Danish royal court used to take so much pride in. And yet her devotion to father and husband in combination with her fame of being an extraordinarily intelligent and educated woman helped to sustain sympathies and respect for Leonora Christina. Contemporary writers (see Chapter 3.1.), but also Danish writers of the ensuing centuries, e.g. Hans Christian Andersen (see Chapters 2.2.1. and 2.2.3.) and Georg Brandes (see Chapter 1.2.1.), expressed strong commiseration in their writings. Considering this point of departure, there is no wonder at the general excitement that surrounded the discovery of Leonora Christina's manuscript *Jammers Minde* in 1868 in Vienna and its subsequent publication in 1869 in Copenhagen.[81] Not only did Sophus Birket Smith publish Leonora

---

79 Cf. Pascal, Roy. *Design and Truth in Autobiography*, p. 61.
80 Lejeune, Philippe. *Le Pacte Autobiographique*, p. 36.
81 When Corfitz Ulfeldt was sentenced to death in 1663, his offspring had to leave the country. After Leonora Christina's death in 1698, the manuscript of *Jammers Minde* remained within Leo Ulfeldt's – one of Leonora Christina's sons, who had emigrated to Austria – family. The descendants of Leo Ulfeldt were thus aware of the existence of Leonora Christina's Danish memoirs, but to the rest of the world, particularly to Danish philologists, the 'discovery' of the manuscript in 1868 was a pleasant surprise. When the manuscript was discovered, it belonged to Leo Ulfeldt's Austrian descendant Count Johann Nepomuk Waldstein-Wartenberg. In 1868, he ordered an examination of the manuscript's authenticity, which was done in Copenhagen. Once the manuscript's authenticity was attested, plans for a publication of the text quickly evolved. Eventually, Sophus Birket Smith, back then a rather inexperienced employee of the Copenhagen University Library, was entrusted with editing this precious material. To Birket Smith's devotional work we owe thus, amongst other things, the first publication of Leonora Christina's magnum opus *Jammers Minde* in 1869. For comprehensive information on Leonora Christina's Austrian descendants and the odyssey of *Jammers Minde*, see Lindegård Hjorth, Poul. '*Jammers Minde*'s udgivelseshistorie'. In Leonora Christina. *Jammers Minde: Diplomatarisk udgave ved Poul Lindegård Hjorth og Marita Akhøj Nielsen under medvirkning af Ingelise Nielsen*, ed. Det Danske Sprog- og Litteraturselskab. Copenhagen: Reitzel, 1998, pp. xiii-xvi.

Christina's autobiography, he also went through the trouble of comparing her own accounts with historical documents and letters in order to compose a complete and very detailed life story. However, Birket Smith seems to have been more interested in Leonora Christina's biography than in her autobiography. He did not discern the literary and, in particular, autobiographical patterns reproduced in *Jammers Minde* and, in line with his century, idealised her life and persona. Even when he could not help but admit that at times she had lied during her countless enquiries, he romanticised this fact by emphasising that she did it for her beloved spouse,[82] instead of highlighting the implications of these lies for the creation of Leonora Christina's life narrative. Clearly, he took *Jammers Minde* for a historical document rather than the product of a writer. Many followed Birket Smith's verdict, but his statements did not remain without dissenting votes for long. In 1888, Julius Lange published his famous article 'Contra Leonora Christina'.[83] Julius Lange contends that although Leonora Christina is not solely to blame for her inaccurate rendering of the truth since without further evidence one must assume that she did it in faithful service to her husband, she is far from being the innocent martyr depicted by Sophus Birket Smith. Back then, scholars had already caught a glimpse of autobiographical truth, but the following discussions on Leonora Christina's challenged innocence demonstrate that the time for critical literary research on *Jammers Minde* had not come yet. One could simply not combine the historical Leonora Christina and the author of *Jammers Minde*. As long as autobiography was still considered to be nothing but historical narrating, it could not possibly be literature and therefore, its author could not possibly be granted the title of an actual writer. So if autobiography was not considered to be literature and consequently not fictional at all, any departure from the truth had to be perceived as a mere lie. Therefore, initial research on *Jammers Minde* rarely concerned the autobiography itself, but the life of the traitor's wife.

1.1.2. A Very Brief History of Autobiography

Time and again, scholars have stressed the West as the place of origin for autobiography, with reference to Augustine's *Confessiones* as the first autobiography and to Heraclitus as »the first theoretical autobiographer«.[84] However, dissentient votes, as taken by Sidonie Smith and Julia Watson,[85] have challenged the formerly

---

82 Birket Smith, Sophus. *Leonora Christina Grevinde Ulfeldts Historie 2*, p. 162.
83 Lange, Julius. 'Contra Leonora Christina', Tilskueren 5 (1888), pp. 721-739.
84 Olney, James. *Metaphors of Self: The Meaning of Autobiography*. Princeton University Press, 1972, p. 4.
85 Smith, Sidonie and Julia Watson. *Reading Autobiography*, p. 84.

undisputed conviction of the West as the origin of the self-reflective genre. French philosopher Georges Gusdorf furthermore contends that the first step toward the emergence of autobiography was human historical awareness (i.e. a consciousness of the difference between now and then, or a similar understanding of the principle of development).[86] According to Paul Delany, Europe did not fully reach this historical awareness until the Renaissance. There were autobiographical products to be found in ancient and medieval times, but to the contemporaries of these life writings the past was a mythological concept rather than a different period of time to their own. Thus, autobiographical writings were scarce prior to the Renaissance, when interest in the past increased.[87]

However, the first autobiography of unchallenged importance came well before this period through Augustine's *Confessiones* from the end of the 4th century. Augustine's conversion to Christianity serves as the all-dominant leitmotif and the reason behind all of his actions. From the newly converted author's point of view, the protagonist's life before conversion cannot be anything but sinful. Augustine understands that the autobiographer's task is not to randomly present readers with details of one's life, but to focus on those events that seemed to have a significant meaning for the author's later life or character. Therefore, Augustine must present all events as having significance, either in being representative of his former corrupt character, or of his redemption. His rigorous and judgemental separation of life before and after the conversion is rooted in the need for justification of the conversion itself. Life after conversion must necessarily be a better one, otherwise the conversion itself lacks a well-founded motivation. Accordingly, life before conversion must have been entirely misled, in order to justify the direct intervention of God. Furthermore, it is God's call that justifies the conversion and thus the conversion narrative; for only the accounts of the few chosen ones can be deemed worthy of written fixation.[88]

Other than Augustine's *Confessiones*, there are hardly any autobiographies before the Middle Ages, in a modern sense of the meaning.[89] Along with the socio-political changes that occurred during the Middle Ages came along a changed perception of the individual and its relation to society. The advent of self-managed cities

---

86 Gusdorf, Georges. 'Conditions and Limits of Autobiography'. In *Autobiography: Essays Theoretical and Critical*, ed. James Olney. Princeton University Press, 1980, pp. 28-48.
87 Delany, Paul. *British Autobiography in the Seventeenth Century*, p. 8.
88 Cf. Sturrock, John. *The Language of Autobiography: Studies in the First Person Singular*. Cambridge University Press, 1993, pp. 20-48. On conversion narratives, see Hodgkin, Katharine. *Madness in Seventeenth-Century Autobiography*. Basingstoke: Palgrave Macmillan, 2007 (Early Modern History: Society and Culture), pp. 19-26.
89 Delany, Paul. *British Autobiography in the Seventeenth Century*, p. 111.

in Europe from the 13th century onwards gave rise to a new notion of the extent of the community, comprised of the individual. This new independency abetted a local awareness, manifesting itself in countless city chronicles, flourishing from the 13th century onwards.[90] In addition, the introduction of private studies in domestic houses gave a new notion to the concepts of and correlation between privacy and authenticity.[91] Medieval autobiographies occurred almost exclusively in the form of conversion narratives or spiritual autobiographies. Only few exceptions are known to have been preserved, such as Peter Abelard's autobiography *Historia calamitatum mearum* (English title: *The Story of My Misfortunes*). The modern concept of individuality appears to have been unknown to pre-Renaissance times. Thus, the physical individual could only tell their story through a higher force, whether it be God or the Holy Church as the second-highest authority. The individual was not perceived to be developing by themselves, as if in a social and mystical vacuum, but rather as being directed by and together with the entirety of humankind.[92]

According to Georges Gusdorf[93] the turn came in 1507, when Venetian clear glass mirrors displaced their darker, more pigmented predecessors, which merely reflected shades. This unprecedented opportunity to see and inspect one's own face is assumed to have given rise to a modern kind of self-consciousness and, consequently, to the proliferation of autobiography.[94] This view, plausible though in its essence, has been challenged by Debora Shuger. For example, Shuger contends that the man in the street would have used this in fact inexpensive innovation to take a closer look at his own face (mostly for grooming reasons). However, early modern literature suggests that mirrors were used in a great deal of less practical ways. Literary mirrors were to be understood in a metaphorical way, either depicting an exemplary positive or negative image of humanity,[95] and even physical mirrors were

---

90 Misch, Georg. *Geschichte der Autobiographie 4/2: Von der Renaissance bis zu den autobiographischen Hauptwerken des 18. und 19. Jahrhunderts*. Bern: Francke, 1969, p. 583.
91 Goodall, Peter. 'The Author in the Study: Self-Representation as Reader & Writer in the Medieval and Early Modern Periods'. In *Early Modern Autobiography: Theories, Genres, Practices*, ed. Ronald Bedford et al. Ann Arbor, Michigan: University of Michigan Press, 2006, p. 104.
92 Kondrup, Johnny. *Levned og tolkninger*, p. 44.
93 Gusdorf, Georges. 'Conditions and Limits of Autobiography', p. 32.
94 Cf. Martina Wagner-Egelhaaf, who refers to the early modern times as the »Erfindung des Individuums« ('invention of the individual'). See Wagner-Edelhaaf, Martina. *Autobiographie*. Stuttgart and Weimar: Verlag J. B. Metzler, 2000 (Sammlung Metzler 323). However, Wagner-Edelhaaf advises against premature views of the early modern times as having born an understanding of 'subject' or 'individual' as comparable to the modern times (see, e.g. ibid. p. 128f.).
95 Shuger, Debora. 'The »I« of the Beholder: Renaissance Mirrors and the Reflexive Mind'. In *Renaissance Culture and the Everyday*, ed. Patricia Fumerton and Simon Hunt. Philadelphia: University of Pennsylvania Press, 1999 (New Cultural Studies), p. 22.

»instruments of correction«,⁹⁶ rather than reflection. The literary use of mirrors with the purpose of reflecting an ideal to aspire to was already known from medieval texts such as the so-called King's mirrors, the most famous Northern European example of which is likely *Konungs skuggsjá* from the 13th century. Also, the image of the devil or devil-like figure reflected in the mirror, warning the beholder against vanity, was not entirely new to the Renaissance. Shuger concludes that »the preponderance of evidence suggests that the Renaissance self lacks reflexivity, self-consciousness, and individuation, and hence differs fundamentally from what we usually think of as the modern self«.⁹⁷ This true and yet somewhat hasty judgement of early modern personality seems to regard premodern self in purely quantitative terms, when the comparison to modern reflexivity should comprehend qualitative differences as well: »It is necessary, therefore, that we read these texts in ways that are cognizant of their times, understanding that formality of style does not necessarily mean impersonality, and, moreover, that impersonality does not mean lack of personhood«.⁹⁸

Another historical novelty favouring the advent of autobiography was the rise of the new class of the merchants and their travel diaries. There have certainly been merchants travelling across Europe long before Renaissance times, however, the 15th and 16th century brought a new need for careful accounting and documentation of travel expenses.⁹⁹ Along with the need for keeping record of events and expenses came the natural desire for documenting cultural differences, which required a certain amount of self-reflection. Thus, the travel report constitutes a type of mother-genre to modern autobiography. The novel conditions of this age of the rising middle class, especially the merchant class, brought about other documentary writings, which, as Adam Smyth contends, formed the basis for later attempts at actual autobiographical writing. Annotated almanacs, financial accounts, commonplace books and parish registers were all means of record keeping fairly typical of the early modern West. Moreover, all provided a network of written life documentation whereby »Early Modern autobiographical writing can […] best be read through this conception of a dense network of life-writing texts, where notes were moved from text to text«.¹⁰⁰

---

96 Kelly, Philippa. 'Dialogues of Self Reflection: Early Modern Mirrors'. In *Early Modern Autobiography: Theories, Genres, Practices*, ed. Ronald Bedford et al. Ann Arbor, Michigan: University of Michigan Press, 2006, p. 68.
97 Shuger, Debora. 'The »I« of the Beholder', p. 35.
98 Bedford, Ronald et al. 'Introduction'. In *Early Modern Autobiography: Theories, Genres, Practices*, ed. Ronald Bedford et al. Ann Arbor, Michigan: University of Michigan Press, 2006, p. 4.
99 Misch, Georg. *Geschichte der Autobiographie 4/2*, p. 584.
100 Smyth, Adam. *Autobiography in Early Modern England*, p. 2.

The humanistic movement and the increasing literacy in the aftermath of the invention of printing played another critical role in the emergence of the autobiographical genres in Europe. Not only did this novel level of general education lend the newly emerged group of literates a stronger sensation of self-determination, but also the augmented audience helped to spread and establish autobiography as an independent genre.[101] Especially to the history of women's autobiography, the early modern age was a crucial period. Since they usually had received good education, more and more upper-class women began to write down their life narratives – often incorporated in their husband's biographies – during the 16th and 17th centuries. By the mid-17th century, around ten percent of the hitherto published autobiographies had been written by women.[102]

Even though autobiographical concepts of self, individuality and self-consciousness do not apply to premodern and early modern times, the 16th century was indeed the age when autobiography was finally established as a genre, although people were not aware of it. Humanism triggered an increased historical consciousness and interest in the individual. Accordingly, most of the great Renaissance scholars composed autobiographies, e.g. Hieronymus Cardanus and Benvenuto Cellini. Jørgen Sejersted refers to the early modern times, especially the 17th century, as the era that gave birth to the modern individual, »en tid da natur og naturlighet fremdeles var truende og kultur, dannelse og sosialisering anerkjent som de viktigste bestanddelene i formingen av et sivilisert jeg«.[103] The early modern times were also the era during which autobiography was to be found for the first time in Scandinavia. As with the rest of the continent, one could find pre-stages of the autobiographical genre in Scandinavia as early as in the Middle Ages. In a specific Scandinavian context, Saint Birgitta's *Revelationes* from the 14th century constitute an essential prototype to the ensuing body of spiritual autobiographies, especially of women writers.[104] Yet it was not until 1650, that autobiography had its definite breakthrough in the North,[105] with Agneta Horn's *Beskrivning över min vandringstid* (1657) being one of the first autobiographies to enter Scandinavia's literary ca-

---

101 Hodgkin, Katharine. *Madness in Seventeenth-Century Autobiography*, p. 22.
102 Jelinek, Estelle C. *The Tradition of Women's Autobiography: From Antiquity to the Present*. Boston, Mass.: Twayne, 1986, p. 23.
103 Sejersted, Jørgen. '»Naar jeg mig fra Top til Fod Betragter«. Barokk Framstilling af Selvet', Edda 97 (1997), p. 243.
104 Mitchell, Stephen A. 'Women's Autobiographical Literature in the Swedish Baroque'. In *Skandinavische Literaturen der frühen Neuzeit*, ed. Jürg Glauser. Tübingen: Francke, 2002 (Beiträge zur nordischen Philologie 32), p. 271: »Despite the fact that such writing, however deeply personal it may be, fails to encompass in a technical sense what has come to be recognized as the autobiographer's art, Birgitta's revelations nevertheless stand as the most intensely interior writing of the Swedish Middle Ages«.
105 Kondrup, Johnny: *Levned og tolkninger*, p. 106.

non. The plentiful Scandinavian life writings by women writers of the early modern times such as Queen Christina of Sweden, Christina Regina von Birchenbaum and Leonora Christina attest to a rapidly growing tradition of female autobiographers from the 17th century onwards. Following previous statements on this account, Stephen A. Mitchell contends that »religious reflection was a socially sanctioned arena where women writers might attain legitimacy«,[106] thus rendering spiritual, or semi-spiritual, autobiographies a fit domain for women to express themselves in an early modern society. Hence, questions of legitimacy and authority posed no serious problem to a female writer of (semi-)spiritual autobiography in the early modern times. In subsequent centuries, when spiritual autobiographies had gone out of fashion, female autobiographers had to conceive of other ways to justify their attempts at personal writing. As far as Leonora Christina is concerned, she surely had no reason to struggle with a justification for writing her life account. She was a public figure who could count on her life story meeting great public interest. This alone gave her reason enough to write not only one, but two autobiographies. Beyond that, there are reasons to consider *Jammers Minde* a spiritual, or at least semi-spiritual, autobiography, which will now be turned to.

17th-century autobiography in general can be organised into two groups: spiritual and secular. Is *Jammers Minde* to be classified as a spiritual autobiography? The first part of *Jammers Minde* (pp. 1*–78/92)[107] – written in 1674 and partially continued and rewritten in Maribo – certainly exhibits traits of the spiritual autobiography or conversion narrative, namely the period of doubt and despair just before the moment of acceptance and trust in God's mysterious ways (*Jammers Minde*, pp. 77-83). According to Katherine Hodgkin, a profound discrepancy between the old and the new self is imperative to the spiritual autobiography, since it is defined by transformation.[108] In the case of the first part of Leonora Christina's narrative, there *is* a point of transformation, causing her to change her attitude towards her miserable position. And yet *Jammers Minde* taken as *one* text is no conversion narrative as provided by Augustine, since Leonora Christina does not regret any of her previous actions (except her recent mistrust in God's greater will) and since issues of faith do not pose a central topic in the rest of the narrative. Nor does she seem to find herself changed in a substantial way. On the contrary, Leonora Christina prides herself in the steadiness of her character. She might have been forced to change her domicile, but she is still the daughter of the great King Christian IV. She never stumps when

---

106 Mitchell, Stephen A. 'Women's Autobiographical Literature in the Swedish Baroque', p. 270.
107 The manuscript essentially consists of three parts, written in three different periods spanning over more than two decades. The genesis of the manuscript will be discussed in further detail in Chapter 1.2.
108 Hodgkin, Katharine. *Madness in Seventeenth-Century Autobiography*, p. 20.

being reminded of her social degradation, as will be discussed further below. In addition, a 'checklist' of deceased enemies (the so-called *dødsliste*) loosely connected to Leonora Christina's prison narrative[109] exposes her account to be rather an act of vindication than a confession.

Another spiritual feature of the otherwise very secular autobiography of Leonora Christina is its near-eradication of the author's past. Unlike in her French autobiography, there is hardly any mention of her life before prison. Especially conspicuous is the scarce mention of husband and children. Spiritual autobiographies often annihilate the life before conversion by demonising it; Leonora Christina annihilates her previous life quite literally. Also, spouses and children, the »details of everyday life«,[110] usually find no mention in spiritual autobiographies, as is already known from Augustine. Nevertheless, *Jammers Minde* remains a very secular autobiography, even considering its more spiritual first part.[111] Scant mention of family members is very common to Baroque autobiographies. A characterisation of Leonora Christina's children – some of whom died during their mother's imprisonment – might have struck her contemporary readers to be as interesting as a description of her clothes (or perhaps even less so). Much more intriguing, on the other hand, is her daily life in prison, an experience more unique than marriage or giving birth. Modern readers might be taken aback by the scarce mention of her children, since according to scholars like Estelle C. Jelinek,[112] female autobiographers demonstrate a stronger focus on family than most male writers of autobiography. But Leonora Christina was not only a woman, she had also enjoyed an exceptional education which allowed her to follow certain literary patterns known from spiritual autobiographies. The most common reading in Baroque times was indeed of a spiritual nature. Therefore, one must assume a basic degree of (spiritual) intertextuality in

---

109 The pages containing a list of Leonora Christina's deceased enemies, i.e. *dødslisten*, as it is now commonly referred to (see for example Wamberg, Bodil. 'Det Ydre og det Indre Fangenskab'. In *Gulnares Hus: En Gave til Hendes Majestæt Dronning Margrethe den Anden på Fødselsdagen, den 16. April 1990*, ed. Annelise Bistrup et al. Copenhagen: Samleren, 1990, p. 78), as well as the names of a few people whose kindness Leonora Christina wished to commemorate, i.e. *Jammers Minde*, pp. 259-266, were stitched together with the same thread used for the core manuscript, but never connected to it. Since Leonora Christina left no indications as to where to place these separate pages, they are positioned towards the end of the *Jammers Minde*-edition used in the present study, but inserted in between *Fortalen Til mine Børn* and the main account in other editions, for example in *Jammers Minde og andre selvbiografiske Skildringer* published by Johannes Brøndum-Nielsen and Carl Olaf Bøggild-Andersen in 1949.
110 Hodgkin, Katharine. *Madness in Seventeenth-Century Autobiography*, p. 25.
111 In fact, Leonora Christina shows just as much interest in outward events as in her own spiritual condition. Finn Stein Larsen called Leonora Christina's style in *Jammers Minde* impressionistic, due to her very secular observations of the everyday-life in the Blue Tower. See Larsen, Finn Stein. 'En impressionist fra baroktiden? En tekstlæsning i Leonora Christinas Jammersminde', Kritik 25 (1973), pp. 17-33.
112 Jelinek, Estelle C. 'Introduction: Women's Autobiography and the Male Tradition', p. 7.

Jammers Minde. Furthermore, it would be an anachronism to characterise *Jammers Minde* as spiritual based on its frequent references to the Bible and similar readings. That would be as accurate as to characterise every person from the 21st century capable of writing a book as being educated. To the typical 17th-century noblewoman profound knowledge of clerical writings was imperative rather than a sign of devoutness above the average.

Meanwhile in France, the formerly spiritual autobiography took on the form of a novel reflecting courtly society and the development of its single members. This new form of autobiography would later contribute to the evolution of the modern novel.[113] Equally popular was a special kind of memoirs recounting amorous adventures, certainly culminating in Giacomo Casanova's *Histoire de ma vie* about a century later. The French seemed to have an exceptional lust for scandal, especially when it involved prominent people. Thus, it comes as no surprise that France should remain the birthplace of the *mémoires*.

The 18th century was a time of increased interest in biography, including literary biography.[114] To be sure, biographies of politicians and/or war heroes (»det menneske, som man kunne kalde det heroiske«[115]) enjoyed great popularity ever since antiquity. However, as soon as the European middle class was fully established, thus leaving the old feudal system behind, biographical interest switched to the less publically present »heroes« and their accomplishments, e.g. writers, philosophers and scientists.[116] Public focus began resting on the personal life and thoughts of the individual, the so-called 'man of ideas'. After Augustine's *Confessiones*, Jean-Jacques Rousseau's autobiography from 1782, likewise titled *Les Confessions*, is the next masterpiece in the canon of great autobiographies. The reason for Rousseau to write down his life story is not novel at all, as he is defending himself against a criminative public. Yet his defensive approach was new as a definite renunciation of the formerly imperative conventions of the spiritual autobiography: »Si je ne vaux pas mieux, au moins je suis autre«[117] – he might not be the best of men, but he is unique and entirely himself. Rousseau's apologia is not built on the claim of being misunderstood or of being wrongly accused. Instead, his singularity constitutes the basis for his defense. After reading parts of his autobiography to a selected audience, Rousseau met nothing but silence. His confessions were too

---

113 Misch, Georg. *Geschichte der Autobiographie 4/2*, p. 739.
114 On the first biographical texts of Leonora Christina, written in the 18th century, see Chapter 3.1.
115 Kondrup, Johnny: *Livsværker: Studier i dansk litterær biografi*. Valby: Amadeus, 1986, p. 34.
116 Ibid.
117 Rousseau, Jean-Jacques: *Oeuvres completes 1: Les Confessions. Autres texts autobiographiques*, ed. Bernard Gagnebin and Marcel Raymond. Paris: Gallimard, 1959 (Bibliothèque de la Pléiade 11), p. 5.

candid for his delicate auditors, and even some scholars of later centuries took offence in some of Rousseau's character traits.[118] However, no scholar would appeal against the literary, historical and psychological importance of Rousseau's product, the *Confessions*. Modern autobiography starts officially with Rousseau's conscious and proud individualism. In addition to his unprecedented confidence, Rousseau's focus on childhood would come to influence the following generations of autobiography. Rousseau's ardour of the uncorrupted years in life declared childhood the privileged age of the ensuing 19th century.[119]

Along with an increased interest in life narratives came the first use of the term *autobiography*.[120] Prior to this point, alternative denominations such as *Vita* or simply *memoirs* had been in use. Shortly afterwards, Johann Wolfgang von Goethe's *Dichtung und Wahrheit* (1811-1831) heralded a new perception of the relationship between truth und fiction in autobiography, thus paving the way for a modern concept of autobiographical truth:

> Hvad Goethe mente med sandhed, var netop ikke livets enkelte fakta, men den udviklingslov, som han øjnede bagved, - ikke overfladen, men »das eigentlich Grundwahre«, som han også kaldte det. Det mest interessante er imidlertid, at dette begreb ikke skal forstås som modsætning til titlens første, »Dichtung«, men som konsekvens eller resultat. Sandheden blotlægges først, idet den huskede virkeligheds stof gennemlyses af en fortolkende, imaginativ evne.[121]

The fifty years that separated Rousseau's *Confessions* (1782) from the last volume of Goethe's *Dichtung und Wahrheit* (1811-1831) are assumed to have polished autobiography and gave it its final, modern appearance. Roy Pascal contends that these years laid the foundation for what today is called autobiography, while the following centuries offered »little more than modifications«.[122] It might strike many a reader familiar with the history of autobiography as utterly curious that Goethe's *Dichtung und Wahrheit* should have come to constitute a milestone in the history of

---

118 Wethered, Herbert Newton. *The Curious Art of Autobiography: From Benvenuto Cellini to Rudyard Kipling*. London: Johnson, 1946, p. 68.
119 Accordingly, Patricia Meyer Spacks declared full maturity the privileged age of the 18th century, and adolescence that of the 20th; see Meyer Spacks, Patricia. 'Stages of Self: Notes on Autobiography and the Life Cycle'. In *The American Autobiography: A Collection of Critical Essays*, ed. Albert E. Stone. Englewood Cliffs, NJ: Prentice Hall, 1981 (A Spectrum Book: Twentieth Century Views), p. 45.
120 Laura Marcus mentions the review of Isaac d'Israeli's *Miscellanies* (1796) as the »birthplace« of the term autobiography. See Marcus, Laura. *Auto/biographical Discourses*, p. 12.
121 Kondrup, Johnny: *Levned og tolkninger*, p. 69.
122 Pascal, Roy. *Design and Truth in Autobiography*, p. 50.

autobiography, considering that it is not a typical representative of this genre. And yet, Goethe seemed to have understood the very essence of autobiography and its proper place in the wide range of fictional and non-fictional writings. In the course of one of his many conversations with Johann Peter Eckermann, Goethe stated about his autobiography that the 'facts' of his life could only be considered valid not in terms of being factually true, but insofar they served to confirm a higher truth.[123]

Being almost two centuries old, Goethe's statement about the essence of autobiography and life itself seems to conform only partially to current notions about the justifiability of publishing one's own life story. Life narratives keep flooding the book market, all on the grounds of being either unique or at least exemplary. From abused women and struggling minorities to ordinary workers,[124] all of these stories are now easily available. Some of these lives may not appear especially significant, but they all do tell life 'as it is'.

With the Industrial Revolution and its implicated end of aristocratic patronage came along a new life perspective for writers and artists. Now, self-sufficiency was not only an opportunity, it was an imperative of the new age. With everybody having the (theoretical) option of making a living out of writing alone, and a constantly growing readership due to improved education levels, the competition in the book market grew ever stiffer. For the 19th-century romantic autobiographer it must have been a wise choice to take »Rousseauian radical individualism«[125] to heart, for now singularity was a bestselling trademark. One of the most outstanding autobiographies from this century was without a doubt William Wordsworth's celebration of the creative spirit: his autobiographical poem *The Prelude; or, Growth of a Poet's Mind* from 1850. However, the interest in the individual and its development was not limited to the purely autobiographical genre. The 19th century was also the blooming age of the autobiographical novel and accordingly, the Bildungsroman. A classic among English fictional literature, Charlotte Brontë's *Jane Eyre* (1847), although published under the pen name »Currer Bell«, even bears the subtitle *An Autobiography*.

---

123 Eckermann, Johann Peter. *Gespräche mit Goethe in den letzten Jahren seines Lebens*, ed. Otto Schönberger. Stuttgart: Reclam: 1998 (Reihe Reclam), p. 509.
124 On specific currents in current autobiographical writings, see Stanley, Liz. *The Auto/biographical I*, p. 12.
125 Smith, Sidonie and Julia Watson. *Reading Autobiography*, p. 99.

In the late 20th and 21st century, autobiography and memoirs took on a popularity of pandemic extent, especially in the Anglo-American space.[126] Sidonie Smith and Julia Watson ascribe this to the historically conditioned ideal of the »self-made individual«.[127] The 1990's, on the other hand, demonstrated a growing interest in trauma memoirs.[128] After hundreds of years of modern autobiography, success stories of more or less famous authors were no longer deemed enthralling enough to call for broad public interest. The reading public wanted to hear the hitherto untold stories of ordinary people they might be able to identify with or indeed read a story so exceptional it would even shock the jaded turn-of-the-millennium reader.

As the 'rules' for content are blurred, so are the conventions regarding the titling of autobiography. Modern autobiography tends to ignore Lejeune's autobiographical pact for the sake of more playful titles. Two examples for a creative handling of modern autobiography titles include the autobiographies of Gertrude Stein: *The Autobiography of Alice B. Toklas* (published in 1933 without an author's name on the title page and in fact being the biography of Stein's partner Alice B. Toklas written in the first person by Stein) and *Everybody's Autobiography* (1937). This trend and the naturally imprecise line between autobiography and novel have caused some researchers, such as Annegret Heitmann,[129] to surrender on their search for the 'absolute' autobiography. After centuries of writing and decades of research on autobiography, there are still few established definitions of typically autobiographical features.

1.1.3. Classic and Current Theories on Autobiography
Fiction in Autobiography
Johnny Kondrup is one of the most prolific researchers of Scandinavian auto/biography. His academic contribution lies, amongst other areas, in thoroughly pre-

---

126 This concerns not only readers of autobiography, but also literary scholars interested in the genre. In 1980, James Olney opened his anthology *Autobiography: Essays Theoretical and Critical* with an essay on 'Autobiography and the Cultural Moment', which ascribes scholarship's sudden interest in autobiography to the high potential in terms of self-reflection inherent to this genre. While scholars before and after Olney showed themselves delighted by Rousseau's claim of absolute individuality, Olney stresses autobiography's potential representativeness of common human experience (Olney, James. 'Autobiography and the Cultural Moment: A Thematic, Historical, and Bibliographical Introduction'. In *Autobiography: Essays Theoretical and Critical*, ed. James Olney. Princeton University Press, 1980, p. 13). As autobiography combines features of historical documents and fictional writing, it can very well serve similar purposes: to document human history and open a window to the human's thoughts on watching the course of history.

127 Smith, Sidonie and Julia Watson. *Reading Autobiography*, p. 109.

128 On this matter, see Gilmore, Leigh. 'Limit-cases: Trauma, Self-representation, and the Jurisdictions of Identity'. In *Autobiography: Critical Concepts in Literary and Cultural Studies*. Volume IV, ed. Trev Lynn Broughton. London: Routledge, 2007, pp. 229-240.

129 Cf. Heitmann, Annegret. *Selbst schreiben*, p. 57.

senting the development of autobiography and biography in Scandinavia, therewith serving as a basis for the ensuing research on Scandinavian autobiography, as conducted by scholars such as Eva Hættner Aurelius. However, research on autobiography is by no means a Scandinavian domain. Americans seem to be the most eager readers of autobiography – for pleasure as well as for academic purposes. Hardly any extensive scholarly work on autobiography would thus be complete without a mention of names such as Roy Pascal or Estelle C. Jelinek.

After the German historian Georg Misch, who published the first detailed history of autobiography, i.e. his unfinished multi-volume work *Geschichte der Autobiographie* in which he challenge the suppositional absence of fiction in autobiography,[130] Roy Pascal was the next scholar to present an extensive history of autobiography, including theoretical groundwork and minute analyses of the most exceptional representatives of this genre. Similar to his predecessor, Pascal emphasises that autobiography always contains fiction. However, his approach of advocating the use of fiction in autobiography is slightly different: by contrasting autobiography to its neighbouring genres (see Chapter 1.1.1.), Pascal marks the difference between the actual event and the experience of that event. The depiction of events in diaries and letters are marked by the recent impressions of the writer, whereas many autobiographers look back at the same events with very different feelings. Events form pieces for the puzzle that constitutes life, and documents such as letters and diaries help the autobiographer to put the pieces in a suitable order and place. Yet not all puzzles are complete; the autobiographer can hardly remember or recreate his entire life. In this instance, fiction comes into play, as it helps to fill in the gap left by the missing pieces. In Pascal's view, autobiography is thus an attempt to find meaning and magnitude in life.[131] In most cases, this meaning is not inherent to the external events, but rather implanted by the author in an effort to select those events in life that had an effect on the later life of the autobiographer. In exposing this process of self-invention, Pascal lent a higher reason to the use of fiction in autobiography and, hence, made it acceptable.

Marc Eli Blanchard adopted and continued Pascal's notion of fiction in autobiography as a means to create a coherent picture of the past. Like Pascal, Blanchard considers the narrated 'I' and the narrator to be two different persons, which makes it practically impossible for the narrator to fully recreate the protagonist's life and thoughts. However, to Blanchard, fiction in autobiography does not appear on single pages, whenever the author feels the need to fill in a gap in order to make

---

130 Misch, Georg. *Geschichte der Autobiographie I/1: Das Altertum*. Frankfurt: Schulte, 1976 (1907), p. 13.
131 Pascal, Roy. *Design and Truth in Autobiography*, p. 16.

Leonora Christina's Jammers Minde

sense out of an otherwise random scene. Autobiography is in itself fiction – »the fiction of self-writing«,[132] an illusion claiming that the narrated 'I' and the narrating 'I' are one and the same person. If it is agreed upon that these two persons are usually very different from each other, the logical consequence is to declare recreating one's own history impossible.

The notion of autobiography as always containing a certain degree of fiction spread since Misch's and Pascal's groundbreaking work and reached its final breakthrough with Paul John Eakin's *Fictions in Autobiography*. Eakin links the often-criticised autobiographical fiction to processes of individual self-invention. This self-invention is to be understood not only as a creative process of writing, but also as a result of human development.[133] In order to exemplify his notion of autobiography being the natural result of human development, Eakin determines language as being the most important mode of self-reference since, together with the emergence of language came the idea of the »self«.[134] Autobiography is thus the natural result of this development, as it constitutes a written fixation of human self-reference. Finally, fiction is a natural part of this process of self-creation, as previously discussed in Chapter 1.1.1. above. On the other hand, years of advocating the occurrence of fiction in autobiography led to the misconception that autobiography *is* essentially fiction, or even 'failed' fiction. Barret J. Mandel's essay 'Full of Life Now' overturned these considerations by highlighting the often overlooked role readers play in such a context: »It is simply a fact that readers turn to autobiography for the kind of satisfaction that one derives from reading something true rather than fabular. It would also be misleading to label autobiography nonfiction«.[135]

Closely linked to the occurrence of fiction in autobiography is the question of the author's motive for writing their life story. Ever since antiquity the connection between style, topic and intention or addressee became commonly known and has been, at times rigorously, applied by authors of all epochs. Autobiography is no exception to this rule. Like any other literary genre, autobiography follows a purpose, which the author can either express directly, or conceal in the narrative. If the autobiographer chooses to do the latter, however, this might affect his portrayal of events.

According to Manfred Fuhrmann, one of the basic reasons for writing an autobiography is justification. When Socrates was accused of blasphemy, he built his

---

132 Blanchard, Marc Eli. 'The Critique of Autobiography', Comparative Literature 34/2 (Spring 1982), p. 101.
133 Eakin, Paul John. *Fictions in Autobiography*, p. 8.
134 Ibid., p. 195.
135 Mandel, Barrett J. 'Full of Life Now', p. 55.

apologia on two basic claims: the claim of individuality or rather exception, and the claim of identity. The former, adopted many centuries later by Jean-Jacques Rousseau, was discussed Chapter 1.1.2., and will thus not be repeated here. The latter, however, his claim of identity or autobiographical claim, is more complex. By repeating to his audience his development and his ideas, and by reminding them of their previous encounters whilst they would still listen to him, Socrates rejects all accusations. His life and doctrines demonstrated nothing but steadiness, so why would anyone condemn him now? His formerly cherished teachings have not changed, therefore he must be considered innocent.[136] Even though this apologia did not save Socrates' life, many writers who found themselves in a similar situation have adopted this same strategy. Amongst them is Leonora Christina, whose apologia will be the topic of a following chapter.

Women's Autobiography
Together with the feminist movements of the 20th century came an increased interest in women's literature. This applies especially to the case of women's life writings, since readers of autobiography could expect to receive the most (accurate) information about the troublesome lives of pre-emancipation women.[137] Accordingly, female autobiographers of the 20th century stopped justifying their need of writing down their life story, whereas in earlier centuries this female custom appeared to have been imperative.[138] Patricia Meyer Spacks, a pioneer in the research on autobiographies of women writers, comes to a similar conclusion. Since patterns and topics of autobiography were predetermined by male writers, only few women were in the position to follow this autobiographical pattern. As given by one of the autobiographical prototypes, the *res gestae*, autobiographies used to include a certain claim of significance. This could hardly trouble authors such as Goethe or Darwin, but it proved to be an obstacle for their female contemporaries. Meyer Spacks stresses that until recently female autobiographers demonstrated difficulties in justifying

---

136 Fuhrmann, Manfred. 'Rechtfertigung durch Identität: Über eine Wurzel des Autobiographischen'. In *Identität*, eds. Odo Marquard and Karlheinz Stierle. Munich: Fink, 1979 (Poetik und Hermeneutik 8), pp. 685-690.
137 Linda Anderson, too, argues on behalf of autobiography's importance to feminist discourses within literary criticism. See Anderson, Linda R. *Autobiography*. London: Routledge, 2001 (The New Critical Idiom), p. 87: »Autobiography has been one of the most important sites of feminist debate precisely because it demonstrates that there are many different ways of writing the subject«.
138 Mason, Mary G. 'The Other Voice: Autobiographies of Women Writers'. In *Autobiography: Essays Theoretical and Critical*, ed. James Olney. Princeton University Press, 1980, p. 107. On the same matter, see Winston, Elizabeth. 'The Autobiographer and Her Readers: From Apology to Affirmation'. In *Women's Autobiography: Essays in Criticism*, ed. Estelle C. Jelinek. Bloomington: Indiana University Press, 1980, pp. 93-111.

a narration on their private lives. Instead, women often turned to writing diaries and journals, where no such justification was required. Moreover, those who did write an autobiography often »fail directly to emphasize their own importance, though writing in a genre which implies self-assertion and self-display«.[139]

The claim of these verdicts, that female autobiographers should have felt the need of a direct or indirect justification of their own existence, affirms John Sturrock's definition of the genre. Based on Paul de Man's assertion of autobiography's purpose being to give the public a textual face and thus claim singularity,[140] Sturrock counter-argues by referring to the actual living author. In his definition, autobiographies are always written by those who are already known and to put a story to a name.[141] However, throughout history, more men than women had the privilege of performing historical, publically revered deeds. Hence, it appears logical that female autobiographers should feel the need to justify their decision to make their life story public.

Despite Leonora Christina's fame, she is no exception, since both her French autobiography and *Jammers Minde* commence with a statement regarding the motivations to write down her life's story. In the French autobiography, it is to »satisfaire [la] curiosité«,[142] i.e. to satisfy the curiosity of the Monsieur addressed in the French autobiography, i.e. Otto Sperling the Younger (1634-1715) to whom she gave the manuscript[143] with the justified expectation of him publishing it in some form (see below). In *Jammers Minde*, in which Leonora Christina could not refer to a direct request for another autobiographical text and hence to a less immanent possibility of the text being published,[144] she addressed her children (*Fortalen Til mine Børn*)

---

139 Meyer Spacks, Patricia. 'Selves in Hiding'. In *Women's Autobiography: Essays in Criticism*, ed. Estelle C. Jelinek. Bloomington: Indiana University Press, 1980, p. 113.
140 For faces, in this instance the manifestation of a personal history, are unique whereas words are imitable and reproducible. See De Man, Paul. 'Autobiography as De-facement', pp. 919-930.
141 Sturrock, John. *The Language of Autobiography*, pp. 3 and 5.
142 *Leonora Christina Grevinde Ulfeldts Franske Levnedsskildring*, p. 1a (Translation p. 3).
143 In their study on Leonora Christina's French vocabulary, Jan Lindschouw and Lene Schøsler state that it is unknown, how Leonora Christina managed to get the manuscript of her French autobiography out of the Blue Tower (Lindschouw, Jan and Lene Schøsler. 'Leonora Christinas franske ordforråd: En didaktisk og diakron analyse af hendes *Franske selvbiografi* (1673)', Danske Studier (2016), p. 7). While this is true, there is, however, no reason to assume that she had *not* simply handed it over to Otto Sperling the Younger, particularly considering the extremely lax security measures in the Blue Tower, as depicted in *Jammers Minde*.
144 It is important to keep in mind that *Jammers Minde* was written in the course of approximately two decades, with – sometimes long lasting – periods of inactivity in between and with differing dimensions of retrospection. It is thus justified to assume that Leonora Christina's motivations for writing the first part of *Jammers Minde* differed significantly from those that prompted her to continue and finish the manuscript. Be that as it may, when Leonora Christina handed her manuscript over to her eldest daughter Anna Catharina she left the decision of what to do with it to Anna Catharina (see Chapter 1.2.1.), rendering the possibility of her autobiography never becoming public a conceivable option.

Theory of Autobiography

with a detailed explanation for her reasons to eternise her life in the Blue Tower (*Jammers Minde*, pp. 1*-5*). Leonora Christina furthermore claims significance of historical proportions through *Hæltinners Pryd*. In this catalogue of honourable women in the tradition of Plutarch's *De mulierum virtutibus*, Leonora Christina praises selected women taken from both history and mythology for specific virtues, who suspiciously resemble Leonora Christina's own characterisation in *Jammers Minde*.[145]

Perhaps due to this pressure to justify any potential interest in a woman's life story, there is a considerably lower number of universally appraised autobiographies written by women, even though women did of course not completely abstain from passing on their stories. In addition, scholarly focus on women's autobiographies is relatively new. Estelle C. Jelinek initiates her criticism of this previous disregard of women's autobiographies with a claim of absolute otherness of women's life studies. She contends that the reason for research to consider women's life and life writings to be (comparatively) insignificant lies in a fixed body of theories on autobiography, which was designed to fit men's autobiographies only.[146] While autobiographical features such as embedding one's personal life in a broader historical context and focus on professional achievements might be typical for autobiographies of male writers, this does not automatically hold true for women's life stories. Thus, Jelinek advocates a broader range of criteria in the assessment of autobiography, as opposed to belittling those that do not resemble the confined body of autobiographies considered to be classics of the genre.[147]

Jelinek's view of autobiographies written by women being different from those written by men was eventually challenged by Sharon Cadman Seelig and Liz Stanley. Emanating from previous, mostly belittling notions of women's autobiographies antedating Gertrude Stein, Cadman Seelig engaged in the question of how women's lives in early modern times were essentially different from those of their male contemporaries and how this difference translates into their texts. Due to the diversity of these texts, Cadman Seelig pleads for a renunciation of generalisations on women's literature of any period. Furthermore, she concludes that categorical gender differentiations regarding literature (at least in this instance) are counterproductive altogether, since literary conventions had been formed based on texts written by men, which renders »those by women the exception, even an aberration«.[148]

---

[145] Aasen, Elisabeth. 'Grevinnen i fangetårnet: Leonora Christina (1621-1698)'. In *Den skjulte tradisjon: skapende kvinner i kulturhistorien*, ed. Kari Vogt. Bergen: Sigma, 1982, p. 133.
[146] Jelinek, Estelle C. 'Introduction: Women's Autobiography and the Male Tradition', p. 5.
[147] Ibid., p. 19.
[148] Cadman Seelig, Sharon. *Autobiography and Gender in Early Modern Literature*, p. 5.

Liz Stanley holds the same view since a sex-based categorisation of autobiographies is too generalising to apply to such a variety of lives reflected in the plentiful »transtextual«[149] autobiographies written by women. One of Stanley's most innovative contentions is the claim that research on autobiography should include neighbouring genres, such as biography, as well. Thus, Stanley advocates closer attention to *bios*, instead of merely focussing on *autos* and *graphē*. Even though former research engaged in the obvious differences between autobiography, biography, letters and diaries, Stanley is convinced that »the same epistemological, theoretical and technical issues arise, in relation to the ontological claims of each of these apparently distinct genres as do for autobiography«.[150] Just as a biographer can hardly succeed in depicting another person's life as it happened, so must autobiographers fail in 'accurately' portraying their lives. The biographer does not know everything, but neither does the autobiographer. Ultimately, memory is not reliable, emotions might link formerly unrelated events to each other, and finally, in eager search for a meaning, the autobiographer might create one.

By further blurring the lines between auto/biographical and fictional genres, Stanley also highlights the role women played in the development of the novel through their fictional autobiographies, e.g. Sarah Fielding's *The Governess* (1749). While women writers were neither dominant in the sphere of fictional, nor autobiographical literature, Stanley hints at their essential part in establishing a topical focus on the unfolding of one particular life, which is not only the autobiographical, but also one of the favourite subjects of novels. Introducing individual, ordinary, and even fictional lives as a possible topic of public interest paved the way for further, self-conscious writing by female authors – »for made through fiction these could be presented as less seditious, and less seductive for women readers, than actually seems to have been the case as witnessed by women's contemporary letters, journals and diaries, and journalistic writing«.[151]

Early Modern Autobiography
Within the autobiographical genre, works written in the early modern period have long been either neglected and dismissed by the literary research community on the grounds of not being subjective enough,[152] or, at best, assigned importance of *some* kind for

---

149 Stanley, Liz. *The Auto/biographical I*, p. 247.
150 Ibid., p. 3.
151 Ibid., p. 59.
152 Shuger, Debora. 'The »I« of the Beholder', p. 35: »[...] the preponderance of evidence suggests that the Renaissance self lacks reflexivity, self-consciousness, and individuation, and hence differs fundamentally from what we usually think of as the modern self«.

being »influential 'prequels'«.[153] While from a modern point of view this verdict is fairly authorised, critics of premodern literature might deem it lacking nuances. Among these critics were Philippa Kelly, Lloyd Davis and Ronald Bedford. In the introduction to their study on early modern autobiography they argue that whereas a contrasting historical view on early modern personality and its manifestations in the arts, i.e. in direct comparison to a modern-day perspective, may easily mislead the critic, or reader, of these early life writings into considering it one-dimensional, a closer look at early modern testimonies of reflection on the self and life might prove to be far more abundant:

> [...] early modern writing displays a constant interplay between two poles: the grand ideals of selfhood (immortality, stability, presence), and the everyday terrain of passing observations, travels, daily records, household expenditures, pleasures and the like. Moreover, the incessant pressure of spiritual beliefs on secular life means that access to »real« selves is granted not through one pole (the spiritual) or the other (the secular and everyday) but rather through a complex personal, spiritual, and social interweaving of these perspectives.[154]

Closely linked to the topic of early modern personality is the question of how authentically a personality is portrayed in an autobiography. As Conal Condren points out, premodern autobiographies were by no means intended for print, yet neither can they be considered private (in terms of intended authenticity).[155] Our modern-day differentiation between public and private sphere does not apply to a world in which many offices were accorded based on moral qualifications. However, this does not exclude the possibility of translucent authenticity, as will become apparent through the example of Leonora Christina's life writings.

When Otto Sperling the Younger, the son of the Ulfeldt family's doctor and friend Otto Sperling the Elder, solicited the imprisoned Countess for a written record of her life in order to incorporate it into a compilation of stories on remarkable women, *De fœminis omni ævi doctis*, a gynæceum following the tradition of Boccaccio's *De virtutibus et vitiis feminarum*,[156] Leonora Christina had good reason to

---

153 Davis, Lloyd. 'Critical Debates and Early Modern Autobiography'. In *Early Modern Autobiography: Theories, Genres, Practices*, ed. Ronald Bedford et al. Ann Arbor, Michigan: University of Michigan Press, 2006, p. 23.
154 Kelly, Philippa, Lloyd Davis and Ronald Bedford. 'Introduction', p. 2.
155 Condren, Conal. 'Specifying the Subject in Early Modern Autobiography', p. 37.
156 In the ancient world, the term *gynæceum* denominated a space in a household designated for womanly work and activities. In the Renaissance, however, the term was transferred to a literary genre narrating all kinds of female deeds worth of (positive) mention. For more information on this topic, see Alenius, Marianne. 'Om alleslags Roosværdige Quindis Personer: Gynæceum – en kvindelitteraturhistorie'. In *Nordisk kvindelitteraturhistorie 1: I Guds navn: 1000-1800*, ed. Elisabeth Møller Jensen. Copenhagen: Rosinante/Munksgaard, 1993, pp. 217-232.

believe that the portion of the public capable of reading would thus be able to learn about her story. It was for this purpose that she made a first attempt to compile an autobiography in 1673, which was a text of mediocre literary quality now commonly referred to as her French autobiography.[157] Sperling's compilation was never finished, but when Leonora Christina began to work on her second autobiography, *Jammers Minde*, shortly after finishing the French autobiography, she might have already acquired a taste of potential fame. Nevertheless, *Jammers Minde* opens with an address to her children, thus indicating privacy: »Hierte Kiere Børn« (*Jammers Minde*, p. 1*). While this address might well have been heartfelt, it must have been obvious to Leonora Christina that this manuscript may not reach her children without passing through the hands of a third, potentially hostile, party first. At the moment of her imprisonment, all of her children were already in exile and spread across Europe. Furthermore, with the high mortality rate of the 17th century and a slightly younger Sophie Amalie co-reigning Denmark, it is quite astonishing that Leonora Christina managed to survive all of her enemies, and even most of her children, and deliver her autobiography to one of her remaining children.[158] In summa, even if *Jammers Minde* was indeed written for Leonora Christina's children, she must have anticipated at least the possibility of someone else reading it first. One might even go as far as to propose that the intended readership, i.e. the children addressed in *Fortalen*, was a fiction created to raise interest in this supposedly honest and intimate record. Solely writing for her children functions both as a justification for composing an autobiography in the first place, and it adds a hint of potentially scandalous authenticity to the text, which the reading public was certainly hoping for.[159] However, whether Leonora Christina's address to her children was the innocent hope of a mother to communicate with her family, or whether it was an opportunistic calculation, she does not verbalise her true feelings about the

---

157 Anne-Marie Mai points to another reason for Leonora Christina's decision to write the French autobiography. Otto Sperling the Younger also asked his father – Otto Sperling the Elder, who was also imprisoned in the Blue Tower – for an autobiography, probably in the hope of drawing the public's attention to the unjust fate of the two prisoners. By the end of the 17th century, copies of Leonora Christina's French autobiography were indeed circulating throughout Europe (while the original was lost at an unknown point in time and rediscovered in the mid-20th century), albeit in vain. Subsequently, Otto Sperling the Younger intended to include the autobiography in his gynæceum, but as mentioned above, this manuscript was never finished. Disregarding the result, the initial motivation for composing the French autobiography was thus »politisk og taktisk« (Mai, Anne-Marie. 'Troskab, lidelse og lidenskab: Om Leonora Christina'. In *Nordisk kvindelitteraturhistorie 1: I Guds navn: 1000-1800*, ed. Elisabeth Møller Jensen. Copenhagen: Rosinante/Munksgaard, 1993, p. 292).

158 On the publication process of *Jammers Minde*, see Chapter 1.2.1.

159 Willumsen, Dorrit. 'En terrorists mod og en engels tålmodighed: Leonora Christina: *Jammers Minde*'. In *Læsninger i dansk litteratur 1: 1200-1820*, eds. Ulrik Lehrmann and Lise Præstgaard Andersen. Odense Uni. Forlag, 1998, p. 128: »»Hierte, kiære Børn!« Sådan begynder forfatterinden Leonora Christina fortalen til sit værk, og den anonyme læser bliver straks hendes fortrolige«.

Theory of Autobiography

events of the past years, even though they shine through. Fully in line with her past tactic of deceitful denial,[160] Leonora Christina still claims not to have taken part in any of her husband's betrayals against his home country. Similarly, *Jammers Minde* contains no negative remarks about Frederik III. However, the text leaves no doubt about who is to blame for Leonora Christina's unjust punishment:[161]

> Den 25. *Aug. importunerte* Slozf. mig flux med sin *discours*, meente ieg haffde Ond Troe til Dronningen: Hand tog ded der aff; thi dagen til forne, haffde hand sagt mig, att hs Kl. Mt haffde befalet, at huis ieg aff Køckenet og Kelderen begierte skulde de mig lade følgactig were, huor til ieg da suarte, Gud beware hs Mt: hand er en goed Herre, maatte hand were goed for onde Mennisker: Og sagde hand da, Dronningen er oc saa goed; huortil ieg intet Suarte; Huorfor hand nu Dronningen wille føre paa tale, oc see om hand nogen Ord aff mig kunde drage: Sagde, Dronningen Beklager eder, att I saa haffuer laded eder forføre, I haffuer wult eder selffuer den Vlycke; ded giør hender Ont; Hun er eder icke Wreed, hun haffuer Medliidenhed med Eder. Oc saa som ieg intet Suarte *repeterte* hand ded igien, oc alt imellem sagde hand, Ia, Ia, mein liebes Frewlein, es ist so wie ich sage. Ieg var meget fortrøden offuer den Snack, sagde *Dieu vous punisse*.
> (*Jammers Minde*, p. 76)[162]

With these and similar statements, Leonora Christina's mind and character are visible throughout the entire text. Without any explicit comments from her side, the reader of *Jammers Minde* becomes acquainted with the stubbornly proud and unforgiving, but also witty and humorous Leonora Christina.

---

160 Even her greatest admirer, Sophus Birket Smith, had to acknowledge that Leonora Christina lied whenever the truth was working against her interest. However, he excuses her use of »meget stærke Forsikringer til Bevidnelse af vitterlige Usandheder«, for example in the course of the Malmö trial, on the ground of her specific situation. First, she had to resort to downright lying in order to save her husband's life. And second, her lies did not interfere with her declared religiousness since she was not under oath at this time. See Birket Smith, Sophus. *Leonora Christina Grevinde Ulfeldts Historie 2*, p. 162.

161 Given her situation, Leonora Christina bewares any open criticism of Frederik III. Only the French autobiography contains one explicitly negative remark on her half-brother. Shortly after the death of Christian IV, Frederik III found his half-sister in tears. He consoled her and promised to be like a father to her. Retrospectively, Leonora Christina's sole comment on this scene is that there have been fathers »dènaturé envers leurs Enfans (il pourroit estre conté au nombre de ceux la)«. See *Leonora Christina Grevinde Ulfeldts Franske Levnedsskildring*, p. 5c (Translation p. 21: »Jeg finder, at der har været fædre, som var unaturlige imod deres børn; (han ville kunne regnes med i disses tal)«). In her manuscript, the last part of this phrase, reproduced above in parentheses, was crossed out, yet not rendered illegible. This indicates that Leonora Christina had felt a need to express her resentment towards her half-brother, but was wary of the potential consequences.

162 Unless otherwise indicated, all italics in quotations from *Jammers Minde* were undertaken by the editors in order to indicate that the respective words were either written using latin, instead of the usual gothic, letters, or abbreviated in the manuscript (see Lindegård Hjorth, Poul. 'Nærværende udgave'. In Leonora Christina. *Jammers Minde: Diplomatarisk udgave ved Poul Lindegård Hjorth og Marita Akhøj Nielsen under medvirkning af Ingelise Nielsen*, ed. Det Danske Sprog- og Litteraturselskab. Copenhagen: Reitzel, 1998, p. lxxi)

While Conal Condren, amongst others, sought to examine the personality creating the early modern text, other scholars examined the texts creating the autobiography. In the Middle Ages, writing was a privilege granted only to a very specific estate: the clergy. When this monopoly was broken in the 16th century, literary production was opened to a new public, and to new contributors and topics. It was at this point that records on common life emerged, e.g. printed almanacs or parish registers, all together forming a »dense network of life-writing texts, where notes were moved from text to text«.[163] Thus, the antique dictum of significance no longer applied to the autobiographical genre (or at least to autobiographies written by men). The newly emerged merchant class ruled the cities, with new writing centres gradually replacing monasteries, as such.

However, these novel ways of documenting life do not only demonstrate a different awareness of self-significance, but also of the writer's dependence. Whereas the medieval autobiographer would regard his life from an unearthly perspective, and the modern autobiographer from within, the early modern writer would always take his position in society into account.[164] The afore-mentioned documents, such as the parish register, confirm that place in society. Similarly, the financial account, another example of early modern ways of documenting life, enlists possessions and thus affirms the writer's status.[165] Accordingly, what is today considered a personal life record used to be a rather public business in the early modern times: »To write and circulate one's memoirs was to produce a public document testifying to a historical period or event«.[166] While extraordinary accomplishments worthy of a Roman emperor were no longer a precondition for writing an autobiography (or memoirs), significance in a much broader context became indispensable. Early modern autobiographers did not simply reproduce their life, but a period in time. It was their role as witnesses which entitled them as writers to publish their stories.

Once this new ground was broken to subsequent scholars, research on early modern autobiography became more specific and diverse as well. Not only did Katherine Hodgkin, the author of *Madness in Seventeenth-Century Autobiography* – to mention only one example – engage in the topic of early modern spiritual autobiography, but she also engaged in the rather specific matter of madness depicted in and inspiring these texts. Others have (re-)examined the role of early modern novel-

---

163 Smyth, Adam. *Autobiography in Early Modern England*, p. 2.
164 Accordingly, Lloyd Davis speaks of a »spatial conception of autobiographical selfhood« (Davis, Lloyd. 'Critical Debates and Early Modern Autobiography', p. 23).
165 Ibid., p. 11.
166 Goldsmith, Elizabeth C. *Publishing Women's Life Stories in France, 1647-1720: From Voice to Print*. Aldershot: Ashgate, 2001 (Women and Gender in the Early Modern World), p. 2.

ties that sparked the proliferation of the autobiographical genre, such as the mirror (Philippa Kelly) or the private study (Peter Goodall). And some have engaged in the autobiographical subgenre of prison writing, e.g. Dosia Reichardt. While a large part of prison literature consists of declarations and petitions, Reichardt contends that writing constituted a way to reunite with the outside world and, for some social groups, a way to be heard for the first time, while it simply was a part of courtly culture for the many noble prisoners of that time.[167] Furthermore, as was already assessed in the case of Leonora Christina's *Jammers Minde*, typical prison narratives depict the inmate's personality as being static. As Leonora Christina prides herself in her rock-solid constancy,[168] writers in similar situations portray personal change as something »having happened offstage and in a vague past«.[169] This strategy of implied innocence has a long-running tradition – Socrates applied the same argument (see above), albeit in vain.

Another typical trait of early modern prison writing is the importance assigned to the simultaneousness of prison and writing experience.[170] While many authors of early modern prison writings stress their being in gaol at the moment of writing, Leonora Christina even went to such lengths as to pretend to still be incarcerated while finishing her text (see Chapter 1.2.1.). This indicates her awareness of the positive implications of arrest for a writer. Furthermore, her intuition proved to be correct. Not by coincidence did her two life accounts, the French autobiography and *Jammers Minde*, receive diverging attention from scholars, with the latter text emerging as the uncontested winner, as will be highlighted in Chapter 1.2.

Leonora Christina's first attempt at an autobiography, the French autobiography, made her a person of interest to historians. Her temporary role as First Lady of the Danish court certainly made her an above average-person and her biography, marriage and possible complicity with the greatest traitor in Danish history, along with her ensuing confinement in the Blue Tower undoubtedly provided material for a great story. Thus, Leonora Christina's role as a crucial witness of her time, and the struggles that characterised this time, caught the public's interest in her life account. After all, Leonora Christina was among the last representatives of the

---

167 Reichardt, Dosia. 'The Constitution of Narrative Identity in Seventeenth-Century Prison Writing'. In *Early Modern Autobiography: Theories, Genres, Practices*, ed. Ronald Bedford et al. Ann Arbor, Michigan: University of Michigan Press, 2006, p. 115f.

168 She even utilises her father's death to clarify her greatest asset. Looking back at this crucial day, she remembers her father's last words to her: »[J]e t'ay mise si ferme que personne ne te peut branler«, see *Leonora Christina Grevinde Ulfeldts Franske Levnedsskildring*, p. 5b, (Translation p. 21).

169 Reichardt, Dosia. 'The Constitution of Narrative Identity in Seventeenth-Century Prison Writing', p. 121.

170 Ibid., p. 123.

Danish *adelsvælde*.[171] She and her family were in the centre of the conflict between nobility and King, which resulted in the introduction of absolutism in 1660 and her imprisonment three years later, and it was this position that made her an important witness of this age of upheaval, for contemporaries as well as for subsequent generations. Hence, it comes as no surprise that Leonora Christina was asked to write down her life story, the result of which is now known as the French autobiography. This account is rather typical of its time and literary context; its focus is based on public events and on the time preceding Leonora Christina's imprisonment, the time when she was a member of the still powerful Danish nobility. Like many authors of early modern (auto)biographical writings,[172] Leonora Christina uses the third person, perhaps in order to suggest the objectivity and historicity of her account, or because she was following the pattern of older texts she had read.[173] In addition, she composed her life story in French, either out of love for this refined language and because it was à la mode, or maybe in order to reach a broader public.[174] Perhaps though, writing her life story in French was also a means of attesting her privileged position, her royal education and, consequently, her authority and reliability.

However, Leonora Christina was not the only witness of this age. The physician Otto Sperling the Elder, who attended the family on a regular basis and thus became a close friend and confidant, supported the Ulfeldt family in their exile. As a consequence, he became Leonora Christina's tower mate. He too wrote down his memoirs, which resemble Leonora Christina's French autobiography both stylistically and thematically. In his *Selbstbiographie* (which includes a distinct *Historia Carceris* focussing only on his life in prison, see Chapter 2.1.2.), Sperling follows

---

171 This term is commonly used to denominate the period 1536-1660. It is characterized by the unusual degree of power which the nobility of that time had and ended in 1660 with the introduction of absolutism.

172 Cf. Goldsmith, Elizabeth C. *Publishing Women's Life Stories in France*, p. 2.

173 Cf. Hougaard, Jens, Toni Nielsen, Erik Vestergaard Rasmussen, Arne Rindom and Peer E. Sørensen. *Dansk litteraturhistorie 3: Stænderkultur og enevælde 1620-1746*. Copenhagen: Gyldendal, 1983, p. 230: »Selvbiografien har et umiskendeligt romanpræg, hun omtaler sig selv i tredje person som ‚Vor dame'«.

174 Danish writer Bodil Wamberg suggests that Leonora Christina chose French »fordi det danske hof med Sophie Amalie var blevet fortysket i en grad, der harmede Leonora. [...] Der lå en direkte demonstration mod den ikke videre intellektuelle Sophie Amalie i Leonoras valg af det franske sprog«. See Wamberg, Bodil. *Leonora Christina: Dronning af Blåtårn*. Copenhagen: Gyldendals Bogklubber, 1992, p. 40. Two facts argue against the first of Wamberg's conclusions. First, Sophie Amalie was not the first, nor the only German 'intruder'. In Leonora Christina's time, the Danish court had been under German influence for centuries. Second, Leonora Christina's frequent use of German in *Jammers Minde* does not indicate any resentment on her part for this language. She declares to have read the bible in German and she composed some hymns in German as well. However, that Leonora Christina's use of French may be interpreted as a disparagement of the not especially educated Sophie Amalie, I find no reason to refute, even though other sources suggest that Sophie Amalie, too, had mastered the French language to an exceptional degree (see, for example, Jørgensen, Ellen and Johanne Skovgaard. *Danske Dronninger*, p. 150). For more information on the diverse languages in Denmark during the *lærde tid*, see Skautrup, Peter. *Det danske sprogs historie 2: Fra unionsbrevet til danske lov*. Copenhagen. Gyldendal, 1947, pp. 265-306.

the biographical pattern, focussing on external events and crucial moments in his life. However, even though Sperling met the same fate as Leonora Christina, he failed to captivate his readers with a narrative like *Jammers Minde*. The only instances in historiography in which Otto Sperling finds mention, are all somehow connected to the Ulfeldt couple. In addition, literary histories classify his text as being mediocre, at best.[175] The comparatively meagre success of parallel texts such as Sperling's *Selbstbiographie*, or the French autobiography, indicates that the popularity and quality of *Jammers Minde* cannot merely be attributed to external factors, such as the historical context or the sensationalist potential of the text. Rather, the biography of Leonora Christina certainly helped to intrigue her contemporaries, with *Jammers Minde* being the reason for her literary breakthrough almost two centuries after her death.

Leonora Christina's magnum opus accorded her a place in every Danish literary history, despite her limited literary activity. Repeatedly, scholars have stressed the modern traits in *Jammers Minde*.[176] Thematically, this text is the continuation of Leonora Christina's French autobiography, as it ignores the very events her contemporaries would probably have cared most to hear about, i.e. those that preceded her imprisonment. Stylistically, *Jammers Minde* is rather the antithesis of its predecessor. Whereas in the French autobiography Leonora Christina uses French, the most courtly of all languages at the time, she did not for *Jammers Minde*, which as a result has been complimented on its use of the Danish language and its authenticity, especially in rendering dialogues. It is in these instances, when Leonora Christina captures her surroundings in such a vivid and relatable way that *Jammers Minde* sets itself apart from the memoir mode and becomes a text of more than merely historical relevance. In the confinement of her dark cell, isolated from the realm of history, politics and society, Leonora Christina resourcefully created a testimony of reflection, comparable to modern autobiography.

When Leonora Christina reconciles herself with God and accepts her fate, after the first part of the account (*Jammers Minde*, pp. 80-83; see Chapter 1.2.1.), she identifies with the biblical figure Job by concluding that her punishment must be a token of God's love for her. Considering all the attention and sympathy her autobiography yielded ever since it was discovered in the 19th century, one might indeed say that for Leonora Christina's literary 'career' the imprisonment in the

---

175 Petersen, Carl S. *Illustreret dansk Litteraturhistorie 1: Fra Folkevandringstiden indtil Holberg.* Copenhagen: Gyldendal, 1929, p. 849: »Sperlings 'Jammersminde' Historia Carceris oder Beschreibung meines Gefängniss etc. udgør kun en mindre Del af Haandskriftet og kan hverken litterært eller rent menneskeligt maale sig med Leonora Christinas Beretning fra Blaa Taarn«.

176 For example Larsen, Finn Stein. 'En impressionist fra baroktiden?', pp. 17-33.

Blue Tower was a blessing.[177] Even though she wrote the French autobiography, *Hæltinners Pryd* and some church hymns as well, Leonora Christina is known as the author of *Jammers Minde,* and extensive interest in her other texts only followed the publication of *Jammers Minde*. It was only when she did not follow the literary conventions of her age, determined by the literary vacuum of her isolation, that Leonora Christina became an author of importance.

1.2. *Jammers Minde*: Confessions Dedicated to the Beloved Ones or Political Apologia?

As was suggested in Chapter 1.1.3., Leonora Christina did not (overtly) compose a statement on the accusations against her family. In exile, her husband had already attempted to present his perspective on his fall from grace (e.g. due to the Dina affair) with the aid of brochures, all of which were only successful to a certain degree.[178] Thus, it must have appeared obvious to Leonora Christina that yet another written defence should have little to no effect, let alone the impracticability of this kind of undertaking during the first years of her imprisonment, when she was not granted any kind of diversion (*Jammers Minde*, p. 99) and thus had no means of obtaining proper writing tools. She did eventually forge ways of writing, however, for example with the help of confectionary paper, wine, ashes and a feather. However, as a prisoner she was in no position to publish a written defence. Even communicating with the King proved to be a difficult matter. At the outset of her imprisonment, Leonora Christina had not yet given up hope. One day, she managed to catch the castellan's interest in her activities by crafting a cup secretly inscribed with a hidden message to the King, which the unsuspecting castellan delivered. The secret supplication was or, rather, is believed to have been »Si il y a un Sinna soyez un Auguste« (cf. *Jammers Minde*, p. 115).

The original manuscript of *Jammers Minde* shows that Leonora Christina had tried to garble the reproduction of the supplication in her manuscript at a later point,

---

177 Accordingly, see Reichardt, Dosia. 'The Constitution of Narrative Identity in Seventeenth-Century Prison Writing', p. 115: »For some social groups – women, millenarian sects, even debtors and merchants from a putative bourgeoisie – prison provided an opportunity to be heard in print for the first time«.

178 Victor Lange elaborates on the polemics between Ulfeldt and his adversaries. However, he concludes that these pamphlets constitute by no means reliable accounts of the preceding events. See Lange, Victor. *Corfitz Ulfeld: Fra Rigshovmester til Landsforræder*. Copenhagen: Jacob Lund, 1931, p. 16.

hence the text contains a lacuna and reads: »Si il y a un ... soyez un Auguste«. Otto Andrup, the editor of two *Jammers Minde*-editions,[179] presumes that after a few years Leonora Christina was ashamed of this attempt and that she feared a false impression resulting from this plea.[180] Despite her efforts to erase all traces of her moment of weakness, the inscription on the cup was deciphered and only one word remained the subject of speculation. Eventually, Andrup proposed to fill the lacuna with »Cinna«/»Sinna«. Thus, the inscription on the cup is presumably as cited above: »Si il y a un Sinna soyez un Auguste«.[181]

Cinna ou la Clémence d'Auguste ('Cinna or the Clemency of Augustus', 1639) is the title of a tragedy by Pierre Corneille. The play was a success all over Europe, thus it seems likely that Leonora Christina was familiar with its plot, which – to a certain degree – resembles the situation of the regal couple and the Ulfeldt family. The eponymous hero, Cinna, forms a literary parallel to Corfitz Ulfeldt, as he finds himself tragically torn between his obligations towards his benefactor, Emperor Augustus, and his love for Émilie, the vindictive adopted daughter of the Emperor and the sole remaining descendant of a dispatched rival to Augustus. Augustus himself is an ambiguous character, since he seized the throne with brutal force (mind the parallel provided by Frederik's own coup d'état, which introduced absolutism in Denmark); but he also cares about the casualties of his accession to the throne. Émilie is the driving force behind Cinna's treacherous plans to murder Augustus, since she craves to see her father's death avenged. At a crucial point of the drama, Cinna

---

179 In 1920, Otto Andrup, back then the curator of the Museum of National History at Frederiksborg Castle and subsequently the editor of two *Jammers Minde*-editions, also managed to effect the sale of the manuscript and transfer it to Leonora Christina's birthplace – Frederiksborg Castle – where it is exhibited until this day (Lindegård Hjorth, Poul. '*Jammers Minde's* udgivelseshistorie', p. xxiii).

180 Andrup, Otto. 'Noter'. In Leonora Christina. *Grevinde Leonora Christinas Jammers Minde*, ed. Otto Andrup. Copenhagen: Gyldendal, 1926, p. 261 (endnote p. 122). Sigvard Skov comes to a similar conclusion: »Men nu er jo det farlige, at paralleliteten med Cinna som legalitetens forsvarer også kunne udstrækkes til at gælde anslaget mod kejserens liv« (Skov, Sigvard. 'Leonora Christina – helgen eller højforræder', Jyske Samlinger 14 (Ny række, 1981), p. 212).

181 Andrup, Otto. 'Noter', p. 261 (endnote p. 122). Andrup's decryption remained mostly uncontested ever since. However, Hans Aage Paludan raised some concerns regarding phonology and spelling of this appeal. He refers to the hiatus »Si il«, as well as the un-Roman spelling of Cinna (»Sinna«) as rather astounding mistakes for a person that had written an entire book in French. See Paludan, Hans Aage. 'Corneille i Danmark: En tilføjelse', Danske Studier (1926), pp. 174-176. Despite these dissonances, no other plausible interpretation has yet been presented as an alternative to Otto Andrup's reading. Furthermore, Leonora Christina's German, too, is adjusted to Danish spelling (e.g. »König«). Sophus Birket Smith (as well as later editors) had corrected many of Leonora Christina's inconsistencies and mistakes which resulted in a portrayal of »Leonora Christinas beherskelse af fremmede sprog som sikrere, end den egentlig var« (Lindegård Hjorth, Poul. '*Jammers Minde's* udgivelseshistorie', p. xx). Paludan may thus not have been surprised about the two mistakes mentioned above, if the early editors of Leonora Christina's works had reproduced her exact spelling.

clearly states that Augustus' fate lies in her hands (Act 3, Scene 3).[182] Augustus, on the other hand, was already apprised of Cinna's and Émilie's plans. He thus consults his wife, Livia, and she advises him to temper justice with mercy (Act 4, Scene 3).[183] Augustus follows Livia's wise counsel and the play ends with a reconciliation of all persons involved. Furthermore, Livia predicts a bright future lying ahead of the Emperor, as a direct result of his clemency (Act 5, Scene 3).[184]

In this play, clemency does not simply serve as an end in itself, but also as a means to augment the Emperor's glory. By referring to *Cinna ou la Clémence d'Auguste*, Leonora Christina tried to appeal to both the brother and the politician Frederik IV. And in many respects, Livia's predicament did indeed apply to Frederik's and Sophie Amalie's fate, albeit *ex negativo*. While Leonora Christina became the heroine of many a writer and historian, the unforgiving Queen Sophie Amalie has predominantly been remembered as a villain and Frederik III as her puppet. The most famous example is perhaps a painting of Kristian Zahrtmann (1843-1917)[185] titled *Dronning Sophie Amalies død* (1882). The painting, although already being a second, more flattering version,[186] depicts the dying Queen in a rather unfavourable position. The aged dowager is surrounded by treasures and shrouded in rich clothing. A blanket, her shoes and what appears to be a feathered fan lie on the ground in front of her, next to an adorned box spilling gold coins. The agitated death scene forms a blatant contrast to the peaceful passing of Leonora Christina, depicted in the painting *Leonora Christinas død*. Both versions (1897 and 1901) show her on her deathbed in Maribo, in which the only riches surrounding her are her books, a cloud of people are gathered around her, and Leonora Christina herself appears to be content and ready to meet her final destiny. Her body posture resembles that of an Orans. This scene conveys an atmosphere of dignity, whereas

---

182 Corneille, Pierre. *Cinna: Tragédie 1643*, ed. Alain Riffaud. Geneva: Droz, 2011 (Textes littéraires français 614), p. 105.
183 Ibid., p. 121.
184 Ibid., p. 146.
185 After reading *Jammers Minde*, the Bornholmian painter Kristian Zahrtmann dedicated a large portion of his work to scenes of Leonora Christina's life. His paintings are considered to be among the most influential media in shaping Leonora Christina's fame, particularly since popular biographies of Leonora Christina (see, for example, Petersen, Margrethe. *Kongedatteren Leonora Christina Ulfeldt og hendes Husbond. Med Kr. Zahrtmanns Leonora Christina Billeder*. Copenhagen: Reitzel, 1928) were adorned with his work.
186 The first version of Sophie Amalie's death scene shows the widowed Queen in a dazzling pink dress, perhaps an allusion to Leonora Christina's disparaging view on the Queen's vanity during her final days (»loed sig see til Taffels meget udsmøcket«, *Jammers Minde*, p. 234). Kristian Zahrtmann, however, changed the Queen's dress in a second version, as it would have been inappropriate for a widow to dress in such a flamboyant manner. See Dissing Paulsen, Trine and Jan Gorm Madsen. 'Zahrtmanns Leonora Christina motiver'. In Ære være Leonora: Kristian Zahrtmann og Leonora Christina, ed. Den Hirschsprungske Samling. Copenhagen: 2006, p. 64.

Sophie Amalie, surrounded only by one person and with her foot sticking out from underneath her splendorous dress, evokes pity at best.

This poor depiction of Sophie Amalie is not a single case. The title of a 1986 publication of the Rosenborg Castle in Copenhagen – *Sophie Amalie: Den onde dronning?*[187] – indicates a widespread perception of Sophie Amalie as 'evil Queen'. In this respect, the character dynamics in *Cinna* are rather peculiar, since Livia, in this instance the literary equivalent of Sophie Amalie, emerges as the prudent and benignant sovereign and thus as the clandestine heroine of the play. Yet even more curious is the role of Émilie, the literary counterpart of Leonora Christina. She is unforgiving and even willing to sacrifice Cinna for her own cause (Act 1, Scene 2).[188]

Be that as it may, when Leonora Christina accorded Frederik III the cup with the hidden supplication, it only resulted in a dismayed castellan, since the King discovered the text immediately (*Jammers Minde*, p. 116). From this moment onwards, the castellan would never inquire about her pastimes again.

This anecdote should serve to illustrate the difficulties of spreading a written defence under such conditions. However, *Jammers Minde* does not entirely lack statements about the new government and its way of reshaping national policies. In the course of a description of her encounter with the King's inner circle, Leonora Christina's comments are rather blunt:

> G. Rantzow suarte som før, att der ware *Documenter*, oc att der saed aff mine Wenner i Raaded, føyede ded der til, att alle haffde offuereens stemmet, icke En haffde hafft der imod att sige. Ded ieg tenckte torde ieg icke sige, Ieg wiste wel huorledis i saadanne *Absolute* Regieringer tilgaar, der tør intet imod sigis, ded hedder Skriff vnder, Kongen wil ded saa haffue, oc Spør icke huor for, ellers est du vdi lige Fordømmelse.
>
> (*Jammers Minde*, p. 55)

Being a representative of the former Danish *adelsvælde*, Leonora Christina was certainly not in favour of this new proportion of power, which stripped her of all former privileges. *Hæltinners Pryd*, too, is considered to contain criticism of Frederik III's enforcement of absolutism, which lent the King absolute authority over the law.[189] In Leonora Christina's account of the regency of Margrethe I of Denmark,

---

187 Hein, Jørgen and Katia Johansen. *Sophie Amalie: Den onde dronning?* Copenhagen: Rosenborg, 1986.
188 Corneille, Pierre. *Cinna*, p. 70.
189 Brøndsted, Mogens. 'En dansk virago'. In *Kvinnor och Skapande: En Antologi om Litteratur och Konst tilägnad Karin Westman Berg*, ed. Birgitta Paget et al. Malmö: Författerförlaget, 1983, p. 115.

the Queen commits herself to the law, thus offering a counterexample to Frederik III's approach. Had the King abode by the law, Leonora Christina could never have been kept in prison: she was being retained without a verdict, thus her captivity was unlawful. Accordingly, Bodil Wamberg – perhaps Leonora Christina's keenest critic – contends that *Jammers Minde* was indeed meant to be its author's very own way of defence: »Leonora Christine foretog sig sjældent noget, uden at der var en mening i videre forstand med det. Jeg skulle tage meget fejl, om ikke *Jammers Minde* netop var *hendes* form for forsvar«.[190]

While Wamberg does not believe in Leonora Christina's ignorance of her husband's attempts of treason, she does not contest her literary talent.[191] Like Julius Lange (see Chapter 1.1.1.), Bodil Wamberg does not consider Leonora Christina to be innocent, as presented to us by Sophus Birket Smith. Yet this should not affect any judgement of her artistic achievements. In her demand to distinguish between the person and the artist,[192] Wamberg was amongst the first reviewers of *Jammers Minde* to approach the text in a way similar to modern standards of literary criticism.

Lone Fatum takes a similar view. According to her, Leonora Christina's writings are to be considered as a way of defence against the Queen's attempts to annihilate her opponent's public status.[193] The first measure of this kind was taken by Frederik III rather shortly after his father's death, when he stripped his half siblings, and thus Leonora Christina, of their peerage and their right to use a carriage to reach the front gates of the Royal Palace. Instead, they were requested to arrive on foot. Moreover, keeping Leonora Christina in a prison shared by inmates of the lowest social rank[194] and subsequently ordering the *in absentia*-execution of Corfitz Ulfeldt to take place in front of his wife's cell served as the icing on the cake. Leonora Christina had certainly had her share in fuelling the Queen's hatred, but in the early days of Leonora Christina's imprisonment, when she showed signs of desperation and doubt,[195] it seemed as if Sophie Amalie had triumphed for good. The inactivity forced upon Leo-

---

190 Wamberg, Bodil. 'Det Ydre og det Indre Fangenskab', p. 80.
191 Ibid.
192 Ibid., p. 76.
193 Fatum, Lone. 'Kongedatteren og Gudsfrygten'. In *Gulnares Hus: En Gave til Hendes Majestæt Dronning Margrethe den Anden på Fødselsdagen, den 16. April 1990*, ed. Annelise Bistrup et al. Copenhagen: Samleren, 1990, p. 196.
194 In fact, Leonora Christina's cell had previously been the accommodation of three farmers, who did not leave their shelter in a decent condition (cf. *Jammers Minde*, p. 13).
195 »Skal ded da were til forgieffues, att mit Hierte wandeler vstraffelig;? oc ieg toer mine Hænder vdi V-skyllighed? oc ieg er dagligen plaget, oc min Straff huer Morgen der?« (*Jammers Minde*, p. 78).

nora Christina at the beginning of her imprisonment made it impossible for her to react at first, but as she gathered writing material she obtained means of retaliation:

> Hendes bedste våben i magtkampen var hendes skrifter, og deres personfremstilling rummer netop en karakteristisk blanding af moralsk selvforsvar og religiøs selvbekræftelse for kongedatteren og grevinden, for den trofaste hustru og ikke mindst for den oprigtige kristne, der må lide uskyldigt, men som dog fastholder tilliden til Guds retfærdige forsyn.[196]

Marita Akhøj Nielsen furthermore classifies Leonora Christina's French autobiography as another attempt at a hidden apologia.[197] As this prequel to *Jammers Minde* was written in French, a language Leonora Christina mastered only to a certain degree, it must be and has been considered inferior in comparison to *Jammers Minde*.[198] The content of the French autobiography differs very much from the one narrated in *Jammers Minde*, as the topics are as courtly as the language chosen to deliver the content. The French account narrates the childhood, youth and adventures of Leonora Christina and ends with her imprisonment in the Blue Tower, whereas *Jammers Minde* begins with her transport from England directly to Copenhagen. While the plots are thus different, *Jammers Minde* and the French autobiography share one theme, i.e. »the persecuted heroine«.[199] In the course of her childhood, Leonora Christina bests her siblings in education and virtuousness, just as she outshines her maids in the Blue Tower in every respect.[200] Even her marriage to the halting,[201] and initially poor, Corfitz Ulfeldt serves the purpose of triumph over her brothers and sisters, as it exceeds all others in mutual affection.[202] Whereas the French autobiography is thus indeed a rather interesting text, as con-

---

196 Fatum, Lone. 'Kongedatteren og Gudsfrygten', p. 196.
197 Akhøj Nielsen, Marita. 'Leonora Christina: An Imprisoned Princess'. In *Female Voices of the North: An Anthology*, ed. Inger M. Olsen. Vienna: Praesens, 2002 (Wiener Texte zur Skandinavistik 1), p. 94.
198 Cf., for example, Heitmann, Annegret. 'Feministischer Umgang mit Literatur'. In *Auf-Brüche: Uppbrott och Uppbrytningar i Skandinavistisk Metoddiskussion*, ed. Julia Zernack. Leverkusen: Literaturverlag Norden, Reinhardt, 1989 (Artes et litterae septentrionales 4), p. 58.
199 Akhøj Nielsen, Marita. 'Leonora Christina: An Imprisoned Princess', p. 93.
200 In the years Leonora Christina spent in the Blue Tower, she had many different maids, each one with different vices and shortcomings. All of their flaws, however, serve to highlight Leonora Christina assets, as will be demonstrated below.
201 Corfitz Ulfeldt suffered from a chronic leg wound, the potential reasons and implications of which will be discussed in further detail below.
202 Historians agree that amongst Kirsten Munk's children Leonora Christina was the only one who could pride herself in a happy marriage. Cf., for example, Bjørn, Hans. 'Leonora Christina – Christian IV's datter'. In *Leonora Christina: Historien om en heltinde*. Århus: Arkona, 1983 (Acta Jutlandica 58, Humanistisk serie 57), p. 36.

cluded by Akhøj Nielsen,[203] it has received little to no attention. Not only is this due to Leonora Christina's deficient mastery of the French language, but possibly to the circumstances of the creation of the text as well. The French account was written on demand and was thus perhaps perceived as contract work, rather than authentic artistic creation. Moreover, the text recounts childhood memories, rather than the part of Leonora Christina's life, which aroused the most attention: her imprisonment and its circumstances. This is undoubtedly the main reason why the French autobiography was not properly published until 1871/72.[204] Finally, this lack of interest in Leonora Christina's other autobiography was the motivation for the exclusion of her French life account from the core bibliography of the present study. Yet as demonstrated in the paragraph above, the French autobiography can very well serve as a supporting primary text to the evaluation of *Jammers Minde* and Leonora Christina's authorial approach.

While some scholars have disputed *Jammers Minde*'s apologetic design altogether,[205] others have posed the question as to whom this apologia was directed at. The title of the present chapter indicates that Leonora Christina wrote *Jammers Minde* either for her children, as *Fortalen Til mine Børn* at the beginning of the manuscript suggests, *or* for a broader audience, since she was a political prisoner and

---

203 Akhøj Nielsen, Marita. 'Leonora Christina: An Imprisoned Princess', p. 94.
204 See Leonora Christina. *Leonora Christina (Ulfeldt)s Selvbiografi. Udgivet efter et Håndskrift i det store Kgl. Bibliothek*, ed. Sophus Birket Smith, Danske Samlinger for Historie, Topografi, Personal- og Litteraturhistorie 1/2 (1871-72), pp. 129-231; and *Memoirs of Leonora Christina. Daughter of Christian IV. of Denmark. Written during her Imprisonment in the Blue Tower at Copenhagen 1663-1685*, transl. F. E. Bunnètt. London: King, 1872, pp. 31-84. However, the original manuscript was not found until 1952, when it was miraculously discovered in the school library of the Gymnasium Christianeum in Hamburg-Altona. It was subsequently sold to a Danish private collector in 1955, resold to the Royal Library in Copenhagen in 1958 and published in the same year. All publications and references to the French autobiography predating the mid-20th century are based on copies and transcripts of the lost manuscript. For more information on the manuscript's composition and odyssey, see Haupt, Hans. 'Das Leonora-Christina-Manuskript des Christianeums in Hamburg-Altona', *Zeitschrift der Gesellschaft für Schleswig-Holsteinische Geschichte* 80 (1956), pp. 73-92. See also Lindegård Hjorth, Poul. '*Jammers Minde's* udgivelseshistorie', p. xxxi.
205 Bjerg, Svend. 'Leonora Christinas Jammers Minde'. In *Selvbiografien*, ed. Lise Bek et al. Viby J.: Centrum, 1983, p. 56: »Formentlig har Leonora Christina heller ikke følt noget større behov for at forsvare sig«.

Jammers Minde: Confessions Dedicated to the Beloved Ones or Political Apologia?

the circumstances of her imprisonment were a rather public affair.[206] As contended by Marita Akhøj Nielsen, the text delivers no reason to believe *Jammers Minde* was written for anybody else than the author's children: »For the future of the family it was crucial to claim that the death sentence on Ulfeldt and the incarceration of Leonora Christina were both without justification«.[207] However, as explicated in Chapter 1.1.3., there was even less reason for Leonora Christina to believe her text would reach her children without passing through someone else's hands first (or to be convinced that she would manage to deliver her account to her children in person). The possibility, or risk, of a publication of *Jammers Minde* was inherent. Thus, the audience Leonora Christina had in mind while writing *Jammers Minde* must at some point have extended beyond her remaining family.

Whoever attempts to determine Leonora Christina's authorial intention in writing *Jammers Minde* must also keep in mind that when she started her memorandum, she still had eleven years of imprisonment ahead of her. Frederik III had already died in 1670 and against all odds Leonora Christina remained in the Blue Tower, where she began the composition of *Jammers Minde* in 1674. When Sophie Amalie of Brunswick-Lüneburg died in 1685, her archenemy was still lusty. Leonora Christina spent the years after her release in Maribo Abbey, where she continued to work on her literary enterprises, including *Jammers Minde*. Altogether, she had thus approximately twenty years to continue and perfect *Jammers Minde*. Thanks to the groundbreaking work of Otto Glismann, who analysed paper and style of the manuscript, it is now commonly known that *Jammers Minde* is a stylised and

---

206 There is, of course, a third option, which has been mentioned before by several scholars, but constitutes a minor consideration in this study, since it hardly accounts for the countless corrections undertaken by Leonora Christina years after her release (see below): that Leonora Christina wrote *Jammers Minde* primarily for herself. Silvia Müller, for example, suggests that writing might have been therapeutical to Leonora Christina (Müller, Silvia. '»Herren sargar och läker, han slår och hans hand helar«: Konfliktbewältigung in den autobiographischen Texten von Marta Hagman (1765), Sophia Elisabet Brenner (1722) und Christina Regina vom Birchenbaum (1651)', Skandinavistik 30/1 (2000), p. 1), while Thomas Seiler contends that the objective of *Jammers Minde* was to preserve its author's autonomy and status (Seiler, Thomas. *Im Leben verschollen*, respectively pp. 69 and 67). That Leonora Christina continued to be concerned with these issues – autonomy and status – is evidenced by her narrative of her exit from the Blue Tower. Even after more than two decades in the Blue Tower, dignity commanded Leonora Christina's conduct and has thus immensely kindled her admirer's esteem for her. When Leonora Christina received the news of her release on 19 May 1685 at 8 o'clock in the morning, she decided not to rush into freedom, but to wait until dark to leave »med manner« (*Jammers Minde*, p. 245). At 10 o'clock in the evening, Leonora Christina left the tower, eagerly awaited by a crowd of people. Her insistence on leaving her arrest with style found its way into several novels featuring her as the central heroine. Accordingly, the opera *Leonora Christina* (1926) by Aage Barfoed and Siegfried Salomon opens with Leonora Christina's last full day in the Blue Tower.
207 Akhøj Nielsen, Marita. 'Leonora Christina: An Imprisoned Princess', p. 94.

elaborate account, rather than a mere prison diary.[208] While Glismann dates the first third of the text, a clean copy, to 1674 (i.e. eleven years after the time of the events described in this part), he asserts that she did not commence with the second part before 1685, the year of her release from the Blue Tower. The third part of *Jammers Minde* was indisputably written during Leonora Christina's final years in Maribo, where she died in 1698. This means that only the first part was composed in prison, the other two after her release from the Blue Tower.

These results were confirmed and specified decades later by Marita Akhøj Nielsen and Ingelise Nielsen. The paper used for the first part of the manuscript (pp. 1*-78)[209] was also used by Otto Sperling the Elder when he wrote his testament in 1674, which is also the date mentioned at the end of *Fortalen*.[210] The second part of the manuscript starts after Leonora Christina's moment of utter despair and subsequent spiritual renewal, when she awakes with an epiphany and decides to accept her fate patiently and stoically. There are a few transitional sheets (pp. 79-92) in between

---

208 Glismann, Otto. 'Om Tilblivelsen af Leonora Christinas Jammers-Minde', Acta Philologica Scandinavica 28 (1966), pp. 75-102. While working on the third edition of *Jammers Minde*, Birket Smith had already noticed that the manuscript essentially consisted of three parts, the latter two of which seemed to have been written in Maribo, as evidenced by Leonora Christina's changing orthography. Birket Smith, however, held the view that the two preserved latter parts of *Jammers Minde* must be copies (written by Leonora Christina) of earlier versions written in the Blue Tower, while Glismann highlighted Leonora Christina's subsequent editing of her own manuscript with the objective of creating the impression of the entire account having been written in prison. Birket Smith believed in the authenticity and immediacy of Leonora Christina's narrative, whereas Glismann uncovered the literary, constructed character of the manuscript and the fictions created by Leonora Christina. For a comprehensive presentation of Sophus Birket Smith's work on *Jammers Minde*, see Lindegård Hjorth, Poul. '*Jammers Minde's* udgivelseshistorie', pp. xiv-xxii. One example of Leonora Christina's creation of fictive immediacy is a later correction undertaken in Leonora Christina's description of her prison cell. A current line in *Jammers Minde*, p. 73 reads: »der vdi staar tuende Senge«; but originally, Leonora Christina had used *stoed*, i.e. past tense. This means that Leonora Christina had described a furniture arrangement that was no longer there, while consciously trying to convey the impression of an immediate description of her current cell (see Akhøj Nielsen, Marita. 'Skrifttræk og blæk'. In Leonora Christina. *Jammers Minde: Diplomatarisk udgave ved Poul Lindegård Hjorth og Marita Akhøj Nielsen under medvirkning af Ingelise Nielsen,* ed. Det Danske Sprog- og Litteraturselskab. Copenhagen: Reitzel, 1998, p. lvi).

209 For a complete register of the diverse types of paper used for the *Jammers Minde*-manuscript, see Nielsen, Ingelise. 'Papir og lægopbygning'. In Leonora Christina. *Jammers Minde: Diplomatarisk udgave ved Poul Lindegård Hjorth og Marita Akhøj Nielsen under medvirkning af Ingelise Nielsen,* ed. Det Danske Sprog- og Litteraturselskab. Copenhagen: Reitzel, 1998, pp. xlvi-lii.

210 For a reconstruction of the genesis of *Jammers Minde* based on the types of paper used for the manuscript, see Akhøj Nielsen, Marita. 'Papirets vidnesbyrd om håndskriftets tilblivelseshistorie'. In Leonora Christina. *Jammers Minde: Diplomatarisk udgave ved Poul Lindegård Hjorth og Marita Akhøj Nielsen under medvirkning af Ingelise Nielsen,* ed. Det Danske Sprog- og Litteraturselskab. Copenhagen: Reitzel, 1998, pp. lii-lv. See also Akhøj Nielsen, Marita. 'The conservator's work and literary history: the example of a 17th-century Danish autobiography'. In *Care and conservation of manuscripts 5: Proceedings of the fifth international seminar held at the University of Copenhagen 19th-20th April 1999,* eds. Gillian Fellows-Jensen and Peter Springborg. Copenhagen: The Royal Library, 2000, pp. 38-47. The results of this paper-based analysis correspond to the conclusions derived from an examination of ink and handwriting in *Jammers Minde*. See Akhøj Nielsen, Marita. 'Skrifttræk og blæk', pp. lv-lxvii.

the first two parts which, due to inconsistencies regarding handwriting and paper, as well as single sheets which have been cut out and replaced by new ones, indicate that Leonora Christina had started with this part of the manuscript in 1674, but continued in Maribo. It further suggests that Leonora Christina had found it difficult to continue her account and create a consistent story, when her living conditions had changed significantly since the time described in the first part of the manuscript.[211] The second part (pp. 93-188) was written in Maribo and its topic covers the years of Leonora Christina's spiritual renewal onwards, until 1674. There is another transitional part (pp. 189-200) in between the last two parts of the manuscript, indicating that Leonora Christina had again found it difficult to continue with her account. The third and final part of the manuscript (pp. 201-258), as well as the separate sheets containing *dødslisten* (pp. 259-266), was written in Leonora Christina's final years, but not too long after finishing the second part of the manuscript, since she had partially used the same paper in the two last parts. A comparison of the orthography in *Jammers Minde* with that used in letters written by Leonora Christina furthermore suggests three different orthographic periods that correspond to the three parts of *Jammers Minde* established through an analysis of paper, ink and handwriting, since Leonora Christina had changed her spelling after 1693 and then again after 1696.[212]

The genesis of *Jammers Minde*, as evidenced by the changing orthography, ink and paper used for the manuscript, indicates that Leonora Christina's narrative mindset must have changed dramatically in the course of the writing process, thus complicating a determination of Leonora Christina's authorial intention.[213] After all, many years passed before Leonora Christina continued the account she had started in the Blue Tower. The analysis of the material exposes the moment of writing in the account as fiction: Leonora Christina wants her readers to believe that she wrote most of the narrative in the confinement of her tower cell. This in turn indicates that at least the last two parts of *Jammers Minde* were not (primarily) written for Leonora Christina's children, since it is rather unlikely that she had created this fictional

---

211 See Akhøj Nielsen, Marita. 'The conservator's work and literary history', p. 44.
212 See ibid., p. 40.
213 For the same reason, Marita Akhøj Nielsen demands that literary scholarship engaging with *Jammers Minde* should not consider and represent the text as one – as has been the norm so far – but as a manuscript comprised of three different texts (ibid., pp. 44-46). Accordingly, Akhøj Nielsen has conducted a separate literary analysis of the three diverse parts of *Jammers Minde* (Akhøj Nielsen, Marita. 'Leonora Christina Ulfeldt: Forfatterportræt': http://adl.dk/adl_pub/fportraet/cv/ShowFpItem. xsql?nnoc=adl_pub&ff_id=36&p_fpkat_id=fskab). Despite the legitimacy of Akhøj Nielsen's observation, a similar approach, i.e. an analysis of *Jammers Minde* in three parts, was not undertaken in the present study since the reproduction of the content of *Jammers Minde* in literary as well as historiographical works depicting Leonora Christina remains unaffected by this awareness of the text's genesis. I have, however, endeavoured to refer to the diverse parts of the manuscript throughout the analysis of the text in Chapter 1.

time of writing for them. Five of them were already dead[214] when she finished the manuscript. Moreover, her eldest daughter, Anna Catharina (1639-1707), came to live with her in Maribo Abbey, hence at least one child is likely to have known that the last two parts of *Jammers Minde* were not composed in prison.[215] It may well be that Leonora Christina was thinking of her children, when she wrote the first pages of *Jammers Minde*, but in Maribo she must have had another readership in mind.

A critical analysis of *Jammers Minde* furthermore shows that Leonora Christina used other literary techniques as well, in order to stylise her account. The apologetic elements in the text are particularly blatant and typical of an autobiography written in prison. A central element of and the organising principle in the first part of *Jammers Minde* is its similarity to a hagiography, primarily due to the previously mentioned spiritual renewal, which concludes the first part of the narrative. *Jammers Minde* as a whole, on the other hand, is a rather profane work, but the title alone predetermines the recipient's expectations. It resembles, probably coincidentally, the title of the autobiography of one of the most influential theologians preceding the 17th century, Peter Abelard's *Historia calamitatum* (probably written in 1132 or soon after), which in turn was influenced by the vita of an even more influential scholar and cleric, Augustine's *Confessiones*.[216] Furthermore, Leonora Christina, as the self-proclaimed new Job, assures both the reader and herself of her immaculacy, which she recognises in an epiphany:

> Endeligen saae Gud til mig med sine Naadsens Øygne, saa at ieg den 31 *Augusti* fick en roelig Søffn om Natten, oc ret vdi dagningen wognede ieg med effterfølgende Ord vdi Munden. Mein Kind verzage nicht, wan du von Gott gestraffet wirst, dan welchen der Herr lieb hatt den züchtiget er. Er steupet aber einen Ieglichen Sohn den er auffnimt.
>
> (*Jammers Minde*, p. 80)

---

214 After 1663, Leonora Christina saw only three of her children again: Anna Catharina, Leonora Sophie and Leo.

215 Based on the letter Anna Catharina sent to her brother together with the manuscript of *Jammers Minde* (see below), Otto Glismann holds the view that Anna Catharina had been entirely unaware of the existence of the manuscript until she found it after her mother's death (Glismann, Otto. *Om at »handle mis« med en klassiker: Sprog og stil i »Jammers Minde« – En tekstkritisk undersøgelse af udgaverne*. Birkerød: 1997, p. 1). Said letter indeed indicates that Anna Catharina had not read *Jammers Minde* before her mother's death. This, however, does not exclude the possibility of her knowing about its existence and her mother's continued work on it. Neither does this information rule out the possibility that Leonora Christina had handed the manuscript over to her daughter in person. Leonora Christina's continued work on the manuscript over the last years of her life rather implies that it had been a dear possession of hers, which renders the idea that she would not submit something of such value in person rather unlikely.

216 For obvious reasons it was impossible for Leonora Christina to follow the tradition established by Augustine and thus call her autobiography *Confessiones*, as she repeatedly insisted on having nothing to confess.

Finally, she lends a new meaning to her name by reinterpreting it as L*iidende Christinne* (*Jammers Minde*, p. 235). Yet the climax of her own sanctification was perhaps reached with a picture drawn by her after her release from the Blue Tower in 1685, today kept in the Museum of National History in Frederiksborg Castle. It depicts Leonora Christina kneeling with a cross in anticipation of a crown, here delivered by what appears to be God. As in Leonora Christina's literary creations, pride and obedience towards God (here illustrated by a crown and a cross) do not contradict, but complement each other, as contended by the theologian Lone Fatum: »I kors og krone forener hun her sin tilværelsens modsigelser, så at de ganske bogstaveligt går op i en højere enhed«.[217] As a woman of faith, Leonora Christina is well aware that her earthly path is separated from and yet connected to her divine destiny. Moreover, the depiction that her final reward must be somehow connected to her years of imprisonment is evident from the background of the scene. It shows her four prisons: Malmö, Hammershus (or »Jammershus«, as Leonora Christina called it in a poem)[218] on Bornholm, Dover Castle in England, and the Blue Tower.

The influence of Leonora Christina's self-portrayal as *Liidende Christinne* was particularly dominant in the 19th century and lingered until the end of the 20th century. Even those (more recent) critics, who eyed her every word with suspicion,[219] could not deny her talent. Whether one decides to consider Leonora Christina a saint, or simply a good writer, *Jammers Minde* was a success in any case. It was indeed a much bigger success than any pamphlet could ever have been. For politics are bound to the moment, but literature – if done well – is of a more general interest, with the possibility of having a more lasting impact. That Leonora Christina, who was so well versed in both politics and the arts, should not have anticipated this success, or at least its possibility, seems rather unlikely.

1.2.1. Research on *Jammers Minde* Since its Discovery in 1868
From Vienna to Copenhagen – The Creation of a Myth

> Det er meget vigtigt at holde sig for øje, at ingen anden gruppe af historisk kildemateriale er så mytedannende som erindringsværker og biografier.[220]

---

217 Fatum, Lone. 'Kongedatteren og Gudsfrygten', p. 198.
218 See Heiberg, Steffen. *Enhjørningen Corfitz Ulfeldt*, p. 200.
219 For example Wamberg, Bodil. *Leonora Christina*, p. 159: »Man træffer på løgnen i alt, hvad hun skriver«.
220 Bjørn, Hans. 'Leonora Christina – Christian IV's datter', p. 9.

When Leonora Christina died in 1698, she was already famous. Writers such as Ludvig Holberg (1684-1754) subsequently took an interest in her fate and reconstructed her life's story with the aid of contemporary records, as well as copies and transcripts of her French autobiography. Even though Leonora Christina's French narrative was not properly published before the mid-20th century, it was known amongst scholars and thus employed as a historical document. When *Jammers Minde* became accessible to a broad public in 1869, it was dealt with in the same manner. A widespread consideration of *Jammers Minde* as historical account postponed much of relevant literary research on the text by decades. However, it was also this ambiguity of the text that encouraged researchers from diverse fields to contribute to current knowledge about Leonora Christina and *Jammers Minde*. Literary scholars, historians, theologians,[221] linguists, and even physicians[222] have all had their share in reconstructing what had happened in the Blue Tower.

Already before the first publication of *Jammers Minde*, Danish historian Oluf Bang sensed the potential for sensation inherent to a life story written by Leonora Christina and made accessible to the reading public. Thus, he published 'Frue Eleonoræ Christinæ Sal. Corf. Ulfelds hendes Levnet af hende selv beskreven den 4. Maji 1697 paa Maribo' and called it a »Rigtig Copi efter det egenhændige Manuscript, som fandtes i Major Becks Giemme i Skaane«,[223] under the assumption – as the title suggests – that the account had been written by Leonora Christina herself. This life account was subsequently declared a forgery by Birket Smith, as well as by Brøndum-Nielsen and Bøggild-Andersen.[224] In hindsight, it appears obvious that this story was not written by Leonora Christina. According to Bang's publication, the original was written in French and in the first person. This indicates that the forger was aware of the existence of her French autobiography, but had probably

---

221 For example Bjerg, Svend. 'Leonora Christinas Jammers Minde', pp. 45-56.

222 For example Frits Tobiesen, who analysed Leonora Christina's account of an intestinal concretion she excreted one day in 1682 (*Jammers Minde*, p. 219) and concluded that Leonora Christina must have suffered from chronical constipation due to the confinement of her cell. See Tobiesen, Frits. *»En steenig Materie«: Oplysninger om Leonora Christina Ulfeldts Helbred*. Copenhagen: 1922 (Særtryk af Ugeskrift for Læger 19).

223 Anonymous. 'Frue Eleonoræ Christinæ Sal. Corf. Ulfelds hendes Levnet af hende selv beskreven den 4. Maji 1697 paa Maribo. Rigtig Copie efter det egenhændige Manuscript, som fandtes i Major Becks Giemme i Skaane'. In *Samling af adskillige nyttige og opbyggelige Materier saa vel gamle som nye II*, ed. Oluf Bang. Copenhagen: 1743, pp. 125-159.

224 Brøndum-Nielsen and Bøggild-Andersen lament that several historians have consulted this document, even though it is a »Falsum«. They also exclude the possibility that a reputable historian like Oluf Bang could have produced the forgery himself. See Brøndum-Nielsen, Johs. and C.O. Bøggild-Andersen. 'Historiske Oplysninger'. In Leonora Christina. *Jammers Minde og andre selvbiografiske Skildringer*, eds. Johs. Brøndum-Nielsen and C.O. Bøggild-Andersen. Copenhagen: Rosenkilde og Bagger, 1949, p. 304.

not actually seen any of the preserved copies. Furthermore, the fake autobiography published by Bang does not do justice to the pleasure in telling usually exhibited by Leonora Christina's accounts. Finally, the opening words of this document are too cynical to stem from Leonora Christina. In 1697, Leonora Christina was living in Maribo, an aged woman who had emerged victorious from her ordeal. However, according to this account, Leonora Christina decided to write down her life story to disillusion others about the cruelties of the world and married life.[225] Yet regardless of the text being a fabrication, this premature attempt at giving the public a life story of the infamous Countess Ulfeldt could only bode well regarding the actual publication 126 years later.

After Leonora Christina's death in 1698, the manuscript titled *Jammers Minde* was initially in the possession of Anna Catharina, who had been living with her mother during her final years in Maribo. Anna Catharina was moved by her mother's testimony and decided to send the manuscript to her brother Leo Ulfeldt, by then an Austrian field marshal. As she explains in a letter sent together with the manuscript, Anna Catharina did not want the narrative to fall into the hands of potential enemies of the Ulfeldt family, as she feared that the account of her mother's calamities would rejoice them.[226] Thus, the manuscript had to be sent out of Denmark. Until 1920,[227] *Jammers Minde* remained in the private possession of Leonora Christina's descendants, one of them being Count Johann Nepomuk Waldstein-Wartenberg (1809-1876), who allowed for the manuscript to be sent from Austria to Denmark in 1868, where it was received by the librarian Sophus Birket Smith. The first edition of *Jammers Minde* was published one year later, in 1869, including a preface by Count Waldstein-Wartenberg himself, in which he attempts to exonerate *both* of his famous ancestors by arguing that such a gifted and noble-minded woman as

---

225 Anonymous. 'Frue Eleonoræ Christinæ Sal. Corf. Ulfelds hendes Levnet af hende selv beskreven', p. 126.

226 Letter written by Anna Catharina Ulfeldt and reproduced in Akhøj Nielsen, Marita. 'Manuskriptbeskrivelse: Manuskriptets ydre'. In Leonora Christina. *Jammers Minde: Diplomatarisk udgave ved Poul Lindegård Hjorth og Marita Akhøj Nielsen under medvirkning af Ingelise Nielsen,* ed. Det Danske Sprog- og Litteraturselskab. Copenhagen: Reitzel, 1998, p. xxxiv.

227 While working on his three editions of *Jammers Minde*, Birket Smith did thus not always have the manuscript in front of him, since it remained private property during his lifetime (Lindegård Hjorth, Poul. '*Jammers Minde's* udgivelseshistorie', p. xvii).

Leonora Christina could never have remained faithful to someone undeserving of her love. [228]

The Count's conviction that Leonora Christina's love for her husband must be considered a token of her husband's positive traits was subsequently adopted by another influential advocate of the Ulfeldt couple, i.e. Hans Christian Andersen (see Chapters 2.2.1. and 2.2.3.). More important, though, is that Birket Smith followed the Count's verdict concerning Leonora Christina's character and that his assessment came to influence generations of artists, scholars and common readers – and spark a long-lasting discussion about her innocence:

> Alt i alt hører Leonora Christinas Skikkelse og Skjæbne til dem, som gjør et uudslette-ligt Indtryk selv paa den sløveste Indbildningskraft, og da nu ogsaa den Kjendsgjerning, at hun væsentlig led for sin Ægtefælles Brøde, maa stemme alle Hjerter til hendes Gunst, forstaar man let Grunden til, at der blandt alle de Kvinder, den danske Historie melder om, ikke findes nogen, hvis Navn Folket holder højere i Ære, eller hvis Minde det gjemmer med større Trofasthed end hendes.[229]

The first publication of *Jammers Minde* was eagerly awaited and subsequently devoured by the scholars and artists who afterwards came to influence Danish perceptions of Leonora Christina to a significant degree, such as the Danish painter Kristian Zahrtmann. Considering that an expansive adoration of Leonora Christina did not commence before 1869, it is rather odd, however, that Birket Smith should refer to Leonora Christina as if she were an undisputed national heroine (and even odder if one considers the misdeeds of the Ulfeldt couple that eventually immortalised their name). Perhaps Birket Smith himself was slightly preconceived due to Hans Christian Andersen's works, which predate the publication of *Jammers Minde* and depict Leonora Christina as a national heroine. If this were the case, one ought to consider the famous fairy-tale writer the rightful source of Leonora Christina's reputation in the 19th century.

---

228 Waldstein-Wartenberg, Johann Nepomuk. Introduction in Leonora Christina. *»Jammers-Minde«. En egenhændig Skildring af hendes Fangenskab i Blaataarn i Aarene 1663-1685 udgivet efter det originale Haandskrift i Grev J. Waldstein Wartembergs Eje. Med et Forord af Hs. Excellence Grev Johan Waldstein Wartemberg*, ed. Sophus Birket Smith. Copenhagen: Gyldendal, 1869, p. VI. The same argument is, coincidentally, produced in the novel *Die Gräfin Ulfeld oder die vierundzwanzig Königskinder* (1834) by Leopold Schefer (see Chapter 2.7.1.) to account for Ulfeld's (fictive) exoneration succeeding his trial in Malmö (Schefer, Leopold. *Die Gräfin Ulfeld oder die vierundzwanzig Königskinder 2. Historischer Roman von Leopold Schefer.* Berlin: Veit & Comp, 1834, p. 97).

229 Birket Smith, Sophus. 'Indledning'. In Leonora Christina. *Leonora Christina Grevinde Ulfeldt's »Jammers Minde«: En egenhændig Skildring af hendes Fangenskab i Blaataarn i Aarene 1663-85*, ed. Sophus Birket Smith. Copenhagen: Gyldendal, 1900, p. 1.

However, another central figure of the 19th-century intellectual milieu in Denmark, as well as in entire Scandinavia, wrote a very favourable review of *Jammers Minde* and its author, thus paving the way for a positive reception of Leonora Christina and her work. After reading the primary publication of *Jammers Minde* in 1869, the Danish critic Georg Brandes (1842-1927) penned the following:

> Denne Bog er den betydeligste, der er udkommet her i Danmark i mange Aar, og en af de betydeligste, der er skrevet paa Dansk. Det Billede af en ædel Charakteer og en overlegen Personlighed, der saa uventet er gjenfundet og som paa et Haar nær var gaaet tabt (se det franske Brev, hvoraf Manuscriptet er ledsaget) denne hele Skikkelse er saa skjøn, at Enhver, selv den, der ingen historisk Sagkundskab har, føler sig bevæget til i al Ærefrygt at lægge sin Krands ved Statuens Fod.[230]

In Brandes' eyes, *Jammers Minde* portrays an exemplary fight between Good and Evil,[231] thus addressing humanity in its entirety. However, he warmly recommends the book to women in particular:

> Skulde man troe det? – Der gives Personer, som løbe i Byen rundt med den Dom, at Bogen paa adskillige Steder er saa uhøvisk, at den ikke kan læses af Kvinder. Er det muligt, at den aandelige Usselhed kan gaae saa vidt, at man for Alvor mener, det skulde kunne skade vore Kvinder at læse, hvad den ædleste og mest udviklede af deres Kjøn her i Danmark har skrevet?[232]

In the same year, Georg Brandes published a Danish translation of John Stuart Mill's essay *The Subjection of Women* (1869). Hence, Leonora Christina also found her way into the foreword to *Kvindernes Underkuelse*: »Det er nutildags umuligt at vide, hvad Kvindenaturen i dens sunde Udvikling, i dens Rigdom og Fylde er; man faar en Anelse derom, naar man læser saadanne Bøger som *Héloises Breve* eller Leonora Christinas *Jammers-Minde*«.[233] Thusly embedded in the contemporary discussion involving women's rights and literature's role within society, *Jammers Minde* was practically guaranteed to be met with great interest.

---

230 Brandes, Georg. 'Leonora Christina'. In *Georg Brandes – den mangfoldige*, ed. Jørgen Knudsen. Copenhagen: Gyldendal, 2005, p. 67.
231 Cf. ibid., p. 68.
232 Ibid., p. 70.
233 Brandes, Georg. 'Kvindesagen'. In *Georg Brandes – den mangfoldige*, ed. Jørgen Knudsen. Copenhagen: Gyldendal, 2005, p. 191.

Fiction or Non-Fiction?
The basic content of Sophus Birket Smith's introduction to *Jammers Minde* is well known, thus his findings shall be reproduced in only a brief summary. It is worthwhile noting that Birket Smith forestalls some of Glismann's work, but that he deemed considerably more of the account to have been written in the Blue Tower.[234] As regards Leonora Christina's authorial intention, Birket Smith plainly follows the author's statements: »'Jammers-Mindet' [er] skrevet for at læses og opbevares af Forfatterindens Børn og for at tjene dem paa én Gang til en Erindring om deres ulykkelige Moder og til en Lære for deres Liv«.[235] Despite any demurs concerning the feasibility of such a transaction and its plausibility, Birket Smith does not question Leonora Christina's declaration of having written this record solely for her children. Birket Smith's evaluation of *Jammers Minde* is, besides its obvious merits, also known for its lack of critical questioning (for example through an extensive use of phrases like »som hun selv siger«). He handles even the most delicate chapter of Leonora Christina's life with an astonishingly carefree credulity:

> At Skriftet saaledes ikke indeholder nogen nærmere Underretning om de Planer, som gav Anledning baade til Mandens Domfældelse og hendes egen Fængsling, maa blandt andet efter min Overbevisning tilskrives den simple Aarsag, *som hun selv et Steds anfører* [my italics], at hvad hun ikke véd, det kan hun heller ikke sige. Hvorledes man nu i øvrigt vil forklare denne hendes Uvidenhed – og jeg mener, at den meget godt lader sig forklare deraf, at han, der visselig elskede sin Hustru højt, ikke har villet gjøre hende delagtig i saa farlige Hemmeligheder, saa længe endnu intet var afgjort – vil dog næppe mange, som har læst denne Bog, tvivle om, *at det forholder sig, som hun siger* [my italics], eller ogsaa maa men én Gang for alle opgive Tanken om at kunne skjelne Sandhedens Sprog fra Løgnens og Hykleriets.[236]

Even though Birket Smith commends Leonora Christina's literary abilities (»Hun, som af Naturen var saa ypperligt udstyret i mange Henseender, havde nemlig ogsaa betydelige Ævner som Forfatter og brugte sin Pen flittigt«),[237] he does not seem to

---

234 See Birket Smith, Sophus. 'Indledning', p. 4.
235 Ibid., p. 3.
236 Ibid., p. 4.
237 Ibid., p. 2.

consider her a writer in the common sense of the word.[238] Birket Smith interprets Leonora Christina's authorial activity as being instigated by motherly love and and a merely documentary interest,[239] which may have led him to the (albeit implicit) conclusion that she was no writer, but simply a person who enjoyed writing. This perception, which ignored the possibility of any occurrence of literary fiction in the account of this writing noblewoman, coined the ensuing assessments of *Jammers Minde* and Leonora Christina.

By the middle of the 20th century, scholarly enthusiasm over *Jammers Minde* sagged and research on the text stagnated. Most academic contributions on the topic would merely aim at presenting, rather than interpreting it. At the same time, Leonora Christina's character and fate still influenced scholarly attitudes towards *Jammers Minde* significantly. One example is Hans Brix's chapter on Leonora Christina in *Danmarks Digtere*. As indicated by the title, Brix's scholarly objective was to present Denmark's poets, rather than discuss them. Thus, he starts his presentation of Leonora Christina with a scholarly commonplace: »Leonora Christina indtager i vor Litteratur et Æressæde som Forfatter af det ypperste danske Prosaværk fra det syttende Aarhundrede«.[240] Despite the aim of his book, Brix does not refrain from inserting some words of admiration for Leonora Christina and thus, for her work: »Man vilde ikke med Rette kunne paastaa, at hendes Bog *Den fangne Grevinde Leonore Christines Jammers Minde* er blevet det den er, mere i Kraft af Forholdenes Magt end hendes egne Anlæg«.[241] Hans Brix's approach, which bases the evaluation of Leonora Christina's works on her character, is characteristic of the research on *Jammers Minde* preceding the last quarter of the 20th century. Brix

---

238 This perception is not unjustified given that Leonora Christina – if one considers her work in the appropriate historical context – was not a writer in the modern sense of the word, but »eine gebildete, lesende und schreibende Frau« (see Heitmann, Annegret. 'Leonora, Gräfin Christina Ulfeldt'. In *Metzler-Autorinnen-Lexikon*, ed. Ute Hechtfischer. Stuttgart: Metzler, 1998, p. 297: »an educated, reading and writing woman«). Sigrid Weigel favours a similar distinction. In her monography on prison literature, Weigel differentiates between »delinquent literature« and literature by imprisoned intellectuals, since for most intellectuals – especially those of previous centuries – writing was a part of the everyday life, instead of being explicitly motivated by their confinement (see Weigel, Sigrid. *Und selbst im Kerker frei...! Schreiben im Gefängnis: Zur Theorie und Gattungsgeschichte der Gefängnisliteratur (1750-1933)*. Marburg/Lahn: Guttandin und Hoppe, 1982, p. 17). According to this differentiation, *Jammers Minde*, being a text written by an imprisoned intellectual cannot be classified as prison literature.

239 Birket Smith, Sophus. 'Indledning', p. 6: »Dertil kommer, at hun, som altid havde en stærk Drift til at optegne, hvad mærkeligt der mødte hende, uden Tvivl ogsaa lige fra Fangenskabets Begyndelse af har været betænkt paa at nedskrive en Beretning om sine Oplevelser i Fængslet og derfor ogsaa maa antages fra Begyndelsen af at have givet nøje Agt paa, hvad der foregik om og med hende [...]«.

240 Brix, Hans. *Danmarks Digtere: Fyrretyve Kapitler af dansk Digtekunsts Historie*. Copenhagen: Aschehoug, 1951 (1925), p. 46.

241 Ibid.

praises Leonora Christina abilities, while at the same time basing his laud on her self-assertions:

> Leonore Christines Vane og Omgang var europæisk og fyrstelig, hun var meget sprogkyndig, hendes Intelligens høit udviklet og hendes Belæsthed udbredt. Tillige var hun skarpsindig og snarraadig. [...] Og hun paabegyndte i Fængslet et delvis bevaret Værk, kaldet Heltinders Pryd, der var inddelt i tre Dele: første Afdeling handler om stridbare Heltinder, anden Del om trofaste og kyske Heltinder, tredje Del om standhaftige Heltinder. Selv havde hun Adkomst til Plads i dem alle tre, idet man med Føie kan kalde hende baade en stridbar, en trofast og en standhaftig Heltinde. [...] Bogen [*Jammers Minde*] er et Mindesmærke i vor Litteratur, lige mærkeligt ved den glimrende Personlighed, der danner Midtpunktet i Skildringen [...].²⁴²

These excerpts from Brix's book illustrate why research on *Jammers Minde* in the mid-20th century was stagnating – it was moving in a circle, instead of advancing. Brix attributes the grandeur of *Jammers Minde* to the character of its author, while at the same time gathering her character from *Jammers Minde*. He also questions the objectivity of Leonora Christina's depiction of events and people in the Blue Tower, yet without pursuing this question in further detail: »Og atter spørger vi: Hvad er Sandhed her og hvad er vrangt? Er Personer og Hændelser helt igennem rigtigt opfattet eller delvis mistydet?«²⁴³ Furthermore, it is quite significant that Brix calls *Jammers Minde* a diary,²⁴⁴ i.e. one of the least literary genres. This miscategorisation of *Jammers Minde* and the focus on its author's personality and the validity of *Jammers Minde* may have hindered its examination to a significant degree.

More current introductions to the topic, on the other hand, such as Vibeke A. Pedersen's article on *Jammers Minde* in the *Dansk litteraturs historie* from 2007, demonstrate an appreciation of the fictional content of *Jammers Minde* by categorising it as »den første moderne selvbiografi«.²⁴⁵ Annegret Heitmann's article on Leonora Christina in the *Metzler-Autorinnen-Lexikon* is equally representative of the perceptional breakthrough concerning *Jammers Minde* that occurred towards the end of the 20th century, as it highlights the constructed character of Leonora Christina's selfportrayal: »Mit dem Einsatz von Fiktionalisierungstechniken zur

---

242 Ibid., p. 47f.
243 Ibid., p. 48.
244 Ibid.: »Af en mærkelig Virkning er i det givne Tilfælde den litterære Form, i hvilken Værket fremtræder, nemlig Dagbogsformen«.
245 Pedersen, Vibeke A. *Dansk litteraturs historie 1: 1100-1800*, ed. Klaus P. Mortensen. Copenhagen: Gyldendal, 2007, p. 398.

Konstruktion eines Selbstbildes legt L. die Grundlagen für die literarische Autobiographie im Norden«.[246]

Birgit Baldwin, too, adopted this new perspective when engaging in the question of whether one should read *Jammers Minde* as a historical document or as an autobiographical narrative. The proportions of historiography and fiction in *Jammers Minde*, as well as in similar texts, still constituted a great conundrum to literary scholars of the late 20th century;[247] but in order to solve it, Baldwin posed a question both innovative and yet curiously reminiscent of Barrett J. Mandel's new perspective on autobiography presented in his essay 'Full of Life Now'[248] (see Chapter 1.1.1.). Just as Mandel referred to the often overlooked role of the reader in the issue of the categorisation of autobiography, Baldwin too decided to tackle the matter from a different direction: »The question of 'how' to read *Jammersminde* presupposes that of 'why' to read it: what have readers looked for in the past, and what may we look for today in order to think again about the work?«[249] As indicated repeatedly in the present study, *Jammers Minde* certainly has been considered and consulted as a historical document (for example as an unquestioned source in reconstructing parts of Leonora Christina's life story) in the past. However, for those readers who had hoped to gather some information on the plentiful memorable events of this time of upheaval in Denmark, *Jammers Minde* must have been a disappointment. The proper question regarding the nature and value of the work must therefore be: why do people *continue* to read *Jammers Minde*? Certainly not for its factual presentation of the events following the introduction of absolutism in Denmark, but rather for its intimate atmosphere and its penchant for detail atypical for its time. Baldwin contends, albeit with a question mark, that the love for detail displayed in *Jammers Minde* is not merely typical for prison literature but »in fact characteristic of literary writing in general«.[250] Thus, *Jammers Minde* – although

---

246 Heitmann, Annegret. 'Leonora, Gräfin Christina Ulfeldt', p. 297: »Through the use of techniques of fictionalisation with the aim of constructing an image, L. [Leonora Christina] lays the foundations for the literary autobiography of the North«.

247 Already in 1970, Jens Aage Doctor attempted to demonstrate that *Jammers Minde* was »en bog der fra første færd er tænkt og skrevet som digtning«; see Doctor, Jens Aage. 'Sandhedens rolle', Kritik 16 (1970), p. 5. That Birgit Baldwin engaged herself in the same issue twenty years later accounts for some reluctance on the reading public's part to accept Leonora Christina's prison account as something else than an objective testimony.

248 Mandel, Barrett J. 'Full of Life Now', p. 53: »Regardless of the rootedness of both novels and autobiographies in a process that binds them together, the very simple point that critics have been missing in their zeal to deal with the 'knotty philosophic and literary question' is that autobiographies and novels are finally totally distinct – and this simple fact every reader knows«.

249 Baldwin, Birgit. 'Jammersminde Remembered: A New Look at the Status of History and Literature', Scandinavian Studies 62/3 (1990), p. 266.

250 Ibid., p. 268.

like all autobiography taking up the position of a hybrid genre – can only be fully understood and appreciated if read as literature.

Closely connected with the issue of classifying *Jammers Minde*, or autobiography in general, is the question of truth in the account. While it is no longer timely to ask about the content of truth in autobiography, it is all the more relevant to examine how Leonora Christina constructs her very own autobiographical truth. Her numerous strategies of establishing authorial authority will be discussed in further detail in Chapter 1.2.2. However, one of those artifices is so rare it demands foreclosing. During her first years in the donjon, Leonora Christina was not allowed to have any tools of entertainment, thus she forged her own. Shortly after hearing about Corfitz's death, Leonora Christina looks for ways to kill time:

> Mit Kaarß war mig saa meget diß tyngere i ded første, efftersom saa høyligen war forbøden icke att tilstæde mig hwercken Kniiff Sax, Traa eller noget ieg kunde fordriffwe tiiden med; Omsider der Sinded kom lit i Roelighed, tenckte ieg paa noget att tage mig til, oc som ieg haffde en Syenaal som melded er, saa løste ieg miine baand op i min Nattrøye, som ware breede tafftis liiffarwe Baand, ded silke syde ieg med paa ded stycke Kluud ieg haffde, adskillige Blomster med smaa sting. Der ded haffde ende, drog ieg traaer vd aff mit Lagen, twant dem oc syde der med[.]
>
> (*Jammers Minde*, p. 99)[251]

After her husband's death, Leonora Christina may have regained some peace of mind and, perhaps, she also realised that she would have to make herself comfortable in the tower. Thus, she kept herself busy by fabricating writing tools, textiles, primitive pottery, and games in the most resourceful manner possible. Now remains the question as to why she deemed it necessary to make a note of those produces for posterity – is it because the ennui tempted her into keeping track of every detail, or, because she perhaps took pride in her own inventiveness? There is nothing to be said against any of the above, but, more importantly, these products constitute a verifiable truth outside the text, as contended by Nichole L. Sterling: »In the *French Autobiography*, she looks to stated claims about truthtelling and memory while in *Jammersminde* the audience is presented with tangible objects that could

---

[251] The words »høyligen« and »oc« are mutilated in the printed edition of *Jammers Minde*, due to a slip in the cropping process. The missing text is provided in Akhøj Nielsen, Marita. 'Leonora Christina *Jammers Minde* i ny udgave – hvorfor? hvordan?' In *Studier i Nordisk 1998-1999: Selskab for Nordisk Filologi: Foredrag og årsberetning*, ed. Selskab for Nordisk Filologi. Copenhagen, 2000, pp. 64-65.

presumably be found in order to support certain specific claims that she makes«.²⁵² Certainly, Leonora Christina could not be sure that the objects she manufactured would be preserved, but it was worth trying and, indeed, the Museum of National History in Frederiksborg Castle, as well as the Royal Danish Collection in Rosenborg Castle, have both retained some of her treasures – thus, at least some parts of her narrative can be proven to be true.

The Manuscript
After the release of *Jammers Minde* in 1869, it still took a century for the manuscript itself to be thoroughly (re-)examined. As indicated in Chapter 1.2., Otto Glismann attended to this task and his results exposed Leonora Christina's perspective on the narrated time as fiction (see above).²⁵³ Leonora Christina's much acclaimed documentary style is sustained throughout the entire account, thus conveying a feeling of immediacy, even though the narrated events date back one decade or longer. Some temporal corrections furthermore suggest that this fiction was much intended and thought-out. For example, Leonora Christina is very careful to use suggestive adverbs of place, such as »ud«, »ind« or »her«.²⁵⁴ Furthermore, her lively and detailed rendition of dialogues creates the impression that the narrated events happened just recently. The original manuscript of *Jammers Minde* reveals that Leonora Christina had sometimes abandoned this literary fiction and later on performed some corrections to re-establish it. This is a perfect example of an autobiography elevating itself from mere documentation, as it features a conscious process of creative construction.²⁵⁵

The first part of *Jammers Minde* ends after the interrogations and a few quotations from the Bible, at the moment of Leonora Christina's spiritual renewal. Once she finished this first part of her account, she put it aside and turned towards other employments, for example the composition of *Hæltinners Pryd*, which – or, as indicated in the introduction, the draft of which – Leonora Christina states to have finished in 1684 (see *Jammers Minde*, p. 226). The question remains as to why Leonora Christina was so eager to finish this first part of her manuscript, while taking

---

252 Sterling, Nichole L. 'Authority and Autobiography: The Case for Leonora Christina': http://www.academia.edu/2368850/Authority_and_Autobiography_Leonora_Christina.
253 Glismann, Otto. 'Om Tilblivelsen af Leonora Christinas Jammers-Minde', p. 99.
254 These and other corrections, such as Leonora Christina's subsequent 'Danisation' of her account, »er således vidnesbyrd om at forfatterindens eminente fornemmelse for sprog og stil skærpes yderligere under det årelange arbejde med teksten«. See Glismann, Otto. *Om at »handle mis« med en klassiker*, unpaginated preamble. Thus, Glismann felt obliged to devote an entire book to these corrections in *Jammers Minde*.
255 Cf. Seiler, Thomas. *Im Leben verschollen*, p. 47.

her time to continue the account. Bodil Wamberg suggests that Leonora Christina's wariness during the first weeks of her imprisonment might have induced her to document the events particularly carefully. The first part of the manuscript contains interactions with carriers of high offices, those men Leonora Christina considered her peers. Once the interrogations were concluded, she was rather isolated and surrounded by people of considerably lower rank. While it was thus comparatively easy for Leonora Christina to overtrump her guards, talking to Count Rantzau and his colleagues was a bigger challenge. Unlike the women attending Leonora Christina in the tower, these men were not simply chatting in order to get information on her husband's affairs – Leonora Christina was in the midst of an unofficial trial. Thus, caution was advisable. Leonora Christina did eventually master the interrogations, but subsequently, her words could still be twisted. Consequently, she felt the need to keep an account of the questioning, to be able to provide *her* version of the examination – if needed:[256] »Bevidstheden om manuskriptet med forhørsreferaterne gav hende ro i sjælen. Skulle hun dø i Blåtårn, så *havde* hun taget sin hævn. Hun havde udødeliggjort dronningens ondskab«.[257]

Leonora Christina's other, less famous autobiographical accounts, such as *Rejsen til Korsør 1656* and *Confrontationen i Malmø 1659*, support this suspicion. In *Rejsen til Korsør 1656*,[258] Leonora Christina narrates her encounter with Ulrik Christian Gyldenløve (1630-1658), one of the illegitimate children Christian IV had with Vibeke Kruse. Leonora Christina undertook this voyage back to her home country in order to achieve reconciliation with her brother Frederik III of Denmark. However, she only met Gyldenløve, who informed her that she was no longer welcome in Denmark. Thus, Leonora Christina headed towards German soil, but was almost detained and robbed by some men in carriages, who were sent to confiscate any letters she was carrying. The account furthermore contains Leonora Christina's

---

256 Similarly, Leonora Christina's meticulous listing of the items, particularly the jewellery that had been taken away from her (*Jammers Minde*, pp. 17-20), suggests that she might simply have wanted to keep an inventory of the injustice she had been subjected to and perhaps a way to retrieve these items in the future. One important reason for her to do so might have been her experience with Adolph Fuchs, who upon the prisoners' arrival in Hammershus had confiscated a casket containing jewellery, letters and value papers. As both Leonora Christina and Frederik III learned months later, he then sent the letters to the King, but kept the valuables to himself. See Birket Smith, Sophus. *Leonora Christina Grevinde Ulfeldts Historie 2*, pp. 10-18 and *Leonora Christina Grevinde Ulfeldts Franske Levnedsskildring*, pp. 9b-9d (Translation pp. 37-39).

257 Wamberg, Bodil. *Leonora Christina*, p. 230. If, on the other hand, one were to assume that Leonora Christina was the one twisting words in order to conceal the truth, Leonora Christina's eagerness to document the first weeks in the Blue Tower, when she was still being interrogated, suggests that she may have tried to remember her own words because they did not entirely match what had actually happened.

258 Leonora Christina. 'Rejsen til Korsør 1656'. In *Jammers Minde og andre selvbiografiske Skildringer*, eds. Johs. Brøndum-Nielsen and C.O. Bøggild-Andersen. Copenhagen: Rosenkilde og Bagger, 1949, pp. 55-68.

long discussion with Gyldenløve about who should come towards whom and, of course, details about the failed attack. It appears as if Leonora Christina intended to keep an account of the poor treatment she received in Denmark. At the same time, *Rejsen til Korsør 1656* could subsequently provide necessary details and facts.[259] *Rejsen til Korsør* is an account of how the Ulfeldts' attempt at a reconciliation with Frederik III failed. Hence, Leonora Christina resolved upon writing down her version of the events – her good intentions and the lack of respect she experienced at the hands of her own family.

Similar motivations must account for *Confrontationen i Malmø 1659*,[260] which reproduces the Swedish trial against Corfitz Ulfeldt. As Ulfeldt was unable to speak on grounds of ill health, Leonora Christina had to defend her husband. Similar to the first part of *Jammers Minde*, the purpose of *Confrontationen i Malmø 1659* was to give an account of the exact course of the interrogation, in case the Swedish authorities decided to falsify the records of this trial.[261] Thus, Leonora Christina's account of the interrogations in Malmö is as detailed as possible.

In addition to having been Leonora Christina's first priority, the first part of *Jammers Minde* is also comparatively long and exhibits a higher plot density than the other two. The most obvious reason for this imbalance is that the first two weeks of her imprisonment were the most eventful of her twenty-two years in the Blue Tower. While Leonora Christina does not seem to omit a single word in the first part of the narrative, leaps in time accumulate as the story proceeds. Whether intended or not, this accelerating advancement of the story conveys a quite natural feeling of the passing of time. One can imagine that Leonora Christina was rather tense

---

[259] Leonora Christina narrates the same episode in her French autobiography, but in a much more adventurous and entertaining manner, which indicates that she had either enhanced her literary talents and ambitions in the meantime, or – and this is more likely – that she was pursuing entirely different goals with these two diverse narratives of the same event. Since the portrayal of her eventful journey to Korsør in the French autobiography is consistent with the overall objective of the French narrative – i.e. to portray her as a heroine admirable in every respect and whose calamities are only caused by the envy of everybody surrounding her – a closer comparison of the two versions of *Rejsen til Korsør* will be provided together with further details on Leonora Christina's self-portrayal in her French autobiography in Chapter 1.2.2.

[260] Leonora Christina. 'Confrontationen i Malmø 1659'. In *Jammers Minde og andre selvbiografiske Skildringer*, eds. Johs. Brøndum-Nielsen and C.O. Bøggild-Andersen. Copenhagen: Rosenkilde og Bagger, 1949, pp. 69-92.

[261] One incident in *Jammers Minde* renders Leonora Christina's decision to pen her own protocols a wise one. The officials who interrogated her included Privy Councillor Erik Krag, who was appointed with the task of documenting the interrogations. However, his initial records do not appear to have been faithful to the actual dialogues: »Der Krag *Protocollet* oplæste, haffde hand skreffuen; Att der ieg bleff tilspurt, om ieg vdi min Mands-Dom deelactig wille were, haffde ieg suaret; Att ieg mig der paa wille betencke. Ieg sagde; huordant war ded? Strax suarte *Canzeler*; Ney hun sagde icke saa, men hun begierte att wide henders Mands Beskyllinger. Ieg *Repeterte* mine Ord igien, wed dog icke, om Krag dennem Skreff eller icke, thi en stoer deel aff ded ieg sagde bleff intet Skreffuen« (*Jammers Minde*, p. 55).

during the interrogations. She did not know what had become of her husband and at the same time, she had to be constantly alert to master the interrogations. In such moments, time often seems to stand still.[262] The first part of the manuscript covers only a period of three weeks, but of these first weeks, Leonora Christina depicts every detail, from her daily routine to the furniture in her cell.[263] Her account of this time almost resembles a documentary in its richness of detail and its comparative lack of personal commentary.[264]

Considering that her account of the first three weeks in the Blue Tower was the only one written in prison, it appears only logical that the same part of *Jammers Minde* should be the most detailed. Two turning points – Leonora Christina's epiphany and her subsequent stoic resignation, as well as the news of her husband's death – change her outlook on her fate and the pace of the narrative. Corfitz Ulfeldt died in February 1664 on a boat on the Rhine. When Leonora Christina learns of her husband's demise, she feels relieved (*Jammers Minde*, p. 98). Leonora Christina knew that her husband would never fall into the hands of his enemies again; and since she remained in prison even after his death, it was obvious that she would not be released in the foreseeable future. Thus, she could set her mind at rest and turn towards other issues, such as how to pass the time (cf. *Jammers Minde*, p. 99). The rest of the account is thus less occupied with political issues, but with anecdotes from the Blue Tower and Leonora Christina's occupational therapy.[265]

Now time advances faster as the days in the Blue Tower become routine and Leonora Christina repeatedly leaps longer periods. For example, in her description

---

262 Cf. Larsen, Finn Stein. *Prosaens mønstre: Nærlæsninger af danske litterære prosatekster*. Odense: Syddansk Universitetsforlag, 2006 (1971), p. 18: »Det fysisk objektive tid forvandles langsomt til oplevet tid. Dette illusionsskabende tidsforhold har naturligvis et bestemt sigte, set i sammenhæng med de beskrevne situationer: Det er en lang, lang dag, der gennemleves, rig på plager og prøvelser for hovedpersonen«.

263 See, for example, *Jammers Minde*, p. 73: »Her wil ieg mit Fengsels Sted beskriffue. Ded er ett Kammers som er 7. aff mine Skrit lang oc 6 breed, der vdi staar tuende Senge, ett Bord oc toe Stoele; ded war Nyß Kalcket, huilcket gaff en stoer Stanck ellers war Gulffuet saa tyck med Skarn, att ieg meente ded war aff Leer, der ded dog er lagt med Muursteen. Ded er 9. allen høyt, Hualt, oc allerhøyest sidder ett Windue som en allen i fiirkant, der er dobbelt tycke Ierntraller for, derforuden ett Sprinckelwerck, som er saa tet, at icke en liden finger kand stickis i Hullerne«.

264 Larsen, Finn Stein. *Prosaens mønstre*, p. 18: »De panoramiske indslag (der frembyder muligheder for skribentens ræsonnerende, vurderende eller lyriserende betragtninger, og som man f.eks. ganske hyppigt finder i et omtrent samtidigt memoireværk som Johan Monrads) forekommer ikke her«. In a subsequent article on the literary style in *Jammers Minde* Larsen commends Leonora Christina again for her impressionist narrative and compares it to Danish impressionism from 1870 onwards. See Larsen, Finn Stein. 'En impressionist fra baroktiden?', p. 28.

265 Cf. Heitmann, Annegret. *Selbst schreiben*, p. 142.

of the year 1668, which she sums up in one short paragraph.²⁶⁶ Moreover, after the death of Frederik III in 1670, Leonora Christina's life becomes almost agreeable. Sophie Amalie, now Queen Dowager, is forced to give way to the new regal couple and is thus unable to ensure that Leonora Christina's living conditions remain insufferable. A *Memory of Lament* offers little room for pleasant occurrences and, consequently, there is not much to tell about those years.²⁶⁷ Only by the end of her imprisonment, when Leonora Christina's release was to be expected after Sophie Amalie's death, she introduces more dates and gives a more detailed account. Again, the account reflects Leonora Christina's tenseness.

A look at the original manuscript also reveals that Leonora Christina had retroactively sought to danisise her account by adjusting the originally German syntax. One might argue this happened due to a natural development of the Danish language. However, in Chapter 1.1.3. it was suggested (by referring to Bodil Wamberg) that Leonora Christina chose French for one of her life narratives in order to set herself apart from her mortal enemy, Sophie Amalie, thus indicating a certain hostility towards everything German on Leonora Christina's part. Her French may have been flawed, but, as suggested by Wamberg, Sophie Amalie did not have much to counter with. In addition, the Queen of Denmark did not speak or even understand (proper) Danish – at least not in the early years of her reign, when Leonora Christina was still frequenting the royal court.²⁶⁸ To Sophie Amalie, this was not even a necessity, since most of the Danish court members of the 17th century were of German origin.²⁶⁹ However, while Leonora Christina wrote nothing that would even hint at the possibility of an animosity towards the German language on her part, it is indeed quite denotative that for her magnum opus she chose a language Sophie Amalie did not master.

Aside from any possible secret motivations for Leonora Christina to danisise her account in retrospect, Finn Stein Larsen pointed to another potential reason for her initially German syntax or, more precisely, her infinitive constructions, such as in this example:

---

266 Her opening account of this year indicates a complete lack of events worth mentioning: »Wii leffte siiden i goed Roelighed, Ieg war *provideret* med adskilligt, til haand-Arbeed, saa Kresten kiøbte intet for mig vden et par Bøger, oc dem maatte ieg betale dobbelt oc meere end dobbelt med Lyß« (*Jammers Minde*, p. 164). Leonora Christina is at peace, almost content, with her fate. The atmosphere in her account of these years forms a blatant contrast to her keen narrative at the beginning of *Jammers Minde*.

267 Cf. Lunde, Katrin and Luise F. Pusch. 'Leonora Christina', p. 89.

268 Cf. Jørgensen, Ellen and Johanne Skovgaard. *Danske Dronninger*, p. 148.

269 Skautrup, Peter. *Det danske sprogs historie 2: Fra unionsbrevet til danske lov*. Copenhagen: Gyldendal, 1947, p. 303.

Den 9. *Augusti* om Morgenen der Klocken war 6. kom Slozfogden ind, bød goed Morgen, oc spurte, om wii wille haffue Brendewiin? Ieg suarte intet. Hand spurte Maren, om ieg Soff? *Hun suarte, icke att wide ded* [my italics], gick til Sengen, oc giorde mig samme Spørßmaal. Ieg tackede, ded war den slags Drick ieg aldrig smagt haffde.

(*Jammers Minde*, p. 27)

While Stein Larsen does not refute the crucial influence of the German language on Leonora Christina's syntax, he emphasises that this construction (»Hun suarte, icke att wide ded«) also allows her to omit any additional use of personal pronouns, the only exception being when *ieg* refers to Leonora Christina herself.[270] Together with Leonora Christina's detailed and realistic depiction of her life in the Blue Tower, this distanced manner of reproducing the attendees' statements indicates that Leonora Christina's overall objective was to render a realistic, almost documental account of her experience, while the selectivity and subjectivity in some of her depictions[271] proves her account to be stylistically heterogenous.[272] That Leonora Christina had tried to correct her German syntax despite its stylistic effect only confirms this last observation. However, considering that *Jammers Minde* was penned over the course of two decades and could hence be considered to comprise three rather different texts, this inconsequence in style is hardly astonishing.

Leonora Christina's Revenge

Once *Jammers Minde* had acquired the status of a Danish classic, a closer examination of Leonora Christina's other literary contributions began. While it was agreed upon that neither her French autobiography nor *Hæltinners Pryd* could live up to the sophistication of *Jammers Minde*, these two works could still serve their purpose as both supplement and contrast to her magnum opus. Research on Leonora Christina has so far only occasionally focussed on *Hæltinners Pryd*. However, when *Hæltinners Pryd* was published for the first and, so far, only time in 1977, its author acquired a new reputation. In this only incompletely preserved compilation of stories of remarkable women, Leonora Christina contests the generally assumed

---

270 Larsen, Finn Stein. *Prosaens mønstre*, p. 20.
271 For example Leonora Christina's depiction of a failed conversation with the castellan: »[…] hand gick vd oc ind i Trappen, Sang en Morgen Psalme, raabte snart paa en, snart paa en anden, som hand dog wel wiste icke war tilstede: Der war paa de tiider en wed Naffn Ion, som bar Madden med Raßmus Taaren-Giemmer, den kalte hand offuer 40 gange paa, oc ded vdi en Sang, tog Tonen høyt oc Law, skreeg stønnem høyeste hand kunde, suarte sig selffuer oc sagde: Far, he iß dar nicht, he iß som Gott dar nicht; Skaagger loe aff sig selffuer, tog saa paa att Raabe igien, enten paa Ion eller paa Raßmus, saa mig syntist, at hand haffde smagt Brendewiinen« (*Jammers Minde*, p. 28).
272 Larsen, Finn Stein. *Prosaens mønstre*, p. 25.

inferiority of the fair sex. As a consequence of this newly provided perspective on Ulfeldt's loyal wife, Leonora Christina was characterised as »dansk virago«,[273] as »kvinnehistoriker«[274] and as »Dänemarks erste Feministin«[275] (even though with a question mark), mostly due to her »Weiblichkeitsentwurf«,[276] i.e. *Hæltinners Pryd*. The notion that the catalogue of female virtues provided in *Hæltinners Pryd* should serve as an aid to appreciate the full scale of Leonora Christina's *own* magnitude (as depicted in *Jammers Minde*), now common opinion,[277] was introduced by the editor of *Hæltinners Pryd*, Christopher Maaløe.[278] The first female virtues accentuated in *Hæltinners Pryd* are *dyd* and *visdom*. While the reader will have to consult *Jammers Minde* and the French autobiography in order to grasp some of the similarities between Leonora Christina and her *hæltinner*, no such browsing is required to find accounts of her wisdom. The design of *Hæltinners Pryd* already attests to its author's prudence, since it follows the models of Pierre le Moyne's *La Gallerie des Femmes Fortes* (1647) and Plutarch's *Bioi Parallelloi* (AD 125).[279] In the Baroque period, the competence of both artists and politicians was often estimated by means of their knowledgeableness. A poet would demonstrate his talent by imitating the antique masters and a ruler's capability would be measured by his knowledge of history. Thus, imitation, instead of creation, was the Baroque passport to fame.[280] Leonora Christina, well versed in the realm of Baroque literature *and* politics, abode by the rules of her time in order to gain credibility and esteem as a writer.

Leonora Christina subsequently utilises the former Danish Queen Thyra as an example of prudence and godliness. Thyra too had to endure the sorrow of losing a beloved one – her son Knud. Yet, with the aid of her strong faith, she did not despair, not unlike Leonora Christina, when she finally accepted her fate in the Blue Tower.

---

273 Brøndsted, Mogens. 'En dansk virago', pp. 109-120.
274 Lervik, Åse Hiorth. 'Leonora Christina som kvinnehistoriker', Edda 78/1 (1978), pp. 11-22.
275 Lunde, Katrin and Luise F. Pusch. 'Leonora Christina (1621-1698): Die Tochter von König Christian IV. von Dänemark und Norwegen: Dänemarks erste Feministin?'. In *Töchter berühmter Männer: 9 biographische Porträts*, ed. Luise F. Pusch. Frankfurt: Insel, 1988 (Insel-Taschenbuch 979), pp. 47-115.
276 Dömling, Anna Katharina. '»Klog i Raad; Keck i Striid«: Leonora Christina Ulfeldts Hæltinners Pryd als Weiblichkeitsentwurf und Diskurskonglomerat'. In *Skandinavische Literaturen der frühen Neuzeit*, ed. Jürg Glauser. Tübingen: Francke, 2002 (Beiträge zur nordischen Philologie 32), pp. 307-318.
277 See, for example, Wamberg, Bodil. *Leonora Christina*, p. 37.
278 Maaløe, Christopher. 'Udgiverens indledning'. In Leonora Christina. *Hæltinners Pryd*, ed. Christopher Maaløe. Copenhagen: Reitzel, 1977, p. 10: »Der er påfaldende mange af heltinderne der har træk tilfælles med Leonora Christina«.
279 Brøndsted, Mogens. 'En dansk virago', p. 114.
280 On that topic, see Hansson, Stina. 'Repertoire und Tradition: Über Schreibformen, Denkformen und Literaturgeschichte im 17. Jahrhundert'. In *Skandinavische Literaturen der frühen Neuzeit*, ed. Jürg Glauser. Tübingen: Francke, 2002 (Beiträge zur nordischen Philologie 32), pp. 41-54.

Other virtues displayed by Leonora Christina's chosen heroines are fortitude and disputability, both qualities usually attributed to men. According to Mogens Brøndsted, it is those masculine strengths that Leonora Christina is most eager to attribute to women and, most importantly, herself.[281] However, since *Hæltinners Pryd* is only preserved in an incomplete copy, determining the actual focal point of this work will always be subject to speculation.

One virtue, however, is conspicuously absent from *Hæltinners Pryd*: clemency. After her own ineffective attempt to appeal to Frederik III's heart, it seems that Leonora Christina dreamed of paying out her enemies in their own coin. In Leonora Christina's (and Herodotus') account of the mythical Massagetean Queen Tomyris, the Persian Emperor Cyrus the Great, once defeated in battle, was decapitated on Tomyris' orders. Subsequently, his head was placed in a tube filled with human blood, in order to quench his thirst for bloodshed. Leonora Christina could have omitted or amended Cyrus' gory end, particularly since she does not always abide by the historical facts anyway.[282] However, it is rather likely that she shared Tomyris' satisfaction over her sanguinary revenge. *Dødslisten* provided at the end of *Jammers Minde* bears the most explicit witness to this character trait of hers, for example when she describes the death of the woman that strip-searched Leonora Christina on her first day in the Blue Tower:

---

281 Brøndsted, Mogens. 'En dansk virago', p. 114. Brøndsted does not provide a proof of his latter assertion; therefore, it is not entirely incongruous to assume a certain bias influencing Brøndsted's judgement. Brøndsted claims that Leonora Christina fancied wearing masculine clothing »for at understrege sin stærke vilje« (ibid., p. 112). While she did indeed travel in men's tailoring on one occasion, it was not in order to accentuate her personality, but for safety reasons. In the course of the Ulfeldt family's escape from Denmark in the year 1651, Leonora Christina disguised herself in masculine clothing. And although retrospectively she did comment on this episode sympathetically as »vne piece digne de Romans« (*Leonora Christina Grevinde Ulfeldts Franske Levnedsskildring*, p. 5d (Translation p. 23: »et eventyr, som er værdigt en roman«)) and kept wearing said masculine garments for weeks after her arrival in Stockholm (perhaps in order to please Queen Christina, who took quite a liking to Leonora Christina's disguise, but not so much to Leonora Christina herself (cf. Hartmann, Godfred. *Kongens børn*. Copenhagen: Gyldendal, 1988 (1981, Gyldendals Paperbacks), pp. 186 and 188), wearing her husband's clothes did not become a permanent habit of hers. In this context, it is important to note that Leonora Christina's use of male clothing is very much in line with contemporary women's practical use of a masculine disguise, i.e. for safety during travels (see Hættner Aurelius, Eva: *Inför Lagen: Kvinnliga Svenska Självbiografier från Agneta Horn till Fredrika Bremer*. Lund University Press, 1996 (Litteratur, Teater, Film 13), p. 173), and not comparable to the likely motives of famous contemporary transvestites, such as Queen Christina, who loathed typically female virtues and employments (ibid., p. 173) and would rather be considered a man, i.e. as hero and ruler (cf. ibid., p. 179). Leonora Christina, on the other hand, was content with being considered equal to a man (as evidenced by *Hæltinners Pryd*) while cherishing her womanhood. Questions of identity and gender did thus not play a relevant part in Leonora Christina's depiction of her Swedish adventure. However, the very same motive mentioned by Brøndsted was widely adopted in literature depicting Leonora Christina – an issue that will be broached in some of the subsequent chapters.

282 Yet certainly not due to a failure of memory or lack of knowledge, since she used Christian V's allowance, granted to her from 1672 onwards, to purchase books, which she then used as source material for *Hæltinners Pryd*.

3. *Able Catharinæ Døe*, war meget Smertelig, haffde hun før søgt hoes mig paa himmelige Stæder effter Breffue; da bleff hun siden aff Balberere meget befølt, efftersom hun haffde Byller paa himmelige Stæder, hun bleff Skaaren oc Brent; All den Piine udstoed hun i Haab att leffwe, men hwercken Batskerns Windskiibelighed eller Dronningens Besøgelser kunde rædde hender fra døden.

(*Jammers Minde*, p. 261)

Leonora Christina does not refrain from pointing out the parallels: while Abel Catharina offended her by examining her »paa ett himlig sted« (*Jammers Minde*, p. 19), she herself came to suffer and die from an illness that befell the same secret place. With satisfaction, Leonora Christina sees God apply the *lex talionis* ('an eye for an eye'), which was rather popular in the 17th century, on her behalf.[283]

Placing the deaths of eleven of her enemies in a separate position of the text (i.e. on separate sheets), instead of spreading these remarks throughout the entire account, sends a marked message – (s)he laughs best who laughs last – which might have got lost if these incidences had been separated and incorporated into the account. Furthermore, Leonora Christina had waited for years until she had gathered an entire list of deceased malefactors. *Dødslisten* is thus not the result of a momentary satisfaction, but of a lasting one.[284] At the same time, she could utilise the deaths of her enemies for a demonstration of her own moral superiority, as exemplified by her description of Jørgen Walter's demise:

9. Ded haffwer behaget Gud, att ieg skulle selffwer wære Widne til att Walter døede en ynckelig Døe, ja att *ieg skulle selffwer beklage hannem* [my italics]; Naar ieg hørte hannem Skriige, da rant mig forrige tiider i Sinde, oc tenckte offte, huorledis et Menniske kand lade sig forføre, at giøre den Ont, *aff hwilcken den alt Gott oc Ære haffwer nyt* [my italics].

(*Jammers Minde*, p. 263)

Leonora Christina emerges as a compassionate Christian in this instance, while at the same time reminding her audience of the misdeeds Walter had committed against her and her family. At the same time, Leonora Christina insists that she was above ignoble feelings of vengefulness. In 1669, Jørgen Walter was brought to the

---

283 Rühling, Lutz. *Opfergänge der Vernunft. Zur Konstruktion von metaphysischem Sinn in Texten der skandinavischen Literaturen vom Barock bis zur Postmoderne*. Göttingen: Vandenhoeck & Ruprecht, 2002 (Palaestra 316), p. 75.

284 Wamberg, Bodil. 'Det Ydre og det Indre Fangenskab', p. 79.

Blue Tower.²⁸⁵ Leonora Christina asked to meet him under the supervision of some authorities, but a higher authority prevented this meeting. Eventually, Leonora Christina has a chance to interact with Jørgen Walter and demonstrate her lordliness:

> Oc som der gaar et Hull aff den Mørcke Kircke ind i ded vderste Rom, saa kand de der er inde raabe opad, saa man kand høre grant hwad de siger; saa kalder *Walter* engang paa Slosf: oc beder hannem giffwe sig et stycke Steeg; Slosf: raaber hannem til; Ia man Skal iu en Rotte Braaden. Ieg sendte ham et stycke Steeg med Chresten, der hand tog ded, oc wiste ieg sendte ham ded, da græd hand.
>
> (*Jammers Minde*, p. 168)

In the course of the following year, Walter's mind and body deteriorate and in 1670, he dies. Leonora Christina does not spare her readers the unappetising details of Walter's madness.²⁸⁶ As demonstrated with *dødslisten*, she regarded those that had been unkind towards her punished for their deeds. The all too realistic description of Walter's final days is only another proof that a higher force fought alongside her.

It is worthwhile noting that Queen Sophie Amalie's death is not on this list. Instead, it is integrated in the chronological account. This may have many reasons, but the most perspicuous one is that the death of Sophie Amalie acts as a catalyst to the events in the narrative. Leonora Christina remained in prison for such a long time, because the Queen Dowager was the only one left alive wanting to see her in gaol. Leonora Christina was well aware of this correlation, thus she paid close attention to her antagonist's state of health:

> I dette 1684. Aar saae ieg Encke Dronningen falde need aff den Stoel, hun hitzis op med til Kongens Gemack; Stoelen løb paa Tritzerne for hastig need, saa hun falt Neeßkrus need, oc støtte sig paa Knæerne; Samme Aar tiltog henders Swaghed, men hun holte sig stærcker end som hun war, loed sig see til Taffels meget udsmøcket; oc imellem Maaltiiderne holte sig inne.
>
> (*Jammers Minde*, p. 234)

---

[285] While his accomplice, Dina Vinhofvers, was decapitated for her wrong accusations against the Ulfeldt family in 1651, Walter was expelled from Denmark. He spent the following years in Lübeck. After Corfitz Ulfeldt's death in 1663, Walter was allowed to enter Denmark again, but he had to refrain from the Royal Court. He returned to Denmark in 1668, but was soon suspected to be involved in yet another poisoning of the regal couple. He was expelled from the city of Copenhagen and immediately imprisoned after returning without permission.

[286] »Walter bleff syg laae lenge heel elendig; Hand war slem imod Chresten; tog Skarnet aff Golffwet, oc kaste i Madden, spøttede i Øllet, oc loed Chresten see derpaa; naar han skulle tage Kanden bort; [...] Naar ieg sendte hannem noget Maed ind, som Saad oc Steeg, da kom Chresten vd dermed igien, og sagde hand wille icke haffwe ded; ieg bad Chresten lade ded staae hoes ham, hand aad wel siden; ded skeede engang, oc loed Chresten mig see ded, att ded war fylt med Snaat oc Skarn« (*Jammers Minde*, p. 173).

Leonora Christina knew that Sophie Amalie's death, and thus her own release from the tower, was close. As she saw that the end of her ordeal was nigh, she admonished herself to be patient (*Jammers Minde*, p. 235: »Ieg begaff mig til ett Gott Taal«).[287] Leonora Christina's name resounded throughout the land[288] and her maid Jonatha addresses her mistress with the news that an anonymous noble person had stated to know for certain that Leonora Christina would still not leave the Blue Tower. This frightening prophecy is only met with laughter and Leonora Christina informs Jonatha that not even Christian V himself knows yet what to do with his prisoner. Jonatha is, understandably, confused until Leonora Christina explains that the King himself »weed ded icke, forend Gud skyder hannem ded i Sinde, oc saa gott som siger til hannem; Nu skalt du lade den Fange komme ud« (*Jammers Minde*, p. 241). Jonatha is immediately silenced, but as the weeks pass, Leonora Christina grows impatient. One month after Sophie Amalie's funeral King Christian V receives a supplication:

> Den 21. April *Supplicerte* ieg Kongl. *Majt:* paa effterfølgende Maade. Ieg haffde Høyloffligste Konning *Christian* den *Fiærdis* Billede i Kaarstycke, lided oc i *oval*; ded haffde ieg *Illumineret* med Farffwer, oc laded giøre en udsnitzet Ramme omkring, den selffwer Forgylt. Bag paa Stycket satte ieg effterfølgende Ord.
> *Min Sønne Søn, oc største Nafne,*
> *Du ligner mig i Mact oc Moed:*
> *Lad ded min Læfning oc nu gafne,*
> *At du som ieg est Naade goed.*
>
> (*Jammers Minde*, p. 241)

Despite Leonora Christina's assertion that God will determine her fate, she boosts her luck by appealing to Christian V through his cherished grandfather.[289] In addition, the picture of Christian IV may have served the purpose of reminding the King who Leonora Christina is – the daughter of an esteemed ancestor and a once influential noblewoman. Unfortunately, history does not inform us about Christian

---

287 Leonora Christina's reaction to the imminent death of her opponent may sound cruel, but it could also refer to the Christian virtue of *patientia*, which constitutes a crucial means for her not to reproach God again. See Dömling, Anna Katharina. '»Billigen kand ieg med Iob sige.« Selbstbilder und Selbstinszenierung in den autobiographischen Texten von Leonora Christina Ulfeldt (1693), Agneta Horn (1657) und Christina Regina von Birchenbaum (1651)', Skandinavistik 31 (2001), p. 28.

288 Even Louis XIV interceded for Leonora Christina (Birket Smith, Sophus. *Leonora Christina Grevinde Ulfeldts Historie 2*, p. 274).

289 Cf. Hein, Jørgen and Katia Johansen. *Sophie Amalie*, image no. 57: »At hun lod Christian IV fremføre sin bøn er næppe tilfældigt, for Christian V nærede stor beundring for sin bedstefader«.

V's reaction. Whether due to her supplication or divine intervention,[290] Leonora Christina left the prison one month later.

Compared to the other death accounts in *Jammers Minde*, the statement on Sophie Amalie's demise is rather dry. While Leonora Christina usually sought to accentuate the misdeeds of the deceased, no such obvious spitefulness is identifiable in this account. It is, however, similarly detailed:

> Den 20. Feb: Døde den Kongl: Frue Moder Dronning *Sophia Amalia*. Hun formodede icke, att Døden skulle saa hastig giæste hender: men der hun aff Doctorn bleff adwaret, att ded syntist Døden icke wille lengre Lænte, adtraade hun att tale med sin Søn; men Døden wille icke biie Kongl. *Majts*. Ankomst, att den Kl. Frue Moder kunde sige hannem et Ord; Liffwet haffde hun enda; saed paa en Stoel, men Maaleløß; oc lided der effter saa siddendis opgaff hun sin Aand.
>
> (*Jammers Minde*, p. 239)

The information that Christian V of Denmark did not arrive in time to hear his mother's last words is insofar worth mentioning, as it indicates that Sophie Amalie might have wanted to prevent Leonora Christina's release even after her death.[291] Hence, it might well be that Leonora Christina included this detail as the proof of her final victory, or perhaps even of God's interference (»men Døden wille icke biie [...]«). Throughout the account of Leonora Christina's last months in the donjon, she invokes God as the ultimate authority in the matter. Yet as a chosen servant of God, it is her right to help along. Her careful bookkeeping of the time periods reveals that she waited approximately one month for divine interference to manifest itself before she took matters into her own hands. Once Christian V had obtained the supplication, one additional month passed before news of her imminent release reached Leonora Christina. Thus, the causality between supplication and release is disputable and leaves the reader of *Jammers Minde* wondering whether it was not a higher force after all that had decided that Leonora Christina had served her time.

---

290 The most likely reason for Christian V initial hesitance is that an immediate release of Leonora Christina may have been regarded tantamount to an admission of his parents', and particularly his mother's, guilt. After reading his mother's testament, however, Christian V had little reason to remain considerate of her reputation, since the document favoured his younger brother Jørgen above himself. Cf. Jørgensen, Ellen and Johanne Skovgaard. *Danske Dronninger*, p. 169 and Hein, Jørgen and Katia Johansen. *Sophie Amalie*, unpaginated preamble.

291 Dissing Paulsen, Trine and Jan Gorm Madsen. 'Zahrtmanns Leonora Christina motiver', p. 64.

Supremacy through Language and Witchcraft

As asserted by Niels Åge Nielsen, *Jammers Minde* does not only constitute an important historical testimony and a Danish literary classic, but »også som sprogværk står det i en særstilling«.[292] Leonora Christina's prison testimony has repeatedly been acclaimed for its lively rendition of dialogues, not least since there are hardly any extant texts, which could convey a trustworthy impression of the 17th century's everyday speech in Denmark.[293] Nielsen, however, also expresses concerns about whether Leonora Christina was indeed able and willing to render the simple life in the Blue Tower in an objective and thus authentic manner.[294] While her use of the diverse languages spoken in the Blue Tower (High and Low German, Danish and French) seems comprehensible and authentic, Leonora Christina's memory and her familiarity with the different sociolects might have deserted her occasionally.

Nielsen's conclusion, that Leonora Christina uses language as an instrument to demonstrate her superiority,[295] is fully in line with all remarks on her self-portrayal made above. *Jammers Minde* abounds with instances in which Leonora Christina establishes herself as predominant in various, yet always subtle ways. For example, when the castellan, Jokum Waltpurger,[296] attempts to involve Leonora Christina in a conversation about her archenemy Sophie Amalie and indicates that her calamities are self-inflicted, she silences him by using a language incomprehensible to him:

---

292 Nielsen, Niels Åge. 'Dansk og fremmed tale i Jammersmindet'. In *Runer og rids: Festskrift til Lis Jacobsen, 29. Januar 1952*, ed. Jørgen Glahder. Copenhagen: Rosenkilde og Bagger, 1952, p. 74.

293 Peter Skautrup especially commends *Jammers Minde* for its variety of style. See Skautrup, Peter. *Det danske sprogs historie 2*, p. 313.

294 Nielsen, Niels Åge. 'Dansk og fremmed tale i Jammersmindet', p. 75.

295 Ibid., p. 81. This is also characteristic of Corfitz Ulfeldt's writings, mainly his letters. He would often switch between Danish, French, Italian and Spanish, sometimes in the same letter, without taking into consideration the language skills of his diverse addressees. Much like Leonora Christina (see below), he also preferred to use a language his addressee was less familiar with than himself in order to establish his own authority, as exemplified by his correspondence with the French diplomat Claude Mesmes d'Avaux, whose French letters Ulfeldt answered in Spanish (see Heiberg, Steffen. *Enhjørningen Corfitz Ulfeldt*, p. 19).

296 In the time of Leonora Christina's imprisonment, the Blue Tower had three successive castellans. The first, Jokum Waltpurger, was replaced by Hans Balcke in early 1665, due to the declining health of Waltpurger. Balcke's successor was Johan Jæger, who took office in June 1665.

> [...] Dronningen Beklager eder, att I saa haffuer laded eder forføre, I haffuer wult eder selffuer den Vlycke; ded giør hender Ont; Hun er eder icke Wreed, hun haffuer Medliidenhed med Eder. Oc saa som ieg intet Suarte *repeterte* hand ded igien, oc alt imellem sagde hand, Ia, Ia, mein liebes Frewlein, es ist so wie ich sage. Ieg war meget fortrøden offuer den Snack, sagde *Dieu vous punisse*. Ho ho (sagde hand) Sie wil Pißen: kalte paa Karen, gick vd oc lucte Dørene.
>
> (*Jammers Minde*, p. 77)

While being proud of her education, however, Leonora Christina is also eager not to be labelled as merely 'book smart'. Several anecdotes in *Jammers Minde* account for her ability to outwit those guarding her. One warm summer day, the woman attending Leonora Christina does not feel well, as she had not received any food or water all day. Moreover, due to the weather, there is no fire in the stove and thus no possibility of cooking her food. Leonora Christina therefore offers to help her prepare *Øllebrød* – of course with the help of witchcraft. Following the orders of her mistress, the woman puts a pot containing the raw ingredients on top of three brick stones. Untiringly, the woman then sits on the ground, stirring the cold porridge and waiting for Leonora Christina to evoke a magic fire, all in complete silence, as she had been ordered to remain quiet during the procedure:

> Ieg saed altiid paa min Seng om Dagen, oc der bleff Borded sat for mig; haffde et Stycke Kriide, oc skreff paa Borded adskilligt, spurte alt imellem om Potten søe? hun keeg flittig til, men wirrede med sit Hoffwet; der ieg haffde spurte tredie gang, oc hun wente sig til mig, oc saae ieg loe, saa tog hun paa som en der war gall, kaste Skeen aff Haanden, oc Stoelen om kuld, reeff atter henders trøye op, oc sagde, gie Fanden være saa narret;
>
> (*Jammers Minde*, p. 132)

The woman is furious after realising her own foolishness, but in the end, Leonora Christina manages to make the day a pleasant one for both of them. Due to her order of silence, Leonora Christina has had a day in peace, and due to some hidden matches, she is also able to make the fire she promised. As usual, Leonora Christina has an ace up her sleeve.

On another occasion, the same woman hears that there were acrobats ordered to perform on the inner yard in front of the Blue Tower. After questioning Leonora Christina about the nature of acrobatic performance, the woman expresses disappointment about not being able to see the acrobats, due to the fact that the only window in their prison cell is out of reach (*Jammers Minde*, p. 133). Yet again, Leonora Christina is able to help her maid. She instructs the woman to build a construction consisting of the cell furniture that would allow them to reach the elevated window and see the performance. This construction can carry only one person at a time. Thus, Leonora Christina generously defers to her maid:

> [...] oc loed ieg hender gaa op først oc ieg stoed oc tog ware paa, om Sengen begynte att knage; hun skulle være paa wact naar ieg war oppe; ieg wiste oc wel att dantzerne i begyndelse icke giorde derris beste Kunster. Ieg kunde see Kongen oc Dronningen i derris øyen, de stoed paa den lange Sael, oc vndrede ieg mig siden paa, att de icke kaste øyet did, der ieg stoed; ieg loed mig icke mercke for quinden, att ieg haffde seet dem.
> (*Jammers Minde*, p. 133)

This anecdote illustrates the different levels of Leonora Christina's authority. First, she is in perfect control of the entire situation. She causes her maid to long for something unknown to her, she conceives of the construction that will allow the maid to see the longed-for performance, and she decides who sees the better part of the show. Second, Leonora Christina can demonstrate her education and courtly experience. As the daughter of Christian IV, she has of course seen acrobats before and is thus able to tell her maid what she has missed so far. In addition, this experience allows her to ensure that she herself will see the better part of the performance. Third, Leonora Christina can demonstrate her shrewdness to her readers, as she uses the maid as a tool to procure the best entertainment for herself while leaving the maid to think that she had just received a favour from her mistress. Fourth, Leonora Christina demonstrates a supremacy on a human level, as she is able to keep a secret (i.e. her thoughts on seeing the royal couple) while the woman reneges on her promises of silence by revealing all those adventures later on (*Jammers Minde*, p. 132).

Leonora Christina is well aware that the women attending her, especially her first maid Maren Bloks, believe that she practises witchcraft – a rumour that might have been promoted by Queen Sophie Amalie herself.[297] However, Leonora Christina encourages this superstition, as she knows how to take advantage of the situation: »[...] ieg gaff oc stønnem med min tale anledning dertil; tenkte som min herre Sl. pleyede att sige (naar hand wille i hands vnge Aar giøre nogen wiiß paa, att hand wiste den Soorte Kunst) att de frycter for dem de haffwer den *opinion* om oc tør icke giøre dem ont« (*Jammers Minde*, p. 111).

Over the course of her twenty-two years in the Blue Tower, Leonora Christina receives twelve different women waiting on her. Her depictions of these women

---

[297] Cf. *Jammers Minde*, p. 23. Furthermore, after Leonora Christina's miraculous escape from Hammershus on Bornholm, Adolph Fuchs concluded that she must have had the assistance of the devil (see *Leonora Christina Grevinde Ulfeldts Franske Levnedsskildring*, p. 10c (Translation p. 44)).

have been commended for their lively description of middle and lower class people, but they also form a contrasting model for Leonora Christina's self-portrayal.[298] These women are all in some way inferior to their mistress: they are either criminal, fallen, alcoholic, superstitious, blasphemic, dull, or simply illiterate.[299]

One episode in particular portrays Leonora Christina as an educated woman suspected of being a witch because of her knowledge. When the Crown Prince of Saxonia, Johann Georg III, celebrates his betrothal to the Danish Princess Anna Sophia in 1663, Leonora Christina knows the entire ceremony by heart:

> Om Morgenen den høitiid skulle angaa, sagde ieg til quinden, i dag skal wii faste indtil imod Afften, thi ieg tenkte nok att de kom icke mig ihue, eller ieg kunde faa nogen læffninger, førend de andre ware tracterede, i ded ringste til Middag; Hun wille wiide Aarsagen, hworfor wii skulle faste, Ieg swarte ded skal i faa att wiide i Afften. [...] Imod Middags tiider der Trommeter oc Herpucher loede sig høre sagde ieg, nu gaar de offwer Platzen til den stoere Sael med Bruden. Huor wed i ded sagde quinden. io ieg wed ded sagde ieg, min geist haffwer sagt mig ded; hwad er ded for en spurte hun; ded kand ieg icke sige eder, (swarte Ieg) Oc saa som Trommeterne blæste hwer gang ett Sæt Maed bleff opborren, oc *Confectet*, saa sagde ieg ded; oc førend der war anrettet, saa slogis paa Herpauckerne naar saa der bleff anrettet, som skeede vden for Køckenet i Platzen, saa sagde ieg effterhaanden; wii faar icke Maed ennu; Der Klocken gik til 3. slet sagde quinden, nu krümper min Maffwe slæt ind, naar skal wii haffwe Maed? ieg swarte ded er endnu langt frem, ded anded Sæt er icke vden for lit siiden opkommen; kand wii faa noget imod 7. slæt da faar wii icke føre, Ded skeede som ieg sagde, klocken 7 ½ kom Slozf: vntskylte sig att hand haffde nock fodret paa Madden, men Kockene haffde alle hænderne fulle. Quinden som altiid Meente att ieg kunde traalle bleff staedfestet i sin meening der om.
>
> (*Jammers Minde*, p. 91)

---

298 Heitmann, Annegret. *Selbst schreiben*, p. 149.

299 From Leonora Christina's point of view, most of these women are corrupt due to their indicated criminal actions (e.g. childmurder). While as a literary work *Jammers Minde* tells us of the hell Leonora Christina finds herself in, as a historical document it also alludes to the options and difficult living conditions for women in those times (see Schmalensee, Lisa and Lene Torp. 'Leonora Christina Ulfeldt: Jammersminde 1663-1685', Litteratur & samfund 30-32 (1979-81), p. 13). Schmalensee and Torp furthermore contend that due to Leonora Christina's own social dependence on (male) custodians she was rather inclined to comprehend these women's actions and thus did not reveal their deeds to the authorities of the Blue Tower (ibid., p. 14). This may well be true, but one ought to keep in mind that within the story line of *Jammers Minde*, Leonora Christina was not in the position to determine the conditions of her prison. Criminal guards are part of her divine ordeal and it would have been a breach of rule to dispose of any of them. Similarly, Annegret Heitmann doubts the occurrence of any feelings of solidarity among the women in the Blue Tower as such an assumption is historically doubtful (Heitmann, Annegret. 'Feministischer Umgang mit Literatur', p. 55).

Leonora Christina is familiar with the wedding protocol, because she has attended quite a few of those ceremonies before (not least, her own wedding in 1636).[300] However, the ignorant maid is not able to draw this deduction and fears her mistress for her mysterious knowledge. Leonora Christina is not unaccustomed to this contemporary topic, i.e. the fear of witches,[301] thus she prevails. The superstitious maid does not grasp the situation and, as she is starving, depends on her mistress' knowledge. Leonora Christina, on the other hand, mocks the ignorant woman for her lack of wit, but again the woman does not comprehend (»io ieg wed ded sagde ieg, min geist haffwer sagt mig ded; hwad er ded for en spurte hun«). In all the episodes depicting Leonora Christina promoting and exploiting the rumours of her being a witch, there is a maid in need of something only Leonora Christina can provide. Being aware of this need, Leonora Christina feels safe enough to support an otherwise dangerous accusation.[302]

All the shortcomings of the women guarding Leonora Christina function as a negative background on which her assets excel even more. This dynamic results in an irony in favour of Leonora Christina's cause, since it essentially suggests a fundamentally wrong conception, i.e. that of a virtuous, faithful noblewoman being guarded by lowly drunkards and adulterers.[303] If the authorities in the Blue Tower are worse scoundrels than the inmate they are guarding, then the entire trial must appear in a dubious light; especially, if those authorities were appointed by the Queen herself (as is the case with Maren Bloks). Thus, the portrayal of the maids in *Jammers Minde* is not a mere tool used by Leonora Christina in order to flatter herself. It is rather a subtly disguised element in her masked apologia.

---

300 This is not the only instance in which Leonora Christina describes a wedding without actually having attended it. One of Leonora Christina's earlier writings, *Kong Karl X Gustavs Bryllup 1654* (Leonora Christina. 'Kong Karl X Gustavs Bryllup 1654'. In *Jammers Minde og andre selvbiografiske Skildringer*, eds. Johs. Brøndum-Nielsen and C.O. Bøggild-Andersen. Copenhagen: Rosenkilde og Bagger, 1949, pp. 51-54), written during the Ulfeldt's years in Sweden, describes its author's impressions of the Swedish ceremony and her amusement over some of the participants' shiftlessness, even though Leonora Christina had to base her thoughts on eye-witness accounts. This indicates that Leonora Christina took pride in her expertise on such ceremonies and thus did not want to waste an opportunity to demonstrate it. Svend Aakjær's theory, on the other hand, according to which Leonora Christina might have taken notes on this foreign celebration in order to prepare for future festivities at a Danish court (see Aakjær, Svend. 'Leonora Christinas skyld – et aktorat', Jyske Samlinger 4 (Ny række, 1957), p. 243), seems a bit far-fetched. For as highlighted by C. O. Bøggild-Andersen, Leonora Christina had been present at *Det Store Bilager* in 1634 and was thus not in need of any further instruction in reveling (Bøggild-Andersen, C. O. 'Kongedatteren for historiens domstol: Nogle bemærkninger til Svend Aakjærs aktorat mod Leonora Christina', Jyske Samlinger 5 (Ny række, 1959), p. 26).

301 Cf. Heitmann, Annegret. *Selbst schreiben*, p. 150.

302 Schmalensee, Lisa and Lene Torp. 'Leonora Christina Ulfeldt', p. 23.

303 Cf. Heitmann, Annegret. *Selbst schreiben*, p. 151.

Leonora Christina's French autobiography likewise depicts its heroine as an inquisitive and talented young lady surpassing everyone around her in intellectuality and other qualities. While her sisters demonstrate only poor knowledge of the female courtly virtues, such as French, Leonora Christina exceeds them all and is thus able to save her negligent teacher, Alexander von Kückelsom,[304] from dismissal. In another episode, Leonora Christina, although still a little girl, finds herself amidst a storm on board of a ship heading towards the Netherlands. While her tutor, Wichmann Haseberd, loses all hope and is already awaiting death, Leonora Christina comforts him with her adamant faith. Further ahead in the narrative, Leonora Christina utilises the account of her first love to portray herself as victim. When the little Countess wins the affection of a highborn nobleboy called Maurits, both of them fall prey to his brother's envy: one day, Leonora Christina contracts smallpox and is thus unable to visit her dear companion. Maurits' brother Vilhelm sends him to her chambers anyway, in the hopes of causing his brother to feel disgust at her sight. Yet, since smallpox is highly contagious, Maurits falls ill as well and dies.

The key information of this account forms a blatant parallel to Leonora Christina's fate in her follow-up autobiography, *Jammers Minde*. Two people love each other, but the siblings of one of them begrudge them their happiness.[305] The result is the same as decades later: one of them (Maurits/Corfitz) dies untimely und undeservingly, while the other one has to suffer the consequences for the rest of her life. In her French autobiography Leonora Christina states to have felt abomination ever since at the sight and smell of rosemary, since the deceased Maurits was adorned with a rosemary crest. The key information of the entire account is the story of her life, the same as narrated in *Jammers Minde*. It is the story of an innocent woman despised and haunted by her own blood relatives due to her manifold talents.

That Leonora Christina maintained to use language as a means of self-affirmation in the Blue Tower indicates that it formed an important part of her identity. While nobleboys received a more historically and diplomatically oriented kind of education, it was essential for their sisters to be instructed in religion as well as in subjects of entertainment, i.e. dancing, painting, music and languages. It is thus con-

---

304 As suggested by Jan Lindschouw and Lene Schøsler, the man was probably a Frenchman and rather called Alexandre de Cuquelçon (Lindschouw, Jan and Lene Schøsler. 'Leonora Christinas franske ordforråd', p. 8).

305 Steffen Heiberg contends that the Maurits-episode reflects the central topic of the French autobiography, i.e. »hendes jævnbyrdighed med de fyrsteligt fødte« (Heiberg, Steffen. *Enhjørningen Corfitz Ulfeldt*, p. 27), in that it places Leonora Christina alongside a princely born child, i.e. Maurits. This interpretation, however, does not account for the countless other episodes in Leonora Christina's autobiographical writings in which she attracts the envy and hatred of her equals and even those of higher rank than herself (such as Sophie Amalie), which in turn leads to unjust tragedies such as Maurits' death or her own imprisonment.

ceivable that the imprisoned Leonora Christina should have perceived her knowledge of these skills as the one courtly relict in her life. With her royal father, her powerful husband and all her belongings vanished, the reassurance of her supreme education must have helped to keep her sanity throughout the years. All abundance displayed in Leonora Christina's French autobiography has disappeared when she wrote *Jammers Minde*, but she could still call herself the daughter of one King and the sister of another.[306] Also, with the aid of simple replies in a foreign language she is able to remind herself and everybody around her of this fact. Whether it was this consideration, or simply the intention to deliver an authentic rendition of her life in prison that made her deliver dialogues in the (assumed) original language, is impossible to determine. However, Nielsen concludes that after finishing the first part of *Jammers Minde*, which contains more translations into Danish than the rest of the account, Leonora Christina decided to reproduce all direct speech in the original language.[307] For reasons presented in Chapter 1.2., we may assume that by the time Leonora Christina started the second part of her life narrative, she might have anticipated the possibility of her account eventually becoming something more than memoirs dedicated to her children. We may also assume that the same kind of considerations motivated her to edit her account in the first place. It is thus not unlikely that Leonora Christina utilised her knowledge of diverse languages: first, to create an atmosphere of internationality within her prison cell similar to her original terrain, the Royal Court of Copenhagen; and second, in order to demonstrate her authority, both as a person and as an author.

As indicated above, *Jammers Minde* constitutes a valuable document for linguists as well. This is especially the case concerning the history of German in Denmark and the prestige of its two main variations, High and Low German. The results of such linguistic examinations provide valuable insights into the creational process that resulted in the final manuscript of *Jammers Minde*. Leonora Christina mastered both High and Low German. Since the Middle Ages, German was one of the colloquial languages of the Royal Danish Court; thus, a Danish noblewoman speaking German was no peculiarity, but rather the norm. It is characteristic of Leonora Chri-

---

[306] Furthermore, soon after being granted an allowance by King Christian V, she acquired golden cutlers – tools that unmistakably testify to her unbroken class-consciousness after a decade in the Blue Tower. Yet also Leonora Christina's frequent references to her father as King illustrate how important her identity as his daughter was to her (see for example *Jammers Minde*, p. 238: »Skreffwen 1684. den 28. Februarii, som er 36. Aars dagen, att Høyloffligste Konning Christian den Fiærde, sagde Werden goede Nat, oc ieg min Wersens welfart«). Kirsten Munk, on the other hand, is practically absent from all of her daughter's writings. While in real life Corfitz and Leonora Christina untiringly tried to mediate between the King and his former consort, the writing Leonora Christina found no affirmation in being the daughter of an unfaithful and thus disowned noblewoman.

[307] Nielsen, Niels Åge. 'Dansk og fremmed tale i Jammersmindet', p. 82.

stina to utilise this skill to set herself apart from (socially and intellectually inferior) others – and to integrate accounts of her supremacy in her autobiography:

> Ieg forbandede med hannem [Job], oc med Ieremia min Fødsels-Dag, oc war meget V-taalmodig, haffde ded dog hoeß mig selffuer, oc talte icke Høyt; Slap stønnem v- forwarendis ett Ord vd, war ded dog paa Tydsk, (efftersom ieg meest Bibelen paa Tydsk læst haffuer) saa att Quinden ey forstoed huad ieg sagde. [...] Endeligen saae Gud til mig med sine Naadsens Øygne, saa att ieg den 31 *Augusti* fick en roelig Søffn om Natten, oc ret vdi dagningen wognede ieg med efftterfølgende Ord vdi Munden. Mein Kind verzage nicht, wan du von Gott gestraffet wirst, dan welchen der Herr lieb hatt den züchtiget er. Er steupet aber einen Ieglichen Sohn den er auffnimt. Ieg talte de sidste Ord høyt vd, tenckte att Quinden Soff, maaskee att hun i ded samme wognede, oc spurte hun mig, om ieg noget begierte, Ieg suarte Ney. Da talte I (sagde hun) oc neffnte eders Strømper, ded anded kunde ieg icke forstaa: Ieg suarte, da haffuer ded werret i Søffne; Ieg begierer intet.
>
> (*Jammers Minde*, pp. 78-81)

In this instance, the two qualities elevating Leonora Christina from her surroundings in the Blue Tower – faith and education – are combined. The short-witted maid Karen Olesdotter does not understand her mistress' quotations from the Bible. This scene depicts a turning point in Leonora Christina's life, since she had found her faith again. Accordingly, she is absorbed in thought and the atmosphere is highly spiritual. So much more crude and comical appears thus the maid's interruption of this meditation. The comicality of the woman's interjection is reinforced when she informs her mistress that she thought she was talking about something as banal as her stockings.[308] Leonora Christina states that she spoke German, since she had mostly read German translations of the Bible. Although she does not specify the type of German, it is most likely that she meant the Luther Bible, which in turn indicates that she spoke High German in front of Karen Olesdotter. As thus concluded by Vibeke Winge, Leonora Christina uses High German to converse with her peers, while Low German and Danish as colloquial languages were restricted to the lower

---

308 Sverre Lyngstad concludes that Leonora Christina's narrative mode changes drastically from this moment onwards: »Leonora's Job-like dispute with God is the turning point of the story, radically shifting the point of view from tragedy to divine comedy. This shift is signaled by the introduction of glaring incongruities that undercut the tragic tone. [...] From this point on, a transcendent, nontragic vision informs the narrative, the Book of Job functioning as the overall paradigm« (Lyngstad, Sverre. 'The Danish Princess Leonora Christina'. In *Women Writers of the Seventeenth Century*, eds. Katharina M. Wilson and Frank J. Warnke. Athens and London: The University of Georgia Press, 1989, p. 382).

classes.[309] Like in the dialogue with the castellan, Leonora Christina can exclude her guards from the conversation by switching into a language above their educational level and thus mark a hierarchy of a different kind.

»Ej noget synes tungt for Ægte-Kærlighed« – Leonora Christina and Corfitz
In addition to being ignorant, Karen Olesdotter also emerges as a fallen woman, flirtatious and vain even in the Blue Tower (cf. *Jammers Minde*, p. 84). Aside from promiscuity being commonly regarded as condemnable, it is a vice completely foreign to Leonora Christina. As it is her duty, she is perfectly loyal to the three authorities in her life: her father, her husband, and her God. As a reward for her loyalty, she is dearly loved by all three of them.[310] Leonora Christina's first authority was her father. As pointed out by Bodil Wamberg, his influence on her cannot be overestimated,[311] for it was by his grace alone that she had attained any power at all. When Leonora Christina claimed to have lost all her fortune with her fa-

---

309 Winge, Vibeke. 'Hochdeutsch und Niederdeutsch im Blauen Turm'. In *Festschrift für Karl Hyldgaard-Jensen: Zum 70. Geburtstag am 3. Februar 1987*, eds. Mogens Dyhr and Joergen Olsen. Copenhagen: Reitzel, 1987 (Kopenhagener Beiträge zur germanistischen Linguistik: Sonderband 3), p. 336. In combination with similar considerations applied to the French autobiography, the following language hierarchy in Leonora Christina's writings becomes evident: the commoner languages Danish and Low German range at the bottom, followed by the languages used at court, i.e. High German and French. Italian and Spanish were more exotic than French and thus more in vogue (see Birket Smith, Sophus. *Leonora Christina Grevinde Ulfeldts Historie 1*, p. 112). Hence, in the French autobiography, Leonora Christina mentions that she had translated a Spanish book during her time in Sweden and that she and Corfitz conversed in Italian while being imprisoned separately in Hammershus, in order not to be understood by the guards (*Leonora Christina Grevinde Ulfeldts Franske Levnedsskildring*, p. 11d (Translation p. 49)) – even though French would probably have sufficed for this purpose. Finally, since knowledge of Latin was a prerogative of the (usually male) intellectually privileged, Leonora Christina also states that she had been instructed in this typically academic language by her friend Otto Sperling (ibid., p. 4d (Translation p. 19)).

310 Following the consensus of earlier centuries, 20th and 21st-century scholarship either repeats the myth that Leonora Christina had been Christian IV's favourite daughter (see Fabricius, Knud. 'Enevældens Dæmring og den ældre Enevælde'. In *Schultz Danmarkshistorie. Vort Folks Historie gennem Tiderne, skrevet af danske Historikere 3*, ed. Aage Friis et al. Copenhagen: J. H. Schultz, 1942, p. 268), or dispels it as a rumour created by Leonora Christina's writings (see Heiberg, Steffen. *Enhjørningen Corfitz Ulfeldt*, p. 56), although neither is entirely accurate. Of course, we do not know for certain if Christian IV loved one of his daughters above the others, since there are no written records indicating that. The origin of this misinformation is not clear either; Leonora Christina's statement »qu'elle estoit estimée de son Pere et Roy« and that her father »la fit des honneurs plus qu'à elle n'estoit due de luy« (*Leonora Christina Grevinde Ulfeldts Franske Levnedsskildring*, both quotations p. 3d (Translation p. 14: »at hun var holdt i ære af sin fader og konge [...] lod hende vederfares æresbevisninger ud over, hvad han var hende skyldig«), as well as her statement regarding her father's last words to her, seem to have sufficed to create the impression that she had been his favourite daughter. However, Christian IV's letters generally depict him as an utterly loving and caring father. He also secured a future worthy of royal offspring for *all* of his children – his and Vibeke Kruse's daughter Elisabeth Sophie Gyldenløve, for example, was married to a high-ranking nobleman from Holstein, despite being the daughter of a former maid and born out of wedlock. Thus, Leonora Christina's statements could be considered truthful; she only forgot to mention that all of her siblings received the same kind of special treatment.

311 Wamberg, Bodil. *Leonora Christina*, p. 18.

ther's death in 1648, it was hardly just a flowery phrase.[312] He *was* her identity, and even after Leonora Christina was stripped of her peerage once Sophie Amalie became Queen of Denmark, she could still call herself a King's daughter. Yet also her loyalty towards her husband, which, according to Mogens Brøndsted, »hører til de leonora-christinske hoveddyder«,[313] is a virtue she cannot stress often enough. When she became engaged to Corfitz Ulfeldt, she introduces this fate-charged marriage with the following significant words: »Elle commençoit á fort bon heure de souffrir pour luy«.[314] Again, it is the envy of those surrounding her that caused her calamities. When one of the ladies at court, together with Leonora Christina's elder sister Sophie, heard about Corfitz Ulfeldt's shortcomings, i.e. his lame leg[315] and his family's impoverishment, both of them tried to spoil the imminent marriage for Leonora Christina by mocking Corfitz. Of course, their attempts were all in vain, but even after the couple's wedding, the mocking did not stop. When rumours of her husband's alleged adultery reached Leonora Christina, she did not grant her enviers the pleasure of seeing any pain at this revelation. Instead, she stated to have given her husband the permission to see other women – as long as she was satisfied.[316]

What is to be learned from this unusually intimate statement is that no matter how hard others tried to make Leonora Christina bemoan her marriage to Corfitz Ulfeldt, she remained the loyal wife her father and God had intended her to be. Repeatedly stressing this loyalty to her husband is an important tool in her apologia.[317]

---

312 »L'an 1648 la Fortune abandonnà nostre femme« (»Aar 1648 veg lykken fra vor dame«). In her French autobiography, Leonora Christina remembers the day of her father's death. She was at his side when he told her the following words: »Je t'ay mise si ferme que personne ne te peut branler«. See *Leonora Christina Grevinde Ulfeldts Franske Levnedsskildring*, both quotations p. 5b (Translation p. 21: »Jeg har sat dig saa fast, at ingen kan rokke dig«). While Leonora Christina claims to have experienced quite the opposite throughout the following years, her three major works are considered testimonies and laudations to her strength.

313 Brøndsted, Mogens. 'En dansk virago', p. 116. Accordingly, Leonora Christina eternalised her motto on an altar cloth made for the Maribo Cathedral: »Ej noget synes tungt for Ægte-Kærlighed, Trofasthed er den Dyd, man ej tør blues ved«. The part of the cloth that contains Leonora Christina's poem can now be seen in Frederiksborg.

314 *Leonora Christina Grevinde Ulfeldts Franske Levnedsskildring*, p. 1d (Translation p. 6: »Hun begyndte i meget god tid at lide for hans skyld«).

315 Ever since his youth, Corfitz Ulfeldt suffered from a cnemial wound, which never completely healed.

316 Cf. *Leonora Christina Grevinde Ulfeldts Franske Levnedsskildring*, p. 4a (Translation p. 15).

317 Bodil Wamberg even questions the couple's love altogether. Instead, she suggests that it might be a myth created by Leonora Christina, for the reasons mentioned above. There is indeed evidence to support this hypothesis. For example Ulfeldt's behaviour in 1656, when he persuaded his wife to go to Denmark to talk to the King. Corfitz did not dare to undertake the journey himself, due to the high risk of being imprisoned. Instead, he sent Leonora Christina – despite her objections and the possibility of her getting arrested. See Wamberg, Bodil. *Leonora Christina*, pp. 113 and 116. The mission turned out to be complete failure, since Leonora Christina was told to leave the country before even seeing her half-brother. Leonora Christina decision to tell her readers who had been in favour of this foolish attempt, and who had not, is also quite indicative.

Loyalty to an allotted spouse could by no means be a vice, as she swore on her wedding day to obey and assist her husband.[318] Consequently, whatever Leonora Christina does out of loyalty towards Corfitz cannot be regarded as an actual offence, »dan welchen der Herr lieb hatt den züchtiget er« (*Jammers Minde*, p. 80). Thus, after her moment of spiritual renewal, Leonora Christina understands that she was one of God's dearest children. Hence the following statement, which she included in one of the last pages of her manuscript:

> Fengsel undertrycker icke eens Ære, men den forøger Æren. Mangen een haffwer i Fængsel faaet stoere Widenskaber,[319] oc erfaret de Ting de før icke kunde naae: Ia Fengsel leeder til Himmelen. Sagde saa offte til mig selffwer; Trøst *dig du Fange du est Lycksalig*.
>
> (*Jammers Minde*, p. 260)

When the Dutch artist Karel van Mander made a painting of Leonora Christina in 1643,[320] he depicted her signature virtue – faithfulness – in the form of two dogs. The fawning pet dog in the left corner of the painting is a symbol of fidelity commonly used in female portraits of the 17th century, while the tame wolf on the other side symbolises Corfitz Ulfeldt.[321] Fidelity, one of the most valued female assets of the 17th century and the one virtue that could absolve her from all questionable deeds, thus had to be made Leonora Christina's life theme and, consequently, a major motif in her life narratives.[322]

---

318 How binding and in fact inevitable these wedding vows were in the 17th century was demonstrated by Bjørn Anders. See Anders, Bjørn. *Ugift eller lykkelig: Kvinden i 1500 og 1600 tallet*. Copenhagen, 1973.

319 Perhaps Leonora Christina refered to herself with this allusion to newly acquired knowledge of scientific significance since in *Fortalen*, Leonora Christina included observations on the diverse critters with which she shared her prison (*Jammers Minde*, p. 14*).

320 This painting is retained at the Museum of National History in Frederiksborg Castle.

321 Mai, Anne-Marie. 'Troskab, lidelse og lidenskab', p. 286. Since the name Ulfeldt resembles the Danish word for wolf (*ulv*), the wolf was the heraldic animal of the Ulfeldt clan and in one instance even Corfitz Ulfeldt's cryptonym. Due to his behaviour after the Swedish victory over Denmark in 1658, Ulfeldt lost the grace of King Karl X Gustav and diverse Swedish noblemen grew suspicious of him. When the conspiracy of a few citizens of Malmö against Karl X Gustav was discovered and ended, the men in charge were captured and interrogated. Those men claimed that Ulfeldt had been involved in the complot against Sweden and that he had furthermore been in contact with Danish officials and revealed the plan of a crucial attack on Copenhagen. The couple denied any involvement in the conspiracy, but documents written by Danish noblemen indicate the opposite. One of these papers contains a reference to a wolf (i.e. Ulfeldt) acting as messenger. Another letter, undeniably written by Leonora Christina despite all her objections, leaves no room for any doubts about an involvement of Ulfeldt in the complot against the King of Sweden (see, for example, Heiberg, Steffen. *Enhjørningen Corfitz Ulfeldt*, pp. 172-191 on this trial).

322 Cf. Heiberg, Steffen. *Enhjørningen Corfitz Ulfeldt*, p. 289.

As is the case with Leonora Christina's education, her loyalty to her husband is what elevates her from her guards in the Blue Tower. She describes her prison as a distorted world, where faithfulness is a crime and where disloyal child murderers (such as Leonora Christina's maid Barbara) watch over abiding wives. This distortion is hardly reconcilable with Leonora Christina's Baroque ideas of godly order. Hence, the question arises why Leonora Christina did not attempt to escape from her prison, as she had done thrice before.

On several occasions in the course of her twenty-two years in the Blue Tower, Leonora Christina had a chance to flee. From 1671 onwards, she received more liberties and amenities due to King Christian V's compassion. Thus, the supervision was not as tight as it used to be and yet she chose to remain in prison. When Leonora Christina alludes to those moments when she probably could have left the Blue Tower without further difficulties,[323] it is hardly just a passing mention. Ever since her moment of spiritual renewal, she had come to terms with her fate. An attempt to abscond would thus have been a contradiction against her previous statements regarding her destiny and equivalent to a guilty plea. Hence, it was crucial to Leonora Christina's credibility that she insisted on enduring this final test willingly. Yet beyond this rather spiritual motivation for her refusal to abbreviate her prison sentence are other, more profane reasons, which render any attempt to escape implausible. First of all, there were purely practical difficulties that hindered any attempt of escape. Even if Leonora Christina had managed to exit the Blue Tower, there would have still remained the question as to what to do next. Her children were in exile, the family's once vast fortune was seized, and Otto Sperling the Elder, once her confidant, was in the Blue Tower as well. Under such circumstances, a flight out of the Tower would have been nothing but shortsighted. And above all, an escape from her prison would have altered Leonora Christina's position only in theory. The world had changed ever since the Ulfeldt couple had left Denmark for Sweden. Denmark had adopted a different kind of monarchy, the name Ulfeldt was accursed in more than one country, and former alliances had forsaken Leonora Christina before. An escape into the outside world could have easily brought a life of constant agitation and persecution for Leonora Christina. In the Blue Tower, on the other hand, she received Rhenish and French wine as well as other delicacies every day, and even the court's pastries were delivered into her cell. Those amenities certainly do not compensate for the otherwise miserable living conditions in a 17th-century prison, but they allude to her – still – elevated status. Furthermore, the imprisoned

---

323 *Jammers Minde*, p. 14*. Otto Andrup furthermore points to letters exchanged between Leonora Christina's children and Otto Sperling (the Younger, I assume), which indicate that her children had thought of diverse flight plans for their mother. See Andrup, Otto. 'Noter', p. 244 (endnote p. 50).

Leonora Christina was not simply a harmless widow, but the last representative of the formerly powerful Danish aristocracy. In addition, she was considered Sophie Amalie's archenemy and could thus be classified as a political prisoner. Her imprisonment has been criticised over the centuries, as it resulted from no verdict,[324] but given the sudden death that befell the Ulfeldt couple's former prison guard, Adolph Fuchs, on the streets of Bruges, Leonora Christina's confinement was a rational decision on behalf of the regal couple. Consequently, if her arrest were to symbolise her remaining power, one need not wonder over her holding on to it.[325] In this context, it is crucial to recall that *Jammers Minde* was finished when Leonora Christina had lost this 'power'.[326] When Leonora Christina was released from the Blue Tower and transferred to Maribo Abbey, she had already outlived most of her children (and all but one son) and there were no enemies left to mind an old, now truly artless woman. In consideration of this perspective, Leonora Christina may have been motivated to finish her autobiography in order to recall once more the old days when she was still a person of significance.

Yet regardless of the underlying reasons, the topic of Leonora Christina's loyalty and her relation to Corfitz Ulfeldt was quite dominant within the first century of research on *Jammers Minde*. Before scholars could engage in questions regarding the literary value of Leonora Christina's work, some other, perhaps historically more relevant issues had to be discussed: Did Leonora Christina know about her husband's final treacherous plans? If she did, is she to blame for her loyalty towards a traitor? Was Corfitz Ulfeldt perhaps insane? And was his insanity caused by syphilis?

While such topics certainly make for good reading, they offer only little assistance to the understanding of Leonora Christina's literary contributions. However, a close reading of selfsame writings can indeed offer some hints regarding the above-mentioned questions, as was demonstrated by Bodil Wamberg, whose readings of Leonora Christina's works suggest a disguised criticism directed towards Corfitz Ulfeldt on his wife's part.

Of course, Julius Lange challenged Leonora Christina's reputed indefeasibility long before Bodil Wamberg. In his essay 'Contra Leonora Christina', he called attention to one specific account in *Jammers Minde*:

An: 1678: den 4. Marti bleff min Naboeske en Quinde weed Naffn *Lucia*, som tiente F.

---

324 Sophus Birket Smith, for example, Leonora Christina's foremost admirer, explicitly disprasies this chapter of Denmark's history. See Birket Smith, Sophus. 'Indledning', p. 11.
325 Cf. Heitmann, Annegret. *Selbst schreiben*, p. 157.
326 Ibid., p. 157.

Rigitze Grubbe, bleff beskylt effter Iomfrue *Agneta Sophia Budde*, att hun haffde werret den, som paa sin fruis wegne haffde offwer-talt hender, att forgiffwe Greffwinnen F. Birrete Skeel, oc *Lucia* haffde bragt hender Gifftet; Der war windisbyrd, att *Lucia* haffde kiøbt Gifftet. Den quinde war en Standhafftig Troefast Tiennerinne; Hun haffde langt et frit Moed, tog imod alt ond hender paalagdis, med allerstørste Taalmodighed: war trøstig i ded Mørcke fengsel, haffde twende Mand-persohner til *Cammerader*, som baade Skreeg, Suckede oc græd; Fra Greffwinne Skeel (som skulle Spiiße hender) bleff hender Sendt Kiød, som krøb fuld aff Maddicker, oc Mullet Brøe. Ieg forbarmede mig offwer hender, (icke for henders Fruis Skyld, thi den haffwer intet gott forskylt aff mig, oc ille belønt forrige tiders welgierninger) Ieg gaff *Lucia* Maed oc dricke, oc penge til att formilde Gert med, som war hender for haard: Hun bleff Piinet, wille dog icke bekiende ded ringste aff ded hender beskyltist; forswarede altiid sin Frue; Hun bleff saa siddendis hen.

(*Jammers Minde*, p. 268)

To Lange this account is »et uimodsigeligt Bevis«[327] that Leonora Christina believed in Lucia's assistance in the attempted poisoning and that she did not perceive it a general duty to speak the truth in the course of an interrogation. The information that witnesses reported Lucia to have bought the poison, may indeed point towards Leonora Christina being convinced of the girl's involvement in the assault. On the other hand, the Dina affair must have taught Leonora Christina that witnesses cannot always be trusted. Thus, the comment cannot count as an irrefutable proof for any opinion on the matter. Leonora Christina does, however, seem to sympathise strongly with this loyal woman, thus leaving it anything but unlikely that she should have deemed obligations towards one specific person more binding than duties towards the public, such as to speak the truth.[328]

---

327 Lange, Julius. 'Contra Leonora Christina', p. 727.
328 Ibid.: »Det vil med andre Ord sige, at hvor Troskabspligten mod en konkret Person kom i Strid med den almindelige Pligt til at bekende Sandhed, særlig lige overfor Statens eller Rettens mere abstrakte Autoritet, der var det førstnævnte Pligtforhold i ethvert Tilfælde det stærkeste og det, som stod ved Magt«. This assumption is reinforced by a childhood account narrated in the French autobiography. Back then, Leonora Christina and her sister Sophie Elisabeth were instructed by their teacher Alexander von Kückelsom, a man who initially paid only little attention to his duties. The consequences were conceivable: the little ladies neglected their homework entirely and gave in to idleness. Kückelsoms rival, the *hofmesterinde*, saw her chance to dispose of her colleague and informed Christian IV about his daughters' lack of skills. When Kückelsom begged Leonora Christina for help, she refused at first, since saving her teacher would have required her to lie. Eventually, she agreed to help him, since he managed to convince her that lying for the purpose of aiding somebody in need of help would not anger, but rather please God. Leonora Christina spent the following three weeks absorbed in her books, thus disproving the *hofmesterinde*'s accusations. This episode is heavy with meaning, as it demonstrates Leonora Christina's extraordinary talent (which was the main purpose of this episode). Additionally, it is another example of her ambiguous perception of the moral dimension behind the concept of truth (see Bjørn, Hans. 'Leonora Christina – Christian IV's datter', p. 28).

This suspicion is substantiated by one specific incident, which gave Leonora Christina cause to address the problem of a double meaning inherent in a text. In the course of the interrogations, which took place during the first days of her imprisonment, Leonora Christina is confronted with a dubious letter written by her husband and subsequently torn and discarded by her. Leonora Christina insists that the letter, or what was left of it, contained nothing but jest. However, Count Rantzau asks her whether there was any deeper meaning behind this frolic, whereupon Leonora Christina responds »icke att kunde wide, att hands Meening anderledis kunde were, end som hand skreff, hand meente vden tuiffuel dennem som saa giorde« (*Jammers Minde*, p. 68). Frederik III's private secretary, Christoffer Gabel, believes her (*Jammers Minde*, p. 69: »ce n'est que raillerie!«), but Count Rantzau and the Empire commander Hans Schack remain sceptical:

> Skack sagde, man meener tit anded vnder Skiemt: oc bruger Naffne huor vnder anded forstaaes: Thi der vdi Breffuet melded bleff, om att dricke vd, war de Schwitzere derris Manner de offuer Borde haffuer, talt oc alle de *Cantons* Herrers Tittel opregnet, huor for Skack formeente, att de Byers Naffn haffde anded att sige; Ieg suarte intet Skack; Men der G. Rantzow trengte immerfort, att ieg skulle sige, huad min Mand dermed meente, suarte ieg, icke att kunde wide, om hand anden Meening dermed haffue kunde, end den som Skreffuen stoed[.]
>
> (*Jammers Minde*, p. 69)

By means of this episode, Birgit Baldwin points out that it is »possible that Leonora Christina herself 'bruger Navne, hvorunder andet forstaaes'«,[329] thus confirming that she might have pursued a specific goal by narrating seemingly random episodes of her life, such as her assisting Alexander von Kückelsom and Lucia.

Lange concludes the same and accuses Leonora Christina of downright lying. However, he softens his criticism subsequently by referring to her conjugal duties,[330] thus following Leonora Christina's instructions as to how to understand

---

329 Baldwin, Birgit. 'Jammersminde Remembered', p. 276.
330 Lange, Julius. 'Contra Leonora Christina', pp. 728 and 739. Another argument Lange provides 'pro Leonora Christina', is women's alleged lack of criminal responsibility, due to their inability to understand justice in an objective manner (ibid., p. 728). Lange underestimated Leonora Christina's abilities; a mistake that did not occur to Bodil Wamberg. Lange's judgement is also curiously reminiscent of the castellan Jokum Waltpurger's opinion of women, more than two centuries earlier, when he tried to persuade Leonora Christina to confess by alluding to her alleged female feebleness: »Ihr seyt ein Frawens Mensh ein Schwaches Werckzeug, Die arme Weibes-Bilder sein bald verführet; Man thut ihnen auch nicht gerne was, wan sie die Wahrheit bekennen« (*Jammers Minde*, p. 42).

her account. Bodil Wamberg, on the other hand, suggests viewing the relationship between the spouses from a different angle:

> Léd hun, fordi hun – som hun forsikrer sine børn – havde været elsket af en dydig herre, fordi hun ikke havde villet forlade ham i ulykken? Eller ligger sandheden snarere i den modsate ende af spektret: var den dydige herre et skvat – stråmand for en hustrus uhyrlige ambition?[331]

It is not inconceivable that Leonora Christina should have had – for her time – an extraordinary amount of influence on her husband. As she does not forbear to mention in her French autobiography, Leonora Christina enquired her husband about his financial situation at the beginning of their marriage. Thus, she learned that Corfitz was indebted. She was very willing to assist him with her fortune; at the same time, this favour might have established a hierarchy in the Ulfeldt estate. *She* was the one in possession of wealth and a powerful family. Thus, it was only in his own interest to preserve those amenities for his wife, for example by lobbying for the King's unfaithful wife Kirsten Munk. The foremost Corfitz Ulfeldt-scholar, Steffen Heiberg, is not disinclined either to attest much of Corfitz Ulfeldt's behaviour to his wife's need for recognition. However, he concludes that they probably spurred each other.[332]

On the other hand, all of Leonora Christina's writings argue for a renunciation of the traditional domestic hierarchy based on an understanding of men as superior to women. The main purpose of *Hæltinners Pryd*, for example, was to demonstrate that it was unjustified to consider women inferior to men:

> Løffuindens Hierte er saa Keckmodig som Løwens: Mangen Quinde haffuer større styrcke end som mangen Mand, Mangen Quinde haffuer oc wel saa Keckt ed mod som Mangen Mand; de suare icke alle til Mands Naffn i Gierningen som bærer Tittel aff Mands Naffn men offte suare Quinder til Helters Naffn i Gierningen, oc bere dog ickun Quinders Naffn: Huoroffte seer man quindactige Hierter i Mands Legemer, oc der imod igien mandelige Kræffter i suage Karr: Ded er Vbilligt, att man maaler Gierningen effter Persohnen, oc skatter icke Persohnen effter Gierningen.[333]

---

331 Wamberg, Bodil. *Leonora Christina*, p. 17.
332 Heiberg, Steffen. *Enhjørningen Corfitz Ulfeldt*, p. 27: »I deres ambitioner og statusjagt var de nemlig afhængige af hinanden. Hans elegance gav hende prestige, og ham gav det ikke mindreværdskomplekser at skulle leve op til hendes behov for at blive anset for jævnbyrdig med de fyrstelig fødte«.
333 Leonora Christina. *Hæltinners Pryd*, ed. Christopher Maaløe. Copenhagen: Reitzel, 1977, p. 21.

Furthermore, it was another purpose of *Hæltinners Pryd* to highlight Leonora Christina's qualities in particular, as noted above. When Leonora Christina was writing about women worthy of a hero's title due to their brave actions, she evidently invited her readers to draw the parallel to the author. One must thus wonder: who was the man with the womanish heart that contrasted the lioness Leonora Christina? For Bodil Wamberg the answer is evident:

> Og når man har gjort sig bekendt med Ulfeldts adfærdsmønster i krisesituationer, som de diskret fremgår af *Den franske selvbiografi* og chokerende afsløres ved studium af andre kilder, får man forståelse for, at en vis aggression må have oplagret sig i Leonora og kommer ud mellem sidebenene engang imellem.[334]

Leonora Christina's portrayal of her husband's shortcomings – conscious or subconscious – is indeed very well disguised. The first among Leonora Christina's few depictions of Corfitz Ulfeldt, i.e. in the French autobiography, portrays him as a limping, poor fellow. The key information in this episode is that Leonora Christina had the magnitude to see beyond those deficits. She emerges as protagonist and heroine, but this is only possible at the expense of Ulfeldt.

One account in her French autobiography, i.e. Leonora Christina's narrative of the couple's attempt to escape from Hammershus and Bornholm, serves more blatantly than any other to depict Leonora Christina's supremacy. On a full moon night on 13 March 1661,[335] the couple, together with their servant Peter Pflügge, commenced their flight. Leonora Christina was the first one to rope down the window[336] towards the cliffs of Bornholm. Throughout the first steps of this adventurous escape, Leonora Christina had to assist her weakened husband. On the way down from the plateau to the seaside, where the fugitives intended to take a fishing boat, the servant fell and got injured. Since he fell in the wrong place, Leonora Christina had to pull him up again with one of the ropes. In her French autobiography, she attributes this risky and miraculous salvation to divine assistance, while others

---

334 Wamberg, Bodil. *Leonora Christina*, p. 39.

335 This is the date declared in a contemporary account, conserved to this day in the Journal for Politik, Natur- og Menneske-Kundskab. See Fuchs, Adolph. 'Underdanigst Relation om Hr. Greve Corfiz Ulfelds Echappade fra Slottet Hammershus paa Bornholm, som skete Torsdag Nat d. 13de Martii 1661. Hvorledes det gik ham paa hans Reise, og den store Ildebrandsfare, som han udentvivl forsætligviis har efterladt sig paa sit Kammer', Journal for Politik, Natur- og Menneske-Kundskab 1816/1, pp. 71-78. In her French autobiography, Leonora Christina wrongly remembers this night as having occured in April.

336 Before the night of their flight, Leonora Christina had forged ropes out of sheets she had received from her children and sewn them together, while Ulfeldt and Peter Pflügge forged further escape tools and prepared the window.

thought that the devil must have had a finger in the pie.[337] Throughout the rest of their path, Leonora Christina had to support her discouraged husband both physically and mentally. When the three of them finally reached the shore, it was already dawning and their efforts were all for naught.

Leonora Christina's account is the main record preserved of this flight. There are other reports of this night, e.g. by Adolph Fuchs, but he did not notice the escape until hours after its start and could thus only by hindsight make sense of the event. There are eyewitness reports from local authorities and fishermen as well,[338] but since the fugitives were not discovered until they had reached the beach, there are only two accounts covering the entire escape. The statement of Peter Pflügge is the other complete account of the flight. It is worthwhile noting that his detailed relation coincides considerably with Leonora Christina's memories of this time.[339] However, Pflügge's presentation of the events also portrays Leonora Christina in a much less heroic manner than her French autobiography and he does not say a word about Corfitz Ulfeldt's despondence.[340] This could, however, certainly be attributed to the nature of the text. Ulfeldt's virility, or his lack of such, was hardly of any concern to the official reconstruction of his attempted escape, but it was to Leonora Christina's portrayal of her own bravery.

Fuchs' version of the escape, the incidents preceding it, and the characters of his notorious prisoners, clearly show that the feeling of aversion depicted by Leonora Christina in her account was mutual. His account differs somewhat from that in the French autobiography and on occasion, Fuchs' report adds information entirely omitted by Leonora Christina.[341] The most significant discrepancy is that in Fuchs' account, Ulfeldt is the driving force behind the escape plan:

---

337 Cf. *Leonora Christina Grevinde Ulfeldts Franske Levnedsskildring*, p. 10c (Translation p. 43).

338 In total, the Journal for Politik, Natur- og Menneske-Kundskab conveys the testimonies of fifteen eyewitnesses, including the statements of Peter Pflügge, who escaped with the Ulfeldt couple. See 'Vidners Udsagn i Forhøret over Corfiz Ulfelds Flugt udaf Hammershuus Fæstning', Journal for Politik, Natur- og Menneske-Kundskab 1816/1, pp. 198-214, and 'Vidnernes Udsagn i Forhøret over Corfiz Ulfelds Flugt fra Hammershuus Fæstning', Journal for Politik, Natur- og Menneske-Kundskab 1816/2, pp. 42-47.

339 Only on one point, the two statements contradict each other considerably. While Leonora Christina said to have left a candle (see footnote below) on the table, the servant – who was the last to leave the cell – remembered her to have put it on the floor next to his bed.

340 'Vidners Udsagn i Forhøret over Corfiz Ulfelds Flugt', p. 208-214.

341 For example, that before escaping through the window, Corfitz Ulfeldt left a burning candle covered in bedstraw in the room – according to Fuchs in the hope of burning down Hammershus and keep their guards from chasing after them. See Fuchs, Adolph. 'Underdanigst Relation om Hr. Greve Corfiz Ulfelds Echappade', p. 77. He further reports that Leonora Christina accused the cat they left in the cell of having dragged the candle towards the straw (ibid., p. 78). However, she did not explain why the same cat was dressed in a red fool's cap and had a tied-up mouth.

> Da Hr. Greve Ulfeld fornam, at han hverken kunde bevæge mig eller mine Officierer, ved Offerter af sine store Penge, der bestode i 100,000 Rdlr., til derved at erhverve sin Frihed, havde han fattet andre Tanker, og ituskaaret de Mobilier, som vare bleven ham sendte fra Kiøbenhavn til hans Beværtning, og giort Seil og Reeb deraf; hvilket det vedgaaende Fartøi udviser; formeendende det kunde ikke mangle ham, at han jo maatte finde nogle Baade ved Stranden, for at betiene sig af dem, efterdi han havde alting færdigt, hvad der var fornødent til Afseiling.[342]

According to Leonora Christina's French autobiography, Fuchs approached *her* with an offer, hoping he could lure the couple into yet another criminal act. Additionally, Leonora Christina's text portrays her negotiating with Fuchs, while Corfitz Ulfeldt was too upset to talk to his guard. Regardless, however the actual events took place, Leonora Christina's version of the story depicts her as a strong, courageous woman leading two men (almost) into freedom. What is even more significant is Corfitz Ulfeldt's portrayal. Already before the account of the escape, he is depicted in a very passive manner – almost all the interaction with Adolph Fuchs is left to Leonora Christina. Then, once the couple has finally left their accursed prison, Corfitz despairs repeatedly, only to be re-encouraged by his wife.

It is hardly a coincidence that Leonora Christina did not omit any of those incidences, all of which present her qualities at the expense of her husband. Marita Akhøj Nielsen, too, expresses some astonishment at Leonora Christina's portrayal of Corfitz Ulfeldt: »Heller ikke hendes dybe kærlighed til Ulfeldt lader sig rokke, men ud fra selvbiografiens skildring af manden er hendes trofaste hengivenhed ret ubegribelig. [...] Gennemgående er han svag, ubehersket og naiv, helt afhængig af sin stærke hustru«.[343] However, unlike Bodil Wamberg, Akhøj Nielsen attributes this implicit criticism to outer circumstances rather than Leonora Christina's true feelings: »Den skæve karakteristik skyldes rimeligvis, at Leonora Christina var nødt til at markere en vis distance til ægtefællen og dermed til hans bevislige forræderi, hvis hun skulle rense sig selv«.[344] Particularly, if compared to historiography's generally positive depiction of Ulfeldt's physical appearance and intellect in his

---

342 Ibid., p. 72.
343 Akhøj Nielsen, Marita. 'Med sod og øl på sukkerpapir: Om Leonora Christina – Årets klassiker 2003', Bogens verden (2003/04): http://wayback.kb.dk:8080/wayback-1.4.2/wayback/20100107153228/http://www2.kb.dk/guests/natl/db/bv/03/4/index1.htm.
344 Ibid.

earlier years,[345] Leonora Christina's portrayal of a tendentially weak, dependent husband is indeed astonishing and may thus be attributed to the overall purpose of her writings, which was to promote her own qualities against the backdrop of everybody else's, perhaps exaggerated, weaknesses.

Regardless of Leonora Christina's true feelings towards her husband, her demeaning portrayal of Corfitz Ulfeldt matches the depiction of her relation to the other sex in *Jammers Minde*. The parade of weak men (with the notable exception of her father) displayed in her French autobiography – Wichmann Hasebard, Alexander von Kückelsom, Adolph Fuchs, and Corfitz Ulfeldt – continues here with even more pathetic specimens: her former enemy, Jørgen Walter, depends on Leonora Christina's grace in order to survive (albeit not for long); the castellan, once again blind drunk, molests her sexually (*Jammers Minde*, p. 140); and the castellan's helper Christian, an inmate on death row for murder, attempts to threaten and daunt Leonora Christina and her maid but is unable to intimidate her (*Jammers Minde*, p. 154). In their presupposed physical supremacy,[346] these men (with the exception of Jørgen Walter, who had been defeated by the Ulfeldts before) represent patriarchy and thus autocracy: »Den enevældige magt og ondskab optræder direkte for Leonora Christina først og fremmest i skikkelse af en række mandspersoner, der forsøger at benytte sig af hendes formodede kvindelige svaghed«.[347] However, in Leonora Christina's opinion, the true driving force behind this absolutist rule is a woman, i.e. Sophie Amalie, which only reinforces Leonora Christina's portrayal of the supposedly stronger sex.

Bodil Wamberg's criticism of Leonora Christina soon evoked a similarly critical response. In answer to Wambergs book, Vilhelm Nielsen published his own, more positive, view on *Jammers Minde* and its author.[348] Nielsen's main objection is that Wamberg's evaluation is biased by an anachronistic perception of Leonora Chri-

---

345 Steffen Heiberg, for example, writes of »den blændende fremtræden« of »den elegante verdensmand« (Heiberg, Steffen. *Enhjørningen Corfitz Ulfeldt*, respectively pp. 21 and 26), while Sophus Birket Smith describes the early Corfitz Ulfeldt (i.e. before Hammershus) as »kraftig« and »imponerende« (Birket Smith, Sophus. *Leonora Christina Grevinde Ulfeldts Historie 2*, both quotations p. 67).

346 Presupposed because Leonora Christina does not believe in any male supremacy, not even a physical one. See Leonora Christina. *Hæltinners Pryd*, p. 21: »Mangen Quinde haffuer større styrcke end som mangen Mand«. Her self-portrayal in her autobiographical accounts confirms this claim. In fact, Leonora Christina takes pride in her own physical strength and is convinced she could overcome many a man, as she informs one of her maids: »[…] ieg kand quæle den stærckeste Karl med miine bare hænder om ieg v-forwarendis fick fat paa ham« (*Jammers Minde*, p. 119).

347 Mai, Anne-Marie and Stig Dalager. '»... et eventyr, som er værdigt en roman«'. In *Leonora Christina: Historien om en heltinde*. Århus: Arkona, 1983 (Acta Jutlandica 58, Humanistisk serie 57), p. 75.

348 Nielsen, Vilhelm. 'Leonora Christines psyke'. Kronik i Kristeligt Dagblad, mandag den 29. juli 1991: http://www.vilhelmnielsen.dk/LeonoraChristinesPsyke.html.

stina's milieu; especially the Law of Jante,[349] with its demonisation of the ego and individual achievement may have played a part in Wamberg's very critical position towards Leonora Christina.[350] While acknowledging that Leonora Christina was far from being a saint, Nielsen demands a more historical validation of her testimonies. While the modern reader may take exception to her self-praise and simultaneous assurances of religiousity, her own aristocratic environment might just as well have expected such a keen self-assessment: »Hun var hverken helgen eller martyr, som senere tider har gjort hende til. Når hun kalder sig ›Kristi Korsdragerske‹ beskriver hun sine lidelser i tidens sprog og tankegang«.[351]

Finally, the question of whether Corfitz Ulfeldt spent the last years of his life in insanity employed much of historical research on the Ulfeldt couple. This issue may appear trivial at first glance, but references to Ulfeldt's sudden illnesses (as well as his misguided decisions) occur frequently in the French autobiography. The timing of these attacks – usually coinciding with professionally or legally challenging times for the Ulfeldt couple – has led to suggestions that they might have been psychosomatic, hysterical paralysis or even mere excuses.[352] This is of course not how Leonora Christina intended to portray her husband. Nevertheless, she utilises this issue in her depiction of the interrogation in the Blue Tower:

Cantzeler sagde; Eders Mand haffuer bøded en fremmet Herre Dannemarckis Riige til. Ieg spurte, om Dannemarckis Riige hørte min Mand til, att hand ded kunde vdbyde? oc efftersom ingen Suarte, foer ieg widre fort oc sagde. I goede Herrer, kiender alle min Herre, I wiide, att hand haffuer werret æstimeret for en Mand aff Forstand, oc ieg kand

---

349 The Law of Jante (*Janteloven*), alternatively referred to as »Who-do-you-think-you-are-law«, was created by the Dano-Norwegian writer Aksel Sandemose. In 1933, Sandemose published his novel *En flyktning krysser sitt spor*, portraying the fictional Danish town Jante and its ten rules, all together forming the Law of Jante. This law de-emphasises personal achievement and self-esteem, while placing emphasis on a collective identity instead. The fictional law with its universally known first rule, »Du skal ikke tro, du er noget«, has since been considered to reflect a typically Scandinavian way of thinking.

350 This suspicion is supported by similar remarks written by the historian Palle Lauring, whose criticism of Leonora Christina is primarily directed at qualities, for which she is usually appraised: »Men iøvrigt var hun en duksenatur. Ug-børn er forældres og læreres fryd, men den kvalitet, at være duks og kunne lære alt til ug, er jo kun noget værd, når den er kombineret med andre gode eller brugelige kvaliteter. Er den ikke det, er alle ug-erne i bedste fald værdiløse. Leonora Christine var kun duks. Alt hvad hun læste og lærte gjorde hende ikke rigere som menneske, men det gjorde hende selvsikker ud over al rimelighed« (Lauring, Palle. *Dronninger og andre kvinder i Danmarkshistorien*. Copenhagen: Høst & Søn, 1990 (1981), p. 71). Palle Lauring is, to my knowledge, also the only historian, who considers Leonora Christina to have got off fairly lightly with her prison sentence: »Som engelsk prinsesse var hun sandsynligvis blevet halshygget. Her slap hun med fængsel« (ibid., p. 75).

351 Nielsen, Vilhelm. 'Leonora Christines psyke', http://www.vilhelmnielsen.dk/LeonoraChristinesPsyke.html.

352 See, for example, Wamberg, Bodil. *Leonora Christina*, p. 125.

Forsickre eder, att der ieg fra hannem skiltist, da haffde hand endnu sin fulle Fornufft; Nu er let att tencke, att ingen Forstandig Mand, ded skulle vdbyde, som icke stoed i hands Mact, oc hand icke for Raade; Hand er io vdi ingen *Charge*, haffuer ingen Myndighed eller Midler; huor skulle hand were saa daarlig, saadan Tilbud att giøre, oc huad for en Herre skulle wille tage der imod? G. Rantzow sagde, ded er dog saa *Madame*, hand haffuer tilbøded Dannemarck en fremmed *Potentat*, i wed ded wel. Ieg ßuarte, Gud skal were mit Widne dertil, att ieg ded icke wed[.]

(*Jammers Minde*, p. 33)

To date, no historian has doubted Ulfeldt's guilt. Extant documents testify to his correspondences and indicate that Ulfeldt did indeed offer the Elector of Brandenburg, Friedrich Wilhelm, the Danish throne, meaning that Ulfeldt suggested creating an insurgency against Frederik III and subsequently using his influence to coronate Friedrich Wilhelm. Whether he did this in a sound state of mind is another issue. To the question, whether Corfitz Ulfeldt has offered the Danish empire to somebody, Leonora Christina answers with a counter-question, thus leaving it to the interrogator to recognise his inquiry as absurd. The following silence demonstrates that her strategy has been a success. Her following remark, that her husband was still in possession of a sane mind when last they saw each other, is rendered an unqualified lay evaluation by her subsequent statement of not knowing anything about her husband's alleged treason. Finally, she closes her statement with yet another question and leaves the choice to her inquisitors: either Corfitz Ulfeldt was insane (and thus legally not responsible) in offering something that did not belong to him, or the recipient of this generous offer would have been insane to accept it. Either way, if this act of treason had indeed happened, at least one mad person[353] was involved in it, thus it can hardly be taken seriously.

---

[353] The issue of Corfitz Ulfeldt's alleged insanity was famously taken on by Johannes Helweg. Due to his frequently irrational behaviour during the last years of his life, Ulfeldt has repeatedly been suspected of lunacy. His uprises against Christian IV and Frederik III may strike a contemporary critic as mad, but they may still be justified by the political system of 17th-century Denmark, alien to the 21st century. However, his attempt to involve the Elector of Brandenburg in his treacherous plan was nonsensical. The Elector of Brandenburg and Frederik III were allies and, as the former Steward of the Realm, Ulfeldt should have been aware of this alliance. The condition that could have caused Ulfeldt's irrational behaviour is another question puzzling many a scholar. Johannes Helweg's theory, which connects Ulfeldt's insanity with his uncurable leg wound and argues that both are symptoms of syphilis, has become particularly popular and is still discussed in scholarship and adopted by 20th-century Leonora Christina-literature. See Helweg, Johannes. 'Var Corfitz Ulfeldt sindssyg?', Tilskueren (1913), pp. 1020-1037.

Den Liidende Christinne

A rather recent contribution by Anna Katharina Dömling is representative of the overall focus of current research on *Jammers Minde* and similar works. In her article on self-perception and self-staging in the autobiographical texts of Leonora Christina, Dömling situates Leonora Christina's act of self-portrayal within the Baroque *theatrum mundi*-metaphor.[354] Yet, if the world is a stage and life a drama, how could one define the protagonist's, i.e. Leonora Christina's, character? Leonora Christina did not wish to be remembered as one type of personality only. In her writings, particularly in the French autobiography, she is a *grande dame*, daughter of King Christian IV; she is also a heroine, with physical and mental skills equal to those of any man; and she is a loving and faithful wife. In the first part of *Jammers Minde*, though, Leonora Christina is a woman of faith as well, a successor of Job and Christ himself. While Leonora Christina's French autobiography thus predominantly portrays her as the *grande dame*, the heroine and the wife, *Jammers Minde* shows us another side of her: the *Liidende Christinne*.

Leonora Christina's self-staging as a martyr begins, as asserted in the preceding chapter, with the title: *Jammers Minde*, which clearly states the theme of her autobiography, thus placing it within the tradition of martyrs' vitae. Throughout the account, but particularly in the first part, the reader finds 'proof' of Leonora Christina's chosenness, for example in *Fortalen*:

> Wil mig alt saa icke alleeneste min Jammer Errindre oc Gud for sin Naadige Bistand i alle tilføyede bedrøffuelige Tilfald tacke: men endoc Eder mine Kiere Børn, Guds Goedhed imod mig Kundgiøre, paa ded i Eder icke alleeneste offuer den Allerhøyestis v-begriibelige Hielps-Gierninger forundre kunde, men endoc med mig der vdoffuer i Tacksigelsen indstemme; Thi med Skiel skal I kunde sige, att Gud vnderlige Ting imod mig giort haffuer: Att hand haffuer wer[r]et [correction by the editors] Mectig vdi mig Suage, oc sin Krafft vdi mig ded allerskrøbeligste Redskab bewiißet: Thi huorledis haffde ded ellers werret muligt, att ieg saa mange offuer stoere, plutzlige oc v-formodentlige Vlyckelige Tilfælle haffde imodstaa kunde, om Hands Aand icke vdi mig sin wirckning giort haffde.
>
> (*Jammers Minde*, p. 3*)

Leonora Christina's main message is that God had assisted her, thus implying that she had suffered undeservingly. However, a closer look at this passage reveals how carefully Leonora Christina watches her diction. Bodil Wamberg draws special

---

354 Dömling, Anna Katharina. 'Billigen kand ieg med Iob sige', p. 25.

attention to the words »pludselige«, »uformodentlige« and »Tilfælde«. All these terms indicate an absence of a causal chain, thus once again presenting Leonora Christina's punishment as entirely unjustified.[355]

In *Fortalen*, Leonora Christina furthermore insists that she could hardly have endured all her calamities without the personal assistance of God: »Gud war den som selffuer traadde ind med mig aff Taarn-Døren, Hand war dend som racte mig sin Haand oc striide for mig vdi Mißdædernis Fengsel, som kaldis den Mørcke-Kircke« (*Jammers Minde*, p. 3*). Anna Katharina Dömling sees Leonora Christina's statement about God's assistance as a reference to the canticle *Magnificat* (or *The Song of Mary*).[356] Thus, Leonora Christina implicitly compares herself to the godchosen woman par excellence, the Virgin Mary.

Moreover, in a reference to the Book of Revelation, Leonora Christina bespeaks seven disasters that fell upon her:

Betencker mine Hierte Kiere Børn, diße haarde Liidelser; errindrer eder oc Guds stoere Goedhed imod mig: Seer, aff Sex Drøffuelser haffuer hand vdfriiet mig, wærer wiß paa att Hand vdi den Syffuende mig ey lader Sticke eller Omkomme; Ney, Hand wil for sit Naffns Ære skyld wældeligen mig Vdriiffue.

(*Jammers Minde*, p. 11*)

The six calamities she has already endured are the following: 1) the Dina affair and the Ulfeldt couple's subsequent flight from Denmark in 1651; 2) her journey to Korsør in 1656 (»huilcken min Herre mig imod mit Sind Befalede *Anno* 1657 [sic]«, *Jammers Minde*, p. 6*); 3) the couple's arrest in Malmö 1659; 4) their arrest in Hammershus 1660-61; 5) their loss of wealth and power; and 6) her imprisonment in Dover Castle.[357] Like Job, Leonora Christina has to endure seven disasters – the seventh being her arrest in the Blue Tower – and like him, she will not be forsaken. In identifying with Job, the distorted world she encountered in the Blue Tower finally receives a higher meaning. On the one hand, her calamities are absurd and meaningless, as they are undeserved. On the other hand, though, they do have a higher meaning, as they consummate her fate. One can presume that this reference to Job would have appeared plausible to most of Leonora Christina's contemporary

---

355 Wamberg, Bodil. *Leonora Christina*, p. 203.
356 Dömling, Anna Katharina. 'Billigen kand ieg med Iob sige', p. 28.
357 Mai, Anne-Marie. 'Troskab, lidelse og lidenskab', p. 294.

readers, as the same motive appears in other autobiographies written in the 17th century, e.g. in *Agneta Horns leverne*, concluded in 1656.[358]

The figure of Job primarily provides Leonora Christina with a consoling story to identify with and hope for better times to come. From all the biblical figures – and we can assume that she was familiar with all of them – she chose Job to disclose her life narrative: »Hierte Kiere Børn, billigen kand ieg med Iob sige; Dersom man min Iammers weye kunde, oc mine Liidelser tilsammen i en Wect-Skaal legge, da skulle de were tyngere end Saand i Haffuet« (*Jammers Minde*, p. 2*).

However, in the second beginning of the narrative, i.e. after *Fortalen*, Leonora Christina abandons Job for a short while by referring to the *Enchiridion* or *Manual of Epictetus*, a manual of Stoic ethical advice from the 2nd century, compiled by Arrian of Nicomedia, a disciple of the Greek philosopher Epictetus:

> Men efftersom alle Ting haffuer saa som tuende Hancker huor wed ded skal hæffuis, som *Epictetus* siger; Den eene Hancke siger hand er Liiderlig, den anden V-liiderlig, oc staar ded vdi worris egen Willie, huilcken Hancke wii wille griibe til att tage fat wed, den Liiderlige eller den V-liiderlige; wil wii tage wed den Liiderlige, saa kand wii alt forbigaaende ihuor smerteligen oc Bedrøffueligen ded endoc werret haffuer, lige saa wel oc føyligere Glædeligen som Sørgeligen Ihuekomme. Huor forre ieg wed den Liiderligste Hancke wil fatte, oc vdi *Iesu* Nafffn min Ihuekommelse igiennem løbe; Errindrendis all Iammer, Elendighed, Bedrøffuelse, Spott, Forhaanelser, Widerwertigheder oc Fortred mig paa dette Sted møtte erre, oc ieg formedelst Guds Naadis Bistand offuerstriid haffuer, ingenlunde mig der vdoffuer Bedrøffue, men tuert imod, wed huer Post i sær mig Guds Goedhed errindre[.]
>
> (*Jammers Minde*, p. 1)

While Leonora Christina's reference to Epictetus attempts to convey a positive outlook, her simultaneous reference to the sorrows she had to endure is reminiscent of her allusion to Job. Yet just as with her reference to Job,[359] Leonora Christina con-

---

358 See Heitmann, Annegret. *Selbst schreiben*, p. 152 and Hættner Aurelius, Eva. 'Under faderens lov: Om Agneta Horn'. In *Nordisk kvindelitteraturhistorie 1: I Guds navn: 1000-1800*, ed. Elisabeth Møller Jensen. Copenhagen: Rosinante/Munksgaard, 1993, p. 275. On the religious language in the writings of 17th century Scandinavian women, see Lindgärde, Valborg. 'Nu skal også Herren optage mig: To selvbiografiske tekster fra 1600-tallet'. In *Nordisk kvindelitteraturhistorie 1: I Guds navn: 1000-1800*, ed. Elisabeth Møller Jensen. Copenhagen: Rosinante/Munksgaard, 1993, pp. 277-285.

359 »Første tildriffuende Aarsage er, Guds Almectigheds Erindring efftersom ieg ey min Iammer, Angst, Nød, Smerte Ihuekomme kand, foruden tillige med mig Guds Allmact att Errindre, som vdi alle mine Liidelser, Elendigheder, Hiertesorrig oc Bedrøffuelser, min Krafft oc Hielp, Min Trøst oc Bistand werret haffuer, thi aldrig lagde Gud mig saa snart en Byrde paa, att hand io med ded samme mig effter Byrdens tyngde Styrcke gaff, saa att Byrden mig wel Krum nederbøyede, mig hart Knuede oc Tryckte, men dog ey slet nederslog, Knusede oc vndertryckte; for huilcket den vbegriibelige Guds Allmectighed skee Loff oc Priis i Ewighed« (*Jammers Minde*, p. 2*).

cludes this maxim with an appraisal of God's omnipotence and, most importantly, assistance. Whether one regards Leonora Christina's fate from a rather negative perspective (Job), or whether one tries to focus on the silver lining (Epictetus), the final say is always granted to God. Thus, God constitutes a much grander authority within this part of the text than meets the eye: »Neither God's written word (the story of Job, among other Biblical quotations) nor the wisdom of the Greeks can usurp the authority of Leonora Christina's personal relationship to God. [...] For no matter how *Jammersminde* is read, the reference to God is the excuse for the writing«.[360]

A manifestation of Leonora Christina's life story is her last sight of the outer world before disappearing in the Blue Tower. When she was escorted from the boat that had returned her to Copenhagen to the Blue Tower, she saw Corfitz's sister, Birgitte Ulfeldt,[361] laughing hysterically at her sister-in-law's misery: »Hun kiørte langs Stranden; der ieg mig om til den Siide wente stoed hun op i wognen, oc loe aff all sin Mact« (*Jammers Minde*, p. 11). At the entrance of the Blue Tower, the castellan, Jokum Waltpurger, deliberately took his time to open the door for his new guest: »[Hand] stoed en Rom Tiid vdden for, oc famlede med Nøglen, loed som hand icke kunde lucke op, for att lade mig lenge Folckis Spetackel were« (*Jammers Minde*, p. 12). In this moment, Leonora Christina is truly alone. Her husband is nowhere to be found, her children are in exile, her extended family has forsaken her, and even the once extraordinary wealth of the Ulfeldt family is gone. Her isolation provides an ideal scenery for the staging of her destiny:

Oc saa som mit Hierte war rettet til Gud, oc min Tilliid war til den Allerhøyeste; opløfftede ieg vdi midler Tiid mine Øyen op til Himmelen, søgende der Styrcke, Krafft oc Redning; huilcken mig oc Naadeligen bleff giffuen. (En hendelse wil ieg ey v-melded lade forbigaa, som er; Att da ieg mine Øyne til Himmelen opslog, fløy en Skrigendis Raffn offuer Taarnet, oc hannem fulte en flock Duer, som oc fløye samme Wey.)

(*Jammers Minde*, p. 12)

---

360 Baldwin, Birgit. 'Jammersminde Remembered', p. 275.

361 In one of his last letters to his friend Otto Sperling the Elder, written shortly before his death, Corfitz Ulfeldt calls his sister Birgitte »den dødeligste Fiende af Madame og af mig« ('Tre Breve, skrevne af den, hos os noksom erindrede, Corfiz Ulfeld, i det sidste Aar af hans Levetid, til Dr. Sperling', Journal for Politik, Natur- og Menneske-Kundskab 1816/1, p. 122). In this letter, Ulfeldt further informs Sperling that his sister had contributed to his wife's imprisonment on Bornholm by forwarding a compromising letter written by Leonora Christina to Joachim Gersdorff (1611-1661), one of Ulfeldt's main opponents at the Danish court.

The raven, an animal typically associated with death and heathen beliefs, is evidently a bad omen: »Den bibelstærke Leonora må gyse for den skrigende ravn, som i Det gamle testamente er en uren fugl og dødsbebuder«.[362] However, the precursor of Evil is followed by doves, a symbol of the Holy Spirit. This could indicate that a better future was awaiting after all and looking back at this incident, Leonora Christina knew that the epiphany was right.

Curiously enough, Leonora Christina calls herself *Christi Kaarßdragerske*, while at the same time identifying with Job, a figure from the Old Testament: »Haffde ieg med Iob talt daarligen, sagde ieg oc med hannem; Att ieg haffde giort v-wiißeligen, oc talt om Ting, som ware mig for høye, oc ieg icke forstoed« (*Jammers Minde*, p. 81). Even though her self-denomination as *Christi Kaarßdragerske* places her within the more conciliatory New Testament, her mindset is altogether echoing the Old Testament, which portrays a more vengeful and unforgiving God:

> Hun pukker stadig, som i Fortalen, på, at Gud holder med hende, *mod* de andre, hendes og dermed Guds fjender. At det er præcis dette indhold, hun udfra Lukas lægger i udvælgelsen, bekræftes af det korresponderende sted i Johannes' Åbenbaring (6.10), hvor der står: »Og de råbte med høj røst og sagde: Hvor længe, Herre, du hellige og sanddru! undlader du at dømme og hævne vort blod på dem, som bo på jorden?«[363]

As a servant of God, Leonora Christina trusts in her final salvation and the punishment of her enemies. Her fate, which had already become much more agreeable when penning the first part of *Jammers Minde*, justifies this conviction. Leonora Christina's identification with Christ is less prominent than the Job theme (perhaps due to the risk of being indicted for megalomania) but none the less suggestive. Her self-designation as *Christi Kaarßdragerske* presents her punishment as an *imitatio Christi*: »Der ware beeske sticker Brød for mig tilskaarren, oc bitter Kaarß-Galle for mig indskenket vdi ded Blaa-Taarn paa Kiøbenhaffns-Slott, did skulle ieg, ded att Æde oc att vddricke« (*Jammers Minde*, p. 10*). According to Otto Andrup, this is a reference to the Gospel of Matthew according to which Jesus Christ, after his crucifixion, receives a drink consisting of vinegar and bile.[364] The self-comparison with Christ in this instance continues when Leonora Christina equates Charles II of England with Judas Ischariot (»huor hand mig med ett Iudas-Kyß Helste«, *Jammers Minde*, p. 10*).

---

362 Wamberg, Bodil. *Leonora Christina*, p. 214.
363 Ibid., p. 230.
364 Andrup, Otto. 'Noter', p. 243 (endnote p. 47).

However, despite the religious tone of the text's first part, *Jammers Minde* is by no means a particularly spiritual text, especially in comparison to other texts of the 17th century. The mindset displayed by Leonora Christina was not optional, but imperative to women of her time. Leonora Christina's identification with Job and her other proofs of chosenness, however, are more peculiar, although not entirely original.

1.2.2. *Jammers Minde* as an Autobiographical Enterprise

The histories of *Jammers Minde* and the autobiographical genre exhibit striking parallels, which substantiate the rather recent notion that *Jammers Minde* is an extraordinary,[365] yet still classic autobiography. The term *autobiography* or, accordingly, *selvbiografi*, with all its side- and sub-genres, did not yet exist in Leonora Christina's times. Autobiographers of the 17th century or earlier had to resort to terms like *Vita* or, as in the more specific case of Danish premodern life writings, *Minder*.[366] Similarly, and as asserted in Chapter 1.2.1., Leonora Christina did not always enjoy the title of a writer and not even her most elaborate work, *Jammers Minde*, has always been perceived as an autobiography. Finn Stein Larsen, for example, called *Jammers Minde* a »memoirebrudstykke, i hvilket det anlagte synspunkt er tilbageskuende«.[367] Similarly, Lisa Schmalensee and Lene Torp categorise *Jammers Minde* as »en blanding af brev og dagbog«,[368] a mix of two highly unliterary genres. However, the work of these three scholars predates the breakthrough of research on life narratives (which occurred in the 1980's), hence the terminological confusion. Today, their evaluations would be dismissed as being either overly simplistic or downright wrong. *Jammers Minde* is evidently neither a diary nor a letter collection. Yet, such terminological confusions were not limited to Leonora Christina's written works; she herself received some alienating denominations as well. For example, the Swiss *Lexikon der Frau in zwei Bänden* simply calls her

---

365 Cf. Mai, Anne-Marie. 'Det danske sprogs inderlige elskerinde: Om Anna Margrethe Lasson'. In *Nordisk kvindelitteraturhistorie 1: I Guds navn: 1000-1800*, ed. Elisabeth Møller Jensen. Copenhagen: Rosinante/Munksgaard, 1993, p. 343: »I 1600- og 1700-tallet fandtes en betragtelig kvindelig litteratur i form af selvbiografier, dagbøger og personlige dokumenter, men denne selvbiografiske eller slægtsbiografiske prosa tjente først og fremmest religiøse eller praktiske slægtshistoriske formål og var kun undtagelsesvis inspireret af den fiktive prosa således som Leonora Christinas selvbiografiske værker«.

366 Heitmann, Annegret. *Selbst schreiben*, p. 120.

367 Larsen, Finn Stein. 'En impressionist fra baroktiden?', p. 19.

368 Schmalensee, Lisa and Lene Torp. 'Leonora Christina Ulfeldt', p. 18.

»dän. Kunststickerin, Schnitzerin, Bildhauerin u. Malerin«,[369] i.e. anything *but* a writer.[370]

However, there are plausible reasons for the eclectic classification of Leonora Christina and *Jammers Minde* dominating in the past. As was asserted in Chapter 1.1.1., it is anything but an easy assignment to draw a clear line between autobiography and memoir, with the level of literacy and/or self-reflection constituting the sole distinguishing feature. Leonora Christina's life did in fact provide enough material for her to put aside the self-reflection required for autobiographical writing and instead get tangled up in the gossipy accounts of all the exciting events that led to her imprisonment. Another issue concerning the classification of *Jammers Minde* in particular is her restriction to the years of her imprisonment in the Blue Tower. As pointed out by Thomas Seiler, a focus on *bios* in autobiography has led to a widespread notion of autobiography having to illustrate the author's entire life, not only parts of it. Leonora Christina, however, starts her account with her transfer from London to a dungeon in Copenhagen called *Mørke Kirke*, where the interrogations took place, and ends it with her release from prison almost twenty-two years later.[371]

However, as far as the narrated time is concerned, one must also consider the autobiographical conventions of the 17th century, which must be assumed to have informed Leonora Christina's understanding of her own endeavour. In the early modern period, only those lives that were either exemplary for a specific group, or extraordinary, were considered worth writing down.[372] As a consequence, entirely unexceptional life stages and events, such as early childhood, usually found scarce mention in life accounts, especially in the case of spiritual autobiographies, the most common type of life writing in the early modern age.[373] Furthermore, delivering a full chronological narrative of one's life was also fairly optional for writers

---

369 *Lexikon der Frau in zwei Bänden 2: I-Z*. Zürich: Encyclios, 1954, p. 1504: »Danish embroiderer, woodcarver, sculptor and painter«.

370 Similarly, Norwegian philologist Elisabeth Aasen contends that »som personlig dokument er *Jammers Minde* enestående« (Aasen, Elisabeth. 'Grevinnen i fangetårnet', p. 142) while it is »interessant også [!] som litterært verk« (ibid., p. 139). The reason for this tentative denomination of *Jammers Minde* might be Aasen's focus on Leonora Christina as »kongedatter«, »tusenkunstner«, »sin egen biograf« and »historiker« (Aasen, Elisabeth. *Fra Gamle Dage: Memoarer, Dagbøker, Salmer og Dikt av Kvinner ca. 1660-1880*, ed. Elisabeth Aasen. Oslo: Universitetsforlaget, 1983, all quotations p. 38).

371 Cf. Seiler, Thomas. *Im Leben verschollen*, p. 43.

372 And, as stated by Annegret Heitmann, Leonora Christina's fate was both exceptional and exemplary. See Heitmann, Annegret. *Selbst schreiben*, p. 157.

373 Hodgkin, Katharine. *Madness in Seventeenth-Century Autobiography*, p. 25.

of spiritual autobiography, since superficialities, such as childhood memories, were thought to only distract from more essential life stages.[374]

One issue, however, that does pose a problem regarding the classification of *Jammers Minde* as autobiography is Leonora Christina's lack of reflection about her current social status in contrast to the one she used to have.[375] Leonora Christina's reluctance to discuss this drastic change – from the most powerful woman of the state to a prisoner badgered by rats and lice – prohibits a coherent tracking of her character development. Whenever she does recollect scenes from her past, it happens to illustrate her superiority, both in an intellectual as well as moral sense, a trait she would never want anyone to regard as something changed, let alone lost. However, if, as suggested above, *Jammers Minde* is to be accepted as an autobiography despite its focus on barely twenty-two years of its author's life, one ought to accept Leonora Christina's development in prison as being representative of her entire life and character as well. As was mentioned in Chapter 1.1.1., selecting and arranging is an integral part of the work of autobiographers (as well as of any writer). Thus, Leonora Christina's »selektive[r] Rückblick«[376] has a legitimate claim on the title of autobiography.

Furthermore, as regards Finn Stein Larsen's reference to *Jammers Minde* as memoir fragment, Otto Glismann's work has long ago unmasked the author's point of view as literary fiction, which elevates *Jammers Minde* above the level of a mere account of events. Thus, it cannot be called a memoir, a category of life narrative which applies much better to Leonora Christina's French autobiography as it exhibits a considerably lower degree of self-reflection (while still being a stylised, literary account). This, in turn, is in part a side effect of Leonora Christina's use of the third person. Annegret Heitmann's interpretation of Leonora Christina's choice not to use the first person for her narrative as an attempt to distance herself from her previous identity and to adopt a new one[377] furthermore attests to this notion of the French autobiography being less reflective than *Jammers Minde*.

Moreover, one ought to take Leonora Christina's primary motivation for writing her French autobiography into consideration. Otto Sperling the Younger requested a short biography of her in order to publish it as a demonstration of her good nature and her applaudable capabilities. Perhaps Leonora Christina was asked, or chose herself to write the biography in the third person, lest it appear as yet another apo-

---

374 Ibid., p. 24.
375 Seiler, Thomas. *Im Leben verschollen*, p. 65.
376 Dömling, Anna Katharina. 'Billigen kand ieg med Iob sige', p. 26: »selective retrospection«.
377 Heitmann, Annegret. 'Feministischer Umgang mit Literatur', p. 58.

logia, but rather as a more impartial account of events. Another possible, perhaps less sophisticated explanation for Leonora Christina's use of the third person is that she was simply following a literary tradition, in this case the use of the third person in Latin literature. In the French autobiography, Leonora Christina herself states to have taken an interest in the Latin language (and thus, perhaps, Latin literature as well). Otto Sperling the Elder volunteered as her teacher, but her frequent pregnancies interfered with her progress.[378] Finally, *Hæltinners Pryd*, too, provides a possible explanation for Leonora Christina's use of the third person in her French autobiography: »In representing herself through the use of the third person and the past tense, her narrative could easily be placed alongside those of the heroines she so admired«.[379] If her French autobiography was meant to present Leonora Christina's life and virtues to a broader public, delivering the account in the fashion of a gynæceum, such as *Hæltinners Pryd*, seems entirely reasonable.

Jammers Minde, on the other hand, and as contended by Annegret Heitmann, exhibits a certain »Doppelheit des Selbst«,[380] and hence a less static character portrayal, which is further reflected in its lack of stylistic homogeneity. While the first part of the text, which in its minuteness resembles an interrogation protocol, was written at approximately the same time as the French autobiography, the second and the third part followed years later, when there was no longer any contact with public figures to provide narrative material for *Jammers Minde*. Thus, Leonora Christina could no longer portray herself in the same courtly, public environment as in her French autobiography.

As regards the specifically literary quality of *Jammers Minde*, the text is exceptionally rich considering its genre and historical environment. As Birgit Baldwin rightly contends, it is »the special predicament of autobiography […] that it demands to be read as history and as literature but refuses to be taken exclusively as one or the other«.[381] Annegret Heitmann denominated *Jammers Minde* as »Zeugnis eines gesellschaftlichen Umsturzes«,[382] thus alluding to the eventful age in Danish history that inspired Leonora Christina in the most aggravating manner to write her autobiography. Since the creation of *Jammers Minde* was embedded in a period of

---

378 See *Leonora Christina Grevinde Ulfeldts Franske Levnedsskildring*, p. 4d (Translation p. 19).
379 Sterling, Nichole L. 'Authority and Autobiography: The Case for Leonora Christina', http://www.academia.edu/2368850/Authority_and_Autobiography_Leonora_Christina.
380 Heitmann, Annegret. 'Feministischer Umgang mit Literatur', p. 59: »duplicity of the self«.
381 Baldwin, Birgit. 'Jammersminde Remembered', p. 277.
382 Heitmann, Annegret. 'Zwischen Macht und Marginalität: Leonora Christines Autobiographie »Jammersminde« als Zeugnis eines gesellschaftlichen Umsturzes'. In *Frauen – Literatur – Revolution*, ed. Helga Grubitzsch et al. Pfaffenweiler: Centaurus, 1992 (Thetis 3), pp. 203-215: »testimony of a societal upheaval«.

upheaval and change directly involving Leonora Christina, the publication of the text in 1869 was met with excitement – assumedly on account of its documentary potential. Nevertheless, one rather ought to position the text on the literary side of the autobiographical spectrum. Leonora Christina uses techniques and follows patterns common to both autobiography and literature in general, for instance Leonora Christina's self-serving portrayal of her maids.[383] Heitmann names *Fortalen* as another such convention.[384] In this preamble, Leonora Christina recounts to her children the unjust calamities that befell the Ulfeldt family in the years preceding her imprisonment, as if they were not already known to them (*Jammers Minde*, pp. 5*-11*). Even though her children are familiar with their parents' past, Leonora Christina finds it necessary to recapitulate her previous life. This method of introducing a character is reminiscent of stageplays, where the opening actor in a lengthy monologue seemingly addressed to another character of the drama, who is often familiar with the content of this monologue, briefs the audience on the events preceding and motivating the plot of the drama. This again strengthens the previously raised hypothesis that *Jammers Minde* was not solely written for Leonora Christina's children.

However, *Jammers Minde* is not the only text in which Leonora Christina imitates the literary conventions of the 17th century. Whereas *Jammers Minde* indisputably outshines Leonora Christina's French autobiography on a stylistic level, the latter crows with a more adventurous content. Stig Dalager and Anne-Marie Mai attribute the venturesome reading provided by the French autobiography to the popular literature of Leonora Christina's age, i.e. »tidens franske halv-mondæne helte- og kærlighedsromaner«.[385] Some writers of the 20th century were very susceptible to this style, e.g. Herta J. Enevoldsen (see Chapter 2.5.1.). The front cover of her historical novel *Leonora Christina og Corfitz Ulfeldt*, published in 1979, shows the book's heroine in a situation reminiscent of the three musketeers: Leonora Christina, a beautiful blond woman, stands in the door frame of a driving carriage. She is apparently in the middle of a wild chase since several men on horseback are pursuing her. But she shows no fear; instead, she alienates them by pointing two pistols at them. This scene is inspired by Leonora Christina's *Rejsen til Korsør 1656*, an event which is also integrated in her French autobiography. Leonora Christina's first draft of her unpleasant encounter with *Ambtskriveren* of Flensburg depicts the

---

383 Cf. ibid., p. 208.
384 Ibid., p. 210.
385 Dalager, Stig and Anne-Marie Mai. *Danske kvindelige Forfattere 1: Fra Sophie Brahe til Mathilde Fibiger*. Copenhagen: Gyldendal, 1982, p. 39.

event in a rather sober manner and the chase appears to be a matter of a few, rather uneventful minutes:

> Han havde vel intet haft at frygte for, thi al mit Gewer udi min hele Suite var et Par Pistoler. [...] Der jeg var Landsbyen forbi, kom de tvende Vogne med de 4 Karle og lange Bysser efter mig i fuld Galop. Jeg lod og køre paa og vilde intet bie derres Komme. Saa rendte vi om Kap en halvanden Mil indtil Fyrstens Gebiet, og der vi var en halv Fjerring-Vejs nær ved Skellet, da havde de mærkeligen vunden, mens Lykken var saaledes, at jeg naaede Fyrsten af Holsteins Gebiet, førend de naaede mig. Dermed blev de holdendes og fulte mig ikke vidre, saa Intentionen kunde sees, og vidre blev intet udrettet.[386]

The purpose of this short account seems to have been merely documental (see Chapter 1.2.1.). However, viewing the same story in Leonora Christina's French autobiography, one cannot help noticing the addition of a few venturesome details:

> Nostre femme qui avoit tousjours quand elle voyageoit des pistolles dans la Carosse, tire un, et luy [Ambtskriveren] presente, disant, retirez vous, ou je vous donneray ce qu'il y a icy dedans; Il ne tardoit pas de quitter, et lacher prise, puis elle jette un pattacon à ceux qui la devoient tenir disoit, voyla pour boire, aydez a faire passer la Carosse le focé, ce quils firent in continent. Pas un demy quart heure apres quelle estoit passée, voici le Gouuerneur qui vient avec encore un autre chariot, deux hommes en chaque chariot, et 4 fucies en chaque chariot, on advertit nostre femme de cette poursuitte, elle fait prier ces deux chattiers quelle avoit pour son page et bagage de leur empescher le chemin tant quils peurent; à Charle elle commende de tousjours ce tenir au costé de la Carosse, si elle voyoit quils gagnassent chemin, pour se jetter sur le cheval, se defis de sa robbe fourée. Ils disputtoient le chemin jusques au pont qui separe la territoire du Roy et du Duc. Comme elle estoit passée le Pont, elle se ferme, remet sa robbe, et met pied à terre. Les autres ce tenoient de l'autre costé le Pont pour la regarder[.][387]

---

386 Leonora Christina. 'Rejsen til Korsør 1656', p. 67.

387 *Leonora Christina Grevinde Ulfeldts Franske Levnedsskildring*, p. 7d (Translation p. 30: »Vor dame, som altid, naar hun rejste, havde pistoler i sin vogn, trækker en frem og viser ham den, idet hun siger: ,Vig tilbage, eller jeg giver eder, hvad der er heri'. Han var ikke sen til at træde tilbage og give slip; derpaa kastede hun en daler til dem, som skulde holde hende tilbage, og sagde: ,Her er noget at drikke for, hjælp at faa vognen over grøften'; hvilket de gjorde uden at tøve. Ikke et halvt kvarter efter, at hun var kørt, kom amtmanden i en vogn og med endnu en vogn, to mænd og fire musketter i hver vogn; man advarer vor dame om denne forfølgelse; hun lader bede sine to kærredrivere, som hun havde til at age hendes page og bagage, om at spærre vejen for dem saa godt, de formaaede; Charles befaler hun stedse at holde sig ved siden af karossen, for at hun, hvis hun saa, at de vandt ind paa hende, kunde kaste sig paa en hest; hun tog ogsaa sin skindkaabe af sig. De stredes om vejen lige til den bro, som danner skellet mellem kongens og hertugens territorium. Da hun havde passeret broen, gør hun holdt, iører sig igen sin kaabe og stiger derpaa ud. De andre blev holdende paa den anden side af broen for at se efter hende«).

Leonora Christina is the unflinching heroine of her French autobiography and, especially in this episode, she does not shy away from anything. She threatens a man with one of her pistols before bringing the other men surrounding her to heel in the most nonchalant manner. At its climax, the wild chase, the account becomes almost bizarre when Leonora Christina prepares to jump directly from her carriage onto a horse in order to shake off her pursuers. In her attempt to evoke the reader's admiration, Leonora Christina's writing resembles formula fiction. The French autobiography's focus on events and action exposes thus a crucial difference between *Jammers Minde* and its French predecessor: the former is a fully-fledged autobiography, while the latter is closer to the less reflective genre of the memoir.

While the two life narratives thus exhibit different stylistic levels, their aim and topic reunite them. Both narratives depict Leonora Christina as a superior person, by virtue of her rank and her natural predisposition. Dalager and Mai ascribe this apparent self-esteem to the advent of Renaissance individualism.[388] In her French autobiography, Leonora Christina herself also highlights a typical Renaissance virtue:

> Elle avoit alors une Memoire pas ordinaire, elle pouvoit en mesme temps lire un sausme par coeur, escrire un autre, et prendre garde à ce qui ce disoit, cela elle à escayée plus d'une foys, mais je croys aussi quelle à gatée la Memoire avec cela. qui n'est pas a heure si bonne.[389]

With this anecdote, Leonora Christina is not only able to excuse any potential aberration from historical facts in her French autobiography, but she can also place herself in line with the early modern ideal of the universal genius: »Denne præstation er så typisk for renæssancetidens opfattelse af det kunstneriske og videnskabelige geni, multibegavelsen, og den afslører på interessant vis en af de mange klichéer Leonora Christina benyttede sig af, da hun sad og redigerede virkeligheden mange år efter i Blåtårn«.[390] Hans Bjørn furthermore alludes to a specific account by Otto Sperling the Elder of Peter Paul Rubens (1577-1640), which portrays the painter's multitasking abilities in a manner suspiciously reminiscent of Leonora

---

388 Dalager, Stig and Anne-Marie Mai. *Danske kvindelige Forfattere 1*, p. 40.
389 *Leonora Christina Grevinde Ulfeldts Franske Levnedsskildring*, marginal note p. 2c (Translation p. 9: »Hun havde paa de tider en usædvanlig hukommelse. Hun kunde paa samme tid læse en salme udenad, fatte en anden i pennen og give agt paa, hvad der blev talt. Dette har hun prøvet mere end en gang, men jeg tror ogsaa, at hun dermed har fordærvet sin hukommelse, som for nærværende ikke er saa god«).
390 Bjørn, Hans. 'Leonora Christina – Christian IV's datter', p. 26.

Christina's self-portrait.[391] Regardless of whether these two testimonies constitute accurate depictions of Leonora Christina or Rubens, they both account for a lingering ideal. From Leonora Christina's French autobiography we learn that she could read simple Latin and that she spoke, albeit not fluently, Italian and Spanish.[392] Especially Italian would prove to be a useful skill: when Adolph Fuchs separated the couple after their failed escape and accommodated them in two separate cells, Leonora Christina and Corfitz had to resort to communicating in Italian, thus excluding their surroundings from their conversation.[393] Just like in *Jammers Minde*, Leonora Christina utilises a courtly language both in order to outsmart her less educated guards and to demonstrate her refined lineage. Of course, Leonora Christina mastered French as well; her French autobiography is the most outstanding proof of this skill. From *Jammers Minde* we also gather that she spoke German and at least some English. Furthermore, she frequently employed in creative as well as adept pastimes, such as sewing, painting, crafting and writing. Thus, Leonora Christina proves to be a true woman of her time.[394] Finally, another typical trait of the Renaissance zeitgeist exhibited in Leonora Christina's work is her interest in the lives of remarkable, educated women, including herself.

In terms of women's autobiography – considered as a subcategory or particular kind of autobiography – the status of *Jammers Minde* is highly equivocal. The question whether *Jammers Minde* can be regarded as a typical work of a female autobiographer has not been answered yet. It even seems impossible to reach a definite conclusion on this matter, since the existence of a typically female autobiography per se has been contested.[395] In addition, the circumstances that led to the creation of

---

391 Ibid.
392 *Leonora Christina Grevinde Ulfeldts Franske Levnedsskildring*, p. 6b (Translation p. 25).
393 Ibid., p. 11d (Translation p. 49).
394 Cf. Bjørn, Hans. 'Leonora Christina – Christian IV's datter', p. 41.
395 See, for example, Heitmann, Annegret. *Selbst schreiben*, p. 97 and Hættner Aurelius, Eva. *Inför Lagen*, p. 66. At the same time, autobiography itself has been named as a specifically female genre, thus again preventing the identification of a female tradition within the autobiographical genre. See Larsson, Lisbeth. 'Kvinnors självbiografier och dagböcker'. In *Lysthuse: Kvindelitteraturhistorier*, ed. Lis Palmvig. Charlottenlund: Rosinante, 1985, p. 156: »Det kvinnliga självbiografiskrivandet har en lång tradition bakom sig. Det är förmodligen den genre där kvinnor varit som mest aktiva både som skribenter och innovatörer. Kanske har de till och med skapat den«.

Jammers Minde are, then as now, not part of a typically female course of life.[396] As regards specific statements concerning common traits of women's autobiography, assessments of *Jammers Minde* are mixed. A focus on family and related matters has been named as such a common trait. In this sense, *Jammers Minde* appears atypical, as it does not even include any reference to the two children that died during their mother's imprisonment.[397] Ignorance of these events – as cautiously suggested by Katrin Lunde and Luise F. Pusch[398] – is hardly the reason for this untypical omission, since all the gossip provided in the account testifies to the existence of informants functioning as links between Leonora Christina and the outside world. At the same time, Leonora Christina does mention the demise of her husband, her father and her half-brother. The death of Frederik III of Denmark is an integral part of the narrative and could thus not have been omitted. First, it considerably improved her life in the Blue Tower since, after 1670, the King of Denmark was no longer under the direct surveillance of Sophie Amalie and could thus grant Leonora Christina a bigger cell, books and other amenities. Second, the death of Frederik III serves as an important 'non-catalyser', as it does *not* lead to Leonora Christina's release from the tower. She could not have chosen a better denunciation of Sophie Amalie, whom Leonora Christina always held to be the true manipulator in the royal household (see *Jammers Minde*, p. 172). While Leonora Christina thus stages herself as mourning sister (»Ieg loed taarene derris frii gang«, *Jammers Minde*, p. 173), the reader necessarily views Sophie Amalie as the true villain. Notwithstanding the fact that not mentioning Corfitz Ulfeldt's death at all would have been absolutely inconceivable, the reference to Corfitz Ulfeldt's death serves a similar purpose. Despite the

---

396 The formation process of *Jammers Minde* hinders a clear subsumption of Leonora Christina's work in most of the discussions concerning women's autobiography. For several, mostly historical reasons, *Jammers Minde* does not form a considerable part in the feminist discourse on autobiography. Other scholars engaging themselves in women's autobiography, who have turned their back on the classic feminist dialogue, have attempted a different approach. One such example is Jane Marcus, whose focus is on female autobiographers, who chose to resign from public discourse: »Enacting a deliberate resignation from the public world and patriarchal history, which had already erased or was expected to erase their names and their works, they re/signed their private lives into domestic discourse. The trajectory of these moves is the opposite of the one feminist historians have chosen to study, the move from private to public« (see Marcus, Jane. 'Invincible Mediocrity: The Private Selves of Public Women'. In *The Private Self: Theory and Practice of Women's Autobiographical Writings*, ed. Shari Benstock. Chapel Hill and London: The University of North Carolina Press, 1989 (1988), p. 114). Since Leonora Christina did not explicitly write *Jammers Minde* for a broad public, nor conducted a »deliberate resignation from the public world«, placing her within any feminist or specifically female autobiographical discussion remains somewhat arbitrary.

397 Her son Ludvig died in 1668 in Greece and her daughter Ellen Christina died in 1677 in Bruges. Most of Leonora Christina's children had already died before she was imprisoned in the Blue Tower, while some of them were still alive when she was released, but died a few years later and never managed to visit her in Maribo.

398 Lunde, Katrin and Luise F. Pusch. 'Leonora Christina', p. 74.

death of the actual offender, his – never convicted – accomplice, Leonora Christina, was not released. Reason to detain Leonora Christina was now, from 1670 onwards, absent in a twofold sense. Again, Leonora Christina exposes the cause for her arrest to be not legal, but purely personal. Finally, Leonora Christina remembers the demise of her father, which occurred long before her imprisonment: »Skreffwen 1684. den 28. *Februarii*, som er 36. Aars dagen, att Høyloffligste Konning *Christian* den Fiærde, sagde Werden goede Nat, oc ieg min Wersens welfart« (*Jammers Minde*, p. 238). Unlike the references to the deaths of Corfitz Ulfeldt and Frederik III, this mention has no direct function within the narrative. However, this would not be the only incident in which Leonora Christina utilises the memory of her beloved father in order to remind herself, her surroundings and her reader of who she really is (see Chapter 1.2.1.).

Why then would Leonora Christina fail to mention the death of two of her children? After all, *Fortalen* indicates that she wished to be remembered as a loving mother. *Jammers Minde* documents plenty of fatalities, most of which, though, concerning enemies of the Ulfeldt family. The reason for Leonora Christina's decision to include a mention of these deaths could potentially shed some light on her motives for omitting any reference to her children's demise as well. As so accurately stated by Lutz Rühling, Leonora Christina divided her world into two sides: the good side or those that were in favour of her family, and the evil side, i.e. her and her family's critics.[399] Leonora Christina's compilation of *dødslisten*, the informative list of her deceased enemies provided at the end of *Jammers Minde*, is so telling it must exceed a mere documentary intention. Leonora Christina's life story teaches that grand, devotional people like Leonora Christina prevail in life while common, wicked individuals eventually meet a painful, sometimes even shameful death. The reader of *Jammers Minde* cannot help but being struck by the fact that Leonora Christina, a woman well past her prime by Baroque standards when she stepped into the Blue Tower, survived every single one of her enemies, some of them even younger than her. These deaths thus benefit Leonora Christina's cause. Yet, there are friends and members of the Ulfeldt clan, whose untimely deaths are reported as well. Corfitz Ulfeldt's passing is one such instance; not mentioning his death at all was no option, for reasons stated above. Otto Sperling the Elder, who had been a close friend of the family, also met his end in the Blue Tower in 1681. In the case of both of these men, death could be interpreted as a blessing, since they had already

---

399 Rühling, Lutz. *Opfergänge der Vernunft*, p. 70.

fallen into the hands of the enemy.[400] Leonora Christina's children, however, were still free (albeit in exile), thus their deaths would have disturbed the worldview constructed in *Jammers Minde*. Hence, the passing of Ludvig and Ellen Christina Ulfeldt was simply swept under the carpet.

Lunde and Pusch further name Leonora Christina's realistic and simple portrayal of her everyday life in the Blue Tower as another typically female characteristic of autobiography.[401] However, since Leonora Christina's surroundings left her with not much of a thematic choice, one can argue whether the realistic tendencies exhibitied in *Jammers Minde* are a typically female autobiographical trait, or just perforce an aspect of Leonora Christina's prison account. A comparison with Otto Sperling's autobiography, provided in Chapter 2.1.2., may shed further light on this matter.

The search for typically female traits in *Jammers Minde* is also closely connected with the feminist discussion centring on Leonora Christina. She does, either implicitly or explicitly, address the topic of the relationship between the sexes in all of her writings, albeit with a differing intensity: in *Hæltinners Pryd*, she explicitly states that women can be just as brave and strong as men (if not even more so), in the French autobiography she mostly opposes her own virtues with her husband's weaknesses, while particularly the latter two parts of *Jammers Minde* offer only sporadic interaction with men. However, such discourses have also been criticised for being anachronous.[402] Yet, apart from the question of whether one can even speak of a 17th century feminist discussion, *Jammers Minde* in particular poses an even bigger problem: aside from Leonora Christina herself, the text offers no female role models. The narrative depicts only one other positive female figure, i.e. Queen Charlotte Amalie, spouse of Christian V of Denmark, who in 1670 paid a visit to the Blue Tower (*Jammers Minde*, pp. 177- 179). This young, empathetic woman constitutes a positive counter character to her predecessor, thus enhancing Leonora Christina's silent accusation. From 1670 onwards, Charlotte Amalie is the new Queen of Denmark, but even she is powerless against Sophie Amalie. Her function in the text is thus to incriminate Sophie Amalie and the previous regal generation once again. One may even interpret Leonora Christina's rendition of

---

400 Bodil Wamberg furthermore suggests that Leonora Christina may not have been as well-disposed towards her old friend as historians believe: »Sperling havde betalt en høj pris for sin loyalitet mod Ulfeldt. Han havde hoppet og sprunget for hende selv, også stået hende nær i hendes yngre dage. Havde han været så hengiven, at hun foragtede ham lidt for det? [...] Når alt kommer til alt, var han jo bare et tyende, ansat i hendes herres brød – og nu irriterede han hende med sin bitterhed og sine lamentationer!« (see Wamberg, Bodil. *Leonora Christina*, p. 250).

401 Lunde, Katrin and Luise F. Pusch. 'Leonora Christina', p. 89.

402 See, for example, Seiler, Thomas. *Im Leben verschollen*, p. 45.

this confrontation of the two reginas as another instance of criticism of Frederik III's introduction of absolutism in 1660. When her half-brother became Denmark's first autocrat, Leonora Christina, who grew up in an elective monarchy, naturally had her thoughts on this new kind of government: »Ded ieg tenckte torde ieg icke sige, Ieg wiste wel huorledis i saadanne *Absolute* Regieringer tilgaar, der tør intet imod sigis, ded hedder Skriff vnder, Konge wil ded saa haffue, oc Spør icke huor for, ellers est du vdi lige Fordømmelse« (*Jammers Minde*, p. 55). However, when Frederik III died and a new autocrat succeeded, Sophie Amalie seemingly remained in charge. When Charlotte Amalie was pregnant with her first child in 1671, she wrenched the promise from her husband that he would release Leonora Christina if the child turned out to be a boy (*Jammers Minde*, p. 182). Sophie Amalie's reaction upon hearing about this agreement compels Christian V to renege on his promise when he obtained the desired crown prince:

> Encke Dron: harmede sig saa, att hun fik ont, løste op om sig; oc sagde hun wille hiem; wille icke biie intil Barnet bleff Christnet, hendis Caret kom paa Slos Platzen; Kongen *persuaderte* hender endeligen att biie, intil daaben war forrettet, maatte loffwe hender wed Eed, att ieg skulle icke komme løß.
>
> (*Jammers Minde*, p. 182)[403]

The dowager's influence overtrumps all the power the regal couple is entitled to exercise. Thus, when Frederik III declared himself the sole ruler of Denmark, it seems that he did not consolidate the authority of the King, but of himself and his wife. This in turn reveals Leonora Christina's punishment not to be the result of a legal affair, but of a private enmity.

The appearance of Charlotte Amalie constitutes thus an integral part of Leonora Christina's apologia. Even the Queen's prophetic last words to her mother in law are perfectly incorporated into the plot of *Jammers Minde*: »Wil Gott so wird Sie wol auß kommen, wan shon Ihr *Majt:* es nicht wollen« (*Jammers Minde*, p. 183). And since she is merely a supporting character in Leonora Christina's *theatrum mundi*, Charlotte Amalie does not reinforce the notion of a feminist discourse evolving in *Jammers Minde*. Furthermore, the impact of this one positive female figure is easily outweighed by Peder Jensen Tøtzløff, who remained Leonora Christina's

---

[403] Leonora Christina's statement regarding the reasons for her continued imprisonment is confirmed by a manuscript, whose author must have been involved in catering to the Blue Tower, since his summary of Leonora Christina's imprisonment is accompanied by particulars concerning the costs of Leonora Christina's meals (see 'Noget om Grevinde Eleonore Ulfelds Arrest i Blaataarn', Journal for Politik, Natur- og Menneske-Kundskab October 1815, pp. 282-284).

loyal friend and frequently visited her in Maribo. Overall, *Jammers Minde* offers no indication for a vanguard feminist discussion. Both the French autobiography and Leonora Christina's chief work do not depict an antagonism between men and women, but between Leonora Christina and the world. As far as *Hæltinners Pryd* is concerned, diverse scholars have already suggested that this list of laudable women may have been intended to provide the proper adjectives to describe Leonora Christina (see Chapter 1.2.1.).

Furthermore, there is the question whether *Jammers Minde* belongs to other subcategories of the autobiographical genre, i.e. the spiritual or conversion narrative, (i.e. the prototype of autobiography) or perhaps the prison autobiography. The first part of *Jammers Minde* does contain spiritual features,[404] namely the crisis and the ensuing stoic acceptance of her fate. Thus, *Jammers Minde* follows an agelong tradition of autobiography. Moreover, Leonora Christina's imprisonment is undoubtedly the dominant topic and cause of *Jammers Minde*. However, *Jammers Minde* lacks other, essential features to qualify for the classification of either prison or conversion narrative. Thomas Seiler, for example, does not consider *Jammers Minde* a fully-fledged prison autobiography, but rather a hybrid form, since it was started in captivity, but finished in liberty.[405] Seiler furthermore characterises prison autobiography mainly by its purpose, i.e. by its entity as a communicative, social act.[406] In addition, prison literature must necessarily constitute a – direct or indirect – examination of the autobiographer's confined situation, the person or accusation that led to this confinement, and/or the autobiographer's guilt.[407] In summary, Seiler defines prison literature as direct or hidden polemic;[408] and in the case of *Jammers Minde,* the text may be regarded as the latter. Explicitly negative remarks about the regal couple occur only rarely in the text. Usually, Leonora Christina conveys her opinion about Frederik III, and about his wife in particular, in the following subtle manner:

---

[404] Hans Bjørn, to name only one example, specifically called *Jammers Minde* Leonora Christina's »helgenbiografi«. See Bjørn, Hans. 'Leonora Christina – Christian IV's datter', p. 18.

[405] Seiler, Thomas. *Im Leben verschollen*, p. 11. Additionally, according to Sigrid Weigel's definition of »delinquent literature« (see Chapter 1.2.1.), *Jammers Minde* would not count as such, but rather as the common pastime of an intellectual noblewoman (see Weigel, Sigrid. *Und selbst im Kerker frei...!*, p. 17).

[406] Seiler, Thomas. *Im Leben verschollen*, p. 19.

[407] Ibid., p. 23.

[408] Ibid., p. 25.

> Den 25. *Aug. importunerte* Slozf. mig flux med sin *discours*, meente ieg haffde Ond Troe til Dronningen: Hand tog ded der aff; thi dagen til forne, haffde hand sagt mig, att hs Kl. Mt haffde befalet, att huis ieg aff Køckenet oc Kelderen begierte skulle de mig lade følgactig were, huor til ieg da suarte, Gud beware hs Mt: hand er en goed Herre, maatte hand were goed for onde Mennisker: Oc sagde Hand da, Dronningen er oc saa goed; huortil ieg intet Suarte[.]
>
> (*Jammers Minde*, p. 76)

Leonora Christina is careful not to let any bad word about the King slip; instead, she praises him with formulaic compliments. However, she completely refrains from the conversation as soon as it concerns Sophie Amalie. When the castellan tries to draw a good word about the Queen from Leonora Christina, he is only met with a curse: »Dieu vous punisse« (*Jammers Minde*, p. 77: »May God punish you«). Usually, Leonora Christina would simply document the Queen's behavior towards her prisoner and let the reader be the judge of the matter. However, she does not always succeed in remaining impartial. When the castellan conducts the King's order by delivering to Leonora Christina whatever she demands, the Queen interferes by executing a seemingly random veto right:

> Hand [the castellan] kom oc noget der effter med en befaling fra Kongen att ieg skulle begiære hwad ieg wille haffwe til Klæder oc Linnet, hwilcket bleff optegnet, oc ieg siden bekom, foruden Snørliiff, ded wille Dronningen icke tilstæde, Aarsagen kunde ieg ingen tiid faa att wiide. Ded war oc Dronningen imod att ieg bekom et Flaskefoder med sex smaa flasker der vdi war Slag Wand, Hoffwitwand, oc hiærtstærckende Wand; alt ded sagde hun maatte hun nok være foruden, men der hun saae att der staar et Kaabberstycke i Laaget, Herode Daatter med S. Johanne Hoffwet paa et Faed, da loe hun, oc sagde, das wird ihr ein Hertz stærckung seyn; Ded Kaabberstycke kom mig til att betencke att *Herodias* haffde endnu Søstre i Werden[.]
>
> (*Jammers Minde*, p. 114)

As usual, Leonora Christina's polemic is rather subtle, but her reference to Herodias, the woman who is said to have instigated the beheading of John the Baptist, unmasks her reputed indifference towards her sister-in-law.

While Leonora Christina is thus eager not to rail against Sophie Amalie, she is equally keen to maintain the impression of her feeling like a sibling and a loyal subject towards her half-brother. She criticises Frederik III only on one single occasion, i.e. in her French autobiography. In this account, Leonora Christina recollects the death of Christian IV in 1648 and the subsequent succession of Frederik III. On his deathbed, Leonora Christina's father tried to console his daughter by reminding her of her adamant strength (»Je t'ay mise si ferme que personne ne te peut branler«).[409] Upon these last words, Leonora Christina remembers how her own family would subsequently test her strength:

> Elle n'à que trop senti le contraire, comme aussi le contraire de la promesse du Roy qui le succedà; car lors que luy estoit Duc et la vicitoit en sa Maison; peu de jours apres la mort du Roy, la trouuant tout en pleurs, il l'embrassoit disant, je vous serez un Pere, ne pleurez point, elle luy baisa la main, sens pouuoir dire mot. Je trouue qu'il y à esté des Peres dènaturé envers leurs Enfans.[410]

The last words of this paragraph, which state that Frederik III could be classified as a father who has been unnatural towards his children (see Chapter 1.1.3.), were struck out. At this time, in 1674, Frederik III was already dead. Perhaps Leonora Christina eliminated her last words because she did not deem it appropriate to criticise the dead; or maybe she considered it unwise for a woman in her position to disparage the late King. What is conspicuous though, is that she struck out the remark with a thin line, thus still rendering the words legible. If she had been afraid of any consequences resulting from her reproval, she would have probably made sure to leave this last phrase indecipherable. Since the manuscript of her French autobiography was meant to be handed over to Otto Sperling the Younger, Leonora Christina probably relied on him to deal with this last phrase as he thought best. At all events, she preferred to stay on the safe side by keeping her criticism as subtle as possible. However, this subtlety hinders a classification of *Jammers Minde* as what Thomas Seiler considers a true prison autobiography, which tends to be more polemic than classic autobiography.[411] Leonora Christina's polemic is present throughout the entire text, yet (almost) always indirect and rarely obvious. Leonora Christina avoids any reference to her previous life and the reason for her imprisonment. Seemingly, the allegations against her and her husband are too absurd to cause a response from her side. Since the text thus seems to focus on anything but her dispute with the regal couple, it is not a classic prison autobiography.

Equally difficult to resolve is the question whether *Jammers Minde* is a spiritual autobiography. For Katharine Hodgkin, spiritual writing is defined by »intense

---

409 *Leonora Christina Grevinde Ulfeldts Franske Levnedsskildring*, p. 5b (Translation p. 21: »Jeg har sat dig saa fast, at ingen kan rokke dig«).
410 Ibid., p. 5b (Translation p. 21: »Hun har kun alt for meget erfaret det modsatte, som ogsaa det modsatte af det løfte, hun fik af den konge, som fulgte efter ham. Thi da denne var hertug og besøgte hende i hendes hus, faa dage efter kongens død, og fandt hende opløst i graad, tog han hende i sin favn og sagde: ‚Jeg vil være en fader for eder, græd ikke'. Hun kyssede ham paa haanden uden at kunne sige et ord. Jeg finder, at der har været fædre, som var unaturlige imod deres børn«).
411 Seiler, Thomas. *Im Leben verschollen*, p. 26.

emotion [...] and periods of despair and misery«.[412] Due to Leonora Christina's emotional breakdown occurring within the first part of the text, *Jammers Minde* has occasionally been compared to spiritual writings of the early modern times. However, *Jammers Minde* has not yet been analysed on the assumption of it being a fully-fledged spiritual autobiography – its author's eventful life has so far always prevented such an approach. Furthermore, the two latter parts of the text do not exhibit or depict intense emotions. Since Leonora Christina is recollecting events, which date back eleven years or longer, she is only able to describe her (once strong) emotions, but not to convey them. Thus, a stoic tune dominates her reminiscences. Another significant feature of the text that prevents a classification as spiritual is its heterogeneity: the first third of the manuscript tells a different story than the rest and it was written by a different Leonora Christina. This first part may indeed qualify for the denomination as prison narrative since it was indeed written in prison and because it narrates a time in which Leonora Christina was directly confronted with the allegations against herself and Corfitz. Due to the content of the narrative, Leonora Christina was forced to document her dispute and thus deal with it. At the same time, this part describes Leonora Christina's strong emotions upon hearing about the accusations against her husband and his subsequent in effigy-execution. It also contains her moment of despair and her passively attempted suicide. This failed suicide is followed by a period of meditation, which constitutes a main feature of spiritual autobiography: »Since to know the self fully is to know it inwardly, spiritual writers have little time for events in the external world, and little interest in presenting a full chronological narrative of their lives«.[413]

If Leonora Christina had concluded her autobiography with the first part, *Jammers Minde* might thus indeed be considered a spiritual (prison) autobiography; but the entire text is no such thing.[414] The other two thirds exhibit an immense interest for all the banalities occurring in the external world. At the same time, there is no direct polemic since Leonora Christina is no longer compelled to defend herself. The matured Leonora Christina has come to terms with her fate and is thus taking an interest in the humble world surrounding her.

Finally, a word about Leonora Christina's innocence, or guilt, as depicted in *Jammers Minde*, would not be amiss. While historiographical discussions about Leonora Christina's involvement in her husband's plots have largely overshadowed

---

412 Hodgkin, Katharine. *Madness in Seventeenth-Century Autobiography*, p. 5.
413 Ibid., p. 24.
414 Cf. Heitmann, Annegret. 'Formen der Selbstdarstellung in dänischen Texten des 17. Jahrhunderts'. In *Skandinavische Literaturen der frühen Neuzeit*, ed. Jürg Glauser. Tübingen: Francke, 2002 (Beiträge zur nordischen Philologie 32), p. 293.

any acknowledgement of the literary quality of *Jammers Minde* and have led to a misuse of the text, the topic itself is not entirely irrelevant to a deeper understanding of the text. After all, the question of Leonora Christina's guilt is closely connected with what Manfred Fuhrmann calls the root of autobiography itself, i.e. justification (see Chapter 1.1.3.). As argued in Chapter 1.2., Leonora Christina's writings lack stylistic homogeneity while exhibiting coherence regarding the heroine's portrayal. In *Jammers Minde*, Leonora Christina avoids reflecting on her life before the Blue Tower and the events that led to her imprisonment, perhaps in order not to provoke any breaches in her self-representation. Upon being directly confronted with her past, she usually does her best to silence her challenger:

> Paa de tiider som worris forrige Gaard her i Byen, (huilcken wii haffde forskreffwen oß fra paa Borringholm der wii der ware fangen) bleff neederbrut, oc en Støtte (eller hwad ded er) til min Herris Wanære opsat, kom Slosf. ind der til Middag bleff opluct, oc satte sig paa min Seng (ieg war da noget Vpaßelig) begynte att snacke om forrige tiider (Ieg wiste alt att der bleff bryt neer paa Gaarden) regnet op alt ded hand meente kunde smerte mig att haffwe mist; [...] Hand bleff alt wed, att beiamre ded shiønne Huuß oc Woninger; med den Haffwe der war hoes; Ieg spurte hannem, Wo der Tempel *Salomones* wehre gebliehen? das shiøne Gebew, da wehre kein Stein von mehr zu finden, man wuste nicht die stelle zu weißen wo der Tempel, vnd das kostbahre Kønigs Hauß gestanden. Hand swarte icke et Ord; hengte med hoffweded, grundede et tag, oc gik vd.
>
> (*Jammers Minde*, p. 113)

This conversation results in another victory for Leonora Christina, therefore it was integrated into the account. Yet unless she is forced by outer circumstances, Leonora Christina does not mention her previous life. Nevertheless, *Jammers Minde* has been regarded as an apologia, e.g. by Anna Katharina Dömling. She also contends that *Jammers Minde* was intended to convey a sentiment of coherence regarding the protagonist's personality, even though it shows the protagonist in a very specific period of life. Subsequently, Dömling raises the question whether or not this coherence derives from what Manfred Fuhrmann assessed to be the root of all autobiographical writing, i.e. »einem Bedürfnis nach Rechtfertigung der eigenen Untadeligkeit durch eine konsistente Persönlichkeitsgeschichte«.[415] Considering that all of Leonora Christina's writings depict a strong, superior woman, resourceful in a way that she can make the best of every situation and environment, *Jam-*

---

415 Dömling, Anna Katharina. 'Billigen kand ieg med Iob sige', p. 37: »a want for a vindication of one's own irreproachability through a consistent personal history«.

mers Minde may justly count as a classic autobiography – in Fuhrmann's sense of the term. The text contains hardly any reference to the accusations raised against her. *Fortalen* constitutes an exception to this rule, as it contains an unusually blunt statement regarding the Ulfeldt affair:

> Den anden tilskyndende Aarsage er, den Trøst ded Eder mine Kiære Børn wil were, att I formedelst denne *Iammers-Minde* forsickris, att ieg vskyldeligen Liider, att mig icke ringeste Sag er tillagt, oc att ieg intet er bleffuen Beskylt, for huilcket I mine Kiære Børn tør Bluis oc Øynene skammeligen nederslaa: Ieg liider for att haffue werret ælsket aff en dydig Herre oc Hoßbonde, for att ey haffue Hannem i Vlycken forlat wilt.
>
> (*Jammers Minde*, p. 4*)

In this rare instance, Leonora Christina explicitly rejects the accusations against her and her husband. Usually her counter-attacks and claims of innocence are more subtle, as demonstrated above. Her apologia is based on demonstrations of her superiority, both before and in the Blue Tower (thus conveying coherence). Throughout her life, this supremacy has made her the target of enviers. However, the first scene of Leonora Christina's French autobiography, her sea journey to relatives in the Netherlands in 1628,[416] establishes her to be of immaculate faith:

---

[416] At that time, Denmark was involved in the Thirty Years' War. Out of concern for his childrens' safety, Christian IV sent all of them out of Denmark. When Leonora Christina arrived in Leeuwarden at the house of a relative, her sister Sophie Elisabeth and her brother Valdemar Christian were already there.

Elle alloit par Mer, avec un des vaisseaux de Guerre du Roy; ayant esté deux jours et une nuiet en Mer, il se levà vers mis-nuiet une Tempeste si furieuse, que tous avoient perdues l'esperance d'échapper. Son Pracepteur qui la conduisoit, Wichman Hassebart (qui devint apres Esvecque de Fyn) la vint éveiller, et la prendre entre ces bras, disant avec des larmes qu'eux deux moureroient ensemble, (car il l'aymoit tendrement), il la parloit du danger, que Dieu estoit irrité, et que tous seroient noyez. Elle le caressoit, le traitant de Pere (comme elle fit ordinairement) le prioit, de ne s'affliger, elle estoit asseurée que Dieu n'estoit pas fâché, qu'il verroit quils ne se noyeroient pas, luy pryant diverse foy de la croire. Wichman versoit des larmes de cette bonne simplicité, et prioit Dieu de sauver le reste pour lamour delle, et pour l'espoir quelle innocente avoit en luy. Dieu luy exsausà[.][417]

As a reward for the little girl's faith and the consolation she offered, the ship is spared. This scene sets the tone for the rest of Leonora Christina's life story. While Leonora Christina has done only good on her dangerous transit, she is met with envy upon her arrival in Leeuwarden: her sister Sophie Elisabeth is furious when she learns that Leonora Christina's entourage and luggage are bigger than her own. However, all these mundane obstacles, culminating in Leonora Christina's imprisonment in the Blue Tower, only strengthen the bond between her and her Lord, which serves as the ultimate proof of her innocence.[418]

---

[417] *Leonora Christina Grevinde Ulfeldts Franske Levnedsskildring*, p. 1a (Translation p. 3: »Hun rejste til søs med et af kongens orlogsskibe; da hun havde været to dage og en nat paa søen, opløftede der sig imod midnatstid en storm saa rasende, at alle havde mistet haabet om at undkomme. Hendes præceptor, som ledede hendes rejse, Wichmann Hasebard (som siden blev biskop i Fyn), kom og vækkede hende, tog hende i sine arme og sagde med grædende taarer, at de begge vilde dø med hverandre (ti han elskede hende inderligt); han talte til hende om faren og sagde, at Gud var fortørnet, og at alle vilde drukne. Hun kyssede og klappede ham, kaldte ham fader (hvilket hun havde for vane at gøre) og bad ham ikke være bedrøvet; hun var vis paa, at Gud ikke var vred; han skulde faa at se, at de ikke druknede; flere gange bad hun ham forlade sig derpaa. Wichmann udgød taarer over denne gode enfoldighed og bad Gud redde de andre af kærlighed til hende og for den fortrøstnings skyld, som hun, den uskyldige, havde til ham. Gud bønhørte ham«).

[418] Cf. Dömling, Anna Katharina. 'Billigen kand ieg med Iob sige', p. 38.

2. The Literary Reception of Leonora Christina and the Interdiscursivity of *Jammers Minde*

2.1. Contemporary Literary Portrayals

> Oc efftersom vtallige Folck sig haffde forsamled ded Spetackel att ansee, ia en stoer deel haffde sig paa Baade begiffuen, for mig til nøye att Beskue […].
>
> (*Jammers Minde*, p. 10)

When Leonora Christina was transported from Dover to Copenhagen and arrived at her former home on 8 August 1663, the public saw her for the first time in twelve years. In the time following the Ulfeldts' sudden, and secret, departure from Copenhagen in 1651, she had lived at the court of the notorious Queen Christina of Sweden; waged a war against her home country that became famous for the Swedish troops' audacious crossing of the frozen Belts in early 1658; been imprisoned and escaped from Sweden; been imprisoned again and escaped from a relatively well fortified prison in a remote corner of Denmark (Bornholm); and, finally, been associated with a planned coup. Before writing autobiographical texts, Leonora Christina had thus already attained a quasi-mythical fame through her biography, which explains the extensive public interest in her return to Copenhagen. In 1663, she was a celebrity, for better or worse. When Leonora Christina arrived at the pier back then called Skt. Annæ Bro (approximately today's Toldbodgade in central Copenhagen), switched to a smaller boat, disembarked at »Slotz-Broen« (*Jammers Minde*, p. 11; probably today's Marmorbroen) and walked across the palace square to the Blue Tower, she was followed by a massive crowd of spectators, some of them rejoicing in the anticipation of the captive's punishment, others showing signs of commiseration; but most of the onlookers had merely come for the spectacle – if Leonora Christina's testimony is to be given any credence (*Jammers Minde*, pp. 10-12).

When the Dina affair heralded the Ulfeldts' downfall in 1650, the public stance on the Ulfeldt couple seems to have been less composed. A lampoon – *Fru Kirsten Munks Ballet*, which will be the topic of Chapter 2.1.1. – published around 1650 indicates that, at least in certain circles, the entire Munk clan and their associates had courted a widespread resentment. Perhaps more than the alleged planning of an attempt against King Frederik III's life, the execution of Dina Vinhofvers had stirred the public (see Chapter 3.2.4.), while her opponent, the powerful Countess

Ulfeldt, must have seemed truly infernal. Even though Dina was a prostitute, most literary portrayals of the affair focus on her status as collateral damage – the sole victim in a power struggle between two influential parties. Through her death, the harlot was thus turned into a tragic, at times even heroic (see Chapter 2.3.2.) figure. Leonora Christina, on the other hand, appears as a demonic dancer in her earliest literary portrayal.

However, the antipathy against Leonora Christina soon ebbed away and was turned into adoration when she disappeared behind the walls of the Blue Tower for nearly twenty-two years. Yet not all the tower's inmates associated with Corfitz Ulfeldt managed to turn their reputation upside-down. Leonora Christina was soon joined by Otto Sperling the Elder, another prominent figure in *Fru Kirsten Munks Ballet*, who, though also loyal to Corfitz Ulfeldt and industrious in the Blue Tower, did not gain as much fame as his tower companion – neither before nor after writing his memoirs. Sperling's *Selbstbiographie*, written at the same time and under similar conditions as Leonora Christina's French autobiography, will be the topic of Chapter 2.1.2., which will engage in the issue of Leonora Christina's depiction in Sperling's text and in the vastly differing success of both authors.

2.1.1. Anonymous: *Fru Kirsten Munks Ballet* (ca. 1650) – The Infernal Egocentric

> Elle pourroit pour marque de sa qualité un petit chapeau de velours noir, que les seules filles de leur Roi avoient droit de porter. Elle le dit ainsi à la Reine, qui d'abord qu'elle la vit lui demanda si c'étoit la mode de son pays, et si toutes les Dames en portoient? Du reste, elle étoit habillée à la Françoise, et avoit bonne mine.[419]

During the last years of Christian IV's life, Leonora Christina and Corfitz Ulfeldt experienced the height of their power. The old King had become weak and he was no longer able to defy his most influential son-in-law. At the same time, the couple had alienated many members of the Royal Danish Court and thus still depended on the patronage of the King. Soon after Christian IV's death and the accession of Frederik III in 1648, the situation grew more acute, eventually culminating into the so-called Dina affair and the Ulfeldts' flight to Sweden in 1651. Yet by then, the conflict had expanded. An anonymously published satire from around 1650 at-

---

[419] Motteville, Madame de. 'Madame de Mottevilles Skildring af Leonora Christinas Optræden ved det franske Hof 1647'. In *Leonora Christina (Ulfeldt)s Selvbiografi. Udgivet efter et Håndskrift i det store Kgl. Bibliothek*, ed. Sophus Birket Smith, Danske Samlinger for Historie, Topografi, Personal- og Litteraturhistorie 1/2 (1871-72), p. 219.

tests to a more general animosity towards the entire circle around Kirsten Munk: *Fru Kirsten Munks Ballet*. The text dates itself to the year 1650, but Sophus Birket Smith contends that – based on the content of the satire – it must have been written a few years later.[420]

Due to its vulgarity and ribald language,[421] the satire is certainly not the finest exhibit of 17th-century writing, but even Sophus Birket Smith concedes that some of the descriptions provided in the text are quite fitting.[422] The 'ballet' opens with a short introduction to the scene. Kirsten Munk is residing at the Royal Court of Hell (»i Helfuediß hofuit Recidentz«),[423] where she recently arranged a ballet to the amusement of a selection of invited guests, consisting of various ladies and gentlemen of Danish, Swedish and French origin. Kirsten Munk is the first of a series of individuals arriving at the scene. In total, twenty-five attendees enter the stage; some clearly identifiable, some not, but all »[e]ffter Helfuediß orden og viß i efterfølgende maade«;[424] the twenty-sixth attendee, the Icelander Torben Warmund, identifies himself as a mere observer. The exact meaning of this infernal order is obscure. It could refer to the severity of sins committed by the ballet's participants. Considering that Kirsten Munk is the first one to appear (as the mother figure and the starting point of all the following evil characters), the order of the figures' appearance could also depend on the relationship between the individuals involved. Around 1650, when Frederik III had first ordered investigations on Ulfeldt's financial transfers, Leonora Christina was hardly considered to be more corrupt and depraved than her husband. However, her connection to the King and to Kirsten Munk was closer and without her, Ulfeldt may never have reached his high position at the Danish court. Accordingly, Leonora Christina enters the stage before her husband. Thus, the »Helfuediß orden« may reflect a spider web with Kirsten Munk at its center. A definite analysis of the ballet's progression is further complicated by the fact that some of the figures remain unidentified, i.e., Sophus Birket Smith contests some of the identifications provided on the margin of the manuscript. Instead of attributing every figure in the ballet to one specific historical character, Birket Smith suggests that some of the figures (such as Briareus, according to Greek mythology

---

420 Birket Smith, Sophus. Introduction in Anonymous. 'Fru Kirsten Munks Ballet', ed. Sophus Birket Smith, Danske Samlinger for Historie, Topographi, Personal- og Literaturhistorie 1/6 (1870-71), p. 348.
421 See for example Kirsten Munk's description: »[A]f hendiß Patter, himmelighed, Nafle og BagEnde udgich En sagte ild« (Anonymous. 'Fru Kirsten Munks Ballet', ed. Sophus Birket Smith, Danske Samlinger for Historie, Topographi, Personal- og Literaturhistorie 1/6 (1870-71), p. 349).
422 Birket Smith, Sophus. Introduction, p. 348.
423 Anonymous. 'Fru Kirsten Munks Ballet', p. 349.
424 Ibid.

one of the Hekatonkheires ('Hundred-Handed-Ones')) may simply symbolise the vices that afflicted the Danish court when Ulfeldt and the rest of *svigersønnerpartiet* became more influential.[425]

Thus, the arrival of Kirsten Munk at court (first the Danish, then the infernal one in the satire) is followed by greed (Briareus) and discord (Discordia). The fourth figure is a French woman, a skilled dancer, who animates another woman, either of Swedish or Danish origin, to dance like a maniac. Sophus Birket Smith speculates whether these two ladies could represent Anne of Austria (1601-1666, from 1643 until 1651 Queen consort of France) and Queen Christina of Sweden, since both women had taken a liking to either Corfitz or Leonora Christina.[426] The fifth character is Leonora Christina, undoubtedly the most famous and successful child of Kirsten Munk. She is easily recognisable by a black velvet hat encircled by two rows of pearls and with a white feather attached to the side – contemporary portraits of Leonora Christina also show her wearing this alleged status symbol:

> Strax fulte En anden Damme med En liden Fløielß hat paa og En hvid plummatz derudi, hafde gode menß hofferdige miner; paa hindiß bryst stod schrefuen: Regnabo pro lubitu (Jeg vil regere efter egen villie); med dend Ene Arm pegte hun paa dend Damme, som schichede sig saa ilde i dantzen, og stod schrefnit paa Ermit: Sic nobis saltatur (Saalediß blifuer der dantzit for oß); paa hendiß Ryg: nu faar vi Revance. Pichelhering[427] Vente sig om til dem i forsamlingen og sagde: du magst Vat Svidschen lechen![428]

When the Ulfeldt couple visited the above-mentioned Queen of France, Leonora Christina received plenty of attention. The Queen was particularly interested in the distinctive looking hat flaunted by her guest from Denmark, and Leonora Christina was all too willing to explain that only the King's daughters were allowed to wear this type of fashion.[429] By the middle of the 17th century, when Ulfeldt had declared himself more powerful than the King himself (most explicitly with the *håndfæstning* Frederik III was forced to sign in order to become King of Denmark), the public must have become annoyed by Leonora Christina's eagerness to insist on

---

425 Birket Smith, Sophus in Anonymous. 'Fru Kirsten Munks Ballet', p. 350 (footnote).

426 Ibid., p. 351 (footnote).

427 The *Pickelhering*, a fool, belonged to the travelling comedy groups of the 17th century and thus found his way from England via Germany until Denmark, hence his remark in Low-German (»Du magst Vat Svidschen lechen!«), which most likely alludes to the Ulfeldt couple's newfound sympathy for the Swedes (cf. Middle Low German *swētsch* or Low-German *sweedsch*).

428 Anonymous. 'Fru Kirsten Munks Ballet', p. 351.

429 See introductory quotation at the beginning of the chapter – an account of Leonora Christina's stay at the royal court in France, written by a French court lady.

her status, represented by this hat.[430] There is furthermore a conspicuous absence of historical records attesting to any wearable status symbol accorded to the King's daughters. The preserved correspondence of Christian IV is extensive and exhibits an interest in even the most menial aspects of the daily life in his realm,[431] but it contains no letters concerned with an exclusive headdress for his daughters. Visual records do not support Leonora Christina's claim either, since she is the only one among Christian IV's daughters to be depicted with this hat.[432] In fact, there are hardly any contemporary portraits of Leonora Christina *not* wearing her famous hat,[433] which supports the Danish writer Maria Helleberg's theory that this hat and its alleged exclusivity had been the invention of the head evidentially wearing it (see Chapter 2.6.3.).

The next person in line is still not Ulfeldt, but M. Simon Hennings, who had been Corfitz's priest. He also played a significant role in the Dina affair. He is followed by Corfitz Ulfeldt:

Fremkomb en stor anseelig Cavallier med en stor Svitte, dog formummed, klæd I en lang Kiortel af adschillige Colører. Somme sagde, dette maatte vist vere Grefuen af Ulfeld; paa hanß hat hafde hand it Smyche med en Crone og En half gylden Maane og diße ord: Fatis jactamur varijs (Jeg blifuer selsom omdrefuen af lychen); paa brystet i et Kosteligt Smyche var udstuchet en flyende Ørn og diße ord: supra Reges et fortunam (ofuer Konger og lychen); menß paa hanß Ryg Var Claus Nar megit artig udstuchet, og saa egentlig som hand gich her i verden. En som en liden diefvel, dog langtfra som et menische til siune, var alt ved siden hoß same Cavalier med En gloende puster, hvorpaa stoed schrefuen: instigo (Jeg schiunder til).[434]

---

430 Cf. Anne-Marie Mai, who interprets the reference to this hat as »et symbol på Leonora Christinas og hendes søstres hoffærdighed og magtbegær« (Mai, Anne-Marie. 'Troskab, lidelse og lidenskab', p. 286).

431 See Christian IV of Denmark. *End lever jeg: Et udvalg af Chr. IVs breve*, ed. Godfred Hartmann. Copenhagen: Reitzel, 1987, which reproduces letters by Christian IV including, among other things, instructions regarding the colour of his children's clothes, and even their stockings (Christian IV of Denmark. *End lever jeg: Et udvalg af Chr. IVs breve*, ed. Godfred Hartmann. Copenhagen: Reitzel, 1987, pp. 10-31), as well as orders concerning his poultry, cows and mills (ibid., pp. 32-53).

432 Among the women of the Munk clan, only Leonora Christina's grandmother Ellen Marsvin is portrayed wearing a hat that resembles that of her granddaughter – a black hat, perhaps made of velvet, circled by a single row of pearls. Ellen Marsvin's headpiece might thus have been a source of inspiration to her granddaughter.

433 Only a portrait of Kirsten Munk together with four of her children – exhibited today in Frederiksborg Castle – shows Leonora Christina without her hat. She was, however, a toddler when the painting was made, i.e. in 1623, and, as was the custom at that time, the three daughters of Kirsten Munk are depicted as miniature versions of their mother (cf. Gotfredsen, Lise. 'Maleren som øjenvidne og digter'. In *Leonora Christina: Historien om en heltinde*. Århus: Arkona, 1983 (Acta Jutlandica 58, Humanistisk serie 57), p. 102).

434 Anonymous. 'Fru Kirsten Munks Ballet', p. 352.

Unlike many of the other figures, Corfitz Ulfeldt is identified by the author of the satire instead of by a more recent note on the margin of the manuscript – perhaps due to the evident nature of his offenses. His characterisation suggests corruption as his main vice (»Jeg blifuer selsom omdrefuen af lychen«) and his motto, »Supra reges et fortunam« indicates that he tends to elide whatever higher power could oppose him. Furthermore, Ulfeldt's semi-lunar headdress alludes to the »månekejser, den onde negation af den guddommelige (sol)konge«.[435]

Corfitz is followed by his doctor, Otto Sperling the Elder. Although historiography reports no actual misdeed committed by Sperling, the pure association with the Ulfeldt family was enough to condemn the medic. The statements attributed to him by the satire indicate that Sperling was considered an opportunist and perhaps involved in Ulfeldt's shady transactions:

> Iblant same Cavalliers Svite lod sig En til siune, som var Doctor Medicinæ, men Klæd som en Kiøbmand eller biße Kremmere; paa hanß Ryg stod schrefuen: in utraque excercitatus (øfuet i begge), paa hanß hat: practicus mirabilis (En selsom Konstner), paa hanß bryst: supra artem alte spiro (Mit sind er langt høyere end til læge Konsten), Paa hanß Fødder: Medicus Politicus (En Stats-Læge).[436]

This mockery of Otto Sperling is a rather isolated case and seems to be induced by the strong contemporary outrage over Corfitz Ulfeldt and his entourage – Sperling may just have been collateral damage. After all, Dina had accused him of brewing the poisonous cocktail meant to rid the Ulfeldt couple of the King and once his best clients had moved to Sweden, Sperling fancied a position as Queen Christina's personal medic. The contemporary Danish public had thus reason enough to blaspheme Otto Sperling the Elder. However, later historiography and literature portray him as a harmless man, who just happened to befriend the wrong people.

Otto Sperling is followed by a scene, which could be interpreted as Kirsten Munk's lack of respect for the Crown (i.e. the former King of Denmark, her husband).[437] Subsequently, Ellen Marsvin enters the stage, followed by Valdemar

---

435 Pedersen, Vibeke A. *Dansk litteraturs historie 1*, p. 400.
436 Anonymous. 'Fru Kirsten Munks Ballet', p. 352.
437 Ibid., p. 353: »Paa Theatro var sat En Krone, som schinnede herlig af Guld og stene, dend dantzede hun Runden om Kring, og i dantzen vilde hun alt til at træde paa samme Krone, menß der laae en liden diefvel paa gulfuet med En gloende Jldtang, som hand stach frue Kisten mellem benene, saa tit hun kom dend for nær[...]«. The little devil's obscene gesture could refer to Kirsten Munk's offence against her husband, i.e. her infidelity involving one of the King's subjects, Otto Ludvig of Salm (1597-1634).

Christian (1622-1656, Leonora Christina's brother), Hannibal Sehested[438] and his wife Christiane, Leonora Christina's sisters Elisabeth Augusta (1623-1677) and Hedevig, and the latter one's husband Ebbe Ulfeldt. Once these persons, mainly consisting of Kirsten Munk's daughters and their powerful husbands, have entered the scene, a flock of ladies perform a dance symbolising the secret matriarchy (»Imperium Muliebre«)[439] that has infested the Danish kingdom. In between, a couple of figures appear, who either could not have been identified, or who were not directly involved with the Ulfeldt couple. Finally, Kirsten Munk reappears, targeting the crown anew.[440] She and her surrounding women mix with a group of dancing trolls and the Greek god of the underworld, Pluto, who shoots fireworks. Confusion arises and Kirsten Munk's derrière catches fire, prompting her to cry for water. Pluto comments on the scene: »[…] hindiß Naade og dendiß anhæng har tent for megit an i verden; derfor faaer hun nu sampt de andre brende i helfuede«.[441]

The lack of information about the text's author poses a problem insofar as it hinders a determination of the text's diffusion. The satire itself mentions a certain Torben Warmund who acted as a transmitter of the events: »At Jeg dette i en siun har seet indværende aar 1650 ved middagß tider d. 24. Julij, Widner jeg med egen haand Torben Warmund islender«. Whether this – probably fictional – eyewitness and the satire's author are the same person, however, is unknown. Sophus Birket Smith does not mention Torben Warmund at all, nor does he bespeak any author of the satire. If any information on the author of the text was available, it might be easier to determine whether the text portrayed the opinion of an individual or the broader public.

The manuscript situation offers just as little enlightenment regarding the text's degree of familiarity, as there are only two extant manuscripts of the satire. The text

---

438 Sophus Birket Smith rightly comments that »H. S. synes ikke vel at kunne savnes i denne Satire« (Birket Smith, Sophus in Anonymous. 'Fru Kirsten Munks Ballet', p. 355 (footnote)). In fact, more recent novels depicting Leonora Christina's life attribute a much more central role to Hannibal Sehested than history granted him. In the historical novel *Eleonora Christine und Corfitz Ulfeldt* by Margarete Boie (1936), Hannibal helps to rid the Danish empire of Corfitz Ulfeldt for both political reasons, but also out of deep and possessive love for Leonora Christina (see Boie, Margarete. *Eleonora Christine und Corfitz Ulfeldt: Der Lebensroman einer Königstochter*. Oldenburg and Berlin: Stalling, 1944, pp. 84-93). The historical Hannibal Sehested was married to Leonora Christina's younger sister Christiane (1626-1670), thus (as part of the infamous *svigersønnerparti*) obtaining one of the highest political positions of 17th-century Denmark, that of Governor of Norway. Hence, he was a companion and rival to Corfitz Ulfeldt, and thus naturally involved in his overthrow.

439 Anonymous. 'Fru Kirsten Munks Ballet', p. 359.

440 This could be interpreted either as a final attempt to regain her lost influence over the King (through a reconciliation), or as an attack against him. Christian IV never forgave Kirsten Munk for her unfaithfulness and she in turn was indignant over her punishment, thus they never reconciled.

441 Anonymous. 'Fru Kirsten Munks Ballet', p. 360.

could have been written for the amusement of a small circle of people or for a broader public, since a lack of extant manuscripts does not necessarily attest to a lack of contemporary reception. Only the coarse language of the satire serves as an indicator as to how well known the text was. Considering the appearance of Latin phrases, the references to classic mythology and the levels of illiteracy in 17th-century Europe, the text must have been restricted to a courtly environment. The frequent references to intimate body parts, however, suggest an even further restricted group of recipients within this courtly environment.

This list of people invited to the ballet includes not only the Munk clan, but also their enemies, such as Anders Bille, and people, who had no direct connection to them. Thus, the text portrays a general rottenness that had befallen the Danish court by mid-century, rather than a small circle of individuals. However, Leonora Christina is clearly at the centre of this circle since she appears even before the powerful statesmen Corfitz Ulfeldt and Hannibal Sehested, and, just as her companions, is doomed to burn in hell. The explicitness of the anonymous author's closing words leaves nothing to be said about this contemporary reception of Leonora Christina.

2.1.2 Otto Sperling the Elder: *Selbstbiographie* (1673) – Marital Appendage

> Ieg fordreff saa skiæls min tiid i Roelighed, indtil Doctor *Otto Sperling* bleff fort Fangen her ind i Taarnet, hwis Fengsel er neden vnder den Mørcke Kircke; Hands Skiæffne er beklagelig, Der hand bleff ført i Taarnet war hand spænt i Iernlencker om hænder oc Fødder[.]
>
> (*Jammers Minde*, p. 106)

In the year 1664, the Ulfeldt couple's former family physician, Otto Sperling the Elder, was brought to the Blue Tower in Copenhagen to share his friend's fate. In the years preceding his imprisonment, the physician had left Denmark shortly after the Ulfeldts' flight, had resided in the Netherlands, and thereafter in Sweden, in the hopes of obtaining a lucrative position at the Swedish court. After a few restless years, he decided to move back to his home country, Germany. There, the Danish authorities finally got a hold of Sperling and he was brought to his final residence, where he died in 1681.

In 1673, the Blue Tower thus housed two famous prisoners, both hurrying to finish their life narratives in order to hand them over to Otto Sperling the Younger, who in 1670 had come to Copenhagen to effect his father's release. When this request was refused, he asked his father and Leonora Christina to pen their life stories, which he intended to spread, each in the form of an apologia. Otto Sperling the Elder and Leonora Christina were thus in the same position[442] and yet their autobiographical approaches are substantially dissimilar. Both Sperling and Leonora Christina wrote about their life before and in prison. Leonora Christina decided to include only little information about her life after her arrest in Dover in her French autobiography; instead, she dedicated a much longer manuscript, i.e. *Jammers Minde*, to the years after 1663. Otto Sperling, however, rendered a very detailed account of his life until 1659, to which he added a comparably short *Historia Carceris*. This conspicuous disparity was first pointed out by Sophus Birket Smith, who in 1885 edited the first, and so far only, edition of Otto Sperling's memoirs.[443] The exact reasons for the text's lack of proportion are unclear. Sperling was in a hurry to finish the manuscript and by the end he may simply have run out of time. However, the purpose of the text may offer an alternative explanation. Sperling must have written his apologia with a particular audience in mind, one that is familiar with everything that had happened after 1659. Regarding this context, recounting all those universally known events would have been a waste of precious time. Hence, Ulfeldt's death deserves only passing mention,[444] while Leonora Christina's arrest in Dover is completely ignored. If we assume that time famine was not the only reason for Sperling to hurry through his *Historia Carceris*, we can regard his text as a rather typical apologia, i.e. a text written for a contemporary audience with no need of a reminder of recent occurrences. Finally, there is another conspicuity, which separates Sperling's work from Leonora Christina's life narratives. Unlike the French autobiography and *Jammers Minde*, which depict their author as a strong character independent of her husband, Otto Sperling's *Selbstbiographie* demonstrates a peculiar focus on Corfitz Ulfeldt. Leonora Christina's apologia bases itself on the grandness of her own character, while Sperling's text is a more conventional

---

442 However, one major difference between Sperling and Leonora Christina's situation was that he had been properly sentenced while Leonora Christina remained in the Blue Tower without an accordant verdict.

443 Birket Smith, Sophus. Introduction in Sperling, Otto. *Dr. med. Otto Sperlings Selvbiografi (1602-1673)*, oversat i Uddrag efter Originalhaandskriftet med særligt Hensyn til Forfatterens Ophold i Danmark og Norge samt Fangenskab i Blaataarn, ed. Sophus Birket Smith. Copenhagen: Selskabet for Udgivelse af Kilder til dansk Historie, 1974 (1885), p. III. Otto Sperling's original manuscript, titled *Selbstbiographie biz auf d. J. 1673 (Autogr.)* – *Historia Carceris oder Beschreibung meiner Gefängnis, Examinis, Anklag, und darauf erfolgten Sententz (Autogr.)*, is rendered in German. Because the German text was never published, I resolved upon contenting myself with the Danish translation conducted by one of the foremost Leonora Christina-researchers, as it proved to meet this study's needs and will facilitate any future revisal.

444 Sperling, Otto. *Dr. med. Otto Sperlings Selvbiografi (1602-1673)*, oversat i Uddrag efter Originalhaandskriftet med særligt Hensyn til Forfatterens Ophold i Danmark og Norge samt Fangenskab i Blaataarn, ed. Sophus Birket Smith. Copenhagen: Selskabet for Udgivelse af Kilder til dansk Historie, 1974 (1885), p. 201: »[…] og havde vi imidlertid bekommet den Tidende, at Hr. Ulfeldt var hastigen død paa Rhinen, i hvor vel Mademoiselle Helene [Ellen Christina Ulfeldt] skrev til mig, at han var død af en Pleuris«.

apologia in that it attempts to exculpate Ulfeldt and thus himself. In fact, Sperling's *Selbstbiographie* contains entire pages narrating Corfitz Ulfeldt's life with barely a mention of Sperling's share in it. The result is a rather blank character portrait of the autobiographer, further resulting in a subsequent lack of interest in the manuscript until Sophus Birket Smith decided to publish the text as a supplement to his *Leonora Christina Grevinde Ulfeldts Historie*.[445]

Research, too, has so far refrained from undertaking an in-depth analysis of the text. Most remarks on Sperling's *Selbstbiographie* are contained either in Danish literary histories or in academic publications on Leonora Christina's autobiographical work – both of which agree that Sperling's text is inferior. Thomas Seiler, for example, criticises Sperling's focus on public events and the accusations raised against him, which prevented him from writing a potentially intriguing account of his prison experience. At the same time, Leonora Christina had better preconditions for attracting interest in her life story, i.e. the drastic depth of her fall.[446] Annegret Heitmann, too, concludes that Sperling's text has only historical-documentary value[447] and attributes his lack of personal reflection to his nationality and, hence, his position as outsider, or rather onlooker.[448]

Also in terms of ascertaining Leonora Christina's portrayal, the *Selbstbiographie* poses a problem, as it is a classic memoir rather than an autobiography. Sperling's character remains an enigma and could at best be described as opportunistic. His text chronicles events to a degree, which would justify a classification as historiography – if only it were reliable historiography. Sperling's account is both faulty – especially regarding his dating – and selective. For example, Sperling does mention that Ulfeldt fled to Sweden after Dina's execution, as soon as he heard of another warrant against him. However, he fails to mention the reason for this second warrant, i.e. embezzlement.[449]

Considering the degree to which Sperling's and Leonora Christina's lives were intertwined, their life narratives are not only surprisingly divergent but they also make strikingly little mention of each other. However, the mere nature of the doc-

---

445 Accordingly, Birket Smith did not publish a translation of the complete text but omitted passages focussing entirely on Sperling.
446 Cf. Seiler, Thomas. *Im Leben verschollen*, p. 61.
447 Heitmann, Annegret. 'Zwischen Macht und Marginalität', p. 210.
448 Ibid., p. 211.
449 Sperling, Otto. *Selvbiografi*, p. 168.

tor's text explains Leonora Christina's meagre appearance.[450] Otto Sperling intended to exonerate himself by exonerating Corfitz Ulfeldt, and in order to achieve this Sperling simply recounted the public events leading to their condemnation. Due to the focus on public life resulting from this strategy, Leonora Christina appears only on rare occasions and plays a rather passive role. At the same time, Sperling must have been aware of Leonora Christina's French autobiography, which was well under way above his own cell. This circumstance may at least partially account for their both disregarding one another in their respective narratives – Leonora Christina, too, rarely mentions her old friend in both of her autobiographical writings. Unless they received the unlikely chance to revise each other's manuscripts, each of the two prisoners never knew what the other one wrote and since their lives had been intricately connected, it was perhaps best to conceal each other in order not to undermine each other's story.

In this light, it is not at all surprising how Sperling's text presents Leonora Christina and her husband forming a unit mostly represented by Corfitz Ulfeldt alone. Leonora Christina's actions usually aim at reinforcing those of her husband, such as in the following example.

Ulfeldt's tremendously dominant role in Sperling's life forms one of the pillars of the physician's apologia. Their friendship is portrayed as being primarily initiated by Ulfeldt:

> Herren fik derudover en saadan Affection til mig, at omendskjønt jeg ingen videre Hjælp kunde yde ham og derfor begjærede at maatte rejse, bad han mig alligevel at blive lidet hos ham, hvilket jeg heller ikke vilde nægte ham, men det lidet varede 4 hele Uger, thi før vilde han ikke lade mig fare. [...] Saaledes blev jeg først bekjendt med denne Herre, og var mit Selskab ham ikke ubehageligt.[451]

Due to his education, the physician enjoyed great popularity in the Ulfeldt mansion, but whether this feeling had always been mutual remains unclear. Later on in his account, he does commend Ulfeldt's qualities yet in the beginning all sympathy between the two men is represented as being one-sided. Thus, it appears as if Sperling could only be convinced to remain in close contact with the Ulfeldt couple through

---

450 Under different circumstances, Sperling's autobiography might have exhibited a different focus. He and Leonora Christina are reported to have spent a lot of time with each other; so much, in fact, that Danish writer Godfred Hartmann was inclined to suspect an infatuation on Sperling's part, as repeatedly betokened in *Kongens børn* (see, for example, Hartmann, Godfred. *Kongens børn*, p. 108).
451 Sperling, Otto. *Selvbiografi*, p. 62.

very generous gifts,[452] and because Corfitz and Leonora Christina persuaded him. When Sperling was offered a position in Copenhagen in 1637, he initially refused. Ulfeldt, however, wanted his friend to move closer to his own domicile and thus pressed Sperling to follow the King's call. When his arguments failed to impress, he asked his wife to step in:

> Alt dette kunde dog intet Indtryk gjøre paa mig. Da sagde han til sin Frøken: »Se Frøken Leonora, han vil slet ikke tage mod denne Lejlighed, og jeg har allerede lovet Kongen det for vist.« Da begyndte Frøken Leonora, hvem jeg aldrig tilforn havde set, ogsaa at tale og formanede mig med mange Ord; spurgte, om jeg havde Børn, og hvor mange? [453]

Sperling emphasises that it had never been his intention to move to Copenhagen and thus start his illustrious career as Ulfeldt's protégé, hence his objections. However, Ulfeldt does not intend to be defeated, so he draws the King into the argument. At this point, Sperling's career-enhancing decision to follow Ulfeldt to the capital turns into an act of attending for duty. As if this were not enough for Sperling and his readers, Ulfeldt prompts his wife to step in and convince the physician with arguments of a more personal nature. She acts according to her husband's explicit wish but whether this reflects the actual relationship between Corfitz and Leonora Christina, or whether it is an attempt to exculpate her in the same way as Sperling, is open to interpretation. What is conspicuous, though, is Sperling's remark that he had just met *Frøken Leonora* at that time, indicating that she demonstrated a resoluteness in character similar to Ulfeldt's. Eventually, it is Leonora Christina's determined demeanour that convinces Sperling, but her words comply with her husband's ambition.

Both Sperling and Leonora Christina are thus exonerated since all decision-making is left to Ulfeldt. As a consequence, both consider their lasting loyalty towards him (and God's mysterious ways) the only reason for their punishment, as stated in both of their life narratives:

---

[452] Ibid. As Sperling is eager to point out, Leonora Christina is equally generous. For instance, after giving birth to her first child the young woman suffered from a neoplasm on one of her breasts. Sperling was able to remove the swelling »[...] uden at der blev noget Ar, hvilket var hende synderlig kjært, og forærede hun mig for Curen 100 Slet-Daler i en Fløjels Pung« (ibid., p. 84). The meticulousness of his account could simply be the result of his personality and profession, or it could have the purpose of confronting the readers of his memoirs with the question of whether *they* could have resisted such a profitable friendship.

[453] Ibid., p. 78.

Thi disse Breve, i hvor vel der ikke indeholdtes andet i dem, end hvad en Ven plejer at skrive til en anden, er ikke alene Aarsag til min Fængsling, næst Guds synderlige Forføjning, Raad og Vilje, men ogsaa til, at man har erfaret, hvad der stod hos mig af Ulfeldts Gods, og til, at Resten af hans Apologi er kommen i fremmede Hænder.[454]

Both autobiographers perceive their evident fealty towards Corfitz Ulfeldt to be innocent; however, it may just be the true cause of their calamities. As regards Otto Sperling, Ulfeldt appears to have played such a dominant role in his life that there was little left to be said about Leonora Christina. Sperling portrays her as an educated, intelligent and wilful woman, but all this comes naturally with being the wife of »en meget from, huldsalig og god Herre, af meget stor Forfarenhed, synderligen i Statssager,[...]«.[455]

2.2. Leonora Christina as Subject of Patriotic Debate

Ieg liider for att haffue werret ælsket aff en dydig Herre oc Hoßbonde, for att ey haffue Hannem i Vlycken forlat wilt[.] *Susspiceris* derfor att wide om ett Forræderi hand aldrig er bleffuen for Tiltalt, mindre offuerbewiist, huis Beskyllings Aarsage mig ey bleff forstendiget ihuor smaaligen oc weemodeligen ieg ded begierendis war.

(*Jammers Minde*, p. 4*)

From July 1660 until December 1661, Leonora Christina and her husband were imprisoned in Hammershus on the island of Bornholm – a former fortress used as a prison for particularly troublesome offenders – due to their previous wrongdoings against the King of Denmark and against Denmark itself (most recently, their involvement in the Dano-Swedish War of 1657-1658). Thus, as a result of the approximate seventeen months that Leonora Christina spent on Bornholm, Danske Færger A/S announced in early 2010 that a new ferry connecting the Swedish town of Ystad with Bornholm's capital Rønne (i.e., the most common means of transport for Danes to reach Bornholm, due to a lack of a direct connection), would be called *Leonora Christina*. This decision was motivated by the company's wish to name the

---

454 Ibid., p. 199. Cf. *Jammers* Minde, p. 4*: »Ieg liider for att haffue werret ælsket aff en dydig Herre oc Hoßbonde, for att ey haffue Hannem i Vlycken forlat wilt«.
455 Sperling, Otto. *Selvbiografi*, p. 93.

new ferry after a woman – since all previous ferries had been named after men[456] – with a historical connection to Bornholm. Due to the inclusion of *Jammers Minde* in Denmark's Cultural Canon in 2006 (see Chapter 2.5.) and because of the interest the Bornholmian painter Kristian Zahrtmann had shown in Leonora Christina, this name seemed like a good choice.[457] The announcement, however, caused a heated debate about history, patriotism and accountability.

Most of the criticism concerned Leonora Christina's famous loyalty towards her husband who, after all, had been co-responsible for the Treaty of Roskilde (1658) and the preceding war, which brought Bornholm under Swedish rule (a rule many Bornholmians rebelled against) – at least until 1660, when Bornholm was returned to Denmark under the Treaty of Copenhagen. The historian Steffen Heiberg, who also published the Corfitz Ulfeldt-biography *Enhjørningen Corfitz Ulfeldt*, referred to this part of Leonora Christina's life story when he remarked that naming a Bornholm ferry after this woman was »en hån mod de bornholmere, der i 1659 kæmpede for, at deres ø kom tilbage til Danmark«.[458] Others expressed their indignation through sarcasm, for example by suggesting that another ferry could be named after Eva Braun (Adolf Hitler's mistress and wife for one day), who »lige som Leonora Christina [var] loyal mod sin mand og blev heller aldrig dømt for landsforræderi«,[459] or by proposing that an Oslo ferry should be called *Vidkun Quisling*.[460] Other bones of contention were Leonora Christina's »noget dysfunktionel familie, som i dagens Danmark nok ville være sat under observation af de sociale myndigheder«,[461] as well as the somewhat loose historical connection linking Leo-

---

456 Qvitzau, Dan. 'Så enkelt er det: Klare stemmeregler': http://tidende.dk/?Id=23708, originally published on 11 February 2011.

457 Qvitzau, Dan. 'Helt ny version: Afstemning om navn': http://tidende.dk/?Id=23608, originally published on 8 February 2011.

458 Heiberg, Steffen. 'En magtsyg kvinde': http://www.b.dk/kommentarer/en-magtsyg-kvinde, originally published on 15 December 2015. One incident in 1661 furthermore suggests that the inhabitants of Bornholm bore hatred towards Ulfeldt due to this war. When Leonora Christina, Ulfeldt and Peter Pflügge escaped from Hammershus and were discovered and caught the morning after their flight, the guards sent to recapture the three escapees eventually had to protect them from the gathering townspeople, who might have struck the traitor Ulfeldt dead if the guards had not been there (see, for example, Birket Smith, Sophus. *Leonora Christina Grevinde Ulfeldts Historie 2*, p. 35 and Heiberg, Steffen. *Enhjørningen Corfitz Ulfeldt*, p. 199).

459 Ejsing, Jens. 'Historisk ballede om færgenavn': http://www.b.dk/danmark/historisk-ballede-om-faergenavn, originally published on 24 November 2010.

460 Ejsing, Jens. 'Skal Oslo-færgen så hedde Vidkun Quisling?': http://www.b.dk/danmark/skal-oslo-faergen-saa-hedde-vidkun-quisling, originally published on 19 December 2010. Vidkun Quisling (1887-1945) was the founder of the fascist party Nasjonal Samling, which collaborated with the National Socialists during the occupation of Norway from 1940 until 1945. Quisling furthermore proclaimed himself Prime Minister of Norway when Johan Nygaardsvold and his government retreated into exile.

461 Christensen, Jan. 'Burgundia igen…': http://tidende.dk/?Id=22819, originally published on 11 January 2011.

nora Christina to Bornholm, a place she hardly mentions in the work that secured her central place in Denmark's cultural history[462] (see *Jammers Minde*, pp. 7*-9*).

Due to this fervid response to the company's decision to name the ferry after a traitor's wife, Danske Færger A/S in collaboration with the Bornholm-based newspaper *Bornholms Tidende* advertised a competition to submit naming suggestions (including *Leonora Christina*) on 10 February 2011. Subsequently, five shortlisted names, led by *Leonora Christina* with 40.5 %, were announced and on 28 February the winning name was made public: *Leonora Christina* won the final voting, albeit barely, with 50.2 %.[463] Even though all Danes interested in the ferry controversy could vote online, only 9,340 people participated[464] – not even near to half of the total population of Bornholm – which suggests that the controversy had largely been led by a relatively few, yet very committed, number of individuals. Nevertheless, the debate demonstrates that the mere name of Leonora Christina is connected to issues of historical awareness, cultural and ethical merits, and, most of all, patriotism.

The following three chapters illustrate that this discourse has a tradition that commenced long before the publication of *Jammers Minde*. The author discussed in Chapters 2.2.1. and 2.2.3., Denmark's famous fairy tale-writer Hans Christian Andersen, establishes an intricate connection between Leonora Christina and Denmark's history, hence presenting her as an icon of Danishness. Mathilde Fibiger, the author of the novel discussed in Chapter 2.2.2., on the other hand, adds a feminist and hence more polemic dimension to the patriotic discourse prevalent in Hans Christian Andersen's tales. Fibiger addresses an issue that has also been central to the Bornholm ferry controversy, namely that of a woman's colliding obligations towards her home country on one side, and her husband on the other side.

---

462 Ibid.

463 For a summary of the process of naming the *Leonora Christina*, see Danske Færger's official statement published on the Folketing's website: Danske Færger A/S. 'Redegørelse vedrørende afstemning om navnet på den nye hurtigfærge til BornholmerFærgens rute Rønne-Ystad': http://www.ft.dk/samling/20101/ almdel/tru/bilag/225/970075.pdf.

464 Ibid.

2.2.1. Hans Christian Andersen: *Holger Danske* (1845) – Defender of the Author's Fame

Den 21. *April Supplicerte* ieg Kongl. *Majt:* paa effterfølgende Maade. Ieg haffde Høyloffligste Konning *Christian* den *Fiærdis* Billede i Kaarstycke, lided oc i *oval*; ded haffde ieg *Illumineret* med Farffwer, oc laded giøre en udsnitzet Ramme omkring, den selffwer Forgylt. Bag paa Stycket satte ieg effterfølgende Ord.
 Min Sønne Søn, oc største Nafne,
 Du ligner mig i Mact oc Moed:
 Lad ded min Læfning oc nu gavne,
 At du som ieg est Naade goed.

(*Jammers Minde*, p. 241)

In 1685, after the death of Sophie Amalie in February, Leonora Christina was awaiting her release from the Blue Tower. Yet Christian V remained inactive, while Leonora Christina grew impatient. Hence, she accorded the King a written supplication including a short poem reminding him of their family ties. By referring to her father Christian IV who, despite his many defeats, had been a rather popular monarch, Leonora Christina invokes a bond that connects her to the royal house and to Denmark, in spite of the previous accusations of treason against her. Leonora Christina's evocative reference to a Danish icon was repeated 160 years later, when Hans Christian Andersen was also facing accusations of disaffection for his home country. The famous fairy tale-writer, however, appropriated the image of the suffering daughter of the King to his defence.

In 1845, Andersen was already an established member of the Danish literary community. However, it is no secret that Andersen did not always feel like he had been accepted as a writer. The ugly duckling, one of Andersen's most popular figures, is known to be a self-portrayal of its author. By the middle of the century, when a stagnating political and economic situation in Denmark had been compensated with the arising cultural Danish Golden Age (*Guldalderen*) from 1800 until 1850, one of the points of criticism raised against Andersen was that he did not seem patriotic enough and, perhaps not surprisingly, one of his fiercest critics in this regard was his old enemy Johan Ludvig Heiberg. Immediately following the publication of the travelogue *En Digters Bazar* (1842), Heiberg reprehended Andersen for ignoring the beauty of Denmark and instead writing about the amenities of the exotic world. In his poetry collection *Danmark* from 1842, Heiberg thus published a poem titled *Kronborg*, which contains the following stanza:

Muligt er du slig en Nar, / At, hvad Andersen fortæller / Om de skjønne Dardaneller / I sin tyrkiske Bazar, / Du med Undren grebet har, / Mens du, tung af Inertie, / Gik vort eget Sund forbi, / Som ei mindre Blikket fryder, / Og hvor ingen Klage lyder, / Fra det miskjendte Genie.[465]

In this stanza, Heiberg advises his (Danish) readers not to get distracted by Andersen's wonder tales about faraway countries, but instead pay regard to the marvels in front of their own door. Andersen's own tribute to Denmark, *Holger Danske*, followed in 1845 and it has been suggested that it constitutes an answer to this very same stanza.[466] In this tale named after the mythical hero dwelling in Kronborg's cellar vault, Andersen recounts scenes from the lives of famous Danes, whom he regards to be true Danish heroes, while the legendary knight Holger Danske provides the tale with a frame. The fabled figure Ogier the Dane, known from the medieval French epic *Chanson de Roland*, is sure to catch the attention of patriotically minded Danes while the actual centre personalities demonstrate that a hero can take on more than one form and profession, as stated by the grandfather in *Holger Danske*:[467] »Jo, *Holger Danske* kan komme paa mange Maader, saa at der i alle Verdens Lande høres om Danmarks Styrke!«[468] The Danish coat of arms contains both »de danske Løver og de danske Hjerter, [...] Styrken og Mildheden«.[469] Hence, the three Danish lions remind *den gamle Bedstefader* of three Danish monarchs, all people who held and executed great power: Cnut the Great, Valdemar I, and Margaret I of Denmark.[470] »[M]en idet han saae paa de røde Hjerter, saa skinnede de endnu stærkere end før, de bleve til Flammer som bevægede sig, og hans Tanke fulgte hver af dem«.[471] Despite the heroic deeds of the three lions, it is the hearts that catch the old man's eye – these symbols of Danish kindness will now guide their observer through the cornerstones of Denmark's history.

---

465 Heiberg, Johan Ludvig. 'Kronborg'. In Heiberg, Johan Ludvig. *Poetiske Skrifter 8: Blandede Digte. Første Afdeling.* Copenhagen: Reitzel, 1862, p. 224.
466 E.g., Hovmann, Flemming. 'Holger Danske'. In *H. C. Andersens Eventyr 7: Kommentar*, ed. Flemming Hovmann. Copenhagen: Reitzel, 1990, p. 107.
467 Elkington, Trevor G. 'Holger Danske as Literary Danish Identity in the Work of H. C. Andersen and B. S. Ingemann'. In *Hans Christian Andersen: A Poet in Time. Papers from the Second International Hans Christian Andersen Conference. 29 July to 2 August 1996*, ed. Johan de Mylius et al. Odense University Press, 1999, p. 249.
468 Andersen, Hans Christian. 'Holger Danske'. In *H. C. Andersens Nye Eventyr 1844-48, eventyr optagne i* Eventyr 1850 *samt Historier 1852-55*, ed. Erik Dal. Copenhagen: Reitzel, 1964 (H. C. Andersens Eventyr 2), p. 101.
469 Ibid.
470 Ibid., p. 99.
471 Ibid.

Leonora Christina represents the first of the hearts of the Danish coat of arms:

> Den første Flamme førte ham ind i et snevert mørkt Fængsel; der sad en Fange, en deilig Qvinde, Christian den Fjerdes Datter: Eleonore Ulfeld; og Flammen satte sig som en Rose paa hendes Bryst og blomstrede sammen med hendes Hjerte, hun den ædleste og bedste af alle danske Qvinder. »Ja, det er et Hjerte i Danmarks Vaaben!« sagde den gamle Bedstefader.[472]

By showing Leonora Christina in her dark prison cell, Andersen portrays her as the woman the Danish know and had learned to respect. Unlike Queen Margaret I, she did not win her battle with the help of an army, but instead she persisted out of love for her husband. On the other hand, the picture serves Andersen's purpose of demonstrating how a true Danish hero may not always seem heroic at first glance. This message is reinforced by another one of Andersen's chosen heroes: »Tyge Brahe, han var ogsaa een, som brugte Sværdet; ikke til at hugge i Kjød og Been, men hugge en tydeligere Vei op imellem alle Himlens Stjerner!«[473] Surely, Andersen felt a special connection to these two heroes since they had also experienced maltreatment at the hands of their fellow countrymen: Leonora Christina was kept in the Blue Tower by her own half-brother and the astronomer Tycho Brahe (1546-1601) was forced to continue his ground-breaking research in Bohemia, since he no longer felt supported in Denmark.

Readers of Andersen's (semi-)autobiographical narratives repeatedly encounter Leonora Christina. Already in 1829, when Andersen debuted as a writer with his *Fodreise fra Holmens Canal til Østpynten af Amager i Aarene 1828 og 1829*, he seemed strangely drawn to the image of the princess in the tower:

> Allerede tittede det store Bryggerhuus frem ved Hiørnet, allerede hørte jeg Bølgernes Pladsken mod Bropælene blande sig med Skildvagtens Snorken. – Blaataarn laa foran mig; i Tankerne saae jeg der det snevre lille Kammer, hvori en Datter af Danmarks største Konge, uskyldig hensmægtede i 23 lange Aar. Væggene vare sorte af Røg, og Lysningen faldt kun ind igjennem det lille Lofts Vindue, som den barske Slutter aabnede, naar Røgen truede med at dræbe den arme Fange.[474]

---

472 Ibid., p. 100.
473 Ibid., p. 101.
474 Andersen, Hans Christian. *Fodreise fra Holmens Canal til Østpynten af Amager i Aarene 1828 og 1829*, ed. Johan de Mylius. Valby: Borgen, 1986 (1829; Danske Klassikere), p. 34.

Whether it is the story of a real-life Rapunzel, or the eerie atmosphere induced by the vicinity of the Blue Tower[475] and *Druknehuset*[476], Andersen »følte [s]ig ganske underligt stemt midt i denne levende Omgivelse«.[477]

Over the years, Hans Christian Andersen advanced his idea. In September 1833, he travelled through Switzerland and during a restless night in the train to Lausanne, the thought of a work about Leonora Christina crossed his mind again, as he reveals in his diary.[478] Four years later, he seems to have translated this scheme into a tragedy called *Dina*. Andersen's friend Henriette Hanck (1807-1846) is amongst the first people to hear of his latest creation and her reaction is both enthusiastic and oddly prophetic:

> Deres ny Tragedie spøger ret om i mit Hoved: »Dina« skal den hedde, det er formodentlig af Ulfeldts Historie? Som Hovedpersoner deri tænker jeg mig da Frederik d: 3die, Ulfeldt, Eleonore Kirstine, Oberst Valter, Dina, o s v. Er det rigtigt? Heltinden der nok bliver en Rolle for Fr Heiberg maa da idealiseres grumme meget, eller maaske Ulfeldts tro Hustru skal staae som et lyst Billed ved Siden af hende, dog derved taber vel Hovedpersonen for meget? Alligevel vilde jeg gjerne høre Dem skildre en Leonore, hun vilde sikkert blive ligesaa elskværdig som Flaminia, ligesaa kvindelig som Louise i »O T«, det forstaar sig der maatte jo blandes nogle kongelige Træk ind i dette Billede, ogsaa det vil De forstaa.[479]

This letter's first lines almost seem to be directed at Adam Oehlenschläger,[480] who turned Dina's and Ulfeldt's fate into a stage play nine years later. Andersen will later on reveal that he had been advised against staging his version of Dina's story due

---

475 Based on the description provided in the tale, Flemming Hovmann concludes that Andersen must have confused the location of the original Blue Tower, which was part of the Copenhagen Castle (1370-1731), with the new Blue Tower (1731-1848), which was originally called *Frederiksholm arrest* and was located on the backside of today's Christiansborg Palace. See Hovmann, Flemming. 'Gudfaders Billedbog'. In *H. C. Andersens Eventyr 7: Kommentar*, ed. Flemming Hovmann. Copenhagen: Reitzel, 1990, p. 329.

476 *Druknehuset* was a warehouse at Langebro in Copenhagen, which acted as a storage place for unidentified victims of drowning from its erection in 1809 until its demolition in 1902.

477 Andersen, Hans Christian. *Fodreise fra Holmens Canal*, p. 34.

478 Andersen, Hans Christian. *H. C. Andersens Dagbøger 1825-1875 I: 1825-1834*, ed. Helga Vang Lauridsen. Copenhagen: Gads Forlag, 1995 (1971), p. 176: »Søndag den 15 September. Jeg sov ikke den hele / Nat, den ene Idee til et Arbeide krydsede mig efter den anden, nu stod Jerusalem Skomager til mig, mystisk og sælsom, nu Eleonore i Fængslet, nu von Qvoten komisk og fornem. –«.

479 Letter addressed to Hans Christian Andersen and dated 22 September 1837, reproduced in *H. C. Andersens brevveksling med Henriette Hanck*, ed. Svend Larsen. Copenhagen: Ejnar Munksgaard, 1941 (Anderseniana 9), p. 201.

480 Andersen, however, stated that his version of Ulfeldt's *historie*, would have been entirely different from Oehlenschläger's stage play (see Andersen, Hans Christian. *Mit Livs Eventyr 1*, ed. H. Topsøe-Jensen. Copenhagen: Gyldendal, 1975, p. 356).

to its delicate subject matter (see below). Nevertheless, the fate of Ulfeldt's women, especially his wife, continued to haunt him.

A passage from Andersen's *Märchen meines Lebens ohne Dichtung* from 1847 reveals the extent of his sympathy for the traitor's wife. In this autobiography, Andersen recounts his third journey to Italy in 1846, one of his stopovers being Trieste. There he remained for five days and, while visiting the opera, made the acquaintance of the Governor of Trieste, Count Johann Nepomuk Waldstein-Wartenberg,[481] who was also a descendant of Leonora Christina, »der edelsten aller dänischen Frauen«.[482] Only for a short while, though, Andersen's thoughts dwell on 'the noblest of all Danish women', for they quickly turn to the object of her own admiration:

> Schon bevor Oehlenschläger seine Dina schrieb, welche eine Episode aus Ulfeld's Leben behandelt, beschäftigte mich dieser Stoff, ich wollte ihn auf das Theater bringen, aber damals glaubte man, daß es nicht gestattet werden würde, und ich gab es auf; über Ulfeld sind seitdem nur vier Zeilen von mir geschrieben worden:[483]
> Verschwiegen ward die Tugend, nicht Dein Fehler,
> So daß die Welt nicht Deine Größe kennt;
> Doch setzte Dir die Liebe Prachtdenkmäler,
> Da sich von Dir das beste Weib nicht trennt.[484]

Andersen's ardour for Leonora Christina is well known and fits the national romanticism of the 19th century. All the more surprising are the lines dedicated to Corfitz Ulfeldt, the traitor. However, of all the writers admiring Leonora Christina, Hans Christian Andersen was probably the one who was also most inclined to sympathise

---

481 Cf. Rossel, Sven Hakon. »Do You Know the Land, Where the Lemon Trees Bloom?« Hans Christian Andersen and Italy. Rome: Edizioni Nuova Cultura, 2009 (Intersezioni. Testi, Culture, Religioni: Pubblicazioni del Dipartimento di Studi Storico-Religiosi 1), p. 154.

482 Andersen, Hans Christian. *Das Märchen meines Lebens ohne Dichtung*. Leipzig: Lorck, 1847, p. 131.

483 Here, Andersen is most likely alluding to the drama he mentioned in a letter to Henriette Hanck. It is, however, curious that he admits to have written not more than four lines about Ulfeldt so far, while in his letter from 1837 he promised his friend that she would hear the entire tragedy soon (see letter addressed to Henriette Hanck and dated 20 September 1837, reproduced in *H. C. Andersens brevveksling med Henriette Hanck*, p. 200). His work must have come to a halt almost immediately after this letter to Henriette Hanck.

484 Andersen, Hans Christian. *Das Märchen meines Lebens ohne Dichtung*, p. 131: »Already before Oehlenschläger wrote his Dina, which narrates an episode of Ulfeld's life, I was captured by this topic, I wanted to stage it, but back then it was thought that that would not be accepted, and I gave up on the idea; ever since I have only written four lines about Ulfeld: Concealed was your virtue, not your vice / and thus the world is unaware of your grandeur / but love is your monument / since the best of all women would not leave your side«.

with her husband. The world-famous fairy-tale writer, who is internationally known as a Danish icon, often felt rejected and misunderstood by his fellow countrymen and was thus always happy to travel (for example to his beloved Italy). In 1843, when Andersen was in Paris and heard about how his play *Agnete og Havmanden* had received catcalls at home, he sent a resentful letter to his friend Henriette Wulff:

> De Danske kunne være onde, kolde, sataniske! – et Folk der passer for de vaade skimmelgrønne Øer, hvorfra Tycho Brahe blev forjaget, hvor Eleonore Uhlfeldt sad i Fængsel, Ambrosius Stub var Herremændenes Nar, og endnu mange, som hine ville behandles ilde, til Folkets Navn klinger som et Sagni [sic!].[485]

Due to his own bad experience, Hans Christian Andersen would not judge Corfitz Ulfeldt based on his reputation amongst Danes. Instead, and just like Count Waldstein-Wartenberg (see Chapter 1.2.1.), Andersen names Leonora Christina as a warrantor of Ulfeldt's character. For Andersen, raising attention to Ulfeldt's good sides through his wife may also have been a pragmatic decision. Oehlenschläger's *Dina*, though generally received with favourable criticism, had demonstrated how a Danish audience could take a reinterpretation of commonly accepted history amiss (see Chapter 2.3.2.). Already before the practice proved the theory, Andersen was assured that an entire stage play on Corfitz Ulfeldt could only cause outraged reactions.[486] He did eventually publish his lines on Ulfeldt, yet he only dared to do so by appeasing his potential readers with the memory of the daughter of the Danes' beloved Christian IV.

---

[485] Letter addressed to Henriette Wulff and dated 29 April 1843, reproduced in Andersen, Hans Christian and Henriette Wulff. *H.C. Andersen og Henriette Wulff. En Brevveksling*, ed. H. Topsøe-Jensen. Odense: Flensteds Forlag, 1959, p. 330.

[486] In *Mit Livs Eventyr* (1855), Andersen elaborates on the reasons for his decision not to stage Ulfeldt's story: »Alt før Oehlenschläger tænkte paa at skrive sin ‚Dina', beskjæftigede dette Stof mig, jeg vilde behandle det for Scenen og havde alt samlet en Deel historiske Materialier dertil, da der blev sagt mig, at det laae vor Tid for nær, og at Kong Frederik den Sjette ikke tillod, at nogen af hans Forfædre, senere end Christian den Fjerde turde bringes paa Theatret; ved Grev Rantzau-Breitenburg fik jeg Vished om, at det forholdt sig saaledes, Christian den Ottende, som da var Prinds, opmuntrede mig imidlertid til at udarbejde Digtningen, ‚den kan jo læses!' sagde han, men jeg opgav den. Da Kong Christian den Ottende kom paa Thronen, faldt disse Hensyn bort, og en Dag sagde Oehlenschläger til mig: ‚Nu har jeg skrevet en Dina, som De jo engang tænkte paa!'« (see Andersen, Hans Christian. *Mit Livs Eventyr 1*, p. 356).

2.2.2. Mathilde Fibiger: *En Skizze efter det virkelige Liv* (1853) – Impulse for Nationalistic Debate

> *An:* 1678: den 4. Marti bleff min Naboeske en Quinde weed Naffn *Lucia*, som tiente F. Rigitze Grubbe, bleff beskylt effter Iomfrue *Agneta Sophia Budde*, att hun haffde werret den, som paa sin fruis wegne haffde offwer-talt hender, att forgiffwe Greffwinnen F. Birrete Skeel, oc *Lucia* haffde bragt hender Gifftet; Der war windisbyrd, att *Lucia* haffde kiøbt Gifftet. Den quinde war en Standhafftig Troefast Tiennerinne; Hun haffde langt et frit Moed, tog imod alt ond hender paalagdis, med allerstørste Taalmodighed: war trøstig i ded Mørcke fengsel, haffde twende Mand-persohner til *Cammerader*, som baade Skreeg, Suckede oc græd; Fra Greffwinne Skeel (som skulle Spiiße hender) bleff hender Sendt Kiød, som krøb fuld aff Maddicker, oc Mullet Brøe. Ieg forbarmede mig offwer hender, (icke for henders Fruis Skyld, thi den haffwer intet gott forskylt aff mig, oc ille belønt forrige tiders welgierninger) Ieg gaff *Lucia* Maed oc dricke, oc penge til att formilde Gert med, som war hender for haard: Hun bleff Piinet, wille dog icke bekiende ded ringste aff ded hender beskyltist; forswarede altiid sin Frue[.]
>
> (*Jammers Minde*, p. 268)

Leonora Christina's description of the steadfast, loyal and brave maid Lucia is overtly sympathetic with the offender. Despite the serious accusations raised against Lucia, Leonora Christina praises the quality that connects these two women, i.e. an allegiance that is stronger than any other commitment and that overlooks the concern for one's own safety. The colliding obligations towards ethics or the rule of law on one side, and towards a master or mistress on the other side do not appear to trouble Leonora Christina in the least. She considers a commitment to a master or, in other words, a husband to be unconditional. The absoluteness of Leonora Christina's loyalty has since astonished many a scholar and writer,[487] including Mathilde Fibiger, who utilises Leonora Christina's name and reputation to engage her protagonists in a polarising discussion regarding a woman's obligations towards either fatherland or husband.

Mathilde Fibiger (1830-1872) is known as one of the foremost Danish feminist writers.[488] Her radical ideas on women's emancipation provoked a nationwide de-

---

[487] See, for example, Julius Lange's reading of Leonora Christina's statement on Lucia (Lange, Julius. 'Contra Leonora Christina', p. 727).

[488] Cf. Busk-Jensen, Lise. 'Romantikbegrebet og feministisk litteraturhistorieskrivning'. In *Nordische Romantik: Akten der XVII. Studienkonferenz der International Association for Scandinavian Studies 7.-12. August 1988 in Zürich und Basel*, ed. Oskar Bandle et al. Basel and Frankfurt: Helbing & Lichtenhahn, 1991 (Beiträge zur nordischen Philologie 19), pp. 314-316.

bate, which eventually was not resolved in her favour. Despite the public support of Johan Ludvig Heiberg, who also published her novel *Clara Raphael* and provided it with a favourable preamble, the alternative marriage and relationship models depicted in Fibiger's novels aroused mostly negative reactions, which in turn forced the young writer to abandon her literary career after publishing only three books and henceforth earn her living with a more modest profession. *En Skizze efter det virkelige Liv* was Fibiger's second novel and it received the least attention of all her work. This is perhaps due to the fact that *En Skizze* was neither as innovative as *Clara Raphael* (1851)[489] nor as shocking as *Minona* (1854).[490]

Despite Mathilde Fibiger's fame of constituting the Danish vanguard of feminism, *En Skizze* does not primarily provide additional material for the discussion concerning Leonora Christina's position within the feminist discourse presented in Chapter 1.2.[491] Fibiger was not only an advocate of the women's movement, but she had also been under the immediate impression of the historical events of Denmark's 1840's – the First Schleswig War (1848-1851) and the abolition of absolutism in 1848 – and was thus also a fierce patriot.[492] It was this subject matter – an individual's obligation to their home country as opposed to other obligations – that provided an impetus to discuss the actions of Leonora Christina.

All of Mathilde Fibiger's novels address the topic of loyalty towards one's fatherland and when dealing with this topic, the protagonist, usually a partial

---

489 Cf. Jørgensen, Aage. 'Mathilde Fibiger og damernes emancipation'. In Jørgensen, Aage. *Kundskaben på ondt og godt: En Studiebog*. Aarhus: Akademisk Boghandel, 1968, p. 102: Jørgensen deems Clara Raphael to be of mediocre artistic quality but at the same time »må det dog stå fast, at Clara Raphael var startskuddet til den stedsevarende diskussion om kvindens stilling i det danske samfund«.

490 Fibiger's idea of a married couple living like brother and sister, first developed in *Clara Raphael*, receives a problematic twist in *Minona*, where the protagonists, brother and sister, indeed fall in love with each other.

491 By 1853, Mathilde Fibiger had of course not yet been familiar with Leonora Christina's own thoughts regarding equality between men and women, which in some ways resemble those of Mathilde Fibiger in its consolidation of biblical doctrines and new ideas. Cf. Clara Raphael's sixth letter to Mathilde: »Mand, Kvinde, er intet Heelt for sig, men ved en aandelig Forening bliver hvert et Menneske i Ordets ædleste Forstand: Gud skabte Mennesket i sit Billede. Var det nu kun Kvindens Bestemmelse, at være Mændenes Husholdersker, eller et smukt Legetøi, hvormed de beskjæftigede sig i ledige Timer, da vilde Menneskeslægten aldrig opnaae nogen Enhed« (Fibiger, Mathilde. *Clara Raphael*. In Fibiger, Mathilde. *Clara Raphael. Minona*, ed. Lise Busk-Jensen. Valby: Borgen, 1994 (Danske klassikere), p. 50).

492 This aspect of Mathilde Fibiger's writings has so far been neglected, as it was entirely overshadowed by the impact of the author's feminist ideas. However, Lise Busk-Jensen does mention Fibiger's political ardour in an article on *Clara Raphael*. There, she also highlights the connection between Fibiger's feminist ideas and her nationalism. See Busk-Jensen, Lise. 'Kvindebevægelsens første manifest': Om Mathilde Fibigers Clara Raphael'. In *Nordisk kvindelitteraturhistorie 2: Faderhuset: 1800-tallet*, ed. Elisabeth Møller Jensen. Copenhagen: Rosinante/Munksgaard, 1993, p. 313: »Hendes [Clara Raphael's] opbrud var inspireret af den nationale begejstring, som krigen og de politiske omvæltninger havde vakt. Nu sidder hun ude på landet uden at have fundet den livsopgave, hun søgte. Hun får den idé, at det er kønnet, det står i vejen; var hun blot en mand, ville der være opgaver nok at løse«.

self-portrait of the author,[493] always takes up a decidedly patriotic position.[494] By unfolding discussions of public interest in her writings and making female characters actively take part in them, Fibiger discreetly negates the formerly common notion of women belonging to the private sphere, whereas the public was reserved for men.[495] In Fibiger's diverse writings, Corfitz Ulfeldt is concordantly regarded as the epitome of a traitor,[496] whereas in *En Skizze*, the debate is extended to the traitor's spouse and the potentially colliding obligations of a married woman. When the four main characters of the novel spend the evening at a soirée, Volmer initiates a game, which requires the participants to name their personal human ideal, both male and female. Without hesitation, Victoria names »,[d]en tappre Landsoldat' og ,Dronning Margrethe'«,[497] whereas the other young ladies choose Frederik Høedt and Alma,[498] Wiehe and Johanne Luise Heiberg,[499] the composer Niels W. Gade (1817-1890) and »Jomfru Lehmann«,[500] and finally Frederik Christian Sibbern and »Fru Jerichaus Danmark«.[501] At this point, Margrethe is about to leave the gathering when Victoria reveals her sister's ideals: »,Holger Danske' og – ja det er haardt at skulde sige det – ,Eleonore Ul-

---

493 Although the protagonist of *Clara Raphael* addresses her letters to a friend called Mathilde, it is Clara Raphael herself, who constitutes a hidden (albeit only partial) self-portrait of her creator. In his preamble to *Clara Raphael*, Johan Ludvig Heiberg made no secret of the fact that many of the ideas stated by Clara Raphael reflected its anonymous author's own thoughts (Heiberg, Johan Ludvig. 'Udgiveren til Læserne'. In Fibiger, Mathilde. *Clara Raphael. Minona*, ed. Lise Busk-Jensen. Valby: Borgen, 1994 (Danske klassikere), p. 10). Lise Busk-Jensen, on the other hand, advises against a complete equalisation of Clara Raphael and Mathilde Fibiger because as it seems too simplistic a conclusion (see Busk-Jensen, Lise. 'Efterskrift'. In Fibiger, Mathilde. *Clara Raphael. Minona*, ed. Lise Busk-Jensen. Valby: Borgen, 1994 (Danske klassikere), p. 256).

494 See, for example, Fibiger, Mathilde. *Clara Raphael*, p. 56.

495 Cf. Dalager, Stig and Anne-Marie Mai. *Danske kvindelige Forfattere 1*, p. 187.

496 E.g., Fibiger, Mathilde. *Clara Raphael*, p. 67.

497 Fibiger, Mathilde. *En Skizze efter det virkelige Liv*. Copenhagen: Reitzel, 1853, p. 102.

498 Frederik Høedt (1820-1885) was a Danish actor, who debuted as Hamlet at the Royal Theatre in Copenhagen in 1851. Alma is a character in Frederik Paludan-Müller's epic poem (1809-1876) *Adam Homo*, published in parts in 1841 and 1848.

499 This is most likely a reference to one of the Wiehe brothers – Michael, Wilhelm and Johan Wiehe. All three were Danish actors, but Michael Wiehe (1820-1864) was the most famous one amongst the trio, especially due to his popular interplay with Johanne Luise Heiberg (e.g., as Romeo and Juliet).

500 Since these two names were chosen by »den musikalske Frøken Staffeldt« (Fibiger, Mathilde. *En Skizze*, p. 103), this must be a reference to a female member of the contemporary Danish musical milieu. Lise Busk-Jensen kindly informed me that this is most likely a reference to Caroline Lehmann (1825-1879), an opera singer, who debuted in 1848 and went abroad in 1852 to pursue a career in Germany and subsequently in America, where she was indeed successful. Caroline Lehmann furthermore remained unmarried, hence the title *Jomfru*.

501 Frederik Christian Sibbern (1785-1872) was a Danish writer, who had his literary breakthrough with *Efterladte Breve af Gabrielis* (1826), whereas »Fru Jerichaus Danmark« (ibid., p. 104) refers to a painting by Elisabeth Jerichau Baumann (1819-1881) called *Moder Danmark* (1851).

feld'«.⁵⁰² Volmer does not quite understand Victoria's attitude towards Leonora Christina; however, the choices of the surrounding women may shed some light on Victoria's contempt. A great deal of the names dropped in this game belong to contemporary actors and actresses, until Volmer finally steps in and tells one of the participants, a young lady who cannot decide on two ideals since all of the names suggested by Volmer belong to people »enten gamle eller comiske«, that she does not need to restrict her choice to the theatrical circle: »Frøken Staffeldt gik allerede et Skridt udenfor denne Regel, idet hun opsøgte sit Ideal i en Bog, og skulde det ikke være mueligt at der i *det virkelige Liv* [my italics] fandtes een bekjendt Mand eller Kvinde.«⁵⁰³

On the background of Victoria's predictions regarding the evening, one may achieve a better understanding of Victoria's depreciatory conduct throughout this conversation. In a private talk preceding the soirée, she had warned Volmer about the attending women's superficial interest in art and culture:

> Dernæst har jeg den Fornøielse at forberede Dem paa at lære Byens to Autoriteter, Skjønheden og Geniet at kjende. Den Ældste har baade af Natur og Udseende meget tilfælleds med utillavet Havresuppe. Den Yngste ligner Damerne paa de allerfineste Spillekort. De ere begge aandrige – hjemme i Æsthetiken, hvor de kjende hver moderne Forfatters Navn, Titelen paa hans Skrifter og Navnene paa de Personer deri, som Conversationen har gjort til sit Bytte. Desuden spille, synge og dandse de naturligviis til Fuldkommenhed.⁵⁰⁴

As anticipated by Victoria, her companions choose their ideals only from the contemporary literary and theatrical scene. Their uniform taste – also predicted by Victoria⁵⁰⁵ – soon causes trouble when some ladies have the same ideals in mind. Margrethe and Victoria are the only ones who do not choose contemporary people to personify their respective ideals, but Victoria does not approve of her sister's choice either:

---

502 Ibid., p. 105.
503 Ibid., p. 103.
504 Ibid., p. 96.
505 Ibid., p. 97.

»At Eleonore Ulfeld var en Heltinde for Mænd, forstaaer jeg godt!« svarede Victoria med spottende Stemme. Thi en Mand var hendes Guddom! Naar vi saaledes dyrke dem, og ligge paa Knæ for deres Fuldkommenhed – saa faae vi Heltinderang. Men naar Ære, Fædreland og Religion er os helligere end deres Kjærlighed – saa er vi svage, hjerteløse, ufølsomme Væsner. Jeg kan tænke mig at en Mand i sin Forfængelighed dømmer saaledes, men at et Fruentimmer ikke har mere Følelse for sit menneskelige Kald, at Du Margrethe, der ellers er saa stolt, kan beundre at Christian den Fjerdes Datter forlod sit Fædreland, for at tale en Forræders Sag ved fremmede Hoffer – det har jeg tidt undret mig over![506]

Victoria's sister Margrethe, on the other hand, does not understand the former's antipathy towards Leonora Christina:

Troer Du da at han i hendes Tanker var en Forræder? Nei – en miskjendt Mand, forurettet af sit Fædreland. Havde hun da Forpligtelser derimod, kunde hun slutte sig til hans Fjender? Selv om hun elskede Danmark som en Moder, maatte hun jo forlade det for at følge sin Mand. Det er ikke alene en Kvindes gode Ret, men en guddommelig Lov, hun skal adlyde.[507]

Victoria's main point of criticism is Leonora Christina's compliance with her husband and his role in Denmark's history. Despite Fibiger's central position in Denmark's feminist movement, Victoria's view is not restricted to this context, but instead extended to the question of the relationship between the individual and its country. Victoria's very own ideals are Margrethe I of Denmark and »[d]en tappre Landsoldat«,[508] both of which portray active forces shaping Denmark's history – hence Victoria's dismissive comment following the addition of Jerichau's *Moder Danmark* to the list of ideals: »Hun troede vist at jeg mente Bissens Landsoldat!«[509] Between 1850 and 1858, the Danish sculptor Herman Wilhelm Bissen (1798-1868) had been working on a statue called *Den tapre Landsoldat* (or *Landsoldaten*), which commemorates the effort of the common soldier during the First Schleswig War and Denmark's subsequent victory. The statue was erected in 1858, but already in 1850 Bissen, as well as Jens Adolf Jerichau (1816-1883), were asked to hand in their sketches for a potential memorial in Fredericia, in commemoration of the Danish

---

506 Ibid., p. 105.
507 Ibid., p. 106.
508 *Landsoldat* is an older term designating Danish men liable to military service, as opposed to foreign soldiers enlisted by the Danish army.
509 Fibiger, Mathilde. *En Skizze*, p. 105.

victory in the Battle of Fredericia (1849). Thus, knowledge of this nascent statue must have already spread by 1853. Judging by Victoria's comment on Bissen's *Landsoldat*, she must indeed have had the living soldier in mind, not his effigy. Hence, her criticism is directed at both her sister and the rest of the women present, for idealising static, representative, fictional, and largely unpolitical fashionable figures instead of living individuals who changed the course of Danish history.

This criticism may be viewed as being directed at the ideologies of the preceding Danish Golden Age. The leading artists and writers of this period, especially those of the first three decades of the 19th century, were notoriously unpolitical. Inspired by the French Revolution of 1830 (also known as the July Revolution), Denmark eventually experienced a re-politicisation of public life which resulted in the formation of two schools: the traditional school, still focussing on purely aesthetic topics, and the modern, politicised school.[510] This re-politicisation of public debate is reflected in Fibiger's novel not only through its protagonist Victoria, who – like Clara Raphael – is a very polemic character, but also through her sister Margrethe. Otherwise a rather indifferent character, she is revealed to have been a passionate observer of the First Schleswig War. Upon being asked about her unusual enthusiasm during that time, Margrethe answers the following:

> Jeg troede at den Tids Bevægelse ikke alene var en Kraftyttring, men en Livsyttring. Jeg ansaae den ikke alene for et Beviis paa at det danske Mod er bevaret, men paa et Varsel fra den danske Aand, til Tegn paa at den snart vilde afkaste sit Skjul under Tidens Usselhed og Sløvhed og træde frem som en Kjæmpe til lysende Bedrifter i Aandens Verden. Det første var sandt: slaaes kan den danske Mand endnu, og Slesvig vandt vi i Striden. Men det andet var en Feiltagelse, thi alt hvad vi have tilbage af Holger Danskes Aand er hans Søvnighed, hvormed vi rimeligvis miste Slesvig igjen.[511]

At this point, the dispute turns into a discussion about the question of *Danskhed*, about what it means to be Danish. It would exceed the objective of this study to analyse the diverse positions taken by Fibiger's fictional characters, especially since it appears to be futile to determine, which of the positions reflects Fibiger's own thoughts on the matter. However, as defined by the post-1830 re-politicisation movement, the debate itself may just as well portray Fibiger's attitude: a desire for an open discussion on the most delicate national subjects. Furthermore, research on Fi-

---

510 Nygaard, Bertel. 'Anti-Politics: Modern politics and its critics in Denmark, 1830-1848', Scandinavian Journal of History 36/4 (2011), p. 420.
511 Fibiger, Mathilde. *En Skizze*, p. 107.

biger's discourses has not yet yielded clear results in terms of which character may constitute a hidden self-portrait of the writer. As stated above by Lise Busk-Jensen, it would be an oversimplification to equate Mathilde Fibiger with her female protagonists alone. In his countless discussions with Victoria, Volmer, too, utters many a freethinking idea on the relationship between the sexes. Fibiger's novels are full of heated debates; hence, it appears most conceivable that the authoress provided her works with plentiful dialogues in order to give her own thoughts enough space by unfolding them through her characters' diverse voices.

Nevertheless, there always seems to be one character, which bears a more pronounced mark of Fibiger's own experiences. In *En Skizze* it is Victoria, the character bearing the closest resemblance to Clara Raphael. In his preamble to *Clara Raphael*, Johan Ludvig Heiberg did not disclose the identity of the person who wrote this epistolary novel, but he could not forbear to hint at the author's sex and age:

> Hvad jeg allerførst maa begynde med, og ligesom stille i Spidsen for mine Meddelelser, er, at Skriftet er forfattet af en ganske ung, omtrent tyveaarig Pige, og at Læseren her modtager det, ganske som det er kommet fra hendes Haand, uden at jeg har forandret en Tøddel deri. Naar jeg betragter denne Meddelelse som den første og vigtigste for den Læser, som vil have den rette Nydelse af Bogen og bedømme den rigtigt, da er det ikke [...] for at lade Forfatterindens Ungdom tjene til Undskyldning for Bogens mulige Mangler; tvertimod, det er, for at ikke den stærkt udprægede Characteer med sin store udadvendte Energie og sin ligesaa store inadvendte Resignation, i Forbindelse med den ualmindelige Modenhed i Fremstillingen, Foredraget, Stilen, skal bringe Læseren paa den vildledende [...] Tanke, at Forfatterinden er en bedaget Dame, der har et mangeaarigt Livs Erfaringer og Betragtninger at øse af.[512]

While Heiberg commented on the author's age with the sole intention of commending her for the results of her reflections, her articulateness and her renunciation of passivity,[513] other readers of *Clara Raphael* took exception to a damsel's criticism of long-established notions. In her second novel, *En Skizze*, Fibiger unfolds a discussion regarding a woman's reputation, which may have been inspired by her own experiences following the publication of *Clara Raphael*. In this scene, Volmer attempts to console his friend Fredrik, who fears Victoria's unconventional ideas may harm her renown:

---

512 Heiberg, Johan Ludvig. 'Udgiveren til Læserne', p. 9.
513 Ibid., p. 10.

Lad os først og see at komme ud over den gamle Overtro at en Dames Rygte er andet end hvad vort Rygte ogsaa er: af al rørlig Eiendom den man mindst selv er Herre over, og som man derfor mindst af alt maae lade sin Velfærd beroe paa. […] I den Henseende vilde jeg raade til en kvindelig Emancipation, jeg vilde sige til dem: Emancipeer Dig fra ethvert Hensyn der generer Dig, fra Moden, fra Rygtet og – om muligt – en lille Smule fra Forfængeligheden; saa vil Du ingen Frihed savne![514]

While most critics of Mathilde Fibiger did not deny her literary talent, many conservative writers did not take kindly to her ideas on women's emancipation.[515] It is worthwhile noting that not only men, but also some women rejected Fibiger's call for equal life choices for men and women. Accordingly, in *En Skizze* it is a young woman, who disclaims Clara Raphael's (i.e., Mathilde Fibiger's) achievements: »'Clara Raphael er den eneste bekjendte Dame jeg har hørt Tale om i det virkelige Liv, naar jeg undtager Skuespillerinder. Men hende kan jeg da ikke sværme for!' afbrød hun ham«.[516] Whereas one single character in Fibiger's novel is thus hardly identical with Mathilde Fibiger, the autobiographically inspired notions and statements in *En Skizze* are too abundant to be dismissed as purely incidental. Hence, it is by all means possible that Victoria's opinion on Leonora Christina was shared by her creator. But whatever Fibiger's own attitude towards the traitor's wife, by 1869 it had changed.

When *Jammers Minde* was published, Mathilde Fibiger had already given up on her literary career and contented herself with a position as a telegrapher in Aarhus, which she occupied until her death in 1872. She, too, was eager to learn about Leonora Christina's experiences in the Blue Tower and despite her depreciatory comment in *En Skizze*, the aged Mathilde Fibiger seems to have enjoyed *Jammers Minde* a great deal.[517] In 1870, Fibiger wrote a review of *Jammers Minde* for the Swedish *Tidskrift för hemmet*, which could not have been any more divergent from Victoria's opinion almost two decades earlier: »Ja, hun er Danskheden selv, kunde man sige! Derfor möder vistnok enhver Dansk i denne Bog noget længe kjendt,

---

514 Fibiger, Mathilde. *En Skizze*, p. 45f.
515 In the epilogue to her edition of *Clara Raphael*, Lise Busk-Jensen gives a detailed account of the so-called *Clara Raphael*-feud. See Busk-Jensen, Lise in Fibiger, Mathilde. 'Efterskrift', pp. 267-274. A great deal of the criticism directed at Fibiger's first novel dispraised her lack of realism, i.e., the escapist nature of her ideas. Hence, the title of her second novel, *En Skizze efter det virkelige Liv*, could constitute an answer to these accusations. Even some of the characters in *En Skizze*, such as Fru Staal, criticise Victoria's lack of realistic thinking: »'Victoria har Ret i mange enkelte Punkter!' sagde hun engang, 'men selv der har hun Uret i Maaden, hvorpaa hun vil forandre det. […]'« (Fibiger, Mathilde. *En Skizze*, p. 29f).
516 Ibid., p. 103.
517 Cf. Andersen, Vilhelm. *Illustreret Dansk litteraturhistorie 4: Det nittende Aarhundredes anden Halvdel*. Copenhagen: Gyldendal, 1925, p. 112.

elsket, ofte *savnet*, endskjöndt vel neppe nogen har tænkt sig Leonore Christine netop saaledes«.[518] One can only guess how Fibiger imagined Leonora Christina to have been, but her following statement indicates that she had previously considered her Ulfeldt's accomplice: »Saaledes soner hun paa dobbelt Maade hvad Ulfeldt forbröd. Jeg har behövet Tid til at skille de To fra hinanden i min Opfattelse, eller rettere: til at faae dem saaledes forenede, at hendes Uskyld hæver hans Skyld«.[519]

Mathilde Fibiger openly reflects on her change of mind and delivers thus a valid example of how the publication of *Jammers Minde* affected Danish notions of Leonora Christina, especially in connection with her husband. Both Count Waldstein-Wartenberg and Hans Christian Andersen (and, in a more complex way, Adam Oehlenschläger) perceived Leonora Christina's love for her husband to act as a warrantor of his character. However, those three men's thoughts on the affair were published before the broad public became familiar with Leonora Christina's autobiography. As stated in his preamble to the first edition of *Jammers Minde*, Count Waldstein-Wartenberg was hoping that by giving a voice to Leonora Christina, that voice would indirectly speak on behalf of Corfitz Ulfeldt, thus exonerating him. However, *Jammers Minde* did not yield the desired result, as demonstrated by Mathilde Fibiger's reaction: »Ligesom *hun* skjuler Ulfeldts Bröde i sin Kjærlighed til ham ved *ikke at tro paa den*, skjule vi den i vor Kjærlighed til hende ved at *glemme den*. Og saaledes udsletter ›Jammers-Mindet‹ Corfitz Ulfeldts Eftermæle«.[520] By witnessing Leonora Christina in a context independent of her husband, the readers of *Jammers Minde* quickly learned to separate her from Ulfeldt – with ambiguous effects on the reception of both spouses. Instead of resulting in a re-evaluation of her husband, Leonora Christina's fate and character have thus overshadowed Corfitz Ulfeldt's reputation.

Fibiger's unchanged evaluation of Ulfeldt after reading Leonora Christina's legacy is exemplified by her thoughts on Ulfeldt's very own residue in Copenhagen, *skamstøtten*. This 'pillar of shame' was erected in 1664 on Gråbrødretorv (called *Ulfeldts Plads* for the ensuing two centuries), Ulfeldt's former place of residence. In 1842, the pillar was removed and is now displayed at the inner yard of the National Museum of Denmark (*Nationalmuseet*) in Copenhagen, while a plaque on Gråbrødretorv indicates the pillar's former location. Unlike others – e.g. Hans Christian Andersen, who regarded the removal of this pillar as a token of Danish kindhear-

---

518 Fibiger, Mathilde. Letter reproduced in E. K. 'Nordiska Qvinnor. Leonora Christina Ulfeldt', Tidskrift för hemmet 12/2 (1870), p. 108.
519 Ibid.
520 Ibid., p. 110.

tedness (see Chapter 2.2.3.) – Fibiger attributes no deeper meaning to this act, as it does not signify any change of attitude towards Ulfeldt:

> Nu som för, klæber »Spot, Skam og Skjændsel« ved Landsforræderiet, og at Stötten ligesom er faldet af sig selv, ligger ene i at Straffen var barnagtig i Forhold til Bröden, skjöndt den i sin Tid var betydningsfuld nok, som et Udtryk for Folkets retfærdige Vrede, og deri: at den ulykkelige Mands Eftermæle har gjort Skamstötten overflödig og stillet den i Skygge.[521]

Whereas Fibiger was thus steadfast in her notion of Corfitz Ulfeldt, she proved to be all the more receptive towards Leonora Christina's self-portrayal. Some of Fibiger's statements are reminiscent of Leonora Christina's own suggestive terminology, such as Fibiger's denomination of Leonora Christina's imprisonment as »Martyrium«[522] and her clear contrasting of Leonora Christina and her enemies.[523] While Fibiger criticised Leonora Christina's passive submission under Ulfeldt's will against her fatherland and her own father's heritage, the testimony of the same woman uncoupled from her husband seems to have altered the picture. *Jammers Minde* did not change history – Leonora Christina was still the woman who had followed the military campaign against her home country. However, Leonora Christina's very own representation of herself (rather than of the affair) made the motivation for her actions appear in a different light. As stated in Chapter 1.2.2., Leonora Christina followed the autobiographical principle of identity through consistency. Mathilde Fibiger may have been highly receptive towards this strategy, as it allowed for an identification of integrity and conviction as Leonora Christina's primary motives for supporting Corfitz Ulfeldt – two virtues, which against all odds were compatible with Fibiger's patriotism.

One scene in *En Skizze* supports this hypothesis. When Margrethe defends Leonora Christina's actions by referring to her conjugal duties, this explanation is belittled by Victoria: »Jeg forstaaer mig ikke paa den Gud, der kan forlange at en christen Mand skal tage sin Hustrue med i Skjændsel og Vanære – Hedningen lod dog

---

521 Fibiger, Mathilde in E. K. 'Nordiska Qvinnor', p. 108.
522 Ibid., p. 110.
523 Ibid., p. 109: »Og ligesaa afmægtig som han var i sit Forsög paa at skade Fædrelandet – [...] ligesaa afmægtig var hendes Fjenders Ondskab – ja *saa* magteslös, at alt hvad der var udtænkt for at fornedre hende, kun tjente til at gjöre hendes Storhed aabenbar, og den bittre Kalk, de rakte hende, blev til en Livsensdrik paa hendes Læber«. Note the resemblance to Leonora Christina's own analogy of her situation with Jesus' martyrdom: »Der ware beeske sticker Brød for mig tilskaarren, oc bitter Kaarß-Galle for mig indskenket vdi ded Blaa-Taarn paa Kiøbenhaffns-Slott, did skulle ieg, ded att Æde oc att vddricke« (*Jammers Minde*, p. 10*).

kun sin Hund og sin Træl begrave med sig«.⁵²⁴ Margrethe answers with an unusual defence of Ulfeldt's actions:

> Gives der kun een Slags Forræderi: at føre Krig – vel at mærke Hevnkrig, mod sit Fædreland? Det er en græsselig Forbrydelse, men dog menneskelig, begribelig! Og den Mand der faldt saa dybt, kan have staaet høit! Derfor agter jeg en saadan falden Kjæmpe mere – eller foragter ham mindre, om Du vil – end de Utallige der ikke svigte, fordi de aldrig have svoret til nogen Fane, aldrig have været seet i noget Helteforbund, eller været opflammet af en stor og skjøn Idee! De ere ikke udsatte for Fald – thi de søge ifølge deres Trællenatur altid instinctmæssigt det laveste Punct.⁵²⁵

Both Victoria and Margrethe oppose the hero (i.e., the ideal) to the slave (*træl*), but they express very diverging ideas of slavish behaviour. Victoria equates Leonora Christina's behaviour, or the ideology attributed to her by Margrethe, with canine or slave status. In Margrethe's eyes, however, all those who dared not even think about turning against their flag resemble slaves. Corfitz Ulfeldt represented and followed an idea of his own and is thus a very own kind of ideal, which Margrethe later on conferred to Leonora Christina, due to their conjugal bond. Leonora Christina's fall from the highest position to the lowest, due to her adherence to her ideals, is what impressed Margrethe – and later on readers of *Jammers Minde*, such as Mathilde Fibiger, as well.

2.2.3. Hans Christian Andersen: *Gudfaders Billedbog* (1868) – By Order of an Optimistic Town History

> [D]en sig glæder i Dag, kand icke were wiß paa, att hand icke Græder i Morgen[.]
> (*Jammers Minde*, p. 10)

As was demonstrated in Chapter 2.2.1., Hans Christian Andersen had always been fascinated by the Ulfeldt couple, but particularly by Corfitz Ulfeldt. The time had not yet been ripe to dedicate an entire tale or stage play to Ulfeldt, thus Andersen's focus shifted to Leonora Christina. Throughout the years, the image of Leonora Christina in the Blue Tower, a lonesome woman in a dim, fuliginous cell, sporadically occupied a few lines in his works. In 1868, Andersen turned this picture into a

---

524 Fibiger, Mathilde. *En Skizze*, p. 106.
525 Ibid.

story. Abiding by the tale's name, *Gudfaders Billedbog* presents static scenes from Leonora Christina's (among other protagonists) life, hence subduing the sense of constant development and consequently increasing the immediate impression of change. Every page of *Gudfaders Billedbog* is a different picture and a different situation; and the erratic life of the Ulfeldt couple provided a perfect chapter for Andersen's *Billedbog*: »Nu vende vi Bladet, som Lykken vender sig for de To«.[526]

The first series of pictures concerning the Ulfeldt couple shows Leonora Christina as an admittedly privileged, but otherwise regular child (»hun faaer ogsaa Riis af sin strenge Hofmesterinde«):

> Der dandser et Kongebarn paa Kongens Slot, hvor er hun yndig at see! Hun sidder paa *Christian IV*'s Skjød, hans elskede Datter *Eleonore*. I kvindelige Sæder og Dyder hun groer. Den mægtige Adels fornemste Mand *Korfits Ulfeldt* er hendes Brudgom. Hun er Barn endnu; hun faaer ogsaa Riis af sin strenge Hofmesterinde; hun klager for Kjæresten og hun har Ret. Hvor er hun kløgtig, danis og oplært, kan Græsk og Latin, synger Italiensk til sin Luth, veed at tale om Paven og Luther.[527]

Whoever is familiar with Danish history will anticipate drastic change in this child's life at the appearance of the next picture: Christian IV is dead and Frederik III is now King of Denmark. Yet, all is still right with the world, even when Sophie Amalie enters the scene: »Hvo styrer sin Hest saa vel som hun? Hvo har i Dandsen en Majestæt som hun, hvo taler med Kjendskab og Aand som Danmarks Dronning?«[528] Andersen does not speak ill of Denmark's former Queen – it would have been unwise to do otherwise. Helge Topsøe-Jensen, who has delivered a detailed analysis and a separate edition of *Gudfaders Billedbog*, relates a massive correction undertaken by Andersen regarding the later Queen Sophie Magdalene (1700-1770). A manuscript containing a first draft of *Gudfaders Billedbog* shows that Andersen had struck a criticism of the Queen and her German roots: »Nu er det den tyske Adels Tid, den strømmer herind, den fattigste Deel, den klædes i Silke faaer Huus og Gaard og Dronningen boer i det høie Slot: *Sophie Magdalene*, hun lider ei Dansk, knap sin egen Søn fordi han taler det danske Sprog, det gjør ei hans

---

526 Andersen, Hans Christian. 'Gudfaders Billedbog'. In *H. C. Andersens Nye Eventyr og Historier: 3. Række 1872 og andre sene eventyr*, ed. Erik Dal. Copenhagen: Reitzel, 1967 (H. C. Andersens Eventyr 5), p. 59.
527 Ibid., p. 58.
528 Ibid., p. 59.

Fader og Moder«.[529] Since Sophie Amalie was another Queen of German origin and is said to have never become fluent in Danish, Andersen may have consciously refrained from animadverting Leonora Christina's opponent – out of political caution. On the other hand, Andersen may simply have been impartial regarding the two women's bilateral animosity. After all, one of Andersen's main sources regarding historical events was Ludvig Holberg's *Dannemarks Riges Historie*,[530] which also indicates that Sophie Amalie may not have been the sole offender in this quarrel (see Chapter 3.2.1.). This suspicion is reinforced by a statement made by Esther, the love interest of Andersen's protagonist in the novel *At være eller ikke være* (1857):

> Hun [Esther] forstod ved et *Mønster for Qvinder*, som *Eleonore Ulfeld* nævnes i Historien og Skolebøgerne, ikke at være blød, yndelig, rørende. Det var *Eleonore* ikke, sagde hun; det var ved sin Kjærlighed og Troskab til sin Gemal i Livets Kamp og Prøvelser, at hun blev dette Mønster. Hun havde en Villie, Ord, der udtrykkede denne, menneskelige Lidenskaber, Characteer; *Esther* forlangte i Digtningen og Fremstillingen den historiske *Eleonore Ulfeld.*[531]

Whether Esther and her creator indeed held the same point of view must remain subject to speculation. In the same novel, the narrator explicitly states not to share some of Esther's notions;[532] however, in this instance Esther's criticism primarily concerns Oehlenschläger's portrayal of Leonora Christina in the drama *Dina*[533] which, as stated by Andersen, *he* would have constructed in a manner entirely different from Oehlenschläger's version (see Chapter 2.2.1.).

Be it out of personal conviction or professional consideration, Andersen chose to not appoint a specific villain in the story of Leonora Christina. Accordingly, the

---

529 Topsøe-Jensen, H. 'Efterskrift'. In *Gudfaders Billedbog. Med Efterskrift af H. Topsøe-Jensen, illustreret af Alex Secher.* Copenhagen: Nordlyndes Bogtrykkeri, 1966 (Udsendelse fra Nordlundes Bogtrykkeri 35), p. 60.

530 As well as L. J. Flamand's *Kjøbenhavn, dens ældre og nyere Historie, samt Beskrivelse* (1855). See Hovmann, Flemming. 'Gudfaders Billedbog', p. 323.

531 Andersen, Hans Christian. *At være eller ikke være*. In *H. C. Andersen. Romaner og Rejseskildringer 5: At være eller ikke være. Lykke Per,* ed. H. Topsøe-Jensen. Copenhagen: Gyldendal, 1944, p. 197.

532 Ibid.: »Esther kom paa Udstillingen, men hun var ikke enig med de Andre, og da vi her ikke ere det med hende, skal hendes Udtalelse ikke høres«.

533 Ibid., p. 197: »Hun [Esther] fandt hans [Oehlenschläger's] nordiske Qvinder for bløde, *Thora, Signe, Valborg,* de bleve ømme, rørende, astralklare christelige Qvinder, de rørte os i deres qvindelige ideale Aabenbarelse; men saaledes meente hun de ikke kunde have været i Virkeligheden. Historien og Kjæmpeviserne viste os dem anderledes, og derfor maatte Fremstillerinden kunstnerisk vide at accentuere efter det historiske, sande Forbillede. *Eleonore Ulfeld* i Dramaet ‚Dina' kaldte hun særligt forfeilet«.

origin of the following malignancy towards Eleonore[534] – triggered by the challenging words of the French legate – remains unspoken of:

> »*Eleonore Christine Ulfeldt*!« de Ord blev sagt af den franske Gesandt. »I Skjønhed, Kløgt overstraaler hun Alle.« Fra Slottets bonede Dandsegulv voxte Niddets Borre; den hængte sig fast, den filtrede ind og hvirvlede om sig Krænkelsens Haan: »Det Slegfredbarn! Hendes Karm skal holde ved Slottets Bro; hvor Dronningen kjører, skal Fruen gaae!« Det fyger med Sladder, med Opspind og Løgn.[535]

The same dance floor that had witnessed Eleonore's innocent childhood now turns into a hostile environment. The crass contrast between the two pictures is the essence of *Gudfaders Billedbog*, as the tale was inspired by Andersen's interest in the visible changes of the Copenhagen cityscape throughout the years.[536] Accordingly, the tale starts with a reference to a citywide change that occurred in the year 1858, when Copenhagen's train-oil lanterns were replaced by gas lamps: »›See det er Placaten!‹ sagde Gudfader; ›det er Indgangen til Historien, Du skal faae. Den kunde ogsaa være givet som en heel Komedie, naar man kunde have givet den: ›*Tran og Gas eller Kjøbenhavns Liv og Levnet*‹. Det er en meget god Titel!‹«.[537]

After introducing the daughter of Christian IV and her changing luck, the picture book's focus turns to Corfitz Ulfeldt, as he takes action: »Og *Ulfeldt* tager sin Hustru ved Haand i den stille Nat. Nøglerne har han til Stadens Porte; han aabner en af dem. Hestene vente derudenfor. De ride langs Stranden, og seile saa bort til det svenske Land«.[538] With the Ulfeldt couple gone, things look dim in Copenhagen as well – the city has visibly changed. Its bleak windy streets contrast with the glamour prevailing in the time when Eleonore was still visiting the Royal Palace.[539] Many a house once belonging to an influential man has been abandoned or repurposed.

---

534 In the present chapter, »Eleonore« specifically refers to the character in H. C. Andersen's text, particularly when referring to passages that do not correspond to historical events, whereas »Leonora Christina« refers to the historical person.
535 Andersen, Hans Christian. 'Gudfaders Billedbog', p. 59.
536 Hovmann, Flemming. 'Gudfaders Billedbog', p. 321.
537 Andersen, Hans Christian. 'Gudfaders Billedbog', p. 47.
538 Ibid., p. 59.
539 Cf. ibid.

Such is the case with Peder Oxe, Kaj Lykke[540] and Corfitz Ulfeldt's respective residences:

> Høit tuder Vinden og farer hen over den aabne Plads, hvor Rigshovmesterens Gaard har staaet; nu er kun tilbage af den een Steen, »den drev jeg som Rullesteen herned paa den seilende Iis,« suser Vinden, »Stenen strandede hvor siden *Tyvsø* skød op, forbandet af mig; saa kom den med i Hr. *Ulfeldts* Gaard, hvor Fruen sang til den klingende Luth, læste Græsk og Latin og kneisede stolt, nu kneiser kun Stenen[541] her med sin Inskrift: »Forræderen *Corfitz Ulfeldt* / til ævig Spot, Skam og Skjændsel.«[542]

Andersen's image of the empty Gråbrødretorv curiously resembles one scene in *Jammers Minde*: one day in 1664, after Ulfeldt's former residence had been torn down, the tower's castellan paid Leonora Christina a visit – apparently just to mock her loss of belongings and fortune:

> [The castellan] begynte att snacke om forrige tiider (Ieg wiste alt att der bleff bryt neer paa Gaarden) regnet op alt ded hand meente kunde smerte mig att haffwe mist; til min *Caret* oc hæste til; Aber (sagde hand) das alles ist nichts gegen den shønnen Hoff, (strøg den vd paa ded herligste) der liegt nu darnider vnd ist kein Stein auff den andren; ist das nicht zu beklagen mein liebes Frewlein?
>
> (*Jammers Minde*, p. 113)

The castellan's double-tongued speech does not yield the intended result, as Leonora Christina appears indifferent towards these drastic changes: »Ieg spurte hannem, Wo der Tempel *Salomones* wehre geblieben? das shiøne Gebew, da wehre kein Stein von mehr zu finden, man wuste nicht die stelle zu weißen wo der Tempel, vnd das kostbahre Kønigs Hauß gestanden« (*Jammers Minde*, p. 114). Despite Leonora Christina's imperturbable reaction, the image of her changed home obviously left an impression deep enough for her to remember this conversation. Two centu-

---

540 Kaj Lykke (1625-1699) was a Danish nobleman, who was executed in effigy in 1661, after writing a letter to one of his mistresses which contained ribald jokes about Queen Sophie Amalie, who – according to this letter – fornicated with her footmen. He lived in exile until Sophie Amalie's death in 1685; subsequently, he moved back to Denmark. As regards Kai Lykkes Gaard, Andersen is mistaken. Lykke's family had taken over Peder Oxe's (1520-1575; former Steward of the Realm) residence, which was neither in Christianshavn, nor ever turned into a penitentiary (see Hovmann, Flemming. 'Gudfaders Billedbog', p. 329). Oxe, too, was forced to spend some time in exile (from 1558 until 1566 in Germany), due to a disagreement with King Frederik II.
541 This is a reference to Corfitz Ulfeldt's *skamstøtte*.
542 Andersen, Hans Christian. 'Gudfaders Billedbog', p. 59.

ries later, the very same impression was adopted by Hans Christian Andersen, who had not even read *Jammers Minde* at this point.

Ulfeldt's story has – for now – come to an end, but what happened to his wife? Andersen has not forgotten the image of the princess in the dark tower;[543] for it is the same picture he drew in *Holger Danske* and his *Fodreise*:

> Hu-ih-hu-ih! piber Vinden med skærende Røst. I »*Blaa Taarn*« bag Slottet, hvor Havvandet slaaer mod den slimede Muur, der har hun alt siddet i mange Aar. Der er i Kamret mere Røg end Varme; det lille Vindue er høit under Loftet.[544]

Just as Holger Danske served as a frame for Denmark's alternative heroes (see Chapter 2.2.1.), Leonora Christina now provides one for her husband. She herself enters the scene in connection with her much-loved father, who now again serves as a reminder of this heroine's noble origin. The striking contrast between her former and current situation forces her to reflect on the change – another scene reminiscent of Leonora Christina's own memories:[545]

> Kong *Christian IV*'s forkjælede Barn, hun den fineste Frøken og Frue, hvor sidder hun ringe, hvor sidder hun slet! Erindringen hænger Gardin og Tapet om Fængslets tilrøgede Vægge. Hun husker sin Barndoms deilige Tid, sin Faders milde, straalende Træk; hun husker sin pragtfulde Bryllupsfærd: hendes Stoltheds Dage, hendes Trængselstid i *Holland*, i *England* og paa *Bornholm*.[546]

Although Leonora Christina's magnum opus had not been published in 1868, Andersen was familiar with some of her other work and could thus quote his heroine: »›Ei Noget synes tungt for ægte Kjærlighed!‹ Dog, da var hun hos ham, nu er hun ene, for altid ene! Hun veed ei hans Grav og Ingen veed den. ›Troskab mod Manden var al hendes Brøde.‹«.[547] The two citations are a reference to an altar cloth inscribed by Leonora Christina and donated to the Maribo church, followed by a line

---

543 Andersen is again mistaken about the location of Leonora Christina's prison (cf. Chapter 2.2.1.), as he envisions the tower behind a castle and in direct vicinity to seawater.
544 Andersen, Hans Christian. 'Gudfaders Billedbog', p. 60.
545 Cf. *Jammers Minde*, p. 92, when the nearby wedding of the Crown Prince of Saxonia, Johann Georg III, and Danish Princess Anna Sophia in 1663 induces Leonora Christina to remember the day of her own wedding: »Ieg laae oc tenkte paa den vstadige lycke, att ieg, som for 28. Aar siden haffde hafft lige saa stoer statz som nu Princeßen haffde, laae nu fangen, oc nest op til den wæg som mit Brude Sengkammers haffde wærrit, tacker Gud att ieg mig ickun lided det offwer bekümrede [...]«.
546 Andersen, Hans Christian. 'Gudfaders Billedbog', p. 60.
547 Ibid.

taken from one of the earliest literary monuments dedicated to Leonora Christina: »Hun sad i Aaringer, lange og mange, mens Livet rørte sig udenfor. Det staaer aldrig stille, men det ville vi et Øieblik her, tænke paa hende og Sangens Ord: ›Min Huusbond holdt jeg tro min Eed / I Nød og stor Elende!‹«.[548] Decades and centuries go by, until *Gudfaders Billedbog* arrives in the 18th century, in the reign of Frederik VI (1768-1839). The next visible change the city of Copenhagen undergoes is the erection of the Liberty Memorial (*Frihedsstøtten*) in 1792, in memory of the abolition of *stavnsbåndet* – a type of serfdom that bound men aged between 18 and 36 to their birthplace – in 1788. Andersen links this memorial to another historical pillar:

> Paa *Ulfeldts* Plads stod den Skjændselssteen; hvor reistes i Verden vel en som den? Ved Vesterport blev en Støtte reist, hvor mange i Verden er der vel som den? Solstraalerne kyssede Rullestenen, Grundlaget under »*Frihedsstøtten*«. […] *Lysaanderne* sang: »Det Gode groer! Det Skjønne groer! Snart falder Stenen paa *Ulfeldts* Plads, men«*Frihedsstøtten*»skal staae i Solskin, velsignet af Gud, Konge og Folk.«[549]

Andersen had indeed witnessed the removal of Ulfeldt's pillar of shame in 1842, when it was relocated following public demand.[550] Herewith, Ulfeldts Plads also retrieved its former name, Gråbrødretorv, which it carries until this day. Andersen's daring connection of the two completely unrelated memorials lends a positive outlook to the end of his tale. Ulfeldt's pillar of shame, a reminder of a dark period in Copenhagen's history, has been removed whereas the Liberty Memorial, the symbol of a major improvement and step towards a better society, prevails: »Forbandelsens Ord ere veirede hen, men hvad Sollysets Børn i Glæde sang om en kommende Tid, er blevet opfyldt. Saa mangen Storm er faret hen, den kan komme igjen og vil atter henfare. Det Sande og Gode og Skjønne har Seiren«.[551]

In 1868, *Jammers Minde* had not been published yet, but news of its imminent disclosure soon reached Andersen. In June 1869, he informed his friend Henriette

---

[548] Ibid. This last citation is taken from Christian Wilster's (1797-1840) poem *Eleonore Ulfeldt* (1827; see Wilster, Christian. 'Leonora Kristina Ulfeldt'. In Matzen, M. *Dansk Læsebog 3 (For de højere Klasser)*. Copenhagen: Gyldendal, 1875 (1865), pp. 89-90).

[549] Andersen, Hans Christian. 'Gudfaders Billedbog', p. 64f.

[550] On the occasion of this act of goodwill by King Christian VIII (1786-1848), Andersen dedicated a poem to this monarch: »Til Danmarks ædle, oplyste Konge, Christian den Ottende, da han lod Ulfeldts Skamstøtte tage ned. / Man opskrev Ulfeldts Feil, hans Dyd man dulgte, / Om denne dog de danske Hjerter veed; / Den ædleste af Qvinder tro ham fulgte, / Hans Monument er hendes Kjærlighed, / Det stande vil – ! hvad Jordens er, maa svinde, / Hiint mørke Tegn sees ikke meer i Nord; / Fred i sin Grav fik hun, den bedste Qvinde, / Du gav den, Konge! ved dit milde Ord. / Hav Tak for det! – nu sees kun Troskabs Minde« (see Andersen, Hans Christian. *Mit Livs Eventyr 1*, p. 357).

[551] Andersen, Hans Christian. 'Gudfaders Billedbog', p. 66.

Collin that he had heard about some recently discovered prison memoirs written by Leonora Christina, which he would read at the first opportunity.[552] In July, he had already purchased an edition of *Jammers Minde* and encouraged friends to read it as well: »Her er i Besøg Frøken Frenckel og Frøken Kjellerup; vi læse dagligt i en meget interesant Bog, som jeg særligt vil anbefale Dem og Deres Mand, det er Eleonore Ulfeldts Erindringer fra hendes Fængsels Tid i Blaa-Taarn, nedskrevet af hende selv«.[553] Considering Andersen's long-standing interest in Leonora Christina, it is odd to observe that this interest was no longer expressed in any writings succeeding the publication of *Jammers Minde*. In *Mit Livs Eventyr*, Andersen explains his interest in Ulfeldt and his family, by way of his ambition to write a stage play about Ulfeldt and Dina.[554] It is conceivable that Andersen's interest had always been slightly more directed at Leonora Christina's husband than at herself and since her account provides only little information in this regard, his rather dry, albeit positive comment on *Jammers Minde* (»en meget interesant Bog«) may appear less surprising. However, whether it was a preference for Corfitz Ulfeldt, or a fading of energy in the years preceding his death in 1875 that caused this apparently ceased creative interest in Leonora Christina, must remain the subject of speculation.

2.3 *Kvinde er kvinde værst*: Leonora Christina and Dina

> Eder mine Hierte Kiære Børn er icke alleeneste witterligt, men ded er endoc Landkyndig, huad stoere Liidelser, oc effterfølgende Vlycker *Dina* oc Walter med derris Mectige Anhang worris Huuß paaførte *Anno* 1651.
>
> (*Jammers Minde*, p. 5*)

The following group of texts presents diverse literary adaptations of the historical Dina affair spanning over a period of two centuries. This specific topic is perhaps

---

552 Letter addressed to Henriette Collin and dated 26 June 1869, reproduced in *H. C. Andersens brevveksling med Edvard og Henriette Collin 4: 1867-75*, eds. C. Behrend and H. Topsøe-Jensen. Copenhagen: Levin & Munksgaard, 1936, p. 77: »Forleden fik jeg Brev fra Carl Andersen[;] [editors' correction] han fortalte blandt Andet, at om et Par Uger udkom ›Fængselserindringer af Eleonore Ulfeldt‹. Jeg vil haabe at disse ere ægte og ikke digtede, da glæder jeg mig særdeles til at læse samme. Han synes at kjende disse Erindringer og skriver varmt og smukt om Eleonore, bittert om Sophie Amalia«.

553 Letter addressed to Therese Henriques and dated 12 July 1869, reproduced in *H. C. Andersens breve til Therese og Martin R. Henriques 1860-75*, ed. H. Topsøe-Jensen. Copenhagen: H. Hagerup, 1932, p. 112.

554 Andersen, Hans Christian. *Mit Livs Eventyr 1*, p. 357.

the most ideal one for an examination of the changing perception of Leonora Christina throughout the centuries, as the Ulfeldt family figured as both victims and offenders in the affair, hence leaving ensuing writers plentiful inspiration to create a possible explanation for this never fully resolved affair. Leonora Christina and Dina in particular lend themselves to comparison, since both fell prey to a man's ambition while the men, who caused their calamities, i.e. Ulfeldt and Walter, went into exile. At the same time, the intricacy of their relationship lends itself to creative exploitation. Throughout the course of the historical Dina affair, the two women appeared as rivals, accomplices and eventually as companions in misfortune. Finally, the Dina affair offers a unique scope for creative exploitation of the relationship between Leonora Christina and her other female rival, Sophie Amalie. Leonora Christina does not clarify, who Dina's and Walter's »Mectige Anhang« were, but contemporary reports of a rather close friendship between Jørgen Walter and the Queen procured differing degrees of royal involvement in literary adaptations of the Dina affair.[555] Beyond such allusions, Leonora Christina does not relate any details of the Dina affair – neither in *Jammers Minde* nor in her French autobiography – as she considered the matter widely known. Hence, authors of literary adaptations of this incident were left with plentiful scope.

The first text in this group, the drama *Eleonora Christina Uhlfeldt* (see Chapter 2.3.1.), was written by Louise Hegermann Lindencrone, who throughout her

---

[555] Leonora Christina herself promotes this suspicion with statements in *Jammers Minde*, which portray an intact friendship between Walter and Sophie Amalie even after his eviction from Denmark in 1651. When Leonora Christina witnessed Walter's arrival in the Blue Tower in 1668, she demanded an interrogation of Walter about the Dina affair and the opportunity to meet Walter herself in the presence of some state officials, as she felt that Frederik III had completely neglected the final elucidation of this complot. But her plea was in vain: »Presten loffwede att forrette ded, giorde ded oc saa; oc bleff *Walter* tredie dag effter sat op i den Mørke Kircke, saa ieg wæntede i en lang tiid hwer dag att wii skulle komme til forhør; men den der laa magt paa forhindrede ded« (*Jammers Minde*, p. 167). Leonora Christina's remark that a powerful person had prevented any further investigation is supported by a later addition on the margin of the same page, documenting Walter's words upon hearing of Leonora Christina's request: »Der Præsten gik fra mig, talte hand med Walter for Traalhullet; sagde hannem / min begiæring, oc hwad der wille følge paa. *Walter* loe saa Sposk oc sagde; Ick hæbbe / nicht en Haar dat dar før bange is, dat de sake skulle gerort werden; De Kønigin / weed dat wol, sagt ii dat ock« (ibid.). Leonora Christina's allusions to a complicity between Jørgen Walter and the royal house are not yet contained in her French autobiography. However, she mentions a certain powerful party, whose anger she feared and wanted to elude: »Comme Ils avoient gaignez leur proces, nostre femme craignoit, que cette forte partie quils avoient surmontées alors, ne cesseroient avant que de les ruiner tout á fait, ce qu'il devoit couster« (*Leonora Christina Grevinde Ulfeldts Franske Levnedsskildring*, p. 5c (Translation p. 22: »Da de havde vundet deres proces, frygtede vor dame, at det ommeldte stærke parti, som de ved den anledning var kommen ovenpaa, ikke vilde give sig til taals, før det ganske havde bragt dem i fortabelse, hvad det end skulde koste«). Leonora Christina's insinuations were not in vain, as even reputable historians like Hans Haupt took her words for face value. In his article on the original manuscript of Leonora Christina's French autobiography, Haupt presents the rumour regarding the Queen's involvement in the Dina affair as an unquestionable fact. See Haupt, Hans. 'Das Leonora-Christina-Manuskript des Christianeums in Hamburg-Altona', Zeitschrift der Gesellschaft für Schleswig-Holsteinische Geschichte 80 (1956), p. 74.

life had been fascinated and inspired by Leonora Christina, and particularly by her symbolic value as a »paradigm of conjugal love and Christian devotion«.[556] Adam Oehlenschläger's drama *Dina* (see Chapter 2.3.2.), published in 1842, however, is undoubtedly the most famous adaptation of the Dina affair. These two texts lend themselves to comparison since the authors were personally acquainted. This circumstance might account for some of the similarities in the texts discussed below. Most conspicuous of all, though, is the striking *dis*similarity created by the titles of their respective dramas: Hegermann Lindencrone's eponymous heroine is Leonora Christina (and accordingly, this text yields more valuable insights into the early phase of Leonora Christina-literature), while Leonora Christina's enemy Dina is the protagonist and undisputed heroine of Oehlenschläger's drama.

The third text discussed below, Rolf Gjedsted's novel *Fordærvede kvinder* (see Chapter 2.3.3.) published in 1991, is typical of the later phase of literary Leonora Christina-receptions, as it portrays her in a less idealised fashion than the versions of Oehlenschläger and Hegermann Lindencrone.[557] His work is also the most committed to the style of the post-revolutionary European historical novel, as it amplifies the historical character scope, hence presenting the lives of other documented inhabitants of 17th-century Copenhagen.[558] *Fordærvede kvinder* thus shows historical characters not only from the aristocratic, but also from the bourgeois and lower class milieu.

2.3.1. Louise Hegermann Lindencrone: *Eleonora Christina Uhlfeldt* (1817) – The Mother

> Hierte Kiere Børn […]
>
> (*Jammers Minde*, p. 2*)

---

556 Cf. Dalager, Stig and Anne-Marie Mai. *Danske kvindelige Forfattere 1*, p. 149.

557 Whether Gjedsted was familiar with the texts of Oehlenschläger and Hegermann Lindencrone is unknown. There is, however, nothing indicating that he was.

558 In general, however, the Leonora Christina-subject matter does not lend itself to reproduction in a classic historical novel, since it emerged out of the autobiographical: »One might suggest an alternative narrative of the rise of the novel focused through historical fiction, for instance, a form concerned with social movement, dissidence, complication and empathy rather than the more individualistic novel form we are familiar with, born of autobiographical, personal, revelatory narratives« (De Groot, Jerome. *The Historical Novel*. London and New York: Routledge, 2010 (The New Critical Idiom), p. 2).

Louise Hegermann Lindencrone[559] (1778-1853) commenced her literary production at a very young age and it was only contained by her frequent pregnancies succeeding her betrothal to Johan Hendrik Hegermann Lindencrone (1765-1849) in 1797. In 1817, Louise Hegermann Lindencrone published her first work: the drama *Eleonora Christina Uhlfeldt*. It received mediocre criticism and far less attention than *Danske Fortællinger*, published in 1825, which also contains two stories dealing with Leonora Christina and her kin: 'Faster Dorothea' and 'Billedet', which will be the topic of a subsequent chapter.

As indicated above, a comparative approach involving Adam Oehlenschläger's *Dina* and Louise Hegermann Lindencrone's *Eleonora Christina Uhlfeldt* in particular yields both astounding similarities and dissimilarities. The most conspicuous discrepancy is, of course, the title. Oehlenschläger dedicated his drama to an infamous woman, perhaps for promotional reasons: as stated by Vilhelm Andersen, »[a]lene Titelen maatte virke som et Trompetstød«.[560] Yet beyond its sensational potential there is little that is exceptional about the title, as Dina Vinhofvers is indeed Oehlenschläger's protagonist. Hegermann Lindencrone, on the other hand, made Leonora Christina her eponymous heroine, despite the fact that without the clue in the title one would have trouble identifying a single main character.[561] Both Leonora Christina and Dina Vinhofvers, as well as Corfitz Ulfeldt and Otto Sperling play dominant and independent roles in the play. However, only one of these characters prompted Louise Hegermann Lindencrone to prefix a foreword regarding her choice of topic:

> For den Læser som maatte forarges ved at see en Mand, hvem en offentlig Skamstøtte er sat, fremtræde som en af Hovedpersonerne i dette Drama, maae her anmærkes: At den Begivenhed i den ulykkelige Uhlfeldts Liv, som foranledigede hiin Skamstøtte, indtræffer 13 Aar senere, end den Tidspunkt, Stykket fremstiller; at han paa denne Tid, i Aaret 1651, erkiendtes som en af de lærdeste og mærkeligste blandt sine Samtidige, ej blot i Danmark men i Europa.[562]

---

559 Hegermann Lindencrone's name can be found both with and without a hyphen between her own and her husband's name. I follow Lise Busk-Jensen's decision to omit the hyphen as Hegermann Lindencrone used to do so herself (see Busk-Jensen, Lise. *Romantikkens forfatterinder 3*. Copenhagen: Gyldendal, 2009, p. 1566, footnote 50).

560 Andersen, Vilhelm. *Adam Oehlenschläger: Et Livs Poesi 2: Manddom og Alderdom*. Copenhagen: Det Nordiske Forlag, 1899, p. 339.

561 Cf. Busk-Jensen, Lise. *Romantikkens forfatterinder 2*. Copenhagen: Gyldendal, 2009, p. 795: »Leonora Christina er dramaets hovedperson, som titlen viser, men hun kan ikke være handlingens hovedaktør, fordi hendes skæbne som hustru bestemmes af ægtemandens skæbne som rigshofmester«.

562 Hegermann Lindencrone, Louise. *Eleonora Christina Uhlfeldt. Historisk Drama*. Copenhagen: Boas Brünnich, 1817, unpaginated preamble.

The authoress is clearly troubled by the public irritation her account may arouse, hence she included some words of consolation, but also a reminder of Leonora Christina's eternal love for her husband, which may seem familiar to the reader:

> At den Mand som en saadan Qvinde elskede saaledes; som fierde Christian (Hvo nævner vel dette Navn uden Ærefrygt?) kaarede til den første i sit Land, maatte i det mindste besidde store Anlæg, vilde enhver finde uimodsigeligt, om Historien end ikke, som den giør, udtrykkelig bekræftede det.[563]

Once again, Leonora Christina's legendary love is presented as a warrantor for Ulfeldt's character.[564] But furthermore, this love is placed at the center of the conflict, thus arousing the reader's empathy. The tragic misunderstanding that would later on change the lives of all people involved is caused by Dina overhearing a fragmented conversation between Corfitz and his wife. In this regard, Oehlenschläger and Hegermann Lindencrone chose the same approach, as both created a more private kind of explanation in relation to a historical state affair. Hegermann Lindencrone, however, went one step further by making the Ulfeldt couple's love for each other the direct catalyst of the misunderstanding. When Dina – who at this point is already in the midst of the intrigue against Corfitz – together with the couple's valet, Langemack, eavesdrop on Eleonora and Uhlfeldt,[565] they misinterpret the former's use of the word 'King'. While Eleonora means to ease her very own King's (»mit Livs Konge«),[566] i.e. her husband's agitation with a calming potion mixed by Otto Sperling that will help him forget his fear of being attacked in his own house, Langemack is convinced that he has discovered a planned poisoning (»ELEONORA. / Som i Dvale, / Fra Sorg han slumre bort, og aldrig vækkes!«).[567] Dina initially disbelieves this accusation as she is captivated by Uhlfeldt's charms:

---

563 Ibid.

564 Corfitz is not the only ambiguous character indirectly declared innocent by love. At the beginning of the drama (Act 1, Scene 1), Walter, Dina and Langemack are equally involved in the conspiracy and despite their private conversation, the reader is left unsure about who initiated it. But Dina's love for Corfitz motivates her to withdraw her false accusations, whereas Langemack's secret love for Dina (Act 3, Scene 3) indirectly declares her to have a noble spirit after all. Thus, only Walter is left out of the love triangle and is promptly exposed as the actual instigator of the complot: »Langemack. / [...] I! som har lokket / I Snaren hende, som har røbet hende!« (ibid., p. 64).

565 In the present chapter, »Eleonora« specifically refers to the character in Louise Hegermann Lindencrone's drama, particularly when referring to passages that do not correspond to historical events, whereas »Leonora Christina« refers to the historical person. Another spelling variation used in the literary source text, and hence in this chapter as well, to refer to Corfitz Ulfeldt is »Uhlfeldt«.

566 Hegermann Lindencrone, Louise. *Eleonora Christina Uhlfeldt*, p. 34.

567 Ibid., p. 35.

> Med Lethed gled jeg hen ad Livets Strøm, / Altid besindig styred jeg forsigtig, / Var stedse Havnen nær om Stormen kom: / Da saae jeg Ulfeldt og – mig selv jeg glemte, / Jeg lod mig tumle om for Vejer og Vind; / Compas og Roer jeg glemte og – forgik! / Og blev selv Offret for min Kierlighed![568]

But Uhlfeldt refuses to even talk to Dina – in line with posterity she is nothing but a »ringe Qvinde«[569] to him. Dina in turn reciprocates his rejection with vengefulness:

> Da kom Grev Uhlfeldt med sin Leonora: / Et Blik af hende smeltede mit Hierte; / Tilstaaelsen alt paa min Læbe svæved; / Men Uhlfeldts Stolthed isnede mit Bryst: / For dybt han lod mig føle sin Foragt, / Han haanlig saae ei, ændsede mig ei; / Da svoer jeg ham et Blik dog at aftvinge, / Og rasende beskyldte ham, forgieves! / Nu – Døden maaske nær – Jeg angrer det, / Og beder Kongen, Uhlfeldt mig tilgive![570]

Dina's behaviour during the trial, erratic in fiction as well as in history, is here explained through human emotions. Her love for him causes her to withdraw her accusations, but in the end her survival instinct prevails: »Fra Døden redder mig! – Jeg døer for ham – / For Uhlfeldt, som saa stolt foragter Døden; / Og jeg – som frygter den, som elsker Livet, / Maae døe! – og – Himmel! – skyldig er han jo, / Nu husker jeg det – Langemack det saae!«[571]

The same reason – love and how it causes people to act irrationally – is, at least partially, provided for as part of Uhlfeldt's own hot-tempered conduct. When he and Sperling talk about the lack of appreciation Uhlfeldt senses from the King's side, Eleonora remains quiet to a point where the reader is tempted to wonder whether she is even in the room. Even when the conversation concerns herself and how she has been mistreated by her own family, Uhlfeldt alone is complaining (»har man der ej haant modtaget / Min ædle Hustroe? Kongens ægte Datter!«),[572] while Eleonora is more reconciliatory (»Tal da, min Uhlfeldt! og forklar Dig for dem«).[573] Naturally, all royal ambitions are attributed to Uhlfeldt alone as well.[574] By removing Eleonora from the dialogue whenever it concerns a sensitive subject, Hegermann

---

568 Ibid., p. 81.
569 Ibid., p. 26.
570 Ibid., p. 84.
571 Ibid., p. 86.
572 Ibid., p. 28.
573 Ibid., p. 29.
574 Ibid., p. 31: »Uhlfeldt. / [...] Men at jeg torde tænke Kronen mig. / Lægger Haanden paa hendes Pande. / Paa denne skiønne, stolte Pande her, / Den eneste i Danmark Kronen værd, – / Det glemmes aldrig!«.

Lindencrone washes her heroine's hands from responsibility. Eleonora is not the proud Countess favoured by the 21st century, but the Madonna-type known from Andersen and Oehlenschläger (see Chapter 2.3.2.), which is so typical of the romantic period. Yet at the same time, Uhlfeldt's love for his high-born wife is thus directly associated with his discord with the royal couple, hence again presenting a commonly comprehensible human emotion as the underlying reason for a much condemned renunciation of Denmark.

Hence love – together with its irrationally destructive capacities – operates throughout the trial. It causes Dina to alter her statements regarding Uhlfeldt, thus creating confusion, which has not been resolved until this day. It provokes the misunderstanding involving Sperling's potion that leads to the accusations raised against the Uhlfeldt couple. And it gives rise to Uhlfeldt's momentous resentment towards Frederik III. Yet, love is not the only destructive human passion informing the beginnings of Uhlfeldt's downfall. Passions are a common topic in Gothic novels, a genre which inspired Hegermann Lindencrone's writings as well.[575]

The tale 'Faster Dorothea', published in 1825 as part of Hegermann Lindencrone's *Danske Fortællinger*, too deals with a historical incident, while attributing it an underlying story involving the obscure side of human passion. 'Faster Dorothea' tells the story of the unresolved death of Frants Rantzau (1604-1632), a former *Rigshofmester* and fiancé of Christian IV's daughter Anna Catharina. Despite his young age, Rantzau – who was a favourite of the King – had been appointed *Rigshofmester* in 1632, but he could not enjoy his new office for long. Seven months after said appointment he drowned in Rosenborg Castle's moat on his way home from a feast. There was no reason to assume that it had been anything but an accident, but the rumours regarding his sudden death ranged from suicide to witchcraft, and the fatality turned even more startling when Anna Catharina died less than a year later.[576] For her adaptation of this incident, Louise Hegermann Lindencrone picked the murder theory: her Frants Rantzau falls prey to his ambitious and fervid valet, the Italian Joseph, who murders his master as he is convinced that Rantzau is willingly hampering his career. Joseph's fiancée Dorothea, the *faster* who narrates the story to her family decades later, initially attributes his wild temper to his south-

---

575 In the tale 'Gjæstekammeret i Præstegaarden' (in *Danske Fortællinger*) a young mother is confronted with the ghost of a miller's widow and the insanity and murder topic in 'Faster Dorothea', too, creates an eerie atmosphere reminiscent of E. T. A. Hoffmann's writings. Overall, the topics ambition, passion and revenge appear in a great deal of Hegermann Lindencrone's non-lyrical writings; thus, Leonora Christina and Corfitz Ulfeldt's story lent itself to creative elaboration on her part.

576 The common opinion was that Anna Catharina had died from a broken heart. See Birket Smith, Sophus. *Leonora Christina Grevinde Ulfeldts Historie 1*, p. 73.

ern provenance,[577] but towards the end Joseph exhibits signs of outright insanity.[578] Here, a pseudo-scientific explanation (Joseph's southern temper) is blended with the mystical character inherent to insanity, as is rather typical of post-Enlightenment literature. A similar composition has been utilised in *Eleonora Christina Uhlfeldt*, where Corfitz Ulfeldt is associated with melancholia. Until this day, writers connect Ulfeldt's chronic shin wound with his irrational behaviour, following his departure from Denmark. Against all medical odds, the theory that this wound may have been a symptom of syphilis, which later on resulted in insanity, remains popular.[579] This motive is not further developed in Louise Hegermann Lindencrone's account, as her intention was to show Ulfeldt at a time when he was still a respectable politician and an asset to Denmark.[580] A certain mental lability that has befallen Ulfeldt is, however, indicated throughout the account. In accordance with Leonora Christina's

---

577 Hegermann Lindencrone, Louise. 'Faster Dorothea'. In Hegermann Lindencrone, Louise. *Danske Fortællinger*. Copenhagen: C. A. Reitzels Forlag, 1862 (1825), p. 113.

578 Ibid., p. 115: »Han var bleg som Døden, hans Underlæber rystede og hans Tænder sloge sammen, saa det varede en rum Tid inden han kom tilende dermed, han knyttede Hænder, græd og lo som en Afsindig, Fraaden stod ham alt imellem paa Læberne, og jeg troede i min Sjæle-Angst at see ham styrte død ned for mine Fødder – jeg anede ikke hvor lyksalige vi begge havde været, hvis det var skeet«.

579 Victor Lange, for example, is not disinclined to believe in the syphilis theory (Lange, Victor. *Corfitz Ulfeld*, p. 163), even though this leads to the conclusion of a rather unlikely scenario, i.e. that Leonora Christina must have been immune to the disease her husband contracted many years before marrying her: »Jeg synes ikke, at der foreligger noget Bevis for at Leonora Christina har havt Mandens Sygdom« (ibid., p. 164). Lange is actually more perplexed by the mere suggestion that there may have been a serious medical reason for Ulfeldt's increasingly erratic behaviour since in his view, Ulfeldt had always had a peculiar character: »Jeg synes, at det af det Foranstaende fremgaar, at vi have at gjøre med en egenartet Karakter, der i Hovedtrækkene bliver sig selv lig saavel i Ungdom som i Manddom; man kan godt klæbe Ordet ›havlgal‹ [sic!] men ›ikke sindssyg‹ [sic!] paa ham; mangen Person met et iltert og stærkt skiftende Temperament erklæres jo i det daglige Liv for uberegnelig, utilregnelig og ›halvgal‹ uden at man tænker paa ham som ›moden til Sct. Hans.‹« (ibid., p. 162). For an example of a more recent text maintaining the syphilis theory, see Hemmer Hansen, Eva. *Den lykkelige hustru*, p. 17. In line with Sophus Birket Smith, who identifies Ulfeldt's condition as venous ulcer (Birket Smith, Sophus: *Leonora Christina Grevinde Ulfeldts Historie 1*, p. 55), the Danish historian Steffen Heiberg has an entirely different theory to explain Ulfeldt's incurable leg, i.e. »at den var gal med kredsløbet, måske et alvorligt tilfælde af årebetændelse« (Heiberg, Steffen. *Enhjørningen Corfitz Ulfeldt*, p. 141) – a more realistic, albeit considerably less juicy explanation for Ulfeldt's symptoms. And as far as Ulfeldt's alleged insanity is concerned, Heiberg shares Lange's conviction in contending that Ulfeldt never *turned* mad, since he had been »manisk eller endog psykopatisk« (ibid., p. 223) throughout his life, albeit with alternating success (ibid., p. 244).

580 Hegermann Lindencrone, Louise. *Eleonora Christina Uhlfeldt*, unpaginated preamble: »Vel var det i Særdelesed under Christian fierdes Regiering, at hans meest glimrende Periode indtraf; dog var han Gienstanden for almindelig Agtelse, om end hist og her Uvenner og Misundere søgte i Smug at nedsætte ham, indtil den ulykkelige Beslutning han tog, at forlade sit Fædreland, blev det første Skridt, som siden drog saa mange andre efter sig«.

self-portrayal in her French autobiography,[581] a comparison between Ulfeldt and his wife, as presented by Hegermann Lindencrone, favours the latter: Uhlfeldt is constantly anxious, whereas his wife, in the fashion of a mother figure, appeases him while being more concerned about him than about the rumour that her own life might be under threat: »Den ængstlige Forsigtighed hvori / Jeg ej min Uhlfeldts høje Mod gienkiender. / Vee mig! – Jeg bragte ham den løse Snak, / Den plat urimelige! – Kun hans Tilstand / Kun ene den forfærder, smerter mig!«[582] Eleonora's maternal stability[583] is contrasted with her husband's disquiet, whose subtle association with keywords such as »sygelig« and »Feberdrøm« alludes to Uhlfeldt's prospective condition. Eleonora and Otto Sperling, whose clear vision of the coming tragedy remains disregarded by their friend and husband,[584] notice that the Count's mental and emotional state is not at its best: both observe a »Taage, [der] giør hans Øje mørkt [og s]taaer som en Skye imellem ham og Solen –«.[585] Uhlfeldt himself is aware of this 'fog': »Lad Sløret falde fra mit matte Øie, / Før Mørkets blege Aand, Tungsindighed / For evig myrdet har mit Hiertes Fred, / Før jeg forvildet reent den Vei forlader, / Som Du mig bød at vandre, Livets Fader!«[586]

In conclusion, human emotions together with their possible destructive implications determine the course of the entire Dina affair, hence subducting some of its political brisance. What maintains this historical incident's fascination to writers today is that the affair was never fully clarified.[587] In accordance with this characteristic of the event, Hegermann Lindencrone remains consciously vague at keypoints of the account. The drama starts with Dina and Langemack arguing about who initiated the affair. While Dina blames Walter and Langemack,[588] the latter imputes Dina (»Du har vel glemt, du selv den første var, / Som har hos Walter Mistroe vakt til Greven, / Som praled af at have snildt opdaget - - / - Jeg veed ej hvad – Du veed

---

581 In the preamble to *Eleonora Christina Uhlfeldt* Louise Hegermann Lindencrone states to have consulted »Eleonora's own biography« (which is probably the forgery published by Oluf Bang), Holberg, »Pau« ([sic!] this is a reference to Hans Paus' *Forsøg Til Navnkundige Danske Mænds Livs og Levnets Beskrivelser, Andet Stykke. Indeholdende Anledning Til den Fra Dannemarkes Riges Hofmester Og Det Romerske Riges Grœve, Forvandlede Til Dannemarkes Riges Forrœder Corfitz Uhlefeld, Hans Livs og Levnets Historie* from 1746), Charles Ogier (*Det store Bilager i Kjøbenhavn 1634*) and Otto Sperling the Younger.

582 Hegermann Lindencrone, Louise. *Eleonora Christina Uhlfeldt*, p. 23.

583 Eleonora's motherly role towards her husband is especially blatant in Act 2, Scene 7, when she spends the night waking over her sleeping husband (ibid., p. 45).

584 Ibid., p. 95.

585 Ibid., p. 25.

586 Ibid., p. 70.

587 Dina did in fact alter her statements in the course of the interrogations and one can only guess that her changing relationship towards Walter may have been the underlying reason.

588 Hegermann Lindencrone, Louise. *Eleonora Christina Uhlfeldt*, p. 12.

det vel ej selv!«).⁵⁸⁹ The beginnings of the intrigue are not part of the drama and not even the people involved seem to remember how it started. The fictional complot thus imitates the haziness of the historical one.

Besides those parts of the Dina affair, which are preserved in protocols and other documents, patriotism is another topic carefully avoided in *Eleonora Christina Uhlfeldt*. Unlike Adam Oehlenschläger and Mathilde Fibiger, who were engaged in the subject of Leonora Christina's colliding obligations towards her fatherland and her husband, Louise Hegermann Lindencrone presents her heroine first and foremost as a mother. Thus, her reflective monologue at the beginning of Act 5 concerns not the country, but the children she must leave behind in order to support her spouse. In this scene, Eleonora takes a last look at her sleeping children, as she must leave them soon.⁵⁹⁰ Both towards her children and her husband, Eleonora takes up the role of the archetypal mother as she watches over her family as they sleep. To Hegermann Lindencrone, Leonora Christina embodies a motherly ideal, which the authoress herself desiderated. In 1793, at the age of 14, she published her first attempt at literary writing called 'Vugge-Vise', a poem depicting a mother waking over her sleeping daughters. The publication of *Eleonora Christina Uhlfeldt* followed the birth of Hegermann Lindencrone's ninth child and still attests to an idealisation of motherhood,⁵⁹¹ implicitly through the portrayal of Leonora Christina, explicitly through Otto Sperling's words: »I! I, den ømmeste blandt alle Mødre, / I vil forlade Eders Børns Vugge!«⁵⁹²

Whenever Eleonora bespeaks a home country, however, she does not refer to Denmark: in Act 2, Scene 6, Uhlfeldt's fatherland is heaven itself⁵⁹³ and in Act 4, Scene 3, home is not defined in geographical terms, but as an intangible ideal: »Høit

---

589 Ibid.

590 Ibid., p. 88.

591 Steffen Auring et al., too, comment on a consistent devotion to husband and especially children, which is reflected in Hegermann Lindencrone's private and published writings: »Fra 1797, da hun indgik i ægteskab med Hegermann, ophørte udgivelserne, og der gik 20 år, inden hun igen ytrede sig på skrift. I mellemtiden synes hendes litterære ambitioner at have ligget underdrejet for de forpligtelser, hun skyldte sin hustru- og moderrolle. Og af hendes korrespondance fremgår det, at hun påtog sig familielivet med stor inderlighed og i hele dets borgerlige rækkevide. Omsorgen for manden og de syv sønner og døtre er et genkommende tema i brevene, ligesom moderkærligheden er et stærkt element hos de kvindeskikkelser, hun senere fremstillede litterært« (Auring, Steffen, Søren Baggesen, Finn Hauberg Mortensen, Søren Petersen, Marie-Louise Svane, Erik Svendsen, Poul Aaby Sørensen, Jørgen Vogelius and Martin Zerlang. 'Den romantiske kvindemyte. Louise Hegermann-Lindencrone'. In Auring, Steffen, Søren Baggesen, Finn Hauberg Mortensen, Søren Petersen, Marie-Louise Svane, Erik Svendsen, Poul Aaby Sørensen, Jørgen Vogelius and Martin Zerlang. *Dansk litteraturhistorie 5: Borgerlig enhedskultur 1807-48*. Copenhagen: Gyldendal, 1990 (1984), p. 444).

592 Hegermann Lindencrone, Louise. *Eleonora Christina Uhlfeldt*, p. 73.

593 »Saa – selv i Lidenskabers Giæring stunder / Din Hu dog stedse til Dit rette Hiem, / Dit Fædreland hvorfra den udsprang – Himlen!« (ibid., p. 47).

elsker jeg mit Danmark, dog jeg veed / Det Gode, Skiønne, trives overalt / Hvor man det elsker, som I [Sperling] selv har sagt; / Det Jordiske kan kun af Støvet bindes, / Det Aandelige skienked Himlen Vinger; / Fra den det kom, did det sig atter svinger«.[594] Thus, the conflicting obligations towards husband and home country do not pose an essential problem in *Eleonora Christina Uhlfeldt*. In Louise Hegermann Lindencrone's writings, (Danish) patriotism and conjugal commitment generally do not collide, but go hand in hand. In the short story 'Gjæstekammeret i Præstegaarden' the protagonist Margrethe and her prospective husband are immediately attracted to each other due to their common Danish roots,[595] and also 'Billedet' (see Chapter 2.4.1.) shows the beginnings of a marriage based on the Danish origin of the suitor, even though the bride is Dutch-born.[596]

Topics of explicitly nationalistic potential are not the only ones avoided in *Eleonora Christina Uhlfeldt*. Since human emotions predetermine the course of the Dina trial, merely political issues call for diversionary tactic, for example in Act 3, Scene 2, when Uhlfeldt and Eleonora enter the royal palace for the first time in a long while. They are now aware of Dina's accusations against them and the mood is heated. Uhlfeldt is infuriated over the King's action and his humour could possibly escalate into lèse-majesty. Hence, Louise Hegermann Lindencrone intersperses references to Leonora Christina deplorable future[597] and – in accord with the environment – her glorious past as the King's daughter.[598] In one of the palace chambers, the couple meets Jacob, a former footman of Christian IV. Eleonora recognises him immediately, thus delighting the old man: »O Gud! I end mig kiender, Eders Naade!

---

594 Ibid., p. 76.
595 Hegermann Lindencrone, Louise. 'Gjæstekammeret i Præstegaarden'. In Hegermann Lindencrone, Louise. *Danske Fortællinger*. Copenhagen: C. A. Reitzels Forlag, 1862 (1825), p. 42.
596 Hegermann Lindencrone, Louise. 'Billedet'. In Hegermann Lindencrone, Louise. *Danske Fortællinger*. Copenhagen: C. A. Reitzels Forlag, 1862 (1825), p. 196: »[D]og kan det tillige ikke nægtes, at den Omstændighed, at han var Dansk, Grevinde Eleonoras Landsmænd, forhøiede hendes Glæde. ‚Saa skal da alt, hvad der er mærkeligt og ærværdigt for mig komme derfra!' tænkte hun«.
597 Hegermann Lindencrone, Louise. *Eleonora Christina Uhlfeldt*, p. 59: »Uhlfeldt. / […] Kongen / Forbyder os jo at forlade Byen / Mod alle Love, mod Haandfæstningen! / Giør mig min skiønne Borg til Fangetaarn, / Den hele store Bye til skummelt Fængsel!« The entire drama is furnished with prophetic statements and other allusions to the imminent events, which is a common feature of literary presentations of Leonora Christina's life.
598 Like many other writers engaging in Leonora Christina, Louise Hegermann Lindencrone utilises the combined fame of Christian IV and his daughter. The foreword of *Eleonora Christina Uhlfeldt* is dedicated to Denmark's past heroes spearheaded by Christian IV and Leonora Christina: »See! – Hvor er han som mon saa herlig stande? / Os mere nær, ej skjult i Oltids Mørke; / Guldkronen hvælvet om den høie Pande / I Blikket Viisdom, Kierlighed og Styrke; / O fierde Christian! hvilket Hierte brænder / Ei høit af Glæde naar det dig gienkiender! / Hos Dig, Din Datter sig af Graven svinger; / Guldkronen blev ei hendes Arvedeel, / Dit Hierte og din Aand hun arved heel; / Ei Purpurkaaben, hvide Engle Vinger / Om Skuldren svæver; hun dem folder ud / Og hæver sig med hellig Flugt – til Gud!« (ibid., unpaginated preamble).

/ Saa veed jeg dog, hvorfor de gamle Been / Endnu i Graven smuldre ei, end engang / Jeg seer min store Konges Yndlingsdatter«.[599]

In other regards, Hegermann Lindencrone's presentation of the Dina affair is less vague, but exhibits an antagonistic structure. This concerns some of the men and women in the proceedings and, of course, Dina and Leonora Christina. The female ideal in *Eleonora Christina Uhlfeldt*, embodied by Eleonora as mother and muse, is committed to two suggestive terminology spheres: the romantic Christian and the adept antique sphere. Both are based on Hegermann Lindencrone's self-image and her striving towards the optimisation of the very same image. For one, the authoress cherished the iconic mother-figure, Madonna. This admiration is expressed in Leonora Christina's portrayal and in Hegermann Lindencrone's lifelong enthusiasm regarding the care of her own family.[600] In scenes showing Eleonora in interaction with her husband and children, she depicts the archetypal Madonna – an affinity her husband is not insensitive towards:

UHLFELDT. / [...] Den fagre Rose i min Urtegaard, / Hvis rene Duft mod Himmelen opstiger, / Den vækker Avind hos den mindre Urt; / Men blomstrer derfor lige skiønt og purt! / Omfavner Eleonora. / ELEONORA. / Hvis Rosen dufter, lad den qvæge Dig: / For Dig den blomstrer og udvikler sig! / UHLFELDT drager hende til sig og siger med Begeistring til Sperling: / See, denne skiønne klare Diamant! / Den Sol som tidlig for mit Liv oprandt, / Den bryder herlig sine tusend Straaler; / Dens Farve-Glands Muldvarpens Blik ej taaler: / Den skinner alt for klar, for stærk, for reen, / Bortskiæmmer jo uægte Glimmer-Steen![601]

The rose is a common symbol of the Virgin Mary, while a further association with purity and light is achieved through the equalisation of Eleonora with the sun and a diamond, together with keywords such as »klar« and »reen«. Dina, on the other hand, is repeatedly equated with another figure known from the testaments: »PETER.

---

599 Ibid., p 60.

600 In Steffen Auring's (et al.) perception, this concerns mostly her children, since some of Louise Hegermann Lindencrone's writings indicate disappointment regarding her marriage: »Både i *Eleonora Christine Uhlfeldt* og i *Troubadouren*, der kom tre år efter i 1820, drejer det sig om ægteskabsproblemer, der, på trods af at de behandles i historisk draperi, nok antyder, at Louise Hegermann-Lindencrone ikke havde fået alle forventningerne fra ungdommen til at gå op i værtindesyntesen. Begge stykkers kvinder har tilpasningsproblemer i ægteskabet, de føler sig ikke hjemme i deres mænds verden. [...] Forfatterindens egne erfaringer om at tilsidesætte personlige ønsker under hensynet til mandens embede skinner igennem i sympatien for Eleonora. Men den underliggende ægteskabskritik kommer aldrig udtalt til orde, Eleonora får netop heltindeformat på grund af den kvindelige opofrelse, hun påtager sig« (Auring, Steffen et al. 'Den romantiske kvindemyte', p. 446).

601 Hegermann Lindencrone, Louise. *Eleonora Christina Uhlfeldt*, p. 29.

/ Seer hun da ud som den der Sandhed taler? / Hun mellem os sig som en Slange snoer, / Og altid spørger hun og fritter os«.[602] Furthermore, a servant of the Uhlfeldt mansion calls Dina a witch (»Gid Satan havde den fordømte Hex!«),[603] but unlike Rolf Gjedsted (see Chapter 2.3.3.), Louise Hegermann Lindencrone makes no further use of this typical 17th-century topic. In another scene, Dina is compared to Melpomene, the Muse of Tragedy.[604] However, Eleonora – whilst defying such a comparison[605] – evokes the memory of Arria Major, a woman that lived in ancient Rome and whose suicide, an act of rebellion against the Emperor Claudius, eternised her name. Arria, like Leonora Christina, is a historical example of a woman whose strength exceeded that of her husband. Thus, Arria's story corresponds to Leonora Christina's self-portrayal in her French autobiography.

The equation of Dina with the serpent that tempted Eve is reinforced by a later scene, in which Eleonora fears for her paradise:

ELEONORA [to Corfitz]. / Dig Herren skienket har et Paradiis, / Hvor Livets Træe sin skiønne Frugt Dig rækker; / Hvor Kierlighed og Selvbevidsthed staae, / Som Engle trindt om Dig, og holde Vagt. / Men Du vil plukke den forbudne Frugt: / Med Magt og List Du bryde vil Din Skiebne, / Og see! – de milde Engle selv sig væbne / Som Cherubim med Straffens Flamme-Sværd, / De Overtræderen er stedse nær / Og trænge ham ud af sit Paradiis![606]

Curiously, it is not a female figure but Uhlfeldt, who is in danger of eating the forbidden fruit. This reversal of a commonly quoted example of female feebleness is part of Hegermann Lindencrone's other antagonistic arrangement: the relationship between the sexes. Despite the men in the drama consistently disdaining Dina's »Qvinde-Sladder«,[607] the women in the drama demonstrate a much more discreet behaviour than the men. After overhearing Uhlfeldt and Eleonora's equivocal conversation in Act 1, Scene 9, Langemack immediately jumps to conclusions while Dina remains tentative: »LANGEMACK yderst bestyrtet. / Jeg selv har hørt det! – Gift

---

602 Ibid., p. 20.
603 Ibid.
604 Ibid., p. 38.
605 Ibid., p. 89: »Uhlfeldt! – Det smerter ikke! – og dog bort, / Bort med den Romerstolthed, som ei passer / Til Moderhiertet, der vemodig bløder!«
606 Ibid., p. 32.
607 E.g. ibid., p. 20. The same deprecatory attitude towards women is sometimes directed at Eleonora as well, for example by the servant Kield Fries: »Nu, – hun er Qvinde – veed ei hvad det gielder; / Greven er klog nok, veed vel hvad han giør / Thi bør hun føie ham« (ibid., p. 19).

til Kongen blandet! / DINA ængstlig. / Troer Du?«[608] Eleonora, too, exhibits a solid sober-mindedness, whenever Uhlfeldt is acting overly dramatic. This, however, is a widespread feature of Leonora Christina-literature.

In the beginning of the drama, the terminology mostly remains in the Christian sphere; yet as the calamity unfolds, the images and metaphors increasingly originate from the Greek tragedy. When Uhlfeldt realises the extent of the hostility against himself and his family, he falls into gloom. In the fashion of a Greek tragedy, Uhlfeldt feels like being persecuted by a dark force rendering the once influential man powerless: »Tungsindighed! / Afgrundens mørke Aand! / Som griber Hiertet med iiskolde Haand, / Forvandler Livets bedste Fryd til Savn, / Forfølger – selv i Leonoras Favn! / [...] Ja, Furie! Dig er det som betvinger / Mit Mod, min Kraft, som matter Sielens Vinger«.[609]

Allusions of this kind accumulate towards the end and even though they seem like foreign matter in this Nordic drama, they accentuate the tragic fate and the powerlessness of all actors involved. Langemack, too, is haunted by his guilty conscience, by visions of blood and revenge, which drive him into suicide.[610] But unlike a Greek tragedy, Louise Hegermann Lindencrone's drama does not depict the hero's final downfall. The authoress did not consider further scenes necessary as the fate of the Ulfeldt family is commonly known and well documented,[611] hence his coming fate remains implied. Despite all prophetic warnings, Uhlfeldt is unable to turn back. In his last attempt at preventing his friend from leaving, Sperling uses terminology reminiscent of the Greek Pandora myth: »Det er ei Nøglen blot til Østerporten, / I der i Haanden holder, Eders Skiæbnes, / det Eders hele Fremtids Nøgle er! / Og hvis I bruger den – I aabner Porten / For Uheld, Smerte, Greve! – og for Anger!«[612] Sperling attempts to end the tragedy by leading Uhlfeldt back onto the righteous path (»Kom! Eders gode Engel vinker Eder!«)[613] but, as predetermined by history, Uhlfeldt would not listen.

The allusions to antique tragedy agglomerate towards the end, yet there are allusions to ancient learned tradition throughout the drama. When Walter attempts to allure Dina with the promise of marrying her upon completion of the complot (Act

---

608 Ibid., p. 35.
609 Ibid., p. 68.
610 Ibid., pp. 93-95.
611 See ibid., unpaginated preamble.
612 Ibid., p. 97.
613 Ibid. Said angel comes in the form of Lars Uhlfeldt, Corfitz's brother. He, too, is unable to deter his brother from leaving. Uhlfeldt's paranoia has won the upper hand as he is even suspecting Sperling of having betrayed his secret plan (ibid., p. 99).

1, Scene 4), Dina sees through his sweet-talk: »Ha! haarde barske / Ha! Trædske, følesløse Mand! alt længe / Jeg var ham til Besvær, min Snildhed nu / Er ham nødvendig til at aabne Dørren / Til Lykkens Tempel for ham, siden kaster / Han mig i Armene paa Langemack«.[614] »Lykkens Tempel« is, of course, a metaphor alluding to Walter's ambition. But in a more literal sense, Dina has already managed to open the door to Uhlfeldt's mansion for Walter, where he intends to obtain the information that will change his life for the better. This negative association of the Temple of Fortune with human vices such as greed and ambition corresponds to an allegorical tale of the same title by Johannes Ewald, published in 1764.[615] In this tale, 'Lykkens Tempel', the first-person narrator recounts a dream featuring two temples: »den evige Lyksaligheds Tempel« ('the Temple of Eternal Bliss') on top of a remote, high and rather uncomfortable mountain, and »Lykkens Tempel«, alternatively called »den timelige Lyksaligheds Tempel« ('the Temple of Fleeting Fortune'), in a valley displaying the most agreeable and inviting natural scenery. Despite having arrived at the Temple of Eternal Bliss, the narrator is intrigued by the sight of the Temple of Fortune down in the lush valley. He pays this enchanted place a visit, thus making, amongst others, the following observation:

> Paa Veien fornam jeg, at Lykkens Tempel havde hundrede Porte, og at de Ankomne, som ikke udvalgte den rette, stode stor Fare for at blive udelukte, og at endog mange af dem, som vare komne ind, stødtes pludselig ud igien. Man sagde mig videre, at endeel af de Udelukte eller Udstødte bleve desuagtet stedse ved Templet, og giorde sig uden Ophør al optænkelig Umage for at komme ind[.][616]

Corfitz Ulfeldt's own fleeting luck corresponds to the above reference to the fickleness of fortune, while the image of the hapless yet unrelenting souls, which have been excluded from the Temple of Fortune, correlates to the documented fate of both Ulfeldt and Jørgen Walter. After all, both men were not content with their initial exiles provoked by the Dina affair, but attempted and failed to regain some success in Denmark in the ensuing years.

Eventually, the narrator of 'Lykkens Tempel' turns his back on the Temple of Fortune, as it augurs no lasting boon. Hence, the Uhlfeldt mansion's association with this cautionary tale adumbrates no happy ending for its inhabitants.

---

614 Ibid., p. 16.
615 Selfsame tale also inspired Nicolai Abildgaard's (1743-1809) mantelpiece-painting *Lykkens Tempel* from 1785.
616 Ewald, Johannes. 'Lykkens Tempel: En Drøm'. In *Johannes Ewalds Samlede Skrifter: Efter Tryk og Håndskrifter 1*, ed. Det danske Sprog- og Litteraturselskab. Copenhagen: Gyldendal, 1969 (1914), p. 66.

This, however, is not the only instance in which the estate of the Uhlfeldt family is associated with a temple. At the beginning of Act 2, Sperling leaves his home in the evening in order to pay a visit to the Uhlfeldt house, which he seems to prefer over his own:

Saa er da Hverdags-Livets Slid forbi! / Ja! som nu denne Dør, jeg lukker i, / For Livets Usselhed et Slør jeg drager, / Med Sygdom, Smaalighed jeg Afsked tager, / Og iler did, hvor Musers hulde Røst / Saa tidt giød Kraft og Tillid i mit Bryst! / Ja! Hist i Uhlfeldts blidt oplyste Sale, / Hvor Kunstens Værker høit til Sielen tale, / Der er i Norden Musers høie Sæde, / Et Tilflugtsted for Skiønhed, Sandhed, Glæde![617]

In his eulogy to the Uhlfeldt house, Sperling blends references to antique culture with Christian terminology. He describes their home as a heaven-like place (»Hvor alle gode Engle holde Vagt / Om Krafts og Skiønheds himmelrene Pragt«),[618] but he also explicitly calls it a temple (»Ja! det er Musers og Apollos Tempel, / Det bærer Evighedens høie Stempel!«).[619] Uhlfeldt is the central deity of this temple (and as most ancient deities, he also has a dark side), but Eleonora is his guardian angel:

Snart som Apol, snart som Mæcen jeg skuer / Den ædle Uhlfeldt under Hallens Buer; / Som Cæsar snart paa Capitolium / Med Herskerblik han stander mørk og stum. – / Held ham! en Engel vandrer ved hans Side, / Sløvt Skiebnens Pile fra hans Hierte glide: / Venus Urania Eleonora! / Du bøder for ham med dit hvide Skiold! / Det er din høie Dyd, din Kierlighed![620]

At the same time, Eleonora exhibits muse-like associations as she – as in all literary representations of Leonora Christina – is portrayed as an unusually erudite and talented woman[621] carrying the nickname Venus Urania.

The presentation of the Uhlfeldt house as a temple of lore and artistry with Eleonora functioning as a muse-like figure may constitute another autobiographical element,[622] as the authoress herself used to host a salon frequented by notable

---

617 Hegermann Lindencrone, Louise. *Eleonora Christina Uhlfeldt*, p. 37.
618 Ibid.
619 Ibid., p. 38.
620 Ibid.
621 Ibid., p. 20: »Grevinden! / Den klogeste i hele Kongeriget!«
622 Cf. Steffen Auring et al., who contend that the female protagonist in Hegermann Lindencrone's second drama *Troubadouren* (1820) displays conspicuous autobiographical features: »I denne kvindebeskrivelse fejrer Hegermann-Lindencrone sin egen udførelse af rollen som muse og moder« (Auring, Steffen et al. 'Den romantiske kvindemyte', p. 446).

literary figures such as Adam Oehlenschläger. Their acquaintance, commencing in the year Hegermann Lindencrone published *Eleonora Christina Uhlfeldt* (1817),[623] may also account for a conspicuous similarity: in a private conversation between Eleonora and Sperling, the latter compares Uhlfeldt to a volcano fertilising the soil, whereas the former fears its destructive powers: »SPERLING. / Vær rolig! / Dumpt giærer i Vulkanens dybe Grund / Den Ild, som varmer, som befrugter Jorden. / ELEONORA. / Dens Udbrud dog er Ødelæggelse! / Vildt strømmer Lidenskabers hede Lava«.[624] Twenty-five years later, Adam Oehlenschläger staged a very similar conversation between Corfitz and his wife:

> ELEONORA. / Ja, Corfitz Ulfeld! du er en Vulcan. / Men det gaaer mig, som i Sicilien / Og i Neapel Bønderne: de elske / Dog Bierget, skiøndt det ofte spruder Ild. / De boe derved, de bygge deres Hytter / Derpaa; thi Grunden er velsignet, frugtbar, / Og skienker deres Viingaard ædle Druer, / Som langt, langt overgaae den sikkre Dals. / ULFELD. / Men – hvis engang der kom et Jordskiælv med / En Lavastrøm, som slugte dig og Bierget? / ELEONORA. / Saa synker jeg, som alle Mennesker, / I Jordens Skiød. Det skal vi Alle dog. / Vogt dig for Udbrud, hvis du elsker Danmark, / Og hvis du elsker mig! Da vil vort Land / Sundt vederqvæges af din ædle Drue.[625]

These two excerpts illustrate the diverging character dynamic devised by the two writers. Oehlenschläger's Corfitz Ulfeld is a more preeminent, but also a more ambivalent character. Hence he is a more self-conscious character that worries about his own deeds, while his adoring and abject wife has a solid trust in her husband. Louise Hegermann Lindencrone, however, indicates a mother-child-relationship between the spouses, which leaves Uhlfeldt slightly inculpable and his mother-like wife in charge. Uhlfeldt takes the decision to leave Denmark but unlike Oehlenschläger's Eleonora, the eponymous heroine of *Eleonora Christina Uhlfeldt* follows her husband not merely out of conjugal conscientiousness but rather out of concern. When Otto Sperling reminds her of her maternal duties, Eleonora assures

---

623 Cf. Oehlenschläger, Adam. *Oehlenschlägers Erindringer 4*. Copenhagen: Andr. Fred. Holts Forlag, 1851, p. 4. Despite Oehlenschläger's declared appreciation of his friend's poetic talent, his letters and memoirs do not attest to a noteworthy acknowledgement of Louise Hegermann Lindencrone as a writer.
624 Hegermann Lindencrone, Louise. *Eleonora Christina Uhlfeldt*, p. 24.
625 Oehlenschläger, Adam. *Dina*. In *Oehlenschläger. Poetiske Skrifter 9: Dramatiske Digtninger*, ed. F. L. Liebenberg. Copenhagen: Det Nordiske Forlag, 1898, p. 28.

him that her children will manage on their own (»Gud dem bevare vil!«).[626] Her husband, on the other hand, needs her assistance:[627]

> SPERLING. / Mon Eders Børn ei vil behøve Eder? / Eleonora. / Mon da ei Uhlfeldt vil behøve mig? / Han har bestemt, at her han bliver ei. / Sæt at han ei det Rette havde valgt, / Om da han staaer, forladt af hele Verden! / Om alle Baand, om alle Forhold brister, / Da [sk]al han føle et Baand dog er evigt, / Et trofast, kierligt Hierte ved ham hænger! / Føler I ei at dette Kald er helligt? / At Moderhiertet selv forstumme maae; Siig kan jeg virke saadan paa de Spæde / Vel, i den føie Tid jeg skilles fra dem?[628]

Hence, Oehlenschläger and Hegermann Lindencrone have devised two rather different spousal couples, with differing implications for the female dynamic in the two dramas. In Oehlenschläger's interpretation of the Dina affair, the principal character is a true heroine. Dina meets her untimely death in a state of complete awareness and with dignity, while the reader is left wondering whether the man, who caused this was deserving of her sacrifice (see Chapter 2.3.2.). Hegermann Lindencrone's version, however, turns the tables. Uhlfeldt – though not portrayed in the most admirable manner – is excused; implicitly by the love of his family and his friend, Otto Sperling, and more explicitly by some implicatory statements.[629] Dina, on the other hand, dies alone and her final outbreak of utter desperation casts a shadow on her aforeclaimed love for Uhlfeldt. When she still considers herself to be safe[630] she intends to undo the harm inflicted upon him: »Men – jeg vil redde Dig! – Dit store Navn, / Af mig bagvasket, skal af mig frikiendes!«[631] However, the scene preceding her execution reveals her predominant survival instinct and Dina's last words in Act 1, Scene 4 allude to a certain degree of opportunism informing her subsequent deeds:

---

626 Hegermann Lindencrone, Louise. *Eleonora Christina Uhlfeldt*, p. 74.
627 Cf. Busk-Jensen, Lise. *Romantikkens forfatterinder 2*, p. 796.
628 Hegermann Lindencrone, Louise. *Eleonora Christina Uhlfeldt*, p. 78.
629 Leonora Christina, Sperling and even Dina (Hegermann Lindencrone, Louise. *Eleonora Christina Uhlfeldt*, p. 15) all notice that Ulfeldt does not seem well, thus alluding to the beginning of his physical and mental deterioration. In addition, the historically aware reader is reminded of the plentiful enemies of the Ulfeldt family, thus indicating that their downfall was perhaps not entirely self-inflicted: »Sperling. / Men I er saa elsket! / Uhlfeldt. / Nej! misundt, frygtet, hadet! – troer I alt mig / Saa ubetydelig at ingen Fjende – –« (ibid., p. 27).
630 A conversaton between Walter and Dina in Act 1, Scene 3 indicates that Dina had hurled herself into this intrigue without realising the gravity of her actions: »Walter med et forskende Blik paa hende. / Husk paa, du kan ej træde tilbage! / En Afgrund har du om dig hulet ud! / Et Skridt af Vejen, – ned i den du styrter! / Dina forvirret. / Hvad mener I?« (ibid., p. 15).
631 Ibid., p. 17.

Mon da ei Uhlfeldt giøre kann min Lykke? – / Ej vil jeg længer' tumles op og ned, / Jeg Livet nyde vil i Rolighed! Med Klogskab hele Værket vil jeg drive, / Ei blot at Uhlfeldt blive skal i Live, / Men han skal indsee hvad for ham jeg vover, / Og skienke mig – langt meer end Walter lover![632]

Eleonora Christina Uhlfeldt does not present a positive image of the lower class (Jacob being the only noteworthy exception). Langemack, who betrays his lordship and Walter, despite his illustrious career as a man of humble origin, is the declared villain of the drama. Dina, though she may indeed be enamoured of Uhlfeldt, does not seem like the most loyal devotee and the other servants of the Uhlfeldt couple, too, appear to be fond of their masters purely based on the advantages gained from their service.[633] The medic Otto Sperling is the only true friend of the Uhlfeldt couple together with Corfitz's brother Lars Uhlfeldt, who appears in the last scene in order to advise his sibling against a secret departure from Denmark.

Eventually, only Eleonora, Otto Sperling and Lars Uhlfeldt (perhaps representative of his otherwise historically ambiguous clan) remain as positive characters. The two former serve as role models in Louise Hegermann Lindencrone's tale 'Billedet' (see Chapter 2.4.1.) as well, whereas Corfitz constitutes the mysterious dark side of the Ulfeldtian magnificence.[634] Yet the ultimate ideal of the drama is, of course, Eleonora, as indicated in the drama's preamble:

Maatte dette lille Stykke (et næsten ufrivilligt Udbrud ved Eleonoras Minde) bevæge en eller anden Læser til nøiere at giøre sig bekiendt med hendes Lidelsers og Taalmodigheds lange Historie, da vil han sikkert ikke fortryde de Timer han offrede til hendes Erindring, hvis hele Liv forkyndte hvad hendes Gravskrift saa skiønt og rørende stadfæster:
»Herre!
»Havde Dit Ord ikke været min Trøst,
»Da var jeg forgaaet i min Elendighed.« – [635]

---

[632] Ibid., p. 18.
[633] Ibid.: »Isak tømmer sit Bæger. / Et herligt Levnet! og et herligt Herskab! / Jeg vaager Aaret om paa dennes Viis / Med Hiertens Glæde! / Holst. / Vel er Vinen god, / Og Greven med, som ikke sparer den«.
[634] This ambiguous perception of Corfitz Ulfeldt is illustrated in a dream fantasy caused by the protagonist Elisabeth's delirious condition and her preceding meeting with the Ulfeldt family (Hegermann Lindencrone, Louise. 'Billedet', p. 165). In this vision, the Countess' presence soothes Elisabeth's feverish heat whereas her husband – although elsewhere portrayed as a loving father – emanates a daunting, almost infernal darkness.
[635] Hegermann Lindencrone, Louise. *Eleonora Christina Uhlfeldt*, unpaginated preamble.

Eleonora represents the ideal wife, a paragon of constancy. She both embodies and cherishes this virtue most blatantly as she takes leave of one of her unsuspecting daughters. The child receives a cross necklace made of sapphires, her mother's favourite gem, as a farewell-present: »Tag det som en Kierminde fra din Moder! / Blaat tyder paa Bestandighed! – Saphiren / Det er en ægte Ædelsteen, min Pige! / Min Kiærlighed til Dig er ogsaa ægte! / Og stærk som Ædelstenen! blaae som Himlen: / Saphiren er; din Moders Yndlingssteen! –«.[636] As demonstrated above, the contrast between Eleonora and Dina is illustrated in manifold ways; but the most preeminent discrepancy is left unsaid in the drama: »Dina Vinhofvers tvetydige personlighed, som først belyver og dernæst betages af Ulfeldt, kontrasteres virkningsfuldt med Leonora Christinas uforanderlige kærlighed til manden og trofasthed mod hans interesser, også hvor hun ikke deler hans synspunkter«.[637]

2.3.2. Adam Oehlenschläger: *Dina* (1842) – A Haven of Domestic Tranquility

> Under Læsningen af denne Bog [*Jammers Minde*] glemmer man hurtigt den gruelige Leonora Christina, som Oehlenschläger har tegnet i »Dina«. En større Afstand end den fra Oehlenschlägers moderne, hysteriske, pedantiske Kvinde til denne mægtige Skikkelse fra det syttende Aarhundrede kan ikke tænkes.[638]

Such were the words of Georg Brandes in his review of *Jammers Minde* in 1869. Evidently, Denmark's most influential critic at that time was not impressed by Adam Oehlenschläger's (1779-1850) presentation of Leonora Christina. Brandes' verdict is not a single case. The Danish scholar Vilhelm Andersen (1864-193), too, was openly disappointed by Oehlenschläger's depiction of Leonora Christina: »Man kan med god Grund klage over, at Oehlenschläger ikke kendte Leonora Christina bedre, da han i *Dina* skulde tegne hendes Billede. [...] Rigtignok er hans tykke, godlidende Frøken Eleonora, der har Taarer i Øjnene og Blækklatter paa Fingrene, ikke Leonora Christina [...]«.[639]

Yet, as is evident by its title, Leonora Christina was not meant to be the iridescent heroine of this tragic drama; rather her nemesis, Dina Vinhofvers, was. Dina's

---

636 Ibid., p. 93.
637 Busk-Jensen, Lise. *Romantikkens forfatterinder 2*, p. 796.
638 Brandes, Georg. 'Leonora Christina'. In *Georg Brandes – den mangfoldige*, ed. Jørgen Knudsen. Copenhagen: Gyldendal, 2005, p. 69.
639 Andersen, Vilhelm. *Adam Oehlenschläger: Et Livs Poesi 2*, p. 347.

wild accusations against the Ulfeldt couple, although withdrawn and disproven subsequently, were the first of a series of official denunciations against Corfitz Ulfeldt and his wife, and their reaction, i.e. the couple's flight to Sweden, initiated their rapid downfall. For a short period in the beginning of the 1650's, Dina's name resounded throughout the land and *Jammers Minde*, too, eternalised the name of this woman, who otherwise had no prospect whatsoever.

When Adam Oehlenschläger staged this less glorious episode in Danish history, much of the play's success had to be attributed to its leading actress, Johanne Luise Heiberg (1812-1890),[640] one of the greatest Danish actresses of her time. However, Dina's character and Oehlenschläger's reinterpretation of her fate also provided the proper *sujet* for a contemporary political discussion regarding Denmark's legal system,[641] thus resulting in mostly favourable critiques. Even the actress' husband Johan Ludvig Heiberg (1791-1860) gave it a rather positive review and defended Oehlenschläger's choice to aberrate from Dina's common image as a loose woman. In his memoirs, Oehlenschläger still remembers the criticism resulting from his all too positive portrayal of Dina:

> Stykket blev meget roest; nu holdt Dadlerne sig til, »at jeg havde forvansket Historien, at jeg havde tegnet Ulfeldt for slet og Dina for god; at hun var en lav Forbryderske.« Men alt, hvad der kan siges til Ulfelds Roes, har jeg ladet ham beholde i Stykket; jeg har kun ogsaa tegnet ham med hans Skyggesider.[642]

Oehlenschläger dismissed any criticism with the explanation that he had chosen poetic beauty over historical accuracy. Heiberg took up a similar position, emphasising that the drama in no way claimed to be historical, but portrayed a private episode in Ulfeldt's life, which had never been fully clarified in the first place.[643]

In *Dina,* Eleonora[644] is merely a secondary character. It is the love triangle involving Ulfeld, Dina and Walter that forms the core of the stage play. Consequently,

---

640 Holm-Hansen, Henrik. 'Dina i 1842'. In *Skitser til Romantikkens Teater: Tilegnet Torben Krogh,* ed. Svend Christiansen et al. Copenhagen: G. E. C. Gad, 1967, p. 101.

641 Bänsch, Alexandra. *»Katholisch im Kopf«: Die protestantische Romantik in Skandinavien und ihre Prätexte zwischen Mündlichkeit und Schriftlichkeit.* Baden-Baden: Nomos, 2011 (Die kulturelle Konstruktion von Gemeinschaften im Modernisierungsprozeß 11), p. 684.

642 Oehlenschläger, Adam. *Erindringer 4*, p. 172.

643 Heiberg, Johan Ludvig. 'Oehlenschlägers »Dina«'. In Heiberg, Johan Ludvig. *Prosaiske Skrifter 3.* Copenhagen: Reitzel, 1861, p. 378f.

644 In the present chapter, »Eleonora« specifically refers to the character in Oehlenschläger's drama, particularly when referring to passages that do not correspond to historical events, whereas »Leonora Christina« refers to the historical person. Another spelling variation used in the literary source text, and hence in this chapter as well, to refer to Corfitz Ulfeldt is »Ulfeld«.

Eleonora's character is rather dull, hence Brandes' evaluation above; and while Eleonora is a thoroughly positive character, Ulfeld's affectionate description of his wife reflects a female ideal, which was not befitting for a drama's heroine: »Hendes Fromhed, Troskab, / Deeltagelse, Forstand – og Modren til / Mig kiære Børn – Ledsagersken paa Livets / Tidt tornefulde, farefulde Vei – / Har ganske vundet Corfitz Ulfelds Hierte«.[645]

In order to turn Dina Vinhofvers into a character worthy of the audience's admiration and compassion, Oehlenschläger added, amongst other things, education to Dina's virtues. Thus, his eponymous heroine is both multilingual and well-read, despite her low social status.[646] By narrowing the intellectual gap between Leonora Christina and Dina, Oehlenschläger enables a direct comparison of the two women.[647] Their respective readings, however, mark a clear distinction between the two: Eleonora reads Latin and is thus fully in line with her time, the early modern period, whereas Dina is still attached to medieval courtly and heroic literature as well as folk poetry.[648] The latter genres were less fashionable in the 17th century, but even more so in Oehlenschläger's time. Several scenes give additional impetus for a direct comparison:[649] 1) Dina in the Blue Tower, a scene in the fifth act, which is inevitably reminiscent of Leonora Christina's fate and likewise provoked by Corfitz Ulfeldt's actions; and 2) Two diverse scenes, respectively in Act 3 and 5, show Eleonora and Dina in disguise (as fishermaid and *Amagerpige*), both times as a result of Ulfeld's double life.

When Dina, disguised as flower-selling *Amagerpige*, visits Ulfeld's mansion in Copenhagen, she reflects on the visibly changed surroundings compared to the last time they saw each other:

O, hvor forskiellig er Naturen her / Fra den, hvor sidste Gang vi saaes! Der kiendte / Det vilde Sand- og Vandstøv ingen Skranker; / Her drømmer Blomsten bag den snevre Muur, / Som om den sad i Fængsel. – Dina! hvis / Du i din Blomsterungdom saadan sad / Indsluttet af den skumle Fængselsvæg![650]

---

645 Oehlenschläger, Adam. *Dina*, p. 72.

646 Ibid., p. 34.

647 As contended by Alexandra Bänsch, this erudition is, by itself, not portrayed as a signature trait of a positive character, or even as a useful skill. Ulfeld, Eleonora, Dina and Otto Sperling are all fairly educated characters. This does, however, not prevent them from actively contributing to the unfolding of the tragedy (Bänsch, Alexandra. »*Katholisch im Kopf*«, p. 705).

648 Dvergsdal, Alvhild. *Adam Oehlenschlägers tragediekunst*. Copenhagen: Museum Tusculanums Forlag, 1997, p. 258.

649 Ibid., p. 258f.

650 Oehlenschläger, Adam. *Dina*, p. 65.

Dina's most preeminent feature is passion[651] (represented by »det vilde Sand- og Vanstøv«), whereas Eleonora impresses with qualities of a more practical nature. Dina, by nature an impractical and tragically unconventional character,[652] does not see or understand practical qualities and equates her former lover's new life and love with a prison (»Her drømmer Blomsten bag den snevre Muur, / Som om den sad i Fængsel«). Eleonora, on the other hand, is perfectly content in her 'prison'. Even on the evening of her family's flight to Sweden, the unsuspecting Countess does not see the coming storm, but engages in plans to regain her enemy's, i.e. the Queen's, favour:

> ELEONORA. / Hvilket herligt Indfald – / Du har dog mange gode Indfald, Corfitz! – / At i den store Maskerade, holdt / Paa Slottet, Deel vi tage, klædt som Fisker / Og Fiskerinde. Jeg mig nærmer ydmygt / Da Dronningen, og overrækker hende / Det lille Dannebrog, hvori med Perler / Er stukket hendes Navnetræk med Krone. / Jeg synker paa mit Knæ, og rækker hende / Det lille Vers. / ULFELD. / Har du det færdigt? / ELEONORA. / Ja, / Her er det. / Rækker ham Papiret. / ULFELD / læser det. / Det er smukt, men alt for ydmygt.[653]

Leonora Christina's pride, which has evoked dispraise by both contemporaries as well as later generations, has completely vanished from Oehlenschläger's depiction: upon being informed that she is no longer entitled to drive her carriage into the castle courtyard, Eleonora reacts equanimously, rather than taking exception to this public withdrawal of her privileges: »Og om saa var – hvad er det da vel meer? / At gaae et Par Skridt længer. Ei jeg finder / Min Fader længer i min Faders Borg, / Om agende jeg kommer, eller gaaer; / Det veed jeg nok«.[654] Eleonora even shows herself appreciative of her rival: »Sandt nok, / Mig har man krænket; men det siger Intet. / Sophia, Dronningen, er fremmed her, / Hun troer, jeg trænger mig hovmodig

---

651 Cf. Billeskov Jansen, F. J. 'Passion og Skæbne: Studier i Oehlenschlägers Æstetik og dens Kilder'. In *Nordisk litteraturhistorie – en bog til Brøndsted: 12. november 1978*, ed. Hans Bekker-Nielsen et al. Odense Universitetsforlag, 1978, p. 137: »Som drivende Kraft i stor Digtning har Oehlenschläger da fra 1800 regnet Lidenskaben«.
652 Cf. Møller, P. L. 'Dina, tragisk Drama i 5 Acter'. In Møller, P. L. *Kritiske Skizzer fra Aarene 1840-47.* Copenhagen, 1847, p. 41: »Og især maa det fremhæves, at Digteren her til Trods for dem, der mene, at han ikke er fulgt med Tiden, i sin Hovedperson har med Begeistring og ungdommelig Varme grebet en af de Ideer, der stærkest bevæge sig i den moderne Tidsalder, nemlig den kvindelige Aands Frihedsberettigelse, idet han viser den ædel og interessant, og vækker vor Deltagelse for den, selv i de Forvildelser, hvortil den føres af en lidenskabelig Natur og Mangel paa klart Indblik i Tilværelsens høiere Orden og Sammenhæng«.
653 Oehlenschläger, Adam. *Dina*, p. 121.
654 Ibid., p. 25.

frem. / Maaske jeg stundom var lidt utaalmodig; / Hver har sin Feil. Det vil nok give sig«.[655]

Towards her husband, Eleonora is equally abject[656] – at the expense of *his* likeability.

> ELEONORA. / Min Gud! hvad fattes dig? / ULFELD. / Alt, Alt maaskee, / Og derfor takker jeg din latterlige, / Urimelige Følsomhed. At du / Bestandig i det timelige Liv, / Med al din Lærdom, Viisdom, bærer dig / Saa keitet ad – det styrter mig til Helved. / ELEONORA. / Igien du raser. / ULFELD. / Hvorfor hader os / Vel Dronningen? Fordi til hendes Kroning, / Da vi besøgte Juveleren, du, / Der endelig skal prøve hendes Krone, / Laer Kronen falde, saa en sielden Perle, / Den bedste, springer af, og sønderknuses. / At det var Hændelse, det vil Sophia, / Det vilde Kongen selv ei troe; de troede, / Det var af Ondskab, af Misundelse, / Du lod den unge Dronnings Krone falde – / Og Hevnen fletter os en Tornekrone.[657]

In his outburst, Ulfeld alludes to an incident, which has been conveyed, among others, by Ludvig Holberg in his *Dannemarks Riges Historie* (1732-35).[658] Ulfeld's angry reproach causes Eleonora to break into tears, thus highlighting the negative aspects of his character. Accordingly, while the King himself never believed in the allegations raised by Dina, he does openly criticise Ulfeld on a personal level:

---

655 Ibid., p. 28.

656 Particularly curious is the fact that during the interrogations, Eleonora is considerably weaker than her husband. Shortly before escorting Dina to the torture rack, Otto Krag informs her that Eleonora's health had suffered severely from the allegations raised against her husband. Thus, Ulfeld has to testify on her behalf, before Krag can assure himself of Eleonora's state of health (ibid., p. 90). Additionally, Ulfeld repeatedly calls his wife too delicate: »Min Hustru kan ei heller trives her [in Denmark]. / Hun er for øm, for blød; af lutter Omsorg / Hun vilde vist forraade mig. – Afsted!« (ibid., p. 102). This evaluation contrasts (ensuing) history which reports Leonora Christina to have testified on behalf of her husband (for example in the trial of Malmö), not to mention Leonora Christina's own numerous accounts which, among other things, depict her carrying her weakened husband down a rocky cliff.

657 Ibid., p. 78.

658 According to Holberg, the royal goldsmith Caspar Herbach ('Kunst-Caspar', 1600-1664) was almost finished manufacturing the crown designated for Sophie Amalie's coronation ceremony in 1648 when Leonora Christina suddenly entered his workshop in Lyngby-Mølle and demanded to see the gem. One can imagine the smith's flurry when Leonora Christina placed the costly item on her own head in order to see how it suited her, but he must have lived through his worst nightmare when the crown suddenly fell to the ground and one of the bigger jewels got destroyed. Ludvig Holberg narrates this anecdote in order to explain Sophie Amalie's subsequent behaviour towards her sister-in-law; and while he does not even attempt to determine whether this incident was an accident, he expresses some understanding of the Queen's conviction that it was none. See Holberg, Ludvig. *Dannemarks Riges Historie 3. Med et tilstrækkeligt Register over alle III. Tomer*. Copenhagen: Hans Kongl. Majests. og Universitets Bogtrykkerie, 1735, p. 593.

I Cabinettet var du altid klog; / D'Avaux, La Thuillerie, samt Oxenstierna, / Ja Mazarin gav dig fortiente Roes. / Men – du mig forekommer, som en Qvinde, / Alt for forelsket i din egen Skiønhed. / Ja, du er en forfængelig Narciss. / Hvor du kom frem – i Haag, Paris, i London, / Du holdt et Indtog, som det kunde været Mig selv.[659]

Oehlenschläger does not mention the historical allegations of embezzlement against Corfitz Ulfeldt that contributed to his flight, thus his motives in the drama remain entirely personal. When Frederik III refuses to pardon Dina at the request of Ulfeld, the latter sees no other way to save her but to bribe the prison guards and help her flee to Sweden. Despite his flaws, Ulfeld emerges as a noble character, whose biggest imperfection is a quick temper. This vice causes him to act and talk rashly, thus leaving his audience in the dark about his sincere motives. Thus, the tragedy unfolds in the third act, when Ulfeld's audience – Dina hiding behind the hedge – overhears Eleonora quoting her husband's previous hasty words about poisoning the King. Unlike his wife, Dina does not know Ulfeld (quite literally, since she did not even know his name for a long time) and as a consequence, she misinterprets the situation and takes him at his word.[660] This scene is paralleled by one in the fourth act, when Ulfeld, once again angered by the King, resolves upon leaving for Sweden:

Men han begriber ikke Corfitz Ulfeld, / Han skiønner ikke paa ham. Nei, det har / Han aldrig giort. Kun den Udmærkede / Forstaaer, hvad er udmærket er i Verden. / [...] Han lader sig ei rokkes, aldrig ledes; / Det passer sig godt for den store Hob, / For Pøblen, som han giøre vil til Folk, / Men ei for hvad der ædlest er og herligst. / O, hvor forskiellig er dog du, Christina! / Du er en Dina – men i større Stiil, / Som Magt har til at bringe Ridderaand / Og Poesie og Eventyr tilbage. –[661]

This praise of Queen Christina of Sweden leaves the audience, who – just like Dina – do not know Ulfeld's enigmatic personality, wondering whether his flight was ultimately provoked by his noble attempt to save Dina, or by his argument with Frederik III. This scene also offers a last word of admiration for Dina, thus revealing that Ulfeld's reasons for cheating on his wife were not all too base. And even though Eleonora eventually wins the fight for Ulfeld's heart, this victory is not necessarily a compliment to her person, since her husband is not portrayed in

---

659 Oehlenschläger, Adam. *Dina*, p. 96.
660 Cf. Bänsch, Alexandra. *»Katholisch im Kopf«*, p. 686.
661 Oehlenschläger, Adam. *Dina*, p. 101.

the most positive manner. The incertitude regarding Ulfeld's motives for fleeing is even reinforced by his wife's sorrowful monologue in the fifth act: »Og saa til Holland! hvor du vil, kun ei / Til Danmark atter! – Corfitz Ulfeld! o, / Du elsker ei dit Fædreland, som jeg«.[662] Eleonora does indeed love her fatherland, but even more so her father: »Den store Mand, / Som leved og som hersked der, er død; / Dog glædte det mig, og det trøsted mig, / At gaae i Hallerne, hvor Christian leved. / […] Elskte Fader! / Hvi kan dit Billed ikke følge mig?«[663] The fact that Eleonora is the daughter of Christian IV is an asset of hers repeatedly mentioned throughout the text, for example when Ulfeld states his love for his wife to Walter (»Jeg elsker Leonora, Christians Datter«).[664] While Eleonora's ancestry may certainly seem appealing to Ulfeld, it must have mattered even more to the drama's audience. Accordingly, the first of these references to the former King of Denmark occurs almost immediately before Ulfeld's hasty death threat, thus potentially enhancing understanding of Ulfeld's anger: »Fierde Christians elskte Datter, / Ham af hans Børn det allerkiæreste, / Christin' Eleonora maa ei meer / I Karmen age til sin Faders Gaard, / Hun skal staae af i Skarnet udenfor«.[665]

The highest praise Oehlenschläger accorded to Corfitz Ulfeldt is his love for this grand woman. In turn, the mutuality of this feeling acts to Ulfeldt's credit. Eleonora is the person closest to truly knowing her husband. Thus, her assessment of his character is not to be disregarded:

ULFELD / stirrer rørt paa hende. / Leonora! / Tidt undrer jeg mig over, hvordan du / Kan elske mig saa høit. / ELEONORA. / Jeg kiender dig. / ULFELD. / Mit Sind er vildt og stolt, jeg tilstaaer det. / Det hede Blod, det løber af med mig; / Dog hersker Aandens Kraft, naar Blodet køles. / ELEONORA. / Ja, Corfitz Ulfeld! du er en Vulcan. / Men det gaaer mig, som i Sicilien / Og i Neapel Bønderne: de elske / Dog Bierget, skiøndt det ofte spruder Ild. / De boe derved, de bygge deres Hytter / Derpaa; thi Grunden er velsignet, frugtbar, / Og skienker deres Viingaard ædle Druer, / Som langt, langt overgaae den sikkre Dals. / ULFELD. / Men – hvis engang der kom et Jordskiælv med / En Lavastrøm, som slugte dig og Bierget? / Eleonora. / Saa synker jeg, som alle Mennesker, / I Jordens Skiød. Det skal vi Alle dog. / Vogt dig for Udbrud, hvis du elsker Danmark, / Og hvis du elsker mig! Da vil vort Land / Sundt vederqvæges af din ædle Drue.[666]

---

662 Ibid., p. 124.
663 Ibid., p. 125.
664 Ibid., p. 108.
665 Ibid., p. 25.
666 Ibid., p. 28.

Eleonora's unconscious prophecy of her own demise simultaneously acts as a guarantor for Ulfeld's good character, since she identifies his eruptive nature as his only flaw. Interestingly, this dialogue mirrors the notions of Hans Christian Andersen (see Chapter 2.2.1.) and Count Waldstein-Wartenberg, who both thought Corfitz Ulfeldt to have been a great man, but a misunderstood statesman, and regarded Leonora Christina's loyalty as a proof of his grandeur. Oehlenschläger's presentation, however, is more nuanced, since Eleonora casts a slight shadow over this dynamic by inadvertently challenging the sincerity in Ulfeld's intentions: »Vogt dig for Udbrud, hvis du elsker Danmark, / Og hvis du elsker mig!«. Once again, Oehlenschläger's audience is left wondering about the true nature of Denmark's most infamous traitor, and about why he was unable to follow his wife's advice. While Oehlenschläger thus portrays a Corfitz Ulfeldt typical of the 19th century, his version of Leonora Christina serves as a comment on his age's conciliatory image of an allegedly misunderstood man.

Despite their personal and professional acquaintance, the conformity of the event depicted in their dramas and the congruencies listed above, Hegermann Lindencrone and Oehlenschläger have thus nevertheless devised two very different interpretations of the Dina affair and in particular of the – partially invented – love triangle involving Leonora Christina, Corfitz Ulfeldt and Dina Vinhofvers. One way to illustrate the diverging character dynamics in the two dramas is the configuration model originally developed by the Romanian mathematician Solomon Marcus and subsequently simplified by the German literary scholar Manfred Pfister.[667] A configuration[668] series (»Konfigurationsfolge«)[669] is a matrix summarising the presence of the dramatis personae scene by scene, by signifying a figure's presence in a scene with '1', its absence with '0'. This model is a simple and illustrative way to depict a figure's relationship with other characters in a drama.[670] It is important to note, however, that in this context, scene (»scène«[671] in the German edition whereas unfortunately, the English edition makes no such distinction) is not synonymous with the English word denoting a subdivision of an act, but corresponds to one configuration, i.e. to one set of figures being present on stage.

---

667 Pfister, Manfred. *Das Drama: Theorie und Analyse*. Munich: Wilhelm Fink, 1984 (1982), pp. 235-240. For the English translation, see Pfister, Manfred. *The Theory and Analysis of Drama*, transl. John Halliday. Cambridge University Press, 1991 (European Studies in English Literature), pp. 171-176.
668 Pfister, Manfred. *Das Drama*, p. 235.
669 Ibid., p. 238.
670 Ibid., p. 236.
671 Ibid., p. 235.

	1	2	3	4	5	6	7	8	9	10	11	12	13	14
Dina	1	1	1	1	0	0	0	0	0	1	0	1	0	1
Langemack	1	1	0	0	1	0	0	0	0	1	0	0	0	1
Walter	0	1	1	0	0	0	0	0	0	0	0	0	0	0
Holst	0	0	0	0	1	0	0	0	0	0	0	0	0	0
Kield Fries	0	0	0	0	1	0	0	0	0	0	0	0	0	0
Isak	0	0	0	0	1	0	0	0	0	0	0	0	0	0
Peter	0	0	0	0	1	1	0	0	0	0	0	0	0	0
Sperling	0	0	0	0	0	1	1	1	0	0	1	1	1	0
Eleonora	0	0	0	0	0	0	1	1	1	0	0	0	0	0
Uhlfeldt	0	0	0	0	0	0	0	1	1	0	0	0	0	0
Sperling's servant	0	0	0	0	0	0	0	0	0	0	1	0	0	0
Jacob	0	0	0	0	0	0	0	0	0	0	0	0	0	1
Lene Boiesen	0	0	0	0	0	0	0	0	0	0	0	0	0	0
Ellen Christine	0	0	0	0	0	0	0	0	0	0	0	0	0	0
Jacobsen	0	0	0	0	0	0	0	0	0	0	0	0	0	0
Yonger children	0	0	0	0	0	0	0	0	0	0	0	0	0	0
Elder children	0	0	0	0	0	0	0	0	0	0	0	0	0	0
Lars Uhlfeldt	0	0	0	0	0	0	0	0	0	0	0	0	0	0

Fig. 1: The configuration series in Louise Hegermann-Lindencrone: *Eleonora Christina Uhlfeldt* (1817). For the sake of lucidity, mere prop figures were omitted from the matrices depicted in Fig. 1 and 2 (see next page). The leftmost column contains the *dramatis personae* in the order of the figures' appearance, the topmost row contains the *scènes*, or configurations.

15	16	17	18	19	20	21	22	23	24	25	26	27	28	29	30	31	32	33	34
1	0	0	0	0	0	0	0	0	0	0	0	0	0	1	1	0	0	0	0
0	0	0	0	0	0	0	0	0	1	0	0	0	0	0	0	0	1	0	0
0	0	0	0	0	0	0	0	0	1	1	0	0	0	0	0	0	0	0	0
0	0	0	0	0	0	0	0	0	0	0	0	0	0	0	0	0	0	0	0
0	0	0	0	0	0	0	0	0	0	0	0	0	0	0	0	0	0	0	0
0	0	0	0	0	0	0	0	0	0	0	0	0	0	0	0	0	0	0	0
0	0	0	0	0	0	0	0	0	0	0	0	0	0	0	0	0	0	0	0
0	0	0	1	1	1	1	0	0	0	0	0	0	1	0	0	0	0	1	1
0	1	1	1	1	1	1	1	1	0	0	0	1	1	0	0	1	0	0	1
0	1	0	0	1	0	1	1	1	0	0	1	0	0	0	0	0	0	0	1
0	0	0	0	0	0	0	0	0	0	0	0	0	0	0	0	0	0	0	0
1	0	0	0	0	0	0	0	1	0	0	0	0	0	0	0	0	0	0	0
0	0	0	1	1	0	1	1	0	0	0	0	0	0	0	0	0	0	0	0
0	0	0	0	0	0	0	0	0	0	0	0	1	1	0	0	1	0	0	0
0	0	0	0	0	0	0	0	0	0	0	0	0	0	1	0	0	0	0	0
0	0	0	0	0	0	0	0	0	0	0	0	0	0	0	0	1	0	0	0
0	0	0	0	0	0	0	0	0	0	0	0	0	0	0	0	0	0	0	1
0	0	0	0	0	0	0	0	0	0	0	0	0	0	0	0	0	0	0	1

	1	2	3	4	5	6	7	8	9	10	11	12	13	14	15	16	17	18	19	20	21
Ulfeld	1	1	1	1	1	1	1	1	1	1	0	0	0	0	0	0	0	0	0	0	0
Hennings	1	0	0	0	0	0	0	0	0	0	0	0	0	0	0	0	0	0	0	0	0
Sperling	0	1	1	1	0	0	0	0	0	0	0	0	0	0	0	0	0	0	0	0	0
Eleonora	0	0	1	1	0	0	0	0	0	1	0	0	0	0	0	0	0	0	0	0	0
Servant	0	0	0	1	1	1	1	0	0	0	0	0	0	0	0	0	0	0	0	0	0
Lykke	0	0	0	0	0	1	0	0	0	0	0	0	0	0	0	0	0	0	0	0	0
Walter	0	0	0	0	0	0	0	1	0	0	0	0	1	1	0	0	0	0	0	1	1
Dina	0	0	0	0	0	0	0	0	0	0	1	1	1	0	0	0	1	0	0	1	1
Johanna	0	0	0	0	0	0	0	0	0	0	0	1	1	1	1	1	1	1	1	1	1
Child Dina	0	0	0	0	0	0	0	0	0	0	0	1	0	0	0	0	0	0	1	1	1
Paul Gebhard	0	0	0	0	0	0	0	0	0	0	0	0	0	0	0	1	1	1	0	0	0
Rudolf Vinhofer	0	0	0	0	0	0	0	0	0	0	0	0	0	0	0	1	1	1	1	1	1
Sergeant	0	0	0	0	0	0	0	0	0	0	0	0	0	0	0	0	1	1	1	1	0
Gardener	0	0	0	0	0	0	0	0	0	0	0	0	0	0	0	0	0	0	0	0	0
Otho Krag	0	0	0	0	0	0	0	0	0	0	0	0	0	0	0	0	0	0	0	0	0
Frederik III	0	0	0	0	0	0	0	0	0	0	0	0	0	0	0	0	0	0	0	0	0
Prison Magistrate	0	0	0	0	0	0	0	0	0	0	0	0	0	0	0	0	0	0	0	0	0
Monk	0	0	0	0	0	0	0	0	0	0	0	0	0	0	0	0	0	0	0	0	0

Fig. 2: The configuration series in Adam Oehlenschläger: *Dina* (1842)

22	23	24	25	26	27	28	29	30	31	32	33	34	35	36	37	38	39	40	41	42	43	44	45	46	47
0	0	0	0	1	1	1	1	0	0	0	0	1	1	0	1	1	0	0	0	0	1	0	1	1	0
0	0	0	0	0	0	0	0	0	0	0	0	0	0	0	0	0	0	0	0	0	0	0	0	0	0
0	0	0	0	0	0	0	0	0	0	0	0	0	0	0	0	0	0	0	0	0	0	0	0	0	0
0	0	0	0	0	1	0	1	0	0	0	0	0	0	0	0	0	0	0	0	0	1	1	0	0	0
0	0	0	0	0	0	0	0	0	0	0	0	0	0	0	0	0	0	0	0	0	0	0	0	0	0
0	0	0	0	0	0	0	0	0	0	0	0	0	0	0	0	0	0	0	0	0	0	0	0	0	0
1	0	0	0	0	0	0	0	1	1	0	0	0	0	1	1	1	0	0	1	0	0	0	0	0	0
1	1	1	1	1	1	1	0	0	1	1	1	0	0	0	0	0	1	1	1	1	0	0	0	1	1
0	0	0	0	0	0	0	0	0	0	0	0	0	0	0	0	0	1	1	0	0	0	0	0	0	0
0	0	0	0	0	0	0	0	0	0	0	0	0	0	0	0	0	1	0	0	0	0	0	0	0	0
0	0	0	0	0	0	0	0	0	0	0	0	0	0	0	0	0	0	0	0	0	0	0	0	0	0
0	0	0	0	0	0	0	0	0	0	0	0	0	0	0	0	0	0	0	0	0	0	0	0	0	0
0	0	0	0	0	0	0	0	0	0	0	0	0	0	0	0	0	0	0	0	0	0	0	0	0	0
0	0	1	0	0	0	0	0	0	0	0	0	0	0	0	0	0	0	0	0	0	0	0	0	0	0
0	0	0	0	0	0	0	0	0	0	0	1	0	0	0	0	0	0	0	0	0	0	0	0	0	0
0	0	0	0	0	0	0	0	0	0	0	1	0	0	0	0	0	0	0	0	0	0	0	0	0	0
0	0	0	0	0	0	0	0	0	0	0	0	0	0	0	0	0	0	0	0	0	0	0	1	0	0
0	0	0	0	0	0	0	0	0	0	0	0	0	0	0	0	0	0	0	0	0	0	0	0	0	1

The configuration structure (»Konfigurationsstruktur«)[672] of Hegermann Lindencrone's drama (Fig. 1) exhibits an opposition of Dina and lower class representatives on one side and Eleonora and upper class representatives on the other side.[673] There is hardly any interaction between these two classes, the only exception being the sporadic appearances of servants, who help to advance the plot. Accordingly, Eleonora and Dina are alternating figures (»szenisch alternative Figuren«),[674] as they never appear in the same configuration. There is no scenically dominant figure (»szenisch dominante Figur«),[675] as the dominance is shared between Eleonora and Dina. There is a very short scenic distance (»szenische Distanz«)[676] between these two women, as one of them appears in nearly every *scène*. The scenic distance between Uhlfeldt and Dina, on the other hand, is longer. The distance between these two figures is also reflected in Uhlfeldt's alternating relationship with any member of the lower classes. Unlike his wife, he does not interact at all with servants. Hence, in most of the *scènes*, Sperling, who is a rather central figure in the drama, functions as family confidant and as a communicating link between the upper and lower class.

In Adam Oehlenschläger's drama *Dina* (see Fig. 2) there is no need for a linking figure since Dina and her peers have been raised to a higher moral and social level, hence eliminating the premises for an opposition based on social class. Eleonora and Dina are *almost* alternating figures: they share the stage when Dina overhears the equivocal words regarding the poison. Dina, Ulfeld and Eleonora are all present in this central *scène*, but the latter is excluded from this knowledge. From Eleonora's perspective, she and 'the other woman' are alternating figures. Ulfeld and Dina, on the other hand, are alone together twice and share a few more configurations. The scenic distance between Dina and Ulfeld is also much shorter than between Dina and Eleonora, all of which creates the impression of Eleonora being a secondary character, who is excluded from most of the plot. These two configuration structures yield two almost opposing drama concepts: whereas Hegermann Lindencrone staged the tragedy of Ulfeldt and Leonora Christina, Oehlenschläger depicted the tragic love story of Dina and Ulfeldt.

---

672 Ibid., p. 236.
673 The relevance of social class within a configuration structure has also been emphasised by Pfister (cf. ibid., p. 238).
674 Ibid., p. 237.
675 Ibid.
676 Ibid.

2.3.3. Rolf Gjedsted: *Fordærvede kvinder* (1991) – The Wise Witch

> Quinden som altiid Meente att ieg kunde traalle bleff staedfestet i sin meening der om anden dagen bleff giort Riddere, oc ieg icke alleeneste sagde hwær gang Trometerne blæste, nu bleff der giort en Ridder (thi ieg kunde høre *Herolden* raabe ud aff winduet men icke forstaa hwad hand sagde) men endoc hwem der war bleffwen Ridder, thi ded giættede ieg, efftersom ieg wiste, att der ware de i Raaded, som icke føre ware Riddere; oc efftersom ded sic saa befant, saa troede quinden fuld oc fast att ieg kunde Traale[.]
>
> (*Jammers Minde*, p. 92)

Louise Hegermann Lindencrone and Adam Oehlenschläger both aesthetisised the parameter of history, thus lending it more reverence than the matter demanded. According to Dina's (false) testimony, she had overheard a treacherous conversation between Ulfeldt and his wife hidden underneath his blanket. The circumstances of her discovery – her concealment and the possibility of misconception induced by the barrier between her and the speaking couple – have been adapted by the above-mentioned authors with the result of a more dignified course of events. In both cases, Dina hears parts of an ongoing conversation between Eleonora and her husband as she is hiding behind a wall. Contemporary Danish writer Rolf Gjedsted, however, does not care much about a courtly presentation of events – his declared intention is simply to »give et billede af tiden, hvor handlingen foregår«.[677] Consequently, Gjedsted's Dina, as all other historical characters portrayed in *Fordærvede kvinder*, is in no way idealised: hidden underneath Ulfeldt's duvet, she hears parts of a conversation regarding poisoned mint drops. Whether or not the attack would have been realised if Dina had not been present remains unresolved. Unlike Oehlenschläger and Hegermann Lindencrone, Gjedsted does not attempt to present a possible explanation for public events; his objective is to deliver impressions of the time around 1650, as he himself experienced it through historical research. In line with Gjedsted's perception of 17th-century Denmark, Leonora Christina is one of the plentiful *fordærvede kvinder* depicted in his novel.

A typical feature of the time depicted in Gjedsted's novel are the witch trials and the still prevalent popular belief in supernatural powers. Women were not the sole target of the Inquisition, yet a modern association of this chapter in history

---

677 Gjedsted, Rolf. *Fordærvede kvinder: En fortælling omkring året 1650.* Copenhagen: Gyldendal, 1991, unpaginated postface. *Fordærvede kvinder* is the first part of a trilogy published in the years 1991-1992, whose diverse parts focus on the Copenhagen city life of the 17th century. Part 2 and 3, respectively titled *Fandens karle* and *Fastende hjerter*, portray the lives of people from diverse social classes in the pest-stricken Copenhagen of 1652 (*Fandens karle*) and the schemes of the city's nobility in the year 1654 (*Fastende hjerter*).

with mostly female victims prevails. At the same time, both Leonora Christina and history report several women of rather ambivalent fame from this period.[678] Wicked women, albeit as victims of men, are thus the unifying topic of the novel. Frederik III is highly aware of this nuisance. Witchhunters do not play a part in Gjedsted's novel, but the husband of the most powerful woman operating in *Fordærvede kvinder*, Frederik III, takes on inquisitor-like qualities. This characteristic of the King of Denmark originates from his clerical past as Bishop of Bremen and Prince-Bishop of Verden. When Frederik's older brother Christian, the heir to Christian IV's throne (*den udvalgte prins*), died in 1647 as a result of his bacchanal lifestyle and was followed by his father in 1648, Frederik, quite unexpectedly, became King of Denmark. Throughout his reign, Frederik III maintained a devout conduct of life. He kept his interest in science and theology and is said to have never been seen drunk. Accordingly, Gjedsted's Frederik III perceives it as his mission to rid Copenhagen of all vicious women.[679]

Yet, despite the King's devoutness, a major concern of his was the natural sciences as well. All kinds of freaks of nature, human or not, would immediately get his attention. The early modern period was the age of the dark sciences, hence *Fordærvede kvinder* depicts of series of human interactions with nature on the cusp between the mystical and the empirical, such as poisonings,[680] experiments with corpses and, of course, alchemy. A meeting with two whales, back then still perceived as mysterious sea monsters, triggers a series of apocalyptic visions. The arrival of the sea creatures is preceded by the appearance of several misformed precursors[681] and when the King himself arrives at the scene, the removal process, starting with the killing of the animals, causes Frederik III to reflect on the deprivation of the world.[682] In order to remove the stranded whales, a professional whaler has been sent for – a true sea bear, who has even been sailing the waters surrounding Svalbard. The man exhibits permanent damage on his left eye, not induced by a whale,

---

678 *Jammers Minde* documents the lives of several fallen women. Leonora Christina's aged servant Karen Olesdatter is vain and flirts with all kinds of men in the Blue Tower. She, as well as another maid by the name of Karen, has committed infanticide. Another maid, Cathrina, is a crestfallen alcoholic while yet another maid by the name of Inger is a promiscuous woman, thus arousing comparison with Dina (see *Jammers Minde*, p. 185). And another maid aborts her unborn child in the tower.

679 Gjedsted, Rolf. *Fordærvede kvinder*, p. 140: »København er ikke, hvad den har været. [...] Der er flere lastefulde kvinder nu en på min salig faders tid«.

680 The demise of Anna Olesdatter's husband, for example, is induced by the poisonous mushrooms provided by the witch Karen Kruse. However, Anna intends to reinforce the agency of her venomed dish by burying her husband's night shirt on a site of death, such as a graveyard or underneath the city gallows.

681 Gjedsted, Rolf. *Fordærvede kvinder*, p. 85.

682 Ibid., p. 88: »Frederik så pludselig hele menneskeheden koge og martre i sit eget blod på grund af dens synder«.

but by his wife. To Frederik, women in particular are a symptom of the world's moral decay, hence his thoughts turn towards the shrew that broke the man who fights the greatest monsters on earth: »Så tænkte han på, hvilken kvinde det mon var, som havde givet den uforfærdede hvalfanger de voldsomme kramper omkring øjet. Det var en helt anden historie, men den samme. Det havde også noget at gøre med menneskets livslange kamp, vidste kongen«.[683]

Being the most powerful man in the country, Frederik does not only target lower class women, but even the former first lady of the Danish realm. Gjedsted's Leonora,[684] though not a typical witch, exhibits haggish traits as well and, as is known from her own recollections in *Jammers Minde*, there had been rumours regarding her seemingly supernatural talent to always land on her feet (see Chapter 1.2.1.). Rolf Gjedsted's presentation of Leonora Christina follows her own portrayal in *Jammers Minde*, as she attributes her ambiguous fame to her superior talents, first of all her intelligence. In accordance with Leonora Christina's self-portrayal, Rolf Gjedsted ascribes the following thoughts to her: »Det der med hekseriet havde hun jo aldrig troet på. Folk havde også kaldt hende selv ‚heks' flere gange i hendes liv, fordi hun kunne mere end sit Fadervor«.[685]

Leonora is also a loving wife, who considers herself to be much stronger than her physically and mentally weakened husband. At the same time, she is a devout Christian, a *Christi Kaarßdragerske*, who will heal her chronically ill husband with her very own white magic, i.e. her faith, common sense and some household remedies:

---

683 Ibid., p. 89.

684 In the present chapter, »Leonora« specifically refers to the character in Rolf Gjedsted's novel, particularly when referring to passages that do not correspond to historical events, whereas »Leonora Christina« refers to the historical person. Furthermore, Queen Sophie Amalie is consistently referred to as »Sofie Amalie«.

685 Gjedsted, Rolf. *Fordærvede kvinder*, p. 187. The same kind of enlightened attitude towards the contemporary witch trials is repeatedly documented in *Jammers Minde*, where Leonora Christina harnesses her servants' fear of her own seemingly supernatural knowledge (cf. Chapter 1.2.1.). At the same time, Leonora Christina expresses doubt at some of the accusations raised against other women: »Hun [her maid Karen Olesdatter] fortelte oc om en hun holte for en Traaldquinde atskilligt, som dog icke bestoed i anded, end vdi wiidenskab, att læge Fransoser, oc skille Hoerer wed derris Foster oc dißlige vtilbørligheder, med samme quinde haffde hun meget omgaaet« (*Jammers Minde*, p. 93). Coincidentally, Leonora Christina did indeed know a Karen Kruse. She was the wife of a councilman and, before the Ulfeldt couple's departure from Denmark, a good friend of the family (cf. Birket Smith, Sophus. *Leonora Christina Grevinde Ulfeldts Historie 1*, p. 261). Other than the name, however, these two namesakes have nothing in common.

Hun havde helbredt børnene for tyfus og lidende soldater for uhelbredelige sår. Hun var udvalgt af Vorherre. Den kloge kones medicin var måske til nytte for folk, der troede på det. Men når det kom til stykket ... [...] Ikke mere brændevin, og mange bønner i stedet.[686]

Leonora also has a special connection with animals, as demonstrated by her subsequent attempt to domesticate a mouse.[687] Besides being another reference to Leonora's witch-like qualities it is also a parallel to Leonora Christina's life recollected in *Jammers Minde*, where she states that she had tamed a rat to keep her company in prison. In the same cell, Leonora Christina kept and nursed an old dog and a kitten as well. Her loving care for and interest in all the creatures housing her prison cell elevates her from the lower class people guarding her and maltreating these animals. As related in *Jammers Minde*, Leonora Christina's prison pets fell prey to her cruel guardians: the free-ranging inmate Christian persuades the castellan Johan Jæger to throw Leonora Christina's kitten off the tower and one of her maids burns Leonora Christina's tame rat (respectively *Jammers Minde*, p. 154 (marginal note) and p. 202 (marginal note)).

Leonora's attempt to tame a mouse is followed by an omen: the same mouse, which indeed seems to take a liking to her, is eaten by Karen Kruse's – the only true witch among Gjedsted's wicked women – cat. The black cat annihilating the effects of Leonora's white magic is a hint to coming events hardly ever absent in Leonora Christina-literature. Another such hint is Leonora's sighting of three ravens on her way back from Copenhagen to the medicinal spring of Sct. Helene, where she left Corfitz behind.[688] The sight of these ominous birds is furthermore reminiscent of Leonora Christina's vision as recollected in *Jammers Minde*, when she sees a raven followed by a flock of doves on her walk to the Blue Tower (see *Jammers Minde*, p. 12).

Despite Leonora's invocation of God's assistance, however, she does not set herself apart from the other wicked women in Gjedsted's novel. Unlike all previous interpretations of the Dina affair, this version presents the Ulfeldt couple as actual suspects. Leonora's extensive talk about poisoned mint drops in Ulfeldt's bed-chamber implies that she had put a lot of thought into her plan and her ensuing

---

686 Gjedsted, Rolf. *Fordærvede kvinder*, p. 144.
687 Ibid.: »Måske kunne musen blive tam. Hun kunne lære den nogle kunster, mens Ulfeldt kom til sig selv igen. Dyrene havde hun et særligt tag på. De følte sig trygge i hendes selskab. De har hjertets renhed, ligesom jeg, tænkte hun og kaldte hviskende på musen [...]«.
688 Ibid., p. 187. This occurrence is preceded by a dream involving the very same animals: »De tre ravne havde svævet over Blåtårns mure, mens hun selv blev ført i lænker ind i sin fars fængsel. Det havde været en frygtelig drøm« (ibid., p. 188).

statements leave little room for misinterpretation.[689] 19th-century representations of this incident had explained the Dina affair by way of a profound misunderstanding of Leonora Christina's words, hence lending these versions a moral dimension. The reason for this exculpation of the Ulfeldt couple is that due to the similar political situation, Hegermann Lindencrone and Oehlenschläger were obliged to present and judge their adaptations from a 19th century perspective.[690] Rolf Gjedsted, on the other hand, is a renunciation of all previous condemnations of the Ulfeldt era based on modern political and moral standards. His novel is an impressionist collage of mid-17th-century Denmark completely devoid of heroes and villains. *Fordærvede kvinder* portrays the lives of culprits and victims, but – as exemplified by Leonora's and Dina's lives – every culprit has a story and can quickly turn into a victim.

Any dichotomies exhibited by Gjedsted's novel are thus not based on moral evaluation, but on gender and class. The power struggle involving the three castes represented by Frederik and Sofie Amalie as high nobility, Corfitz Ulfeldt and Leonora as middle/lower nobility, and Jørgen Walter and Dina Vinhofvers as emergent lower-middle class, is further fractioned by an everlasting war of the sexes (which renders only Dina – a lower class woman – entirely powerless). Gjedsted's wicked women act on a level detached from the world of traditional, i.e. male power. Poisonings and witchcraft are common practices displayed in *Fordærvede kvinder*.

---

689 Ibid., p. 26f: »– Man ville have meget vanskeligt ved at smage på et pebermyntebolsje, om det var forgiftet. Mynten døver den slette smag af giften. [...] Man skulle forgive den tyske mokke med et pebermyntebolsje, inden hun får slået os andre ihjel! [...] Vi kunne sende Sofie Amalie en æske med pebermyntebonbons, og skrive at det var fra en hemmelig beundrer. [...] De skal selvfølgelig være dødeligt giftige inde under alt sukkeret. Så kan det være intrigerne ved hoffet vil ebbe ud«. The execution of Dina, the result of the King's conviction that her accusations were false, gives some leeway to the reader's speculations regarding Leonora's guilt: »Frederik indrømmede, at Dina Vinhofvers løj. Der var intet, der tydede på, at hun havde ret i påstandene om et giftkomplot mod kronen« (ibid., p. 178). Yet, as contended above, Gjedsted's authorial intention was not to deliver a possible explanation for the Dina affair (unlike his predecessors), but to provide a colourful portrait of the Copenhagen of 1650. Accordingly, there is no omniscient narrator in the novel but the chapters rarely depart from their respective protagonist's perspective.

690 The constancy of Louise Hegermann Lindencrone's 19th century perspective is especially blatant in her short stories collected in *Danske Fortællinger*. Despite the authoress' expressed concern for historical correctness (see, for example, letter addressed to Peder Hjort and dated 13 November 1824, reproduced in *Udvalg af Breve fra Mænd og Qvinder skrevne gjennem en lang Række År til P. Hjort og nu udgivne med biografiske og literærhistoriske Anmærkninger af Modtageren*. Copenhagen: Gyldendal, 1867, p. 326: »[V]ed den Leilighed maa jeg spørge, om det er en Feil imod Tids-Regningen at der i Haag ved Ulfeldts Ophold siges at have været en Mængde Karether samlede?«), both 'Faster Dorothea' and 'Billedet' exhibit countless anakronisms. Lise Busk-Jensen, however, considers Hegermann Lindencrone's occasional departures from historical accuracy to be the product of literary deliberation: »Beskrivelsen af den nyere tids borgerlige dagligliv med skovture og selskaber [in 'Faster Dorothea'] modstilles de dramatiske historiske begivenheder ved hoffet et halvt århundrede tidligere på en måde, som levendegør begge perioder og miljøer« (Busk-Jensen, Lise. *Romantikkens forfatterinder 2*, p. 803).

The catfight between Leonora and Dina constitutes one of Dina's motivations for accusing the Ulfeldt couple (thus annihilating Ulfeldt's own, traditional power), the other one simply being ambition.[691] Frederik and Corfitz are the most powerful men in Denmark, but the King flees his carping wife at every opportunity and Ulfeldt's weakness for women causes his downfall: his affair with Dina exposes his wife's treacherous plan while his physical and mental capacity has long been ruined by his rampant sex life. Moreover, even the whaler that catches the King's attention, a true sea dog, did not obtain his worst injury from some marine monstrosity, but from a woman: »Majestæten forestillede sig, at lidelsen stammede fra hvalfangsten. Men manden fortalte modstræbende og stammende, at det kom af samlivet med en træsk kvinde. Kongen var forstående og talte straks om hvalerne, som de egentlig skulle beskæftige sig med«.[692]

While some of the men bond thusly over a common experience of being henpecked, the women in the novel share a decadent lust for luxurious fashion – a common topic of the Leonora Christina-literature of the 20th and 21st century. Leonora and Sofie Amalie's rivalry reaches a preliminary climax when the Queen decides to place her sister-in-law among low-ranking aristocrats during a ballet evening, which Leonora answers by wearing the most flamboyant outfit she could think of:

> Så slog det hende, at det måske netop var sådan en prangende, slæbende kjole, der ville ærgre dronning Sofie mest, selv om det var udtryk for dårlig smag. [...] Som datter af Christian 4. ville Leonora vise gæsterne, at kun hun kunne tillade sig alt, selv slæbende, pralende brokadeskjoler, når moden dikterede noget andet.[693]

Leonora's dress shows the desired result: her rival boils with rage. Sofie Amalie and Dina, who otherwise have little to say to each other, too, initiate a type of communication alien to the men present. During the first interrogation of Dina, the Queen initially refuses to be in direct vicinity of this widely known concubine. Yet, when Sofie Amalie pays the interrogation committee a surprise visit, she notices Dina's looks of admiration directed at her outfit. Suddenly, the Queen becomes empathetic

---

691 As Dina eavesdrops on Corfitz and his wife, she hears Leonora advising her husband against an acquaintance with Dina, as it may result in an infection with a sexually transmittable disease. Upon hearing this insult, Dina swears revenge.
692 Gjedsted, Rolf. *Fordærvede kvinder*, p. 86.
693 Ibid., p. 179.

towards Dina,⁶⁹⁴ despite their being born on opposite ends of the social spectrum. The two women speak the same kind of silent language; Sofie Amalie interprets Dina's looks correctly, whereas Dina in return reacts appropriately to the Queen's altered behaviour by consciously repeating her marvelling looks. The men in the room, however, do not quite follow this process.⁶⁹⁵

Despite all above-mentioned differences, both sexes in the novel exhibit a striving for power. In some cases, but especially for the women, the aspired power is represented by luxurious goods.⁶⁹⁶ Leonora demonstrates her superiority over the Queen with the help of dresses and other commodities that testify to her own royal taste. Dina, on the other hand, intends to set herself apart from her humble origin with the help of fine goods and in order to achieve this elevated status, she needs to invest in her appearance. Much of this female finery is associated with decadence and deprivation. Hence, Dina discusses ways to advance at court with Walter while unwrapping her freshly cleaned bibelot,⁶⁹⁷ whereas another character in the novel, the amanuensis Jens Skøtte, turns his back on all the frilly ladies he knows from the royal court and courts a much simpler woman, a commoner, instead.⁶⁹⁸

Despite the suggestive title, however, the men in the novel are not immune to depravity either. Gjedsted's Walter is as ambitious as in most literary adaptations of the Dina affair and the King of Denmark spends most of his leisure time pursuing alchemy, even though his wife sees that he has fallen prey to a swindler.⁶⁹⁹ The

---

694 Ibid., p. 98: »Det var ikke så let, når man ikke var født med en guldske i munden, som hun selv, men alligevel tørstede efter pragt og overdådige kjoler«. A comparison with Dina's own thoughts regarding her attempt to rid herself of her inborn social disadvantages reveals that she and the Queen of Denmark exhibit the same type of thinking, despite their different background: »Hun havde gerne stillet sig gratis til rådighed, hvis det ikke var, fordi der skulle så meget til for at leve i København nu, hvor den franske mode havde gjort sit indtog. Der var meget at leve op til i de kredse, hvor Dina Vinhofvers færdedes, når man ikke var født med en guldske i munden« (ibid., p. 15).

695 Cf. ibid., p. 99.

696 Cf. Dina's statement regarding the wealth she sees in the Ulfeldt manor: »Af alle de fornemme herrers soveværelser, hun besøgte i hovedstaden, kunne Dina bedst lide duftene I rigshovmesterens kammer. Der duftede af fine perfumer fra fjerne lande, magt og virkelig velstand, ting, der hang nøje sammen« (Gjedsted, Rolf. *Fordærvede kvinder*, p. 15).

697 Ibid., p. 67: »De skulle bruge Dinas viden om Leonoras og Ulfeldts planer til selv at komme frem i verden, havde Walter forklaret, mens han så hende pakke hyrdinderne ud af deres stofæsker«.

698 Ibid., p. 94: »Anna var helt anderledes end de andre kvinder, han havde kendt fra hoffet. Og hendes kjole var meget lettere at tage af, end en adelsfrøkens. De skjulte altid et hav af bændler, indsnøringer og lag af stof, der kunne få én til at miste lysten til kærlighed, længe inden man var nået ind til den oprindelige hud. – Der er ikke så langt ind til din kærlighed, sagde Jens og knappede Annas kjoleliv op«.

699 Rolf Gjedsted included the Italian jack-of-all-trades Giuseppe Francesco Borri (1627-1695; Burrhis in Gjedsted's novel) in his account, even though, and as stated in Gjedsted's note at the end of his novel, Borri had met Frederik III at a much later time. The same man had consulted Corfitz Ulfeldt himself, when the Ulfeldt couple sought the advice of several medics in the course of their recreational travel to the Netherlands in 1662 (see *Jammers Minde*, p. 15).

riches described in *Fordærvede kvinder* are representative of the time portrayed by Gjedsted, as they attest to the early modern age, one of the few periods in Scandinavian history which could be termed ostentatious in European terms. Louise Hegermann Lindencrone, too, thematised the fascination of the Ulfeldt era with its otherworldly reminiscence of *One Thousand and One Nights* in the tale 'Billedet' (see Chapter 2.4.1.). When Elisabeth spends a few hours with the Ulfeldt family, the Countess Ulfeldt – upon being asked by her eldest daughter – shows the two girls her jewellery collection. The riches hidden in her golden jewel case leave a fairy-tale-like impression on Elisabeth, which would later on contribute to her life-long obsession with the Countess.[700] From their very first encounter onwards, Elisabeth demonstrates a vast interest in her idol's commodities, starting with her clothing.[701] In Rolf Gjedsted's account, Dina demonstrates a similar interest in the possessions of Leonora and Sofie Amalie, but here this concern has mostly negative implications as Dina is seeking to destroy one of the two women in order to obtain such riches herself while her appetite for luxury eventually causes the downfall of both Leonora and herself.

While all the riches of the Ulfeldt house leave an everlasting impression of enchantment on Elisabeth's infantile mind, the same luxury has thus explicitly negative connotations in Gjedsted's account. This alterable perception of excessive wealth is a common feature of the Leonora Christina-literature. Few writers managed to elude the fascination of the extravagance attributed to the Ulfeldt couple, especially as it was promoted by Leonora Christina herself.[702] However, more recent depictions of Leonora Christina's life tend to condemn this indulgence, rather than marvelling it. In Maria Helleberg's *Kongens kvinder* (see Chapter 2.6.3.), the aged Kirsten Munk advertises a natural splendour over one achieved through jewellery,[703] however anachronistic this attitude may be. Rainer Maria Rilke (see Chapter 2.7.2.), on the other hand, was under the dominant impression of 19th cen-

---

700 Hegermann Lindencrone, Louise. 'Billedet', p. 188.

701 Ibid., p. 168: »Hun havde en Guldmoors Kjortel paa, som ved Skinnet af de utallige Voxlys syntes at straale; dog hvad der især havde indprentet sig i Elisabeths Erindring, var et Smykke af blodrøde Rubiner, som hævede Halsens blændende Hvidhed, og endte i et stort Kors. En Rad af store indfattede Rubiner udgjorde hendes Livbælte, og samledes med et Demants Spænde. Omkring Hatten gik et Baand af Diamanter og Rubiner mellem hverandre, hvis Glans Øiet neppe kunde udholde. Hatten var opheftet med en Agraf i samme Smag«.

702 Cf. Leonora Christina's description of her arrival in Copenhagen after being arrested in Dover or of the personal search inflicted upon her in the Blue Tower, when she was bereaved of all her jewellery (*Jammers Minde*, pp. 5-7 and 17-20).

703 Cf. Kirsten Munk's assessment of Sophie Amalie, Queen of a few hours' standing, in Maria Helleberg's *Kongens kvinder*: »Hun var sikker, som Leonora aldrig havde været det. Behøvede ingen slids i sin handske for at vise en særlig kostbar sten frem. Hende skulle alle alligevel respektere og adlyde« (Helleberg, Maria. *Kongens kvinder*. Copenhagen: Samleren, 2013, p. 408).

tury Denmark (not least through his idol Jens Peter Jacobsen), which still idealised these kind of expenses. Accordingly, Leonora Christina's account of her transit from Dover to Copenhagen inspired him to write a moral tale on 'Wealth and Poverty', which depicts her as a person endued with natural grandeur.[704]

The decadence of the nobility in *Fordærvede kvinder*, however, exhibits clear features of the original meaning of the word 'decadence' (lat. *decadere* 'to decay'), as it indicates a type of power devoid of actual might and rather constituted by outward symbols, such as dresses. The two major conflicts in *Fordærdevede kvinder* thus concern gender and social class. Both of them are unified in the lower class women Karen Kruse and Dina. These two characters are most vulnerable to Frederik III's intention to clear the streets of Copenhagen of all depraved women, but their examples expose the actual focal point of the moral decay of society.[705] Karen Kruse falls victim to arson and is eventually found dead and frozen on the side of the road, while Dina is executed. Frederik III, the self-proclaimed sole upholder of moral standards in Copenhagen, on the other hand, is searching the local charnel houses for an adequate corpse for further, alchemical processing.

Despite all indicators, however, it is not primarily Dina's lower class origin that causes her untimely death. Her declared intention in the beginning of the drama is to imitate the life style of the Ulfeldts and eventually rival them,[706] yet her attempt to mingle with the rotten aristocracy causes the downfall of both of them.[707] Leonora Christina figures thus as a typical character of her time (including the Baroque key-terms *vanitas* and *memento mori* directing her life), but also as a deterrent example, as she is but one of many wicked women. In the end, Leonora comes to the same conclusion as Karen Kruse:

---

704 See Rilke's letter addressed to Hermann Pongs and dated 21 October 1924, reproduced in *Briefe 2: 1919-1926*, ed. Horst Nalewski. Frankfurt: Insel, 1991, pp. 359-361.

705 The same applies to Dina, but while Karen Kruse suffers the animosity of the general population, Dina – due to her good looks – tends to receive a milder treatment. Unfortunately for Karen Kruse, she lacks this type of female weapon.

706 Cf. Gjedsted, Rolf. *Fordærvede kvinder*, p. 17.

707 Dina's offence against the laws of society, which eventually leads to her decease, is her rebellion against traditional power relations. Not only does she attempt to dispossess the highborn Ulfeldt couple and replace them with herself and Jørgen Walter, but she also intends to turn the power dynamics between the sexes upside down: »Hun måtte sikre sin stilling, mens hun endnu havde noget at byde på. Senere ville hun have så mange penge, at dette udseende var ligegyldigt. Så kunne hun købe de smukke, unge mænd, der nu var villige til at betale for hendes gunst« (ibid., p. 68).

> Kongen og dronningen, rigsgreven og hende selv, sammen med en håndfuld andre nøglepersoner, var som grådige kortspillere, der kun ventede på modstandernes nederlag, for selv at triumfere og hæve gevinsten. Nu var Leonora i tvivl om, hvad gevinsten egentlig var, mens hun rakte kanekusken pungen og selv tog Karen Kruses bog med sig op på stedet.[708]

But this hindsight comes too late. The women in Gjedsted's account are indeed wicked, but the raw brutality and powerlust of their male counterparts eventually overcomes them. Dina's demise, caused by Jørgen Walter's ambition, is already indicated in the beginning of the account.[709] However, she is not the only victim of male authority. Sofie Amalie is the sole woman in the novel that withstands the legal force of the men she is involved with. Leonora Christina is thus one of many examples of strong women exceeding male domination in the short term, but who is eventually overcome by the conditions of her time.

2.4. Leonora Christina's Via Dolorosa: Stages of a *Christi Kaarßdragerske*'s Life

> Lader ded were Eders Trøst mine Kiære Børn, att ieg haffuer en Naadig Gud, en goed Samwittighed, oc en frii Foed att staa paa, att ieg aldrig nogen Skammelig Gierning giort haffuer: Ded er en Naade hoeß Gud siger Apostelen St Peder, om nogen bærer ded Onde formedelst en goed Samwittighed, oc liider Vret. Ieg liider Ære wære Gud icke for mine Mißgierninger, thi da war ded mig ingen Roeß: men ieg kand Roeße mig aff, att ieg aff Vngdom op Christi Kaarßdragerske werret haffuer, oc hafft vtrolige himlige Liidelser, huilcke effter mine Aar oc Alder ware wel tunge att bære.
>
> (*Jammers Minde*, p. 5*)

---

708 Ibid., p. 188.

709 Ibid., p. 67: »Dina havde haft både fornøjelse og besvær med at stille alle sine nips tilbage på den store kaminhylde igen efter at hendes gamle, langsynede hushjælp havde vasket dem af. Den fine, franske hyrdinde af glas havde knækket et stykke af sin stav. Men det var ikke hushjælpens skyld. Det var oberst Walter, der en animeret aften havde væltet den på gulvet«. The equation of Dina with a doll is encouraged by her own perception of herself: »Hun så godt ud. Det vidste hun. [...] Hun lignede en dukke, der var udført i det kinesiske porcelæn, der var så eftertragtet, og som alle velhavende og kunstforstandige ville eje« (ibid., p. 36).

As stated in the preamble to her children, Leonora Christina saw herself as »Christi Kaarßdragerske«, a martyr following in the footsteps of Jesus Christ himself. Accordingly, the texts presented in the following exhibit a strong emphasis on Leonora Christina's ordeal – thus highlighting the sense of predetermination and unity in her life, rather than contrast and fickleness – or even go as far as insinuating a similarity of Leonora Christina's path to the stations of the Passion of Christ by repeatedly making her run into the respective protagonists of the texts, hence showing her at different stages of her trials and tribulations.

This group of texts features an elevated engagement in the religious nature of Leonora Christina's vita. In Louise Hegermann Lindencrone's tale 'Billedet' (see Chapter 2.4.1.), Leonora Christina turns into a Madonna-substitute for a half-orphaned girl, as she becomes a mother and at the same time an idolised saint to the protagonist of the tale. H. F. Ewald (see Chapter 2.4.2.), on the other hand, presents a true martyr, a woman whose life receives its meaning through loss and suffering, while Ebbe Kløvedal Reich (see Chapter 2.4.3.) presents a holistic history of 17th-century Denmark, integrating the events surrounding Leonora Christina into a larger geographic, historic and religious context.

The literary community's tendency to convert Leonora Christina's life into a work of fiction exhibits two major tendencies, both of which are especially blatant in this group of texts. Some authors were fascinated by Leonora Christina's unsteady biography – her high position as the King's daughter and the wife of the most powerful man in the Danish realm, and her subsequent downfall to the status of a widowed prisoner. Others took a greater interest in the predetermination and consistency of her life, an autobiographical principle also conveyed in *Jammers Minde*. Leonora Christina's *Via Dolorosa* can thus imply two meanings. It can either denote Leonora Christina's self-projection onto the Passion of Christ with the respective text's protagonist observing the diverse stations of Leonora Christina's life and the changes that occurred in between (contrastive disposition); or it can signify a consistent, predetermined life of suffering (consistent disposition), which places Leonora Christina within a tradition of martyrs following the example of Christ.

2.4.1. Louise Hegermann Lindencrone: 'Billedet' (1825) – The Role Model

> Den anden tilskyndende Aarsage er, den Trøst ded Eder mine Kiære Børn wil were, att I formedelst denne *Iammers-Minde* forsickris, att ieg vskyldeligen Liider, att mig icke ringeste Sag er tillagt, oc att ieg intet er bleffuen Beskylt, for huilcket I mine Kiære Børn tør Bluis oc Øynene skammeligen nederslaa: Ieg liider for at haffue werret ælsket aff en dydig Herre oc Hoßbonde, for att ey haffue Hannem i Vlycken forlat wilt.
>
> (*Jammers Minde*, p. 4*)

Louise Hegermann Lindencrone had already demonstrated her interest in Leonora Christina in 1817, when she published *Eleonora Christina Uhlfeldt* (see Chapter 2.3.1.). This drama is the first literary presentation of Leonora Christina's life published in a time succeeding her imprisonment. After years of literary inactivity, Hegermann Lindencrone returned to one of her favourite topics in 1825 and published two tales engaging, albeit to differing degrees, in Leonora Christina's life: 'Faster Dorothea' and 'Billedet', both published in the tale collection *Danske Fortællinger*. Lise Busk-Jensen contends that Hegermann Lindencrone's lasting interest in Leonora Christina derived from a lack of other female literary role models[710] whereas her role as devoted wife and mother appealed to the authoress on a personal level.[711] Accordingly, the two tales 'Faster Dorothea' and 'Billedet' depict Leonora Christina as simply being family-oriented.

'Faster Dorothea'[712] shows »Eleonora Christine« as a 10-year-old child and only in close interaction with her father and her sister Anna Cathrine, who had just lost her fiancé Frants Rantzau. Upon questioning her father about the condition of Count Rantzau, the young girl understands the severity of the situation and in commiseration with her sister, she mourns the death of the young man.[713] Next, she is depicted comforting her sister while reminding her to stay strong out of daughterly duty towards their beloved father.[714]

Overall, the family surrounding Christian IV is portrayed as loving and caring, thus enhancing Dorothea's feeling of guilt (as it had been her fiancé, who had killed

---

710 Busk-Jensen, Lise. *Romantikkens forfatterinder 1*. Copenhagen: Gyldendal, 2009, p. 655.

711 Leonora Christina's family-oriented identity is self-promoted, as she dedicated her life to her husband and her magnum opus to her children. Louise Hegermann Lindencrone did, of course, not know about *Jammers Minde*, but the actions of some of the Ulfeldt children attest to an everlasting devotion to their parents.

712 For a short summary of the tale, see Chapter 2.3.1.

713 Hegermann Lindencrone, Louise. 'Faster Dorothea', p. 131.

714 Ibid.

Rantzau) and connecting this depiction of a warmhearted young Leonora Christina with her ensuing portrayal in 'Billedet'.

This tale, by far the longest one contained in *Danske Fortællinger*, chronicles the life of the Dutchwoman Elisabeth Arentzen,[715] who throughout decades repeatedly meets the Countess Ulfeld,[716] thus following her tumultous career. From their first encounter onwards, Elisabeth exhibits a strange obsession with Eleonora, the occasion for which is surely to be found in her own parental home in The Hague. The marital life of Elisabeth's parents is portrayed as content, yet it resembles a marriage of convenience rather than one of love. Especially the protagonist's father, simply called Arentzen, though later on a caring parent, exhibits a conspicuously unemotional behaviour towards his little family:

> De [Arentzen and his wife] levede stille og indgetogent, hun holdt hans Tøi pent og ordentligt, passede Huset og deres eneste Barn, et udmærket deiligt Pigebarn paa omtrent sex Aar. De gik aldrig ud, undtagen om Søndagen til Kirken, og et Par Spadseretoure om Sommeren, da førte Moderen den lille Pige ved Haanden, og langsomt, Skridt for Skridt, fulgte de Arentzen, som gik foran, iført sin Kistekjole med sin høie guldknappede Stok i Haanden og med store Skospænder af blinkende Sølv.[717]

The narrator's, or perhaps rather Elisabeth's focus on her father's churchgoing outfit in this rare memory of a family moment is conspicuous, yet it corresponds to the girl's later interest in the splendour surrounding the Ulfeld couple.[718] The girl's mother, however, remains a bleak memory throughout the account as she – in her function as role model to a young girl – is soon replaced by the Countess Ulfeld;[719] hence her garment remains undefined.

---

715 Perhaps a Dutch perspective offered an impartiality impossible to a Danish protagonist and was thus preferred. Ebbe Kløvedal Reich, too, makes a Jewish merchant-spy from Hamburg, yet with Spanish roots, his Copenhagen-visiting protagonist for the trilogy *Rejsen til Messias*.

716 In the present chapter, »Eleonora« specifically refers to the character in Louise Hegermann Lindencrone's short story, particularly when referring to passages that do not correspond to historical events, whereas »Leonora Christina« refers to the historical person. Further spelling variations used in the literary source text, and hence in this chapter as well, are »Ulfeld« and »Anna (Cathrine)«.

717 Hegermann Lindencrone, Louise. 'Billedet', p. 143.

718 Cf. the detailed descriptions of Eleonora's clothing whenever the young Elisabeth Arentzen sees her, such as this one: »En Purpurrød Fløiels Kaabe, heelt foeret med Hermelin og med bred Hermelins Kant omkring den, gav hende en kongelig Anseelse, som hendes ædle Aasyn og høie Væsen bekræftede. Det deiligste blonde Haar […] krøllede sig i de yndigste Lokker under en sort Fløiels Hat, som var stærkt opslaaet, med en Agraf af Ædelstene. Hvide Strudsfjær faldt veiende hen over Skyggen, og omkring Hattepullen gik ligeledes et Baand af kostbare Stene« (Hegermann Lindencrone, Louise. 'Billedet', p. 162).

719 Cf. Auring, Steffen et al. 'Den romantiske kvindemyte', p. 447.

When Elisabeth loses her mother at a very young age, Arentzen exhibits signs of grief, but the reasons attributed to this grief do not attest to an especially affectionate marriage either:

> Og da han nu kom hjem, og den lille Pige krøb i Skjul bag Moderens tomme Lænestol, ved hvilken Rokken, første Gang i de syv Aar bedækket med Støv, stod i en Krog, og han selv maatte føre de faa Frænder, der havde fulgt hende til Jorden, til Middagsbordet, selv maatte lægge dem Maden for, og eftersee alt, hvad hans Maria ellers lige saa troligt og ordentligt, som stille og ubemærket, pleiede at besorge: da følte han først tydeligt, at hun var borte, da brast han bitterligt i at græde.[720]

During her lifetime, Maria Arentzen had taken on the role of the dutiful mother and wife, hence she is subsequently missed as such by her newly widowed husband. The little girl, too, had sensed this atmosphere of conscientiousness and reacts accordingly after her mother's death. Neglected by all remaining members of the household, Elisabeth turns into a tomboy:

> At hun ogsaa nyttede denne Frihed, at den lille Pige, som før jomfruelig sædelig sad paa sin grønmalede Skammel foran sit lille Bord, nu foer som den vildeste Dreng fra Loft og til Kjelder, fra Kjøkken til Gadedør, ja vel endog imellem stak sit guldlokkede Hoved ud af Gadedøren, nu, da Ingen formenede hende det, dette vil ikke synes underligt for hvem der kjender den barnlige Natur, som, især naar den har været *mere end tilbørligt indpresset* [my italics], lig en bøielig Vidie slaaer tilbage som en Springfjær, idet man slipper den. Elisabeth var af en opvakt og levende Natur, og kun ved *Tvang, Exempel og Sædvane* [my italics] bragt til den forrige Stilhed.[721]

One place that allows her to roam and romp *ad libitum* is the manor which will house the Ulfeld couple and Dr. Sperling during their official stay in The Hague in 1649 and which her father has been hired to redecorate:

---

720 Hegermann Lindencrone, Louise. 'Billedet', p. 144.
721 Cf. ibid., p. 146.

Forskjellen paa de mange, lyse, store Sale og hendes Faders vel reenlige, men smaa mørke og tarvelige Kamre, samt Madam Berghens endnu mindre, endnu lavere Smaahuller var saa afstikkende, at det var hende som en heel Verden paa engang aabnede sig for hende, en Følelse lig den, der opstaaer naar man efter længe at have været indeklemt i den snævre, qvalme By træder ud i den frie Natur, og drager Aande af fuldt Bryst.[722]

Elisabeth's first encounter with the Ulfeld world thus enduces positive feelings of liberation. Yet, not only the spaciousness impresses the child. In the course of his preparations for the redecoration of the Ulfeld couple's Dutch abode, Arentzen receives a delivery of the finest crimson and golden damask. Elisabeth, who accompanies her father for lack of a nursemaid, cannot help but admire, even caress the gorgeous material. Just like in the bright halls of the Ulfeld mansion, the personal possessions of the Countess Ulfeld, which Elisabeth will see later on in the account, evoke feelings of joy in the little girl and perhaps also suppressed memories of better times, such as the Sunday familystroll reproduced above.[723] Under the watchful eyes of her father and Madam Berghen, her foster mother, Elisabeth dares only occasionally draw a corner of the beautiful cloth over her dull mourning garment: »Imellem, naar de vare fordybede i deres Beregninger, stjal hun sig dog til at brede en Flig af Tøiet over sit lille Skjød, og skjule den forhadte sorte Kjole dermed, forresten forholdt hun sig ganske rolig«.[724]

The splendour of the Ulfeld mansion in The Hague overshadows the mourning for the lost mother,[725] perhaps a feeling unrealised by Elisabeth herself. Due to her young age, the girl copes quickly with the death of a close family member,[726] yet a colourful remnant from the lifetime of her mother had become her most cherished possession: »Kort før Moderens Død havde den lille Elisabeth faaet et rødt Silketørklæde, som hun havde en lidenskabelig Kjærlighed til«.[727] Thus, the acquaintance

---

722 Ibid., p. 152.
723 Accordingly, Elisabeth notices with astonishment her father's elegant clothing upon the arrival of the Ulfeld couple in The Hague, which evokes further associations between the Ulfeld couple's appearance and her family's wellbeing: »[D]og størst blev Elisabeths Forundring da hun blev sin Fader vaer, iført sine bedste Kisteklæder, ligeledes med en Sølvarmstage i Haanden« (ibid., p. 160).
724 Ibid., p. 150.
725 Cf. Lise Busk-Jensen, who highlights the possibility of Maria Arentzen – despite her short appearance in the tale – playing a major role in the development of the plot: »Elisabeths passivitet [later on in the tale] kan [...] forklares som en fiksering til den døde moder, der har hindret hende i at leve et aktivt voksenliv og selv blive moder [note: the adult Elisabeth *does* have two sons]« (Busk-Jensen, Lise. *Romantikkens forfatterinder 2*, p. 801).
726 Cf. Hegermann Lindencrone, Louise. 'Billedet', p. 145: »Den lille Elisabeth følte det naturligviis, ifølge hendes Alder, hverken saa dybt eller saa længe«.
727 Ibid., p. 149.

with the splendidly equipped Ulfeld couple helps Elisabeth and her father cope with the loss of Maria Arentzen in manifold ways.[728] Together with disclosing an entirely new world to Elisabeth, the assignment of redecorating the Ulfeld mansion brings previously unknown wealth to the Arentzen family, as Count Ulfeld is known to pay very well.[729] Consequently, Elisabeth entertains feelings of esteem towards her father's benefactors even before seeing them for the first time.

All the stronger is then the impression left by the first appearance of the Danish ambassador Ulfeld and his wife. Both of them astound with an elegance unknown to their simple audience. Yet, unlike her husband, whose appeal is of a darker and more mysterious nature, Eleonora graces the surrounding people, including Elisabeth, with eye-contact: »Et af hendes Blik traf Elisabeth's lille Hjerte saa dybt, at hun aldrig, end ikke i sit Livs alvorligste Øieblikke, kunde glemme det«.[730] Eleonora combines otherworldly splendour with humane warmth,[731] thus making the young Elisabeth her ever-loyal devotee. Hence, the eponymous picture, *Billedet*, is the picture of Eleonora, forever engrained in Elisabeth's mind and heart:

> Det er ofte sagt, at man, ved jevnligt at efterligne Miner og Gebærder, som udtrykke en eller anden Sindsstemning, virkelig kan fremkalde denne Gemytstilstand; men om det end ikke var saa, da vilde dog upaatvivlelig Billedet af noget virkelig Ædelt og Skjønt hæve Hjertet og Sindet, bevare det reent, og er det ret levende i os, væbne os mod ethvert fordærvende Indtryk. [...] At Grevindens Billede, som saa mægtigt og levende fyldte Elisabeths unge Bryst, havde denne Virkning paa hende, vil det Følgende vise, og bekræfte Sandheden af denne Bemærkning.[732]

---

[728] The above-mentioned silk scarf, for example, is later on replaced by a diamond ring, which Elisabeth receives as a gift from the Countess Ulfeld, and which she subsequently wears with a golden chain around her neck (ibid., p. 191).

[729] Furthermore, seeing her father performing his work causes Elisabeth to see him in a new light as well. During her first visit at the Dutch Ulfeld mansion, she virtually sees this new environment through rose-coloured glasses: »Dette Rosenskjær [induced by crimson curtains] havde noget særdeles muntert og livligt, alting forskjønnedes ved det. Arentzen, som netop gik hen over Gulvet, syntes forynget, hans gustne Ansigtsfarve forvandledes til Sundhedens friske Rødme« (Hegermann Lindencrone, Louise. 'Billedet', p. 153).

[730] Ibid., p. 163.

[731] The gentleness exuded by Eleonora is reinforced by the appearance of Sperling, who arrives a few days later. He heals Elisabeth's burned hand, a wound induced by parental negligence as it is inflicted in a moment when Elisabeth is left alone at home. At the same time, the excitement surrounding the appearance of Eleonora and her husband helps Elisabeth forget the pain in her hand (cf. ibid., p. 159ff.). The multiple meetings with the Ulfeld family, but especially with Sperling and Eleonora, thus compensate for some of the previous lack of parental warmth and care.

[732] Ibid., p. 166f.

Eleonora's picture thus figures as an exemplary ideal, as a role model Elisabeth can comply with throughout her life.[733] In authentic child-like fashion, Elisabeth re-enacts the entrance of Eleonora into The Hague whenever she is left to herself. However, in the course of the ensuing decades, the very same picture remains too omnipresent, as it completely absorbs the tale's protagonist and eventually interferes with her and her husband's life.

Yet, Elisabeth's initial encounters with Eleonora are entirely beneficial to the girl. When Sperling brings his little patient to the Countess Ulfeld, after having cured Elisabeth's burnt hand, the girl is confronted with yet another new world. The single child is left to play with Anna Cathrine Ulfeld, who attempts to cure their guest from her awe-induced paralysis, and the two immediately take a liking to each other. Subsequently, the children overhear the conversation of the adults regarding Corfitz's difficult task to renegotiate a Danish-Dutch commercial treaty[734] and his frustration over the situation at court:

> Hvad som udtales med Varme og med en Grad af Lidenskabelighed, har en forunderlig Kraft til at prente sig dybt i Hukommelsen hos Tilhørerne, især naar disse ere Børn. Endskjøndt Elisabeth, i det Øieblik denne Samtale fandt Sted i hendes Nærværelse, ikke forstod noget af den, kunde hun i sine ældre Aar erindre den Ord til andet, ja endog næsten hver Tonebøining, især den første Deel af den, da Ulfeld var tilstede.[735]

Ulfeld's passionate behaviour must have seemed like an entirely novel world to Elisabeth, whose parents in the description of her youngest years are mostly distinguished by an air of passiveness and, in her mother's case, absence.[736] Thus, Elisabeth meets a previously unknown world of plenty in the Ulfeld mansion: she sees more riches, more space, but also more emotion.

Overall, 'Billedet' presents quite a felicitous description of infant behaviour. Due to her own plentiful childbearing, Louise Hegermann Lindencrone could obtain an intricate understanding of human nature and of the importance of childhood

---

733 Cf. Busk-Jensen, Lise. *Romantikkens forfatterinder 2*, p. 799: »Hegermann forsøgte at skabe en repræsentativ kvindelig livshistorie med især Leonora Christina som det 'billede', alle kvinder kunne spejle sig i på hver deres niveau, et nationalt sidestykke til det romantiske madonnabillede«.

734 This treaty was effected in 1649.

735 Hegermann Lindencrone, Louise. 'Billedet', p. 186.

736 Cf. Arentzen's characterisation: »Strax efter hans Kones Død havde en af dennes Paarørende i Flandern skrevet efter Elisabeth, men Arentzen, som ikke kunde beslutte sig til at skille sig fra sit kjære Barn og som desuden vanskeligt, ifølge *sin naturlige Phlegma* [my italics], kunde bestemme sig til at tage nogensomhelst rask Beslutning, havde takket hende i ubestemte Udtryk, der hverken tilsagde eller bestemt afslog hendes Forlangende« (ibid., p. 146).

impressions.[737] Said impressions dominate Elisabeth's behaviour and thus the tale's plot. Yet, not all statements regarding her role model are left to Elisabeth Arentzen alone. Regarding the ambiguous fame of Leonora Christina and especially Corfitz Ulfeldt (which had obviously troubled the authoress before; see Chapter 2.3.1.), Louise Hegermann Lindencrone gives the floor to some other spectators following the life of this infamous couple. Hence, Arentzen defends Ulfeld's fame upon hearing Madam Berghen taunting Ulfeld's famous haughtiness:

> Fører han sig som en Konge, saa betaler han ogsaa kongeligt, det maa man lade ham. Ogsaa er han mild og nedladende mod alle Ringere, det have vi seet den sidste Gang han var her. Om saa er, at han er stolt i sit Hjerte, hvo er vel Skyld deri? Vises ham ikke fast kongelig Ære hvor han kommer frem?[738]

Leonora Christina's famous pride, too, receives some mention, yet it does not match the character's subsequent behaviour in the novel. When the Dutch mansion is prepared for the arrival of its Danish guests, the servants of the Ulfeld family inspect Arentzen's work in order to ensure that the decor matches their masters' extravagant taste:

> [M]en for alting, Monsiur [sic!] Louis, forlanger Greven, at al den Pragt, det er muligt at anskaffe, anbringes i hans Dames Gemakker. Han selv vil hjelpe sig som han kan, men for Hende maa sørges i alle Maader og ikke glemmes, at hun er en Kongedatter, og vant at behandles som saadan![739]

---

737 Cf. Steffen Auring et al., who commend Louise Hegermann Lindencrone's »psykologisk realisme, der [...] peger frem mod en mere moderne problemorienteret kvindelitteratur« (Auring, Steffen et al. 'Den romantiske kvindemyte', p. 447).

738 Hegermann Lindencrone, Louise. 'Billedet', p. 157. The same explanation is provided later on in the account, when Madam Berghen wonders why Ulfeld would dare to sit in the presence of high-ranking Dutch statesmen. To this, one of Ulfeldt's servants merely replies: »Greven, min Herre, forstaaer at lade Penge rullere, det giver Respekt, helst her i Holland!« (ibid., p. 169). This opportunism exercised by Ulfeld's surroundings parallels the – mostly negative – conduct of lower class representatives portrayed in Louise Hegermann Lindencrone's drama *Eleonora Christina Uhlfeldt* (see Chapter 2.3.1.). 'Billedet', too, portrays the servants of the Ulfeld couple as more snobbish than their masters, best exemplified by the conduct of Ulfeldt's equerry reproduced above or by Arentzen and Elisabeth's reception at the mansion when they enter in order to thank Otto Sperling for his medical advice regarding Elisabeth's hand. While the servants ignore the guests entirely, they receive a much warmer welcome by the hands of Sperling and the mistress of the house herself (cf. Hegermann Lindencrone, Louise. 'Billedet', p. 172). Yet, the behaviour of the lower class depicted in 'Billedet' is at its worst when Elisabeth commiserates the fate of the once so glamorous Countess upon her public arrival at the Blue Tower, while some of the bystanders »yttrede larmende Velbehag og kaad Glæde, som ofte er Tilfældet blandt den lavere Pøbel, naar den seer Dem, den forhen har maattet yde Ærbødighed, i Fornedrelse og Ulykke« (ibid., p. 145).

739 Ibid., p. 156.

Ulfeld and Eleonora are thus preceded by their fame, manifested in their arrogant equerry, who – purportedly on behalf of his masters – treats Arentzen and his entourage in a belittling manner.[740] However, the same meeting reanimates Arentzen's mind, as Ulfeld's equerry motivates him to express his indignation in a – for his terms – lengthy and passionate speech.[741]

The meeting with the Ulfeld couple thus helps Elisabeth and her father cope with the distress caused by Maria Arentzen's death and heralds a new period of life for both of them.[742] Elisabeth's visit at the Ulfeld mansion connects her impression of a loving family with the Countess' otherworldly, royal status, proof of which is the portrait of Christian IV decorating one of the house's hallways.[743] The Ulfelds' position within Denmark's political realm, however, remains a mystery to little Elisabeth: although a bystander of Ulfeld, Eleonora's and Sperling's conversation on Ulfeld's difficulties in Denmark and abroad, the girl is too young[744] to grasp the meaning of this discussion. With the political connotations of the name Ulfeld thusly suppressed, Elisabeth Arentzen is free to admire her role model on a personal level.[745]

The sensitive subject of patriotism is thus first and foremost eluded by Elisabeth's foreign nationality and her infantile worldview, while positive nationalistic aspects of Leonora Christina's persona are subsequently highlighted through Elisabeth's perspective. To her, the Countess has become synonymous with her fatherland, Denmark, and her father, »den af Europa beundrede og ærede Konge og Helt«.[746] Elisabeth's admiration for Eleonora leads to a lifelong interest in anything Danish, eventually culminating in her betrothal to a Dane, a descendant of the Bartholin lineage. Hence, 'Billedet' – through Elisabeth's eyes – portrays Leonora

---

740 Cf. ibid., p. 156f.
741 Ibid., p. 158.
742 Cf. ibid., p. 190: »Saa kort som Elisabeths Møde med Ulfelds Familie, egentligst med Grevinden, havde været, saa vigtig en Indvirkning havde det paa hendes hele Fremtid.«.
743 Accordingly, the authoress considered the mention of his portrait in the tale as absolutely indispensable, as stated in a letter addressed to Peder Hjort and dated 13 November 1824, reproduced in *Udvalg af Breve*, p. 325.
744 Much less is she a native speaker of Danish (or German). Nevertheless, the language discrepancy between the Arentzen family and the Ulfeld family seems to play no role in 'Billedet', as Elisabeth – years afterwards – miraculously remembers and understands each word of the conversation mentioned above.
745 Equally personal is Elisabeth's prospective husband's, i.e. Bartholin's sympathy for the Ulfeld couple. His father had been a close friend of Otto Sperling, who had thus implanted a general benevolence towards the Ulfeld family in the Bartholin house. Furthermore, this acquaintance explains Bartholin's familiarity with the fate of the Ulfeld couple, which he frequently relates to Elisabeth.
746 Hegermann Lindencrone, Louise. 'Billedet', p. 193.

Christina as the legacy of her internationally esteemed father and as an ambassador of Denmark.

Initially, Elisabeth's acquaintance with Eleonora appears to be entirely beneficial to the girl. With the Countess in mind, she develops into the best version of herself.[747] Her noble disposition leads to a romantic bond with a kindred spirit from Denmark, i.e. Bartholin, who one day with expressed sorrow relates the fate of Eleonora to his unsuspecting fiancée. His – historically quite accurate – summary of Ulfeld's life and deeds in the twelve years succeeding Elisabeth's first encounter with Eleonora[748] mostly portrays the latter as the passive appendix of her industrious husband. This concerns even Bartholin's account of their arrest on Bornholm, which Leonora Christina herself had conveyed as her very own adventure story. As it would have contradicted Hegermann Lindencrone's consistent portrayal of Leonora Christina as a domestic icon, she attenuated her 'illegal' activities while exaggerating Leonora Christina's legal efficacy in the Malmö trial. Accordingly, Leonora Christina's primary qualities are »de første af alle qvindelige Dyder, Troskab og Ægtekjærlighed«.[749]

Bartholin and Elisabeth share a distraught feeling upon hearing of the arrest of the Ulfeld couple, which the groom interprets as them being meant for each other.[750] To Bartholin and Elisabeth, the elusive Ulfelds act as marriage brokers and as fate. Both Bartholin and Elisabeth admire a personal experience, a childhood lesson, which taught them sympathy with the Ulfeld couple, even though they are actually strangers to each other: Elisabeth had met the couple only once while Bartholin merely knows them by hearsay. Despite their general ignorance of the physical Ulfeld couple, Ulfeld and Eleonora had played a major role in Bartholin's and especially

---

747 Ibid., p. 195.

748 Louise Hegermann Lindencrone departs – perhaps due to ignorance of the relevant documents kept in the Swedish National Archives – from history only in one episode of Corfitz Ulfeldt's life which allowed his wife to act independently, namely when Leonora Christina was forced to defend her husband in the course of the Malmö trial. Bartholin states that Eleonora had managed to »have beviist hans Uskyldighed« (ibid., p. 218) and that he subsequently – also favoured by Carl Gustav's sudden death in 1660 – had been acquitted by the Swedish Council. This is not quite correct, since Leonora Christina's defence of her husband – though marveled by all statesmen present – could not avert Ulfeldt's ensuing conviction. The proclamation of the sentence was adjourned due to Ulfeldt's illness and only reversed by Carl X Gustav's death, which resulted in an administrative confusion, and by his successor Carl XI of Sweden, who bore no personal grudge against Ulfeldt (cf. Birket Smith, Sophus: *Leonora Christina Grevinde Ulfeldts Historie 1*, pp. 387-420). The minutes and the verdict of the Malmö trial, as well as other records of the Ulfeldt couple's activities in Sweden, are printed in the Samlingar utgifna för De skånska landskapens historiska och arkeologiska förening (see 'Till Corfitz Ulfelds historia', Samlingar utgifna för De skånska landskapens historiska och arkeologiska förening 6 (1877), pp. 26-70).

749 Hegermann Lindencrone, Louise. 'Billedet', p. 220.

750 Ibid., p. 221.

Elisabeth's ethical upbringing. Thus, Eleonora represents an undefined good, whose vicinity Elisabeth instinctively seeks.

As Bartholin and Elisabeth encourage each other's sympathy for the discredited Ulfeld couple, Elisabeth's attention is further drawn to Eleonora's own commiseration:

> »Den bedste Løn har hun faaet!« udbrød Elisabeth med straalende Blik. »Den Eneste fyldestgjørende for et saadant Hjerte: hun har deelt sin Elskedes Lidelser, og lettet dem idet hun delte dem! Hun har befæstet i hans dybt saarede Bryst Troen paa Menneskelighed, paa Hengivenhed og Troskab, hun staaer som et Exempel for sit Kjøn, og Aarhundreder skulle ikke udslette hendes Minde, som skal styrke og husvale mangt et uskyldigt Hjerte.[«]⁷⁵¹

Seeing Eleonora's decision to share her husband's calamities as the ultimate reward life could provide, Elisabeth decides to emulate her role model through an exaggerated involvement in Eleonora's ensuing life. Elisabeth replaces religious icons with Eleonora as a more accessible idol, a Madonna-figure, who in her lifetime had already found a way to enter the realm of eternity:

> Ja! naar hendes berømmelige Slægt, som et fældet Træ forlængst er uddøet af Jorden, naar Intet af hvad der var hendes lever i Tiden, saa skal dog Mindet om hendes Standhaftighed og Kjærlighed, som et herligt sig forplantende Sædekorn bære Frugter for Evigheden!⁷⁵²

Elisabeth's perception of Eleonora as her very own icon is especially blatant in her terminology concerning Eleonora. Once Elisabeth had reached Denmark and heard of her idol's release from Hammershus, she »vilde gjøre en *Valfart* [my italics] over til Fyen og besøge Grevinde Ulfeld«.⁷⁵³ Later on in the account, on her way to the Blue Tower, Eleonora causes responses reminiscent of Christ's Passion. When Elisabeth observes her walking towards the tower and Birgitte Ulfeld bars the way only to roar with laughter at her sister-in-law's misfortune,⁷⁵⁴ the former's carriage is removed by two sympathetic bystanders. Upon Eleonora's looks of appreciation,

---

751 Ibid.
752 Ibid.
753 Ibid., p. 229.
754 Cf. *Leonora Christina Grevinde Ulfeldts Franske Levnedsskildring*, p. 14c (Translation p. 59).

caused by this scene reminiscent of Simon of Cyrene's assistance to Christ, Elisabeth is overwhelmed with emotion:

> Hun styrtede ned for hendes Fødder, omfavnede hendes Knæe og trykkede et brændende Kys paa hendes Haand, som i samme Øieblik blev vædet af de hede, fremstrømmende Taarer. Med himmelsk Mildhed, med et Smiil, som ikke var uden Veemod bøiede Eleonora sig over hende og kyssede hende paa Panden.[755]

Despite a lack of a clear role allocation, the description of this scene is evocative of some of the stations of Christ's Passion, namely the collapse and the weeping, but also Eleonora's stoic conduct during the scene. A look at the same scene in the French autobiography (and in *Jammers Minde*, pp. 10-12) furthermore shows that Hegermann Lindencrone had moved the appearance of Birgitte Ulfeldt both spatially and chronologically in order for it to interfere with Leonora Christina's walk to the Blue Tower, which in the original account is rather uneventful.

In Christ-like fashion, Eleonora's calamities have an inspiring effect on her disciple Elisabeth: »De Lidelser, de Savn og Følelser, der, som hun syntes, bragte dette tilbedte Væsen nærmere til hende, omgave det tillige med en Helgens Straalekrands for hendes Øine«.[756] And finally, the house of the Ulfeldt family on Gråbrødretorv, a temple in *Eleonora Christina Uhlfeldt*, is again depicted as a place of worship, almost a church, in 'Billedet': »Magdalena [...] opregnede de Trængende og Bedrøvede, som der [in the Ulfeldt house] havde hentet Trøst og Hjælp og vidnede, at Ingen var gaaet uhjulpen fra de Porte, som nu vare styrtede i Gruus«.[757]

Bartholin shares his bride's feelings of adoration and on the morning of her wedding day, Elisabeth receives a letter from her fiancé informing her that Eleonora had been released from her prison on Bornholm. The groom had kept these tidings to himself for a few days, as he wanted to give his bride the good news as his »Brudegave«.[758] Elisabeth perceives these news as a sign of her own future wellbeing,[759] yet her sympathy with the Ulfelds soon affects her family's life in a negative way. Former friends of Bartholin, like the scholar Jacob Henrik Pauli,[760] keep aloof due to a difference of opinion regarding the Ulfeld couple. In a subsequent year, when Elisabeth cannot visit her aunt in Bruges, since she had been

---

755 Hegermann Lindencrone, Louise. 'Billedet', p. 250.
756 Ibid., p. 259.
757 Ibid., p. 262.
758 Ibid., p. 222.
759 Ibid., p. 225.
760 Jacob Henrik Paulli (1637-1702) was a Danish physician, historian and politician.

advised to avoid any possibility of meeting Ulfeld, her husband confesses to feeling weariness and misgiving at being so intimately connected with the Ulfeld house, as if its demise was foreboding their own imminent misfortune.[761]

The Bartholin house becomes even lonelier when Bartholin's mother dies of illness. This experience takes Elisabeth and her father back to the unfortunate time when they lost Maria Arentzen and just like in 1649, when Arentzen and Elisabeth needed some distraction from the loss of their wife and mother, respectively, they meet Eleonora, who is again announced by her once haughty equerry Holst. At the custom house of Copenhagen, Elisabeth and Arentzen join a group of curious townspeople awaiting the arrival of the arrested Countess Ulfeld. The much repentant equerry apologises for his former behaviour and informs his unsuspecting listeners about Ulfeld's lot. Terribly unhinged by this news, Elisabeth interrupts Holst's attempt to introduce her and her father to another member of their extended family, whom he found in the crowd, and demands instead to hear of Eleonora's fate. Her wish is promptly granted and soon she sees Eleonora descending from the boat. Unlike her servant, Eleonora has not changed. Despite all these tumultuous and sorrowful years, she is still the incommutable icon Elisabeth needs to rely on.[762]

Elisabeth and her likeminded companions stand out in the mob of »Fiskerkjællinger, Haandværkskarle og Matrosdrenge«,[763] who offend their superiorly educated surroundings with their malicious comments. Elisabeth regains some composure once her idol is out of sight and she finds herself alone on the palace square, only to be rescued by Holst and Thomas Fuiren (Danish scholar; 1616-1673), a relative of Bartholin and admirer of Eleonora and, thus, another companion to Elisabeth and Arentzen. Despite their initial isolation in Copenhagen due to Bartholin's study-related absence, Elisabeth and her father soon find like-minded admirers of Eleonora – like Thomas Fuiren and Eleonora's former maid Magdalena Boiesen – and they form a little community of faith, whose members would give their life for the Ulfeld couple.[764]

Elisabeth's life and her obsession with Eleonora, induced by the Countess Ulfeld's self-inflicted participation in her husband's fate, begs the question as to what extent such a commiseration – however justified it may be – is condign, let alone an ideal, for humankind but especially for women. From the beginning of her marriage, Elisabeth's thoughts dwell on the fate of the Ulfeld family to a degree which

---

761 Hegermann Lindencrone, Louise. 'Billedet', p. 265.
762 Ibid., p. 244.
763 Ibid., p. 246.
764 Cf. ibid., p. 262.

prevents her from enjoying her marital bliss.[765] When the narrator of 'Billedet' thus asks: »Var det vel at undres over, om Elisabeths Tanker dvælede veemodigt ved disse Forestillinger?«,[766] all the while Bartholin shows the wonders of Paris to his doleful wife, one is tempted to give a positive answer. Eleonora's passive involvement in Elisabeth's life climaxes when Bartholin is unable to return to his home country, due to his wife's suspicious public commiseration with the Ulfeld couple. He conceals this reason from his wife and tries to obtain amnesty while feigning a work-related journey. During his repeatedly prolonged absence, Elisabeth's aunt hints at the possibility of Bartholin having abandoned his wife. Elisabeth finds herself unable to turn to anybody for comfort, as this would only confirm her aunt's suspicions and damage her husband's reputation. Only the thought of Eleonora's suffering consoles the young woman and encourages her to emulate her idol's strength:

> Da betænkte hun tillige hvor meget Mere Eleonora havde at udstaae, der bestandig var omringet af dem, der hadede og foragtede Den, hun elskede høiest i Verden, og aldrig hørte det hende saa kjære Navn nævne, uden at Ordene Troløse og Landsforræder ledsagede det. Da lovede Elisabeth, i taalmodig Hengivenhed at vise sig sit Forbillede værdig.[767]

This turn of events confronts the reader with a 'Chicken and Egg'-like causality dilemma: are Elisabeth's sorrows induced by her involvement with Eleonora, or is Elisabeth only able to bear all grief due to her idolisation of Eleonora? After all, and as stated by Leonora Christina, »alle Ting haffuer saa som tuende Hancker huor wed ded skal hæffuis« (*Jammers Minde*, p. 2). Elisabeth's attempt to imitate her idol's strength eventually proves to be beneficial once again: following the advice of an old friend, she decides to openly oppose all slander regarding her husband, thus proving herself to be a loyal partner to Bartholin, who indeed returns soon afterwards. Whether it is of any significance that Elisabeth needs to resort to fabri-

---

765 Elisabeth is not entirely unaware of the difficulties resulting from her distraction. When Bartholin is forced to leave his wife for a few weeks, Elisabeth regrets her past behaviour: »[H]un kunne ikke dølge for sig selv, at hun i de Maaneder de havde levet sammen ikke ganske havde været ham hvad hun kunde og burde; at hun mere havde levet i sine Ideer og Erindringer, end med og for ham. Og selv nu, da hans Kummer og Skilsmissen fra ham syntes at burde opfylde hendes hele Sjæl, opstod hos hende næsten ubevidst og aldeles uvilkaarligt den Tanke, at Eleonoras Skjæbne kaldte Bartholin, og fyldte hende med en Uro og Angst for denne, som blandede sig med Smerten over hendes Elskedes Tungsindighed og Fraværelse« (ibid., p. 306).

766 Ibid., p. 302.

767 Ibid., p. 308.

cation in order to restore her husband's good reputation,⁷⁶⁸ thus again suggesting a parallel to Eleonora's difficult situation, remains to be seen.

What is then Elisabeth's motivation to blur the lines between her idol's and her own life and what is the reader supposed to take from this? Upon hearing of her exile from Denmark, due to her »overdreven og overspændt«⁷⁶⁹ public commiseration with the Ulfeld couple, Elisabeth reacts quite uncomprehendingly. She had become an admirer of Eleonora, the wife and mother, whereas the Countess Ulfeld as a public figure had remained a complete stranger to her. Eleonora had provided the young girl with an ideal and with constancy, when she needed it the most. Moreover, while the reader may share a certain marvelling over Elisabeth's exaggerated behaviour, her most recent obstacle, i.e. her exile, had been a third party's as well her own fault: as can be derived from a letter written by Thomas Fuiren to Bartholin, public opinion had attested an exaggerated importance to Elisabeth's actions,⁷⁷⁰ thus ascribing to her an involvement in a politically ambitious circle of Danes, which Elisabeth had never even met.⁷⁷¹ Hence this letter initiates a discourse on historical significance, i.e. the relevance of one's deeds in the eyes of a distant audience, which will be further exposed in the following sections.

While the overall disposition of the text regarding Eleonora is contrastive,⁷⁷² the exemplary nature of her conduct is provided through constancy, as stated by her devotee Elisabeth: »[J]a! jeg saae hende [Eleonora]: hun var lige saa skjøn og blomstrende, lige saa høi og rolig, som i sin lykkeligste Tid, thi hendes store Sjæl seirede

---

768 When an old friend demands that she defend her husband's honour, Elisabeth admits that she is entirely uninformed about Bartholin's whereabouts and operations. The only thing she can be sure of is »at han ikke kan være skyldig i noget Dadelværdigt« (ibid., p. 310). Upon hearing this, her friend Frantz Stein suggests the use of white lies regarding the details, as long as she can confirm the faultlessness of Bartholin's character towards any of his defamers: »At han er paa det Sted han bør være, det er Sandhed! De øvrige Omstændigheder, om Stedet hedder Berlin, eller Paris, eller Stockholm, det er kun Fjas og Lapperi, det kommer Ingen ved, naar I kun kan overbevise dem om, hvad I selv er vis paa« (ibid., p. 311).
769 Ibid., p. 330.
770 Elisabeth is not the only one whose daughterly sympathy is held against herself. Anna Cathrine Ulfeld, too, had raised the royal house's suspicions with some blatant remarks regarding her mother, as related in Thomas Fuiren's letter: »Da hendes dristige, bestemte Sindelag besuden er noksom bekjendt, og da hun nu er uforsigtig nok til i same Brev at omtale sin ophøiede Frænde paa en uærbødig Maade og anklage ham for Tyrannie, saa, istedet for, som efter min ringe Mening var det rigtigste og billigste, at forklare disse Ord som Udbrud af en hjælpeløs Qvindes Fortvilelse, som en Datters Jamren, i sin Smerte over sine Forældres Ulykke, saa have hendes Huses Fjender søgt at lægge en dybere Betydning deri, end der sandsynligt findes i dem« (ibid., p. 334).
771 Cf. ibid., pp. 329-338.
772 Cf. Busk-Jensen, Lise. *Romantikkens forfatterinder 2*, p. 800.

over Skjæbnen!«[773] In this regard, 'Billedet' conveys a similar ideal as Herta J. Enevoldsen's novels on Leonora Christina: whenever their heroine faces adversaries of any kind in these texts, she reacts by erecting herself (»ranke sig«) and holding her head up high.[774] At the same time, Ulfeld does *not* comply with this ideal – hence highlighting the singularity of Eleonora's examplarity – as he overindulges in self-pity and despair. As a consequence, Elisabeth cannot admire his immutability, but is left to lament his altered condition: »Hvor forandret, hvor aldeles modsat var hans Tilstand, som hans Aasyn, fra den første Gang hun saae ham. Hiint Billed var næsten ganske fortrængt af dette«.[775]

While the image of Ulfeld has a cautionary effect on his observer, the contrast of his fate to that of his wife pulls Elisabeth deeper into Eleonora's life, which to Elisabeth represents a consistent principle (or, also, the principle of consistency). In the aftermath of her meeting with the dying Ulfeld, Elisabeth can no longer distinguish any phases or contrasts in her life. Instead, her entire life appears to her like one entity revolving around a core: »[…] dog Kjærnen, om man saaledes kan kalde det, var Kjærlighed til alt Godt og Skjønt«.[776] The 'Good and Beautiful' is, of course, embodied by Eleonora and all variations in her and Elisabeth's life are thus perceived not as autonomous developments detached from this core, but rather always as contrasts towards it. This worldview allows Elisabeth to reconcile the drastic changes in Eleonora's environment[777] with the comforting constancy assigned to her by Elisabeth. On the other hand, her involvement with the Countess Ulfeld causes disruptions in her own life, which somehow resemble her idol's challenges; for example, when she must defend her husband against defamating comments from her own family, while at the same time being completely in the dark about the actual motives for Bartholin's prolonged absence. The transformation of Elisabeth into an effigy of Eleonora is complete when she returns to The Hague and moves into the

---

773 Hegermann Lindencrone, Louise. 'Billedet', p. 282. Even more than two decades later, when Elisabeth reunites with Eleonora and her daughter in Maribo, she finds Eleonora unchanged: »Fire og tyve Aars Mellemtid, hvoraf de to og tyve tilbragte i Fangenskab, havde vel falmet Kindernes blomstrende Friskhed, men Kjærlighed, Haab og Tro havde holdt Hjertet varmt, derfor var en evig Ungdom i hendes Sind, som i hendes Blik og Smiil, hvilken hverken Aar, Kummer eller Lidelser havde formaaet at udslette!« (ibid., respectively p. 349).

774 For example, during her walk to the Blue Tower in Enevoldsen, Herta J. *Leonora Christina i Blåtårn.* Copenhagen: Gyldendal, 2013 (1979), p. 103.

775 Hegermann Lindencrone, Louise. 'Billedet', p. 288. The same contrast between the spouses is, again, provided by Herta J. Enevoldsen and, not least, by Leonora Christina herself. Both authoresses provide a depiction of the Ulfeldts' sufferings which portrays Leonora Christina as the stronger part.

776 Ibid., p. 289.

777 E.g., the contrast between Eleonora's reception in The Hague, which resembles a triumphal procession, and her arrival at the gates of the Blue Tower, provoking the most diverse comments from the spectators (Hegermann Lindencrone, Louise. 'Billedet', p. 242ff).

former Ulfeld mansion, whose initial decoration has been maintained in the minutest details, even including the portrait of Christian IV. Despite all of Elisabeth's efforts to elevate herself to Eleonora's level,[778] she still finds herself unworthy of taking in her idol's place in The Hague:

> Det forekom hende, næsten som en Vanhelligelse, at disse Mure, der havde indesluttet Mennesker hvis Tilværelse var kjendt og mærkelig over hele Europa, hvis Aandsgaver og Magt havde været ligesaa gigantisk, som deres paafølgende Fald, nu kun skulde høre Gjenklangen af hendes ubetydelige Skjæbnens Løb; [...].[779]

Elisabeth finds her own life and her everyday tasks insiginificant, yet her third meeting with Eleonora years later proves her wrong. After the death of Arentzen and Bartholin, Elisabeth and Eleonora reunite in Maribo and they switch roles. All the while Elisabeth had been thinking about the noble woman, who had granted her a friendly look in a time of sorrow, the very same woman had shared this thought:

> Da sagde Eleonora: »Erindrer Du, Anna, at jeg har fortalt Dig om et lindrende Syn, som formildede et af mit Livs bittreste Øieblik! – Disse Øine var det, hvis medlidende Taarer husvalede mig i det Øieblik, da jeg skulde miste min Frihed, skilles fra alt det, jeg havde kjært i Verden, da Had og Spot omgave mig. Kun et Øieblik saae jeg disse Træk, men saaledes og i et saadant Øieblik, at jeg aldrig glemmer dem!«[780]

Hence, Elisabeth's life, despite being lived for another person, had not been insignificant, as her commiseration had made a difference in Eleonora's eyes. 'Billedet' presents two models of female self-sacrifice, respectively, exemplified by Elisabeth's mother on the one hand, and by Elisabeth herself and her mother substitute Eleonora on the other. Maria Arentzen had lived a life for her husband, house and daughter, and the void left by her death is soon bridged by the appearance of Eleonora – Elisabeth's mother is never mentioned again in the text.[781] Eleonora, howe-

---

778 Said approximation concerns not only some incidents and difficulties in her life, but also her character, which has been formed towards the image of her idol. Accordingly, and despite her ambiguous, at best anachronistic social status, Elisabeth is said to be widely travelled and multilingual (ibid., pp. 310-312).
779 Ibid., p. 323.
780 Ibid., p. 350.
781 In this regard, Hegermann Lindencrone's perspective on Leonora Christina is rather vanguard, since only in the following century, a similar laud of Leonora Christina refinement through isolation would be phrased by the Danish writer Johannes V. Jensen (1873-1950), in his poem 'Leonora Christine' (1906): »Naturen sine Floder / udtømte i dit Blod. / Du bed som Brud og Moder, / men ene var du god« (Jensen, Johannes V. 'Leonora Christine'. In Jensen, Johannes V. *Digte*. Copenhagen: Gyldendal, 1954 (Gyldendals nyklassiske lyrikerserie), p. 53).

ver, abandons her former secure life by following her husband and despite her long ordeal she eventually obtains redemption and eternal fame. Following her idol's example, Elisabeth, too, is rewarded in the end, as she is invited to stay with Eleonora and her daughter Anna Cathrine: »Hendes Barndoms og Ungdoms Drømme og Haab vare nu opfyldte, hun saae sin aldrig rokkede Tro paa Eleonora beseglet«.[782]

Maria Arentzen's efforts had been unilateral, hence supporting the previously raised suspicion that Louise Hegermann Lindencrone saw no fulfillment in marital life alone.[783] Eleonora and Elisabeth, on the other hand, enjoy a bilateral appreciation as both women had had an impact on each other's lives based on their shared beliefs and values. Elisabeth thus dies soon after meeting her idol once again, with peace in heart and Eleonora by her side.

Previous scholarship has mostly perceived Elisabeth Arentzen's strange character as the authoress' criticism of contemporary life schemes available to women:

> Narrativt og poetologisk kan slutningen læses som Hegermanns påpegning af, at de sociale vilkår forhindrede kvinden i at blive subjekt i sin egen livshistorie og heltinde i en roman, med mindre hun havde position og egenskaber som Leonora Christina; fortællingens øvrige kvindelige personer er enten døde som moderen, indskrænkede som nabokonerne og tanten eller fattige enker. I al sin historiske nøjagtighed bliver Leonora Christinas skikkelse i sidste instans et mytologisk billede på det kvindelige subjekt, Hegermann ønskede at skrive frem i sine tekster.[784]

Steffen Auring et al., too, conclude that Elisabeth's need of a maternal figure has an intentionally destructive effect on her own life, whereas the ending of the tale offers no discoursive resolution, but rather an unfulfilling reversal of selfsame discourse.[785] Yet, instead of focussing on the negative implications of Eleonora's appearance for Elisabeth's life, I suggest a conception of 'Billedet' as a plea for a new understanding of historical significance, in terms of women's history, with Hegermann Lindencrone as forerunner. For although all criticism of Elisabeth's life choices is justified, this does not in the least concern Louise Hegermann Lindencrone's own lifelong admiration of Leonora Christina, as it was already expressed in the prologue to *Eleonora Christina Uhlfeldt*:

---

782 Hegermann Lindencrone, Louise. 'Billedet', p. 351.
783 Auring, Steffen et al. 'Den romantiske kvindemyte', p. 446.
784 Busk-Jensen, Lise. *Romantikkens forfatterinder 2*, p. 801.
785 Auring, Steffen et al. 'Den romantiske kvindemyte', p. 448.

Saa stod hun herlig for mit indre Øie, / Med Stierne-Krandsen, som Urania; / Opløst i Harmonie hver Angst og Møie, / Hvert Suk forvandlet til Halleluja. / Og – som alt her – Gratiers Rosenbaand / Omslynged Kraftens Spir i hendes Haand. [...] Fra Himlen skulde Leonora svæve / Forklaret her paa Jorden med os leve![786]

In conclusion, however one chooses to understand Elisabeth's behaviour, Leonora Christina's position as the tale's icon is incontrovertible.

2.4.2. H. F. Ewald: *Leonora Kristina: Billeder af en Kongedatters Liv* (1895) – The *Liidende Christinne*

En Beretning om Minde oc Moed
Gud til Ære optegnet aff den
Liidende Christinne i henders
Alders 63. oc Fengsels nesten 21. Aar.

(*Jammers Minde*, p. 235)

Herman Frederik Ewald's (1821-1908) late work chiefly consists of historical novels, one of them being *Leonora Kristina*, a rather complete presentation of Leonora Christina's life. While the subtitle containing the keyword *Billeder*, i.e. 'Pictures' or 'Images', hints at the possibility of this account providing a certain degree of contrast (i.e. a depiction of Leonora Christina's great wealth and subsequent downfall), this novel is actually the most faithful interpretation of her life in the tradition of the Passion of Christ. *Leonora Kristina* depicts a continuous sequence of tragedies and conflicts, thus exhibiting a consistent disposition.[787] Accordingly, the term *Billeder* corresponds to Louise Hegermann Lindencrone's use of the word in her tale 'Billedet', but also to Hans Christian Andersen's stationary depiction of Leonora Christina in 'Gudfaders Billedbog'.

Leonora Kristina consists of six books respectively dealing with Leonora Christina's childhood in a broken home including the loss of her dearest sister,

---

[786] Hegermann Lindencrone, Louise. *Eleonora Christina Uhlfeldt*, unpaginated preamble.

[787] Ewald does not even perceive any change in Leonora Christina's behaviour during or after her imprisonment in the Blue Tower, as demonstrated by his comment on the list of deceased enemies (*dødslisten*) provided at the end of *Jammers Minde*: »Der er imidlertid en Efterskrift til dette Værk, som man kunde ønske borte. I den nævner hun alle dem af hendes Fjender, som Døden bortrev, mens hun sad i Fængsel. [...] Udfrielsen af hendes Fangenskab synes altsaa ikke at have stemt hende blidt eller gjort hende villig til at tilgive« (Ewald, H[erman] F[rederik]. *Leonora Kristina: Billeder af en Kongedatters Liv*. Copenhagen: Jacob Erslevs Forlag 1903 (1895), p. 382).

the conflict between her husband and her father, the Ulfeldts' clash with the new royal couple, the Ulfeldts' years abroad, including their attempt to settle in Sweden, their fall from grace in Sweden, and their final failure leading to Leonora Christina's imprisonment. Conflict dominates thus the protagonist's life, whether she is part of it (as in her rivalry with the Queen) or in between antagonists (e.g. in the conflict between her parents). The account furthermore depicts her as a victim of other people's power struggle, leaving her conflicted over who to side with. Finally, as in most 19th-century literary depictions of Leonora Christina, Leonora[788] remains the passive appendix of the scoundrel Korfits Ulfeldt for most of the account. Only the last two chapters of the final book provide an opportunity for her to act independently, as her husband is finally out of the picture. At the same time, the plot accelerates towards the end. While Ewald took the time to elaborate conversations between King Kristian and his subordinates, the entire seven months Leonora and her husband spend in Hammershus on the island of Bornholm rush by within a few pages. Furthermore, Ewald's account covering the time spanning from Leonora's departure to England until her imprisonment in the Blue Tower fills merely a page. This hurry may well be due to the dreariness of prisonlife and the poor documentation of the months in between Leonora Christina's incarcerations. Nevertheless, Ewald's – intended or unintended – preference for the first half of his heroine's life leaves the reader with the impression that firstly, Leonora is yet another pretence-heroine[789] and secondly, that her father and husband are the true protagonists (i.e. the tragic and the antihero, respectively) of the novel, while Leonora constitutes a mere epilogue to, or a sort of legacy of, *their* lives.

Ewald's depiction of calamities commences on the first page, which presents the iconic Frederiksborg Castle – otherwise a symbol of Denmark's great past – as a place of sorrow:

---

788 In the present chapter, »Leonora« specifically refers to the character in H. F. Ewald's novel, particularly when referring to passages that do not correspond to historical events, whereas »Leonora Christina« refers to the historical person. Further spelling variations used in the literary source text, and hence in this chapter as well, are »Korfits (Ulfeldt)«, »Kristian (den Fjerde)«, »Anna Katrine« and »Sofie Amalie«.

789 This is also the case in Louise Hegermann Lindencrone's *Eleonora Christina Uhlfeldt*, where Eleonora is the eponymous heroine, but far from being the (sole) protagonist, and, in a different way, in Hans Christian Andersen's tales, which utilise Leonora Christina and her famous love to promote her infamous husband.

Hvad husede dette fortryllede Slot, som var saa rigt smykket? Var der Fryd og Gammen i dets Haller, eller dækkede al denne Pragt kun som en Maske over Elendighed? De stolteste Menneskeværker ere Forfængelighed underkastede; men de ere dog stærkere og staa længer end de Drømmeslotte, som det menneskelige Hjerte opfører. Et Pust kan vælte dem, selv om de synes byggede paa fast Grund, end sige naar de ere byggede paa Sand. Saaledes var det gaaet Frederiksborgs Bygherre, Kristian den Fjerde.[790]

As shall be demonstrated again in some of the subsequent chapters, it has become a common feature of contemporary Leonora Christina-literature to highlight her parents' uncivilised domestic quarrel in order to – implicitly or explicitly – account for her resulting character (e.g., her haughty personality or her need for marital solidarity).[791] Yet, H. F. Ewald has been the first writer to depict Leonora Christina's troubled childhood – a feature quite vanguard for the 19th century, which otherwise tended to glorify Christian IV. Ewald even extends his presentation of this broken home to Leonora Christina's children, who usually play no active part in Leonora Christina-literature – the only nameable exception being Louise Hegermann Lindencrone's tale 'Billedet'. Thus, Leonora's eldest daughter is also deeply affected by the daily family quarrel.[792]

Furthermore, the above passage showing King Kristian as the nation's constructor in chief is reminiscent of Christian IV's famous last words to his daughter, as related in her French autobiography (»Je t'ay mise si ferme que personne ne te peut branler«).[793] Leonora Christina's subsequent comment in her French account, indicating that her father's influence had not lasted long enough, correlates to Ewald's allegory of transience, hereby replacing the usual prophetic references to the Ulfeldts' coming downfall – which every single work dealing with Leonora Christina contains – with the Baroque doctrine of *memento mori*, thus lending the account a darker tone than is common for Leonora Christina-literature. At the same time, Ewald's account is the first to offer a look behind the facade, behind the *billed*, while also illustrating a crack in the veneer:

---

[790] Ewald, H[erman] F[rederik]. *Leonora Kristina*, p. 3. This passage refers to Christian IV's failed marriage with Leonora Christina's mother, Kirsten Munk.

[791] On the other hand, 19th century presentations – as well as Leonora Christina herself – usually discreetly omit any mention of her scandalous mother.

[792] »›Det var i Gaar,‹ sagde Anne, efter at hun havde fældet nogle Taarer, ›at jeg talte til Kay [Lykke, her fiancé] om al det Spektakel og det Skænderi, som her er hver Dag. Da jeg forgangen Dag kom ind i Hallen, hørte jeg, at Oldemoder bandede Kongen, Faster Sofie saa ud som en Heks, og Fader havde ogsaa sine vrede Øjne paa[‹]« (Ewald, H[erman] F[rederik]. *Leonora Kristina*, p. 114).

[793] *Leonora Christina Grevinde Ulfeldts Franske Levnedsskildring*, p. 5b (Translation p. 21).

Silketapeter, hvori der var indvævet skønne Landskaber, dækkede Væggene, og fra det rigt udskaarne, forgyldte Loft holdt Retfærdighed, Klogskab, Taalmodighed, Kærlighed og andre Dyder, fremstillede som en Kreds af svævende Kvinder, Laurbærkranse over hans Hoved, mens Nag og Vrede rasede i hans Hjerte, og Mishaab tyngede hans ellers saa stærke Sjæl.[794]

Apart from such contrasts between outside and inside, Ewald's depiction of Leonora Christina's childhood follows her own implicit statements: all misfortune in her life results from other people's envy and ambition, starting with her privileged position within a flock of royal children: »Det var Leonoras Skæbne overalt at blive foretrukken; endogsaa hendes lunefulde Moder var ofte mild imod hende, hvorfor hendes Søstre ogsaa vare misundelige paa hende, alene Anne Katrine undtagen«.[795] The young girl rewards this motherly sympathy with daughterly love, thus entering the first conflict of her life: as she loves both of her parents dearly, she is unable to lay the blame for their failed marriage on either of them – a conduct commended by the narrator:

> Hun var naturligvis ikke i Stand til at dømme dem imellem; men hendes skarpe og tidlig udviklede Forstand sagde hende, at hun ikke kunde retfærdiggøre sin Moder uden at nedsætte sin Fader. Derfor tav hun. Men Anne Katrine, som var mere vidende og aldrig havde mærket noget til Kærlighed hos Moderen, havde let ved at tage Parti. Hun gav sine Følelser Luft paa en Maade, som viste, at hun tænkte mindre dybt end hendes yngre Søster.[796]

While the auctorial narrator dispraises Anne Katrine for picking sides, he does not hesitate to follow her lead. His unconcealed preference for Leonora is a result of her moral elevation from her historical milieu. Korfits, for example, who cannot help growing fond of his fiancée, eventually wins the favour of the King's daughter by showing her kindness and understanding, thus taking in the place of her first love Maurits (see Chapter 1.2.1.): »Hendes fantastiske Barndomskærlighed døde hen som en Larve, af hvilken den dybe og trofaste Kærlighed sprang frem, som siden skulde gøre hende saa navnkundig«.[797]

---

794 Ewald, H[erman] F[rederik]. *Leonora Kristina*, p. 4.
795 Ibid., p. 10.
796 Ibid.
797 Ibid., p. 18.

Korfits receives eternal loyalty and assistance from his future wife while she will not be rewarded in turn. In fact, she will always be punished for her love as it will sooner or later be held against her. This is not only the case with her marriage to Korfits Ulfeldt, but also when Leonora refuses to turn her back on her mother:

Vel blev han [King Kristian] nu Fru Kirsten kvit, og hun kom aldrig mere for hans Aasyn; men hun skulde vedblive at ærgre ham ved sine Streger, og for hendes Skyld opstod der mellem ham og hendes Frænder, ja siden endogsaa med hans egne Børn en Strid, som skulde holde ham varm lige til det sidste.[798]

Leonora Christina is thus portrayed as the exception from, rather than a representative of her age. This can only bode well for her character as Ewald makes no secret of his disgust for the 17th century.[799] He could neither refrain from explicitly excusing Christian IV's polygamy while condemning Kirsten Munk and Ellen Marsvin on the background of »Datidens sædelige Fordærvelse«,[800] nor from scoffing at *Det Store Bilager*'s »smagløse og naive Brogethed«.[801]

At the same time, his portrayal of Leonora Christina's »tornefulde Ungdomsbane«[802] is not intended to serve as an explanation or excuse of her subsequent character. On the contrary; her wicked milieu nourishes her: »Hun udviklede sig herlig. Hun var lig en kraftig Plante, som Stormen ikke kan oprykke, og som drager Næring selv af Nattefrostens isnende Rim«.[803]

Ewald's novel is not among the most creative pieces of literature considered in this study. Most criticism of his life's work deplores his dry mode of narrating and his fixation on historical accuracy and educational value at the expense of fictional

---

798 Ibid., p. 47.
799 The view that the 17th century had been an infinitely more primitive and vulgar age than the modern one is rather common to the 19th century. Writers and scholars of this classic age of Leonora Christina-literature often draw on this notion whenever they are faced with exceptions to their heroine's otherwise exemplary behaviour. Sophus Birket Smith, for example, refers to the 17th century's general incivility in order to account for Leonora Christina's allegedly open marriage (as implied in her French autobiography, see introductory quotation Chapter 2.4.3.): »[...] et Svar, som, skjønt kun givet på Skrømt, foranlediger mig til én Gang for alle at minde om, at enhver Tid har sin egen Målestok for det passende, og at vi ikke på det 17de Århundredes helt igjennem mere grovkornede Slægt må overføre vor Tids Sømmelighedsfordringer, allermindst hvad den ydre Fremtrædelsesform angår« (Birket Smith, Sophus. *Leonora Christina Grevinde Ulfeldts Historie 1*, p. 96).
800 Ewald, H[erman] F[rederik]. *Leonora Kristina*, p. 20.
801 Ibid., p. 62. *Det Store Bilager* was the betrothal of Christian IV's son Christian to Magdalene Sibylle of Saxony (1617-1668) in 1634 and it was the biggest celebration of 17th-century Denmark.
802 Ibid., p. 48.
803 Ibid.

finesse.⁸⁰⁴ However, in many regards he has been a pioneer of Leonora Christina-literature. His portrayal of the royal household is impious, thus accounting for most of the comedy in the novel,⁸⁰⁵ and he is the first to present Leonora Christina as a child in situations disrobed of their nimbus.⁸⁰⁶ Unlike his predecessors – especially Oehlenschläger and Hegermann Lindencrone, who both presented the Dina affair as a personal conflict between individuals – Ewald presents Leonora Christina in a broader, historical-political context. He is the first to depict Leonora Christina's life in the form of a historical novel and – following the tradition of Walter Scott⁸⁰⁷ – Ewald is also the first to thematise the sociopolitical upheaval of the mid-17th century, which resulted in the overthrow of the nobility and implementation of absolutism in Denmark in 1660. Thus, when Otto Sperling warns Leonora of the revenge of her enemies, he refers not only to the King and Queen of Denmark, but also to the people: »[D]er rører sig meget i Borgerstanden, som vil afryste Adelens Aag«.⁸⁰⁸

Another novelty worth mentioning, albeit not the topic of this study, is that Ewald is evidently not impressed by the political abilities of Corfitz Ulfeldt, whom he considers to have been highly overestimated, most of all by himself: »En stærk Ærgerrighed brændte i hans Sjæl, og han havde en overdreven Forestilling om sine Evner og sit Værd«.⁸⁰⁹ His promotion to the highest position in the kingdom is thus accorded not to his capability, but to the untimely death of his predecessor Frants Rantzau, and the subsequent account presents Ulfeldt as an incompetent snob. At the same time, Ewald emphasises Leonora Christina's talents, thus elevating her intellect over the level of her husband. With this notion of Denmark's most notorious statesman – a complete renunciation of Andersen's defence of Ulfeldt – Ewald's account is entirely unique.

---

804 See, for example, Bauditz, Sophus. 'H. F. Ewald'. In *Dansk Biografisk Leksikon 6: Devegge–Ferdinandsen*. Grundlagt af C. F. Bricka. Red. af Povl Engelstoft. Copenhagen: Schultz 1935, p. 479.

805 E.g., Ewald's description of the »holmgang« between Kirsten Munk and one of her daughters, which ends in the daughter wrestling down her mother while being applauded by King Kristian (see Ewald, H[erman] F[rederik]. *Leonora Kristina*, p. 36).

806 Hans Christian Andersen, too, depicts Leonora Christina as a child, yet his presentation is too static to provide a character portrayal.

807 Cf. Lukács, Georg. *The Historical Novel*, transl. Hannah and Stanley Mitchell. Harmondsworth: Penguin Books, 1976 (1969), pp. 340-342.

808 Ewald, H[erman] F[rederik]. *Leonora Kristina*, p. 150. Equally novel is Ewald's mention of the same kind of ill-humour the Ulfeldts meet upon their flight from Hammershus. Once the fugitives reach the coast of Bornholm in order to look for a fishing boat, they are stopped and threatened by a horde of fishermen, who have not forgotten about Korfits's treachery (ibid., p. 333). This bornholmian grudge against the Ulfeldts seems to have lasted over centuries, as demonstrated by the recent Bornholm ferry dispute.

809 Ibid., p. 54.

Besides exhibiting a contempt for Corfitz Ulfeldt, Ewald's account reverses Andersen's doom over the Ulfeldt couple in yet another sense. While Andersen and some of his contemporaries reckoned Leonora Christina's love to be a guarantor for Ulfeldt's character, Ewald inverts this verdict by lamenting Leonora Christina's devotion *despite* her husband's character. Most interesting and unique is Ewald's formulation of this conviction by means of a direct comparison of Leonora and her enemy Sofie Amalie:

> Dernæst stod hun ingenlunde tilbage for Leonora i diplomatisk Snildhed og i Viljekraft snarest over hende. Kongen laa for hendes Fødder, hun kunde faa sin Vilje med ham i alt undtagen i de store politiske Spørgsmaal, men til sidst var det dog hende, der drev ham til Handling ogsaa i dette Punkt. Leonora derimod var sin Man underdanig, hans Vilje var hendes Lov, og uagtet dette taler til Ære for hendes Hjerte og viser, at hun havde en ædlere Natur og større Kvindeværd end Sofie Amalie, saa lammede det dog hendes Handlekraft. Hun vilde have staaet højere, hvis hendes Kærlighed havde kunnet gaa i Lag med hendes overlegne Evner, og intet vilde have været mere til Ulfeldts Gavn, end om hun havde kunnet faa ham for sine Fødder, saaledes som Dronningen havde sin Husbond.[810]

Despite Ewald's praise of wifely devotion, he sees Leonora Christina's unconditional love and loyalty – usually regarded as her greatest assets – as her greatest flaws.

Ewald's historicised depiction of the Ulfeldt couple resembles Julius Lange's conclusions. The latter's article, published in 1888 and carrying the title 'Contra Leonora Christina', constitutes a caesura in the corpus of research on Leonora Christina (see Chapter 1.2.1.). Lange was not only a forerunner in questioning the objectivity of Leonora Christina's writings and of Sophus Birket Smith's judgement of selfsame writings, but he was also the first to add a historical-cultural perspective to his assessment of Leonora Christina's texts. While most 19th-century authors and scholars perceived Leonora Christina as a romantic Madonna, Lange pulled her out of this static role by highlighting potential historical differences. This academic development may constitute the background of Ewald's novel depiction of Leonora Christina, as both authors – Lange and Ewald – draw on the moral standard of the 17th century, which they did not consider equal to their contemporaries' ethics. Hence, Julius Lange argues:

---

810 Ibid., 141.

> Det kommer nu blot an paa, om Forfatteren regner tilstrækkelig med den store og væsentlige Differens, der skiller det 17de Aarhundredes Moral fra den der gælder, eller i alt Fald skulde gælde for vor Tid. [...] Om end al Ting tyder paa, at Leon. Chr. paa sin Tids Vis var en ypperlig Kvinde, og i det hele af sin Tid anerkendtes for at være det, var der i hendes Handlemaade dog sikkert meget, som vor Tid, naar den vil se klart, efter sine Begreber maa fordømme, endog som Forbrydelse.[811]

This moral relief is repeated in Ewald's depiction of Leonora Christina's contemporaries – the author's countless interjections bear witness to this tendency. Ewald openly condemns some of the actions and customs portrayed in his novel, while conceding Leonora Christina a certain grandness of character, yet without depicting her in an idealised manner – she too has her share of flaws.[812] Most of all, though, Ewald's explanatory comment, that »Lydighed jo *var* [my italics] bydende Pligt for en Hustru« (see above) serves to defend her on the background of *her* age, while in other instances attacking her on the background of his own. Through his elevated position, Ewald disassociates himself from the events in his novel, thus allowing for both praise and dispraise of Leonora Christina to arise – either way the account will evoke lament.

In many ways, the respective portrayals of Julius Lange and H. F. Ewald coincide: both regard Leonora Christina as the superior part of the Ulfeldt marriage (»den overlegne og verdenserfarne Kvinde, som var hans Hustru«);[813] both invoke the female abjectness typical of the 17th century in order to account for any potential moral deviations committed by Leonora Christina (»Efter Tidens rent bibelske Opfattelse af Ægteskabet var Manden Hustruens Herre, som hun ogsaa bestandig kalder sin Mand«);[814] both had their doubts about Leonora Christina's ignorance regarding her husband's schemes (»Hun maatte da ogsaa være baade dum og blind for at tro, at deres overvættes Rigdom skulde være skaffet paa lovlig Maade. Men det kan ikke være faldet hende vanskeligt at finde paa Undskyldningsgrunde. Datidens Moral var slap«);[815] and finally, both concluded that Leonora Christina was prone to resort to lies when it served her husband's cause (»Intet Middel blev vraget af

---

811 Lange, Julius. 'Contra Leonora Christina', p. 722.
812 The same kind of relative perfection is attributed to her father. While Ewald deplores the King's concubinages, he admits that this was no personal flaw, but rather a custom of the 17th century. At the same time, he emphasises the King's faithfulness towards his respective mistresses (Ewald, H[erman] F[rederik]. *Leonora Kristina*, p. 20).
813 Lange, Julius. 'Contra Leonora Christina', p. 725.
814 Ibid., p. 728.
815 Ewald, H[erman] F[rederik]. *Leonora Kristina*, p. 94.

hendes ›trofaste Ægtekærlighed‹, og hvor alt andet bristede, greb hun til Løgn«).[816] Like Lange, Ewald, too, seems to have carefully studied Leonora Christina's writings, weighing her every word. One example is his portrayal of father and daughter at the former's hour of death, which Leonora Christina remembers as follows: »Skreffwen 1684. den 28. *Februarii*, som er 36. Aars dagen, att Høyloffligste Konning *Christian* den Fiærde, sagde Werden goede Nat, oc ieg min Wersens welfart« (*Jammers Minde*, p. 238). This perception is reflected in Ewald's novel, in which an opportunistic Leonora cannot help but seeing her dying father as a fading guarantee of wealth and power: »Men han mærkede, at Leonora ikke græd over ham alene. Hun havde bange Anelser om Fremtiden. […] Hun var mere fremsynet end Ulfeldt, og nu, da Enden nærmede sig, værdsatte hun først til fulde, hvor meget hendes døende Fader havde været for dem«.[817]

Ewald's presentation of Leonora Christina as a faithful yet proud and ambitious woman follows her own self-portrayal in all its seeming inconsistency. Leonora Christina's self-understanding as *Liidende Christinne* in the tradition of Christ derives from her apparent chosenness in gifts as well as in birth. As has repeatedly been pointed out in Leonora Christina-historiography, her abilities had soon surpassed those of her siblings – a notion also promoted by Leonora Christina herself. Those talents are universally considered to have been inherited from her father alone, thus making Leonora Christina the only proper representative and legacy of her father. In *Jammers Minde*, as well as in her French autobiography, Leonora Christina refrains from mentioning her perfidious and less sophisticated mother, thus creating the impression of an immaculate birth onto the throne of Denmark. At the same time, she refuses to renounce her highborn father by declining to bow to her higher-ranking brother and his wife. This insistance on chosenness and providence places her within the tradition of Christ. Ewald adopts this pattern,[818] yet without any glorifying elevation of Christian IV as a starting point. In this, as in many other regards, Leonora Christina has been humanised.

Accordingly, Leonora rages whenever the quality of her origin is drawn into question while the narrator questions the motives for her doing so. The appearance of Vibeke Kruse, another historical character to be utilised for the first time by H. F. Ewald, prompts the following explanation:

---

816 Ibid., p. 303.
817 Ibid., p. 130.
818 Already at the age of eleven, Ewald's Leonora is more knowledgeable than »de fleste voksne og modne Kvinder paa hendes Tid« (ibid., p. 50). At the same time, she is very proud and status-conscious: »Det kongelige Blod, der flød i hendes Aarer, fornægtede sig aldrig. Denne Ætstolthed gav hendes Færd lige fra Ungdommen et storladent Præg; men den skulde ogsaa blive skæbnesvanger for hende« (ibid., p. 70).

> Dog slap de [Leonora and her sisters] ikke altid for at være under Tag sammen med denne Kvinde, som de hadede dødeligt, ikke saa meget af moralsk Finfølelse, som fordi de troede, at hun havde fordrevet deres Moder. Vel elskede de ikke Fru Kirsten; men med Aarene fik de dog Forstand paa, at deres Moders Vanære kastede Skygge paa dem selv.[819]

Leonora Christina's famous pride is thus presented as a concoction of her conflicting parental relations. Her father's high status raises her status-consciousness, while her descent from a lower born mother, whose chastitiy has been challenged, forces her to defend her status against challengers, whose number will increase over the years. Again, a certain likeness to the fate of Christ is detectable, as those who formerly loved and admired her will grow to hate her: »Saaledes kom Leonora i sin Ungdoms første Blomst til at træde en Æresdans med Fyrster og Herrer, som i sildigere tider skulde hade og fornægte hende«.[820] Ewald's word choice imposes an association with the disciple Saint Peter, who denied Christ thrice.

In conclusion, Leonora Christina is portrayed as a tragic figure that fell prey to her own love – thus her sufferings are a choice of hers, as most blatantly demonstrated in the course of the Malmö trial, when Leonora chooses to stay with her husband – but also due to her insistence on providence and chosenness. To a certain degree she sets herself apart from her mean surroundings, but as a consequence of that, her perfection is only relative. Ewald's reinterpretation of Leonora Christina's life story indicates a perception shift from Leonora Christina as national heroine to a figure of public nuisance, from etherial Madonna to profane noblewoman,[821] and from spokesperson of Corfitz Ulfeldt to his sidekick.

The novel's actual heroine is Leonora's daughter Anne Katrine, whose mature character saves her from the negative influence of her temporary fiancé, Kay Lykke, an arrogant yet cowardly young nobleman. This *enfant terrible* follows in the footsteps of Korfits Ulfeldt, but he never wins over his daughter. Unlike her mother, Anne Katrine manages to keep her distance to troublesome suitors, thus preventing a fate shared with them. Despite being courted by yet more fortune hunters in Sweden, she remains unwed for a longer time than her mother finds fitting. Yet, by doing so she achieves independence and eventually happiness. Furthermore, her eventful

---

819 Ibid., p. 49.
820 Ibid., p. 71.
821 Accordingly, her silent farewell before her departure from Denmark is directed not at her homeland (Oehlenschläger) or her children (Hegermann Lindencrone), but at her material possessions, her home on Gråbrødretorv: »Den næste Dag, den 14de Juli, silde om Aftenen, brød han [Ulfeldt] op og forlod sit skønne, pragtfulde Hjem, hvor han havde nydt saa mange Glæder og prøvet saa store Sorger. Mon vi nogen Sinde faa det at se igen?« (ibid., p. 179).

lovelife during her parents' years of struggle compensates for her mother's passivity during selfsame time. Most importantly, though, Anne Katrine is a younger and improved version of her mother – she has all the good qualities of Leonora, yet without the bad influence of her father.[822] However, she is not entirely unaffected by it either. This becomes especially blatant when she reunites with her father and her brothers in Basel, after their final flight from Denmark:

> Paa Veien derhen udspurgte Brødrene hende om hendes Rejse; de hørte i Tavshed paa hendes Fortælling om alle de Eventyr, hun havde gennemgaaet, roste hende ikke for den Kækhed og Snildhed, hvormed hun havde klaret for sig, og udtalte ingen Glæde over den Trofasthed, hun havde vist ved at vove sig ud paa denne farlige Rejse. Det sidste krænkede hende især dybt.[823]

Despite all her efforts to not repeat her mother's mistakes, Anne Katrine still gets drawn into the fatal schemes of the Ulfeldt family's male members and she, too, receives no reward. Only when the two women reunite after more than two decades, Anne Katrine receives gratitude for her love and care.[824] This analogy between mother and daughter is especially evident when considering that Ewald – with all his judgemental interjections – dealt with Leonora Christina as a historical, i.e. pre-written character, while taking great fictional liberties in his rather extensive presentation of Anna Catharina Ulfeldt – of whom otherwise very little is known.

In his depiction of an enduring and caring mother and daughter in opposition to destructive father and sons, Ewald follows a very traditional gender notion.[825] Despite his criticism of this very same endurance Leonora Christina demonstrates for her husband, Ewald simultaneously praises her for this 'female quality'. In general, Ewald's references to 17th-century female obedience leave little room for a feminist discussion. Nevertheless, his – as well as Julius Lange's – resigned comments on Leonora Christina's subordination towards her treacherous husband enabled a discourse on her obedience. Thus, Ewald paved the way for the next generation of Leonora Christina-literature, which presents a much more disputatious Countess – both towards her surroundings as well as her husband.

---

822 While Leonora thus finds herself in Anne Katrine, Korfits's short-tempered character is reflected in two of his sons, one of which murders Adolph Fuchs to avenge his parents, while the other one exposes his father's hideout in Basel by challenging two Swiss officers to a duel, thus attracting unwanted attention.
823 Ewald, H[erman] F[rederik]. *Leonora Kristina*, p. 366.
824 Ibid., p. 385.
825 The same gender pattern will also be the topic of Chapter 2.7.1.

2.4.3. Ebbe Kløvedal Reich: *Rejsen til Messias* (1974) – The Covetable Companion

> [M]ais elle la diroit un secret que peut estre elle ne sçavoit pas, qui estoit, qu'elle avoit donnée permission à son Mari de passer son temps avec d'autres; et quand elle estoit satisfaitte, le reste seroit pour les autres[.][826]

Ebbe Kløvedal[827] Reich's trilogy *Rejsen til Messias* is a literary Chinese box, with ever more stories emerging out of previous ones. At first glance, it is the narrative of a single person, Josef Lazarus, and his life in the years spanning from 1648 until 1670. Yet, by opening each book and by reading each chapter, more stories, elaborately nestled, emerge.[828] Each narrative level has a different narrator, yet – despite their spatial distance to each other – they all tell the same story, thus constituting a compact and rounded history of religion, nobility and power.

As there are several narrators in the novels, one ought to identify Leonora Christina's[829] function in the diverse narrative levels. The first layer belongs, of course, to its first-person narrator. In his preamble, Ebbe Kløvedal Reich calls for a new perspective on past events:

> Jeg foreslår kort sagt et historiesyn, som gør verdenshistorien mere spændende, end den er lige for øjeblikket. I stedet for at studere den under lup uden at vide, hvorfor, kan vi holde Dommedag over fortiden alle sammen på samme tid, når blot vi har nogle faste principper, som vi kan blive enige om.[830]

The novel thus offers a widened understanding of single historical events – however fictionalised they may be in this instance – by implicitly depicting parallelisms

---

826 *Leonora Christina Grevinde Ulfeldts Franske Levnedsskildring*, p. 4a (Translation p. 15: »Men hun vilde nu berette hende en hemmelighed, som hun maaske ikke kendte, hvilket var, at hun havde givet sin mand forlov at tilbringe sin tid med andre, og naar hun var fornøjet, var de andre velkomne til resterne«).

827 Kløvedal is a sort of second family name, as Ebbe Reich, together with fellow hippies, founded the Kløvedal family in 1969 – a flower power collective based in 'Maos lyst' in the Copenhagen suburb of Hellerup. Kløvedal is the Danish name for Rivendell, a paradise-like refuge and seat of the Elven lord Elrond in J. R. R. Tolkien's trilogy *Lord of the Rings*.

828 Josef Lazarus is the novel's protagonist, yet not its first-person narrator. Nevertheless, the narrative provided in the trilogy is based on the (fictive) accounts of the very same protagonist, subsequently transformed into three novels by several anonymous narrators living in the 17th century, the 19th century, and the year 0 (respectively Volume 1-3). In accordance with Ebbe Kløvedal Reich's analogical method (see below), the latter date indicates that history is about to repeat itself.

829 In the present chapter, »Leonora« specifically refers to the character in Ebbe Kløvedal Reich's novel, particularly when referring to passages that do not correspond to historical events, whereas »Leonora Christina« refers to the historical person.

830 Reich, Ebbe Kløvedal. *Rejsen til Messias: Tre bøger fra enevældens tid: Første bog: Herrens rakkere og bødler*. [Copenhagen:] Gyldendal, 1974, p. 10.

between geographically and thematically remote developments. The infighting between magnates of the secular sphere aligns with the struggle of clerical dignitaries, in Protestant Copenhagen as well as in Islamic Istanbul, for example in the depiction of the life of Sultan Ibrahim, who died in 1648, just like Christian IV. He, too, had fallen prey to his polygamy and to the resulting flock of rebellious children,[831] while his son becomes an absolutist sovereign.[832] Reich had already used this analogical method in *Frederik. En folkebog om N. F. S. Grundtvigs tid og liv* from 1972, in which he also explains his approach and source of inspiration: »Der findes to dominerende måder at tænke på. Man kan kalde dem den logiske måde og den analogiske måde, den videnskabelige og den poetiske. Logikken har at gøre med de åbenlyse forskelle, analogikken med de skjulte ligheder. Bogen her er et analogisk eksperiment, ligesom Frederiks værk var det«.[833]

Applied to the historical topics of Reich's novels, the analogical method invites the reader to reflect on contemporary developments and problems; and in the context of Denmark in the 1970's, it is safe to suggest a parallel between the events in *Rejsen til Messias* and the author's scepticism towards the political and economical developments leading to Denmark's accession to the European Communities in 1973.[834]

Despite this demand for a Danish recall of national culture and values free of international intervention,[835] the protagonist of *Rejsen til Messias* is by no means a

---

831 Ibid., p. 79f.
832 Ibid., p. 80.
833 Reich, Ebbe Kløvedal. *Frederik. En folkebog om N. F. S. Grundtvigs tid og liv.* Copenhagen: Gyldendal, 1978 (1972), p. 30. In *Rejsen til Messias*, there is no such explicit reference to his use of an analogical method. However, the implied author connects Josef Lazarus and Leonora's flirt on their way from Copenhagen to Amsterdam with the meeting between Sabbatai Zwi and Miranda in Alexandria in an equally explicit manner, thus sensitising his readers to the ubiquitous presence of hidden analogies – in the story as well as in history: »Og mange, mange mil derfra skete der noget, som endnu intet menneske vidste hang sammen med det, der skete på rigshovmesterens karavel« (Reich, Ebbe Kløvedal. *Herrens rakkere og bødler*, p. 107).
834 Cf. Søren Schou, who thematises Reich's »allegoriserende brug af danmarkshistorien i kampen mod EF/EU« (Schou, Søren. 'En folkelig esoteriker: Ebbe Kløvedal Reich's *En engels vinger* og *Morgendagens mand*', Spring 7 (1994), p. 120). See also *Litteraturhåndbogen*, ed. Ib Fischer Hansen et al. Copenhagen: Gyldendal, 1987 (1985), p. 483, which sums up Reich's political intentions regarding his historical novels as follows: »Kun ved at kende historien kan man få forklaringen på nutidens misforhold«.
835 In his preamble, Reich utilises Isaac Newton's three laws of motion (*Philosophiæ Naturalis Principia Mathematica* 1687) in order to apply the laws of physics (or also metaphysics) to the history he is about to retell, thus suggesting a certain universality of these laws and furthermore connecting history with current events. By replacing Newton's »every body« with »everybody«, Reich turns the first law of motion into the following: »Enhver forbliver i sin tilstand af hvile eller ensartet bevægelse ad en ret linie – medmindre man forhindres i det af indtrængende kræfter« (Reich, Ebbe Kløvedal. *Herrens rakkere og bødler*, p. 10). In the subsequent narrative, Reich applies this law, which states that only invading forces can lead someone astray, to Danish history. Thus, the destructive aspects of heteronomy constitute the moral focal point of the trilogy.

Dane, but a German Jew named Josef Lazarus and employed by the Hamburg-based banking house Teixera, who is sent to Copenhagen to explore business opportunities amidst the struggle between Danish aristocrats. During the course of the trilogy, Josef Lazarus will abandon his task in Copenhagen and travel across continents in search of truth, his true call in life, and a messiah. This turn of events reveals the actual target of Reich's criticism: his plead is not directed against cosmopolitanism, but against globalisation and capitalism.[836] The appearance of Josef Lazarus alone does not constitute a threat to Denmark's cultural and economic independence, but rather the meddling on behalf of his employer Diego Teixera, who attempts to eliminate his competition, the Dutch banking house Marselis, from the Danish market. Gabriel Marselis, on the other hand, had already taken financial control over Denmark and Norway by the time Lazarus reaches Copenhagen in 1648. However, as it was Christian IV, who left the country financially stricken and reliant on foreign magnates, one ought neither interpret the trilogy as a nationalistic depiction of a fight of Denmark against foreign invaders. As in Reich's present, Danish potentates had advanced this interference from outside the realm in order to propel their own agenda. Moreover, as a historian, Marxist *and* Christian, Reich uses the depiction of mid-17th-century Denmark to denounce the age-old threat of capitalism and globalisation in favour of collectivism and altruism. Once his protagonist realises that he is but a chessman in the hands of competing magnates,[837] he leaves the game in search for something more meaningful in life.

In Reich's own words, the historical period presented in *Rejsen til Messias* implies »kapitalismens oprindelse, Danmarks smertensvej til enevælden[,] den danske folkekirkes første tvivl [og] Vesteuropas første skridt mod Fællesmarkedet«.[838] His warning index finger is thus pointing at three intricately connected spheres of influence: economy, politics and religion.

Now, what does this imply for the representation of the wife of a potentate like Ulfeldt, who is deeply involved in this power game? Reich's Ulfeldt is a devil, a businessman, who speaks »den ny tids sprog bedre end de fleste«.[839] But what

---

836 Reich pursues this subject matter especially by the end of the trilogy, when Denmark reinforces its attempts to establish companies in its newly founded colonies, the Danish West Indies (17th-20th century).

837 Throughout the trilogy, Reich alludes an equation of the royal power game with a game of chess by placing chess matches in strategic scenes or by using a cinematic technique by switching to the depiction of a chess match without fading out the previous scene. For example, in his description of the two sides' reaction to the Danish-Swedish war 1657, which almost seamlessly switches from Ulfeldt's delighted response to Sophie Amalie playing chess with her husband (Reich, Ebbe Kløvedal. *Rejsen til Messias: Tre bøger fra enevældens tid: Anden bog: Brudeturen.* [Copenhagen:] Gyldendal, 1974, p. 97).

838 Reich, Ebbe Kløvedal. *Herrens rakkere og bødler*, p. 11.

839 Ibid., p. 100.

about the wife of the businessman, who patiently listens to this modern, globalist language in all its tediousness and lack of focus?[840]

In the beginning of the account, Reich's Leonora Christina is first and foremost a representative of her age and power struggle, i.e. the political sphere: »Danmarks smertensvej til enevælden«.[841] Accordingly, Reich is accurate in the depiction of the historical parameter. Yet unlike H. F. Ewald, who reckoned it his task to reconstruct history in as much detail as possible, Reich takes great liberties in his depiction of Leonora Christina, especially in situations of a more private character.[842] While Ewald thus reanimates history for history's sake, Reich hardly ever turns his focus anywhere but forward. Thus, he presents financial operations that also involve Leonora without an immediate judgement (unlike H. F. Ewald), yet not without subtly highlighting the absurdity and fragility of the financial system the Ulfeldts and their peers' wealth is based on. For example, when Leonora is ordered to decorate her temporary domicile in Amsterdam in the most costly manner, in order to impress potential allies of her husband and perhaps persuade them to help Ulfeldt cover Denmark's debt:

> Der var blevet købt nye dragter til det meste af tjenerskabet, nyt sølvtøj, nye smykker og nyt pelsværk og fire store vægtæpper med motiver fra Danmark, som havde ligget hos en klædehandler, der havde overtaget dem i en forretning med Marselis, der havde fået dem af en dansk købmand, der gik fallit og ikke kunne betale sine fordringer i Amsterdam.[843]

While the Danish merchant selling Danish goods thus goes bankrupt, the Ulfeldts, who buy the Danish products via Dutch merchants, as well as the Dutch merchants themselves profit from this bargain. The internationalised market has turned out to be of no use to the domestic merchant. If this is another example of Ebbe Kløvedal Reich's use of his analogical method, it is clearly a cautionary tale about what Denmark's membership in the European Communities will do to its retail dealers.

---

840 Cf. the following description of the spouses' conversation, which resembles criticism of modern politicians' evasive manoeuvres during speeches: »Derfor havde Leonora lært tålmodighed, når hun stillede ham et svært spørgsmål. Han snakkede lidt videre om de økonomiske aspekter i situationen og de forhandlinger, der endnu stod tilbage, og så kom han til sagen« (ibid., p. 100).

841 Ibid., p. 11.

842 Cf. Uffe Andreasen, who states that the characters in *Rejsen til Messias* »mere er idérepræsentanter end levende, psykologisk tegnede mennesker« (Andreasen, Uffe. 'Ebbe Kløvedal Reich'. In *Danske digtere i det 20. århundrede 5: Fra Anders Bodelsen til Dan Turèll*, eds. Torben Brostrøm and Mette Winge. Copenhagen: Gad 1982, p. 296).

843 Reich, Ebbe Kløvedal. *Herrens rakkere og bødler*, p. 122.

Another important characteristic of Reich's text is that *adelsvælde* and *enevælde* do not form an ideological opposition as in many other representatives of Leonora Christina-literature. Both Frederik III and Corfitz Ulfeldt are depicted as rather untalented politicians, whose power struggle is carried out on the backs of their subjects. Also the rivalry between Sophie Amalie and Leonora Christina is degraded to the level of a catfight, as both women show their strengths and their weaknesses. Even Josef Lazarus cannot pick sides: »Sophie Amalie blev næsten skytshelgen for København. Josef [...] glemte, at han havde en venskabspagt med dronningens bitreste fjende. Han syntes, hun var fremragende«.[844] That Leonora Christina was among the opponents of the upcoming absolutism (regardless of her actual reasons) surely played a role in her post-1848 depictions. Even a rather recent text, namely Herta J. Enevoldsen's novel *Leonora Christina i Blåtårn* from 1979, presents its protagonist as a combatant against tyranny. Reich, however, depicts *enevælde* as the logical consequence of *adelsvælde*, both of which impede the only proper form of human community, which is direct democracy.[845] Accordingly, the title of the trilogy's first volume, *Herrens rakkere og bødler*, is a reference to all types of souvereigns: »Så blev han [Bishop Brochmand] værdigere: ,Thi har ikke mester Luther sagt, at fyrster er Guds bødler og rakkere, og det er Guds vilje, at vi skal kalde Guds bødler for nådige herrer, falde dem til fode og være dem underdanige med al vor ydmyghed[']«.[846]

The historical Leonora Christina is thus a representative of an Evil, against which Reich attempts to warn his contemporaries. However, Leonora, who repeatedly crosses paths with Josef Lazarus and thus belongs to the narrative layer related by Lazarus, takes in an entirely different function within the text. In line with Reich's textualised demand for a universal assertion of female values, or an assertion of feminity itself (»det kvindelige«)[847] with the same significance as masculinity,[848] there are several women in *Rejsen til Messias* leading Josef Lazarus onto the right path, thus ending his service to capitalism.[849] The unexpected meeting with his childhood friend Dina constitutes the first guidepost in Lazarus' life, even though she is already involved in the plot against Ulfeldt at the beginning of the trilogy, leading to her beheading at the end of Volume 1. She introduces Lazarus to

---

844 Reich, Ebbe Kløvedal. *Brudeturen*, p. 107. Josef Lazarus' business partner and friend Hans, however, sees more clearly: »I det hele taget er det blodsugerne, der styrer København lige nu« (ibid., p. 113).
845 In this context, it is worthwhile mentioning that Ebbe Kløvedal Reich was also one of the foremost advocates for the Freetown Christiania, founded in 1971, and its entitlement to autonomy.
846 Reich, Ebbe Kløvedal. *Herrens rakkere og bødler*, p. 93.
847 Reich, Ebbe Kløvedal. *Rejsen til Messias: Tre bøger fra enevældens tid: Tredie bog: Det klare vand.* [Copenhagen:] Gyldendal, 1974, p. 97.
848 Cf. Andreasen, Uffe. 'Ebbe Kløvedal Reich', pp. 286 and 292.
849 Cf. ibid., p. 295.

Heksegitte, whose potent magic potion induces hallucinations, which send Lazarus on his way to selfdiscovery.[850]

Humanity's assertion of feminity in every aspect of life as a cosmic complement to (not substitute of) the dominant masculinity[851] is a demand already voiced in *Frederik*. In this novel, the poet and Lutheran minister N. F. S. Grundtvig proclaims the coming of a female messiah.[852] Reich integrated a hint to this idealistic prophecy in *Rejsen til Messias* as well, namely when Sara, the wife of Sabbatai Zwi, tells Josef Lazarus that she is with child: »[,]Barnet er en søn af Guds søn,' sagde hun. ‚Eller en datter,' svarede Josef«.[853] *Frederik* contains furthermore a denunciation of male dominance over every aspect of life: »Grundtvig udpegede med sikkert instinkt bødlerne i denne usynlige klassekamp: De kønsforskrækkede, bogstavstro, fornuftshovmodige, bjergsomme og ualvorlige mandfolk, som havde tiltvunget sig magten over folkets følelsesliv«.[854] Besides Reich's curious use of the word *bødler*, his accusations against men are most striking, as both terms reappear in *Rejsen til Messias* in a similar context. When Josef Lazarus meets Christoffer Gabel, Frederik III's former right hand, again long after the events involving Dina and Leonora, he confronts him about the role he played in the Dina affair:

> Josef var ved at rejse sig, men Gabel greb ham i ærmet og trak ham ned. »Hun blev dømt under lovlig rettergang!« sagde han kampberedt. »Der er ikke noget dér.« »Hvad er en lov?« råbte Josef. »Et stykke papir, hvor nogle søvnige mandfolk – eller måske bare en enkelt – har sat underskrift og segl på særlig måde. Det er en lov!«[855]

In her analysis of Ebbe Kløvedal Reich's *Frederik*, Susanne Kopp-Sievers identifies several institutions, or power spheres (such as capitalism and imperialism), Reich denunciates on the basis of historical examples. In many regards, he finds a confederate in N. F. S. Grundtvig, who – among other things – also embraced Danishness (as opposed to the overpowering German neighbour) and female peacefulness and

---

850 As one of the most active members of the Danish *græsrodsbevægelse*, a 1960's movement consisting of several social networks fighting for emancipation, social equality, but also for the legalisation of drugs as an instrument in humanity's search for a meaning in life, Reich himself was an advocate of all sorts of consciousness-expanding means. Accordingly, Josef Lazarus has to reach a moment of intoxication in order to see the truth.
851 Reich's demand for absolute and universal equality correlates thus with that of some of his contemporaries, which were united in *rødstrømpebevægelsen*, a Danish feminist movement that started in 1970 and whose members claimed that there could be no social equality without gender equality and vice versa.
852 Reich, Ebbe Kløvedal. *Frederik*, p. 286.
853 Reich, Ebbe Kløvedal. *Det klare vand*, p. 77.
854 Reich, Ebbe Kløvedal. *Frederik*, p. 10.
855 Reich, Ebbe Kløvedal. *Det klare vand*, p. 112.

libido (as opposed to male belligerence and thanatos).[856] On the occassion of the imminent threat posed by the European Communities to Denmark, Reich published his *folkebog* on N. F. S. Grundtvig, in order to remind the Danish public of their national values, before the interferences by the Holy Roman Empire. One of these original Danish values used to be femininity, directly opposed to German masculinity and belligerence, as indicated in *Frederik*:

> Endelig kommer det tyske kapitel, som er tirsdags og krigsgudens, hvadenten han hedder Tyr eller Mars. Nutidens kapitel og kirke er viet til mandag, månens dag, den frugtbare, uudgrundelige, mellem liv og mørke bølgende kvindelige guddom, som vores kultur står i begreb med at glemme.[857]

In this context, Reich's inclusion of one of the female icons of Denmark, Leonora Christina, in the trilogy *Rejsen til Messias* is especially intriguing. The same message pervading *Frederik*, i.e. Reich's demand for a universal assertion of femininity and sexuality (as a way for men to unite with women),[858] is detectable in *Rejsen til Messias* as well, for example in Josef Lazarus' delirious vision in Heksegitte's cottage:

> »Goddag, Josef,« sagde den lille pige. »Du skal føre mig hjem til Solen som hans brud. Og når jeg er blevet Messias' brud, så vil Solen blive skabt om til en halvmåne. Sådan her.« Og hele universet krængede sig ind i hinanden og gik over i det modsatte. Månen blev til Sol og Solen til Måne, mørket blev til lys og lyset blev til mørke. Han [Josef] skreg, men hørte beroligende kvindelatter til alle sider.[859]

The little girl Josef sees in his vision is Sara, the future wife of Sabbatai Zwi. The false messiah is thus the sun. Once Sabbatai Zwi marries Sara, an event which also in history promoted his fame as true messiah, he will convert to Islam (hence the halfmoon). With the union of Sabbatai Zwi and Sara, Josef Lazarus' mission will be accomplished and »moon will turn into sun and sun into moon«. As (half)moon and sun had been mentioned before, this could be another reference to a forthcoming union (or confusion) of the religions, but since nothing in the text indicates such an event, it is more likely to be a reference to the two sexes. In many cultures, the sun

---

856 Kopp-Sievers, Susanne. *Die Wiederentdeckung des Nationalen in Dänemark: Eine Analyse von Ebbe Kløvedal Reichs* Frederik. En folkebog om N. F. S. Grundtvigs tid og liv <*1972*>. Frankfurt: Lang, 1985 (Beiträge zur Skandinavistik 5), p. 63.
857 Reich, Ebbe Kløvedal. *Frederik*, p. 29.
858 Cf. Andreasen, Uffe. 'Ebbe Kløvedal Reich', p. 292.
859 Reich, Ebbe Kløvedal. *Herrens rakkere og bødler*, p. 57.

is a symbol of masculinity, while Reich himself (also in line with much of cultural symbolism) associated the moon with feminine traits (see above). The union of moon and sun is thus a hint to an imminent union in a physical sense (i.e. sex) – which also plays an important role in Lazarus' upcoming life – as well as in a spiritual sense.

As a woman, Leonora is a necessary part of Josef Lazarus' life and she could have been an equally beneficial directive instance in her husband's life, if he had listened to her. Even though Ulfeldt is well aware that his wife is more sensible and astute than himself,[860] he increasingly disregards her advice towards the end. Josef, on the other hand, learns from all the women he meets on his way and is consequently led to happiness:

> Rigshovmester Ulfeldt og Sabbatai Zwi og sultan Muhammed lærte mig, at sejr og offer er det samme, og at vi mennesker aldrig vinder mere end vi ofrer, selv om vi prøver at vinde for at undgå at ofre os. Men det var kvinderne, der lærte mig, at man kan ofre sig og være glad endda. Endda gladere, end hvis man ikke gør det.[861]

Like in Louise Hegermann Lindencrone's tale 'Billedet', Leonora Christina figures as a manifested life lesson leaving an everlasting impression on the protagonist.

At first, Josef does not realise the common trait of all his love interests until he meets another infamous woman of this age – Marie Grubbe (see also Chapter 2.7.2.):

> Mens hun talte, betragtede Josef hendes ansigt med stigende interesse. Der var noget, han kendte igen. En vild trods, der med årene var kølet ned til målbevidsthed. En forventning om lidelse, der var lige ved at blive en lyst. En forventning om kedsomhed, som hun trodsede med al den målbevidsthed og al den lyst, hun kunne finde frem. Han genkendte det fra Dina og Leonora og Kristina og Miranda… nå, han genkendte det i sig. Og han sluttede ud fra det, han kunne genkende, at den smukke adelsfrue flygtede fra Danmark, fordi livet ikke skulle gå hendes næse forbi, fordi nogle mænd stillede sig i vejen for hende hele tiden. Hun skulle ud at føjte. Og hun ville blive skuffet og klogere, når hun kom over skuffelsen. Til sidst ville hun blive nødt til at indrømme, at hun kendte livet til bunds, men det ville næppe gøre hende gladere. Hun manglede evnen til at underkaste sig. Men hun troede, at det hun manglede var den rigtige mand at underkaste sig. Derfor var hun på flugt og på jagt på samme tid altid.[862]

---

860 E.g., Reich, Ebbe Kløvedal. *Det klare vand*, p. 35.
861 Ibid., p. 125.
862 Ibid., p. 104.

Reich's presentation of Leonora Christina's relationship to her husband resembles H. F. Ewald's presentation of the same marriage. Yet while Ewald considers Leonora Christina's femininity proven by her compliance to Ulfeldt, Reich presents an entirely different form of femininity – one that is defined by independence and disengagement from any negative, self-sufficient masculine influence. Leonora can, of course, not be saved – she has been under the spell of her husband for too long when she meets Josef Lazarus. However, Reich still manages to depict Leonora Christina in an unusually independent manner and he does so by sexualising her, as well as the rest of the environment enlightening Josef Lazarus.

The meeting with Dina and Heksegitte opens Josef Lazarus' eyes for the world surrounding him. When the inexperienced, almost boyish Lazarus arrives in Copenhagen, he initially does not recognise its frivolous delights. The aftermath of his terrifying visions at the medicinal spring entails an erotic awakening as well.[863] The same applies to Leonora Christina; she emerges as a covetable companion not only to her spouse,[864] but also to the protagonist. The Ulfeldt marriage is thus in no way romanticised.

Reich's decision to foist an affair with Dina on Ulfeldt – despite all historical likelihood – indicates a general intention on his behalf to de-mystify the depicted age and place, starting with Josef Lazarus' arrival in Copenhagen. The protagonist's first impression of the city is anything but misty-eyed. He arrives at the capital in 1648, when the powershift at court might lead to the opening of a new market for his employer, the Hamburg-based Teixera Bank. He finds his place of investigation dirty, he calls it »Sodoma« and »helvede«,[865] and its upper-class is more ostentatious than naturally elegant. The infernal Copenhagen is ruled by a rebellious devil: Corfitz Ulfeldt. Through her marriage with »Haltefanden«,[866] the limping Corfitz Ulfeldt, who appears to Josef as the devil himself in a delirious vision, Leonora is intricately connected with this hell, even though she may initially seem to be above

---

863 Cf. Reich, Ebbe Kløvedal. *Herrens rakkere og bødler*, p. 63. In the preceding novel *Frederik*, the role of eye-opening sin city devolves upon London (Reich, Ebbe Kløvedal. *Frederik*, pp. 208-210). There, too, the protagonist feels uneasy at first but will eventually meet the woman, who will change his life, i.e. Clara (cf. Kopp-Sievers, Susanne. *Die Wiederentdeckung des Nationalen in Dänemark*, p. 53). The causal relationship between the new, dirty surroundings and sexual awakening leading to a fulfilled and just life – as defined by the hippie motto »Make love, not war!« – is thus a recurring theme in Ebbe Kløvedal Reich's novels.

864 For example, when she helps her husband with his plan to use Josef Lazarus to his own advantage. When Leonora suggests bringing Lazarus to Amsterdam in order to put his rival Marselis under pressure to agree with Ulfeldt's terms and conditions, Ulfeldt rewards his wife with marital attentiveness the following night (Reich, Ebbe Kløvedal. *Herrens rakkere og bødler*, p. 101).

865 Ibid., respectively pp. 62 and 63.

866 Ibid., p. 56.

it. As the wife of Lucifer himself, Leonora is not associated with the Holy Mary, but rather with one of her antigonies: Lilith, a female demon, who can be traced back to Sumerian mythology, and who is otherwise known as Adam's first wife.[867]

In feminist-Jewish tradition, Lilith is a symbol of female emancipation and independence. Following this antitraditional evaluation of a demonic woman, more and more institutions and public places for women carrying the name *Lilith* emerged in the recent past, such as specialised bookstores or shelters for battered women. In her analysis of the Lilith-myth in 19th and 20th-century literature, Swantje Christow attributes the increase in literary Lilith-figures from the 19th century onwards to a substantial shift in the perception and portrayal of women, which eventually led to the development of the *femme fatale*-concept[868] in literature.[869]

According to one interpretation of the creation account, Lilith was Adam's first wife, who left her husband as he demanded her subordination. Since both Adam and Lilith had been created out of ashes, Lilith saw herself equal to Adam and decided never to return to him. As a substitute for Lilith, God created Eve for Adam; but this time he made sure to create a lesser version of a man. While in the conservative Jewish tradition, Lilith is a demon, a succubus and a child murderess, modern interpretations have focussed on her strength, her intelligence and her appeal as an equivalent to men. Some of these traces are present in the character of Leonora, who – at a certain point – can no longer rely on her husband: »,Nu skal jeg prøves helt alene,' sagde hun en dag. „Jeg tror jeg klarer det bedre end sammen med Corfitz ... jeg er stolt af, at Gud har valgt mig til at prøves alene.'«[870] Accordingly, Leonora crosses paths with Josef Lazarus only in the years antedating and succeeding her husband's tumultous schemes against Frederik III, while Josef himself only hears about the Ulfeldts' fate from their common friend Otto Sperling. Once Leonora serves as Ulfeldt's sidekick in his years of travel, she virtually disappears from the narrative only to re-emerge on her way to the Blue Tower. Unlike many authors preceding him,[871] Reich rushes through the years degrading Leonora Christina to her husband's appendix, consequently highlighting her self-reliance instead. Only

---

867 The *Alphabet of ben Sirach*, written some time between 700 and 1000, is the first text that identifies Lilith as Adam's first wife. Many succeeding texts, such as Goethe's *Faust*, followed this interpretation. For a comprehensive presentation of the development of the Lilith-myth, see Christow, Swantje. *Der Lilith-Mythos in der Literatur: Der Wandel des Frauenbildes im literarischen Schaffen des 19. und 20. Jahrhunderts*. Aachen: Shaker, 1998 (Sprache und Kultur).

868 This new contextualisation of Leonora Christina will the topic of Chapter 2.6.

869 Christow, Swantje. *Der Lilith-Mythos in der Literatur*, p. 7.

870 Reich, Ebbe Kløvedal. *Det klare vand*, p. 45.

871 For example H. F. Ewald, whose novel is called *Leonora Kristina*, even though it should justly bear the title *Korfits Ulfeldt*.

from her escape from Hammershus onwards, does Leonora start to re-enter Reich's account. She and Josef meet again in London, when the Ulfeldt couple is already separated for good and when Josef is on his way back from his mission: he has led Sara to Sabbatai Zwi.

Leonora's independence is reinforced by her and her husband's gradual departure from one another. Long before their final physical separation, the two spouses develop lives of their own – Ulfeldt with his affair and by excluding his wife from his latest schemes,[872] Leonora through her flirt with Josef. Here, as in most 20th-century depictions of Leonora Christina, she is no longer the unviolable saint known from Andersen and Hegermann Lindencrone. Yet, Kløvedal Reich takes this development one step further by presenting her as a fleshly woman whose sexuality is not only within reach of her husband, but is recognisable to others as well. Leonora does not commit adultery – nevertheless she and Josef share a moment of temptation.[873] Their flirt leads nowhere, but Leonora's sympathy for Josef arises at the expense of her marital love.[874] Looking back at their first encounter, Leonora's reminiscence years later reaffirms the flair of forbidden young love lying over these years:

> »Jeg tænker en gang imellem på den dag i Amsterdam, da vi begge to var unge og smukke. Men jeg var kongedatter, og du var spion.« »Jeg var ikke spion,« sagde Josef. Men han var hverken indigneret eller overrasket over, at hun sagde det. »Jeg var din ven, men jeg blev brugt til alle mulige formål.« »Det ved jeg godt,« sagde Leonora og lagde sin store hånd på hans. »Men derfor var du alligevel spion. Og nu er vi ved at blive gamle og trætte.«[875]

From the beginning of the novel, her and Josef's lovelives are connected since Lazarus' erotic awakening advances the Dina affair, thus initiating Leonora's downfall, while Dina's execution in turn opens Lazarus' eyes for the evil his work is causing. After his visit at Heksegitte's cottage, Josef Lazarus shuns Dina and spends more and more time with a much cruder, but harmless girl: Anna Buntmagers, his future

---

[872] Reich, Ebbe Kløvedal. *Det klare vand*, p. 36: »,Og her er jeg,' sluttede Leonora, mens de gik ind fra balkonen. ,Jeg ved ikke, hvad Corfitz har for i Brandenburg. Jeg har forklaret ham, at den brandenburgske flåde ikke er stor nok til hvalfangst. Men han kan have fået en endnu værre idé … dagen før han får ligfald siger han somme tider sådan nogle underlige ting.'«

[873] Reich, Ebbe Kløvedal. *Herrens rakkere og bødler*, p. 123.

[874] Ibid., p. 145: »Leonora, som havde fjernet sig en tomme fra ægtemandens nærhed efter den historie med Josef, var mere skeptisk. […] Hun foragtede ham en smule for hans vindblæste pralerier over bordet på skibet«.

[875] Reich, Ebbe Kløvedal. *Det klare vand*, p. 41.

wife. This sudden preference for Anna may be induced by an intuition prior to or knowledge after his revelatory visions induced by Heksegitte's magic.[876] Whatever the reasons, the result is that Dina becomes more susceptible to Walter's advances, which in turn furthers the complot against the Ulfeldts. At the same time, he senses a non-physical approach from Leonora's side: »Han havde nok mærket noget fra hendes retning, men det overskred hans dristighed at tænke på, hvad det var han mærkede«.[877] What he senses turns out to be a revenge-flirt meant to punish Ulfeldt for his liaison with Dina, besides a natural attraction Leonora feels towards Josef. Reich thus highlights a previously disregarded aspect of Leonora Christina's personality, i.e. her zest for life.

Reich is not the only one who noticed a certain spark in Leonora Christina's writings. Carsten Overskov's paraphrase of Leonora Christina's life called *Leonoras latter* (2004), too, emphasises its protagonist's joy, instead of her grief, thus presenting her as a sanguine tumbler:

> Det krævede i hvert fald, at jeg læste »Jammers Minde« først. Og den oplevelse var lidt af en chok. [...] For det andet var læsningen fouroligende lystig. Gang på gang greb jeg mig selv i at sidde og fnise. Kunne det være rigtigt? Intet havde forberedt mig på, at »Jammers Minde« ligefrem skulle være morsom.[878]

Leonora is presented in a similar way. Especially towards the end, she emanates optimism:

> Foran Blåtårn steg Leonora ud. Hun så Josef og blinkede til ham som om det hele kun var for sjov. Så fangede deres ører samtidig en svag, tør raslende lyd, og de så begge op. Fra Blåtårns top lettede en stor ravn med knirkende, raslende vinger. Den kræede et par gange og tog fart ud mod Amager. Og samme sted fra, som den havde siddet, på toppen af tårnet, lettede en flok duer og fløj under hvisken og tisken den samme vej. Det så ud, som om de forfulgte ravnen. Men det kunne jo ikke passe. Leonora trak på skuldrene og gik ind i Blåtårn uden at vende sig.[879]

It almost seems as if the removal of her husband has brought relief to Leonora's life. The Ulfeldtian marriage in *Rejsen til Messias* is thus not as untainted as reported by

---

876 Reich, Ebbe Kløvedal. *Herrens rakkere og bødler*, pp. 52 and 59.
877 Ibid., p. 107.
878 Overskov, Carsten. *Leonoras latter*. Copenhagen: Branner og Korch, 2004, p. 8.
879 Reich, Ebbe Kløvedal. *Det klare vand*, p. 50.

history, yet Leonora is still held in high esteem by her husband. While Reich reinforces the libido of the Ulfeldt couple by making both of them stray, the depiction of their partner bond follows Leonora Christina's lead; both bolster each other and initially, their teamwork is impeccable.[880] Leonora Christina is no longer portrayed as her husband's asexual appendix,[881] but as an adequate partner.

Unlike other novels, *Rejsen til Messias* depicts Leonora Christina not only as a factor in a secular power game, but she is also affected by a religious insecurity that seems to have haunted the century. Josef Lazarus himself is not sure, which confession to consider the right one, and he will eventually convert to Protestantism. Another example in this regard is probably the most famous convert of the North: Queen Christina of Sweden, who avowed herself to Catholicism in 1654. She, too, repeatedly crosses paths with Josef Lazarus, thus making him a part of her religious development. Yet also Sperling and Leonora get involved in a confessional discourse with Josef and the influential rabbi Mesanneh Ben Israel (1604-1657),[882] while Ulfeldt is revealed as a declared enemy of the works of the Reformation.[883] Finally, there is Sabbatai Zwi, a former rabbi and self-proclaimed messiah, who converted to Islam and thusly offended many of his followers. Next to Baruch Spinoza (1632-1677) and Giuseppe Francesco Borri (see Chapter 2.3.3.), he is one of the controversial historical figures depicted in *Rejsen til Messias* that offended religious authorities and whose doctrines are representative of the religious upheaval of the 17th century.

Confessional insecurity and conversion are thus a recurring theme in the trilogy. Leaving Leonora's own loyalty towards her secretly Catholic husband aside,

---

880 Cf. Reich, Ebbe Kløvedal. *Herrens rakkere og bødler*, pp. 67, 101 and 104.

881 Leonora Christina has been presented as a coveted woman before, namely in Ove Rahbek's novel *Ad tornede Veje* (1912). Here, Dina's accomplice Walter attempts to rape Leonora Christina, whom he does not recognise due to the late hour and her cloaked head. But she is quite literally untouchable, as she simply issues a lash on her surprised offender's face, thus driving him off. While Walter, on behalf of Ove Rahbek, thus makes an attempt to sexualise Leonora Christina, he completely fails as she subsequently demonstrates an impeccable amount of transcendence by not even taking this attack seriously. When she meets Walter again and recognises him by his voice, she laughs it off and reacts only later when a friend of hers is about to get involved with Walter: »Ha! ha! Saa det var Kaptajn Walter, der havde været paa Kvindejagt hin Aften. Ja, man sagde jo nok, at han drev den Idræt og var saare øvet i den. Leonora Kristina lod atter Tæppet falde, og hendes Tanker beskæftigede sig ikke mere med Kaptajn Walter« (Rahbek, Ove. *Ad tornede Veje. Historisk Fortælling*. Odense: Søndergaard, 1912 (Søndagsbladets Bogsamling 4), p. 15).

882 Reich, Ebbe Kløvedal. *Herrens rakkere og bødler*, p. 121.

883 There are, in fact, indications that Ulfeldt may have secretly converted to Catholicism during his years abroad. Cf. Helk, Vello. 'Rigshofmester Corfitz Ulfeldts katolske forbindelser', Kirkehistoriske Samlinger 1987, pp. 121-139. There are no indications that Leonora Christina had converted as well, but some sources suggest that she was aware of her husband's new creed and sympathetic to his and the Vatican's cause (i.e. to invigorate the Catholic community in Denmark). See Heiberg, Steffen. *Enhjørningen Corfitz Ulfeldt*, p. 75.

it should be noted that she undergoes a transformation of her own. While the first volume of the trilogy presents her as *Haltefanden*'s wife ruling the Copenhagen hell, the third volume is interlarded with some of the hymns she had written in prison and afterwards, and which are preserved in *Jammers Minde*. Volume 1 and 2 of the trilogy, however, are adorned with hymns and some reformatory songs written by the Danish bishop and poet Thomas Kingo (1634-1703), while most of Volume 3 contains hymns written by Leonora Christina. Towards the end – of the account, but also of Josef Lazarus' journey – her female voice complements that of Thomas Kingo, the predominant male. Once Leonora enters the Blue Tower, she exits the plot. When Josef Lazarus returns to Copenhagen and passes the Blue Tower, he knows that she is inside, but cannot feel her presence.[884] In the third volume of the trilogy, Leonora's body disappears, but her voice remains as the volume provides some of her texts.

Based on Uffe Andreasen's insightful statements that the characters in *Rejsen til Messias* are rather »idérepræsentanter end levende, psykologisk tegnede mennesker« and that »[p]ersonerne er mere typer end individuelle figurer«,[885] one ought to ask what sort of concept or type Leonora represents? Through the use of Leonora Christina's own texts, she is represented as an independent, strong and erudite woman, whose voice eventually complements the dominantly male literary, religious and cultural canon. Her role in the trilogy *Rejsen til Messias* is that of the woman as one half of a – desirable – cosmic union. She enters the trilogy as part of a power sphere Reich attempts to expose in order to educate his contemporary readers on the dangers of current developments in Denmark but ultimately, this is not her primary function. There is no love lost between the newly introduced absolutism and its agrieved party, but nevertheless, Leonora Christina is not primarily a representative of the *adelsvælde* and its opposition to absolutism, but of something much more universal: femininity, as suggested by the 1970's gender role models.

---

884 Reich, Ebbe Kløvedal. *Det klare vand*, p. 105.
885 Andreasen, Uffe. 'Ebbe Kløvedal Reich', both quotations p. 296.

2.5. By Order of Education: Leonora Christina's Admittance into Denmark's Literary Canon

> En klassiker er et værk så velkendt, at de fleste vælger at springe det over. F.eks. Beethovens »Skæbnesymfoni«, Beatles' samlede production, H. C. Andersens eventyr og Leonora Christinas »Jammers Minde«. Berømmelsen får dem til at virke banale. De hænger en ud af halsen på forhånd.[886]

These are the introductory lines of Carsten Overskov's *Leonoras latter* – a paraphrase of *Jammers Minde* published in 2004 – followed by Overskov's own guilty confession that until recently he had never read *Jammers Minde* himself. His subsequent explanation for this grievance also helps to shed some light on recent developments in Leonora Christina-literature: »I Leonoras tilfælde har vi den undskyldning, at hun er forbistret svær at læse«.[887] Due to its antiquated language, *Jammers Minde* is considered to be a tough read, which is why Overskov published his book – a reproduction of *Jammers Minde* in a more contemporary language – in the first place.

Overskov is not alone in his efforts to familiarise his contemporary fellow countrymen with a national classic. As pointed out by Torben Weinreich, Denmark has a commendable tradition of providing children and adults with reading difficulties with books tailormade for their special needs. The upside of these efforts is that they proved successful in enthusing even children with learning disabilities about books. The downside is that the availability of easy versions of rather stern texts tends to tempt even adults with no reading difficulties to reach for the less challenging variant.[888] This tendency serves to explain all the modernised editions of *Jammers Minde* and paraphrases of Leonora Christina's autobiographical works published since the mid-20th century. Besides Carsten Overskov, Inger Bentzon published *Frøken Leonora* in 1946, whose preamble already negates any interest in creative elaboration:

---

886 Overskov, Carsten. *Leonoras latter*, p. 7.
887 Ibid.
888 Cf. Weinreich, Torben. 'I statens tjeneste: Prosaen i dansk børnelitteratur 1945-1990'. In *Dansk Børnelitteratur Historie*, eds. Kari Sønsthagen and Lena Eilstrup. Copenhagen: Høst & Søns Forlag 1992, p. 152.

Enhver af os vil før eller siden erfare, at de romaner, livet skaber, ofte er langt dybere dramatiske end det, forfatterne kan sætte paa papiret; og den, der vil skrive en folkelig roman om Danmarks berømteste kongedatter, opdager hurtigt, at den strenge historiske sandhed – saa vidt som en lægmand kan gribe den – er fuldt tilstrækkelig til at give det, han ønsker at berette. Saa har da dette værks forfatter af al magt søgt at holde sig i baggrunden og sin fantasi i tømme og kun at søge ind til kendsgerningerne[.][889]

Another example is Line Krogh's 2014 edition of *Jammers Minde*, yet another modernised version of Leonora Christina's text, meant to aid those who may otherwise have severe trouble understanding the original. Finally, there is also the second part of the novel presented in the subsequent chapter, *Leonora Christina i Blåtårn* by Herta J. Enevoldsen, whose first half follows the tumultuous life of Corfitz Ulfeldt and Leonora Christina, while the second half presents *Jammers Minde* in a language and elaboration suitable to young readers.

Overskov's introductory statement already addresses two paradoxical facts regarding *Jammers Minde* and its admittance into the Danish literary canon, which served as a source of inspiration to this chapter; namely, that 1) due to its aesthetic quality and unique topic, *Jammers Minde* has been regarded as a classic for most of the 20th century and beyond, and that 2) few people have found it necessary to read *Jammers Minde* or to include it in their school teaching (partially for reasons stated above). These are also the two reasons why Leonora Christina's name resounded throughout the land in 2004 (in the same year Overskov published his book), since – despite the central role *Jammers Minde* has in Danish Baroque literature – it was not part of the *Dansk litteraturs kanon*, published in late September 2004. This prompted many negative reactions, mostly because the number of female writers in the presented canon was strikingly low, but also because Leonora Christina had been part of a Danish literary canon before.[890]

In 1992, Bertel Haarder, at that time Denmark's Education Minister, ordered the creation of a literary canon. The committee assigned with the task of selecting the canon presented its results – a literary corpus consisting of a small and a big canon – in 1994 in the form of the publication *Dansk litteraturs kanon: Skønlitteraturen i skolen*. While the big canon (*den store kanon*) consisted of 100 works meant to serve as a source of inspiration to school teachers, the small canon (*den lille kanon*) was made up of twenty-one works, including *Jammers Minde*, which were already

---

889 Bentzon, Inger. *Frøken Leonora: Udgivet i Forbindelse med Forfatterindens 25 Aars Jubilæum*. Odense: Skandinavistik Bogforlag, 1946, unpaginated preamble.
890 Cf. Lise Busk-Jensen, who calls the 2004 canon a »tilbageskridt« compared to the one from 1994 (Busk-Jensen, Lise. *Romantikkens forfatterinder 2*, p. 1474).

taught regularly in schools and were thus considered to form a sort of natural core to the literary canon.

The debate over a Danish literary canon was readopted ten years later when professor of children's literature Torben Weinreich suggested the formation of a canon for children's literature. This proposal prompted Education Minister Ulla Tørnæs to announce that she had assigned a committee with the formation of a literary canon in January 2004, whose results were presented in September 2004 in the form of a report.[891] This report recommended one list consisting of fourteen works obligatory to all schools and two lists, one for primary schools and one for secondary schools, with additional suggestions. None of these lists contained Leonora Christina and only one woman – Karen Blixen – had made it to the obligatory list.

This report caused many disappointed reactions from literary researchers and feminists alike, who demanded the addition of some nameable female Danish writers, such as Leonora Christina, to the canon's diverse lists. However, Tina Nedergaard, member of the Folketing's Education Committee (*uddannelsesudvalget*), as well as other representatives of the Education Committee, declared that it was not in their power to alter the obligatory canon's gender imbalance while Jørn Lund, chairman orf the canon committee, declared that Denmark had many excellent female writers besides Karen Blixen, »[m]en ikke på kanonisk niveau«.[892] However, many experts, such as Anne-Marie Mai, advanced the view that aesthetic considerations could never justify the deselection of masterpieces such as *Jammers Minde*.[893]

Despite all criticism the Danish literary canon as well as the idea of canonisation itself drew, former Cultural Minister Brian Mikkelsen initiated the creation of a Danish Cultural Canon (*Kulturkanon*) in December 2004. This canon consists of eight categories with twelve works each,[894] one of them being literature, and all of them supervised by chairman Jørn Lund, who had already chaired the Danish literary canon. The diverse expert committees presented their collected results in the book *Kulturkanon*, published in January 2006. This time, Leonora Christina as well as Karen Blixen and Inger Christensen were among the selected.

---

891 This report is available on the Ministry's webpage: http://pub.uvm.dk/2004/kanon/.

892 See the article in *Politiken* from 23 November 2004 on the letter written by Pil Dahlerup, Elisabeth Møller Jensen (director of KVINFO) and Anne-Marie Mai, addressed to the Education Committee, in which they request the addition of several female names to the list and the committee's negative answer: Thorsen, Lotte. 'Kvinderne mangler i den litterære kanon': http://politiken.dk/kultur/boger/ECE100109/kvinderne-mangler-i-den-litteraere-kanon/, originally published on 23 November 2004.

893 Anne-Marie Mai's criticism and her concrete suggestions on the extension of the literary canon were published on the webpage of the educational journal *Folkeskolen*: Mai, Anne-Marie. 'Kvindefattig kanon': http://www.folkeskolen.dk/31590/kvindefattig-kanon, originally published on 8 October 2004.

894 The only exception is the category music, which contains two subcategories (*partiturmusik* and *populærmusik*) with twelve titles each.

Perhaps these choices is what the committee[895] was hinting at with the following statement: »Kanonudvalget for litteraturs arbejde med at finde et fåtal af litterære værker i en 800-årig litteratur har trods medlemmernes forskellige baggrund været mindre brydsomt, end mange har forventet«.[896] The committee defined their overall selection criteria as follows:

> Udgangspunktet for vores valg har været, at smag faktisk lader sig diskutere. Vi har peget på værker, der har vist sig slidstærke i den kulturelle tradition. Blandt disse er valgt værker, som hver og ét af udvalgets medlemmer dels finder af høj kunstnerisk kvalitet, dels spår en fremtid som levende og værdifuld litteratur. I kriterierne indgår altså både tradition, oplevelse og holdbarhed.[897]

Leaving aside its incontrovertible aesthetic quality, *Jammers Minde* is thus also considered persistent enough to recommend it to future generations as well. The committee's justification of this choice focuses mainly on Leonora Christina's formidable personality, captured in her account, as well as her ability to convey 17th-century experiences to the 21st-century reader, which without her work may have been lost forever:

> Værket er uden tvivl det mest respektindgydende værk, den dansk baroktid har efterladt. Som menneskelig præstation er det enestående, at den fængslede kongedatter overhovedet overkommer at berette om og nedskrive de mange års lidelser og ydmygelser, skønt hun i sin fortale med rette overvejer, om det var klogere at skrive det hele i glemmebogen. [...] Værket er myldrende fuldt af realistisk iagttagelse, syn, stank, lyde, ofte gengivet med sanselig væmmelse, men også med grotesk humor, som blot gør detaljerne endnu mere påtrængende. Leonoras evne til at fastholde udseende og karakter hos de mennesker, fængselsopholdet påtvinger hende berøring med, har for eftertiden opbevaret billeder af en række oftest betydningsløse mennesker, især kvinder, som ellers for evigt ville være forsvundet i tidens gang.[898]

---

895 The committee for literature consisted of two professors (chairman Finn Hauberg Mortensen and Erik A. Nielsen) and three writers (Mette Winge, Claes Kastholm Hansen and Jens Christian Grøndahl).
896 Kanonudvalget. 'Om kanon for litteratur', p. 108: http://kum.dk/uploads/tx_templavoila/KUM_kulturkanonen_OK2.pdf.
897 Ibid.
898 Kanonudvalget. 'Jammers Minde: Udvalgets begrundelse', p. 110: http://kum.dk/uploads/tx_templavoila/KUM_kulturkanonen_OK2.pdf.

Based on her perception of *Jammers Minde* as one long letter addressed to Leonora Christina's children,[899] Dorthe Sondrup Andersen, who after the committee's statement provides some excerpts containing background information on Leonora Christina's life and work, highlights another characteristic of *Jammers Minde* – its educational value: »I Jammers minde fortæller Leonora Christina nemlig også om, hvordan man opfører sig kongeligt blandt fangevogtere, spioner, fængselspræster og medfanger«.[900]

Thus, the following chapters are based on the committee's, Dorthe Sondrup Andersen's as well as Leonora Christina's own notion that *Jammers Minde* and, accordingly, Leonora Christina's life story contains valuable life lessons for future generations and will attempt to answer what kind of educational content it provided to subsequent writers. Two of the three authors presented below – Herta J. Enevoldsen and Birgithe Kosovic – wrote their novels on Leonora Christina with a specific pedagogical or didactic context in mind. Hence, their work begs the questions as to what kind of educational value is inherent to *Jammers Minde* and Leonora Christina's life story in general, and how it can be transmitted into an account for children, young adults, and other readers who want to learn more about Leonora Christina and her time. The third author discussed below, Eva Hemmer Hansen, published the first work of Leonora Christina-literature specifically engaging with feminist considerations; that is, aside from Mathilde Fibiger's parenthesis on Leonora Christina's conflict of duties, of course. Hemmer Hansen's work is thus essential to the understanding of the scholarly-feminist discussion provoked by the omittance of *Jammers Minde* in the literary canon of 2004.

Finally, the following three chapters also investigate whether the canon committee (together with Dorthe Sondrup Andersen) and the authors presented below noted the same or a similar kind of educational value contained in *Jammers Minde*. After all, all three parties involved – Leonora Christina, the canon committee and the authors presented below – wrote their texts with regard to some sort of future generations in mind.

Herta J. Enevoldsen composed two novels on Leonora Christina – *Kongedatteren Leonora Christina* and *Leonora Christina i Blåtårn* (see Chapter 2.5.1.), originally published in 1979 and republished in a different format in 2013 – whose simple titles and colourful bookcovers are guaranteed to appeal to a young, mostly female audience, i.e. young teenage girls. At the same time, her presentation of Leo-

---

[899] Sondrup Andersen, Dorthe. 'London, sommeren 1663', p. 111: http://kum.dk/uploads/tx_templavoila/KUM_kulturkanonen_OK2.pdf.
[900] Ibid.

nora Christina's childhood, depicted by Enevoldsen in especial detail, should prove fruitful for an analysis in the context of educational Leonora Christina-literature, as it potentially provides its intended readership with a protagonist to identify with. The second part, *Leonora Christina i Blåtårn*, commences with Leonora Christina's eventful years abroad and in prison, while its second half depicts the novel's eponymous topic, Leonora Christina's imprisonment in the Blue Tower. These last 100 pages reflect the content of *Jammers Minde* in minute detail. Even though this last part is a mere paraphrase of *Jammers Minde*, the interplay between Enevoldsen's extensive depiction of Leonora Christina's childhood and her development to the authoritative figure in the Blue Tower provides ideal preconditions for the determination of a potential educational value contained in *Jammers Minde*.

Eva Hemmer Hansen's fragment,[901] consisting of the two novels *Den lykkelige hustru* and *Den trofaste hustru* (1982 and 1983, respectively; see Chapter 2.5.2.), on the other hand, is directed at an older (adult or young adult) readership. Yet, her novels provide a detailed picture of Leonora Christina's time and contemporaries, thus nevertheless exhibiting an educational approach. Eva Hemmer Hansen's Leonora Christina-novels demonstrate no obvious didactic intent, yet her comprehensive presentation still adds to our understanding of why the lifestory of a 17th-century noblewoman could still be of use today, and hence to the discourse surrounding the admittance of *Jammers Minde* into the Danish Literary Canon and the inherent question of why every Dane should know the story of Leonora Christina. Hemmer Hansen was furthermore known as a feminist,[902] hence her presentation of Leonora Christina carrying such provocative titles such as *Den trofaste hustru* should prove fruitful for an analysis on the background of the 2004-debate on the lack of female writers in the Danish literary canon.

Finally, there is Birgithe Kosovic, whose novel *Leonora Christina* (see Chapter 2.5.3.) was published in 2012 as part of Alfabeta's blue series on characters from Danish history, which is meant to help adult students of the Danish language and Danish adults with reading difficulties learn and practice the language while educating them on the country's history. This function of the product is of particular

---

901 The author was most likely aiming at a trilogy, but her untimely death in 1983 prevented the creation of her final book on Leonora Christina's life. Eva Hemmer Hansen's daughter, Luise Pihl, who edited her mother's manuscript and handed it in for publication, expressed her conviction that *Den trofaste hustru* was finished when she found the manuscript. She also stated that it was unsure, whether her mother ever intended to write a third part (Pihl, Luise. 'Efterskrift'. In Hemmer Hansen, Eva. *Den trofaste hustru: Leonora Christine II*. Copenhagen: Hernov, 1983, p. 216). I, on the other hand, consider Hemmer Hansen's Leonora Christina-novels to be unfinished, for reasons stated below.

902 Between 1968 and 1971 Hemmer Hansen was the chairwoman of the Danish Women's Society (*Dansk Kvindesamfund*). She is also the author of *Blåstrømper, rødstrømper, uldstrømper*, published in 1970, about Denmark's feminist revolution.

relevance on the background of some of the arguments that were produced in favour of the idea of canonisation itself, as they were hints at some of the new challenges Denmark was facing, especially globalisation and immigration.[903]

2.5.1. Herta J. Enevoldsen: *Kongedatteren Leonora Christina* and *Leonora Christina i Blåtårn* (1979) – Ignorance is Bliss

Ded ieg icke wed, ded kand ieg icke sige[.]

(*Jammers Minde*, p. 35)

In terms of historical novels on famous court-affiliated, controversial women in European history, Herta J. Enevoldsen is a 'recidivist'. She is the author of books such as *Caroline Mathilde* (1977), *Marie Antoinette* (1986) and a trilogy on Dyveke Sigbrittsdatter (1978), the mistress of Christian II. Enevoldsen's historical children's books follow a tradition started in the 1950's, when in an effort to escape the contemporary, post-war environment, literature became increasingly historical. This development concerned children's books as well, especially from the 1960's onwards, when the Danish children's book market was tightly connected to the educational sector and its efforts to teach pupils about national history. Accordingly, there is a Danish tradition of writers of children's books being employed in the educational sector.[904]

According to Torben Weinreich, Enevoldsen's works do *not* rank among these educationally committed children's books. Instead, they classify for the term of *kulisseromaner*, which are defined by a vague historical interest and a much more elevated taste for costume and drama:

---

[903] The introduction to *Dansk litteraturs kanon*, for example, contains, among others, the following explanation as to why there is a need for a canon at all: »I disse årtier har udviklingen på national, europæisk og international plan ført til et intensiveret kulturmøde; indflydelsen fra ikke mindst amerikansk kultur er ikke til at ignorere. I den situation er det naturligt, at vi her i landet, som det er tilfældet i andre lande, må spørge os selv: Hvad har vi at byde på, på hvilken måde har vi forvaltet den europæiske og nordiske kulturarv, og hvad er det særlige ved dansk kultur?« (Lund, Jørn. 'Indledning': http://pub.uvm.dk/2004/kanon/, p. 10). Similar arguments were produced in favour of a Danish democracy canon (*demokratikanon*), which was launched in 2008, also following the recommendation of former Cultural Minister Brian Mikkelsen. The most popular argument for the creation of such a canon was probably brought forward by Ove Korsgaard, professor for education and pedagogics at the University of Aarhus, who argued that a democracy canon would help to make Danish citizens of diverse ethnicities or religions Danes »i politisk forstand«, whereas a cultural canon would only divide people (Lenler, Jens. 'Glem kulturkanonen – lav en demokratikanon': http://politiken.dk/kultur/ECE315799/glem-kulturkanonen---lav-en-demokratikanon/, originally published on 30 March 2007).

[904] Cf. Weinreich, Torben. 'I statens tjeneste', p. 140f. Furthermore, Torben Weinreich himself is both professor in and author of children's literature.

Det er kulisseromaner, hvor de historiske hændelser indrammer skildringer af store lidenskaber som kærlighed, jalousi, magtsyge og had. Der er en eksotisme i disse bøger, tæt på ugebladsføljetonerne, som har givet dem en del læsere. Valget af kvinder som hovedpersoner giver sjældent anledning til skildring af kvindespecifikke livsvilkår, men tjener i højere grad til at skabe identitetsmuligheder for de i overvejende grad kvindelige læsere.[905]

Weinreich hence contends that Enevoldsen's novels are not part of the Danish corpus of educationally committed children's books. However, knowledge is a central topic in *Kongedatteren Leonora Christina*, as the young protagonist is portrayed as very knowledgeable and eager to learn. As *Kongedatteren Leonora Christina* is only the first part of a two-volume-novel – the other one focussing on her tumultuous marriage with Corfitz Ulfeldt and her imprisonment in the Blue Tower – questions regarding Leonora's[906] knowledge that run like a thread through the first novel connect both parts, as the same kind of questions cause her imprisonment: What does Leonora know? What can she know? And how can and will she use this knowledge?

Her first novel on Leonora Christina, *Kongedatteren Leonora Christina*, joins Enevoldsen's series on historical women as its subheading prepares the reader for her trademark topic: *Spænding, romantik og store skæbner fra Danmarkshistorien*.[907] The arrival of Leonora into her world augurs something remarkable, as her mother had been more anxious in anticipation of this new child than she had been during her previous pregnancies. When the girl is born, the interplay between father and newborn daughter also seems different than what the previous births must have caused, as attendees of this event seem insecure about his reaction: »Var majestæten skuffet over, at det igen blev en pige? Nej, hans ansigt lyste af glæde, mens han med faderstolt ømhed betragtede sin datter. Hans øjne var fugtige, det var tydeligt, at et eller andet gjorde ham bevæget«. [908]

Father and daughter maintain their special connection throughout their lives. Kirsten Munk, on the other hand, is portrayed as an unloving, violent mother. But unlike H. F. Ewald, whose unreasonable Kirsten Munk resembles the burlesque

---

905 Ibid., p. 182.
906 In the present chapter, »Leonora« specifically refers to the character in Herta J. Enevoldsen's novels, particularly when referring to passages that do not correspond to historical events, whereas »Leonora Christina« refers to the historical person. Another spelling variation used in the literary source text, and hence in this chapter as well, is »Sofie Amalie«.
907 Enevoldsen, Herta J. *Kongedatteren Leonora Christina*. Copenhagen: Gyldendal, 2013 (1979).
908 Ibid., p. 8.

demon in 'Fru Kirsten Munks Ballet' (see Chapter 2.1.1.) rather than a young woman *with* demons, Herta J. Enevoldsen adds a tragic note to this character since the reader is made acquainted with her side of the story as well (nota bene, *before* her adultery):[909] »Kan du ikke forstå det? Forstår du ikke, at man bliver træt af at føde børn – og af at være gift med en halvgammel mand[?]«[910] The subsequent information on the habits regarding child-rearing additionally relativise Kirsten Munk's portrayal, as her mother, Ellen Marsvin, is portrayed as no particularly committed foster mother either, followed by a declaration of the entire century as positively pedophobic: »Og den almindelige mening var, at børn havde bedst at blive voksne så hurtigt som muligt«.[911]

While *Kongedatteren Leonora Christina* thus contains a hint at Kirsten Munk's difficult situation,[912] Enevoldsen lets the matter rest for the remainder of the account. The following clashes between Leonora's parents show the King as a conciliatory and loving husband and father, while all Kirsten Munk can think about is the object of her recent infatuation, Otto Ludvig of Salm. Despite this only rudimental broach of a social problem, the consequences of Kirsten Munk's distress nevertheless become central to the protagonist's life: a parents' divorce would cause any child considerable pain, but in Leonora Christina's case, Kirsten Munk's fall from grace also led to an increasingly questionable social status of her children. This, however, is another topic directly addressed only in the beginning and in the postface of the novel, but not readopted later on in the account, hence it provides hardly

---

909 In Leonora Christina-literature predating the publication of *Jammers Minde*, Kirsten Munk is barely ever mentioned (much unlike Leonora Christina's idolised father), most likely due to her fall from grace. Works published after 1869, on the other hand, initially reflect Sophus Birket Smith's judgement of Kirsten Munk, which is entirely built on statements written by Christian IV about his unfaithful wife. Birket Smith merely attributes the King's failed second marriage to Kirsten Munk's character, which had only shown its true colours once the girl bride turned into an adult woman: »Hun synes at have været ikke blot en stærkt sanselig, men en helt igjennem grov og uædel Natur, uden synderlig Intelligents eller moralsk Sans, og let vakt til ubændig Lidenskab, der da lige så let udladede sig i Ord og Handlinger af ligefrem oprørende Råhed« (Birket Smith, Sophus. *Leonora Christina Grevinde Ulfeldts Historie 1*, p. 6).

910 Enevoldsen, Herta J. *Kongedatteren Leonora Christina*, p. 11. Little Leonora, too, often finds her mother crying, which is why she is more empathetic towards her violent mother than her brothers and sisters.

911 Ibid., p. 12. While Leonora Christina's contemporaries thus dismiss her as an ignorant infantile (»Det er på grund af krigen, og det forstår I jer ikke på«), the omniscient author knows that she is much more capable than the adults assume: »Selv om hun kun var 7 år, forstod hun sig mere på krig, end de voksne troede« (ibid., p. 15f).

912 This reassessment of Kirsten Munk is not exclusive to fiction. Historians, too, eventually began to empathise with Leonora Christina's infamous mother about her situation; see, for example, Palle Lauring's verdict: »Men det var ikke hendes skyld, at hun af skæbnen fik en rolle stukket ud, som hun aldeles ikke magtede. Derfor var hun på forhånd dømt til fiasko. Det er hverken morsomt, pikant eller forargeligt. Det er trist« (Lauring, Palle. *Dronninger og andre kvinder i Danmarkshistorien*, p. 58).

any explanation of Leonora Christina's character, as portrayed by Enevoldsen.[913] Yet despite the lack of psychological depth exhibited by Enevoldsen's characters,[914] her novel and its topic – Leonora Christina's problematic childhood and her parents' broken marriage – constitute forerunners of the current Leonora Christina-literature,[915] which depicts a very ambivalent heroine.

Enevoldsen's novels are littered with motific stumps such as the one mentioned above. The reasons for the conflict between the Ulfeldt couple and the rest of the court, too, remain in the dark, as all hatred towards them seems entirely unmotivated and is only attributed to the envy of rivals.[916] The only noteable exception to this approach are occasional comments by Christian IV regarding »sin svigersøns selvrådighed og provokerende adfærd over for adelsfolket«,[917] which are, however, immediately relativised by his coincidental declining health: »Hendes fars helbred var ikke, hvad det før havde været, og hans humør var ikke altid lige godt. […] Det ene øjeblik gav han Corfitz skylden for, at det var slået fejl. […] I det næste øjeblik kunne kongen slå om og rette heftige bebrejdelser mod sig selv«.[918]

Kongedatteren Leonora Christina is thus indeed not representative of Denmark's Social Realism, or rather »problemrealisme«,[919] as Torben Weinreich calls the chief interest of 1970's children's literature in Denmark. The novel exhibits a binary structure, similar to that of a folk tale, regarding the moral evaluation of the characters: Leonora is an innocent princess, whose beauty and other amenities

---

913 This circumstance is a particularly dissonant element of the novel, as Enevoldsen depicts the course of the family quarrels in great detail and subsequently, in the 'Historisk redegørelse', designates Leonora Christina as »skillsmissebarnet« that grew up in a »splittet verden« (Enevoldsen, Herta J. *Leonora Christina i Blåtårn*, p. 213). Despite this clear indication of a troubled childhood with consequences for the character's adult life, Leonora Christina is a strikingly one-dimensional and flawless character throughout the entire account.

914 Due to her fixation on her father, the removal of Kirsten Munk causes the protagonist only little distress. Furthermore, Vibeke Kruse is not mentioned until Leonora Christina meets her at her father's deathbed and she is much less bothered by Christian IV's civil concubine than Corfitz Ulfeldt (Enevoldsen, Herta J. *Kongedatteren Leonora Christina*, p. 142). Hence, all the domestic trouble indicated in the beginning of the account and that could be of didactic value remains merely superficial and Leonora Christina's life remains virtually carefree until the arrival of Sofie Amalie.

915 However, not only literature depicting Leonora Christina has taken an interest in her troubled childhood. *Indfald og udfald: Ti nye studier* by Bo Elbrønd-Bek, for example, provides a reading of Leonora Christina's autobiographical writings based on the assumption of her life being a series of traumata, starting with the separation from her parents in 1627 (see Elbrønd-Bek, Bo. *Indfald og udfald: Ti nye studier*. [Copenhagen:] Underskoven, 2012).

916 Enevoldsen, Herta J. *Kongedatteren Leonora Christina*, p. 118.

917 Ibid., p. 126.

918 Ibid., p. 136f.

919 Weinreich, Torben. 'I statens tjeneste', p. 164.

attract the hatred of the evil Queen Sofie Amalie[920] and her equally envious husband.[921] However, the novel is not completely bereft of contemporary elements. Little Leonora's exemplary school behaviour and character, for example, match the educational measures of 1970's Denmark and their success. A public discourse started in the 1960's regarding the importance of quality reading for the education of children – both in and after school[922] – was resolved with school and library laws that made quality reading free and accessible to every pupil. This first step towards public regulation of children's reading behaviour was continued in the 1970's and completed with the emergence of the *socialistisk børnelitteratur* in the same decade, hence declaring children's reading behaviour an affair of public importance, as stated by Torben Weinreich: »Man kan sige, at der sker en form for 'statsliggørelse', som omfatter mennesket fra fødsel til død. Også børnelitteraturen kommer på sin måde i 'statens tjeneste'«.[923] This attitude – the central importance of frequent (quality) reading and the library as a recreational space for children – is reflected in *Kongedatteren Leonora Christina*. Leonora is a good pupil and especially fond of books, which attracts the envy of her less gifted elder sisters. And despite being bullied by her jealous siblings, Leonora is no telltale, but rather empathetic towards them since they seem to have a learning disability.[924]

Through her empathy, Leonora demonstrates not only a universal virtue, i.e. sisterly love, but her behaviour can also be regarded in the context of the appearance of Danish *letlæsningsbøger* ('easy reads')[925] from the 1950's onwards, which – together with the 1964-law that declared the establishment of school libraries man-

---

920 Sofie Amalie is an especially malignant creature, since even her husband is afraid of her (Enevoldsen, Herta J. *Kongedatteren Leonora Christina*, p. 182). Her despise for Leonora furthermore seems completely unmotivated, as she is already hostile at their very first meeting, and her animosity is not only directed at Leonora, but also at her father-in-law, as he stands between Sofie Amalie and the throne of Denmark (ibid., p. 140).

921 This Evil, immediately represented by Sophie Amalie and Frederik III, remains rather faceless as especially the King is portrayed as a spineless shadow of a man. The power opposing Leonora and Corfitz Ulfeldt eventually takes on the character of a superiority, rather than human beings with motives governing their deeds. Accordingly, all opposition against the Ulfeldt couple acts out of no specified reason until it takes on a form, whose right to exist ends in itself alone. When Leonora demands to see the documents stating the verdict over Corfitz Ulfeldt, she receives only vague excuses and a reference to the almighty absolutism: »– Der findes måske ikke anden forklaring, grevinde Ulfeldt … end at majestæten er enevældig … og kan gøre, hvad han vil« (Enevoldsen, Herta J. *Leonora Christina i Blåtårn*, p. 128).

922 Cf. Weinreich, Torben. *Historien om børnelitteratur: Dansk børnelitteratur gennem 400 år*. Copenhagen: Branner og Korch, 2006, p. 511.

923 Weinreich, Torben. *Historien om børnelitteratur*, p. 503.

924 Enevoldsen, Herta J. *Kongedatteren Leonora Christina*, p. 14.

925 There is also a *letlæsningsbog* on Leonora Christina: *Leonora Christina* by Agnete Elkjær Laursen, published in 1960. Letlæsningsbøger are characterised by a child-friendly mode of narrating, letter size and line pitch as well as occasional drawings. Furthermore, longer words are divided into shorter units in order to facilitate the reading of potentially unknown words, such as »Grå-brødre-torv« or »be-brej-de«.

datory for all primary schools – was part of a large-scale, institutionalised effort to advance children's reading skills in the second half of the 20th century, with special attention to those with reading difficulties. All these measures soon proved to be very successful as they made Danish children uncommonly diligent readers.[926] Hence, the strikingly superior Leonora does not mock her sisters, but rather offers them her help.[927] Yet her sisters are plainly evil, so Leonora ends up taking refuge in her father's library, whenever she seeks a hideout from her siblings.[928]

Another strength, which is also connected to the discourse presented above, is Leonora's imagination. While she is recovering from smallpox, her fantasy helps her to escape her bedridden and lonely situation.[929] Her rich inner life also allows her to enjoy her strict and monotonous daily grind as a pupil, who receives an education worthy of a princess,[930] and eventually, it will also help her to endure her imprisonment in the Blue Tower, as she explains to one of her maids:

[O]g for resten så rejser jeg stadig. Hver dag. – Rejser? Hvordan skal det forstås? […] – Som jeg siger det. Og du kan også komme på rejse … du kan flyve ud af rummet her, hvis du har kraft til det. […] Jo, på tankens vinger kan man … man kan komme, hvorhen man vil.[931]

Overall, *Kongedatteren Leonora Christina* follows the outline of the French autobiography while amplifying the little Countess' assets. Yet as stated above, Leonora Christina's life narratives, particularly *Jammers Minde*, can also be read as a guidebook on etiquette. In Enevoldsen's account, Leonora's class consciousness wells up every once in a while, particularly whenever she is faced with the question of her status, hence encouraging her to behave in a more dignified manner: »Men kongedatter er jeg dog, tænkte Leonora, mens hun uvilkårligt rettede sig i stolen, – og det vil jeg blive ved med at være hele mit liv«.[932] This is not an uncommon feature of the late Leonora Christina-literature – the 20th-century demand for social equality left its mark on these texts too, thus leading to rather ambivalent and not always likeable depictions of this class-conscious King's daughter. However, many modern

---

926 Cf. Weinreich, Torben. 'I statens tjeneste', p. 152.
927 Enevoldsen, Herta J. *Kongedatteren Leonora Christina*, p. 13.
928 In comparison, Maria Helleberg's presentation depicts the church as its protagonist's choice for a safe haven.
929 Enevoldsen, Herta J. *Kongedatteren Leonora Christina*, p. 38.
930 Ibid., p. 82f.
931 Enevoldsen, Herta J. *Leonora Christina i Blåtårn*, p. 200.
932 Enevoldsen, Herta J. *Kongedatteren Leonora Christina*, p. 46.

novels presenting Leonora Christina as their protagonist also soften her behaviour, which otherwise may be regarded as too elitist. Enevoldsen's Leonora, for example, teaches her younger siblings to never mistreat their subordinates: »De skulle altid tale pænt til tjenerne – lige så pænt som til de fornemme personer«.[933] And in her last years at home with her father, Leonora often accompanies the King on his rides, handing out money and clothing to children and the poor, with the result that both are much beloved by the people. In addition, she advises her father on legal matters, hence effecting the pardon of many an offender.[934] By her father's side, Leonora is thus a popular heroine and of great service to her country.

A hint at a didactic intention is thus indeed detectable in *Kongedatteren Leonora Christina*. The positive image of the bookworm Leonora on the background of the contemporary public discourse on children's reading habits is, however, negated by her knowledge on the background of *Jammers Minde*. In this particular context, knowledge is Leonora's doom. As a young girl, Leonora is very knowledgeable and constantly seeks to improve her education, but once her knowledge could harm her, ignorance is her bliss. When the interrogations in the Blue Tower commence, Leonora can honestly state, that she has nothing to confess, not even regarding her husband: »Hvad jeg ikke ved noget om, kan jeg ikke fortælle om«.[935]

Yet, this is not the only instance, which requires ignorance. At strategic passages in the plot, Leonora asserts her unawareness,[936] and while this behaviour corresponds to Leonora Christina's own assertions, it contributes in no way to the formation of a comprehensible character.[937] Even though in every other instance the protagonist is an omniscient all-rounder and the right hand of her father and her husband, topics that require a familiarity with politics and court schemes and could potentially harm her reputation render her seemingly clueless.[938] This ignorance

---

933 Ibid., p. 99.

934 Ibid., p. 113.

935 Enevoldsen, Herta J. *Leonora Christina i Blåtårn*, p. 113.

936 The same strategy is applied to Corfitz Ulfeldt, albeit this is not a gimmick unique to Enevoldsen's account. Based on the popular theory that Ulfeldt was gradually turning insane, the character in *Kongedatteren Leonora Christina*, too, eventually loses his wit (cf. Enevoldsen, Herta J. *Kongedatteren Leonora Christina*, p. 14) and is thus – like his wife – rendered ignorant of his actions.

937 The account additionally forfeits traceability through occasional leaps in the plot. Many a character's behaviour remains unmotivated and some hints in the novel beg an explanation which is never delivered. This concerns, for example, Leonora's fear of seeing her carriage fall into the hands of her pursuers: »For foruden forsvarsskrifterne til majestæten var der hemmelige breve og dokumenter, som han absolut ikke måtte få at se« (ibid., p. 9). The reader is left wondering what kind of documents the carriage might contain but an explanation never follows.

938 She is, for example, unaware of Hannibal Sehested's plan to marry into the royal family by wooing Leonora's younger sister (ibid., p. 122) or of her father's plan to reoccupy the position of Stewart of the Realm, which will be accorded to Corfitz Ulfeldt (ibid., p. 130).

appears especially dubious in light of her attitude towards inconvenient truths, such as the quarrel between her father and Corfitz, the exact origins of which remain in the dark: »Hun vidste, at der var fejl på begge sider. Men hun ville helst lukke øjnene for disse fejl – for hun elskede dem begge to *trods* deres fejl«.[939] This strategy continues in the second part, *Leonora Christina i Blåtårn*, which on the one hand shows its protagonist utterly guileless when confronted with a reaction from her enemies, whereas she can turn into an omnipotent opponent within seconds. For example, when she travels back home after her and her husband's escape from Denmark. When she receives an unexpectedly hostile reception in the town of Korsør in Zealand, she responds in the most blue-eyed manner: »Men jeg kommer med gode breve til kongen«.[940] When this strategy proves fruitless, she turns into a heroine worthy of a novel by Alexandre Dumas the Elder within an instant. She draws two pistols, escapes while shooting at her adversaries with both hands, and eventually outdistances them due to her astonishing knowledge of horse stamina and her pursuers' training.[941]

This strategy becomes more explicit as the plot progresses. When Corfitz Ulfeldt's actions become increasingly treasonous, his wife decides that she simply does not *want* to know too much: »I den følgende tid blev det Leonora, der lukkede sig til, når hendes ægtemand ville delagtiggøre hende i sine politiske planer«.[942]

Yet eventually, Leonora returns to her previous, educationally committed approach and uses her knowledge to her advantage. Once her indefinite imprisonment has commenced and her ignorance is no longer of any use to her, she demonstrates her superiority by means of her education (cf. Chapter 1.2.1.). The second half of *Leonora Christina i Blåtårn*, which renders the content of *Jammers Minde*, returns to the initial didactic intention inherent to parts of Enevoldsen's account, as Leonora becomes once again the well-meaning teacher of those less privileged beings surrounding her. She uses her naturally rational thinking to help her superstitious maid Karen, all the while Leonora herself learns to understand how privileged her own life had been:

---

939 Ibid., p. 137.
940 Enevoldsen, Herta J. *Leonora Christina i Blåtårn*, p. 6.
941 Ibid., p. 10f.
942 Ibid., p. 13. As the account proceeds, Leonora continues to ignore her husband's thirst for revenge. Corfitz Ulfeldt is partially excused as he gradually turns certifiably insane. Leonora reacts by consciously and sometimes even literally looking the other way: »Leonora så et øjeblik op fra bogen i sit skød, men sænkede så blikket igen. Hun udholdt ikke at se det mærkeligt stirrende blik i sin mands øjne« (ibid., p. 76).

Og Leonora kunne ikke lade være med at have medlidenhed med hende, for det liv hun havde levet. Det havde været så fattigt på venlighed og varme, fattigt på kærlighed, på alt. I sammenligning med hende følte Leonora sig rig. Hun havde haft en god barndom – en blanding af godt og mindre godt ganske vist, men dog mest af det første – og hun havde haft en vidunderlig far. Hun havde også mødt en kærlighed, der var så rig og stor, som noget menneske kunne ønske sig – var blevet viet til verdens dejligste ægtemand og havde været uendelig lykkelig i sit ægteskab.[943]

With this adaptation of the plot provided by *Jammers Minde*, Enevoldsen not only reproduces the original's documentary value, which had been appraised before,[944] but the novel also exhibits a social commitment, which is not present in *Jammers Minde*.

Later on in the account, Leonora's empathy takes on specifically religious forms. The Christian virtues of altruism and forgiveness – already central to *Jammers Minde* – are turned into a more explicit life lesson in Enevoldsen's adaptation. What Leonora Christina only indicates in *Jammers Minde* is directly addressed in *Leonora Christina i Blåtårn*, for example when the castellan Jokum Waltpurger asks Leonora about the reasons for her benevolence even towards enemies: »Jamen, det er heller ikke noget, jeg kan af mig selv ... det er en kraft, der kommer ovenfra, svarede hun«.[945] Enevoldsen removes Leonora Christina's resentment underlying every page of *Jammers Minde* from her own account, hence depicting a character much less ambivalent than Leonora Christina herself managed to portray.

The character's development – absent in *Kongedatteren Leonora Christina* and subsequently caught up on in *Leonora Christina i Blåtårn* – is, however, eventually withdrawn as the topic of predetermination, introduced at the moment of Leonora's birth, dominates again towards the end of the account, hence negating any difference between the little daughter of Christian IV and the aged woman in the Blue Tower:

---

943 Ibid., p. 162.
944 »Leonoras evne til at fastholde udseende og karakter hos de mennesker, fængselsopholdet påtvinger hende berøring med, har for eftertiden opbevaret billeder af en række oftest betydningsløse mennesker, især kvinder, som ellers for evigt ville være forsvundet i tidens gang« (Kanonudvalget. 'Jammers Minde: Udvalgets begrundelse', p. 110).
945 Enevoldsen, Herta J. *Leonora Christina i Blåtårn*, p. 177.

Og tit undrede det hende selv, at hendes sind ikke tog skade og blev formørket af al den råhed, hun så omkring sig. For det stod i skærende kontrast til det liv, hun tidligere havde levet, og den tilværelse hun ved sin kongelige fødsel og rang var bestemt til. Men netop fordi hun var kongedatteren, kom hun igennem det. Hendes medfødte værdighed kunne ingen ydmygelse få bugt med, og hendes store selvbeherskelse kom hende til hjælp.⁹⁴⁶

The bridging of beginning and end of Enevoldsen's Leonora Christina-novels is complete when the protagonist exits the story the same way she entered it – as Christian IV's proud daughter:

Med blomsterne i hånden og sin dyrebare bog Jammers-minde trykket ind mod sig, så hun over mængdens hoveder op mod balkonen overfor, hvor hun så tit havde stået ved sin fars side og modtaget folkets hyldest. Hun syntes, at hun for sit indre øje kunne se hans ansigt for sig, hans ranke og værdige skikkelse. Og hun rankede sig selv. Mere end nogen sinde følte hun sig som hans datter.⁹⁴⁷

The character appears to have undergone no change at all. While this is consistent with the declaration inherent to *Jammers Minde*, it leads to the question whether Enevoldsen perceived any intrinsic life lesson of didactic value to contemporary young readers in her subject matter at all.

In this regard, Enevoldsen's 'Historisk redegørelse' at the end of the novel is not particularly enlightening either, as it is a summary of the preceding novel in the disguise of historical background information. In this postface, Enevoldsen contends, for example, that due to Leonora Christina's »tidlig modenhed«⁹⁴⁸ she soon developed true and everlasting love for her husband. The protagonist's prematurity is a recurring topic in the beginning of the novel and drawn on whenever there is a need to account for Leonora's perfection, despite her young age. Enevoldsen must have drawn on her own fictional account for this 'historical' background information, as this sort of declaration is not present in scholarly writings on Leonora Christina. As a consequence, even the historical Leonora Christina presented at the end of the novel is in no way different from the fictional character presented at the beginning, hence reinforcing the impression of a one-dimensional folk tale-character. The only lesson to be learned from Leonora Christina's life story through the eyes of Herta J. Enevoldsen is thus – in true folk tale-fashion – that Evil does not prevail:

---

946 Ibid., p. 198.
947 Ibid., p. 211.
948 Ibid., p. 213.

Af de to kongelige damer – Leonora Christina og Sofie Amalie – var det statsfangen og kongedatteren, der sejrede til sidst. [...] Denne dronning kan nok så meget have stået på Københavns volde i farens stund (Københavns bombardement 1659). Hun vil dog mest huskes for de 22 år, hvor hun lod en anden kvinde lide – uforskyldt.[949]

As stated above by Torben Weinreich, Herta J. Enevoldsen's mostly female protagonists »tjener i højere grad til at skabe identitetsmuligheder for de i overvejende grad kvindelige læsere«.[950] However, due to her predetermined perfection, Enevoldsen's Leonora is a particularly inaccessible character, hence offering little opportunity for identification. The topic of predestination is present throughout the account, as Leonora is born with some virtues and acquires others at a very young age. When Christian IV feels deeply betrayed by his wife Kirsten Munk, he makes his daughter promise that she will always be faithful to her future husband, Corfitz Ulfeldt: »For troskab i kærlighed er det vigtigste af alt – utroskab er en pine i hjertet«.[951] The historically aware reader knows that she will keep her promise, especially since she had learned another virtue from her father, i.e. always keeping one's promise.[952]

Eventually, Leonora's main virtue, faithfulness in word and deed, spells doom over a virtually immaculate young woman. The reader is soon made aware of the approaching calamity, as prophetic allusions so typical of Leonora Christina-literature are littered over the account at an unusual density. Leonora even addresses her fate herself, when she uses the fireworks launched at her brother's wedding to predict her and Corfitz's future together. When her *skæbneraket* produces only a meek fulmination, while an owl departs from the Blue Tower only to cross the hopeful couple, she takes both as a sign of a dark future. These hints together with Corfitz's subsequent counter assertion that man forges his own destiny[953] add up to a tragic sense of irony lying over this situation, as both of their attitudes turn out to be

---

[949] Ibid., p. 221f.
[950] Weinreich, Torben. 'I statens tjeneste', p. 182.
[951] Enevoldsen, Herta J. *Kongedatteren Leonora Christina*, p. 79.
[952] See ibid., p. 29: »Hendes far havde lært hende, at et givet løfte altid skal holdes – og han holdt altid selv sit ord«. His successor King Christian V, on the other hand, breaks his promise. Forced by his despotic mother Sofie Amalie, he reneges on his promise to release Leonora from prison if his first-born child is a son. Deeply disappointed by his behaviour, the King's mother-in-law upbraids the young father: »Jeg troede ikke, en konge brød sit ord, sagde hun og så ham lige i øjnene« (Enevoldsen, Herta J. *Leonora Christina i Blåtårn*, p. 182).
[953] Enevoldsen, Herta J. *Kongedatteren Leonora Christina*, p. 108.

right.[954] Leonora's resolution to place her fate in the hands of her husband[955] eventually exposes Corfitz as her hangman, yet it does not undo the previously introduced topic of predestination.[956] Hence, it is justified to ask whether Enevoldsen's account contains any didactic value at all.

On the other hand, the novel implies the same message as Leonora Christina's own writings, which tell of envy and unjust punishments. As denoted in *Jammers Minde* and the French autobiography, the authoress' innocence makes the punishment seem all the more outrageous and hence more captivating to a readership unfamiliar with Leonora Christina's fate and its backdrop.

At the same time, the plot recounting the events narrated in *Jammers Minde* uses the same narrative techniques as deployed in the original. Directly opposed to the brutish and malicious behaviour of the people surrounding her in the Blue Tower, Leonora's behaviour seems all the more exemplary.[957] Her self-restraint is opposed to their rampant greed[958] and her endurance overcomes all physical desires and needs, contrary to her servants, who complain in the most snivelling manner.[959] As observed by Dorthe Sondrup Andersen (see previous chapter), *Jammers Minde* does thus possess an educational value, as it adverts potential readers to dignified behaviour in even the most degrading situations. However, in Enevoldsen's folk tale-like account, this is an isolated finding.

By depicting the exotic 17th century with its strange habits and its pompous festivities, *Kongedatteren Leonora Christina* and *Leonora Christina i Blåtårn* primarily provide their readers with all elements of a typical girl's novel: a love story,

---

954 All references to Corfitz's share in his initial fall from grace in Denmark remain mere hints, hence leaving him innocent. In the second part, however, he is mainly driven by a thirst for revenge, even though Leonora does not approve of his decisions. The image of the innocent Corfitz Ulfeldt is thus reversed in the second volume.

955 Enevoldsen, Herta J. *Kongedatteren Leonora Christina*, p. 109.

956 In Enevoldsen's account, the main reason for the fall of the Ulfeldt couple is the – not further explicated – hatred and envy of their enemies, led by Sofie Amalie and her husband. However, Ulfeldt's vengeful actions against the royal couple immediately trigger his and Leonora's arrests.

957 That it is Leonora's destiny and final task to figure as a role model to others is realised by the protagonist in the course of her spiritual renewal, when she understands that her time has not yet come: »Hun kunne stadig bruges i hans tjeneste – blive et lysende eksempel for andre« (Enevoldsen, Herta J. *Leonora Christina i Blåtårn*, p. 139).

958 Ibid., p. 117: »Med grådighed kastede de simple folk sig over den fine mad, som var noget helt usædvanligt for dem at få. Lige så grådigt svælgede de vinen og øllet i sig, og deres opførsel blev derefter«.

959 Ibid., p. 120: »De to kvinder sov begge i en slagbænk, der var sat ind til dem og lige akkurat kunne være mellem bordet og væggen. Men de var syge af stanken og den beklumrede luft. Og især Cathrine var så medtaget, at hun jamrede sig højlydt det meste af natten. Det blev Anne Skomagers voldsomt vred over, og hun skældte ud og råbte op, hvilket var meget værre at høre på end Cathrines jammer. Leonora var selv syg, men hun tav. Selv om hun led af kvalme og opkastning, selvom hun ingenting spiste, men kun drak vand, kom der ingen klage over hendes læber«.

schemes, and an adventurous life. The main character, Leonora, has the potential to serve as a role model, yet due to her absolute faultlessness, especially in her childhood and teenage years, she lacks psychological depth and provides thus little opportunity for identification. The repeated reminders of her physical and mental maturity generate an additional divide between her and the reader, as they constantly force the reader to compare themselves to this unreachable role model. For the same reasons that would captivate a teenage girl's interest in the novel – Leonora Christina's unique fate and the estranged background provided by the 17th century – Enevoldsen's Leonora Christina-novels are thus rather informational than educational books.[960] As such, the text is, however, quite felicitous. Enevoldsen managed to capture the authoritative nature of Leonora Christina's account, the sensations reproduced in *Jammers Minde*, i.e. the filth, the odour and the cold, and even Leonora Christina's humour despite these gruesome living conditions, all the while amplifying the account according to the taste of a young readership.

2.5.2. Eva Hemmer Hansen: The Leonora Christina Fragment (1982-1983) – The Feminist Case Study

Son Mari l'aymoit et honoroit, fit le Galand et pas le Mari.[961]

A first glance at Eva Hemmer Hansen's novels on Leonora Christina – *Den lykkelige hustru* and *Den trofaste hustru* – reveals that they were not (primarily) meant to be children's books, or even intended for a young audience. There are no illustrations, no inviting cover design, and the text is rather dense.[962] Nevertheless, the two novels exhibit signs of didactisation,[963] as they provide their readers with plen-

---

[960] The same kind of informational – as opposed to educational – value is attributed to *Jammers Minde* itself, as it is depicted as merely serving the purpose of informing Leonora Christina's children about their mother's fate: »Og den skulle kun læses af hendes børn, besluttede hun, ingen andre måtte se den. Derfor ville hun i den fortælle *alt*, som det var gået til og ikke skjule noget. For måske slap hun aldrig ud af fængslet i levende live, så hun kunne møde sine børn og fortælle dem det hele. Og så var det godt, at de i bogen kunne læse om deres mors skæbne« (Enevoldsen, Herta J. *Leonora Christina i Blåtårn*, p. 190).

[961] *Leonora Christina Grevinde Ulfeldts Franske Levnedsskildring*, p. 3d (Translation p. 14: »Hendes mand elskede og ærede hende, omgikkes hende som en elsker, ikke som en ægtemage«).

[962] Furthermore, the novels contain rather explicit scenes, such as Leonora Christina's wedding night, which could be considered unfit for a very young readership.

[963] I am referring to Göte Klingberg's use of the term 'didaktisering': »Definition: *Indarbejdning af en intention om at meddele viden og/eller indlære moralske attituder og adfærd*« (Klingberg, Göte. 'Begrebet adaptation', transl. Hans Christian Fink. In *Lyst og lærdom – debat og forskning om børnelitteratur*, ed. Torben Weinreich. Copenhagen: Høst & Søn, 1996, p. 146.

tiful background information on the 17th century.[964] Like Herta J. Enevoldsen, Eva Hemmer Hansen, too, took on the task of educating future generations on Leonora Christina's life, the origination of *Jammers Minde*, on 17th-century Denmark and the lot of women in this period.

Even though the novels bear the subtitle 'Leonora Christine', their focus is much less on their eponymous heroine than is the case with other representatives of Leonora Christina-literature.[965] Instead, Eva Hemmer Hansen presents Leonora Christina's comtemporaries from all social classes, as well as events and habits of the 17th century in great detail, hence creating the impression of her novels being a portrait of a society rather than biographical novels. The chapters 'Efter en krig', 'Præsten' and 'Genopbygning',[966] depicting Ellen Marsvin inspecting the farms belonging to Boller,[967] for example, deal with the lives and fates of Central Jutland's rural population during and after Denmark's participation in the Thirty Years' War, which had hitherto only been portrayed as one of Christian IV's personal defeats. These accounts are interrupted by descriptions of *Det store bilager* 1634, one of the biggest celebrations of its time meant to overshadow the King's ineffective martial engagements, and the diplomatic tangle preceding it. In Leonora's[968] eyes, the diversionary

---

[964] In this regard, Hemmer Hansen's novels resemble that of H. F. Ewald and like him, Eva Hemmer Hansen, too, inserted many a comment in order to help her reader put the events in perspective. For example, when she defends Christian IV's chaotic approach in managing realm, business and family (»Nu gjorde Ulfeldt både kongen og Gyldenløve nogen uret«, see Hemmer Hansen, Eva. *Den lykkelige hustru*, p. 28), followed by an extensive annotation on past developments and conditions.

[965] If it were not for the indicative titles of Hemmer Hansen's novels, both declaring Leonora Christina their protagonist, and some thematic deviations, *Den lykkelige hustru* and *Den trofaste hustru* – especially the former – could justly be called family stories. Like Louisa May Alcott's *Little Women*, published in 1868 (and surely one of the most famous representatives of the family story), *Den lykkelige hustru* focuses on the lives and struggles of the mostly female descendants of one female ancestor, who remains in the background yet acts like a leader of the clan (respectively Marmee and Ellen Marsvin). And while most of the space of the respective novels are not dedicated to one person alone, there is one – more or less declared – protagonist (respectively Jo March and Leonora Christine). Finally, despite all initial struggles, both families learn to cooperate; in the case of the March family, out of Christian duty and love, in the case of the Marsvin clan, in order to defend their common status as relatives of a King and the privileges this status implies. For a short yet comprehensive overview of the family story, see Kimberley Reynolds' chapter on this genre in *Children's Literature: A Very Short Introduction* (Reynolds, Kimberley. 'Genres and generations – the case of the family story'. In Reynolds, Kimberley. *Children's Literature: A Very Short Introduction*. Oxford University Press, 2011 (Very Short Introductions 288), pp. 77-95).

[966] Hemmer Hansen, Eva. *Den lykkelige hustru*, pp. 56-71 and pp. 95-111.

[967] Boller was a seat farm in the Central Denmark Region and one of the many farms belonging to Ellen Marsvin. Following the final separation between Christian IV and Kirsten Munk in 1630, the King ordered his mother-in-law to allocate Boller to his disowned wife, together with the seat farm of Rosenvold. For more information on Kirsten Munk's years as lady of Boller, see Fussing, Hans H. 'Kirsten Munk som frue paa Boller og fange paa Stjernholm 1630-35', Jyske Samlinger 5/5 (1939), pp. 15-60.

[968] In the present chapter, »Leonora« specifically refers to the character in Eva Hemmer Hansen's novels, particularly when referring to passages that do not correspond to historical events, whereas »Leonora Christina« refers to the historical person.

tactic had been a success: »Det havde været en herlig fest. Den havde gjort hendes far ære«.[969] Yet, the ensuing accounts of rape and torture during the war, and of poverty and trauma affecting the rural population, challenge the validity of this assessment.

Eva Hemmer Hansen's authorial intent is thus primarily informative, but also educational as Leonora's life is presented in contrast to those of her civic contemporaries, hence implying an educational intent as well. The legitimacy of a royal title is called into question already at the beginning of *Den lykkelige hustru*, when three young men of equal luck but varying social status meet Fatima, »en fornem elefant, en hvid elefant, en elefantprinsesse, som skal behandles med respekt«.[970] The animal was brought to Denmark at the occasion of *Det store bilager* and when Duke Frederik (the future Frederik III), Corfitz Ulfeldt and Ulrik Christian Gyldenløve, an illegitimate son of Christian IV, meet the elephant, it is formally introduced to the other royal in the stable, Frederik. The protocol requires Frederik to offer an apple to the elephant princess. Despite Corfitz's contemptuous laughter, Frederik performs to everybody's satisfaction and Gyldenløve even bows to the elephant. When Corfitz asks to participate in the charade, Gyldenløve informs him that the elephant princess would only receive presents from equals: »[H]an [the elephant's caretaker] siger, at en prinsesse kun tager imod gaver fra kongeligfødte«.[971] Besides portraying Corfitz as a sadistic man with an inferiority complex,[972] this episode also serves the purpose of implicitly challenging the legitimacy of the elephant's and her human peers' titles. When the offended Corfitz asks why the elephant is called white when its actual colour is clearly »beskidt lysegrå«,[973] Gyldenløve explains that it is all a question of comparison: »›Det kommer af, at du ser hende alene,‹ lo Gyldenløve. ›Hvis du så hende sammen med almindelige elefanter, var der lige så lidt tvivl, som når man ser på os to – og så Frederik.‹ Men han havde sænket stemmen lidt«.[974] Royalty is thus portrayed as an outwardness, a superficiality that only exists in comparison to others, but not per se.[975]

---

969 Hemmer Hansen, Eva. *Den lykkelige hustru*, p. 94.
970 Ibid., p. 10.
971 Ibid.
972 The beginning of the novel shows Corfitz throwing stones at the elephant for no apparent reason but boredom, until he is stopped by Frederik.
973 Hemmer Hansen, Eva. *Den lykkelige hustru*, p. 12.
974 Ibid.
975 Hemmer Hansen's ironically reserved treatment of peerage in her novels becomes more blatant at the end of the chapter, when the elephant princess is left to herself: »Elefantprinsessen Fatima stod tilbage og søgte stadig skeptisk efter noget godt i høet og tænkte sit – eller tænkte muligvis slet ikke« (Hemmer Hansen, Eva. *Den lykkelige hustru*, p. 24). In comparison, Herta J. Enevoldsen's novels still present a national romantic picture of royalty, which regards nobility as both an outward as well as inward quality.

The same applies to Leonora, who exhibits neat behaviour only in noble company. At the beginning of *Den lykkelige hustru*, Leonora is thirteen years old and still a real child. She and the rest of her unruly flock of sisters rag and quarrel at every opportunity and only turn into well-behaved *frøkener* at the appearance of guests.

In its disposition, Eva Hemmer Hansen's two novels on Leonora Christina thus resemble that of H. F. Ewald, yet her character focus is much more amplified than what *Leonora Kristina* offers. Like the great representatives of literary realism, Hemmer Hansen's work depicts the lives of those surrounding Leonora, yet the account is not entirely devoid of social criticism. Just like Ewald, Hemmer Hansen approaches and presents Leonora Christina's life story with a different historical-cultural perspective, yet her comments are much more subtle than the open contemptuousness displayed by Ewald. The thoughts assigned to the diverse characters and exaggerated to the brink of sarcasm substantiate the critical element in Hemmer Hansen's narrative. For example, when Ellen Marsvin arrives in the middle of the night at the seat farm of Boller to pay her disowned daughter Kirsten Munk a visit. After instructing the menial staff on how to receive their surprise guest she sits down to wait for her daughter to join her for dinner: »Ellen Marsvin fandt ikke noget bemærkelsesværdigt i, at dette sløve hus pludselig vågnede op, og at alle gik i gang som lydige marionetter. […] Underordnede gør, hvad de skal. Hvad ellers?«[976]

Similar comments that raise the attention of a modern readership, yet particularly concerning the prospects of women, occur at a higher density, starting with Corfitz Ulfeldt's assessment of his future father-in-law's failed marriage:

> Ulfeldt ventede sig ganske vist noget mere af et ægteskab end en sengefælle og en barneføderske. Jo mere han så til Leonora og hørte om hende, jo mere blev han tilfreds med, at det var hende, der var tilfaldet ham. […] I kyndige, nænsomme hænder er en begavet hustru et aktiv for en mand. Men han kunne ikke se sig selv nogen sinde tabe hovedet over en kvinde sådan som den arme mand der ved skrivebordet. Hvis det kunne tænkes, at Leonora havde arvet noget af sin mors natur, agtede han i hvert fald at styre hende bedre fra begyndelsen.[977]

The notion of women merely serving as bedfellows and childbearers is later on readopted and problematised through the portrayal of Ellen Marsvin and Kirsten Munk, both of whom had to endure exploitation by their relatives and subsequent

---

976 Ibid., p. 40.
977 Ibid., p. 35.

hapless marriages. The proverb »Happy wife, happy life« proves true in a negative sense, as Ellen's and Kirsten's respective marriages both end in disaster. The life stories of Leonora's female ancestors accentuate their victimhood. The cycle commences with Ellen Marsvin's »svagelig, forkuet«[978] mother and it continues with Ellen Marsvin and her handover to a brutish and possibly perverted husband: »Han var ikke en ung piges drøm om en ægtemand. Han var en ond drøm. Han havde ægteskabelige vaner og krav, som forvirrede Ellen en del«.[979]

The victim status assigned to Ellen and her mother (»Ellen og hendes mor blev ikke spurgt«)[980] is passed on to Ellen's daughter Kirsten (»Kirsten var opdraget til at være hjælpeløs«),[981] while the widowed Ellen eventually becomes the Ellen Marsvin known to history – a coldblooded businesswoman,[982] who is independent and liberated from all male dominance. She acquires wealth and status and when she meets King Christian IV, they talk to each other like two men (»og de gik op i deres fælles interesse, byggeriet, som to mandfolk«).[983] Like a man Ellen also settles the issue of her daughter's marriage. Hemmer Hansen's use of blunt language when referring to Kirsten Munk's morganatic betrothal to the King of Denmark resembles that of a business transaction: »En beskadiget adelsjomfru taber katastrofalt i værdi. [...] Forhandlingerne endte med kompromis. Et kontraktægteskab efter gammel dansk skik, hustruen åbent anerkendt, børnene legitime adelsbørn, men uden kongelig rang«.[984]

Only later, when Christian IV's marriage is already dissolved, Ellen realises that her daughter may have been unhappy in her marriage: »Meget var måske gået anderledes, hvis hun havde vidst, hvad Kirsten følte. Men måske havde Kirsten ikke følt noget? Bare været den unge velopdragne lydige adelige datter?«[985] Hemmer Hansen's work is thus the first to extensively put the affair of the hitherto

---

978 Ibid., p. 47.
979 Ibid.
980 Ibid.
981 Ibid., p. 44.
982 Cf. a comment by Godfred Hartmann underneath a portrait of Ellen Marsvin painted by Karel van Mander in 1648 and reproduced in Christian IV. af Danmark. *End lever jeg*, p. 98: »En snu og listig godssamler der havde mere sans for kvægdrift og afgrøder end for de børn som kongen betroede hende at opdrage. Hun købslår og handler – også med den datter der snart kom til at forbitre kongens liv«. See also Lisbeth Weitemeyer's Leonora Christina-biography, which primarily characterises Ellen Marsvin as »følelseskold« (Weitemeyer, Lisbeth. *Leonora Christina – Fra kongedatter til jammer*. Aarhus: Siesta, 2006, p. 27). Ellen Marsvin is known as one of the richest women in Danish history – hence her fame as cunning yet unempathetic tradeswoman.
983 Ibid., p. 49.
984 Ibid., p. 50f.
985 Ibid., p. 51.

demonised second wife of Christian IV into perspective; first, through the prelude depicting Kirsten Munk's female ancestors and their abuse by the hands of the men possessing them and second, through the depiction of Christian IV's own polygamy before,[986] during and after his liaison with Kirsten Munk, which leads his mother-in-law to the resigned conclusion that »[m]ænd kunne åbenbart ikke leve uden at have en at sprælle med i sengen«.[987]

Even though Hemmer Hansen leaves no doubt that political considerations had steered Christian IV's selection process regarding his future sons-in-law,[988] Leonora's marriage compares in no way to those portrayed above. However, the curious titles of Hemmer Hansen's Leonora Christina-novels, *Den lykkelige hustru* and *Den trofaste hustru*, raise the question whether the authoress meant to betoken a pair of opposites with these titles, hence denoting a feminist reading of Leonora Christina's life, or whether they were rather meant to depict a complementary pair, hence commending the protagonist's successful marriage. Unfortunately, the absence of a sequel to *Den trofaste hustru* hinders a definitive conclusion in this regard. Yet, there are indicators in the first two novels – starting with Corfitz Ulfeldt's plan for his future wife reproduced above – countenancing a feminist reading of Hemmer Hansen's text and hence a critical assessment of Leonora Christina's usually glorified marriage.

The title of the chapter containing the account of Leonora's betrothal to Corfitz Ulfeldt – 'Rosmarin', indicating a hapless love story to readers familiar with Leonora Christina's life narratives – augurs badly. Ever since the death of her first love Maurits and the habit at that time to decorate the bodies of the deceased with rosemary, Leonora Christina could not tolerate the herb's smell.[989] When Corfitz uses rosemary ointment on his wedding day in order to heal his STD-induced cnemial

---

986 This feature is absent from Herta J. Enevoldsen's novel *Kongedatteren Leonora Christina*, which provides a first glimpse at Kirsten Munk's situation, yet does not pursue this topic any further. In this text, Christian IV is a perfectly monogamous and obliging husband, whereas Hemmer Hansen provides her readers with a very detailed and suggestive register of births occurring in the royal household. In the year 1611, the former King of Denmark received two children within two days from two different women, one of them being his first wife Anne Cathrine of Brandenburg. Furthermore, his first child with Vibeke Kruse was born only three months after his final separation from Kirsten Munk in 1630. The language Hemmer Hansen uses to recount this chronology betrays sympathy with the repudiated wife: »Dagen efter at kongen havde tilladt – eller bedt – Kirsten gå fanden i vold, var Vibeke Kruse rykket ind i hendes værelser på Frederiksborg. Tre måneder efter havde hun sat en til af kongens små Gyldenløver i verden, og i fjor var der kommet en datter« (ibid., p. 55). Hemmer Hansen's portrayal of Christian IV is harmless compared to some of the other men in the novel, yet his attitude towards his women attests to a deep-rooted egotism: »Hvad disse kvinder selv havde følt og tænkt, havde han vel ikke nogen sinde spekuleret over« (ibid., p. 265).

987 Ibid., p. 55.

988 Ibid., p. 29.

989 Cf. *Leonora Christina Grevinde Ulfeldts Franske Levnedsskildring*, p. 1c (Translation p. 5).

wound,[990] his first advance fails as his wife reacts with apparent terror. Yet in this night, Corfitz proves himself to be a chilvalric and sensitive husband, as he listens to his wife's reasons for her behaviour and decides to postpone the consummation of the marriage. He is, however, lying about the origin of his wound, as he claims to have been injured in battle a long time ago.

After this unconsummated and hence successful wedding night, the couple rejoices in a prosperous marital life. Curiously, it is thus Corfitz Ulfeldt, who uncovers the secret to a happy marriage:

> Han fandt hurtigt ud af, at han havde ret, da han bedømte hende til at være både varm og sanselig, og han tænkte med nogen foragt på grobrianen von Pentz [Leonora (Christina)'s brother-in-law] og andre af hans ret almindelige slags. De snød først og fremmest sig selv og opnåede det, de havde fortjent – at komme til at trækkes med enten en kuet og kedsommelig hustru eller en rappenskralde resten af hendes liv.[991]

Corfitz's wife, on the other hand, shall not become intimidated and dull like Leonora's great-grandmother, and neither a shrew like her mother and her sister Sofie. Like Ebbe Kløvedal Reich, Eva Hemmer Hansen provides a feminist reading of Leonora Christina's life story and her marriage. Yet, while Reich's model is based on a common sexualisation of men and women in order to reach unity, Hemmer Hansen portrays an alternative marriage model disengaged from the demand of female submission and its sexual implementation. Both Leonora and Ulfeldt benefit from their harmonic marriage, based on congeniality rather than sexuality. Even Ulfeldt's shinbone, a reminder of his rampant bachelorhood, recovers as Leonora convinces her husband to continue using rosemary ointment. Hence, both of their wounds heal.

Compared to most of the other men portrayed in Hemmer Hansen's novel, Corfitz Ulfeldt seems thus like an ideal husband. Analogous to historiography's reports of Leonora Christina's marriage being the happiest among Kirsten Munk's children, Leonora, too, finds no flaw in her husband and can only pity her siblings. Yet as was the case with the elephant princess, this perfection exists only in comparison to his immediate surroundings. As indicated prior to their marriage, Corfitz's intention was to mould his wife according to his taste and needs. He did so in terms of her cultural taste (»Et par romaner af dem, Corfitz havde lært hende at le ad som tåbe-

---

990 The actual cause of this chronic wound is unknown, yet Hemmer Hansen opted for the popular theory that it may have been a souvenir of Ulfeldt's time in Paris (cf. Hemmer Hansen, Eva. *Den lykkelige hustru*, pp. 173 and 180).

991 Ibid., p. 192.

lige [...]«),⁹⁹² her attitude towards motherhood (»Leonora elskede sine børn og tog sig omhyggeligt af dem, fordi Corfitz ventede det af hende«)⁹⁹³ and regarding her position in the family: when Leonora tries to mediate between her increasingly offensive father and her husband, Corfitz orders her to keep aloof.⁹⁹⁴

Spousal conflict, instead of its joys, thus turns into a central topic of *Den trofaste hustru*, and so does Leonora herself. As in many representatives of Leonora Christina-literature, Leonora had been a secondary, at times even tertiary character in *Den lykkelige hustru* and it seems as if this secondariness had been the reason for her happiness and popularity. *Den lykkelige hustru* portrays the unhappy lives of the women surrounding Christian IV, the disagreements within the family and the calamities that have befallen Denmark's rural population during and after wartime. In the midst of all this affliction, Leonora seems almost like an anachronism, due to her lack of grievances. As stated in her French autobiography (see above), her husband treated her like a beau, not like a spouse, which raised the envy of the women surrounding her. She perceived herself as the lucky exception from the norm, as marriages were not primarily meant to be happy. Analogous to Leonora Christina's statement, but also to Enevoldsen's Leonora Christina-novels, Hemmer Hansen's account, too, initially portrays Leonora as a happy fool, as explicitly expressed by her sister Christiane, who takes on the role of the omniscient observer: »›De er så lykkelige – Corfitz og Leonora,‹ sukkede Hedvig hen for sig. [...] ›Den ene af dem gør altid, som den anden vil.‹ ›Leonora gør altid, som Corfitz vil,‹ rettede Christiane hende. ›Leonora er et fæ – på den måde.‹«.⁹⁹⁵

Leonora's contentment is also the reason for her father's preference for his second eldest daughter. His wife Kirsten Munk and Gustav Adolf of Sweden had both shown the King of Denmark that he was a failure, in martial as well as in private matters. His children's misery had had the same effect: »Han vidste måske, at nogen af dem var ulykkelige, og at nogen af dem var mislykkede. Men han ville helst ikke erkende det. [...] Men han kunne elske Leonora – mere og mere, fordi hun var lykkelig, harmonisk, smuk, en succes og taknemlig imod ham«.⁹⁹⁶

Throughout *Den lykkelige hustru*, Leonora's role is thus that of the content and thankful wife and daughter and as such, she remains a character of secondary importance – both to the reader as well as within the semi-fictive world created by

---

992 Ibid., p. 219.
993 Cf. ibid., p. 143.
994 Hemmer Hansen, Eva. *Den trofaste hustru: Leonora Christine II*. Copenhagen: Hernov, 1983, p. 55.
995 Hemmer Hansen, Eva. *Den lykkelige hustru*, p. 237.
996 Ibid., p. 266.

Hemmer Hansen. Leonora is, however, becoming an increasingly dominant part of the sequel's narrative, *Den trofaste hustru*, which displays increased dispute in her marriage. All the while, her husband exhibits trouble accepting Leonora's gradual emancipation.[997] Upon their return from a long diplomatic journey across Europe, Corfitz still portrays his wife as the happy fool she used to be in *Den lykkelige hustru*, yet his motives are somewhat questionable: »›Lykkelige Leonora,‹ sagde Corfitz. ›Hun tog komedien for virkelighed.‹ Der var en klang i hans stemme, som fik Sivert Urne til at sende ham et hastigt skjult sideblik. Var Corfitz en smule skinsyg på den virak, der var blevet Leonora til del?«[998]

Leonora's process of becoming more self-determined complements that of her husband's mental and physical weakening. When the conflict between the Ulfeldts and the royal couple turns increasingly apparent, Leonora expects her husband to act; but instead, he withdraws and becomes more and more dependent on his wife.[999]

After Christian IV's death, the task of protecting Leonora falls upon her husband, Corfitz Ulfeldt. When the couple flees from Denmark after the inconclusive resolution of the Dina affair, Leonora repeats her father's words: »›Jeg har sat dig så højt, at ingen kan røre dig,‹ citerede Leonora stille og bittert sin fars ord, mens hun så ind mod landet, der gled forbi. Corfitz lagde armen om hende. ›*Jeg* sætter dig så højt, at ingen får lov at røre dig,‹ sagde han«.[1000] The historically aware reader knows that neither Corfitz nor Christian IV are able to fulfill their promise of protecting Leonora Christina. As is the case with the elephant princess Fatima, Leonora's elevated position is an illusion, a superficiality accorded to her by her surroundings. Like this elephant, who is after all nothing but a pretty, decorated animal trained to perform stunts, Leonora will fall together with the men meant to grant her immunity. Yet towards the end of her life, Leonora will perform the greatest stunt in her repertoire, i.e. becoming an independent woman outlasting everybody in the possession of power.

---

997 This emancipation is not synonymous with a process of growing apart, as portrayed in Ebbe Kløvedal Reich's *Rejsen til Messias*. In fact, Leonora reverses the typical gender roles by becoming increasingly protective towards her husband, as noticed by a friend: »Det havde altid moret ham en smule, at hun lyste af beundring, når hun så på Corfitz. Nu greb han hende i at kaste stjålne, ængstelige blikke på ham ind imellem. Leonora var bekymret for sin mand. Beskyttende. Leonora beskyttende overfor sin Corfitz?« (Hemmer Hansen, Eva. *Den trofaste hustru*, p. 21).

998 Ibid., p. 49.
999 Ibid., p. 81.
1000 Ibid., p. 107.

Like her grandmother Ellen Marsvin had done before – taking on the clothing and thus the role of a man[1001] – Leonora subsequently discards her unpractical, feminine clothes during her journey to Sweden and dresses in men's tailoring instead, despite the wry looks her new appearance attracts: »Corfitz fandt det hverken helt passende eller særlig klædeligt. Men forholdet mellem ham og hans hustru havde langsomt forandret sig«.[1002] In line with her coarse disguise, she hurls herself into typical adventures of men such as sleeping in a sailor's inn, all the while ignoring her husband's moaning. At the same time, Corfitz's flagging health and mind arouse her protective instinct. By and by, Leonora, formerly the King's and her husband's protegée, adopts the mindset of her husband's guardian: »Men Sofie Amalie skulle nu ikke komme godt fra dette her, og ingen havde ret til at miskende og forfølge hendes mand«.[1003]

Part of this process are Leonora's efforts to reach her husband's educational level. During their exile in Swedish Pomerania, she is eager to learn about her husband's world and to become a part of it. When Corfitz thus composes an apologia regarding the Dina affair, she is partaking and engrossed in his defense.[1004] Despite her husband's complaints, Leonora becomes increasingly active and decisive. Notwithstanding Leonora Christina's own statement that her husband had convinced her to return to Denmark in 1657 to try to initiate a dialogue with Frederik III and to collect some debts,[1005] Hemmer Hansen's Leonora is the driving force behind such and similar undertakings, while Corfitz is portrayed as the worrying husband left behind at home.[1006] This development is finalised by Corfitz's behaviour during the second half of *Den trofaste hustru*. During their arrest on Bornholm, Leonora becomes increasingly argumentative while her husband comes to terms with his new fate and role:

1001 As a self-sufficient widow and estate owner, Ellen Marsvin soon takes on the habit of inspecting all of her estates in practical clothing: »Fru Ellen traskede en tur rundt omkring herregården i sine store mandfolkestøvler og sine korte, solide bekvemme skørter, sådan som hun færdedes til daglig hjemme på sine egne ejendomme« (Hemmer Hansen, Eva. *Den lykkelige hustru*, p. 57).
1002 Hemmer Hansen, Eva. *Den trofaste hustru*, p. 111.
1003 Ibid.
1004 Ibid., p. 114.
1005 *Leonora Christina Grevinde Ulfeldts Franske Levnedsskildring*, p. 6c (Translation p. 25).
1006 Hemmer Hansen, Eva. *Den trofaste hustru*, p. 133. In this account, the journey is dated 1656.

> Han sad med pen og blæk og papir og havde fyldt en del ark, men da hun trådte ind, sad han bare og stirrede tomt frem for sig. Han så lige straks på hende, som om han ikke kendte hende. Men så smilte ham [sic!] bedrøvet. »Frankrigs rige og Venezias skatte,«[1007] sagde han. »Jeg skulle ikke have været ulydig mod min hustru.«[1008]

A third novel on Leonora Christina is missing and the second novel, *Den trofaste hustru*, is considerably shorter than the first one and stops at a rather vacuous point of the narrative. Despite Luise Pihl's conviction that the novel and perhaps even the entire project had been finished (see Chapter 2.5.), I thus still find reason to believe that the work was meant to be a trilogy of which a substantial part was never finished. As demonstrated above, there are several indicators in the first two novels suggesting a development of their eponymous heroine from silent sufferer, much in the fashion of the deeply unhappy Vibeke Kruse,[1009] to an emancipated human being, which would culminate in the third part of the trilogy.

What Torben Weinreich thus criticises as being absent in Herta J. Enevoldsen's historical novels, is the principal theme of Eva Hemmer Hansen's work: the living conditions of – mostly married – women in the 17th century, with Leonora Christina serving as a case study. *Den lykkelige hustru*, whose bigger part depicts nearly everybody in detail *but* Leonora, still shows her as a happy and well-behaved wife, cherished but also educated by her husband. At the transition from *Den lykkelige hustru* to *Den trofaste hustru*, she gradually uses her newly acquired skills for her own emancipation's sake and grows to be an equal partner to her husband. As Corfitz and Leonora, as well as all other characters involved, are portrayed as victims of circumstances, the schemes which dominate many other literary representations of

---

1007 »Frankrigs rige og Venezias skatte« is Corfitz's pet name for his beloved wife – a reference to Martin Luther's statement, that he would not yield his wife, Katharina von Bora, in exchange for all of France or Venice (Luther, Martin. *Werke: Kritische Gesamtausgabe: Tischreden 1: Tischreden aus der ersten Hälfte der dreißiger Jahre.* Weimar: Hermann Böhlaus Nachfolger, 1912, no. 49, p. 17). Considering Luther's well-known misogyny (see, e.g., Luther, Martin. *Werke: Kritische Gesamtausgabe: Tischreden 4: Tischreden aus den Jahren 1538-1540.* Weimar: Hermann Böhlaus Nachfolger, 1916, no. 4081, p. 121, where Luther criticises the alleged chattiness of women because, in his view, it suits women much better to stammer and be virtually voiceless), however, this compliment is to be taken with a pinch of salt.

1008 Hemmer Hansen, Eva. *Den trofaste hustru*, p. 196.

1009 Cf. ibid., p. 42. Christian IV's mistress is one of the most tragic characters in Hemmer Hansen's Leonora Christina-novels. Despite fulfilling all wifely duties by being thankful and quiet, the King is unable to protect her and her children from the wrath of his higher-born offspring led by Leonora. Within minutes after her father's death, she orders the evacuation of the fatally ill Vibeke: »»Og det skal være på en af de vogne, de kører skarn og affald væk på,‹ sagde Leonora« (ibid., p. 63).

Leonora Christina's life are eclipsed as they would have distracted from the bigger picture, i.e. the life options of Leonora Christina and her female contemporaries.[1010]

Accordingly, the meaning and implications of a woman's marital life are thematised throughout the account. As stated by Leonora Christina herself[1011] her husband behaved towards her like a lover, not like a husband. The implications of this statement are illustrated by the plentiful unhappy marriages depicted in the novels, hence leading to the question of the nature of marital love, as finally posed by Leonora's level-headed sister Christiane: »»Hvad ligger det i, Leonora? Er det det med sengen? [...] Og du og jeg kunne lige så godt have fået en af dem. Hvem spurgte os?«»[1012] This final realisation – that Leonora Christina's happiness is pure coincidence and that this happy coincidence was initiated by ulterior motives, which never involved the bride's wishes – leads Christiane back to her initial question: How is something like marital love even possible when its preconditions were all wrong?

With Leonora's relationship to her husband being inverted and the nature of her marriage thusly being questioned, one would expect to find a complete renunciation of the protagonist's initial status as happy wife in the missing third novel. But what would have been the title of this missing third novel? The inversion of the first novel on Leonora Christina would, of course, suggest *Den ulykkelige hustru* for a title. Since the second novel ends with the Ulfeldts' redemption after their escape from Hammershus, a third novel would have mostly depicted Leonora Christina's years in the Blue Tower. In line with *Jammers Minde*, this third novel could thus also have been called *Den lidende hustru*. Yet, these suggestions do not quite capture the completion of the development process initiated in the first two novels. Despite her new role, Leonora continues to love her husband. His changed behaviour merely changes the type of love she feels for him,[1013] hence she will hardly turn into an *ulykkelig hustru* like some of her sisters. Leonora Christina's depiction as *lidende hustru* would neither complete the process exposed above, despite conforming to

---

1010 Accordingly, it is of no relevance to the account that in the process of acquiring knowledge about her husband's professional environment, Leonora only learns about her husband's perspective. Hemmer Hansen's Corfitz is a decent enough man and statesman, hence the question whether his and his wife's fall from grace in Denmark was self-inflicted is of secondary importance and overshadowed by the central topic of Leonora's emancipation.

1011 See quotation at the beginning of the chapter.

1012 Hemmer Hansen, Eva. *Den trofaste hustru*, p. 163.

1013 Cf. ibid., p. 174: »For første gang i deres næsten et kvart århundrede lange, lykkelige ægteskab begyndte hun somme tider at se på hans planer og ideer udefra i stedet for bare at beundre dem, støtte dem og opmuntre dem. Det var jo, som om Corfitz somme tider ikke kunne huske det i dag, som han lige havde sagt i går. Havde fjenderne og misunderne endelig fået drevet hendes Corfitz ud i rådvildhed?« As Corfitz – the man who formerly protected her and nurtured her mind – gradually loses his mind, Leonora becomes more nurturing and protective towards her husband. The marital love is thus still very much present, only its implementation has changed.

her self-portrayal in *Jammers Minde*. The predominant topics of Leonora Christina's own writings and of most of the subsequent Leonora Christina-literature – the schemes, Leonora Christina's chosenness and the envy of others – are practically eliminated from Hemmer Hansen's account; especially the second topic is rendered impossible due to the randomness of Leonora's happiness. Eva Hemmer Hansen created her very own reading of Leonora Christina's life, mostly based on the few instances in Leonora Christina's writings in which she renders an insight into her marital life. Thus, I suggest a third novel would have carried the title *Den emanciperede hustru eller kvinden*.

2.5.3. Birgithe Kosovic: *Leonora Christina* (2012) – The Ambitious Manipulator

> Men endeligen haffuer tilskyndende Aarsager mig dreffuen, icke alleeneste min Iammer at ihuekomme, men den endoc vdi Pennen att forfatte, oc eder mine kiære Børn att Tilskriffue; […] Den anden tilskyndende Aarsage er, den Trøst ded Eder mine Kiære Børn wil were, att I formedelst denne Iammers-Minde forsickris, att ieg vskyldeligen Liider, att mig icke ringeste sag er tillagt, oc att ieg intet er bleffuen Beskylt, for huilcket I mine Kiære Børn tør Bluis oc Øynene skammeligen nederslaa[.]
>
> (*Jammers Minde*, p. 2* and 4*)

In 2012, the publishing house Alfabeta, whose works are dedicated to the instruction of adult students of the Danish language and Danish adults with reading difficulties or poor education, issued three new items of its so-called Blue series (*Blå serie*) on outstanding individuals known from Danish history. These three historical novels engage in the life stories of Countess Danner (the morganatic wife of King Frederik VII of Denmark), the writer Karen Blixen and Leonora Christina. As announced on Alfabeta's web site, these three »stærke kvinder« are presented »i deres kompromisløse favntag med livet. Samtidig giver romanerne et spændende indblik i særlige historiske epoker i danmarkshistorien«.[1014]

The exact meaning of Leonora Christina's intransigence (»kompromisløse favntag i livet«) – a word rarely used to characterise the self-sacrificing wife of Corfitz Ulfeldt – is explained by a short description of the novel provided online:

1014 http://www.alfabetaforlag.dk/butik?c=Catalog&category=5279

Leonora Christina kunne have undgået landsforvisning og fjendskab med sin bror, kongen, hvis hun ikke havde insisteret på sin ret til den danske trone. Hun kunne måske have undgået 22 års fængsel, hvis hun havde tilstået at være medskyldig i sin mands forræderi. Men sådan en kvinde var Leonora Christina ikke. Hun var kongedatter, og hun holdt hovedet højt, hvad enten hun førte krig mod Danmark, var på flugt eller i fangenskab.[1015]

For the reader unfamiliar with this chapter of Denmark's history, Leonora Christina is thus presented as a pretender to the throne of Denmark, as an accomplice – basically as a traitor. The potential educational value of this novel[1016] thus seems to be of a less didactic, moral kind. Instead, the novel's main intent seems to be of an informational nature, as it purposes to familiarise its readers with a fascinating character representative of a peculiar chapter in Danish history.

The opening chapter's title, 'Horeunger', a reference to historical reports stating that Kirsten Munk had occasionally called her children 'bastards',[1017] substantiates the impression that the novel's main intent is to captivate even a weak reader's attention, hence facilitating the learning process. The disruption of the usually employed chronological portrayal of events serves to intensify the reader's curiosity, as the account does not commence with Leonora Christina's carefree childhood, her achievements in school, or her glorious father. In the fashion of a cine film, the first scene depicts the adult Leonora[1018] in her dark prison cell, reminding herself not to be afraid: »Ikke at være bange. Det vigtigste i livet er ikke at være bange. [...] Det havde hun lært at holde op med at være allerede som barn«.[1019]

Leonora's childhood had provided plenty of elements of which to be scared. The process of de-mystification started by H. F. Ewald has now reached a preliminary

---

1015 http://www.alfabetaforlag.dk/butik?c=Item&category=5279&item=29147

1016 The main target group of the Alfabeta publishing company are adults: international students of the Danish language, immigrants, and Danish or non-Danish adults with restricted literacy. Alfabeta's blue series can, however, also be used for supplementary reading in school. While the main target group of Birgithe Kosovic's *Leonora Christina* is thus not children, the novel's educational context still calls for a correspondent reading of the text. Furthermore, the novel's potential as crossover fiction is to be taken into account. To children (and international adults) it is the fast-paced and thrilling account of a villain receiving her punishment, while the open ending maintains the reader's curiosity beyond the written story. Yet to Danish adults the name »Leonora Christina« may evoke memories of a historical character whose story they have heard recounted in an entirely different manner. While children can thus enjoy the adventurous plot, adults may indulge in the striking discrepancies between Kosovic's *Leonora Christina* and a parallel story.

1017 Cf. Birket Smith, Sophus. *Leonora Christina Grevinde Ulfeldts Historie 1*, p. 17.

1018 In the present chapter, »Leonora« specifically refers to the character in Birgithe Kosovic's novel, particularly when referring to passages that do not correspond to historical events, whereas »Leonora Christina« refers to the historical person or other literary presentations of this character.

1019 Kosovic, Birgithe. *Leonora Christina*. Copenhagen: Alfabeta, 2012, p. 5.

climax, as every aspect of Leonora Christina's childhood is blemished. The former fairy-tale castle Frederiksborg is now a haunted house,[1020] her mother – previously swept under the carpet but now an abusive fury – forces her presence upon the frightened flock of children, and the royal father, a hopeless alcoholic, is now a snoring animal: »Hendes far skræmte hende kun, når han var 'mærkelig'. Det var han, når han lå og snorkede som en drage eller et vildt dyr over sit skrivebord, eller når han var faldet ned ad trapperne og lå og grinte, selv om han havde slået sig og ikke kunne rejse sig«.[1021]

Kosovic's Leonora is a traumatised child, who subsequently, out of escapist motives, creates the fairy-tale of her own life:

> Men selv om hun kunne være bange for sin far, følte hun altid, at han elskede hende – måske var hun endda hans udvalgte blandt alle hans børn? Det spurgte hun sig selv om så mange gange, at hun til sidst blev overbevist om, at det var sådan, det var: Hendes far elskede hende højest.[1022]

As Leonora reinterprets her life in hindsight, her written memories are in turn challenged by Kosovic's own reinterpretation of her protagonist's life. This interpretation resembles that of Bodil Wamberg, as the topic of Leonora's own royal ambitions is gradually introduced:

> Hun ville gøre ham [her father] glad igen, og det lykkedes, det tvivlede hun aldrig på. Hun tvivlede heller aldrig på, at han altid elskede hende højere end nogen af alle hendes mange andre søskende. Hun var også den af alle hans børn, der havde elsket ham højest. Faktisk havde de aldrig elsket deres far som far eller menneske; kun som en konge, der en dag ville give tronen videre til en af dem.[1023]

Already as a child, Leonora sees her father as her link to the throne of Denmark and as his (favourite) descendant, she sees herself as his natural successor. Her marriage to Corfitz, however, does not constitute a relevant step in this plan. When the two future spouses meet for the first time, she sees her own future as Queen of Denmark

---

1020 Ibid., p. 6: »Men siden hun var lille, havde slottet skræmt hende: de store, rungende sale; de tomme rustninger, som raslede, når man gik forbi. [...] Hun lærte sig selv ikke at se væk fra malerierne med ansigterne af hendes døde forfædre, der stirrede efter hende, men at se tilbage på dem, som om det var dem, der skulle være bange for hende. Men der var én, hun aldrig lærte at holde op med at frygte – og det var hendes mor«.
1021 Ibid., p. 8.
1022 Ibid., p. 9.
1023 Ibid., p. 13.

as already sealed while Corfitz is excluded from this part of the plan, but constitutes a mere expansion of Queen Leonora's territory: »En dag ville hun blive Danmarks dronning – og også denne kammerjunkers dronning«.[1024] Her implied plan is to outperform her future husband, in this chapter ('Leonoras konge') consistently referred to as *kammerjunker*, and to become his Queen, thus *his* superior. Yet, the chapter's title indicates that her plan will fail.

Thus, Kosovic's text abandons most of the previous Leonora Christina-literature, which had either shown both spouses as victims or at least Leonora Christina as collateral damage to her husband's ambitions. Kosovic switches these roles by showing only Leonora scheming and plotting, while Corfitz is still not part of her plans: »Imens planlagde Leonora, hvordan hun – og ikke Frederik – skulle overtage tronen efter deres fars død«.[1025] However, Leonora fails to prove the legitimacy of her birth and status before the arrival of the actual heir apparent, Frederik.

The account proceeds quickly; the next chapter depicts the Ulfeldt couple already 'I Stockholm' and subsequently partaking in the historic Swedish march across the frozen Belts in the winter of 1658, and especially Leonora is enthusiastic about the prospect of conquering Denmark.[1026] Her plan to become the Queen of Denmark, which never explicitly includes Corfitz, advances the plot, whereas there is no mention of Corfitz's ambitions. His aspirations are, of course, implicit, yet his plan to wrest the throne from Frederik seems like a conciliatory promise to his demanding wife rather than a choice of his own: »Da de kom hjem, tog Corfitz hendes hand og sagde: 'Han kommer til at betale alt det, han har lånt, tilbage. Ikke kun pengene. Også tronen'«[1027].

1024 Ibid., p. 16.

1025 Ibid., p. 18. This is an unusually harsh portrayal of Leonora Christina, as it indicates that she may have looked forward to her father's death. It is, however, reflective of a rumour spread by Leonora Christina's contemporaries according to which she and her husband may have poisoned Christian IV. The historian Benito Scocozza – a stern critic of the Ulfeldt couple and their peers – alludes to these allegations, which have been raised in the course of the questioning of Otto Sperling the Elder upon his arrival in the Blue Tower (Scocozza, Benito. *Christian 4.* Copenhagen: Politikens Forlag, 1988 (1987), p. 265), and concludes that these accusations are not as absurd as most writers and scholars seem to think and express through a complete disregard of these rumours in their writings: »Det er vel mest sandsynligt, at kongen døde af sin mavesygdom, men det er ikke utænkeligt, at Ulfeldt'erne har hjulpet ham på vej, eftersom kongen jo ikke ligefrem frivilligt havde sat dem så urokkeligt fast. Det er da heller ikke besynderligt, at parrets fjender, som selv kendte til magtkampens mislige metoder, under forhøret af Sperling spurgte denne, ›om fru Leonora ikke hjerteligen havde glædet sig, da kongen var død?‹« (ibid., p. 266).

1026 Kosovic, Birgithe. *Leonora Christina*, p. 29.

1027 Ibid., p. 22. A similar view has been advanced by the historian Steffen Heiberg, who considered Leonora Christina a major driving force in the behaviour of her husband: »I sin fremturen blev Ulfeldt pisket frem af sin hustru« (Heiberg, Steffen. *Enhjørningen Corfitz Ulfeldt*, p. 92).

As had been the case in much of the 19th-century literature on Leonora Christina, Leonora's relationship to her husband now turns into something resembling a mother-child-relationship with her husband being entirely dependent on her. The major difference between this and previous accounts is, however, that this dependency is not the result of a depiction of Leonora as a motherly type, but rather of a portrayal of Corfitz as increasingly pathetic (another parallel between Kosovic's and Wamberg's presentation of Leonora Christina's life).[1028] The account following the Ulfeldts' exile in Sweden depicts Leonora as the active part, travelling, negotiating and scheming, while Corfitz is marked by inactivity imposed upon him by higher forces. In some instances, the higher force binding him to the bed is an inborn weakness, whereas in other instances, it is Leonora: »Leonora var ikke overrasket over hans sygdom. Sådan var det altid, når der var problemer: Så blev Corfitz syg, og så måtte hun passe godt på ham«.[1029] While Corfitz thus »hulkede ind mod væggen« and eventually becomes paralysed,[1030] Leonora takes action by travelling to Stockholm to talk to King Karl X Gustav. When the next calamity, i.e. the Swedish death sentence over Ulfeldt, strikes, Leonora decides to protect her husband from the harsh truth by concealing the actual verdict from him. Instead, she tells him that their fate was to be deported to Finland. This drastic departure from historical records and Leonora Christina's own writings allows the protagonist to prevail as the account's dominant actor, while Corfitz is suppressed further into the role of a minor. For example, when Leonora virtually grounds her husband when he asks to accompany her to Copenhagen to talk to Frederik III: »'Jeg vil med,' sagde Corfitz. 'Nej,' sagde hun bestemt. 'Det er for farligt for dig'«.[1031] In this instance, Leonora is the higher force overpowering her husband and forcing him into inactivity.

The turn occurs towards the end of the novel when Corfitz convinces his wife to travel to England to collect the debt owed to them by Charles II of England. Her arrest and deportation to Denmark follow. On her way to Copenhagen, where she receives her punishment, Leonora's character changes. Her ensuing reflections on life expose a new side of this hitherto unlikeable figure:

1028 Bodil Wamberg sees proof of Corfitz Ulfeldt's weakness in his tendency to become sick (or simulate an illness) whenever faced with a difficult situation. Even his face illustrates – in Wamberg's eyes – that he had been a weakling, as expressed in a caption provided underneath the reproduction of a portrait of Corfitz Ulfeldt preserved until this day in Frederiksborg Castle: »Den ukendte kunstner har formået at formidle et ansigtsudtryk, som selv på 300 års afstand appellerer stærkt med sine fortolkningsmuligheder. Er dette ikke en mand med en stor svaghed i sig? – Umiddelbart synes svagheden at være det fremherskende træk i dette fysiognomi« (Wamberg, Bodil. *Leonora Christina*, p. 89).

1029 Kosovic, Birgithe. *Leonora Christina*, p. 31.

1030 Ibid., p. 34.

1031 Ibid., p. 36.

Hun nægtede tårerne at komme frem, mens hun tænkte: »Hvor er det smertefuld stadig at være i verden, når man ved, at man skal tage afsked med den. Hvad er det, der gør, at vi elsker verden på den måde? Hvad er det, der gør, at vi kæmper for at blive i den, selv om alting er tabt?«[1032]

Unlike Louise Hegermann-Lindencrone's heroine, who is depicted taking leave of her sleeping children (see Chapter 2.3.1.), and unlike Adam Oehlenschläger's Eleonora, whose farewell is directed at her home country (see Chapter 2.3.2.), Birgithe Kosovic's protagonist is not primarily a citizen or a mother, but an individual bidding farewell to the world – perhaps an implication of the diversity of Kosovic's intended readership. This tribute to life offers a more conciliatory picture of this anti-heroine, just like the starting scene which showed her enduring her punishment and to which the account now returns. In this desolate situation, Leonora decides to write down her story in order to recall her own identity: »Med fjeren førte hun sodet på papiret – bogstaver blev formet og dannede de ord, der hjalp hende med at huske, hvem hun var«.[1033] And who is she? »Hun var kongedatter. Hendes værdighed var noget, som hun var født med. Den kunne ingen tage fra hende«.[1034]

Curiously, the following account does not render the content of *Jammers Minde* in order to illustrate Leonora Christina's laudable combat against desperation and lunacy during her imprisonment. Instead, it provides a metatext juxtaposing the infant's strategy of dealing with her fears with that of the adult Leonora: »Hun tvang sig selv til at se op mod det vindue, ganske ligesom hun engang havde tvunget sig selv til at gå langsomt forbid de tomme rustninger på Frederiksborg Slot og stirre tilbage på malerierne af alle de døde«.[1035] As in her childhood, Leonora projects her fears to the objects of selfsame misgivings as she presents herself as a despot's innocent and clueless victim. This process of re-remembering her sorrows leading to the composition of *Jammers Minde* involves the rewriting of her life story starring herself as Denmark's national heroine: »Alt, hvad hun havde gjort, det havde hun gjort for Danmark. Hun havde altid elsket Danmark – ved Gud, det havde hun!«[1036]

1032 Ibid., p. 52.
1033 Ibid., p. 62.
1034 Ibid., p. 58.
1035 Ibid., p. 60.
1036 Ibid., p. 61. Kosovic's depiction of Leonora Christina's own *re*interpretation of her life's story is remarkable in using a perception of Leonora Christina that was born in the 19th century, i.e. Leonora Christina as Denmark's national icon, but completely absent in *Jammers Minde* and the French autobiography. These works do not bespeak Denmark, neither as a home country, nor as a place connected to her beloved father. Leonora Christina's self-portrayal is rather that of a citizen of the (European) world.

This direct confrontation of Leonora Christina's self-portrayal with Kosovic's twisted re-reading emphasises the self-reflective, metafictional elements in the novel, hence highlighting the revisionist, innovative tendencies of this new type of historical novel. Kosovic's account is short and anything but subtle, but also representative of the currently predominant literary portrayal of Leonora Christina. She is ambitious and manipulative, but perhaps *because* of this negative depiction she has become such a popular figure in contemporary historical literature on famous Danish women. Both of these characteristics have allowed Leonora Christina to step out of her husband's shadow and to be portrayed as an individual driven by self-sufficient motives. This side of her character had been present and visible all along, in the form of *Jammers Minde*, a text ultimately dedicated to its author alone. While most authors preceding Kosovic have used *Jammers Minde* to supplement their own narrative, hence accentuating the value of its content, Kosovic completely excludes the narrative of *Jammers Minde* from her own while highlighting the value of its creational process, namely in the novel's postscript:

> I denne tekst, der er formet som et brev til hendes børn, fortæller hun om sit liv i Blåtårn og om sin uskyld. Sandsynligvis var hun ikke helt så uskyldig, som hun skrev. Men hun er respekteret for sin imponerende fortælling om at overleve med værdighed, når livet er sværest. Og hun er moderne og interessant for læsere i dag, fordi hun med sit selvportræt viser, hvordan et menneske selv kan skabe sin identitet.[1037]

Unlike Herta J. Enevoldsen and Eva Hemmer Hansen, Kosovic portrays a Leonora Christina that is in no way exemplary. Her only, but very explicit, commendation is directed at her protagonist's decision to become creative, thus recreating her life and creating a new identity for herself. Kosovic's metatext is thus a laudation of the creative process of writing and as such (and in line with Alfabeta's purpose of promoting reading among all ages), a very subtle invitation to the novel's readers to engage with this process, or at least its products.

1037 Ibid., p. 64.

2.6. A Chip off the Old Block: Denmark's Century of *Femmes Fatales*

> Den 12. Aug: dette Aar, fuldente ieg mit forretagende Werck; oc saa som miine Klat-Skriffter ware om alleslags Dydige Quindis Persohner, baade. Om Striidbare; Om Fornufftige Regentinner, Om Troefaste; Om Kyske; Om Gudfryctige; Om Dydige, Om Ulyckelige, oc Om Lærde oc Om Standhafftige.
>
> (*Jammers Minde*, p. 226)

As indicated above, the present chapter deals with the current trend of presenting Leonora Christina as a *femme fatale*. This thematic approach may seem alienating, as she is nowhere presented as a predatory temptress, which is probably the most common understanding of the term *femme fatale*.[1038] Yet, this analysis is not inspired by a purely sexual understanding of said term, but by its eclectic tendencies.[1039]

In her study on the *femme fatale* in Danish literature of the 19th and 20th century, Lise Præstgaard Andersen identifies this figure by means of the following characteristics:

> Der indgår jo så modsætningsfyldte elementer i hende som beregning og instinkt, høj bevidsthed og umiskendelig seksualitet, invitation og afvisning, dampende sex og dødelig stivnen – og vel at mærke uden at disse elementer kan blande sig eller eksistere fredeligt side om side.[1040]

Despite the current trend of sexualising the former saint Leonora Christina, she is certainly not a succubus like the one described above. However, there *is* a dichotomy inherent to her character and life story that allowed for a portrayal as multifaceted as presented in the present study. One case in point is Leonora Christina's self-portrayal through the interplay of her own writings. *Hæltinners Pryd*, for example, though not an autobiography but a collection of biographical texts on, among other things, »battlesome, prudent, and faithful« female rulers is commonly

---

1038 See, for example, Hilmes, Carola. *Die Femme fatale: Ein Weiblichkeitstypus in der nachromantischen Literatur*. Stuttgart: Metzler, 1990, p. 10, which describes the typical *femme fatale* as a young woman whose erotic appeal leads to the partial or complete destruction of a man.
1039 Lise Præstgaard Andersen furthermore distinguishes diverse types of the *femme fatale*, some of which are fatal – and hence captivating – due to their (feigned or factual) unavailability to their idoliser's desires. See Præstgaard Andersen, Lise. *Sorte damer: Studier i femme fatale-motivet i dansk digtning fra romantik til århundredskifte*. Copenhagen: Gyldendal, 1990, p. 18ff. Hence, negated sexuality is also a typical trait of the fatal woman.
1040 Ibid., p. 19.

regarded as a hidden third self-portrayal of its authoress.[1041] In turn, her repeated self-portrayal (yet always with a different angle and approach) offered subsequent writers multifarious ways to present Leonora Christina. In the literary presentations of Leonora Christina presented above, she is a demonic dancer, a national heroine, a mother, a saint, a role model, and a Machiavellian criminal. This variety leaves »dobbelthed«[1042] as the one permanent and defining characteristic of Leonora Christina – and the *femme fatale*:

> Den traditionelle Madonna-luder-spaltning er her indbygget i *samme* kvinde. Med det resultat, at hendes tiltrækningskraft ikke beror på, at hun enten er den tilbedelsesværdige og ophøjede renhed eller den altopslugende lyst. Hun er begge dele på én gang. Og derfor dobbelt så attråværdig. Den principielt uforenelige sammenstilling af raffineret bevidsthed og ren sanselighed gør hende både indladende og afvisende og således låst inde i sig selv.[1043]

Due to this twofold characterisation of the *femme fatale* it has been possible for writers and artists of the past century to see and utilise her both as an incarnation of men's fear of women, which usually results in a portrayal of toxic and destructive female characters, but also as a symbol of female empowerment.[1044] Evidently, those are two antithetic tendencies, but the same development can be detected upon following the appearance of Leonora Christina in Danish literature.[1045] Here, she has gradually been turned into an absolutely detestable character, an elitist and self-righteous aristocrat. However, this recent development has not in the least derogated

---

1041 Cf. Aasen, Elisabeth. 'Grevinnen i fangetårnet', p. 133. See also Chapter 1.1.3. Sven Holm's drama, which will be discussed in Chapter 2.6.1., thematises the variety of Leonora Christina's self-portrayals, even though Holm does not exploit the topic in its full potential. His protagonist mentions *Hæltinners Pryd* (Holm, Sven. *Leonora. Tre scener for en heltinde*. Copenhagen: Rhodos, 1982, p. 95) and betokens a self-classification as yet another heroine (»Jeg har det vist som det anstår sig for en af de mindre heltinder«; ibid., p. 78).

1042 Præstgaard Andersen, Lise. *Sorte damer*, p. 108.

1043 Ibid., p. 19. See also Silke Binias, who after a short yet comprehensive review of the most central definitions of the *femme fatale* concludes that, in a nutshell, the *femme fatale* defies definition apart from one, rather un-defining, characteristic: ambivalence (Binias, Silke. *Symbol and Symptom: The Femme Fatale in English Poetry of the 19th Century and Feminist Criticism*. Heidelberg: Universitätsverlag Winter 2007 (Anglistische Forschungen 379), p. 38f).

1044 Cf. ibid., p. 18.

1045 Accordingly, Lise Præstgaard Andersen's description of Georg Brandes' »mørke dame« (as described in *Shakespeare II*) matches Leonora Christina's portrayal in current Danish literature: »Hun er nøjagtig, som hun skal være med al sin dobbelthed: ›skabt til at skjænke Lykke og Kval af fulde Hænder,‹ med evnen til at besnære på trods af al fornuft, det omskiftelige sind, et vist præg af luksus – ›aristokratisk Kvindelighed‹ – og hun er åndfuld, vittig og intelligent. Med andre ord: ånd, krop, elegance, sindrigt koketteri og grusomhed, forenet i én og samme kvinde« (Præstgaard Andersen, Lise. *Sorte damer*, p. 108).

her popularity as a literary character. On the contrary; current writers of Leonora Christina-literature, such as Maria Helleberg, are tirelessly attempting to illuminate her character from all possible angles in order to penetrate her mind ever deeper. This has resulted in a very ambivalent character portrayal which offers the reader an opportunity to both loathe and marvel Leonora Christina.

The current portrayal of Leonora Christina is thus not a complete renunciation of the 19th-century Madonna-like depictions, but rather their completion. The Madonna and the harlot respectively representing spirit (ånd) and flesh (krop), in earlier texts opposed through Leonora Christina and Dina, are now juxtaposed in one and the same woman.[1046] The target of this versatile woman is, however, in these instances not a languishing, fictive man, but the reader. Furthermore, the object of the reader's attention and fascination is no longer a monolithic character like the asexual, caring mother-type, the *femme fragile* preferred in the 19th century. The new Leonora Christina is multifarious, at times even enigmatic and dangerous and hence very different from the innocuous Madonna-type as, for example, portrayed by Adam Oehlenschläger.[1047]

Considering that the *femme fatale* is a character unifying several types of women within one body and mind,[1048] placing this particular chapter at the end of this part dealing with Danish literary portrayals of Leonora Christina[1049] proves to be a sound choice. More than three centuries of presenting Leonora Christina have demonstrated that a woman with a life story as volatile as hers can be depicted in all ways imaginable. Accordingly, some of the portrayals dealt with earlier contain one or more features of a *femme fatale*, while not explicitly depicting her as such. Ebbe Kløvedal Reich's Leonora, for instance, already exhibits traits of one variety of the *femme fatale*, i.e. Lilith (see Chapter 2.4.3.). In the 19th century – as well as

---

1046 Lise Præstgaard Andersen's illustration of C. G. Jung's positive and negative anima projections shows the same opposing confrontation of »Madonna« (positive, type I, mind) and »skøgen« (negative, type II, body). See ibid., p. 67.

1047 This is perhaps what Georg Brandes was deploring when he criticised Oehlenschläger's »gruelige«, »moderne, hysteriske, pedantiske Kvinde« (Brandes, Georg. 'Leonora Christina', p. 69), i.e. Eleonora in the drama *Dina*. Although most texts, both literary and historical, dealing with the Dina affair label Dina Vinhofvers as *skøge*, based on Lise Præstgaard Andersen's classification system, I would term Oehlenschläger's Dina as *hetære/kurtisane*: »Den elskværdige, åndfulde og sexede kvinde« (Præstgaard Andersen, Lise. *Sorte damer*, p. 49). Either way, her antithesis is Eleonora, the Madonna: »aseksuel, men moderligt elskende og kvindelig smuk« (ibid., p. 66).

1048 In this context it is important to note that Præstgaard Andersen insists that the *femme fatale* is ultimately only a fantasy created by and for men, even though it was readily adopted by many modern-era females. See ibid., p. 41ff.

1049 The subsequent chapter on international literary portrayals of Leonora Christina is merely based on the (non-Danish) nationality of authors dealing with Leonora Christina and not on any thematic intersections.

at present – Leonora Christina was and is mostly complimented for her unfading loyalty towards her husband. *Rejsen til Messias*, however, abandons this image by provoking an emotional distance between the spouses through the appearance of the protagonist Josef, hence suggesting a re-evaluation of Leonora Christina, not as the tame and self-sacrificing wife of a traitor, but as a disobedient and emancipated partner claiming equality, i.e. as a Lilith-type. Herta J. Enevoldsen's Leonora Christina, on the other hand, is an impeccable folk tale princess, but even she takes on attributes of the belligerent Diana – a type of *femme fatale* – with her pistols and her wild chase through Holstein until the Danish border. This part of Leonora Christina's French autobiography was adopted and amplified in the most vivid manner in *Kongedatteren Leonora Christina*. This variety of the *femme fatale* is fatal because she is armed and has hence entered a male domain.[1050] Another type of *femme fatale*, the witch, is portrayed as being dangerous and yet fascinating for the same reasons, i.e. for intruding into the (male) dominion of medicine or, more generally speaking, professional education.[1051] As it was a topic prevalent in 17th-century Denmark and especially under Christian IV's rule,[1052] witchcraft plays a central role in some of the literary works presented above. One case in point is Rolf Gjedsted's novel *Fordærvede kvinder* which, based on Leonora Christina's own exploitation of her fame as witch, associates Leonora Christina with witchcraft. It is important to note that all of the characteristics mentioned above are inspired by Leonora Christina's own statements, where they all serve to underline her own proto-feminist aspirations.

Hence, the texts discussed below constitute a summary as well as a culmination of the preceding ones. On the one hand, they combine some of the modes of representation implemented in previous centuries. Leonora Christina is no longer purely malicious (like the demon depicted in the 17th-century text 'Kirsten Munks Ballet'), nor is she a saint as seems to have been the common notion throughout much of the 19th century; the new Leonora Christina is portrayed with virtues as well as vices. On the other hand, though, the following texts represent the currently dominant perception of Leonora Christina as a woman with more vices than virtues, whose unscrupulous strength made her the object of everlasting respect. This modern-age

---

[1050] Præstgaard Andersen, Lise. *Sorte damer*, p. 33. Præstgaard Andersen mentions Ibsen's Hedda Gabler as an example of the Diana type.

[1051] Cf. ibid., p. 51. At the same time, Præstgaard Andersen disputes a connection between the medieval witches (the herb hags) and the sexually active and hence dangerous witch-types of later literature, such as the girl seducing the narrator of Umberto Eco's *Il nome della rosa* (ibid, p. 50).

[1052] Through her enlightened attitude towards witchcraft, Leonora Christina presents herself as rather progressive in *Jammers Minde*. However, her father persecuted alleged witches and was still bound to archaic ideas of jurisdiction, such as trial by fire. He even suggested to his mother-in-law Ellen Marsvin to undergo such a trial in order to prove her daughter's fidelity, even though at that time trials by ordeal were already considered humbug (Scocozza, Benito. *Christian 4.*, p. 235).

admiration for a true anti-heroine is new and clearly distinguishes the later wave of texts on Leonora Christina from the early ones, which utilised every means possible to exculpate their heroine and, preferably, also her husband.

In the following, four texts by three authors will be discussed and, as usual, one of them breaks ranks. In this case, it is Sven Holm's drama *Leonora Christina. Tre scener for en heltinde* (see Chapter 2.6.1.), which does in fact match my use of the term *femme fatale*, yet not the approach used by the two other texts, which present Leonora Christina together with her female contemporaries. At large, Holm's text is absolutely singular, as its outline and conclusion are entirely original. Unlike any other of the works presented in the present study, Holm's drama focuses on the years following its heroine's imprisonment in the Blue Tower, i.e. Leonora Christina's 'retirement' in Maribo. Yet, the past is regularly invoked through nightmares, a visit by her exiled son Leo Ulfeldt, but also through the protagonist's unwillingness to forgive and forget. Her meetings with her son Leo (the past) and the bishop and poet Thomas Kingo (the present) produce a portrayal of Leonora Christina as sinner and saint and thus, as a *femme fatale*.

However, Holm's text is not the only one with a new approach to this old subject matter. Helle Stangerup and Maria Helleberg, too, have turned their backs on the conventional biographical novel starring Leonora Christina. Like Rolf Gjedsted (see Chapter 2.3.3.), these two authors pursue the 20th century's interest in Leonora Christina's female contemporaries, hence dedicating their respective works to them alone.[1053]

A common feature of all four texts discussed below is their focus on the poetic characteristics of textiles, clothing and/or fashion. On the one hand, this understanding of the creative potential of fibre craft is a reverberation of the early modern age's relationship with materiality and, in particular, clothing:

> To understand the significance of clothes in the Renaissance, we need to undo our own social categories, in which subjects are prior to objects, wearers to what is worn. We need to understand the animatedness of clothes, their ability to »pick up« subjects, to mold and shape them both physically and socially, to constitute subjects through their power as material memories.[1054]

1053 While constituting a rather central force in the portrayed women's lives, the male characters in these novels have mere peripheral positions. Their characterisation solely accords with the way their respective women perceive them. Accordingly, the King in *Kongens kvinder*, i.e. Christian IV, is barely called by his birthname – he is simply »Han«.

1054 Jones, Ann Rosalind and Peter Stallybrass. *Renaissance Clothing and the Materials of Memory*. Cambridge University Press, 2000 (Cambridge Studies in Renaissance Literature and Culture 38), p. 2.

The identity-generating impact of clothing is a recurring theme in the following three chapters. Chapters 2.6.2. (Stangerup) and 2.6.3. (Helleberg) deal with a costume's suitability to convey, construct and deconstruct its bearer's personality. The texts discussed in these chapters seemingly use luxury garments exclusively as a way for female rivals to steal each other's thunder. As best illustrated by Helleberg's novels, however, clothing also constituted its early modern bearer's identity in assessing her value and position in a highly hierarchical and materialist society.[1055] In the modern world, descriptions of clothing, whether in literature, magazines or catalogues, assume a large portion of this connotative function of costume, which is why the French philosopher Roland Barthes has published an extensive analysis of the *Système de la mode*. In this work, Barthes contends that only the written garment has no practical or aesthetic function, but is pure denotation.[1056]

Sven Holm's text is seemingly not involved with questions of luxurious garment as a means of constructing identity. However, the protagonist of Holm's drama, Leonora, knits a metaphorical garment in order to influence the fate of her archenemy, i.e. the Queen whose life span had determined the length of Leonora's prison sentence. Leonora's – albeit only fictive – attempt to avenge her imprisonment is reminiscent of a long tradition of mythical females fibre-crafting fate, the Nordic version of which is the Norn. According to Old Norse mythology, these supernatural women determine the fate of every human being through explicitly female occupations, such as weaving or spinning; they are thus related to the Greek Parcae – three women controlling a human's thread of life. This pagan belief has long been a motive in Nordic literature. For instance, the Old Icelandic *Eyrbyggja saga*, whose oldest preserved manuscript dates back to the 13th century, depicts the sorcery of a wise woman named Katla[1057] through acts of weaving and spinning. Another epi-

---

1055 Cf. ibid., p. 11: »The sixteenth and seventeenth centuries […] are of particular interest in the history of clothing because clothes were still material mnemonics in metropolitan centers even as they were becoming the commodities upon which international capitalism was founded«.

1056 Barthes, Roland. *Système de la mode*. Paris: Éditions du Seuil, 1967, p. 18.

1057 Due to her knowledge, her age and her interest in the much younger Gunnlaug, Katla is what the 21st century would call a 'cougar'. In Lise Præstgaard Andersen's terminology, however, she is clearly a witch, i.e. a type of *femme fatale*: »Heksen«: den ældede, hærgede, depraverede kvinde, der dog besidder magisk (erotisk magt. Slægtskabet med middelalderens og renæssancens virkelige hekse er ikke ganske klart. Litterært: […] kvinden, der i og med sin stærke og krævende erotiske udstråling rummer en fare for mandens udødelige sjæl […]« (Præstgaard Andersen, Lise. *Sorte damer*, p. 49). In this context, it is important to note that Katla is indeed both feared and shunned by her neighbours, which does not prevent her from taking what she desires. After Gunnlaug's repeated refusal to spend the night with her, Katla attacks him by night and 'rides' him half to death (whereas Katla's son Oddr claims that Katla's rival Geirríðr »mun hafa riðit honum« (Anonymous. 'Eyrbyggja saga'. In *Eyrbyggja saga. Brands þáttr ǫrva. Eiríks saga rauða. Grœnlendinga saga. Grœnlendinga þáttr*, eds. Einar Ól Sveinsson and Matthías Þórðarson. Reykjavík: Íslenzka fornritafélag, 1957 (Íslenzk fornrit 4) p. 29)). In this instance, the account is as vague as the connotations are explicit.

sode in this saga involving another middle-aged woman with witch-like qualities, and a penchant for young men and weaving, results in a blood rain occasioning the death of a rival.[1058] As is the case in both episodes of the *Eyrbyggja saga*, Holm's Leonora, too, directs her 'magic' at a female rival with death in mind as the desired outcome.

The Norn is, however, only one of many examples of a cultural-historical connection of women's creative power through fibre craft, which soon developed into a metaphor of writing and memory. Starting with the mythological thread Ariadne used to guide Theseus through the labyrinth harbouring the dangerous Minotaur,[1059] and continuing with the tapestry crafted by the weaver Arachne which incurred the wrath of Athena,[1060] women's fibre craft has become a common metaphor for – often autobiographical – writing itself. In some instances, mythological craftswomen have even assumed an unequivocally virtuous fame, such as Odysseus' wife Penelope, an icon of female loyalty and virtue. She kept the suitors besieging her at bay during her husband's absence, with the promise of accepting one of them, once the shroud she was weaving for her father-in-law was finished. Every night, however, she would undo the work of the day, hence averting the otherwise inevitable fate of betraying her lost husband.[1061] Such positive associations with the originally female work of fibre craft were, however, inverted in the 18th century, when female textile workers were replaced by machines.[1062] A re-evaluation of fibre craft as a – positively connoted – metalanguage of femininity[1063] and as a symbol of emancipation and societal change (due to its involvement in the broader 'Do it yourself'- movement)[1064] has only occurred recently, i.e. within the so-called *craftista* (alternatively called *craftivista* – an amalgamation of 'crafting' and 'activism') movement.

1058 On the origin of the Norn-motive and its use in Old Icelandic literature, see Lionarons, Joyce Tally. 'Women's Work and Women's Magic as Literary Motifs in Icelandic Sagas'. In *Constructing Nations, Reconstructing Myth: Essays in Honour of T. A. Shippey*, ed. Andrew Wawn, with Graham Johnson and John Walter. Turnhout: Brepols, 2007 (Making the Middle Ages 9), pp. 301-317.

1059 In a review of Gilles Deleuzes' *Différence et Répétition* (1969), the French philosopher Michel Foucault refers to Ariadne's thread made of »l'identité, de la mémoire et de la reconnaissance« (Foucault, Michel. 'Ariane s'est pendue'. In Foucault, Michel. *Dits et Écrits 1954-1988 1: 1954-1969*, eds. Daniel Defert and François Ewald. Paris: Gallimard, 1994, p. 767), hence connecting the mythical thread to issues of identity, memory and recognition.

1060 Cf. Jones, Ann Rosalind and Peter Stallybrass. *Renaissance Clothing and the Materials of Memory*, p. 32.

1061 Cf. ibid., p. 110.

1062 Ibid., p. 106.

1063 Gaugele, Elke. 'Revolutionäre Strickerinnen, Textilaktivist_innen und die Militarisierung der Wolle. Handarbeit und Feminismus in der Moderne'. In *Craftista! Handarbeit als Aktivismus*, ed. Critical Crafting Circle. Mainz: Ventil, 2011, p. 18.

1064 Freiß, Lisbeth. 'Handarbeitsanleitungen als Massenmedien. D.I.Y und Weiblichkeit im 19. Jahrhundert'. In *Craftista! Handarbeit als Aktivismus*, ed. Critical Crafting Circle. Mainz: Ventil, 2011, p. 41.

However, due to her vengeful intentions, Holm's Leonora is a highly ambiguous craftswoman and hence a true *femme fatale*, but at the same time she emerges as a woman using her creative skills to craft her own life story. The protagonist of Holm's drama constitutes thus an archetype of a female writer.

Curiously, the four texts presented below largely avoid those years of Leonora Christina's life which made her famous, namely the almost twenty-two years she spent in the Blue Tower. Perhaps the respective authors took this unusual approach in order to not have to deal with the problematic gaps between Leonora Christina's life before, during and after prison. Literary works that attempt to present Leonora Christina's life in a comprehensive, chronicled manner, usually find themselves forced to comply with Leonora Christina's self-portrayal conveying predetermination and consistency. This approach worked quite well for Leonora Christina's own diverse texts (the French autobiography, *Jammers Minde* and *Hæltinners Pryd*), as they all convey the same message, yet always in an entirely new form, by portraying her own life from an ever new perspective. Yet for an author to try to blend the diverse phases of Leonora Christina's life into a single progressive account is a bold venture and the result is usually a bleak one – one case in point being Herta J. Enevoldsen's novels on Leonora Christina, which follow the biographical method.

Artistic deliberation aiming at originality as a reason for the choice of timeframe may only be surely attributed to Sven Holm as his plot is truly singular. Holm avoids Leonora Christina's tumultuous past and her famous incarceration altogether. Instead, he outlines solely those years of her life, in which most scholars and writers have showed little to no interest, i.e. the final years of her life spent in Maribo. Helle Stangerup, on the other hand, tackles her subject-matter from the conventional point of departure, i.e. starting the account with the protagonist's childhood yet proceeding only until her first day in the Blue Tower. The literary account ends with Leonora asking herself how long she would remain in this place, while a postscript educates potential historically unaware readers on what happened subsequently. In this instance, a further advance in the account was perhaps abandoned in order to avoid a marginalisation of the stories of the other female characters (Ellen Marsvin, Kirsten Munk, Vibeke Kruse and Sophie Amalie). Finally, Maria Helleberg's *Kongens kvinder* approaches the life of Leonora Christina in yet another way. As Helleberg had published several texts dealing – exclusively or partially – with Leonora Christina (one of them being the second text discussed in Chapter 2.6.3., the biographical novel *Leonora Christine*), *Kongens kvinder* deals with the King's infamous daughter only as a secondary character, while the other women that had dominated Christian IV's life – Ellen Marsvin, Kirsten Munk and Vibeke Kruse – come to the fore.

Hence, two of the three authors presented below do not deal exclusively with Leonora Christina, but also with her female contemporaries, whose equivocal reputations marked Denmark's 17th century as much as its most celebrated female representative. They, as much as Leonora Christina herself, are *femmes fatales*[1065] and the objective of the following three subchapters will thus be to examine how postmodern Danish literature processes Leonora Christina's ambiguous fame, to investigate if and how she is presented as setting herself apart from her family and surroundings, and finally to attempt to ascertain a reason for her lasting popularity despite the fact that her fame as national heroine has been abandoned many decades ago. All of these problem statements act on the assumption that Leonora Christina is a typical *femme fatale*, a woman that is defined through her ability to both allure and repulse. The alienating aspects of Leonora Christina's life and actions are blatant, hence the question remains why she still attracts so many readers and writers.

2.6.1. Sven Holm: *Leonora Christina. Tre scener for en heltinde* (1982) – The Writer or How to Craft the Story of Your Life

Men efftersom alle Ting haffuer saa som tuende Hancker huor wed ded skal hæffuis, som *Epictetus* siger; Den eene Hancke siger hand er Liiderlig, den anden V-liiderlig, oc staar ded vdi worris egen Willie, huilcken Hancke wii wille griibe til att tage fat wed, den Liiderlige eller den V-liiderlige; wil wii tage wed den Liiderlige, saa kand wii alt forbigaaende ihuor smerteligen oc Bedrøffueligen ded endoc werret haffuer, lige saa wel oc føyligere Glædeligen som Sørgeligen Ihuekomme. Huor fore ieg wed den Liiderligste Hancke wil fatte, oc vdi Iesu Naffn min Ihuekommelse igiennem løbe[.]

(*Jammers Minde*, p. 1)

1065 As already indicated in Chapter 2.5.2. on Eva Hemmer Hansen's Leonora Christina-novels, Ellen Marsvin enters the world of men by becoming a fully-fledged manorial lady and constructor, hence replacing her late husband instead of acquiring a new one. By thusly contesting men's position and privileges in her environment while remaining unmarried, she can be classified as the Diana-type of a *femme fatale*, who is characterised by strength, aggression and – most notably in this context – asexuality. Vibeke Kruse is at the other end of the spectrum. She is – depending on the portrayal – either a courtesan or a harlot, both of which are pure sexuality with varying degrees of intellect and kindness. Due to her noble parentage but somewhat dubious marriage to the King, Kirsten Munk is preconditioned to be classified as something in between her mother and her rival. She is – also depending on the portrayal – either a Cleopatra (sensual but cruel) or a witch (old and depraved, yet still magically intriguing). 19th-century portrayals were less merciful – Ewald and his contemporaries depicted Leonora Christina's mother either as a mermaid-type (the *havfrue* known from Danish folk ballads who draws men under water) or even as a harlot (pure body, no (detectable) mind). The classification of Sophie Amalie, however, is plain and rather consistent; she is a typical 'evil queen'. All the typifications used above follow Lise Præstgaard-Andersen's classification of the *femme fatale* (see Præstgaard Andersen, Lise. *Sorte damer*, p. 49).

Following Epictetus' stoic doctrine, Leonora Christina declares at the beginning of *Jammers Minde* that in retrospection of her past calamities she had nevertheless chosen to remain cheerful and to focus on the positive aspects of her fate. This statement is part of her autobiography's earliest section, which she commenced in prison, but revised in Maribo. While Leonora Christina's text preaches humility and frugality, it is no secret that the subtext betrays deeply rooted bitterness. Sven Holm's (*1940) drama *Leonora Christina* – three scenes dedicated to the *heltinde* Leonora Christina – is an extraction of this subtext. Its heroine[1066] is a cynical old woman who does not perceive her 'retirement' in Maribo as a compensation for, but rather as a modification of her punishment. Accordingly, and in line with Leonora Christina's statement reproduced above, the theme of Holm's drama is perspective. In a broader sense, however, *Leonora Christina* is concerned with the same topic as Birgithe Kosovic's novel of the same title, namely the opportunity that literature, and particularly autobiography, can provide to its authors as a means for rewriting their life and identity (see Chapter 2.5.3.) thereby – even retroactively – taking charge of their life and image.

A scene reproduced in *Jammers Minde* and central to Holm's play is the day of the in effigy-execution of Corfitz Ulfeldt in 1663, which – just like Leonora's dramatic reproduction of her life's story in Maribo (see below) – blurs the lines between reality and its re-enactment:

> Der til Middag bleff opluct oc quinden haffde wærret i Trappen, oc talt med Kudsken, kom hun ind, gik til Sengen til mig, stillede sig som forbaset. oc sagde med en hast, O. Jesus Frue der kommer de med eders Mand, Den tiiding forskræckede mig, hwilcket hun læt formerckede, thi i ded hun sagde ded, da reiste ieg mig i Sengen, oc racte min høyre Arm oc Haand vd, oc mæctede icke att tage den strax til mig igen; Ded haffwer maaskee fortrød hender i ded samme, thi ieg bleff saa siddendis oc talte icke et Ord, huorfor hun sagde; Min hierte Frue, ded er eders Mands Affwiißning; Derpaa sagde ieg Gud straffe eder[.]
>
> (*Jammers Minde*, p. 93)

In this scene, Leonora Christina finds herself deceived in a twofold way. First, her maid betrays her intentionally by omitting the information that it was not her actual husband, but merely a wax doll made to resemble Corfitz that was being led to its execution. Second, and perhaps worse, is the trick played by Leonora Christina's

---

1066 In the present chapter, »Leonora« specifically refers to the character in Sven Holm's drama, particularly when referring to passages that do not correspond to historical events, whereas »Leonora Christina« refers to the historical person.

own body on her mind that forces her to forget her physical separation from the site of the execution by instinctively reaching out for her husband. Yet eventually, as Leonora Christina reflects on the disparity between reality and its effigy, she finds consolation in this type of public punishment: »Ieg laae saa stille hen talte intet, slog mig med mine egne tancker, snart trøstede ieg mig, oc haabte att ded som war skeed wed Billeded war et tegn, att de icke kunde faa Manden« (*Jammers Minde*, p. 95). Holm's Leonora, however, is haunted by this memory, which she remembers throughout the play together with other traumatic experiences of her years in the Blue Tower. In these instances, she is not able to distinguish reality from its effigy.

The first of the three scenes shows the aged Countess lying in a bed in Maribo, as it is too cold to leave the bed on this chilly autumn day. She is still asleep, yet she talks to an absent auditor: »Ja. Ja. Nu kommer jeg ned til jer. Er I der? I har måske ventet på mig? Så kan vi begynde! (*Sætter sig op i sengen og stirrer sig omkring som om replikken var henvendt til tilskuerne* [...])«.[1067] Holm blurs the lines between external and internal communication, leaving the recipients wondering whether they are observing reality or whether the fiction has already commenced. The play begins with Leonora catching fleas and cracking them with her teeth:

> Det var en af de store i dag, Leonora. Fyldt til bristepunktet med æg. På vej ned i Maribo Klosters gulvskarn for at anlægge en ny slægt. Et dynasti. Udstyret til rejsen med dit personlige blod, Leonora. En kongelig loppeslægt ville det såmænd være blevet. Nå, ja, en adelig! Nu fik du sat en stopper for det. Tand for tand. Bid for bid.[1068]

Leonora's strange soliloquy continues up until a point which renders the question whether she is still talking about fleas highly pressing: »Alt det panser på sådan et lille dyr. Bitte små plader ligesom kobberpladerne på Børsens tag. En hel lille loppefæstning. Og så er det alligevel nok med et enkel bid. Færdig«.[1069] Yet, the confusion is soon dissolved when Leonora begins to reminisce about her husband's in effigy-execution:

> Det var en af de unge. På vej ud i verden, fuld af forhåbninger. Drømme. Smukke tanker inde i loppehjertet. Og så lige en sæk af *mit* blod på nakken. (*Spytter igen*.) Det gælder om at få det hele med. En samlet henrettelse. Jeg vil ikke have dem på hjul og stejle. Som den gang de splittede trædukken ad. Arme og ben, hænder og fødder, de pegede i

---

1067 Holm, Sven. *Leonora*, p. 7.
1068 Ibid., p. 8.
1069 Ibid.

hver sin retning. Og hovedet sad alene på en stage. Når de dør skal de stadigvæk hænge sammen. Ligge i kiste. Låget skal ligge hen over dem. Stilheden skal ligge hen over dem. Ellers glemmer du dem aldrig, Leonora.[1070]

Again a line is blurred, as Leonora blends past with present and reality with fantasy.[1071] The arbitrariness of her comparison (and thus her despair at the face of these, albeit fictive, memories) is further highlighted by the fact that the crude intrusion of reality into her dream, i.e. the unpoetic appearance of fleas, is not capable of waking her from her fantasy. Leonora simply takes the presence of fleas as an occasion to return to the past. However, Leonora does not acknowledge that it is herself who prolongs her pain by repeatedly invoking the past. As is the case with the fleas she had snatched the week before, the pest is long dead (long in due proportion to a flea's life expectancy), but Leonora still feels the itch:

> Et par gange om dagen vil de give sig til at klø. Jeg kender dem. Et par gange om dagen kommer jeg i tanke om netop de to lopper. Det er også et kunstart. Først om et par uger kan jeg glemme dem. En hel lille evighed. Loppen er et klogt dyr. Dens liv er kort. Men erindringen om den er lang.[1072]

In front of others, especially patriarchal authority figures such as the priest visiting Leonora on a regular basis, she needs to suppress her craving for reaction and the expression of her true feelings:[1073] »Jeg ville ikke klø mig lige op i præstens åsyn. Jeg måtte altså både høre på præsten og klø på halsen uden at svare igen. Han gik

---

1070 Ibid.

1071 In this context it is important to note that Leonora Christina had not been able to witness the effigy's execution with her own eyes, as the only window in her cell had been too high for her to see through. The castellan, however, had access to another window and reported the progress of the execution live. This event constitutes thus not a memory, but an imagination of a memory. Just as Holm's Leonora deals with the diverse images through which her life has been made known to the public – images over which she had not had any control until the publication of her works – Corfitz Ulfeldt's death is only known to Leonora Christina through images, i.e. scenes recounted to her by another person.

1072 Holm, Sven. *Leonora*, p. 9.

1073 Leonora is, however, highly critical of the institution represented by the priest and by Thomas Kingo, who visits Leonora in the third scene. When Kingo asks Leo to free his mother from the net he had cast over her before Kingo's arrival (see below), Leonora thanks her liberator, albeit with cynical undertones: »Tak for friheden, biskop. Det er første gang kirken har hjulpet mig i mit fangenskab« (ibid., p. 78). Kingo is also representative of the religious requirements and patterns to which the women of his time were subjected. Hence he does not acknowledge Leonora's likening of spousal adoration to Kingo's spiritual devotion: »Leonora: Både I og jeg tager Jesu legeme i vores mund og lader det indgå i vores krop. [...] Kingo: Det er et billede. Leonora (*eftertænksomt*): Et billede, ja. Men hvad er det da andet end et billede at Artemis væder sin elskede mands aske med sine tårer og optager den i sit legeme [a subsequently addressed mythical parallel to Leonora's own absorption of her husband's story into her own]? Kingo: Jeg vil ikke se ligheden« (ibid., p. 97).

klokken fire. Så kløede jeg mig«.[1074] Only later, in a double scene[1075] created by a play within the play (see below), Leonora is able to express her true feelings towards the enemies she could never face. Leonora is, however, overtly aggressive towards people she does not esteem highly enough. One of these people is Maribo's administrator (*amtsskriveren*):[1076]

> AMTSSKRIVEREN: Det er muligt grevinden ser ned på os der lever efter landets love og søger at gøre vores pligt over for kongen. Jeg er bange for at jeg skal forstå grevindens ord på den måde. LEONORA: Såh? AMTSSKRIVEREN: Jeg er villig til at ændre min opfattelse, hvis – LEONORA: Det skal De ikke. AMTSSKRIVEREN: Vil det sige at det er efter grevindens hjerte at følge andre love end kongens og fædrelandets? LEONORA: Ja.[1077]

Leonora has two antagonists in the play: the administrator with whom Leonora involves in constant conflict, and Jomfru Urne, Leonora's housekeeper, who is also a sort of confidante to her mistress.[1078] Both of these antagonists notice that Leonora lives by her own rules (see the administrator's insinuation above) and that she tends to create her own reality – hence Jomfru Urne's sarcastic comment in the first scene:»JOMFRU URNE: Det er godt at Gud har gjort grevinden så hellig«.[1079] Leonora herself is well aware that she gave herself the power to turn fiction into truth and wrong into right. When she tells her two companions, the housekeeper Jomfru Urne and the maid Agnete, about the story reproduced in Leonora Christina's French autobiography, which relates how she saved her teacher Alexander von Kückelsom

---

1074 Ibid., p. 9.
1075 My use of the term 'double scene' is inspired by Lars Lönnroth's study on *Den dubbla scenen* (even though Lönnroth deliberately excludes the dramatic genre from his corpus): »I alla de nu givna exemplen bygger den dramatiske illusionen på att det faktiskt finns en viss korrespondens mellan scenen för framförandet och den framförda textens fiktiva värld« (Lönnroth, Lars. *Den dubbla scenen: Muntlig diktning från Eddan til ABBA*. Stockholm: Bokförlaget Prisma, 1978, p. 9).
1076 This is a historical detail exploited by Holm. As reported by Sophus Birket Smith, the original administrator of Maribo had had reason enough for hostile feelings towards Leonora Christina as she had simply evicted him from his former office and home. Since the 17th century, a part of Maribo called Nykloster, a two-storey building lying North of the church of Maribo, had been the seat of Maribo's administrator. According to Birket Smith, King Christian V's original intention had been to leave only a part of this building to Leonora Christina. Yet, Leonora Christina was not pleased with the prospect of sharing a building with a stranger and the administrator was forced to clear his former home. See Birket Smith, Sophus. *Leonora Christina (Ulfeldt) på Maribo Kloster*, p. 11.
1077 Holm, Sven. *Leonora*, p. 28.
1078 Sophus Birket Smith's biographical work on Leonora Christina's final years – *Leonora Christina (Ulfeldt) på Maribo Kloster* – contains accounts by Leonora Christina's housekeeper in Maribo, Dorthea Sophie Urne, as well (Urne, Dorthea Sophie. 'Frøken Urnes Meddelelser om Leonora Christinas Liv på Maribo Kloster'. In Birket Smith, Sophus. *Leonora Christina (Ulfeldt) på Maribo Kloster: Et Bidrag til Oplysning om hendes sidste Leveår*. Copenhagen: Gyldendal, 1872, pp. 77-86).
1079 Holm, Sven. *Leonora*, p. 17.

from dismissal by lying about his achievements in the classroom she prides herself in her ability to figure as judge about the truth:

> Og eftersom han kun blev på slottet fordi jeg havde løjet, så forvandlede løgnen sig til en anden slags sandhed. Sprogmesteren holdt nemlig op med at slå os [...]. JOMFRU URNE: Det var ikke desto mindre en løgn, selv om det var en barnlig løgn. Leonora: Det er ikke det der er det vigtige. Det vigtige er at jeg fik magten over løgnen og vendte den til sandhed.[1080]

Despite Jomfru Urne's criticism of such and similar statements, Leonora adheres to her insistence on absolute power. Strangely though, Leonora is not able to use this power for her own good. In defiance of her self-awarded ability to turn the world upside down, she insists on being trapped in the self-implanted, fictionalised memory of her prison years. Subconsciously she is fully aware that one cause of this prolonged captivity is her own gratification at the face of injustice. She admits, for example, that it gives her pleasure to continue bearing her cross:

> Jeg har båret korset og jeg havde ingen Simon fra Kyrene til at hjælpe mig. Men min ryg er blevet stærk, Leo, og de to der i begyndelsen sad overskrævs på korsets tværbjælke, de faldt fra før jeg selv mistede kraften. Nu er der kun det tomme kors tilbage og det føles næsten *som en lyst* [my italics] at bære det det sidste stykke. [...] Kong Frederik, min halvbror, der så skammeligt glemte vores fælles blod og hans gemalinde Sophie Amalie, slangedronningen. De sad på hver sin halvdel af tværbjælken og tyngede mig.[1081]

In the second scene, the arrival of Leonora's son Leo,[1082] who is forced to visit his mother under a false name – »som et billede«[1083] – due to the bad reputation attached to his real name, brings both joy and disruption to the life of the previously sole survivor of the Ulfeldt-affair. It also confronts Leonora with her past (personified by Leo Ulfeldt), thus forcing her to reflect on whether she has chosen the right manner to process the loss of fortune and family. Holm's overall adherence to documented

---

1080 Ibid., p. 32.
1081 Ibid., p. 51.
1082 This meeting between mother and son – the first since Leonora Christina's imprisonment – occurred in 1691.
1083 Holm, Sven. *Leonora*, p. 90.

companions and visitors in Maribo[1084] – Leo, Jomfru Urne, Thomas Kingo (see below)[1085] – begs the question why Leo Ulfeldt became a character in the drama, but not Anna Catharina Ulfeldt, who lived with her mother in Maribo[1086] – especially since Anna Catharina would have complemented the women's collective in Maribo presented by Holm. Since the plot could easily have accommodated Anna Catharina as well, or even instead of her brother, Leo's appearance must be motivated by his function as a carrier and preserver of his mother's monument, *Jammers Minde*. Anna Catharina did *not* fulfill this task since she had conflicted feelings about her mother's testimony and decided to leave it to her brother (see Chapter 1.2.1.).

When Leonora's son Leo tells his mother that shortly before his death Corfitz had admitted to have conspired against the King of Denmark, Leonora refuses to accept the truth as it contradicts the story she had created of her and her husband's life. Instead, she blames her son for believing his father's words:

Over for sine tre sønner og over for Gud ville han give det udseende af at han havde tilgivet sine fjender, blot fordi han aldrig nåede at få hævn over dem. Jeg kan høre at han er blevet fejg i sidste øjeblik. Han troede han kunne slå handel af ved at påtage sig skylden. Men han får den ikke![1087]

Before Leo's arrival in Maribo, Leonora had been the only person alive and thus able to tell what had happened more than two decades ago. Yet, Leo is another witness and his counter-testimony is immediately silenced: »Leonora (*rejser sig*): Jeg har ingenting hørt«.[1088] The reasons for her insistence on Corfitz's innocence

---

1084 Several details in the drama indicate that Holm had informed himself well about Leonora Christina's everyday life in Maribo. The monastery garden – central in providing many important props throughout the course of the play – was one of Leonora Christina's first demands upon her arrival in Maribo. Originally there had been two separate gardens respectively belonging to the monastery's monks and nuns, but when Leonora Christina arrived in her new domicile (which had been closed by Christian IV in 1621), King Christian V. granted her wish to preside over both gardens. And, as depicted in the beginning of Holm's drama, Leonora Christina was often forced to stay in bed until noon since starting a fire was too dangerous of an affair, due to the building's acute state of disrepair. See Birket Smith, Sophus. *Leonora Christina (Ulfeldt) på Maribo Kloster*, pp. 12-14. Finally, the drama within the drama (see below) may be a reference to a play (the title and topic of which are unknown) composed by Leonora Christina and staged on 27 February 1688, starring the Maribo staff (ibid., p. 54).
1085 In the 17th century, Lolland – and hence Maribo – still belonged to the diocese of Funen, which is why the bishop of Funen, Thomas Kingo (1634-1703), paid occasional visits to Maribo, as well as to Leonora Christina (ibid., p. 63).
1086 In 1688, at the latest, the widowed Anna Catharina came to Maribo to live with her mother and stayed there until Leonora Christina's death in 1698 (ibid., p. 20). Hence, Anna Catharina was present when her brother Leo came to visit his remaining family. After her mother's death, Anna Catharina spent her final years in Vienna, most likely in a monastery (ibid., p. 22).
1087 Holm, Sven. *Leonora*, p. 55.
1088 Ibid., p. 54.

A Chip off the Old Block: Denmark's Century of Femmes Fatales

are connected to the identity she had acquired for herself over the past decades: her husband cannot be guilty as it would contradict the life story she had constructed. If Corfitz was to blame for a committed crime, her own identity as innocent martyr would crumble: »Helheden mellem Corfitz og mig kan ikke deles op i to halvdele, hvoraf den ene kan påtage sig skylden. Vi er i fællesskab uskyldige. Uskyldige og straffede, så ondt og enkelt er det«.[1089] She cannot separate her own guilt from that of her husband either, as it would declare the object of her faithfulness unworthy of it and, consequently, Leonora would have been wrong.

Leo is both terrified and confused by his mother's refusal to accept his words. Leonora's following explanation helps to clarify her reaction to her estranged son, but it does not minimise his astonishment. Leonora now vividly remembers the day when her husband's effigy was publically executed. She remembers her horror and her pleas to stop the dismantling of the doll, an image of Corfitz created by his enemies – until she had an epiphany which from that moment onwards would determine her philosophy, i.e. the potence and simultaneous impotence of an image:

> For i det øjeblik forstod jeg at det jo kun var en figur der forestillede Corfitz Ulfeldt de havde anklaget lige fra begyndelsen, ligesom det også var en figur af Corfitz Ulfeldt de henrettede til sidst. Så tydeligt havde Gud gjort det for mine og alle andres øjne: de anklagede og straffede kun et billede og virkeligheden så de ikke.[1090]

God's assistance would from now on be the force to which Leonora would ascribe all subsequent events, even those occasioned by humans. Through this act of re-ascription, Leonora would regain control over the narratives of her and her husband's lives. For example, when King Frederik III would not allow his vengeful wife Sophie Amalie to have the effigy carried into Leonora's cell, in order for her to have one last 'wedding night' before the execution:

> Den var dagen før ved at blive båret over i Blaataarn for at jeg kunne holde bryllupsnat sammen med den. Dronningen havde bestemt det sådan. Men det forbød Gud hende. Og han brugte kongen, hendes egen gemal, som redskab. Sådan kom jeg aldrig til at se det modbydelige skambillede.[1091]

1089 Ibid., p. 56.
1090 Ibid., p. 57.
1091 Ibid.

Leonora's interpretation of the King's decent behaviour – a reference to Leonora Christina's own explanation for King Christian V's clemency after his mother's death[1092] – serves to illustrate Leonora Christina's international fame to her son Leo, who had not met his mother in decades and to whom she was thus a stranger:

> LEO: Selv om jeg ikke forstår jer, mor, så forstår jeg nu bedre hvad der bliver talt om jer, også i udlandet. LEONORA: Hvad siger man da? LEO: At jeres styrke er af en anden verden. LEONORA: Men jeg giver den til denne her verden. Sådan gør jeg min egen historie. LEO: Far ville elske jer for det. LEONORA: Det er jo også min måde at elske ham, Leo.[1093]

Leonora is complicit to her husband's treason and hence just as guilty as him. As stated by her maid Agnete, guilt requires a certain level of consciousness: »Det er også lettere at tie stille med sandheden når man rigtigt kender den«.[1094] Yet, despite her guilt, she does not cease to astonish and captivate.

The supernatural strength attributed to Leonora by her admirers (»At jeres styrke er af en anden verden«), exposes her as a true *femme fatale*: »Denne kvindes præg af ønskedrøm afsløres af den umådelige – og umenneskelige – styrke, hun tillægges«.[1095] Furthermore, and notwithstanding my previous remark that the term *femme fatale* is used here in a way excluding its explicitly sexual connotations, one driving power controlling the character and life story of Holm's Leonora is indeed explicitly sexual: »Når jeg ikke mere kan slå mine arme om ham og åbne mit skød for ham, så kan jeg elske ham gennem min historie. Det har nogen gange givet mig en fryd der er lige så stor og enkel som den Corfitz og jeg havde sammen i sengen«.[1096] In Holm's drama, Leonora Christina's famous love for her husband is first implemented in a specifically carnal (*krop*), later in a specifically spiritual (*ånd*) way, i.e. through her love and faith, that both seem to be »af en anden verden«. Furthermore, Leonora is not only a bitter, self-righteous woman, but also kind and forgiving. Because its protagonist can be a living dichotomy, Holm's play constitutes a rejection of all previous attempts to define the historical Leonora Christina through binary categories. Holm's Leonora is a true *femme fatale* as she embraces contradiction. She captivates through her own contrariness as she herself remains enchanted by a fatal man, i.e. her husband Corfitz Ulfeldt:

1092 Cf. *Jammers Minde*, p. 241.
1093 Holm, Sven. *Leonora*, p. 57.
1094 Ibid., p. 60.
1095 Præstgaard Andersen, Lise. *Sorte damer*, p. 28.
1096 Holm, Sven. *Leonora*, p. 58.

Han var en klog og alligevel hævnlysten mand. En retfærdig og alligevel sårbar mand. En varmblodig og alligevel hensynsløs man. Hver gang han havde fået en egenskab i dåbsgave, havde han også fået dens modsætning. Det var som om han var sat sammen af to brødre, en lys og en mørk. Og de lod aldrig hinanden i fred.[1097]

Leonora's seemingly supernatural strength and her sex drive are, however, not the only features characterising her as a *femme fatale*. Holm's Leonora is, in fact, a very specific and unique variant of this artistic motive. The third and last scene of the play shows Leonora in the midst of another reproduction of reality. In this instance, she, together with her two maids, is staging a play about Elizabeth I of England (played by Jomfru Urne) and her imprisonment by the hands of her half-sister Mary I, also known as Bloody Mary (played by Agnete), due to suspicions regarding Elizabeth's involvement in the Wyatt rebellion of 1554. Besides the obvious parallels provided by the opponents' close kinship (Leonora Christina, too, was imprisoned by a half-sibling) and the reasons for Elizabeth's imprisonment (alleged treason), there are other hints as to why Leonora would have composed such a play.[1098] Jomfru Urne, i.e. Elizabeth (and thus a representation of Leonora), is equipped with oversized knitting needles – a symbol of Leonora Christina's own imprisonment in the Blue Tower as her resourcefulness during these years continues to astonish readers of *Jammers Minde*. Yet, as argued above, these accessories are denotative of a whole array of powerful mythical females crafting fate – often that of a rival – through fibre. The earliest representatives of this type of myth furthermore connect female fibre craft with creative activities of another kind, such as writing (cf. text/ile) and identity constitution. Hence, Elizabeth is a metafictional and metabiographical representative of Leonora.

Elizabeth's artisan magic is occasioned by and directed at a female rival, namely her half-sister Mary, who is responsible for the imprisonment and who is known to have been outlived and succeeded by Elizabeth: »JOMFRU URNE [who plays Elizabeth]: Du skal se at jeg kun bliver siddende i Tower til jeg har strikket dit ligklæde

---

1097 Ibid., p. 75.
1098 A comparison of Leonora Christina with enemies of Mary I is in fact a recurring approach to her life story. Before Sven Holm, Ludvig Holberg had compared Leonora Christina and Lady Jane Grey (see Chapter 3.1.), Queen of England for less than two weeks and hence executed as unwanted competition for her cousin Mary. Norwegian writer Ingrid Lang, on the other hand, chose the same analogy as Sven Holm, due to the women's reversed dramatic fall: »Når fengselsdørene en dag ble åpnet, gikk ikke veien til skafottet; men til oppreisning og ære. Slik gikk det med dronning Elisabeth I av England. Like fra Towers skumle mørke, blev hun ført i triumf på en hvit hest til Englands trone. Og slikk gikk det Leonora Christina Ulfeldt, Christian IV's datter« (Lang, Ingrid. *Prinsessen i fengsel: Leonora Christina*. Oslo: Lutherstiftelsen, 1956, p. 7).

færdig«.¹⁰⁹⁹ As later on stated by Leonora's son Leo, the character of Elizabeth is clearly inspired by Leonora herself: »LEO (mildt ironisk): Eller også var det jer der skulle spille Elisabeth, mor! LEONORA: Åh, hende har jeg spillet i 22 år«. After all, Leonora Christina herself had made – among other things – a shroud in prison, albeit for herself (cf. *Jammers Minde*, p. 212).

Holm's Leonora, alias Elizabeth, however, is determined to drive her opponent into an early grave: »Jeg strikker med store masker. Så går det hurtigere. Så går det hurtigere«.¹¹⁰⁰ In this double scene, Leonora expresses her thirst for revenge in increasingly explicit ways, which in her reality would not be possible due to her situation. While Leonora cannot scratch herself in front of the priest and while the presence of the administrator does not permit her to express her rage in its full extent, staging a drama about Elizabeth and Mary allows her to exclaim all the threats and curses she – though released from prison – is still not able to say. Such as this cannibalistic fantasy succeeding the scornful bidding of a piece of meat by Mary, played by Agnete:

> Kød smager mig ikke. (*Sænker strikketøjet.*) Det skulle da lige være hvis det var dit. Dine rygstykker, dine nyrer, dit hjerte, det ville smage mig, Mary. Jeg ville riste det selv og jeg lover dig at jeg ville riste det længe. Du skal blive så mør med tiden at kødet falder fra dine knogler.¹¹⁰¹

In this double scene, Leonora indulges in ideas of revenge instead of following the Christian dogma of turning the other cheek. Elizabeth's triumphant last words finalise the analogy:

> Kort tid efter døde Mary en forsmædelig død og jeg blev dronning: Elisabeth af England, Skotland og Irland. Og al senere tid kom til at huske mig mens ingen kærede sig om Mary, min halvsøster. Sådan viste Gud hvordan retfærdigheden binder sit eget mønster i det skjulte. Thi det er bedre at være fængslet uforskyldt end at være fri og have forskyldt fængsel.¹¹⁰²

Once the curtain falls, the similarity between the two scenes still overpowers their differences. The maid Agnete senses the intrusion of the play into real life: »Men

---

1099 Holm, Sven. *Leonora*, p. 67.
1100 Ibid.
1101 Ibid., p. 68.
1102 Ibid., p. 70. Cf. *Jammers Minde*, p. 259: »Att ded er bedre [att] wære uskyllig Fengselet, end att wære frii oc [for-]skyldt Fengsel [both addenda by the editors]«.

det er alligevel som om jeg bliver en smule til Mary«.[1103] Leonora, too, eventually attributes the role of the fibre crafting, creative woman to herself. In prison, she herself had created the *text*ile comprising the image, and the story, of Leonora Christina:

> Leonora Christina Ulfeldt er der kun een af. Og billedet af hende, det har jeg selv vævet og broderet på hver eneste dag, stykke for stykke, tråd for tråd. Og selv om det er Gud der har æren for billedet, så var det mig der havde hænderne og hjertet. Og hjernen, Leo, den vil jeg ikke være så beskeden at jeg glemmer.[1104]

This association of Leonora with a mythical, omniscient life-crafting woman has a twofold implication. For one, these new attributes make her threatening and mystical – like the sphinx[1105] – and hence fatal. Her vengefulness as well as her seemingly supernatural willpower (»At jeres styrke er af en anden verden«) make her a dangerous opponent. Yet, on the other hand, Holm's focus on the products of Leonora Christina's imprisonment such as her handicraft and the manuscript, rather than its prehistory and progress, perpetuate the implicit conclusion provided by Birgithe Kosovic's novel *Leonora Christina*: that *Jammers Minde* continues to be of relevance to readers today as it exemplifies literature's identity-constituting potential. Both of the products thematised in Holm's drama – Leonora Christina's fibre craft and *Jammers Minde*, i.e. textile and text – have lasted until this day and provide her with an opportunity to forge her own life story (or, in the case of the fibre craft in the double scene, the fate of others which will then have an immediate impact on her own).

When Leo eventually addresses this division between his physical mother and her image (*billed*), he learns about the real Leonora, the aged woman deported to Maribo and forgotten by history, and about the image she had created of herself, the immortal Leonora: »Det er hendes livsværk, Leo. Det er hendes klædedragt. Hendes hat og fjeren i hatten. Det er hendes hytte og slot, hendes lysthus og fæstning. Det er hendes handlinger, spundet sammen tråd for tråd. Det er det der er hendes historie og rygte«.[1106] Leonora's peculiar use of the third person indicates that she, the living Leonora, has transferred all her creative power to her image. Her own

---

1103 Holm, Sven. *Leonora*, p. 71.
1104 Ibid., p. 72.
1105 Lise Præstgaard Andersen names the sphinx as one type of *femme fatale*, due to her inscrutability and the threat she poses to approaching (male!) heroes, such as Oedipus (Præstgaard Andersen, Lise. *Sorte damer*, p. 49).
1106 Holm, Sven. *Leonora*, p. 73.

effigy, just as those created by others (»det er tungt med alle de forvandlinger«),[1107] seems to have developed a life of its own. The rest of Holm's play is thus concerned with the question of how to recuperate control over this autonomous image.

Towards the end of the play, before Leo returns to his exile in Austria,[1108] he, together with the Danish bishop and poet Thomas Kingo, who visits Leonora in the third scene,[1109] occasions his mother to acknowledge and fight her own impotence at the face of her effigy's power and to regain control over the image (»det [*Jammers Minde*] er mit billede jeg har givet jer«)[1110] she had created of herself.[1111] Towards Thomas Kingo Leonora admits that she had grown tired of the past and of the image her life story had created: »Men alligevel er det en fristelse at tænke sådan. Verden uden farver. Uden godt og ondt. Uden retfærdighed fordi uretten slet ikke findes. Uden billeder fordi farven hvid er tilstrækkelig«.[1112] She longs for a life in which these *billeder* have disappeared, but once again fleas remind her of a reality, in which these images are still present (»den satans yngel til lopperne og deres bid, det var dem der erindrede mig om min krop«).[1113]

Leo eventually reproaches his mother for her creation. Once he knows that Leonora had always known Corfitz's dark side but could not have cared less, he takes the fishing net which in her play had served as a prison for Elizabeth I – on a

---

1107 Ibid., p. 103.

1108 In 1691 and 1693 Leo Ulfeldt obtained the permission of the Danish King to visit his mother in Denmark. However, since the sons of the Ulfeldt family were still reckoned with suspicion in Denmark (not least due to the vengeful murder of Adolph Fuchs by the hands of Christian Ulfeldt in the streets of Bruges in 1662), Leo could initially only visit Leonora Christina incognito (he was recommended to assume the identity of one of Anna Catharina's stepsons, i.e. one of her late husband's Jan Wigilius Cassetta's sons) and only for three days (see Birket Smith, Sophus. *Leonora Christina (Ulfeldt) på Maribo Kloster*, p. 22). Unlike in the drama, however, Leo did not visit his mother under the name of Cassetta; instead he used the alias 'Faber' (Urne, Dorthea Sophie. 'Frøken Urnes Meddelelser', p. 86). On top of these strict requirements, the King's consent to Leonora Christina's request was only attained when news of a serious illness, that had befallen her, reached the court in Copenhagen (Birket Smith, Sophus. *Leonora Christina (Ulfeldt) på Maribo Kloster*, pp. 22 and 24).

1109 Holm's Kingo advances the same view as Leo Ulfeldt, namely that Leonora had imposed an image upon herself (unlike Leo, who was forced to use an alias, i.e. a fictive identity, upon coming to Denmark), which she is now more unwilling than unable to discard: »Jeg viser kun at vi allesammen har brug for at rejse i forklædning. Ind imellem et billede der bliver pålagt os ved tvang, ind imellem et billede vi har mulighed for at vælge. Men kun sjældent et billede som vi selv har bygget op med de mangler og fejl der kan være i vævningen. Og det er jo sådan et billede Leonora Christina har skabt. Efter 22 år i kulde og mørke mens de fleste af hendes medfanger brød sammen efter bare et enkelt år« (Holm, Sven. *Leonora*, p. 91). Kingo's first statement is a reference to the incognito-arrival of Leo Ulfeldt in Maribo.

1110 Ibid., p. 88.

1111 Cf. ibid., p. 82, where Leonora suggests towards Kingo that sometimes written words take on a life of their own and gain control over their originator: »Men så talte I om feberen. Ganske vist kan I både skrive salmer og have halsonde, men det kan jo også være at feberen kommer fra ordene selv og at de omtåger ens hoved og ophidser ens blod, så man ikke længere kan se fuldstændig klart«.

1112 Ibid., p. 83.

1113 Ibid., p. 86.

metaphorical level the yarn, i.e. the net of fiction, or lies, she herself had fabricated – and throws it over his mother: »Her har I så jeres evighedsfængsel. I vil jo bære det rundt som eremitkrebsen bærer sit hus«.[1114] He blames her for all the hardship he and his brothers and sisters had to endure because of his mother's insistance on the innocence of both her and Corfitz. Notwithstanding Leonora's protests against his accusations, she reacts to his words by crafting reality in the service of others, rather than herself. When Jomfru Urne calls Leonora's attention to the maid Agnete's growing stomach, Leonora initially denies this protruding reality by attributing this dubious transformation to her maid's late fondness for candy. Yet, since Jomfru Urne does not quite believe in this theory, and since Agnete is unwed, Leonora is advised to dismiss Agnete. Despite Leonora's growing suspicion that Agnete may indeed be with child, the visit of her son Leo propitiates her and she suggests to let Agnete have her child in Maribo and to pass it off as her own grandchild. When Jomfru Urne insinuates that this might not be the right thing to do, Leonora simply declares herself the absolute judicial authority in this case: »Leonora: Når vi bestemmer os for at gøre det, så har vi gjort det til det rigtige. Jomfru Urne (forbavset): Det er kun grevinden der kan få verden til at stå på hovedet uden at den vakler«.[1115]

By allowing Agnete to bring a new life into Maribo, Leonora simultaneously lets go of her own old life and adopts a more future-oriented outlook. Upon the realisation that she has the power to change even though it might contradict her previously created self-image, Leonora eventually relinquishes her hold on the past. She casts away the fishing net that represented Elizabeth's as well as her own prison and she orders Agnete to go out into the herb garden to fetch some rosemary.[1116] By letting go of her old fears and habits, she becomes »et helt menske [...], [e]t billed som hele tiden kan forandre sig«.[1117] Holm's drama is thus a complete renunciation of the autobiographical principle of unity, which *Jammers Minde* abides by. Leonora Christina's understanding of her self-portrayal as a portrait, i.e. an invariable picture, receives a twist through a new understanding of selfsame picture as expressed by Holm's Leonora:

1114 Ibid., p. 77.
1115 Ibid., p. 63.
1116 In the first scene, Agnete had unsuspectingly brought her mistress a bouquet which contained, among other herbs, rosemary – a reminder of the death of Leonora Christina's first love Maurits (see Chapter 1.2.1.). This innocent mistake had caused a little drama in Leonora's bedroom.
1117 Holm, Sven. *Leonora*, p. 105.

JOMFRU URNE: I har altid den samme rolige styrke, Leonora. LEONORA: Det er kun billedet af Leonora. Men der er jo ingen der kan se at et billede forandrer sig hver gang der bliver føjet et nyt ord til historien eller et nyt sting til broderiet. I verdens øjne skal et billede være så fast at man kan fange det og sætte det i fængsel eller fange det og henrette det.[1118]

By revising her past, Leonora turns back time. She becomes a new human being, almost a child. Consequently, her relationship with her former critic Jomfru Urne, too, is rejuvenated: »LEONORA: Lad mig hvile mit hoved i dit skød, Dorthea. Jeg føler selv at det er tungt med alle de forvandlinger. (*Hun sætter sig på sengen og lægger hovedet halvt op mod jomfru Urne, som gør plads.*)«[1119]

Before Leo departs, Leonora gives him the manuscript of *Jammers Minde*. Through the example of Artemisia II of Caria, wife and sister of the Persian Satrap Mausolus (4th century BCE), who occasioned the construction of the Mausoleum at Halicarnassus in memory of her late husband (and who is said to have swallowed her husband's ashes to protect them from tomb raiders),[1120] she explains to her son and to Kingo the eternal value of *Jammers Minde* as a monument to her husband, but most of all to herself:

Og sådan kan man se at en heltindes rygte kan modstå stærkere storme end den største og prægtigste bygning. Også selv om rygtet kun er bygget op af så ubetydelige ting som ord og ordenes bogstaver. For nok er ordene små og svage, men når de står sammen, helt tæt som de gør i en bog, så kan de bære de største og tungeste ting på deres skuldre.[1121]

Hence, Holm's Leonora emerges as a writer and as an advocate for literature. Through the publication of *Jammers Minde*, which Leonora had laid in the hands

---

1118 Ibid., p. 103.
1119 Ibid.
1120 In Leo's view, Leonora, too, has swallowed her husband's metaphorical remains in order to nourish her own life, i.e. to legitimize her life's story, i.e. her autobiography: »LEONORA: Leo kaldte mig en Artemis. Han mente at jeg havde ædt min husbonds aske for at give næring til mit eget liv, jeg tror det var sådan han sagde det. […] Kingo: Og så skulle I have skabt jeres Jammersminde – (*tøvende*) – fordi I har optaget Corfitz i jeres legeme? Leonora: Fordi han lever videre i mig, ja« (ibid., p. 99).
1121 Ibid., p. 74.

of her son Leo, Leonora had built herself her very own paper mausoleum.[1122] Leonora's effigy lives on in the printed book, even when the physical Leonora had already moved on from this image.[1123] Through her fibre craft and her texts, Leonora can fabricate and hence influence the life story of her opponents, but eventually also her own life story. She determines to end her old life, to trap it in a manuscript and to send it off into an independent existence. In the meantime, the real Leonora stays behind, liberated from the prison she – in her almightiness – had cast upon herself. Finally, Leonora is also a heroine, as indicated by the drama's title. A summary produced in *Litteraturhåndbogen* on Sven Holm's work indicates that Holm had accorded Leonora Christina the status of a heroine for sociopolitical reasons:

> De historisk-aktuelle teaterskuespil »Struensee var her« (1977), »Hans Egede eller Guds ord for en halv tønde spæk« (1979) og »Leonora. Tre scener for en Heltinde« (1982) skildrer således mennesker der reagerer imod den tvang som udgår fra deres politiske og sociale vilkår.[1124]

Yet the above analysis of the text exposes clearly that Holm's Leonora is no heroine because she rebels against authorities. Instead, her heroic deed is the eventual overcoming of her past and of herself.

2.6.2. Helle Stangerup: *Spardame* (1989) – Baroque Fatalities

> Her hoes wil ieg Ihuekomme Dennem hwis Dødelig affgang mig wærende mit Fængsel bleff beretet.
>
> (*Jammers Minde*, p. 261)

1122 Literature's potential to mobilise and create beyond the written word is a recurring motive in Sven Holm's authorship. For example, Holm's experimental novel *Min elskede*, published in 1968 and hence at a time of revolution and protest against established authorities, depicts the difficulties of various social groups and individuals in urban Copenhagen. The text represents thus a city collage but, in a metatextual way, also a collage city, in that it debates »the status of language in relation to the extratextual world« (Wischmann, Antje. 'Collage City – City Collage: On the Relation Between Aesthetic and Political Mobilisation in Sven Holm's *Min Elskede – En Skabelonroman*', Forum for World Literature Studies 4/1 (2012), p. 126). Similar to *Min Elskede*, a »text [which] is to perform itself and become a reading event which goes beyond a mere constition of meaning« (ibid., p. 127), Holm's Leonora, too, has created a text, which had taken on a life of its own and – in creating a seemingly unchallengeable effigy of its creator – outgrown her.

1123 Cf. Thomas Bredsdorff, who contends that art as an implementation of power is a recurring theme in Holm's work (Bredsdorff, Thomas. *Sære Fortællere. Hovedtræk af den ny danske prosakunst i tiåret omkring 1960*. Copenhagen: Gyldendal, 1967, p. 57).

1124 *Litteraturhåndbogen*, p. 427.

These are the introductory lines to Leonora Christina's *dødsliste*, the list of her deceased enemies provided at the end of *Jammers Minde*. *Dødslisten* is not an integral part of *Jammers Minde*, but rather a chapter by itself, detached from the rest of the account through its separate position and content, which in turn highlights its central place within Leonora Christina's memory. Within the corpus of research on *Jammers Minde* and its author, this list has thus served as an exemplification of Leonora Christina's personality which – according to common opinion – was characterised by a maliciously long memory. Postmodern examples of Leonora Christina-literature, one of them being Helle Stangerup's (1939-2015) novel *Spardame*, are profoundly coined by this now common notion of Leonora Christina as an unforgetting fury.[1125] What has been mostly ignored, though, is the fact that *dødslisten* expresses not only rage and vengefulness, but also Leonora Christina's zeitgeist, i.e. her awareness of the volatility of earthly existence and fate, in her age phrased through the key terms *vanitas mundi* and *memento mori*. Together with their variations, these two Baroque mottoes are the leitmotives pervading *Spardame*.

The outline of Helle Stangerup's novel is the same as that of Eva Hemmer Hansen's novels on Leonora Christina. Stangerup, too, presents Leonora Christina together with her female contemporaries – Ellen Marsvin, Kirsten Munk, Vibeke Kruse and Sophie Amalie. All of these women made history, either through their unconventional ways of living (e.g. Ellen Marsvin) or through their – sadly – all too representative life stories (e.g. Vibeke Kruse). However, the disposition of Stangerup's novel is entirely different from that of Eva Hemmer Hansen. As the title *Spardame* (i.e. the card game Black Lady, which in turn is a reference to the card *Spar Dame* ('Spade Lady')) indicates, Stangerup's women are no victims but cold-blooded gamblers. Ellen Marsvin is not married to a brutish pervert, but to a fragile and rather un-libidinous elder man, and the only thing they have in common is a lack of carnal interest. Kirsten Munk is not a victim either, exploited and sold by her own mother, but a woman who was young and naïve when she accepted the King's proposal. And lastly, Vibeke Kruse is not a better version of Kirsten, benign and magnanimous, although mistreated by Kirsten's children, but a calculating gold-digger who is all too willing to replace her former mistress as the King's partner.

1125 Cf. Stangerup, Helle. *Spardame*. Copenhagen: Gyldendal, 1991 (1989), p. 13: »Leonora havde to hemmelige lister. Den ene med navne på de mennesker hun elskede, og den anden over dem, hun hadede«. Stangerup's Vibeke Kruse, too, writes a *hadeliste* inside her head, which seems to be almost as potent as Leonora Christina's *dødsliste*: »Hver eneste høflighed, der blev sprunget over, hver lyd, hver bevægelse og hvert eneste navn. Hun pakkede det hele sammen inde i sig som små endnu ubetydelige gældsbeviser, der med tiden og med renter og renters rente skulle vokse sig til en kæmpe skat« (ibid., p. 63). Vibeke's memory and the according measures taken by her through the King soon effect the dismissal of some of her dispraisers and the ensuing promotion of those, who have shown her kindness. And of course, Leonora's sister-in-law, too, keeps a similar record in her head: »Det gode skulle huskes såvel som det onde« (ibid., p. 134).

Stangerup's Leonora[1126] joins this group of fatal women perfectly. At least in her rival's, i.e. Sofie Amalie's eyes, Leonora is a true *femme fatale*. She is tall, beautiful, sophisticated and dangerously eloquent, but also greedy and domineering.[1127] One of Sofie Amalie's greatest fears is to find herself in a soirée bestridden by her sister-in-law, thus being outshined by her husband's lowerborn half-sister. Even when the Ulfeldts are already outlaws in Denmark, she worries about Leonora's engaging air, for »[h]vem kunne hun ikke charmere, denne Leonora?«[1128]

Stangerup's Leonora is the most conventional *femme fatale* provided in Chapter 2.6. She is not only sexually appealing and fully aware of her effect on the opposite sex, but she has other typical traits of a dangerously magnetic rival as well:

> Hun [Sofie Amalie] kunne se Leonora for sig. Glidende ned gennem al forgyldningen, smilende til højre og venstre, kommenterende, komplimenterende, med perlekrans i sin lille sorte hat, der var så anderledes, at alle bemærkede den, og med hånden rakt frem til kys, som var hun det officielle Danmarks fornemste kvindelige repræsentant. Spejlene ville mangedoble Leonoras person. Den, der blev fokuseret på i denne verden blev uendeliggjort. Hun stod der, midt på gulvet, midt i kredsen af de fornemme og de magtfulde, der var tryllebundne ved hendes latter, indsuget af charmens og magiens lange fangearme.[1129]

Leonora's serpentine (»glidende«) and demonic qualities have a profound effect not (only) on any man, but primarily on Sofie Amalie. The Queen remains obsessed with her sister-in-law until the very last minute of her life: »I bestemte belysninger og fra bestemte vinkler så Sofie Amalie i sit ansigt noget hæsligt gro frem. Det var Leonoras værk. Alle disse furer, disse poser, og hagens tyngde. Det var skabt af Leonora«.[1130]

1126 In the present chapter, »Leonora« specifically refers to the character in Helle Stangerup's novel, particularly when referring to passages that do not correspond to historical events, whereas »Leonora Christina« refers to the historical person. Another spelling variation used in the literary source text, and hence in this chapter as well, is »Sofie Amalie«.

1127 Cf. Stangerup, Helle. *Spardame*, respectively pp. 126 and 138: »Alle de italienske sætninger og behændigt anbragte franske citater var ikke nok til at dække over blikkets griskhed, mundens streg og det urene blod, for rådenskab kan ikke holde forgyldning. [...] Sofie Amalie nød Leonoras fravær fra hoffet. Vist kunne hun tale fransk. Men når dette kvindemenneske turede frem, var det som en maskine, der spyede metal ud, naglede Sofie Amalies sætninger fast til gulvet og hældte bly i hendes konversation«.

1128 Ibid., p. 166.

1129 Ibid., p. 251.

1130 Ibid., p. 255.

However, all *femmes fatales* are merely projections of their (traditionally male) counterparts' fears; they are embodiments rather than actual human beings.[1131] The same applies to Leonora and Sofie Amalie as the latter – if only for a fraction of a moment – must come to realise. When Frederik and his wife hear of Ulfeldt's attempt to involve the Elector of Brandenburg in a conspiracy against the King of Denmark, Frederik is terrified, but his wife is not. She is excited; not in view of the potential final destruction of Corfitz Ulfeldt, the actual perpetrator, but in the face of the possibility to once and for all put Leonora in her place.[1132] Yet in the midst of her anticipation, Sofie Amalie senses something else; something less pleasant: »Den kom i glimt, som små bid, frygten for hvad der fulgte efter. Leonora fanget og hvad så?«[1133] At this point, the Queen has long lost the once intimate connection to her husband and while now it is still possible for her to blame her increasing resemblance to an evil hag on Leonora, her wrinkles, her malicious gaze and her double chin will still be there once Leonora is locked up and rendered innocuous. Even when the two women have not met each other in more than twenty years and Leonora is already in the Blue Tower, Sofie Amalie still attributes almost supernatural powers to her adversary, hence creating Leonora's fatalness out of her own fears. Sofie Amalie is somehow conscious of this process, yet she has already given in to her dark side:

Når nætterne kom, og længselen efter Frederik ville være ved at tage magten fra Sofie Amalie, agtede hun at stå op, gå til et vindue og finde trøsten i, at derovre sad Leonora i så snævert et rum, bag så tykke mure og i selskab med rotter og skarn. Hver gang skulle der findes på nye ydmygelser. Nye veje til fornedrelse. Heras milde smil var tabt for evigt og blev til en grimasse.[1134]

In these moments, the two women are involuntarily connected; both long for what is lost forever,[1135] and both attribute this loss to their respective adversary. The

---

1131 Cf. Binias, Silke. *Symbol and Symptom*, p. 12.
1132 Stangerup, Helle. *Spardame*, p. 255.
1133 Ibid.
1134 Ibid.
1135 Decadent world-weariness is also a trait typical of classic *femme fatale*-literature (cf. Carola Hilmes on the so-called *Mal du Siècle*: Hilmes, Carola. *Die Femme fatale*, p. 9). This apocalyptic sentiment associated with the *femme fatale* renders the Leonora Christina-subject matter an ideal candidate for the construction of a *femme fatale*, as the Baroque age – especially in Denmark where this era culminated in the fateful introduction of absolutism – is generally perceived as a symptom of cultural (as implicated by a political and economical) diminution (cf., for example, Barner, Wilfried. *Barockrhetorik: Untersuchungen zu ihren geschichtlichen Grundlagen*. 2., unveränderte Auflage. Tübingen: Max Niemeyer, 2002 (1970), p. 19).

Baroque topic of transience pervades the entire novel. For most of the later years portrayed in *Spardame*, Leonora perceives her own life in nostalgic terms. Even though Leonora Christina was only in her thirties when the conflict with Frederik III and Sophie Amalie escalated, Stangerup's Leonora – like Sofie Amalie – subsequently begins to long for the years when she was young and carefree and when she and her husband only seemed to live for each other. Stangerup's use of the seasons enhances this notion of finitude. When the exiled Leonora turns melancholic, she remembers the days when she was still sixteen and became the newly-wed wife of the upstart Corfitz Ulfeldt, both of whom lived in the secluded yet idyllic fiefdom of Møn. In these moments, Leonora remembers the first months of their marital life, which culminate in Corfitz's promotion in the springtime and their subsequent emigration to Copenhagen (curiously, Sofie Amalie and her husband share a similar experience of their honeymoon weeks).[1136] Twenty years later, during their exile in Sweden, these spring days are long gone and Corfitz and Leonora see signs of seasonal deterioration on their walk:

> De var dog sammen, hun og Corfitz. Og de gik over broen gennem haven og ud i skoven. Det regnede let, dråberne prikkede ned gennem sneen, og det knasede under deres fødder. Der var nøgne grene, visnet løv hang som gammel slidt forgyldning fra underskovens vækster, og da de nåede lysningen var mere end tyve år forsvundet. [...] De tog handskerne af og følte med deres hænder ind under trærødderne, hvor Kaka [Leonora's cockatoo, shot dead by Corfitz the day he met Leonora] blev lagt. [...] Og dér ved skovstien, hvor troldnødden blomstrede løftede han hende op på sin hest og red hende hjem. Så han også hende som dengang? Hun vidste det ikke og tiden var knap.[1137]

The past and the passing are evoked at this part of the forest glade, where their life together began. Their first, accidental meeting had also been a hint at the future as the entrance of Corfitz into Leonora's life had brought about her first experience of loss and death, i.e. the killing of her cockatoo. In this moment, when they return to the location where their story began, the place under the tree turns into a place where time has never passed (»var mere end tyve år forsvundet«). The witch-hazel (*troldnød*), a typical winter and spring bloomer, simultaneously evokes memories of Leonora and Corfitz's early marital life on Møn. Such nostalgic moments occur at a higher density towards the end of the account – for example, when the Ulfeldt couple's attempted flight from Hammershus fails, which occasions Leonora to long

---

1136 Cf. Stangerup, Helle. *Spardame*, p. 87.
1137 Ibid., p. 177.

for the reversal or absence of time, embodied by a tree: "[...] hun fik en pludselig længsel efter at se et træ. Et højt, højt træ, med grene, der bredte sig ud over dem med en kæmpestor krone og mængder af store grønne blade. Bare en mærkelig tanke midt i det hele.[1138]

Sic transit gloria mundi,[1139] another Baroque motto cautioning its contemporaries against profane indulgence, is not just expressed implicitly by the narrator in *Spardame*, but also by its characters. Leonora, in particular, experiences the validity of this saying through suddenly emerging images of the past and possessions. When Leonora experiences imminent perishability for the first time, namely during a sea journey from Denmark to the Netherlands, which is interrupted by a sea storm, she processes this novel threat only subconsciously while her superego would not allow any breach in the facade:[1140] »Hun havde drømt om den røde kjole. Den havde krave med stivere, kniplinger og masser af bånd i guldtråd syet på silken, og Anne Kathrine havde den på. Hun var den ældste. Hun ejede kjolen«.[1141] The silk dress she once coveted so much eventually turns into a worn-out rag »efter at have været lagt først ind og så ud til Sofie og så ind og ud til hende selv, og guldtrådene var løse og bulede på både liv og skørt«.[1142] Such failed escapism occurs whenever Leonora's status quo is in peril; for example, when she returns from the Netherlands and senses hostility between her parents: »Leonora huskede på en dukke, hun engang havde. Det var hendes bedste eje, men en dag gik der hul på den, og så var det bare savsmuld det hele. Men hun kunne ikke forstå, hvorfor hun tænkte så meget på den dukke netop nu«.[1143]

Leonora's fixation on possessions is mirrored by the other women presented in *Spardame*. Yet in the case of Leonora, this obsession is distinctly aimed at luxury items.[1144] The protagonists' vanity is at the same time one of the novel's keywords:

1138 Ibid., p. 239.
1139 Curiously, this phrase is introduced in reference to little Leonora, who has temporarily lost her infantile beauty during an outbreak of smallpox (ibid., p. 15).
1140 »Gud elsker mig, jeg elsker Gud. Gud vil ikke lade mig dø og heller ikke magisteren. Han skal jo undervise, så jeg bliver endnu klogere« (ibid., p. 9).
1141 Ibid., p. 7.
1142 Ibid.
1143 Ibid., p. 37.
1144 Ellen Marsvin, on the other hand, follows her dream of building an empire of seat farms whereas Vibeke Kruse, to name another example, is content with less refined items, due to her humble background. After her first night with Christian IV, she is simply delighted about being in a proper bed, albeit for questionable reasons: »Da solen stod op og sendte morgenens første grå lys gennem vinduerne havde Vibeke helt glemt sin kongelige elsker. Hendes tanker koncentrerede sig fuldt om, hvem af de andre tjenestepiger, der mon skulle skolde fingrene og brænde hænderne på at vaske og stryge det linned hun, Vibeke, havde ligget i« (ibid., p. 32f).

vanitas, i.e. the Baroque conviction that all profane ado is perishable and hence futile.[1145] One symbol of Baroque vanitas is gambling,[1146] including all of its variations such as playing dice or cards.[1147] Hence, the novel's title *Spardame*, an allusion to one of such vices, is an indication to its protagonists as exemplifications of this Baroque principle. They are all utterly vain in every sense of the word, as they exhibit a peculiar fixation on materialistic symbols of wealth, such as clothes or manors. Yet, all of their possessions fade, as clarified above (e.g. Leonora's doll and her red silk dress), and so does their luck. One case in point is Kirsten Munk, once the proud and austere mistress of Vibeke Kruse. Her privileged position would not last: »Den højadelige fru Kirstens sidste datter var nu en horeunge, men hun, Vibeke, var ikke længere tjenestepige, for hun bar et kongebarn i sit skød«.[1148] Further examples are, of course, Leonora Christina, who went from the top of the Danish hierarchy to its very bottom, but also the men and women chronicled in *Jammers Minde*. Most of Leonora Christina's adversaries, even those of low birth, had wielded power over their noble prisoner. However, this power could not save them from dying a painful and often demeaning death, as Leonora Christina was eager to highlight through her *dødsliste*.

Fortuna is capricious, as all of the women depicted in *Spardame* will eventually learn. All material possessions as well as the human body itself will eventually fade and rot. Kirsten learns this through her own fading love for Christian IV and through her drooping beauty, prematurely occasioned by numerous births: »I et glimt indså hun, at alt måske ikke var givet, at det utænkelige var tænkeligt. Angsten rakte ud over øjeblikket«.[1149] Ellen sees her life's work slip out of her hands when the King forces her to leave two of her very own monuments, the seat farms of Boller and Rosenvold, to her daughter Kirsten and when she loses the fiefdom of

---

1145 Leonora Christina herself addresses this motive in *Jammers Minde* upon being provoked by the castellan about the loss of her mansion (*Jammers Minde*, p. 113).
1146 Cf. Rosmarie Zeller's study on the German Baroque writer Georg Philipp Harsdörffer (1607-1658), in which she states that games of skill were condoned by the 17th century, whereas any kind of gambling was condemned (Zeller, Rosmarie. *Spiel und Konversation im Barock: Untersuchungen zu Harsdörffers »Gesprächsspielen«*. Berlin and New York: Walter de Gruyter, 1974 (Quellen und Forschungen zur Sprach- und Kulturgeschichte der germanischen Völker 58 (177)), p. 147ff).
1147 A vanitas still life by the Dutch painter Jacques de Claeuw (1623-1694) from 1677, for example, depicts cards as symbols of the perishability of human fortune, next to withered flowers and an hourglass.
1148 Stangerup, Helle. *Spardame*, p. 36.
1149 Ibid., p. 54.

Dalum.[1150] To Leonora, the realisation of the omnipresence of deterioration comes in the form of Vibeke, standing in the place that had once belonged to her mother and – fittingly – dressed in green, the colour of decay:

> Hun stod der grøn og skinnende som råddenskab, der var groet op gennem stengulvets fugninger og truede med at sprænge fliserne. [...] Hun græd, tårer løb ned ad hendes kinder og ned i rillerne på hans [Christian IV's] krave, men Vibeke stod stadig foran hende, en skinnende svamp, rådden, stinkende og giftig.[1151]

Two decades later, during Leonora and Corfitz's exile in Sweden, she gradually comes to terms with the volatility of fate. In these years, Leonora longs for stability, for the familiar, and for family.[1152] Eventually, her world's transition goes to such lengths that Leonora tries to embrace her inverted environment in order to regain her balance. While Corfitz plots against Sweden in order to facilitate the Danish victory over its adversary in 1658, his wife longs for the opposite. Yet, as she cannot act in public or against her husband, she manipulates her immediate environment. She refurnishes her house in Sweden in a fashion mirror-inverted to her old manor in Copenhagen, in order to accommodate herself in this twisted world: »Kister og skabe og spejlet var flyttet, fra østvæg til vestvæg, og fra vestvæg til østvæg. Det var blevet en mani hos hende, og hun lod en globus snurre omvendt rundt«.[1153] Due to her sex[1154] and her husband's oppositional hopes for the Dano-Swedish War of 1658, Leonora cannot influence world affairs but her recent pastime of turning her globe from East to West[1155] – hence inverting world order – strongly indicates that she would certainly like to. When Corfitz is accused of treason against the King of

---

1150 Ellen subsequently decides to invest her money in Christian constructions, as a measure of obtaining an eternal life: »Ellen hengav sig til fromme tanker, og det hinsides ventede. Hun sad der dog stadig, søndag efter søndag og år efter år og glædede sig over mester Dreiers skønne billedskæringer under krydshvælvene i kapellet i Ellensborg sydfløj. Og hun glædede sig over at hendes initialer umuligt kunne fjernes uden at ødelægge panelerne som helhed« (ibid., p. 83).
1151 Ibid., p. 38.
1152 Iibid., p. 155.
1153 Ibid., p. 212.
1154 As a woman, Leonora is forced to remain passive during the war. Curiously, her rival Sofie Amalie experiences the same kind of frustrating restriction and is hence also disappointed when the Danish victory over Sweden is declared, yet for different reasons. During the siege of Copenhagen, the Queen tries to participate as much as possible, but eventually peace is declared without her having had the opportunity to become a heroine: »Det var en af de tolv danske faldne under stormen på København. Og hun kunne være blevet den trettende. De ville have båret hendes lig op. Hvilket øjeblik! Hvilken storhed! [...] Hun ville blive husket. Hun ville blive hyldet, ikke som nu kun i nogle timer, dage, højst måneder.« (ibid., p. 209). Like Kirsten Munk and Ellen Marsvin, Sofie Amalie is at this point much preoccupied with questions of death and afterlife, and with options to secure her very own monument.
1155 Cf. ibid., p. 213.

Sweden and reacts with a stroke, Leonora finally gets the chance to take action – *she* will exonerate her husband. Once her resolution is initiated, she feels as if she had regained control over the entire world: »Da Corfitz sov tungt, og hun endelig lagde sig til ro, var det med en følelse af at være så stærk, at hun kunne bære verden på sine skuldre«.[1156] But of course, this feeling of sovereignty is not meant to last.

Finally, *memento mori* becomes a central topic to the novel as well as to the diverse female characters in it. Ellen Marsvin provides for a comfortable afterlife by donating chapels and altars to the church, all adorned with her initials. Her daughter Kirsten, on the other hand, is torn between her lust for life and her concerns regarding her approaching death. She dreams of a funeral befitting her rank as dowager, shrouded in a beautiful gown and laid down in a tomb made of black and white marble – »Det var hendes alderdoms drøm. Men der var stadig ønsket om at høre dans og musik i den firs alen lange sal«.[1157] Leonora, for her part, senses the vicinity of death when she notices Corfitz's changed shape. His exile in Sweden has stooped him and Leonora sees this for the first time while beholding her husband from a distance: »Skibet gled fra kaj. Han vinkede og hun vinkede, og som han stod derinde og blev mindre, blev han også duknakket. Hun havde ikke bemærket det før. Modgangen havde tæret også på ham«.[1158] Little by little, Leonora's world breaks apart in front of her eyes as she and Corfitz approach their doom. Vanity, volatility and finiteness all come together when she realises that the world she has been living in is merely a farce:

> Pludselig slog det ned, som det lyn der flækkede træet. Havde hun og Corfitz, med al deres klare logiske tænkning bevæget sig ind i en verden, som ikke fandtes og aldrig havde eksisteret. For verden var ikke logisk. Men hun så Sofie Amalies skarptskårne ansigt for sig og hun råbte, så det gjaldede gennem vinterskoven: – NEJ.[1159]

The fraction of the Danish society presented by Stangerup is best summarized through the Baroque term of *theatrum mundi* – the world as sheer illusion.[1160] As was the norm among educated noblemen at that time, they seemingly share this

---

1156 Ibid., p. 214.
1157 Ibid., p. 160.
1158 Ibid., p. 155.
1159 Ibid., p. 178.
1160 The most typical target of this Baroque term is the court, as »Theater in höchster Potenz« (Barner, Wilfried. *Barockrhetorik*, p. 117: »theatre in its highest potency«). Accordingly, all members of the Danish court as portrayed in Stangerup's *Spardame* are conscious albeit reluctant actors on their royal stage; cf. Stangerup, Helle. *Spardame*, p. 191: »Sofie Amalie stod ved et vindue. Hun havde spillet sine roller så perfekt på teatrets scene, og dette var også en scene. En forrykt scene. En afskyelig scene«.

ideology. Accordingly, the young and unmarried Corfitz is eager to nonchalantly express his own weariness at social gatherings – yet ironically, even this is an act:

> – Hvad er verden andet end en farce? kom det livstræt henkastet, men i de få øjeblikke, han var alene med Leonora, var forandringen total. Han blev fortrolig, han fortalte om rejsen over Alperne, om det anatomiske teater bag den øverste loggia i Padovas skønne universitet.[1161]

Leonora, like her husband, is another master of dissimulation, as observed by Sofie Amalie: »Dette smil, disse mundvige med deres falske løft og blikkets intense varme, når det var rettet mod mennesker af værdi. Forstillelsens kunst på virkelighedens scene […]«.[1162] Both are cunning actors familiar with the roles required of them. Even when life forces them to improvise, they adhere to their characters. When Denmark ends the Swedish siege of Copenhagen in 1659 with the help of Dutch allies, Sofie Amalie cannot find rest as her rival is still not removed from the stage: »Men fryden og begejstringen var væk. Den var smeltet, som sneen under hende ville smelte senest til april. Og derovre, bare et uendeligt lille punkt på den fjerne kyststribe, var en anden kvinde, som evnede smilets selvfølgelige charme, hvad der end skete«.[1163] Even though all seems lost for Leonora and her husband when the Swedish prosecution of Corfitz Ulfeldt has begun, Leonora is convinced of their imminent triumph as long as Corfitz stays in character. When Corfitz slowly recovers from his stroke and regains his ability to move and speak, he is instructed to conceal this development.[1164] Again, irony exposes the Ulfeldts' self-righteousness as Leonora advises her husband to feign a complete paralysis all the while she denounces the act that accorded her her current role: »Leonora fik rystelser. Alene i mødet med Gud kunne man vente at finde retfærdighed. Jordelivet bød kun på skinprocesser«.[1165]

Both Leonora and Sofie Amalie are hence aware of the theatrical nature of life and both condemn it. The Baroque *homo eloquens* is by nature an actor: *parler, c'est agir* – to speak is to act.[1166] Play, affectation, and fiction itself hence constitute the

---

1161 Ibid., p. 72. »Verden er en farce og styres af fordomme« – as a common topic of Baroque literature and worldview but also as a reference to his favourite author François Rabelais (1483/94-1553) – was Ulfeldt's motto (Heiberg, Steffen. *Enhjørningen Corfitz Ulfeldt*, p. 221).
1162 Stangerup, Helle. *Spardame*, p. 194.
1163 Ibid., p. 208.
1164 Ibid., p. 215.
1165 Ibid., p. 215.
1166 Barner, Wilfried. *Barockrhetorik*, p. 89.

Baroque human's right to exist. Sofie Amalie's fantasy to deny Leonora her right to act is thus more than an episode in the two women's catfight; it is an existential struggle. Consequently, Sofie Amalie's fear of Leonora is no hysterical paranoia, but a legitimate concern. The Baroque obsession with rhetorics derives from its understanding as effective speech,[1167] i.e. as the ability to create and to destroy.[1168] Hence, Stangerup, like Holm, portrays Leonora Christina once again as a powerful female writer, who had used her speech to construct her own identity and to deconstruct that of her enemy (the latter effect was not least aided by Sophie Amalie herself, who chose to remain silent and had thus yielded her constructive power to Leonora Christina), as clarified in the novel's postscript.

As indicated in the introductory chapter, *Spardame* concludes with the moment that initiates Leonora Christina's prison years: Leonora is left alone in the part of the Blue Tower called *Mørke Kirke* and wonders how long she will remain in this place. The subsequent twenty-two years are summarised in a postscript which renders Leonora the inofficial protagonist of *Spardame*. Selfsame postscript also provides some final words on Leonora Christina's afterlife, i.e. *Jammers Minde*:

> Jammersmindet vakte dengang [in the 19th century] enorm opsigt både for dets store litterære kvaliteter og for dets rystende beskrivelse af kongedatterens lange og ydmygende fangenskab. Leonora fremstod som den ædle, begavede og tragiske heltinde. Sofie Amalie som den onde dronning. Først i vore dage har vi et mere nuanceret billede. Spørgsmålet har meldt sig, om ikke hun først fik sin styrke og sin storhed gennem fornedrelsen.[1169]

The rather explicit message of this postscript, in combination with the preceding, volatile life stories, is that Leonora Christina was able to bequeath to her children and the public a monument more expressive and influential than any chapel donated by one of the richest women in Danish history, i.e. Ellen Marsvin. Even the powerful Queen Sophie Amalie, whose name graces the current residence of Danish monarchs (Amalienborg), could not prevent her enemy from blemishing her reputation almost irrevocably. While Stangerup's *Spardame* is thus first and foremost a rather conventional historical novel depicting the lives and struggles of five fascinating women, while at the same time providing its readers with a taste of Denmark's Baroque age, Stangerup's more implicit authorial intention is of a literary-advisory kind. Leonora Christina is thus presented as a historical example of a woman who

---

1167 Ibid., p. 90.
1168 Ibid.
1169 Stangerup, Helle. *Spardame*, p. 263.

tried to secure her afterlife with every means possible and who had only succeeded in doing so by choosing the humblest of media.

2.6.3. Maria Helleberg: *Kongens kvinder* (2013) and *Leonora Christine* (2014) – Fine Feathers Make Fine Birds: The Construction and Deconstruction of a *Femme Fatale*

> Elle pourtoit pour marque de sa qualité un petit chapeau de velours noir, que les seules filles de leur Roi avoient droit de porter. Elle le dit ainsi à la Reine, qui d'abord qu'elle la vit lui demanda si c'étoit la mode de son pays, et si toutes les Dames en portoient?[1170]

In the years of 1646 and 1647, Leonora Christina accompanied her husband on his journey to the Netherlands where he was sent to negotiate the future of Danish-Dutch trade and military relations. Before returning home, the couple decided to pay a visit to the French court in Paris. The memoirs of Madame de Motteville – one of Queen Anne's (Anne of Austria, 1601-1666) confidantes – quoted above give an account of Leonora Christina's reception at the court. Upon being introduced to Queen Anne, the *reine* enquires about her guest's curious little hat, which gives Leonora Christina the opportunity to state that it was an accessory exclusive to the Danish King's daughters. Ever since, this hat, flaunted by the Countess Ulfeldt in almost every portrait, has been considered her trademark; even the 17th-century satire 'Kirsten Munks Ballet' (see Chapter 2.1.1.) distinguishes Leonora Christina through this hat. Maria Helleberg, however, questions whether this status symbol was actually accorded to Leonora Christina and her sisters by King Christian IV. Instead, she portrays it as a more recent creation:

> Og den hat, Leonora bar, var den hendes egen opfindelse? En lang og smal mandehat med fjer? Damerne stimlede sammen om hende, for hendes lille mandehat sad fast i håret, som var friseret op i en knude på issen. Den gjorde hende højere end de fleste, fordi hun i forvejen var høj. – Den er et tegn på, at man er den danske konges datter, løj Leonora, de ville aldrig kunne afprøve hendes påstand.[1171]

1170 Motteville, Madame de. 'Madame de Mottevilles Skildring', p. 219.
1171 Helleberg, Maria. *Leonora Christine*, p. 146. In the complementary novel *Kongens kvinder*, Helleberg furthermore alludes to this hat through the eyes of Kirsten Munk: »Brevet var fra Leonora, og pigebarnet skrev på fransk side op og side ned, jeg gjorde sådan, og jeg blev modtaget med glæde af folk, og far siger, at jeg er utrolig, og alle klappede, og jeg havde fået lavet en lille hat som en, jeg så på et portræt fra Spanien. *Jeg er kongens yndlingsdatter«* (Helleberg, Maria. *Kongens kvinder*, p. 329).

Helleberg's *Kongens kvinder* and *Leonora Christine* turn each and every one of Leonora Christina's famous statements upside down. These two novels play with the dynamic created through the interplay between character perspective, quotations and public image of the diverse characters. *Kongens kvinder* offers only glimpses of Leonora Christina (even though the novel's last pages contain more frequent appearances of Leonora,[1172] hence disposing the reader for the follow-up novel *Leonora Christine*) and she is only portrayed through the eyes of other women. In this context, Helleberg's use of intertextuality is most illuminating as her other texts dealing with Leonora Christina serve to scrutinise her from different angles.

Among writers of fiction, Maria Helleberg, often promoted as the Queen of the Danish historical novel, is also the uncontested Leonora Christina-expert. In 1997 and 2002, respectively, she published two books entirely or partially concerned with Leonora Christina: *Leonora* and *Danmarkshistorier for børn*.[1173] In the years 2013 and 2014, Helleberg published three additional books – two novels and one non-fictional work – dedicated to, or partially dealing with, Leonora Christina. The two novels are *Kongens kvinder* (2013) and *Leonora Christine* (2014), while the latest non-fiction deals with *Kvinder der forandrede Danmark* (2013), which characterises Leonora Christina as »en af Danmarkshistoriens første skilsmissebørn«.[1174] This is a trait rather common of the recent Leonora

---

[1172] In the present chapter, »Leonora« specifically refers to the character in Maria Helleberg's novels, particularly when referring to passages that do not correspond to historical events, whereas »Leonora Christina« refers to the historical person.

[1173] The 'adult versions' of Leonora Christina's life – *Kongens kvinder* and *Leonora Christine* – are revoked in Helleberg's *Danmarkshistorier for børn*. This collection of stories accompanied by colourful illustrations presents the traditional fairy-tale variant of Leonora Christina's life. Leonora is presented as her father's favourite child and the one meant to carry on his legacy after his death (Cf. Helleberg, Maria. 'Leonora Christine'. In Helleberg, Maria. *Danmarkshistorier for børn*. Illustreret af Christian Würgler Hansen. Copenhagen: Sesam, 2005, respectively pp. 164 and 166: »I 1621 fik han med Kirsten Munk datteren Leonora Christine, som han kom til at holde særlig meget af – hun lignede ham, syntes han. Leonora Christine skulle have det sikreste, smukkeste liv, han kunne skabe for hende. Men det kom til at gå helt anderledes. [...] Det tog ikke Leonora lang tid at opdage, at hun var den eneste kvinde, som kunne gøre livet smukt ved hendes fars hof«). The only notable exception to the usual pattern is Helleberg's socialist perspective on Leonora Christina and Sophie Amalie: »Til sin rædsel opdagede Leonora, at Sofie Amalie havde en fordel i sin fattigdom og i den tid, hun havde levet sammen med sin mand uden anden storhed end en tom titel. Sofie Amalie havde intet imod at færdes til fods i byen. Hun talte med alle, høj og lav, og hun var nysgerrig, venlig og vittig. Hun lærte endda hurtigt dansk. Leonora havde aldrig færdedes til fods i byen. Hun havde aldrig nedværdiget sig til at tale med håndværkere og borgere. Hun vidste godt, de mente, hun var arrogant, men hun var jo kongedatter og måtte hele tiden passe på sin værdighed« (ibid., p. 168).

[1174] Helleberg, Maria. 'Leonora Christine Ulfeldt'. In Helleberg, Maria. *Kvinder der forandrede Danmark: Ildhu, vilje og engagement*. Rødovre: Sohn, 2013, p. 42.

Christina-literature[1175] as most biographical novels dealing with her focus on her parents' undignified separation and her character as a result of it. What is entirely new, however, is Helleberg's categorisation of Leonora Christina as politician.[1176] She argues, for example, that »[d]er er ingen tvivl om, at Christian den Fjerde uddannede hende og hendes mand, således at de kunne regere bag om hans alkoholiserede, sløvsindede søn, Den Udvalgte Prins«.[1177] Helleberg's assertion that Christian IV had educated his daughter to govern is an exaggeration. Leonora Christina had obtained the same education as her sisters, i.e. music, languages, painting and religion. Her subsequent, more elaborate education was the work of her husband, of Otto Sperling the Elder, and of her own ambition and natural curiosity. Helleberg further classifies Leonora Christina's fight against the introduction of absolutism as political activity: »Kæmpede imod enevælden, men hendes politiske virke førte til, at enevælden måtte indføres«.[1178] Leonora Christina was certainly involved in a political struggle which resulted in the replacement of one form of government by another. Yet, her reasons to become politically active were of a purely personal, even selfish nature (Helleberg, too, is aware of this and adapted her literary depictions accordingly). While it is thus inaccurate to categorise Leonora Christina in modern terms, such as 'politician', especially considering her motives, Helleberg's bold and fresh views are nevertheless highly delighting, particularly in consideration of her manifold literary portrayals of Leonora Christina. In addition, Helleberg highlights some aspects of Leonora Christina's political activity which have hitherto been mostly or even completely overlooked.

First, she emphasises the particular political implications of the *causa Leonora Christina*, i.e. that as a consequence of her case, the Danish *Kongelov* of 1665 was expanded by one section (§ 25, which Helleberg calls »Lex Leonora«)[1179] stating that members of the royal family should receive the verdict for their respective offences from the King alone (which in practice meant that Leonora Christina could

---

1175 Helleberg herself had dedicated the novel *Leonora* (1997) to this aspect of Leonora Christina's life. This book deals exclusively with Leonora Christina's childhood and the – at times rather anachronous – issues children of divorced parents have to cope with, such as identity issues (as a result of being the child of two seemingly incompatible people), resentment towards the parents' respective new partners and even eating disorders. Due to its blunt language and subject matter, Helleberg does not seem to be addressing children at all, but rather adults, who can experience the destructive effects of an unhappy marriage and subsequent divorce through the eyes of Leonora Christina.

1176 In the book's index, which lists the diverse women portrayed in the following including their respective occupations, Leonora Christina's name is followed by »politiker, forfatter«.

1177 Helleberg, Maria. 'Leonora Christine Ulfeldt', p. 44.

1178 Ibid., p. 42.

1179 Ibid., p. 49.

legally remain in prison without ever receiving a proper trial or an official verdict). This section of the *Kongelov* is also one of the few laws which are still valid today, namely as the first law in the second chapter of the first book of the *Danske Lov* of 1683.[1180]

Another fact emphasised by Maria Helleberg are the political and cultural implications of Leonora Christina's rivalry with Sophie Amalie. Some authors (such as Herta J. Enevoldsen) have portrayed Leonora Christina as a rebel against absolutism and hence as a freedom fighter and a martyr. While this particular conception is a matter of perspective, Helleberg's statement that Leonora Christina had become a representative of Denmark's fight against absolutism, due to the fact that she had published an apologia (i.e. *Jammers Minde*) while Sophie Amalie never commented on the topic, sounds all the more convincing. Furthermore, the publication of *Jammers Minde* in 1869 coincided roughly with the time of the Danish momentum to abolish absolutism (which occurred in 1848). While Leonora Christina had thus exculpated herself through the publication of a hidden apologia, Sophie Amalie remained silent and thus an unapproachable figurehead of tyranny.[1181]

Finally, and most important for this chapter's purposes, Helleberg highlights that despite Leonora Christina's initial symbolic value, she is still a highly ambivalent character with a paradoxical past:

> Hun og Corfitz tog faktisk store dele af det danske folk som gidsler. Leonora blev egentlig – med sin person og skæbne – også et bevis på, at enevælden kunne være nyttig. Om ikke andet kunne enevælden bremse elitens politiske amokløb. Og adeliges politiske hasard. Hun kom til at hjælpe indførelsen af det politiske system, hun afskyede og havde sat alt ind på at hæmme. Den første store politiske taber i Danmark.[1182]

Despite Leonora Christina's rare appearances in *Kongens kvinder*, this novel provides an enlightening prearrangement for its complementary novel *Leonora Christine*, as Leonora gradually consorts the line of women shaping Christian IV's private life. On her official website, Maria Helleberg characterises her three protagonists as follows: »De er tre stereotyper, som vi også kender i dag: Den politiske kvinde, Ellen Marsvin. Den dårlige mor, Kirsten Munk. Og golddiggeren Vibeke Kruse. De har på

1180 Cf. https://www.retsinformation.dk/Forms/R0710.aspx?id=59516. This website contains those laws of King Christian V's *Danske Lov* which are still valid today. The first of these laws states that »Printzerne og Printzesserne af Blodet skulle for ingen Underdommere svare, men deris første og siste Dommere skal Kongen være, eller hvem hand særdelis dertil forordner«.
1181 Helleberg, Maria. 'Leonora Christine Ulfeldt', p. 49. The same view is produced by Helle Stangerup (see Chapter 2.6.2.).
1182 Ibid.

mange måder samme grundlæggende behov og følelser som os«.[1183] Notwithstanding Helleberg's subsequent statement that »heller ikke kvinder er ens«,[1184] these three types are variations of the *femme fatale*. The politician and businesswoman Ellen Marsvin has clearly invaded a male domain and is hence a threat to patriarchy, while her loneliness also exposes her husband's inability to perform his physical duties. On a professional and a personal level, Ellen eventually overpowers her husband: she develops a keen sense of economy, she defies him sexually and nevertheless, she manages to foist a cuckoo's egg on Ludvig Munk, i.e. her daughter Kirsten.[1185] Helleberg's Ellen Marsvin is a feisty and sensual woman. This unusual portrayal is the result of the authoress exploiting the poor documentation of Ellen Marsvin's life in the years before she became Leonora Christina's grandmother.[1186] This, along with other examples of Helleberg's bold reinterpretation and elaboration of the lives of the women surrounding Christian IV, was perhaps the main reason why *Kongens kvinder* was nominated for DR Romanprisen 2014, which was, however, eventually won by Erling Jepsen (for his novel *Den sønderjyske farm*).

The bad mother, Kirsten Munk, on the other hand, constitutes an archetype of the *femme fatale*, i.e. Lamia, who according to Greek mythology was one of the mistresses of Zeus. When Zeus' jealous wife Hera discovers her husband's affair, she kills his and Lamia's offspring, which results in Lamia turning into an insane, child-murdering demoness.[1187] Kirsten Munk's own shortcomings as a mother to her plentiful children are first and foremost exposed by the comparison to her own

---

1183 Helleberg, Maria. 'Spørgsmål & Svar': http://www.mariahelleberg.dk/qa/, originally published in 2013.
1184 Ibid.
1185 Ludvig Munk's recognition of Ellen's only child as Kirsten Munk – despite her being the result of his wife's affair with his accountant – is the conclusive demonstration of his cowardice compared to his wife Ellen, who risked the worst of punishments with this transgression, but who nevertheless pursued what she craved: »Ludvig Munk var ikke farlig. Det ville aldrig falde ham ind at udstille sin skam« (Helleberg, Maria. *Kongens kvinder*, p. 62). Years later, after Ludvig Munk's death, Ellen continues to take what she wants. She takes a new husband without involving her male siblings in the decision, she takes over her husband's seat farms and leads them to prosperity and finally, after her second husband's demise, she takes a young and attractive peasant into her bed. As a twofold widow, Ellen becomes a 'cougar' – a fatal intrusion into male territory as it is suddenly *her*, who seduces a young, inexperienced and dependent human being. Helleberg portrays Kirsten Munk's affair with Otto Ludvig of Salm in a similar way. He is not the sadistic Don Juan depicted in Helle Stangerup's *Spardame*, but a young, innocent and naïve man, who happens to fall passionately in love with the King's wife. Her next lover, Nørlund's parish clerk, is coincidentally also a young, inexperienced man.
1186 Cf. Helleberg, Maria. 'Ellen Marsvin'. In Helleberg, Maria. *Kvinder der forandrede Danmark: Ildhu, vilje og engagement*. Rødovre: Sohn, 2013, p. 35: »Ellen Marsvin blev malet i hvert fald to gange i sit liv – da hun indgik sit andet ægteskab, og da hun som gammel kone mærkede livet ebbe ud. Det er desværre kun portrættet af den gamle kone, som er offentligt kendt. Den unge, men modne, lykkelige og frodige kvinde kender vi ikke«.
1187 Cf. Binias, Silke. *Symbol and Symptom*, p. 49. Binias also refers to similarities of this story to other examples of the early *femme fatale* (e.g. Medusa) in order to highlight their victimhood and hence the ambivalence of the *femme fatale*-motive.

upbringing. Despite Ludvig Munk's rather comprehensible request to send the cuckoo-child to Ellen's siblings once Kirsten turns three (as was the norm in the 17th century), Ellen is determined never to give her only child into the care of her estranged family: »Han var den eneste, hun aldrig havde trodset direkte. Men i dette ene ville hun stå imod. Hendes datter skulle ikke anbringes hos fjerne slægtninge«.[1188] Kirsten Munk herself is no such lioness. When she meets King Christian IV, the spoiled middle-aged man is immediately attracted to her Lolita-like qualities[1189] and he turns into a fool in the presence of this 13-year-old child.[1190] Eventually, Christian marries Kirsten, but the relationship remains one-sided. According to Helleberg, she was inspired to write *Kongens kvinder* upon seeing a real-life *femme fatale*:

> Kongens kvinder voksede ud af min undring. Jeg blev på en tur til Tyskland fascineret af et ægtepar, som jeg observerede på færgen. Manden var tydeligvis meget forelsket i konen, mens hun egentlig ikke vær [sic!] særlig interesseret i ham. Hun kunne dog godt lide, at han var vild med hende. Det er lidt det samme med Christian den Fjerde og hans første kone, Kirsten Munk [note: Kirsten Munk was Christian IV's second wife].[1191]

Thus, Helleberg sees Kirsten Munk as a classic *femme fatale*: anxious for admiration and hence helplessly vain, but also cold and dismissive. Yet, like the classical *femme fatale*, she is also a victim – the King's bedfellow and a mere birth machine. Outside the King's private chambers she fulfills no function: »At tie og være. Det var, hvad hun kunne få lov til«.[1192] Kirsten feels repulsed by her much older, inattentive husband and would hence prefer purely verbal interactions, while Christian had never learned how to talk to his child-bride and is hence only interested in the nocturnal delights she has to offer. Kirsten finds no confidants in her children either, as they remain strangers to her. In order to be at her husband's disposition as much as possible, each and every child is sent to Ellen Marsvin. As a consequence, Kir-

---

1188 Helleberg, Maria. *Kongens kvinder*, p. 64.
1189 Whether Kirsten's conduct is genuine or acumen, is diffucult to determine: »Kirsten så endelig over på sin mor, og tilbage på ham, og strakte sig, og strakte ben og fødder, vippede med fødderne. Et barn, en barnekvinde. Det var jo hendes datter, formet af hende, hun lignede sin mor, og måske sin far. Men denne lille dame var helt sig selv. – Når jeg gifter mig, får min mand retten over alt, hvad jeg ejer, sagde Kirsten fromt og så på ham, og videre til sin mor, og tilbage på ham« (ibid., p. 124).
1190 Ibid., p. 124: »– Følger hun til daglig sin mor rundt for at se, hvordan man styrer et gods? spurgte Han. Denne mand plejede at være så god til at tale med kvinder, Han roste sig selv af sit held med kvinder, og her stod en yndig ung pige foran ham. Hvad sagde Han så? Stillede et fjollet spørgsmål«.
1191 Helleberg, Maria. 'Spørgsmål & Svar': http://www.mariahelleberg.dk/qa/, originally published in 2013.
1192 Helleberg, Maria. *Kongens kvinder*, p. 135.

sten is afflicted with domestic loneliness – like Ellen used to be – even in the midst of her children: »Jeg er tilovers, slog det ned i Kirsten, jeg er ingens foretrukne selskab. Den eneste, som holder af mig, kender mig ikke«.[1193] She looks for human company wherever she sees an opportunity, even in her later rival Vibeke, who has been sent to Frederiksborg to serve as Kirsten's maid: »– Jeg er ikke min mor, du skal ikke gå og knikse hele tiden, det er ikke til nogen nytte. Tal til mig, tal med mig, jeg har ikke andre«.[1194] Once she finds a confidant, i.e. Otto Ludvig of Salm with whom she shares more than a purely physical relationship, Kirsten is willing to defend this liaison against intruders like Ellen had defended her daughter. Her children, on the other hand, are as unwanted as their father.[1195] Yet eventually, when Otto Ludvig is gone, Kirsten's loneliness takes over again: »Hun savnede dem alle: Christian, Vibeke, sin mor og børnene«.[1196]

Finally, the gold-digger Vibeke Kruse is fatal due to her overtly sexual allure and her ability and intention to use her victim's carnal weakness to her own, non-physical advantage. Helleberg's Vibeke had always liked Christian IV, as he had shown her kindness when she arrived at Frederiksborg to serve Kirsten. She also adores his children, for whom she became a mother substitute. Yet, she is also lonely and hence longing for a family, even if it should be an illegitimate one.[1197] She has a soft, vulnerable side like Kirsten and Ellen, but she has also learned from her former mistress:

> Vibeke kopierede fru Ellens bevægelse, tomme for tomme, uden at slippe hendes blik. Uden at bøje nakken. De var skilt ad nu, som barnet fra moderkagen. Han [King Christian IV] havde foræret sin Vibeke et gods i Holsten. Hun kunne spærre vejen for fru Ellen. Hun havde lært spillet, og hun havde en flig af magten i sine hænder.[1198]

In conclusion, these three women have two things in common: their loneliness and their attempts to achieve freedom. Ellen frees herself from male dominance by becoming her own master, Kirsten tries to follow her mother's path while establishing

---

1193 Ibid., p. 140.
1194 Ibid., p. 169.
1195 Ibid., p. 211: »De børn var sandelig ikke hendes valg, de blev plantet i hende, som når gartneren tog en ny potte i brug, hun havde aldrig bedt om dem«.
1196 Ibid., p. 251.
1197 Cf. ibid., p. 246.
1198 Ibid., p. 296.

an identity detached from that of her mother,[1199] and Vibeke does her best to elevate herself from her former position as servant without family or fortune. Regardless, all three women eventually fail. Kirsten's fall from grace affects her mother as well and, in the end, these two women have little to say to each other. Vibeke's sad fate is no secret either – the minute Christian IV is declared dead, she loses all protection from his vengeful daughters and their husbands.

The protagonists of Helleberg's novel are thus characterised in similar ways as the same women in Helle Stangerup's *Spardame*. The greatest difference between these two works is the degree to which Leonora Christina plays a part in them. *Kongens kvinder* portrays Leonora Christina mostly from Kirsten Munk's perspective and only through the eyes of other women; and even her mother cannot find it in her heart to ignore Leonora's hopeless vanity. One inconspicuous yet central scene delivering a hint at Leonora's character is provided towards the end of *Kongens kvinder*, which shows Kirsten Munk blossoming into an autonomous and very insightful woman, i.e. a younger version of her mother. In this scene, Kirsten observes her daughter's carefully constructed outfit:

> Leonora stod midt på gulvet med hænderne samlet foran sig. Selv indendørs gik hun med handsker, de var irgrønne, broderet med sølvtråd og besat med bittesmå perler. Venstre hånd havde en fin slids, så en særlig skøn rings sten kunne beundres gennem handsken. Hendes datter beskyttede sig mod verden med rigdom. Og lige nu var hun rolig, kold, uimodtagelig. Politisk uangribelig.[1200]

This scene appears to be a reference to, or at least inspired by, Queen Charlotte Amalie of Hesse-Kassel's visit to the Blue Tower in 1670. As recorded in *Jammers Minde*, the Queen did not introduce herself to Leonora Christina and left all conversation to her court ladies. Nevertheless, the prisoner recognised her highborn visitor by her facial features and by an especially precious ring: »Oc sidst worris allernaadigste Dronning, som ieg meest beskuede, oc fant de *liniamenter* i henders Ansict saaledis som Peter Iensen hender haffde beskreffwen, saae oc en stoer Demant paa

---

1199 This is a psychological trait exploited and amplified by Maria Helleberg, who has elsewhere stated that Christian and Ellen would have made a much better match (cf. Helleberg, Maria. 'Ellen Marsvin', p. 41: »Skade, at Christian forelskede sig i hendes datter og ikke i moderen. Ellen Marsvin havde nogle af de evner, han selv manglede«). The same story is readopted in *Kongens kvinder* and verbalised through the character of Kirsten Munk. See Helleberg, Maria. *Kongens kvinder*, p. 317: »Han [Christian IV] troede, jeg var min mors billede som ung, og at jeg elskede ham eller ville komme til at elske ham, hvis Han elskede mig tilstrækkeligt meget og hedt. Det skete ikke, og Han hader mig til sin dødsdag for at have svigtet ham. Men jeg er ikke min mor, jeg er Kirsten Munk, og jeg vil have min frihed«.

1200 Ibid., p. 406.

henders Armlaas, oc en paa Fingeren huor Handsken war opskaarren« (*Jammers Minde*, p. 178). Leonora Christina describes the Queen as being speechless at the face of all the hardship she sees. She further reports that Queen Charlotte Amalie had persuaded her husband to promise to release Leonora Christina if their firstborn child should be a boy. Sophie Amalie's successor is thus portrayed as a kind and noble spirit, unmasked by her jewellery. Maria Helleberg, however, adds an ironic twist to this scene by alluding to it in a context that exposes Leonora's passion for finery, as a nervous attempt at shielding herself.[1201] To Kirsten, Leonora's motives become even more obvious in comparison with Sophie Amalie: »Hun var sikker, som Leonora aldrig havde været det. Behøvede ingen slids i sin handske for at vise en særlig kostbar sten frem. Hende skulle alle alligevel respektere og adlyde«.[1202]

Leonora Christine, which is narrated from its protagonist's perspective, confirms Kirsten's conviction. Even the famous black velvet hat, Leonora Christina's trademark, is nothing but a homespun remedy against insecurity: »Måske skulle hun have iført sig den lille mandehat, som hun plejede at gå med. Den var hendes særpræg, det billede, hun ønskede at vise andre. Ikke denne usikre kvinde, som stod og gav sig hen til kuldegysningerne og til sin egen frygt«.[1203]

Leonora's sullen use of expensive clothing and gems is of particular interest to this chapter as it, on the one hand, exposes her as a staged character, who uses artful ways of cloaking (e.g. with gloves) and uncloaking (such as the exposure of a ring through the gloves) in order to construct her body and hence her image. In this regard, Helleberg's Leonora is potentially dangerous as she is presented as one of the most fatal types of the *femme fatale*, i.e. Salome. Lise Præstgaard Andersen refers to Salome as obtaining her lethal appeal through a carefully calculated construction of the body by covering and uncovering at the same time,[1204] »således at det bliver meget svært at skelne, hvad der er kvinde (natur), og hvad der er påklædning, smykker, sko og andre kunstfærdige virkemidler (unatur)«.[1205] On the other hand,

---

1201 Cf. ibid., p. 420: »Leonora fulgte Sophie Amalie med blikket – hun drejede ikke hovedet, hun brugte kun øjnene, som en kat. Der var ikke det sted på Leonora, hvor man kunne få anbragt endnu en perle eller en fjer. Tværtimod virkede det, som om hun havde iført sig demonstrativ, overlæsset rigdom«.

1202 Ibid., p. 408.

1203 Helleberg, Maria. *Leonora Christine*, p. 167.

1204 Following this tradition, the transparent veil has become a classic means for women to generate an atmosphere of exotic eroticism.

1205 Præstgaard Andersen, Lise. *Sorte damer*, p. 28.

though, Leonora's dependency on her glittering armour[1206] gradually exposes her as the weaker woman; eventually, Sophie Amalie manages to strip her adversary of all her luxury items, hence bereaving Leonora of her identity – for the time being, this is a complete victory for Sophie Amalie.

Kirsten Munk recognises the young Queen's advantage over her daughter much sooner than Leonora herself. She attributes her daughter's overtly territorial behaviour[1207] to the substantial threat posed by Sophie Amalie: »Fru Kirsten ville ikke tysse på sin datter. Men hun kunne da glimrende forstå Leonoras skinsyge. Hun havde *konstrueret sig selv* [my italics] ud af lutter detaljer, mens Sophie Amalie nu fik alt foræret«.[1208] Kirsten Munk's judgement inverts most previous portrayals of Leonora Christina and her rival Sophie Amalie. While authors like Herta J. Enevoldsen and Helle Stangerup depict Leonora Christina as personified self-confidence and the Queen as a desperately vain scarecrow, Maria Helleberg reverses this characterisation. Her Leonora is insecure and lonely,[1209] and depends hence on details, while Sophie Amalie is anything but that – for she has it all.

In *Kvinder der forandrede Danmark*, as well as in *Leonora Christine*, Helleberg contends that Corfitz Ulfeldt had had an aversion to real estate: »Han havde ikke

---

1206 Cf. Carola Hilmes, who identifies the 'holy courtesan' as another type of *femme fatale* due to her body, shielded by gems and hence virginal (Hilmes, Carola. *Die Femme fatale*, p. 20). Hilmes' analysis confirms Helleberg's portrayal of Leonora Christina, as well as her female contemporaries, as secretly vulnerable. Hilmes' implicit reference to the shield maiden, or the amazon (but also to Salome), is of especial significance to this chapter as the combination of the masculine attribute of armament together with maidenhood ascribed to this type of woman matches Helleberg's Leonora, as will be explicated below.

1207 Cf. Helleberg, Maria. *Kongens kvinder*, p. 405: »– Hun kommer fra Braunschweig, sagde Leonora endelig. Hendes stemme var tilkæmpet neutral, men meningen var klar, Sophie Amalie var en fremmed fugl. Hendes hjemby var latterlig, målt med København, et stort kongeriges hovedstad. [...] Men fru Kirsten vidste, at Braunschweig var en prægtig by med rigtigt hofliv, en vældig kunstsamling, selvbevidsthed og styrke. Sophie Amalie var givetvis både selvbevidst og stolt. Men også ganske alene og isoleret i familien. Leonora måtte læse noget andet og værre hos den unge kvinde, hvis hun opførte sig arrogant«.

1208 Ibid., p. 421.

1209 In this regard, Leonora resembles her mother more than she would like to admit to herself. To Corfitz, infidelity is an ideology, especially during his wife's numerous pregnancies. In the hopes of recapturing her husband, Leonora is constantly trying to better herself with every means possible. As a result, she has little time for her children and is left isolated in her home. All of Helleberg's women are lonely individuals with a bad fame. Her use of a change of perspective challenges the diverse women's fame, hence rendering a more eclectic portrait of an age and its inhabitants. This technique is no novelty; Carola Hilmes points to a similar literary method used by some *fin de siècle*-writers, such as Heinrich Mann. His trilogy *Die Göttinnen oder Die drei Romane der Herzogin von Assy* (1903) produces the story of the Countess of Assy from its protagonist's point of view, hence allowing its recipient to learn about the fatal woman's loneliness (»Als Idol ist sie zur Einsamkeit verdammt«; see Hilmes, Carola. *Die Femme fatale*, p. 70).

sat formuen i jord, han havde den i kontanter, smykker og lån«.[1210] Instead, he and his wife preferred portable and presentable wealth. The reasons for this mindset are, in summary, determined by Corfitz's will and need to represent, exemplified by his wife as well. Leonora, too, follows the motto 'Dress to impress': »Hvor hendes mor og mormor havde reinvesteret i godser og jord, var Leonora og Corfitz's velstand særdeles synlig. Velstand skulle bæres, drikkes, vises frem, være spændt foran ens vogn og pryde vægge og gulve«.[1211] This attitude is not only produced in Helleberg's novels. Louise Hegermann Lindencrone's tale 'Billedet', too, deserves especial mention in this context, as Eleonora's clothes and the riches produced in her temporary home in The Hague capture the protagonist's mind to a degree that would come to determine the rest of Elisabeth's life. This sort of poetics of clothing[1212] is a central topic in Rolf Gjedsted's novel *Fordærvede kvinder* as well, where attire and jewellery serve as a means to implement women's desires and their rivalry among each other.

In *Leonora Christine*, the competition between Leonora and Sophie Amalie is once again implemented through a secret fashion show which turns the Queen's hunting ground into a catwalk. In this environment, Leonora is completely out of her element, yet she tries to blend in with her scenically matching outfit. Despite her averseness to hunting and her lack of equestrian practice, she dresses for the occasion: »[H]un havde fået syet en grøn dragt med pynt, som hun nød at vise frem. Med ulveskind overalt, hvor det var muligt, som en hilsen til Corfitz«.[1213] Sophie Amalie, on the other hand, has turned the forest into her home and playground. She adores hunting and can easily use her pastime to accentuate the image she is

---

1210 Helleberg, Maria. 'Leonora Christine Ulfeldt', p. 45. The Ulfeldts' lack of interest in real estate as a form of investment is in fact historically well-grounded as clothes and other portable valuables constituted a major portion of the pawnbroking business up until the 19th century (cf. Jones, Ann Rosalind and Peter Stallybrass. *Renaissance Clothing and the Materials of Memory*, p. 30). This implies that the notion of clothing as constituting basic assets (instead of mere luxury, i.e. superfluous items) was more widespread in the Ulfeldts' age than Helleberg's novel conveys.

1211 Helleberg, Maria. *Leonora Christine*, p. 127.

1212 I am referring to Roland Barthes' use of the term »Poétique du vêtement« ('poetics of clothing') in his influential study *Système de la Mode*, published in 1967. In his book, Barthes assigns the language and terminology used in texts describing fashion – he conducted his study by means of French fashion magazines – a rhetorical value, i.e. an effective function. See Barthes, Roland. *Système de la Mode*, pp. 239-248. Andreas Kraß' study on the identity-constituting function of clothing in chivalric romance, too, presupposes the theory of clothing as a symbol of social identity, with garment, body and person semiotically mirroring the trinity of *signifiant*, *signifié* and *signe* (see Kraß, Andreas. *Geschriebene Kleider: Höfische Identität als literarisches Spiel*. Tübingen and Basel: Francke, 2006 (Bibliotheca Germanica 50), p. 2).

1213 Helleberg, Maria. *Leonora Christine*, p. 188.

about to create for herself. She appears as multiple *femme fatale* – as a goddess[1214] and as an unconquerable maneater. As Leonora approaches while concentrating on reining her horse, Sophie Amalie is surrounded by a flock of young, attractive men, all hanging on her lips. As if this had not been enough to steal Leonora's thunder, Sophie Amalie wears the most flamboyant outfit:

> Men jakken, jakken. Den var fuldkommen overbroderet med guld og farvet silke. Syet sammen af rester, så vidt hun vidste, en gave fra dronning Elizabeth i England, da Christians søster Anne blev skotsk dronning. Selv da hendes far var allerfattigst, havde han sparet og skånet denne sidste rest pragt og storhed. På ærmer og bryst voksede der blomster, som skjulte symboler og alskens snurrepiberier.[1215]

Leonora is aghast at Sophie Amalie – who seems to not have noticed her arrival at all – and her unequivocal fashion statement, hence she is left with no other choice but to leave the battlefield:

> Så havde den lille kvinde fra Braunschweig alligevel smag og sans for at bruge alt i sin nærhed, slog det ned i hende. God smag og tilbedende unge mænd omkring sig og en hengiven ægtemand – og en vrimmel af smukke børn. Sophie Amalie ville ikke være tilfreds, før hun havde erobret alt andet.[1216]

Unlike the women's fashion rivalry depicted in *Fordærvede kvinder*, this scene is not symptomatic of a century's hopeless decadence and depravity. In their study on the constructive functionality of Renaissance clothing, Ann Rosalind Jones and Peter Stallybrass emphasise the semantic shift the word 'fashion' has undergone in the early modern age. Initially,

> [...] »fashion« did not have changing styles of clothing as its naturalized referent; rather, it commonly referred to the act of making, or to the make or shape of a thing, or to form as opposed to matter, or to the enduring manners and customs of a society. It was thus the goldsmith's »fashion« (what would later be called »fashioning«) which added value to the raw material that he worked upon.[1217]

1214 Ibid., p. 189: »Bondepige, krigens gudinde, jagtens gudinde, spansk dame, græsk gudinde, altid en hovedrolle. Således åbenbart også under jagten, som hun elskede så højt, at hun gerne ville fremstilles som selveste den kyske Diana«.
1215 Ibid., p. 189.
1216 Ibid., p. 190.
1217 Jones, Ann Rosalind and Peter Stallybrass. *Renaissance Clothing and the Materials of Memory*, p. 1.

Based on this original meaning of the term 'fashion', the early modern human used clothes in order to shape body politics. Rank and gender were constituted through fashion,[1218] to an extent which renders many early modern portraits as records of their sitters' clothing, rather than the sitters themselves: »These portraits, then, are as much the portraits of clothes and jewels as of people – mnemonics to commemorate a particularly extravagant suit, a dazzling new fashion in ruffs, a costly necklace or jewel«.[1219] This is in part due to the circumstances of how these portraits were made. The sitter's service was usually required for only a fraction of the time that went into creating the endresult, whereas the clothes and jewels would have to be worn by a body double during every session. This has resulted in some of these portraits showing the sitters' faces as something that resembles a background to their much livelier attire.[1220] One case in point is the earliest portrait of Leonora Christina, painted by Jakob van Doordt in 1623 and portraying her together with her mother, her two elder sisters and her brother Valdemar Christian.[1221] The faces of the three girls depicted in this portrait are representative for this era's style, as they are merely miniature versions of their mother's face instead of portraying four different individuals. Maria Helleberg depicts this scene in *Kongens kvinder*. Kirsten Munk had received the opportunity to be painted together with a dress worthy of a Queen, as a reward for giving the King a son, the first one after three daughters. The dress is the undisputed centrepiece of the painting. The sitters, however, are only needed for a first sketch: »Det skulle ikke tage meget af deres tid, lovede maleren. Han ville blot gerne have et indtryk af dem alle, og han krattede løs […]«.[1222]

One scene in particular illustrates the identity-constituting function of clothing as well as the reversal of Leonora's gender through a change of garment. In 1655, when Leonora Christina and Corfitz had been forced to flee from their home in Barth (Swedish Pomerania) due to an impending conviction for treason, Leonora Christina and her husband travelled incognito, with Leonora Christina dressed as a man. In this scene, as portrayed in the novel, Leonora's new appearance as well as her new identity lend her a type of freedom previously unknown to her and she is prepared to sample all of its pleasures. She enjoys the firm step of her boots, the authority conveyed by her arms and the freedom provided by trousers. Yet, there are many more delights to be savoured in this kind of disguise: »Mænd tørnede ikke

---

1218 Ibid., p. 2.
1219 Ibid., p. 34.
1220 Ibid., p. 35.
1221 This painting is preserved in Rosenborg Castle in Copenhagen.
1222 Helleberg, Maria. *Kongens kvinder*, p. 139.

bare ind, når de kom til et nyt logi, vidste hun. Mænd gjorde sig det behageligt. De drak, og de horede. Leonora havde intet imod at gøre som mænd«.[1223] By taking on her husband's clothing, Leonora takes on his role[1224] – that of an irresponsible, pleasure-seeking man, who only lives for himself: »Hun nød at sidde og iagttage andre, skjult i sit falske køn. Uden ansvar for hverken mand eller børn«.[1225] From this first experience onwards, Leonora enjoys wearing men's clothing.

In these years of abscondence, Leonora increasingly questions her own identity and that of her husband. As they are outlaws, they lack a referential environment and, as a consequence, their gender-reversal accelerates until it culminates with Leonora's imprisonment: »Hun var hovedet, han var kroppen. Hun var blevet mand, og han kvinde. Hun sad fængslet, mens han vansmægtede i landflygtighed, sammen med deres børn«.[1226]

This gender-confusion is rendered obsolete when Leonora reaches the Blue Tower. Her initial refusal to expose her bare body to this new referential environment[1227] is a futile attempt to sustain her self-constructed identity. When Sophie Amalie's maid Abel Cathrine (whom Leonora Christina included in her death list) thus urges Leonora to take off her own dress and put on a simple grey chemise instead, the prisoner cannot think of a worse punishment: »Hvis hun iklædte sig den, aflagde hun al sin værdighed. Så ophørte hun med at være Leonora og blev statsfangen fru Ulfeldt«.[1228] Over the years in prison, her stylised body, her image is gradually deconstructed until only her natural body is left: »Hun havde engang været optaget af, om de kunne genvinde deres boliger og ejendomme. Nu stod det

---

1223 Helleberg, Maria. *Leonora Christine*, p. 225.

1224 Leonora herself observes that in this inn, the rules of the outside world do not apply: »Dette var den omvendte verden, en kvinde, som udfordrede, og en mand, som veg tilbage« (ibid., p. 226). As a consequence, Leonora and her former husband and master change roles as soon she dresses accordingly, while Corfitz appears in this scene only dressed in a »natskjorte [probably not a very manly sight] og søvnighed« (ibid., p. 227), both attributes of passive femininity: »De havde byttet køn. Nu forstod hun det. Corfitz gemte sig bag døren, mens hun trak blank« (ibid.).

1225 Ibid., p. 226.

1226 Ibid., p. 11.

1227 »Ikke røre gulvet med fødderne, med nøgen hud. Fandt sine strømper frem og tog dem på og stak fødderne ned i sine sko. Ikke røre ved noget med nøgen hud« (ibid., p. 9).

1228 Ibid., p. 14. See also ibid., p. 12: »Omsider kom sorgen til hende, som gråd og pine, ikke sorgen over tabet af mand og børn og frihed, men en spids smerte over tabet af de sølle juveler, hun havde forsøgt at gemme«. This seemingly superficial feeling has, however, deep roots in the late medieval and early modern literary-cultural canon. One famous example of a woman, who was stripped of her clothes and hence her identity is Griselda, as pointed out by Ann Rosalind Jones and Peter Stallybrass. Griselda is a character in Boccaccio's *Decamerone*; she is a simple peasant girl and in order to turn her into 'noble wife material', Griselda's future husband strips her naked and redresses her (see Jones, Ann Rosalind and Peter Stallybrass. *Renaissance Clothing and the Materials of Memory*, pp. 220-244).

om livet«.[1229] Even Corfitz, who had become a part of her identity, without whom she feels incomplete,[1230] is gradually excised out of her body. She is eventually left with only her body, while Sophie Amalie undergoes the opposite development until she is nothing but a grotesquely decorated entity, whose body barely resembles a human anymore:

> Kurven, hvor enkedronningen lod sig hejse op og ned, faldt til jorden, mens Leonora iagttog den farefulde færd, og hun kunne følge, hvordan dronningen raslede ud af sin kurv og havnede på alle fire som et dyr. Overpyntet og oversminket fik hun sin straf. Hofdamerne måtte besværligt rejse den kæntrede flodhest og halvt bære, halvt skubbe hende ind i huset igen.[1231]

Despite all escapist efforts,[1232] Leonora eventually sees and accepts the degree to which she has been stripped when the new Queen of Denmark, Charlotte Amalie of Hesse-Kassel, together with her mother and some court ladies enters Leonora's bubble (i.e. the Blue Tower), where time seems to have no power or meaning and where the progress of the outside world goes unnoticed.[1233] They all resemble highly stylised dolls with their angelic curls and their crimson cheeks whereas Leonora has nothing but herself to offer: »Engang havde hun selv været som dem, men alt overflødigt var fjernet fra hendes personlighed, og de trivedes kun i overflødighed. Hun kunne ikke holde dem ud«.[1234]

After Leonora's release from the Blue Tower, her biological body, too, begins to dissolve. She becomes overweight, indolent and old. Notwithstanding her newly-granted freedom, her damaged body is still forced into inactivity: »Leonora havde forventet, at det var hendes sind, som vanskeligst ville vænne sig til frihed«.[1235] Eventually, Leonora – as she used to be – is gone. Everything that used to be a recognisable part of the construct called *frøken Leonora* has disappeared by the time she has made her home in Maribo; what is left is a *tabula rasa*. Gloves, formerly one of her favourite tools to cover herself in mystery and luxury, now serve

---

1229 Helleberg, Maria: *Leonora Christine*, p. 316.
1230 »I løbet af de første ti år sammen var han gledet så dybt ind i hendes liv, at hun egentlig ikke længere kunne skille dem ad« (ibid., p. 257).
1231 Ibid., p. 280.
1232 »Hun forsøgte at holde sig hel og ren og velklædt. Hun forsøgte at ophøje sit fængsel, havde fået guldmaller syet på sit snøreliv, havde fået guldbestik at spise med og pyntede sig hver dag, friserede håret op og satte det med små kamme og smykker« (ibid., p. 186).
1233 Cf. ibid., p. 361: »Verden var alt det, som befandt sig uden for hendes celle«.
1234 Ibid., p. 288.
1235 Ibid., p. 412.

merely as working garment. Her formerly written clothes conveying meaning are now replaced by merely worn or 'real' clothes,[1236] which provide nothing but trivial coverage.[1237] What is left is not the Leonora she had constructed by herself decades ago, nor the biological Leonora that was unsheathed when she was stripped of all her belongings:

> Hver gang hun kom til at se sig selv i spejlet, studsede hun over det næsten selvlysende, klumpede ansigt. Dette havde jo intet at gøre med Leonora. Dette var en aldrende, værdig og tung kvinde, som bar alle sine oplevelser offentligt til skue i sit ansigt. Dette var en ny Kirsten Munk. Hendes mor var genopstået inde i sin datters ansigt. Men hendes far var ganske forsvundet.[1238]

Despite all efforts to dissociate themselves from their estranged ancestors, Ellen Marsvin, Kirsten Munk and Leonora have become one.[1239] Like the little girl depicted by Jakob van Doordt, Leonora has become an effigy of her mother, ripped of a separate identity. When Leonora reunites with her eldest daughter in Maribo, she and her child share the same experience: »Hendes datter var blevet hendes skygge, det vidste hun«.[1240] With this meeting between Leonora and the next generation of Ulfeldts, the cycle closes while Leonora Christina's lineage and fame are bereaved of all the myths that were built up during *Kongens kvinder* – for both are dismantled in *Leonora Christine*: »Leonora var reduceret til et nøgent sandskorn, men ikke desto mindre var hele personen alligevel til stede i dette ene korn«.[1241]

[1236] Cf. Roland Barthes, who distinguishes »vêtement écrit« from »vêtement reel« (Barthes, Roland. *Système de la Mode*, p. 18).

[1237] Helleberg, Maria. *Leonora Christine*, p. 421: »Her [in Maribo] gik hun i have og urtegård for at gøre nytte. […] Til lejligheden havde hun iført sig et par lange handsker, der havde kendt bedre dage, men som passede til havearbejde, der involverede jord og seje rødder«.

[1238] Ibid., p. 417.

[1239] Towards the end of the novel *Kongens kvinder*, Kirsten Munk, too, turns into her mother's doppelgänger. Her successor Vibeke sees this all too clear when the two women see each other again after many years. When the two women's carriages almost clash on a narrow country road in Holstein and the two rivals face each other, Vibeke is distraught by how much her former mistress has changed: »I den anden vogn sad en kvinde, som lignede fru Ellen Marsvin slående: et enormt, måneagtigt ansigt, gråblegt fedt og to smalle øjne. Al den askeblonde skønhed var borte, æltet til dej af tiden. […] De to kvinder var ved at gro sammen, de havde fået de samme træk; alderen skilte dem ikke længere, men bandt dem sammen« (Helleberg, Maria. *Kongens kvinder*, p. 384).

[1240] Helleberg, Maria. *Leonora Christine*, p. 420.

[1241] Ibid., p. 428.

Leonora (Christina)'s father had been a, if not *the* constitutive aspect of his daughter's identity.[1242] The other half of her body and character, her mother, was regularly swept under the carpet. The conspicuous lack of mention of her mother in Leonora Christina's writings as well as the very same sentiment attributed to Helleberg's Kirsten Munk reaffirm this suspicion:

> Hun måtte ikke vise sig i Roskilde, og fru Kirsten forstod med en bitter smag i munden: Leonora og de andre ønskede ikke at huske folk på, hvem og hvad deres mor var. De var alene kongens børn, avlet og født ved Helligåndens hjælp. De var kongebørn, af ædel byrd, og de holdt sammen, for de havde ingen andre at støtte sig til. Og de var den nye konges søskende.[1243]

Leonora's insistence on flaunting her black velvet hat as a public link to her royal father suggests the same. When the aged Leonora is thus no longer able to detect her father when observing herself, Sophie Amalie – despite being outlived by her enemy – seems to have achieved her goal, i.e. the complete annihilation of Leonora.

However, Leonora has not given up just yet. She resorts to her magnum opus, *Jammers Minde*, in order to rebuild herself:

> Hun byggede perspektiv ind i sin tekst som i et intrikat moderne brevskab, fulde af spejle og skuffer, hvor hver åbning var en fiktion, et fikserbillede af dybde. Hun ville tilbage til teksten og fortiden og genskabe sine koner, slotsfogeden og Mørke Kirke. Det var hendes tryghed, den lillebitte teaterscene, hvor hun i årtier havde improviseret sin hovedrolle som hr. frøken.[1244]

Helleberg's novels address diverse subject matters, which are constantly inverted and reaffirmed through the interplay of the two texts and the change of perspective obtained through the respective protagonists' separation through chapters in *Kongens kvinder* on the one hand, and the distorted chronology of Leonora's life narrative in *Leonora Christine* on the other. The novels deal with gender-conflicts and its early modern implementation in the form of witch hunts, and the topics of unhappy marriage and lonely wives. The thusly implied feminist

---

1242 Not even her role as the wife of the powerful Corfitz Ulfeldt seems to have coined her self-conception to a similar degree: »– Fru Ulfeldt, sagde han [Karl X Gustav of Sweden, with whom Corfitz is about to conspire against Denmark], men hun havde aldrig kaldt sig Leonora Christine Ulfeldt. Hun var alene frøken Leonora, kongens datter« (ibid., p. 251).
1243 Helleberg, Maria. *Kongens kvinder*, p. 407.
1244 Helleberg, Maria. *Leonora Christine*, p. 433.

dimension of the two texts receives staggered redemption through the delayed emancipation of the diverse female characters. If, however, one conceives of the two complementary novels as one autobiographical novel on Leonora Christina including an extended preview – as the promotional appearance of Leonora towards the end of *Kongens kvinder*, as well as Helleberg's lifelong interest in Leonora Christina, would suggest – one major topic of these two novels is also constituted by Leonora's own attempt at rebuilding and emancipating herself, i.e. through the use of literature.

When Leonora is released from the Blue Tower, she has lost all identities that had been suggested before as options for females. She is no longer a mother since her children are completely estranged from and at times even hostile towards her. Her father, her husband, and even her royal half-brother are dead, hence she is no longer part of any family or social group, since even her former position as noblewoman has been rendered insignificant by the introduction of absolutism. Not to mention that Leonora has neither the financial means, nor the proper audience to parade any luxury items in Maribo. Hence, she is left to resort to literature. Instead of carrying the outward symbols of her former social group she inscribes herself, the *tabula rasa*, with a new identity.[1245] Once this new life is set out in writing, Leonora is ready to leave this world: »Der var ikke mere at gøre i livet, så hun lod det ebbe ud, befriet og reduceret«.[1246] Leonora's voluntary disengagement from the world in her reduced form is, however, not equal to Sophie Amalie's obliteration of her enemy. Leonora had written her immortal identity into a text. Her daughter's closing words testify to her mother's afterlife: »– Nej, der er stadig liv i hende, hørte hun sin datter hviske, splittet mellem fortrydelse og glæde«.[1247]

2.7. International Leonora Christina-literature

The three texts discussed in the following share no thematic approach to the topic of Leonora Christina and her writings. Instead, they serve as a comparative group to those presented above and their only common feature is the non-Danish nationality

---

[1245] »Alene for at kunne forstå hende måtte Leo overtage hendes manuskript, det eneste, hun havde skrevet, som hun ikke ønskede publiceret. Han ville beskytte hendes værk. Det var stilet til børnene, og det var en forklaring af, hvordan fangenskabet havde formet hende« (ibid.).
[1246] Ibid., p. 446.
[1247] Ibid., p. 447.

of their respective authors. The following three subchapters are thus concerned with the question whether this group of texts features similar topics and dispositions as identified above, and whether the non-Danish background of author and intended audience could have instigated entirely new approaches to the topic. As most notably demonstrated by Chapter 2.2., the name of Leonora Christina is associated with issues of patriotism and loyalty. Chapter 2.5. illustrates how Leonora Christina and *Jammers Minde* have taken up a central place in Denmark's cultural history, the implication of which is the monopolisation of her story by one country. A complementary look into the representation of Leonora Christina in international literature thus seems expedient, particularly since only very few non-Danish authors have engaged in the topic.

Corresponding to the chronological approach within the subchapters, the German writer Leopold Schefer's novel *Die Gräfin Ulfeld oder die vierundzwanzig Königskinder* (see Chapter 2.7.1.), published in 1834 and hence prior to most of the Danish texts engaging with Leonora Christina, is the first of the three texts presented below. Next is the Bohemian-Austrian writer Rainer Maria Rilke's autobiographically inspired novel *Die Aufzeichnungen des Malte Laurids Brigge* (see Chapter 2.7.2.), published in 1910. This work exhibits a transitional quality the two other texts do not, as *Malte* is the product of Rilke's Scandinavian, particularly Danish 'phase'. As a tribute to one of his literary role models, the Danish writer Jens Peter Jacobsen, Rilke's eponymous hero Malte Laurids Brigge is a Dane, the last living representative of an old Danish dynasty. Accordingly, the publication of *Malte* was preceded by intensive and protracted studies abroad, especially in Copenhagen, and the result is a plethora of allusions to Danish history in the novel. The historical framework outlined in *Malte* was furthermore inspired by Jens Peter Jacobsen's own research for his naturalistic historical novel *Marie Grubbe* (1876), which relates the story of the eponymous noblewoman, who was also a distant contemporary of Leonora Christina. Hence Chapter 2.7.2. commences not with an analysis of Leonora Christina's literary function in *Malte*, but with a presentation of Jens Peter Jacobsen, the 'middleman' of the Leonora Christina-subject matter, and his interest in *Jammers Minde*.

The final literary text discussed in this study, the historical novel *Kungligt blod* by the Swedish writer and translator Karin Johnsson (see Chapter 2.7.3.), published in 1919, is a biographical novel. *Kungligt blod* is thus one of the earliest biographical novels, and *the* earliest biographical novel written by a woman, about Leonora Christina. Historical women's literature in Denmark experienced a breakthrough only in the second half of the 20th century, which is why Karin Johnsson's early representative of this genre is of particular interest in this context.

2.7.1. Leopold Schefer: *Die Gräfin Ulfeld oder die vierundzwanzig Königskinder*[1248] (1834) – Boys Will Be Boys or Mathilde Fibiger's Nightmare

»At Eleonore Ulfeld var en Heltinde for Mænd, forstaaer jeg godt!« svarede Victoria med spottende Stemme. Thi en Mand var hendes Guddom! Naar vi saaledes dyrke dem, og ligge paa Knæ for deres Fuldkommenhed – saa faae vi Heltinderang. Men naar Ære, Fædreland og Religion er os helligere end deres Kjærlighed – saa er vi svage, hjerteløse, ufølsomme Væsner. Jeg kan tænke mig at en Mand i sin Forfængelighed dømmer saaledes[«.][1249]

While regarded as some of German poetry's forgotten treasures, the literary works of the writer and composer Leopold Schefer (1784-1862)[1250] have regularly been characterised as obscure. Most contemporary criticism dealing with Schefer's prose writings commend the thoughts presented in his work, while at the same time resigning to try to understand them. The *Damen Conversations Lexikon* (1834-1838), for example, pronounces a comparably favourable judgement by complimenting Schefer's aphorisms which are »die feinsten Entdeckungen auf dem Gebiete des menschlichen Herzens in einem eigenthümlichen, idealen Gewande«.[1251] Other critics have been less kind; such as Karl Gutzkow, who spurns Schefer's female ideology, his »Uteruspoesie«.[1252] Considering such critiques, it should come as no surprise to learn that both Schefer's target audience and his preferred subject matter were women.[1253]

In his analysis of Schefer's prose writings, Albin Lenhard connects this circumstance – the general (albeit mostly male) perplexity in the face of Schefer's literary products – to the author's finite popularity,[1254] while Gutzkow, among many

---

1248 'The Countess Ulfeld or the Twenty-Four Royal Children'.
1249 Fibiger, Mathilde. *En Skizze*, p. 105.
1250 Perhaps Schefer's (among contemporaries known under the pen name Pandira) most famous publications are the short story 'Palmerio' (1823) and *Laienbrevier* (1834/35), which made Schefer a celebrity until the mid-19th century, when his work began to be considered obsolete.
1251 *Damen Conversations Lexikon 9: Rubens bis Tabernakel*, ed. C. Herlosssohn. Adorf: Verlags-Bureau, 1837, p. 85 ('the finest discoveries in the field of the human heart in a peculiar, ideal form').
1252 Gutzkow, Karl. *Beiträge zur Geschichte der neuesten Literatur 1*. Stuttgart: Balz, 1839, p. 259 ('uterus poetry').
1253 Lenhard, Albin. *Zur Erzählprosa Leopold Schefers*. Cologne and Vienna: Böhlau, 1975 (böhlau forum litterarum 4), p. 220.
1254 Ibid., p. 51.

others, attributes the latter to his Biedermeier subject matters.[1255] Notwithstanding his at times misogynist reasoning,[1256] Gutzkow produces a sound argument in referring to Schefer's mystical understanding and appraisal of women as the ultimate reason for his literary failure: »Kurz, die Klippe, an welcher der Dichter scheitert, bleibt seine Sucht nach Zartheit und seine Anbetung des Weibes, als eines ganz abstrakten Begriffes, und im Weibe wieder die Anbetung der Mutter«.[1257]

Despite being his first novel, *Die Gräfin Ulfeld* constitutes no great exception to Schefer's oeuvre. Like most of his prose writings, the novel engages in presenting »[d]ie einfachen Bande der Familie, die Leiden und Freuden eines Gatten, eines Vater-, eines Mutterherzens«.[1258] F. G. Kühne's criticism of the novel, stating that Schefer had been unable »uns [...] ein Gesammtbild von einem absoluten Herrscherhause aus dem siebzehnten Jahrhundert zu entwerfen«[1259] is thus rather unwarranted, inasmuch as it had hardly been Schefer's intention to produce a historical novel of 'Walter Scottish' calibre. Instead, his declared objective was »die Geschichte auf das menschliche Herz zu basiren«.[1260]

Like most of Schefer's writings, *Die Gräfin Ulfeld* also refuses to disclose its innermost meaning to its readers. Accordingly, a review of *Die Gräfin Ulfeld* published in the literary magazine *Blätter für literarische Unterhaltung* calls the recently published novel »ein neues Geheimniß, ein neues inhaltreiches und kost-

---

1255 Cf. F. G. Kühne, who also indicates that Schefer's historical and at times even exotic literary topics would always remain bounded by the author's disposedness to domestic deliberation (Kühne, F[erdinand] G[ustav]. Review of *Die Gräfin Ulfeld, oder die vierundzwanzig Königskinder* by Leopold Schefer, Jahrbücher für wissenschaftliche Kritik 1835/1, p. 496).

1256 »Das ist die Noth: Schefer's Phantasie glüht nicht, sie erwärmt nur, sie ist mild und linde und hält sich auf einer Stufe der Weltanschauung, welche nie zureichend ist, auf der weiblichen« (Gutzkow, Karl. *Beiträge zur Geschichte der neuesten Literatur 1*, p. 256: 'That is the issue: Schefer's phantasy does not blaze, but only warms, it is mild and gentle and remains at the level of an ideology which will always be insufficient, and this level is female').

1257 Ibid., p. 259 ('In short, the cliff at which he fails as a writer is his longing for tenderness and his adoration of women as an entirely abstract concept, which comprises his worship of motherhood'). Incidentally, Heinrich Laube, a less fierce critic of Schefer, comes to the same conclusion (Laube, Heinrich. *Geschichte der deutschen Literatur 4*. Stuttgart: Hallberg, 1840, p. 163). For an understanding of the following quotes from Schefer's work, it is important to note that the (antiquated) German word *Weib* means both 'woman' and 'wife'.

1258 *Damen Conversations Lexikon 9*, p. 85 ('simple family matters, the sorrows and joys of a husband, of a father's, of a mother's heart').

1259 Kühne, F[riedrich] G[ustav]: 'Leopold Schefer'. In Kühne, F[riedrich] Gustav. *Portraits und Silhouetten 1*. Hannover: C. F. Kius, 1843, p. 166.

1260 Letter addressed to Hermann von Pückler-Muskau and dated 9 February 1832, reproduced in *Briefwechsel und Tagebücher des Fürsten Hermann von Pückler-Muskau 7: Briefwechsel des Fürsten Hermann von Pückler-Muskau*, ed. Ludmilla Assing-Grimelli. Berlin: Wedekind & Schwiger, 1875, p. 401 ('to base the story on the human heart').

bares Räthsel, das er seinen Lesern zum Rathen aufgibt«.[1261] Furthermore, most of the appraised mystification is provided by the novel's eponymous heroine, whose imprisonment in the Blue Tower forms the core plot's framework.

Schefer's most ingenious gimmick regarding this novel is his construction of a double story by making his incarcerated heroine receive her own life's story written by an anonymous author, one chapter each second week,[1262] hence duplicating the narrator. The initial narrator might thus appear to be unreliable due to his temporal distance to the events narrated, while the second narrator receives immediate credibility through the protagonist herself: »Eleonore heftete die Lagen und verbarg sie aus mancherlei Gründen; denn dem Hofe, dem Lande, ihr selbst und ihrem Corfitz war darin auf den Grund gesehn«.[1263]

This is not the only instance in which Schefer resorted to manuscript fiction in order to create a sense of immediacy concerning events dating back hundreds of years. Albin Lenhard, for example, refers to one of Schefer's most prominent short stories, 'Künstlerehe' ('An Artist's Matrimony') published in 1828, which tells the story of the German painter Albrecht Dürer's (1471-1528) marriage, partially through a book written by Dürer himself and subsequently edited by his friend Willibald Pirckheimer (1470-1530).[1264] The narrative's core story furthermore coincides with that of *Die Gräfin Ulfeld*; it is that of an ambivalent, ultimately unhappy marriage between two persons whose love for each other is eventually capped by their incompatible ideologies. It also coincides with the plot of Schefer's short story 'Die Düvecke, oder die Leiden einer Königin'[1265] about the lives of King Christian II of Denmark's two women, his mistress Dyveke Sigbritsdatter and his wife Isabella of Austria, who are both betrayed by the King and his double life. In many of Schefer's marriage narratives, the reader is thus confronted with the – at times

---

1261 Anonymous. Review of *Die Gräfin Ulfeld oder die vierundzwanzig Königskinder* by Leopold Schefer, Blätter für literarische Unterhaltung 1/21 (21 January 1835), p. 81 ('a new secret, a new comprehensive and precious mystery, for his readers to figure out').

1262 Perhaps inspired by the literary practice of Schefer and his age, which tended to publish short stories or even chapters of longer stories in literary magazines, this editorial procedure was meant to allow its fictive recipient to reflect on her life's course and coherence more anxiously (Schefer, Leopold. *Die Gräfin Ulfeld oder die vierundzwanzig Königskinder 1*. Historischer Roman von Leopold Schefer. Berlin: Veit & Comp, 1834, p. 57). The fictitious suspension created by this gimmick (see also Lenhard, Albin. *Zur Erzählprosa Leopold Schefers*, p. 144) furthermore enhances the reader's sense of immediacy while the focus on the chapter-wise 'publication' of the account stresses the coherence and supra-literary truth contained in this semi-fictional story.

1263 Schefer, Leopold. *Die Gräfin Ulfeld 1*, p. 58 ('Eleonore attached the sheets to each other and hid them for various reasons; because their author had penetrated the very soul of the court, of her country, of herself and of her Corfitz'.

1264 Lenhard, Albin. *Zur Erzählprosa Leopold Schefers*, p. 83.

1265 'Düvecke, or the Sorrows of a Queen'.

disastrous – consequences of a husband's double life (in the case of 'Künstlerehe', the duplicity is created by the husband's life as an artist *and* as a husband)[1266] and its effects on his wife. However, in their readiness to submit to their respective husband's will, Schefer's raises his female characters above those of their husbands – their affliction evokes sublimity. Schefer's philosophy of the female psyche adores models of subservience and self-abandonment, as verbalised in the final words of the short story 'Die Düvecke':

Für Andr'e [sic!] fürchten und für And're sorgen, / Statt And'rer leiden und unglücklich sein, / Den bittern Kelch, den ihren Lieben strafend / Das Schicksal vollgegossen – heimlich leeren / Und schweigen…ja statt And'rer selber sterben, / – Das kann ein edles, zartgesinntes Weib![1267]

As the words of Mathilde Fibiger's leading character (see introductory quotation at the beginning of the chapter) in the novel *En Skizze efter det virkelige Liv* (see Chapter 2.2.2.) resonate in Schefer's words in the most ironic way, his conclusion and its display in the novel *Die Gräfin Ulfeld* turn into a challenge, not just of a feminist reading of Leonora Christina's story, but also of itself. For one, the male counterparts to his appraised female characters are rarely worthy of their wives' sacrifices[1268] and in the case of *Die Gräfin Ulfeld*, both protagonist and narrator are painfully aware of this circumstance:

Sie litt zuletzt aus Starrsinn und Eitelkeit: leiden zu wollen, um ein treues, untadliches, also löbliches Weib zu sein und zu scheinen, und gewissenhaft strenge die Pflicht zu erfüllen, die ein liebendes Herz schon sich selber verspricht, noch eh' es sie vor dem Altare der Gottheit gelobt.[1269]

1266 Cf. ibid., p. 87.
1267 Schefer, Leopold. 'Die Düvecke, oder die Leiden einer Königin'. In *Leopold Schefer's ausgewählte Werke 4*. Berlin: Veit & Comp, 1845, p. 233 ('To worry about others and take care of others, / suffer and be hapless on someone else's behalf / to secretly empty the cup of sorrow that destiny had filled to punish her loved one / in silence…even to die to spare others, / that is what noble, gentleminded women do!').
1268 Schefer's tendency to portray men, but especially husbands as worse humans than their female counterparts might be rooted in the author's experience with his own father (Clausen, Bettina and Lars Clausen. *Zu allem fähig: Versuch einer Sozio-Biographie zum Verständnis des Dichters Leopold Schefer 1.* Frankfurt: Bangert & Metzler, 1985, p. 159).
1269 Schefer, Leopold. *Die Gräfin Ulfeld 1*, p. 56 ('Towards the end she suffered out of stubbornness and vanity: to want to suffer, to be and to look like a faithful, irreproachable and hence commendable woman, and to conscientiously fulfill the duty which a loving heart swears to itself, already before repeating these vows in front of the heavenly altar').

Most dubious, however, is Schefer's authorial intention in depicting what in his portrayals seem like wasted yet glorified lives. Thus, the question arises whether his readership was justifiably confused or perhaps not ready for a subversive portrayal of romantic novel characters.

The novel commences with Eleonore's[1270] enforced return to Copenhagen in 1663, where the wildest rumours regarding the arriving ship's cargo have been circulating: one bystander announces that a merwoman caught in Dover was to be revealed. This expectation of a woman shrouded in myth and legend[1271] is immediately countered by the picture of a very human Countess – somebody's daughter (in this case the »liebste Herzenstochter« [1272] of a cherished deceased King) or sister – created by the words of her friend and mentor Sperling, the death-dreading medic providing occasional humour in this otherwise tragic account,[1273] and by a subsequent, bilaterally emotional encounter with her brother, which is only interrupted by her sister-in-law.[1274] Simultaneously, Sperling delivers a quick recap of Eleonore's life before the Blue Tower. This eclectic picture of Eleonore on her way to the Blue Tower is completed by a subsequent confrontation with her foremost victim, Dina – reincarnated in her daughter, who is also called Dina and who happens to be employed as a maid in the Blue Tower.

On the one hand, this collage of conflicting images provided by the different perspectives on Eleonore – the uninvolved-observing (bystanders and audience), the affiliated-loving (family and friends) and the legal-punitive (Dina) perspective – serves to illustrate the inner conflict besetting Eleonore regarding her image and her role. Eventually, she relents to a »eingelernte und eingeprägte falsche Ehre«[1275] attributed to an unnatural, courtly environment.

The image chosen by Eleonore, that of a chaste, loving and sacrificing woman, is, however, also Schefer's thematic focus of choice, which eventually reopens the question regarding her conflicting roles. While Schefer thus merely touches upon

---

1270 In the present chapter, »Eleonore« specifically refers to the character in Schefer's novel, particularly when referring to passages that do not correspond to historical events, whereas »Leonora Christina« refers to the historical person. Another spelling variation used in the literary source text, and hence in this chapter as well, is »Friedrich«.

1271 This image is reinforced by her husband's seemingly preliminary absence, who – much like the mythical King Arthur – could return at any given moment to eject the usurpers. The threat posed by Eleonore and Corfitz as potential regents substituting the current royal couple lingers over the scene (Schefer, Leopold. *Die Gräfin Ulfeld 1*, p. 14).

1272 Cf. ibid., p. 2 ('most beloved daughter').

1273 Cf. Kühne, F[erdinand] G[ustav]. Review of *Die Gräfin Ulfeld*, p. 496.

1274 Schefer, Leopold. *Die Gräfin Ulfeld 1*, p. 21.

1275 Ibid., p. 55 ('studied and engrained false honour').

the aspect of the mythical in Danish historiography[1276] and upon questions of guilt and atonement regarding Eleonore, his narrative's core plot – as produced on the mysterious sheets delivered to Eleonore – focuses on the private aspect of the protagonist's life, i.e. her conflicting roles as wife, mother and as a woman.

Schefer portrays Eleonore's marriage as doomed from its very beginning. Once she decides to accept Corfitz as her husband if he is able to save her repudiated mother, »verfehlte [so] ein gutes Kind sein Leben höchst mitleidswürdig«.[1277] Eleonore's subsequent habit of turning both of her blind eyes to her husband's activities – initially for her mother's, later on for her own sake – as well as Corfitz's secret love for a girl called Jolessa,[1278] who unlike Eleonore would never fall for a scoundrel like Corfitz,[1279] challenge the spouses' famous bond and hence the legitimacy of Eleonore's decisions.

Despite, or perhaps *because of* an eerie awareness of her fate, Eleonore turns her future into a self-fulfilling prophecy. By putting her life into her husband's feckless hands, she fosters his most despotic character traits. Corfitz gradually turns into a tyrant, dreaded by his entire household and even by his own sister Dorothea, who dies after only six months of living under her brother's roof because she was too afraid of her brother to ask for another doctor but Sperling: "und wenn Eleonore die arme Kranke bedauert, hatte Dorothea nur Eleonoren bedauert und ihr die Hand gedrückt".[1280]

Notwithstanding Schefer's scrutinising depiction of a traditional marriage model, Albin Lenhard insists that as an author of the Biedermeier period, Schefer would not directly challenge the modulatory function of marriage as an institution, neither the legitimacy of the partriarchal system per se.[1281] At the same time, however, Lenhard emphasises that many of Schefer's short stories present arranged marriages or those of convenience with disastrous outcomes, for example in 'Künstlerehe'. Hence, the author's philosophy posed a problem for his presentation of the Ulfeldtian marriage (which presents an equally contradictory pattern), which

---

1276 Cf. ibid., p. 58 and the two subsequent chapters about a demonic, giant sea snake landing on the Danish island of Funen simultaneously with the prodigal son Corfitz Ulfeld.

1277 Ibid., p. 152 ('a good child tragically ruined her own life'). These words receive further confirmation through an accompanying footnote implying that the narrator had construed Eleonore's life correctly: »Diese Worte waren vielleicht im ganzen Manuscripte der bitterste Stich durch Eleonorens Herz, denn sie machten ihre Liebe zur Täuschung« (ibid., footnote: 'Within the entire manuscript, these words were probably those that hurt Eleonore the most, for they revealed her love as mere deception').

1278 Jolessa is the only daughter of King Christian IV's secretary Günther, one of Ulfeld's earliest victims.

1279 Cf. Schefer, Leopold. *Die Gräfin Ulfeld 1*, p. 161.

1280 Ibid., p. 193 ('and while Eleonore had deplored her poor, sick sister-in-law, Dorothea had only pitied Eleonore and held her hand').

1281 Cf. Lenhard, Albin. *Zur Erzählprosa Leopold Schefers*, pp. 67 and 90.

Schefer attempted to solve by separating Leonora Christina's diverse female roles as wife, mother and woman (»ja wenn sie ihn als Frau auch gehaßt hätte, so mußte die Mutter der Kinder doch schweigen«).[1282] The final resolution, Corfitz's death through the hands of his son and – unconsciously – his wife, concludes Eleonore's life as the wife of an unworthy husband and leaves her to be completely absorbed in her remaining roles as loving woman and mother.

Schefer initiates this resolution through a first open conflict between Eleonore's role as a wife and that of a mother. After a show of force between Corfitz and Friedrich, the new King, Corfitz succumbs and appoints his eldest son Christian to be his avenger – an evident affront against Eleonore's maternal heart: »Der Vater […] drückte ihn an sein Herz und versprach dem gerührten, kindlich gehorsamen Knaben: ihn einst zu seinem Rächer zu machen und schenkte ihm einen Dolch. Der Mutter schauderte«.[1283] As this request entails no action, Eleonore remains submissive. Nevertheless, Eleonore begins to muse about the nature of her diverse roles and about which one to adopt for her marriage's sake: »Nur wirklich als Frau habe ich wirklich einen Mann, sonst keinen, nur ein riesengroßes Kind eines Riesen. […] Nun thut man ihm Unbill an und Herzeleid … und mir wird leichter um's Herz! Diese Nacht träumte mir sogar: ich ward mit meinem Manne wieder getraut«.[1284]

The second breach against her maternal conscientiousness occurs when Eleonore is forced to take leave of her home country and her female children, as she needs to leave them behind while following her husband and their sons into exile. The effects of this first major sacrifice remain mostly internal (»[a]ber ihre Augen weinten nicht Thränen, ihr schönes Gesicht verzog sich nur zum Weinen«); nevertheless, Corfitz sees her pain and interprets it as love (»aber ihre Brust schluchzte und sie war so schön, so rührend unselig, unaussprechlich unselig, wie er noch kein Weib aus Liebe zu ihm gesehn«).[1285] At this occasion, Eleonore drinks herself into a comatous passivity – which not only spares her from allegations of treason but

---

1282 Schefer, Leopold. *Die Gräfin Ulfeld 1*, p. 238 ('even though she might have hated him as a woman, the mother in her had to be silent').

1283 Ibid., p. 255 ('The father embraced his son and promised the emotional, childishly obedient boy to make him his avenger one day and gifted him a dagger. The mother shuddered').

1284 Ibid. ('Only as a woman I truly have a man, no other, only a gigantic child of a giant. […] Now he is suffering rigour and heartbreak…and my heart feels lighter! This night I even dreamed about remarrying my husband').

1285 Ibid., both quotations p. 287 ('but her eyes cried no tears, only her beautiful face contorted in the manner of crying'; 'but her chest sobbed and she was so beautiful, so heart-warmingly distraught, unspeakably distraught, as he had never before seen a woman out of love for him').

also eliminates this topic from Schefer's account once and for all[1286] – only to be reawakened by a subtle reminder of her duties, i.e. her sons, sent by their father.[1287] While Eleonore bows to her parental instinct, no such credit is awarded to Corfitz. In times of need, he would not even let his seasick sons have a single lemon: »Also hatte er nur, wo Ueberfluß war, davon Etwas gegeben. Wo ihm nun fehlen sollte, da mußten selber die Kinder darben. So sehr betrachtete er sie als sein Eigenthum und sich als ihren Herrn«.[1288]

Encouraged by her encounter with Christina, Sweden's amazon Queen who had refused to marry in order to avoid a fate as »Weib, eines Mannes Tag und Nacht und Wochen und Jahre stets unterthänige, erbärmliche Sklavin«,[1289] Eleonore initiates a process of gradual yet silent dissociation from her husband.[1290] However, to read feminist ideas into Schefer's interpretation of Leonora Christina's life would be premature, since only one particular event constitutes the last straw that breaks Eleonore's loyalty: »Wie tief ein Mann, der Liebe unbeschadet, / Sein Weib darf kränken? – bis auf's Mutterherz! / Noch selbst die Tochter läßt sie ihn verderben; / Am Sohn erst übt er ihr den ersten Frevel – – / Aus Männerliebe! Stets liebt sie den Mann«.[1291]

This last straw is the irrevocable corruption of Eleonore's son Christian at the hands of his father. After observing the presence of Fuchs, his tormentor at Hammershus prison, Corfitz calls upon his son Christian to meet him at an inn in Bruges carrying the prophetic name *zu Vater und Kind* ('At Father and Son's').[1292] Christian follows his father's request as well as the subsequent demand for revenge as

---

1286 Schefer actually advises his reader on several occasions to disregard the political-legal dimension (i.e. the Danish perspective) of his characters' story altogether. At the beginning of the account, the recently imprisoned Eleonore states that her decision to follow her husband on his treacherous path was not to be interpreted as infidelity towards her country, but rather as the opposite because: »im Herzen des Mannes ist des Weibes Heimath« (ibid., p. 25: 'a woman's home country is her husband's heart'). Even Corfitz is exculpated as he turns out to be not a Dane, but Bavarian in origin (ibid., p. 64).

1287 Ibid., p. 288.

1288 Schefer, Leopold. *Die Gräfin Ulfeld 2*, p. 8 ('Only in times of abundance he had shared. In times of need even his children had to starve. He viewed them entirely as his property and himself as their master').

1289 Ibid., p. 19 ('woman, a man's persistently submissive, wretched slave throughout day and night and weeks and years').

1290 Cf., for example, ibid., p. 109: »denn sie merkte, daß sie anfing, sich seiner zu schämen, weil sie sich in ihre weibliche Ehre flüchtete und flüchten mußte« ('she noticed that she started to be embarassed by him, because she took refuge in her female honour and had to take refuge there').

1291 Ibid., p. 161 ('How deeply can a man, without reducing her love / hurt his wife? – it even comprises the maternal heart! / She would even let him spoil the daughter; / but at the son's harm she takes offense - - / Out of love for men! She always loves men').

1292 The inn's guiding words – »Ein Kind spielt mit nichts lange, ein Mann hält an der Stange« (ibid., p. 164: 'A child does not persist in playing, a man keeps at it') relegate further to Corfitz's fatal relentlessness as opposed to his son's fickleness.

he murders Fuchs at the next opportunity. When Christian flees to his mother and reveals his deed to her, she resolves upon leaving her husband:

> Das hat Corfitz gethan! stöhnte sie schwach, wie lebendig begraben und jetzt erwachend. Und ihre Liebe zerflog und zersprang ihr in der Brust wie ein langes, schwer durch das Leben getragenes Uebel, und Kälte und Tod und gefühlloses Starren verbreitete sich langsam schleichend durch all' ihre Glieder.[1293]

Not grasping the content of Christian's following question (»Mutter, soll ich ihn tödten?«)[1294] due to her agitation, she answers positively, hence sending out her eldest son to remove his father. Eleonore remains thus faithful to traditional, patriarchal despotism as she secures her family's male line while sacrificing her daughters[1295] before departing to England alone:

> Doch sandte sie noch dem Vater vorher zum Trost die Töchter; aber mit klopfendem Herzen, mit abscheuverbergender Furcht ihre zweite, bildschöne, reizende, aber auch leicht zu bethörende Tochter Ellen, die oben darein zur Erleichterung des Unglücks beinahe vollkommen so aussah, wie die Mutter in ihrer schönsten Blüthe ausgesehen.[1296]

Eleonore's solution, the subliminal incest between Corfitz and his daughter Ellen Christina,[1297] is Eleonore's recognition of her husband's claim to a submissive and

---

1293 Ibid., p. 178 ('Corfitz did this! she moaned faintly, like buried alive and now awakening. And her love evaporated and burst in her chest like a long, severe malady she had lived with, and cold and death and insensible numbness slowly crept through her limbs').
1294 Ibid ('Mother, shall I kill him?').
1295 Despite Eleonore's decision to flee from her husband, this escape is by no means an act of scrutiny of the existing patriarchal system which she herself had submitted to so willingly for decades. When Eleonore's eldest daughter Anna Catharina confesses that she had recently given birth to a child out of wedlock, Eleonore remains silent at her husband's designs to restore his honour. Despite Corfitz's own philandering tendencies and the honest intentions of the child's father, Corfitz resolves upon the most archaic reaction: he disowns his daughter and intends to give her to his loyal servant Sperling. Eleonore attempts to appease Corfitz only halfheartedly while secretly acknowledging the legitimacy of his partriarchal mindset (ibid., p. 67). The execution of Corfitz's sentence is only averted by the sudden entrance of Cassette, Corfitz's equerry and the father of Anna Catharina's child, while Eleonore mourns the deprivation of both spousal and maternal joy (ibid., p. 69).
1296 Ibid., p. 180 ('But to appease the father she sent their daughters to him; but with a trembling heart, with abhorrence-covering fear she sent her second, ravishingly beautiful, lovely, yet also easily beguiled daughter Ellen, who on top of that, to ease the misfortune, looked almost entirely like her mother in her fullest bloom').
1297 This turn of events might be inspired by Schefer's own experiences with his environment, where fathers preying on their daughters appears to have been not entirely unacceptable (Clausen, Bettina and Lars Clausen. *Zu allem fähig: Versuch einer Sozio-Biographie zum Verständnis des Dichters Leopold Schefer 2*. Frankfurt: Bangert & Metzler, 1985, p. 317).

caring wife. Furthermore, by initiating her husband's death at the hands of his eldest son, she acknowledges the abiding validity of patriarchy, as Christian is taking in his father's place as the head of the family, ruling over its remaining members' fate. This new arrangement is readily assumed by both son and abandoned husband. Corfitz flees and meets Ellen, whom he subsequently passes off as his wife, in Basel, »angeblich ihrer Sicherheit wegen«.[1298] The substitution process initiated by Eleonore's sacrifice of the daughter, who carries her own, truncated name, gradually evolves into a connubially inclined relationship between father and daughter. The relationship moves further from the official (i.e. Corfitz's pretended marriage) to the private level, at which Ellen, as her father's caretaker, shares his bedroom,[1299] and further again to an intimate level, until any further development is prohibited by Ellen's escape. Before Ellen follows her mother's fate, she flees Basel on a hay wagon – a bed usually associated with secret meetings between domestics – together with her father.[1300]

Despite Schefer's subsequent optimistic conclusion – »Des Weibes Doppelleben ist nun aus! – / Die Mutter waltet geltend noch im Haus«[1301] – Eleonore's remaining function as a mother continues to evoke incomprehension. The incestuous tonality of the arrangement contrived by Eleonore adds to the problematic nature of Schefer's resolution – i.e. isolating and subsequently eliminating Eleonore's role as the wife of the perfidious Corfitz – and eventually renders an account that fails to convince, let alone enlighten its readers about the nature of womanhood and marriage. Schefer's actual narrative focus, which is motherhood, miscarries to account for itself as it revolves around the wayward son and husband Corfitz instead of its alleged heroine. One case in point is Corfitz's mother Brigitta Brokkenhuus, who, despite having given birth to a large number of children, dies alone in a house in co-inhabitation with her husband's bastard daughter.

Eleonore's unconditional love for her son forms a stark contrast to her husband's lack of concern for his own mother,[1302] who has spent a lifetime worrying about and

---

[1298] Schefer, Leopold. *Die Gräfin Ulfeld 2*, p. 188 (»allegedly for safety reasons«).
[1299] Ibid., p. 190.
[1300] Ibid., p. 192.
[1301] Ibid., p. 200 ('The woman's double life has come to an end! – / the mother remains to preside over the household').
[1302] »Und wenn alle Weiber meine Mütter wären, oder meine Mutter als alle Weiber vor mir auf die Kniee fielen! sprach Ulfeld in Grimm. [...] die Erweichung eines Sohnes durch seine Mutter ist also da gewesen – in der Welt muß nun etwas Neues sein: die Versteinerung des Herzens« (Schefer, Leopold. *Die Gräfin Ulfeld 1*, p. 269: 'And if all women were my mothers, or my mother knelt down in front of me on behalf of all women! Ulfeld said grimly. [...] a mother had thusly softened her son before – this world needs something new: the hardening of the heart').

even dreading her wayward child.[1303] When Corfitz and Eleonore enter the house of Brigitta Brokkenhuus, whose recent death had gone unnoticed by her son and his wife, they meet the same Dutch painter, who had produced a sudarium depicting Corfitz's likeness, which Eleonore had ordered in her worst time of doubt. A new order had brought the painter into this house as he is now working on a portrait of Brigitta Brokkenhuus in her coffin. While the plot presents this encounter as purely coincidental, it can by no means be discarded as such on a structural level since Corfitz's mother had turned her son into a religious matter as well. Upon venturing further into the sitting room, Eleonore finds a reliquary casket dedicated to Corfitz or, to be accurate, to his sins. Brigitta's shrine contains, among other keepsakes, Corfitz's public apologia concerning the Dina affair, a handkerchief immersed in Dina's blood, candles and a bouquet remaining from the funeral of Corfitz's sister Dorothea, a cookery book that Christian V had received from Corfitz (before dying of gluttony and hence, theoretically, paving the way for Corfitz's election for the post of King of Denmark), as well as Jolessa's torn neckpiece. The meaning of this shrine is revealed to the reading, imprisoned Eleonore in the same way as it is visualised to the written Eleonore, who beholds the shrine in terror: »Ueber dem Tische jedoch hing ein Bild mit lebensgroßen Menschen. Auf einer Seite stand der König Christian V. [sic!], auf der andern der alte Kanzler und Beide sahen zu, wie Eleonore als Engel mit Zärtlichkeit ihren Ulfeldt anbetete, der mit einem Pferdefuße abgebildet war«.[1304] Corfitz dismisses this display of his mother's sorrows as eccentricity and misguided attention, knowing that his words, and their inherent irony, would confirm Eleonore's worst suspicions (»ein Weib hat auch Freude am Manne – eine Mutter hat nur den Sohn«).[1305]

To Eleonore and her mother-in-law, one misguided son weighs thus heavier on their conscience than the fate of all the other children. This equivocal conclusion is, however, interrupted by Schefer's urge to resolve the reverberations of Eleonore's marriage: »Doch auch das heimliche Verklären / – So fragt der Tod – wie lange soll es währen?«[1306] The last chapter ('Die Wittwe', i.e. 'The Widow') leaves the fictional manuscript closed and finished, hence returning to the imprisoned widow, whose initial reaction to the news of Corfitz's death is to blend out all previous ma-

---

1303 Ibid., p. 148.
1304 Schefer, Leopold. *Die Gräfin Ulfeld 2*, p. 150 ('But above the table there was a painting of life-sized people. On the one side stood King Christian V [sic!], on the other side the old Chancellor and both looked on, as the angel-like Eleonore tenderly adored her Ulfeldt, who was depicted with a horse's foot'). Based on the logic of the account (and historical progression), Christian IV should be depicted in this painting.
1305 Ibid., p. 152 ('a wife also has the joys of marital life – a mother has only her son').
1306 Ibid., p. 200 ('But also this secret glorification / death asks – how much longer shall it last?').

ternal feelings and to declare her life finished.[1307] The inevitable realisation – »Und durch Wen bin ich Wittwe?«[1308] – reignites the previous struggle between »die empörte Mutter« and »das verzweifelte Weib«,[1309] whose only conceivable solution seems to be a complete annihilation of Eleonore, the vessel containing these two conflicting roles: »Sich selbst also wollte sie vergessen«.[1310] Nevertheless Eleonore, the complete human, is eventually saved. A stirring encounter with Eleonore's daughters petitioning for mercy sends Sophie Amalie to an early grave and her successor, the aggrieved wife of the serial adulterer Christian V, Queen Charlotte Amalie, enforces Eleonore's release after a considerable (and fictitious) suspension of three years. Eleonore's discharge from the Blue Tower, achieved not solely by her rival's death, but by her daughters' love and another mistreated wife's empathy, gives Eleonore the chance to wipe the slate clean and restart instead of abandoning her existence or any aspect of it altogether – the act of grace is directed at both the mother and the wife. As Eleonore relocates from the Blue Tower to Maribo, the process of integration continues and culminates in sublimation. Corfitz's widow dies joyfully and with a pure heart:

> Denn so sehr sie auch ihren Mann geliebt, so war doch ihr Herz ohne ihn wieder zum Kinderherzen geworden. Sie hatte ihre über Alles geliebte Mutter zu sich an ihr Sterbebette kommen gesehen, sie hatte sich aufgerichtet, vor Entzücken geschluchzet und war an der Mutter Brust gestorben.[1311]

Several contemporary critics have identified Schefer as a pantheist[1312] and the infantile as the celestial manifestation of immaculacy and eternity[1313] is one implementation of Schefer's pantheistic ideology, the other one being women: »Am liebsten wühlt Schefer in der Unergründlichkeit des weiblichen Herzens, wie ihm überhaupt das Weib als die eigentlichste Menschwerdung der namenlosen Naturgot-

---

1307 »[D]as beugt sie vollends zur Erde – mit dem Gesicht und der Brust auf den schweigenden Hügel des Todten, der Alles ihr war, wie sie klar jetzt sieht, als wären tausend Schleier von ihren Augen gefallen« (ibid., p. 201: 'This makes her break and bend down to the ground – her face and chest on the silent hill holding the man that had been everything to her, as she now clearly sees, as if a thousand veils had been lifted off her eyes').
1308 Ibid., p. 202 ('And by whose hand am I a widow?').
1309 Ibid., both quotations p. 203 ('the indignant mother' and 'the desperate wife').
1310 Ibid ('Thus herself she wanted to forget').
1311 Ibid., p. 215 ('For as much as she had loved her husband, her heart had nevertheless become that of child without him. She had seen her most beloved mother come to her deathbed, she had sat up, sobbed out of delight and died at her mother's chest').
1312 Cf., for example, Kühne, F[riedrich] Gustav. 'Leopold Schefer', p. 169.
1313 Lenhard, Albin. *Zur Erzählprosa Leopold Schefers*, p. 174f.

theit erscheint«.¹³¹⁴ Eleonore, especially in her final form, personifies thus Schefer's conviction; even her self-centered husband snatches a glimpse of her sublimity: »Und einen Augenblick geschah es, daß ihm das Weib und die Mutter als bloße, aber unläugbar wahre, vorhandene und leibhafte Erscheinung der Natur als heilige Natur selbst hervor glänzte und da stand«.¹³¹⁵

With so much indicating that Eleonore was to be understood as an ideal archetype of a woman, a divine embodiment of celestial creation,¹³¹⁶ it would hence seem obvious to dismiss all previous confusion regarding the quintessence of Schefer's prose writings, including *Die Gräfin Ulfeld*.¹³¹⁷ However, Schefer's dismissal of the second narrator (who remains anonymous), i.e. the switch from within to without the fictional manuscript narrating Eleonore's story, leaves the final conclusion to a different, slightly contradictory narrator.¹³¹⁸ The end of the manuscript concludes Eleonore's story, i.e. her development, and transports the reader back to the point of departure.¹³¹⁹ Eleonore has regained her infantile balance:

1314 Schmidt, Julian. *Geschichte der deutschen Literatur im neunzehnten Jahrhundert 2: Das Zeitalter der Restauration*. Leipzig: Herbig, 1856 (1853), p. 414 ('Schefer's favourite subject is the inscrutability of the female heart, just like women in general seem to be the most intrinsic incarnation of the innominate Nature-God').

1315 Schefer, Leopold. *Die Gräfin Ulfeld 1*, p. 209 ('And for a moment the wife and the mother stood before him in a shining light, as a pure, but undeniably true, existing and incarnate apparition of nature as sacred nature').

1316 Cf. Kühne, F[erdinand] G[ustav]. Review of *Die Gräfin Ulfeld*, p. 496: »Er hat hier eine Apotheose des Weibes bezweckt und allen Zauber seiner unerschöpflichen Herzensergießung darauf verwendet, nach seiner Art eine moderne Alceste zu schildern« ('His intention was to create an apotheosis of womanhood and he used all the enchantment of the inexhaustible expressions of his heart to depict a modern Alceste of his style').

1317 Cf., e.g., Laube, Heinrich. *Moderne Charakteristiken 2*. Mannheim: Löwenthal, 1835, p. 329: »Leider schreckt sein neuster Roman [...] durch jene unselige Manier wieder ab, welche oben erwähnt ist. Alles, jedes Wort soll bedeutend sein, aller Fluß, alle Bewegung wird dadurch gehemmt, und aus solcher Unnatur entwickelt sich ein verstopfender Schwulst« ('Unfortunately, his latest novel alienates [...] through that unfortunate habit which has been mentioned above. Everything, every word is meant to carry significance, every flow, every movement is being constrained by that, and this artificiality creates a choking magniloquence').

1318 An abrupt, slightly inconclusive ending seems, however, to have been a trademark of Schefer's prose writings (cf. Mundt, Theodor. *Geschichte der Literatur der Gegenwart: Vorlesungen über deutsche, französische, englische, spanische, italienische, schwedische, dänische, holländische, vlämische, russische, polnische, böhmische und ungarische Literatur. Von dem Jahre 1789 bis zur neuesten Zeit*. Leipzig: Simion, 1853 (1842), p. 663).

1319 This seems to be another signature trait of Schefer's style: »Der orientalische Pantheismus kennt keine Entwickelung. Darum ist Schefer's letztes Werk, wie sein erstes; er ist ein Dichter ohne Entwickelung« (Gottschall, Rudolph. *Die deutsche Nationalliteratur in der ersten Hälfte des neunzehnten Jahrhunderts: Literaturhistorisch und kritisch dargestellt 2*. Breslau: Trewendt & Granier, 1855, p. 137: 'The oriental pantheism knows no development. This is why Schefer's last work is just like his first one; he is a writer without development')

Doch es blieb Alles so, wie der Tod und das Schicksal es festgestellt. Sie hatte vergeben, ja sie fing wieder an, das Gute und Edle in ihrem Manne zu lieben, und mit diesem wieder den ganzen Mann, wie sie es im Leben leicht mit dem Lebendigen gekonnt, und geübt.[1320]

Whether the novel is thus to be interpreted as a cautionary tale or as a narrative legitimisation of patriarchy – that is, patriarchy as a law of nature and hence part of Schefer's pantheistic ideology – remains to be seen. One last clue, however, may lie in Schefer's presentation of a consistently neglected aspect of female existence, that of a daughter; and as a daughter Eleonore remembers the following exigent request to stay faithful, produced by her father on her wedding day:

Mann, Mensch! Hier ist Dein Weib! Es ist meine liebste Tochter, mein Kind – und, guter Freund, noch Jemandes Kind! Das, bitte ich, als ein armer Mensch auf Erden, zu sehn, zu fühlen und stets zu bedenken. [...] Mann, Mensch, Vater ... mein Sohn, dem ich mein Liebstes auf der Erde gebe, zu freiem, ganzem, ewigem Eigenthum, in Deine Gewalt gebe, wie der Mensch nichts Anderes auf Erden in eines andern Menschen Gewalt geben kann und gibt – dann denke noch: sie ist ein armes Kind der Erde! [...] Sei ein gutes Weib, mehr kannst Du nicht werden; und glücklicher kannst Du nicht werden, als – sei eine gute Mutter; das rührt und bezwingt und beherrscht den Mann, so sehr er ein Mensch ist[.][1321]

According to Eleonore's omniscient father, Eleonore is thus to faithfully commit herself to her husband and master, hence following a traditional gendermodel. However, several scenes involving Sperling and Eleonore crossdressing seem to challenge the gendermodel presented and supposedly promoted by Schefer. Eleonore's quasi-unconditional and hence 'naturally female' loyalty towards her husband

---

1320 Schefer, Leopold. *Die Gräfin Ulfeld 2*, p. 204 ('But everthing remained just as death and destiny has determined it. She had forgiven, yes she began anew to love the good and the noble in her husband, and with that the entire man, as she in life had done, and practiced, with the living man'). One last critical comment by the initial narrator enhances the discord between the manuscript's resolution and the lack of development in the narrative's framework: »Ja, sich selbst für eine mütterliche, treue Heldin haltend, schrieb sie auch mit ihres jungen Freundes, des Doctors Sperling Hülfe das Buch: Preis der Heldinnen« (ibid., p. 214: 'Yes, seeing herself as a maternal, faithful heroine, she also wrote the book: Heroines' Praise, with the help of her young friend, Doctor Sperling').

1321 Schefer, Leopold. *Die Gräfin Ulfeld 1*, pp. 167-169 ('Man, human! Here is your wife! And it is my dearest daughter, my child – and, good friend, still someone's child! This, I beg of you, as but a deplorable human, to see, to feel, and always to consider. [...] Man, human, father, my son...to whom I give my dearest thing on earth, as your entire and eternal property, give in your governance, as a human cannot do with anything else – so consider: she is a poor child of this earth! [...] Be a good wife, you cannot become more than that; and you cannot become happier than – be a good mother, that touches and conquers men, as much as they are humans').

forces her on numerous occasions not only to abandon her maternal instincts, but also her femininity altogether. For example when Corfitz orders his wife to conceal her sex while travelling in order to protect his own honour and identity: »[...] damit Du, als so schönes Weib, keiner Beleidigung ausgesetzt bist, welche ich, als Dein Mann, nicht rächen kann, da ich mich nicht entdecken, nicht einmal meinen Namen nennen darf«.[1322] Eleonore's uneasiness at being forced to doff her true identity for the sake of her husband's fake one is taken to an extreme when Corfitz's handsome younger brother, i.e. Eleonore in disguise, is being stalked by a Russian widow, who resides at the same inn chosen by Corfitz for a temporary refuge. That the widow badgering Eleonore carries the telling aptronym »Madame Unverdorben« ('Madam Unspoiled'), whereas Corfitz enhances his wife's embarrassment to deflect attention from his own identity,[1323] perpetuates any previously raised challenge of his behaviour's legitimacy. Eventually, Eleonore agrees to flee with and subsequently marry her worshipper, only to discover her true identity to Madame Unverdorben on a ship to Jutland, where the couple intends to seek out Eleonore's troubled mother. Nevertheless, the madame's loyalty towards Eleonore remains unbowed despite the sudden sex change. After recognising Eleonore's true nature, Madame Unverdorben saves her friend by allowing herself to be arrested in Eleonore's place. The irony is rather blatant: despite being deliberately fooled, Madame Unverdorben acknowledges Eleonore's identity in an instant and even sacrifices herself for her – both services Eleonore could never expect from her original spouse.

Sperling, on the other hand, Corfitz's other loyal follower,[1324] has – in the past – transgressed a sacred rule verbalized by Christian IV in being excessively unfaithful to his wife. As he had perverted the idea of what it means to be a man and husband to a degree which drove his wife into suicide, he was doomed to lose whatever was left of his virility: to substitute the lost mother, the widowed Sperling would often

---

1322 Schefer, Leopold. *Die Gräfin Ulfeld 2*, p. 17 ('so that you as a beautiful woman are not exposed to any insult, which I, as your husband, cannot avenge, since I cannot reveal myself, cannot even say my name').

1323 Ibid., p. 23.

1324 Schefer's Otto Sperling is not just a comical, but at times also pathetic character. In the novel, Sperling joins his friends »wie eine Schlingpflanze [...] einen schönen, beschützenden, sie tragenden Baum, obgleich die Nähe eines solchen Baumes die Schlingpflanze bedingt, und vielleicht nur auch so dergleichen Menschen. Sittlichkeit, Sitte, Ruhe, eigenes Leben und Wollen schien bei ihm ganz still zu stehn, ja verschwunden, so lange er Corfitz Reden und Wünsche anhörte« (Schefer, Leopold. *Die Gräfin Ulfeld 1*, p. 175: 'like a twiner [...] a beautiful, protecting, supporting tree, even though the vicinity of such a tree conditions the twiner, and perhaps only this kind of people. Morality, mores, calmness, his own life and wishes seem to stand still, gone even, as long as he listened Corfitz's talk and wishes'). As a doctor, however, Sperling is presented as being rather incompetent. Christian IV, whose physician Sperling had become through Ulfeldt's agency, would only consult him in times of health and Corfitz's sister, Dorothea, eventually wastes away while receiving no other doctor but Sperling.

dress up as a woman in order to console his child and as the account progresses, this private habit would turn more pronounced as he travels to find his exiled friends disguised in female apparel.[1325] Thus, Sperling constitutes not only a parallel to his crossdressing friend Eleonore, but also to his equally emasculated master Corfitz, in that both men have misapplied their male prerogatives and duties. Over the course of the account, Corfitz proves to have misconceived his own function as a husband, father and man while at the same time disdaining his wife's identity:

> Er achtete kein Weib. Er hatte nur Eines kennen gelernt. Wie er als Kind alle Blumen gegessen, ja, kleine Puppen in den Mund gesteckt, so war er erwachsen geblieben, denn seine Sinnlichkeit hielt jeden Anstoß zu dem Gedanken, daß Etwas...also auch das Etwas: ein Weib...hoch und geistig sei, in ihm nieder.[1326]

Corfitz's failure to recognise his wife, or any woman, by her true identity resonates in his reaction to her escape. The moment he realises that he has lost his better half, his soul adopts the shape of a »häßlicher Zwerg oder [...] eine, noch dazu zertretene, Schlange«.[1327] This diminution resulting from Eleonore's departure, in turn, contrasts with Eleonore's ideal understanding of her husband as implanted by her father, who appeared to her in a dream:

> Sie blickte hin, und sah einen *Riesen* [my italics] in so furchtbarer Gestalt vor sich stehen und erkannte an seinem Gesicht doch ihren Ulfeld, so daß sie mit Schrecken rief: Das ist der Teufel! Dummheiten! sprach der Vater lächelnd. Das ist ein Mann. Schaue nur durch seinen Harnisch hinein![1328]

In the same dream, Christian IV describes man and woman as one entity, both being separate divine creatures,[1329] yet meant to complete each other like yin and yang:

1325 Schefer, Leopold. *Die Gräfin Ulfeld 2*, p. 3.
1326 Ibid., p. 21 ('He had no respect for women. He had only known one thing. As he ate all flowers as a child, and stuck little dolls in his mouth, he had remained as an adult, because his sensuality prevented every spark of a thought that something...including the something: a woman...could be sublime and intellectual').
1327 Ibid., p. 187 ('ugly dwarf or [...] a, scrunched even, snake').
1328 Ibid., p. 86 ('She looked and saw a *giant* [my italics] in such a terrifying shape stand in front of her and recognized her Ulfeld in his face, so in terror she cried: That is the devil! Nonsense! spoke her father, smilingly. That is a man. Just look through his armour!').
1329 Ibid., p. 87.

Du aber, als Weib, sollst Dein Leben an ihm dadurch gewinnen und haben, daß Du ahnen lernest – eine lange, lebenslange Ahnung, wie ein Seufzer von der Wiege bis in's Grab, daß der Mann frei ist, und darum nur frei geboren und darum über alle Furcht und Schrecken erhaben...und durch ihn sollst Du ahnen, was Freiheit ist – was die Liebe nicht weiß.[1330]

Eleonore had taken her father's advice to heart; she had adopted her husband as a part of herself, but Corfitz had remained thoroughly himself: »[D]enn seit dem Besuche in dem Gerichtszimmer seiner Mutter bedünkte es ihm, wie seiner Seele, so auch seinem Leibe nach: er lebe nicht mehr, er habe nicht gelebt, denn ihm habe ein Etwas bei allem seinen Wirken und darum in seinen Werken, im Herzen gefehlt«.[1331] While Eleonore had thus remained true to her nature, Corfitz had completely misinterpreted his own. Finally, her father's claim that a woman should learn freedom from her bond with a man resonates cynically in Leonora Christina well-known fate as a prisoner. While Eleonore's story is that of coherence, that of Corfitz is one of coherent failure. Hence, Schefer's account is less the narrative of one woman, but of two complementary ideological counterparts. The realisation of this extra-literary pantheistic law[1332] allows Schefer's Eleonore to die full of »Freude und Seligkeit«[1333] and to reinitiate the infinite loop of human existence: »Denn so sehr sie auch ihren Mann geliebt, so war doch ihr Herz ohne ihn wieder zum Kinderherzen geworden«.[1334]

1330 Ibid., p. 88 ('But you, as a wife, shall earn and have your life through him, to learn to sense – a long, lifelong sense, like a sigh from the cradle to the grave, that men are free, and are only born free and elevated above all fear and terror...and through him you shall sense what freedom is – what love does not know').

1331 Ibid., p. 157 ('For since the visit in his mother's judgement room he, and his soul as well as his body, had the feeling: er lived no more, he had not lived, for he had in all his doing and hence in his deeds lacked a something in his heart').

1332 One of the main points of criticism regarding Schefer's narrative mode is the author's literary implementation of his pantheistic worldview. According to this philosophy, every aspect, every detail of life is a manifestation of the divine. This – and this is the bone of contention for many contemporary critics – means that both small and great deeds, both Good and Evil have equal value (see, e.g., Schmidt, Julian. *Geschichte der deutschen Literatur im neunzehnten Jahrhundert 2*, p. 410). Some critics did indeed grasp Schefer's philosophy (»Corfitz und Eleonore würden nicht so ergreifen, und so viel, ich möchte weniger sagen zu schauen, als zu ahnen geben, wenn sie nicht durchweg apologetisch und in sich eben als Mann und als Weib und als Beides in seiner Ganzheit gerechtfertigt aufgefaßt wären« (Gutzkow, Karl. *Beiträge zur Geschichte der neuesten Literatur 1*, p. 257: 'Corfitz and Eleonore would not touch us like they do, and, I am tempted to say, give us less something to see than to divine as much, if they were not conceived as entirely apologetic and in themselves man and woman and as both in its wholeness)); but only few approved of it.

1333 Schefer, Leopold. *Die Gräfin Ulfeld 2*, p. 216 ('joy and bliss').

1334 Ibid., p. 215 ('For as much as she had loved her husband, without him her heart had become a child's heart again').

2.7.2. Rainer Maria Rilke: *Die Aufzeichnungen des Malte Laurids Brigge*[1335] (1910) – A Figurehead of Northern Stoicism

> Ieg Klædde mig, oc satte mig vdi en aff Bodzmendenis Koyer paa Offuerlaaget med en Stadig *Resolution* friimodeligen att tage imod alt ded mig war forrelagt, dog wentede ieg ingenlunde ded mig hendede[.]
>
> (*Jammers Minde*, p. 3)

When the Danish writer Jens Peter Jacobsen (1847-1885) started his research on the historical environment of the infamous Danish noblewoman Marie Grubbe (1643-1718) in 1873, he came across the newly published autobiography of Leonora Christina, which provided Jacobsen with the necessary local colour he would later on integrate in his novel *Fru Marie Grubbe*,[1336] published in 1876.[1337] Danish philologist Ole Restrup has even suggested that *Jammers Minde* may have posed a profound source of stylistic inspiration to Jacobsen and his successors, due to its simple and realistic style, which would come to define the Danish historical novel.[1338] Jacobsen's initial inspiration for writing a novel like *Fru Marie Grubbe* is unknown, but some sources point to Hans Christian Andersen and Georg Brandes, two early admirers of Leonora Christina, as instigators. In 1869, the same year *Jammers Minde* was printed, Hans Christian Andersen published *Hønse-Grethes Familie*, Marie Grubbe's story in the form of a fairy-tale. In a character-portrait of Andersen published by the critic Georg Brandes the following year, Brandes contends that a life story in the form of a fairy-tale could never do justice to an enigmatic character such as that of Marie Grubbe.[1339] As noted by Vilhelm Andersen,[1340] Jacobsen accepted the implicit challenge of publishing Marie Grubbe's life story in a more fitting form and started his work shortly afterwards. Frederik Nielsen, on

---

1335 The commonly used English title of this novel is *The Notebooks of Malte Laurids Brigge*.
1336 Nielsen, Frederik. 'Om at læse Marie Grubbe'. In *J. P. Jacobsen: Samlede værker*, ed. Frederik Nielsen. Copenhagen: Rosenkilde og Bagger, 1972, p. 12.
1337 The first two chapters, however, were already published in 1874 in the cultural periodical *Det nittende Aarhundrede*, published from 1874 until 1877 by Edvard and Georg Brandes.
1338 Restrup, Ole. *Leonora Christina: Ein Frauenschicksal des 17. Jahrhunderts*. Bonn: Bonner Univ. Buchdr., 1943 (Friedrich-Wilhelms-Universität Bonn am Rhein 120), p. 14.
1339 Brandes, Georg. 'H. C. Andersen som Eventyrdigter'. In Brandes, Georg. *Kritiker og Portraiter*. Copenhagen: Gyldendal, 1870, p. 360: »En Kvinde, som den Marie Gruppe, af hvis interessante Liv Andersen giver en Skizze i ‚Hønse-Grethe fortæller', er altfor meget Charakter, til at det skulde være en Eventyrdigter muligt at fremstille eller forklare hendes Væsen; forsøger han derpaa, fornemmer man et Misforhold mellem Gjenstanden og Formen«.
1340 Andersen, Vilhelm. 'Marie Grubbe'. In *Omkring Fru Marie Grubbe*, ed. Jørgen Ottosen. Copenhagen: Hans Reitzel, 1972, p. 239.

the other hand, points to Ludvig Holberg – another early promoter of Leonora Christina's fame – as another source of inspiration to Jacobsen: »Med en vis rimelighed kan man gætte på Holbergs epistel, der peger på det driftsbestemte og irrationelle i kvindens væsen, som det der har afgjort valget af netop Marie Grubbe som hovedfigur i digterens første roman«.[1341] A letter from 7 March 1873 to the politician and critic Edvard Brandes (1847-1931) contains Jacobsen's first reference to his nascent novel:

> Tænk dig jeg staaer op hver Dag Kl. 11 og gaaer paa kgl. Bibliothek og læser gamle Dokumenter og Breve og Løgne og Billeder om Mord, Hor, Kapitelstakst, Skjørlevnet, Torvepriser, Havevæsen, Kjøbenhavns Belejring, Skilsmisse-Processer, Barnedaab, Godsregistre, Stamtavler og Ligprædikener. Alt det skal blive til en vidunderlig Roman der skal hedde:
>
> »Fru Maria Grubbe«.
> Interieur fra det 17de Aarhundrede.[1342]

In the course of his research, Jacobsen inevitably must have come across Leonora Christina's *Jammers Minde*, which had been printed only a few years earlier. Considering Jacobsen's extensive historical studies, his interest in Leonora Christina's text must have primarily been motivated by the observing character of this autobiography, as well as by the plentiful dialogues rendered in the respective original language.[1343] Leonora Christina's own fate seems to have impressed the writer to a lesser degree, although he had obviously taken some interest in it. In a letter to his friend Vilhelm Møller (1846-1904), dated 16 April 1877 and concerning the improvement of the lower social classes' education, Jacobsen suggests to »give de Samfundslag, der høre til 16 17 osv Aarhundrede, Bøger fra de nævnte Aarhundreder

---

1341 Nielsen, Frederik. 'Om at læse Marie Grubbe', p. 11.

1342 Jacobsen, Jens Peter. *Samlede Værker 5: Breve: 1863-1877*, ed. Frederik Nielsen. Copenhagen: Rosenkilde og Bagger, 1973, p. 80. Upon publication Jacobsen slightly modified the title of his novel, thus entitling it *Marie Grubbe: Interieurer fra det syttende Aarhundrede.*

1343 Leonora Christina herself is mentioned merely *en passant* in *Fru Marie Grubbe*, namely as the person Queen Sophie Amalie hated the most (»Dronningen, der mere hadede Ulfeldts Hustru end hun hadede Ulfeldt selv […]«; see Jacobsen, Jens Peter. *Fru Marie Grubbe*. Copenhagen: Gyldendal, 2006, p. 81). However, the fact that the Queen's archenemy is a friend of Sofie Urne's, who was the first, and secret, wife of King Frederik III's lovechild Ulrik Frederik Gyldenløve (1638-1704), prompts Sophie Amalie to convince her husband to prohibit his son from seeing »den virkelig intriguante Sofie Urne« (ibid.) any longer. Despite the couple's defiance and the secret marriage, Ulrik Frederik eventually grows weary of the secrecy imposed upon him and his wife. He declares the marriage invalid and agrees to marry the wealthy Marie Grubbe instead. Despite her absence from the novel, Jacobsen's Leonora Christina hence actuates its core plot.

at læse; jeg tror de vilde læse dem«.[1344] In Jacobsen's eyes, *Jammers Minde* »helt omskreven og forkortet vilde være brillant«[1345] as common reading.

Despite this rather blurry trace leading from Jacobsen and Grubbe to Leonora Christina, there is one clear thematic correlation connecting the two women which had been manifest to 19th-century critics, yet not so much to their successors. Frederik Nielsen's mention of »det driftsbestemte og irrationelle i kvindens [i.e. Marie Grubbe's] væsen« – which according to him is the novel's key theme – is to be understood as a reference not only to Marie's emotion-based decision to leave the King's son only to end up with a brutish peasant, but also to her tendency to resort to physical solutions when faced with an emotional crossroad. Besides Marie's obvious partiality for belligerent machos, she, too, has a violent streak:

> Naar Marie næsten ubevidst med Kniven støder efter Ulrik Frederiks Bryst, naar hendes første Indskydelse overfor Karen Fiol er at slynge en Sten i Hovedet paa hende, saa handler hun absolut forskelligt fra den Maade, paa hvilken i vort Aarhundrede en Dame i hendes Situation vilde handle, men hun handler overensstemmende med sin Natur og man kan i Leonore Christines Jammers Minde finde talrige Beviser for at selv en Dame af et hende stik modsat Naturel, en der var ligesaa rationel som hun var hysterisk, kunde handle paa samme rent uoverlagte og haandgribelige Maade.[1346]

Brandes refers to the few incidences of Leonora Christina threatening and eventually chastening her maids in the Blue Tower.[1347] Despite her initial assurance that she had never struck a single maid,[1348] the new milieu soon taints her character.

1344 Jacobsen, Jens Peter. *Breve*, p. 182.

1345 Ibid., p. 183. Jacobsen's suggestion to completely rewrite *Jammers Minde* was not meant as a direct criticism of Leonora Christina's work per se. In order to arouse the lower classes' interest in (good) literature, Jacobsen recommends the following procedure for the works in question: »I det hele taget ved Almueliteratur: ingen Pietet for Forfatteren, rask Skæren bort, Omsætning af en ulykkelig Slutning til en lykkelig, derimod nødigere Omlokalisering og Forandring af de Agerendes Stand« (ibid.).

1346 Review by Georg Brandes of *Fru Marie Grubbe* by Jens Peter Jacobsen, published 1877 in the January/February-edition of the periodical *Det nittende Aarhundrede* and reproduced in *Omkring Fru Marie Grubbe*, ed. Jørgen Ottosen. Copenhagen: Hans Reitzel, 1972, p. 49.

1347 See for example *Jammers Minde*, p. 119: »[M]eener i att ieg nu icke kunde gjøre ont om ieg wille, saa wel som da, om der giorde mig nogen noget som ieg icke kunde liide? nu langt bedre; de haffwer icke behoff att necte mig kniiff for den skyld, att ieg icke skulle myre eder, ded kand ieg giøre med miine bare hænder, ieg kand quæle den stærckeste Karl med miine bare hænder om ieg v-forwarendis fick fat paa ham [...]«. See also Leonora Christina's reaction to her maid Inger's repeated misbehaviour of dumping drinking water on the ground: »[F]oruden nogen Ord slog ieg hender først paa den eene oc saa paa den anden Kiæffte, saa Bloded stoed vd aff Næße oc Mund, oc hun falt imod sin Slabenk oc støtte sit Skinnebeen hudden aff[.]« (ibid., p. 186).

1348 »Ieg kunde icke wiide, huorledis ieg hoeß dronningen war kommen i den Tancke att slaa, der ieg dog aldrig nogen aff mine Kammer-Piiger en Ørfigen giffuen haffde« (ibid., p. 24).

Just as Marie Grubbe's new surroundings at Palle Dyre's seat farm transform the formerly educated and refined Marie into a more ignoble human being,[1349] Leonora Christina, too, eventually adapts to her environment consisting of murderers, adulterers and lunatics. This modern verdict of the 17th century as an utterly primitive age – a reminiscence of similar comments in H. F. Ewald's novel *Leonora Kristina* (see Chapter 2.4.2.) – was enough for 19th-century critics to highlight even the most arbitrary congruence between these two women, who otherwise could not have been more different. Hans Brix's blatant disappointment at finding the aged Marie Grubbe to be different from Leonora Christina, for example, testifies to this circumstance:

> Nu vilde man tro, at en Bog om Marie Grubbe maatte anlægges saaledes, at man efter hendes Livs mangfoldige Oplevelser og Omskiftelser saa hende som Færgekone paa Falster opfyldt af dyb og rig Viden om høje og lave Ting og med Livets Visdoms Krone om sine Tindinger, et Sidestykke til Leonore Kristine, hvis Mindebog J. P. Jacobsen har gjort flittig Brug af til sin Skildring; man vilde vente et Billede af hollandsk Djærvhed med denne storslaaede Skikkelse som Midtpunkt. Det er imidlertid slet ikke saaledes J. P. Jacobsen ser paa sin Heltinde.[1350]

Nevertheless, Brix remains adamant in his literary perspective on the two protagonists in *Jammers Minde* and *Fru Marie Grubbe* when he continues to consider these two women as the same type of character (»Marie Grubbe i Borrehuset, en Søsterskikkelse til Leonore Kristine i Maribo Kloster«[1351]).

Notwithstanding the arbitrariness of such analogies, Jacobsen himself had provided the very same notion. The author's statement of a text like *Jammers Minde* being representative of the 17th century – an age of peasants and lower commoners – reproduced above, in combination with Jacobsen's reflections on said social classes'

[1349] »Som en skjøn og ædel Bygning i Barbarers Hænder forsømmes og fordærves, idet de dristige Spir trykkes ned til plumpe Kuppelhatte, de kniplingsfine Ornamenter brydes Led efter Led, og den rige Billedpragt dækkes Lag paa Lag med dødende Kalk, saaledes forsømtes og fordærvedes Marie Grubbe i disse seksten Aar« (Jacobsen, Jens Peter. *Fru Marie Grubbe*, p. 221).

[1350] Brix, Hans. 'Marie Grubbe'. In *Omkring Fru Marie Grubbe*, ed. Jørgen Ottosen. Copenhagen: Hans Reitzel, 1972, p. 205.

[1351] Ibid., p. 206. Vilhelm Andersen could be named as another example of a critic, who adjudged Leonora Christina a disputable amount of influence on Jacobsen: »Et Forbillede [to *Fru Marie Grubbe*] var nyligt givet ved Fremdragningen af Leonora Christinas Jammersminde, hvis mægtige Realisme, som det fremgaar af en Anmeldelse, ogsaa først havde aabnet Brandes' Øjne for det uvirkelige i Livsbillederne i den ældre Tids historiske Kunst« (Andersen, Vilhelm. 'Marie Grubbe', p. 239).

behaviour,[1352] had created a hyper-analogy of Leonora Christina, Marie Grubbe, epoch and social class. Not least due to the profound impression the publication of *Jammers Minde* had on its immediate literary environment, Leonora Christina had now come to be understood as a representative of an entire age, i.e. that of Baroque Denmark, with Marie Grubbe constituting a more base version of this paradigm. This notion was eventually seized by the Bohemian-Austrian writer Rainer Maria Rilke (1875-1926), whose attention was drawn to the Danish Countess through Jacobsen, and who – despite his admiration for Jacobsen[1353] – completely converted the material provided by Leonora Christina and her age.

As contended by George C. Schoolfield, Rilke's journey to Scandinavia in 1904, especially to Copenhagen,[1354] may have drawn Rilke's interest towards Leonora Christina for the first time. The works of Jens Peter Jacobsen undoubtedly motivated Rilke's initial interest in Northern Europe, its history and cultural contributions, but during his visit at the art museum Ny Carlsberg Glyptotek on 24 June 1904, Rilke may have also become (more) acquainted with Leonora Christina through the work of the Danish painter Kristian Zahrtmann.[1355] Rilke's own literary treatment of Leonora Christina and her illustrious family would at least indicate so, since, in *Die Aufzeichnungen des Malte Laurids Brigge*, the protagonist meets Leonora Christina and her circle in the form of paintings.

Rilke's only novel, *Malte Laurids Brigge*, has puzzled researchers and readers alike since its publication a few years after its author's first – and only – encounter with Scandinavia. To date, the bigger part of Rilke-critics focussed on Malte's disturbing city-impressions of Paris and the process of self-discovery and reinvention of human existence and language expressed through these impressions. During the

---

1352 For example, when Marie finds herself in an abusive relationship with a violent alcoholic, she accepts it as part of the social class she had married into: »[...] og om han end tidt drak sig fuld og slog hende, saa gjorde det ikke saa meget; Marie vidste jo, det var Hverdagsbrug i det Samfundslag, i hvilket hun havde ladet sig indskrive« (Jacobsen, Jens Peter. *Fru Marie Grubbe*, p. 262).

1353 On Jens Peter Jacobsen's influence on the works of Rainer Maria Rilke, see Baer, Lydia. 'Rilke and Jens Peter Jacobsen', Publications of the Modern Language Association 54/4 (December 1939), pp. 1133-1180.

1354 In a letter dated 3 July 1904 and addressed to his long-term confidante, the writer and psychoanalyst Lou Andreas-Salomé (1861-1937), Rilke comments on the city in an exceptionally romanticised manner: »Eine Stadt ohnegleichen, seltsam unaussprechlich, ganz in Nuancen vergehend; alt und neu, leichtsinnig und geheimnisvoll –, überall, nirgends zu fassen« (Rilke, Rainer Maria. *Briefe aus den Jahren 1902 bis 1906*, ed. Ruth Sieber-Rilke. Leipzig: Insel, 1929, p. 186: 'A unique city, strangely unpronounceable, entirely made up of nuances; old and new, frivolous and mysterious –, everywhere, nowhere to grasp').

1355 Schoolfield, George C. 'Rilke and Leonora Christina', Modern Language Quarterly 14/4 (1953), p. 425. During the same or a different visit to Copenhagen, Rilke may have also visited the National Gallery of Denmark (Statens Museum for Kunst), thus encountering more of Zahrtmann's depictions of Leonora Christina's life (ibid.).

years Rilke spent tinkering with *Malte Laurids Brigge*, he underwent a fundamental artistic crisis which could not be resolved through the completion of the novel.[1356] This crisis of the modern human, the artist, as expressed in the novel's metropolitan part, occupied the critics' attention to a degree which left the Scandinavian chapters of *Malte Laurids Brigge*, the Danish protagonist's childhood memories, to go mostly unnoticed. The fact that the Danish episodes grow scarce as the novel proceeds – as did Rilke's short-lived passion for Scandinavia[1357] – as well as the ghost episodes, which seemed like a romantic artefact in a novel that otherwise belonged to modernity, contributed to this imbalance.

Malte Laurids Brigge is the outcome of Rilke's examination of his own fears and shortcomings. The topic of death and decay, i.e. the frailty of the human body, is discussed both in the Danish as well as the Paris-episodes as human existence and its finitude coalesce throughout the novel. This becomes apparent in the ghost episodes, which belong exclusively to Malte's Danish past. Malte's grandfather, who has been identified as the protagonist's ideal reflection on numerous occasions,[1358] constitutes the focal point for these scenes as he manages to overturn the temporal aspect of human existence. Past, present and future converge in his realm Urnekloster, the ancestral home of Malte's maternal family, the Brahe dynasty. Not only ghosts, who died centuries before the plot's time, are considered family members; Malte's grandfather can even foresee future events and converse about them with an implicitness terrifying to his surroundings.[1359] At the same time, these ghost episodes represent an integral part of Malte's search for a new language, for a new,

---

1356 Rilke's painful anticipation of the moment of epiphany and redemption is evident from the novel's final words: »Er war jetzt furchtbar schwer zu lieben, und er fühlte, daß nur Einer dazu imstande sei. Der aber wollte noch nicht« (Rilke, Rainer Maria. *Die Aufzeichnungen des Malte Laurids Brigge*. Herausgegeben und kommentiert von Manfred Engel. Stuttgart: Reclam, 1997, p. 213: 'He was now terribly difficult to love, and he felt that only one person was capable of that. But that person was not yet willing').

1357 Cf. Schoolfield, George C. 'Rilke und Skandinavien'. In *Rilke – ein europäischer Dichter aus Prag*, ed. Peter Demetz et al. Würzburg: Königshausen & Neumann, 1998, p. 125: »Zur selben Zeit, als der allgemeine Enthusiasmus für skandinavische Literatur in Deutschland nachließ, ließ auch der Rilkes nach«.

1358 See, for example, Rilke's own statement in a letter dated 10 November 1925 and addressed to Witold von Hulewicz: »Malte ist nicht umsonst der Enkel des alten Grafen Brahe« (reproduced in *Materialien zu Rainer Maria Rilke >Die Aufzeichnungen des Malte Laurids Brigge<*, ed. Hartmut Engelhardt. Frankfurt: Suhrkamp, 1974, p. 131: 'Malte is truly the grandchild of the old Count Brahe'). Moreover, some of the grandfather's skills – his ability to ignore the temporal restrictions of human existence and his narrative gift (cf. Rilke, Rainer Maria. *Malte Laurids Brigge*, p. 124) – reflect Malte's substantial shortcomings.

1359 Cf. ibid., p. 29.

adequate and significant way to express modern existence,[1360] to which attempts are rendered in the Paris episodes.[1361]

In his study of the ghost episodes in *Malte Laurids Brigge*, Hans Richard Brittnacher connects Malte's imperative of writing[1362] with past incidences of Malte encountering something that could not be expressed. The fact that Malte repeatedly remembers seeing something that should not be seen further connects Malte's Danish past with his experience of elevated sight in Paris. The first of a series of spiritualist episodes occurs immediately following Malte's absolute resolution to write. In these instances Malte encounters death intruding into life – a threat Malte, as well as Rilke, would not manage to confront throughout the entire novel – without learning to express and hence apprehend the experience. One scene central to Brittnacher's analysis of these phenomena is that of Malte accidentally dropping a pen – a writer's utensil – while drawing a picture of a knight, crawling underneath the table in search of said pen and encountering a foreign hand looking for the pen next to his own. Yet, instead of accepting the helping hand and retrieving the pen, the young boy is petrified. He pulls back his hand, hence leaving the pen behind, and is unable to narrate the incident: »Ich schluckte ein paarmal; denn nun wollte ich es erzählen. Aber wie? Ich nahm mich unbeschreiblich zusammen, aber es war nicht auszudrücken, so daß es einer begriff. Gab es Worte für dieses Ereignis, so war ich zu klein, welche zu finden«.[1363] Brittnacher concludes that as long as Malte is unable to seize the inexpressible, he will also remain unfit for the challenge of picking up the pen in pursuit of a new kind of writing.[1364]

1360 Cf. Brittnacher, Hans Richard. 'Gespenster aus Dänemark. Okkultismus und Spiritismus in Rainer Maria Rilkes *Die Aufzeichnungen des Malte Laurids Brigge*'. In *Strahlen sehen: Zu einer Ästhetik des Emanativen*, eds. Roland Innerhofer und Rebecca Schönsee. Vienna: New Academic Press, 2015, p. 60.

1361 See, for example, Malte's description of a stranger, a woman sitting outside while resting her face in her hands: »Die Frau erschrak und hob sich aus sich ab, zu schnell, zu heftig, so daß das Gesicht in den zwei Händen blieb. Ich konnte es darin liegen sehen, seine hohle Form.« (Rilke, Rainer Maria. *Malte Laurids Brigge*, p. 10: 'The woman got startled and lifted herself out of herself, to quickly, too violently, so her face remained in her two hands. I could see it lie in there, its hollow form').

1362 Cf. ibid., p. 24: »Dieser junge, belanglose Ausländer, Brigge, wird sich fünf Treppen hoch hinsetzen müssen und schreiben, Tag und Nacht: ja er wird schreiben müssen, das wird das Ende sein« ('This young, insignificant foreigner, Brigge, will sit down five steps above and write, day and night: yes he will have to write, that will be the end').

1363 Ibid., p. 82 ('I gulped a few times; because now I wanted to tell. But how? I gathered myself beyond words, but could not find a way to express it in a way comprehensible to others. If there were words for this incident, then I was too little to find them').

1364 Brittnacher, Hans Richard. 'Gespenster aus Dänemark', p. 70. Brittnacher's sound analysis of Rilke's novel does not fail to convince, yet his interpretation of the ghost hand episode raises additional questions. The red colour of the dropped pen, for one, poses a non-negligible problem as it is atypical of a writer and at the same time unobvious considering the motive depicted by Malte. The very same motive, the knight – a typically romantic motive – on the other hand, begs the question whether it is to be considered a mere reflection of infantile interests or whether it carries a deeper meaning; especially in consideration of Malte's attempts to meet the literary requirements of his post-romantic environment.

At the same place where Malte encounters all these unspeakable incidents, he comes across portraits of Leonora Christina and her kin. One night, when young Malte decides to investigate whether a portrait of the deceased Christine Brahe, who is now haunting Urnekloster, is to be found in his grandfather's ominous gallery, he comes across several paintings depicting characters of Danish history, such as Christian IV, Kirsten Munk, Ellen Marsvin and, of course, Leonora Christina: »Da waren König Christians Kinder: immer wieder frische aus neuen Frauen, die ›unvergleichliche‹ Eleonore auf einem weißen Paßgänger in ihrer glänzendsten Zeit, vor der Heimsuchung«.[1365]

Despite Leonora Christina's insignificant role in Rilke's account, her position within it is anything but that. For one, she is placed in the midst of Malte's childhood memories composed of metaphysical and historical elements, both of which may be directly attributed to Rilke's Scandinavian and, in particular, Danish phase. When the entire German-speaking realm of Europe had fallen prey to a Scandinavia-hype created by the international success of Henrik Ibsen, Jens Peter Jacobsen and August Strindberg, Rilke followed this trend. Already in 1902, Rilke delved into the history of the Reventlow family, whose members upheld close connections to the Danish royal house and whom Rilke vaguely attaches to Malte's semi-fictive family. Two years later, Rilke's extended stay in Denmark and Sweden provided the opportunity for further research on Danish history. The final result – *Malte Laurids Brigge* – testifies to its author's diligence: notwithstanding Leonora Christina's position at the utmost periphery of Rilke's literary spiritualism, the author included her recollections, i.e. *Jammers Minde*, in his work queue (*Arbeitsliste*) for *Malte Laurids Brigge*.[1366] Rilke furthermore worked through an account by Otto Sperling the Elder of King Christian IV's final hours, which is rendered in *Malte Laurids Brigge* in the form of a copy written by Malte's deceased father, found by Malte in his father's wallet.[1367]

Another central source for many Danish details in *Malte Laurids Brigge* was *Danske malede portrætter – En beskrivende katalog*, edited by E. F. S. Lund and C. C. Andersen and published in ten volumes between 1895 and 1914. From this

---

1365 Rilke, Rainer Maria. *Malte Laurids Brigge*, p. 97 ('There were King Christian's children: ever-fresh ones out of new women, the >incomparable< Eleonore on top of a white ambler in her most glorious period, before the haunting').

1366 This work queue is originally preserved in Rilke's so-called *Berner Taschenbuch*, a notebook including a draft of the novel's second part as well as Rilke's work queue, a rather random-looking list of work titles (such as *Jammers Minde*, which Rilke calls »Jammerminde«), names and ideas. A reproduction of this work queue is provided in Engel, Manfred. 'Dokumente III: Die Arbeitsliste aus dem >Berner Taschenbuch<'. In Rilke, Rainer Maria. *Malte Laurids Brigge*. Herausgegeben und kommentiert von Manfred Engel. Stuttgart: Reclam, 1997, pp. 304-307.

1367 Rilke, Rainer Maria. *Malte Laurids Brigge*, p. 136.

source, Rilke obtained not only references to further reading and autobiographical information (Otto Sperling's above-mentioned text, for example), but also visual material subsequently transcribed into Malte's eerie observations at the Urnekloster gallery.[1368] Malte's spectral encounters, on the other hand, are restricted to the protagonist's Danish past as these elements constitute another constituent of Rilke's 'Scandinavian fever', as the author explains in a letter to his publisher dated 21 October 1924:

> Übrigens war hier einer der Gründe, warum die erfundene Figur des M. L. Brigge zu einem Dänen gemacht wurde: weil nur in der Atmosphäre der skandinavischen Länder das Gespenst unter die möglichen Ereignisse eingereiht erscheint und zugegeben (:was meiner eigenen Einstellung gemäß ist).[1369]

Despite, or perhaps *because of* Rilke's intensive research on Leonora Christina's age, *Malte Laurids Brigge* suggests that the material provided on Leonora Christina in particular did not fit what Rilke required from the Danish episodes. His detailed comments on some of the historical characters immortalised on the walls of the Urnekloster gallery attest to Rilke's love for the anecdotal. In this context, and considering that Leonora Christina and Rilke had both practiced – more or less successfully – remedial writing,[1370] the absence of any explicit reference to her

---

1368 For a comprehensive elucidation of Rilke's sources, see the correspondent annotation in Rilke, Rainer Maria. *Prosa und Dramen*, ed. August Stahl. Frankfurt and Leipzig: Insel, 1996 (Rainer Maria Rilke. Werke 3), pp. 866-1054.

1369 Letter addressed to Hermann Pongs and dated 21 October 1924, reproduced in Rilke, Rainer Maria. *Gesammelte Briefe in sechs Bänden 5: Briefe aus Muzot 1921 bis 1926*, eds. Ruth Sieber-Rilke and Carl Sieber. Leipzig: Insel, 1937, p. 323 ('By the way, this is one of the reasons why the fictive character of M. L. Brigge is a Dane: because only in the atmosphere of the Scandinavian countries the appearance of ghosts could seems like a possible occurrence (:which coincides with my own attitude'). In his analysis of the very same apparitions in *Malte Laurids Brigge*, Hans Richard Brittnacher – following Salman Rushdie's definition of a ghost as »unfinished business« (in the novel *The Satanic Verses* (1988)) – refers to literature's most famous ghost, i.e. Hamlet's (Danish) father, to Henrik Ibsen's use of the term 'ghosts' in his homonymous drama, and to the ghosts distressing Rilke's Malte as literary elements carrying one intertextual symbolic value: that of haunting protagonists for whatever they fail to do. This functional correspondence and the Scandinavian origin of the former two (Hamlet and Ibsen's *Gengangere*) underscore the plausibility of Rilke's conviction that ghosts should naturally occur in Scandinavia (see Brittnacher, Hans Richard. 'Gespenster aus Dänemark', p. 52f).

1370 The diverse functions fulfilled by the writing of *Jammers Minde* have been discussed at length above. As far as Rilke and *Malte Laurids Brigge* are concerned, the latter is commonly perceived as having failed to produce the relief sought after by the former. Rilke himself spoke of his novel as »ein unendlicher Schmerz« (letter addressed to A. Baumgarten and dated 27 June 1911, reproduced in *Materialien zu Rainer Maria Rilke >Die Aufzeichnungen des Malte Laurids Brigge<*, p. 87: 'infinite pain').

International Leonora Christina-literature

exceptionally long imprisonment and *Jammers Minde* would strongly indicate that Rilke was, at least at this time, not quite familiar with her fate.[1371]

The Rilke-material on the years after *Malte Laurids Brigge* shows that he eventually caught up on his lecture of *Jammers Minde*. Rilke's somewhat mysterious remark »Und Jammers-minde?«[1372] in a letter from 1911 to the publisher Anton Kippenberg indicates that Leonora Christina still haunted his mind. In his article on Rilke and Leonora Christina, George C. Schoolfield further claims that Rilke had incorporated some of the impressions imprinted upon him by his reading of *Jammers Minde* into his cycle of poems *Duineser Elegien* (1923; English title: *Duino Elegies*).[1373] I must, however, join Steffen Steffensen's verdict that Schoolfield sees similarities where there are none.[1374] Schoolfield ascribes, for example, Rilke's fifth elegy an undeniable resemblance to Leonora Christina's account of a band of acrobats, who one day performed on the castle square in front of her window (see Chapter 1.2.1.). If Rilke had indeed drawn immediate inspiration from *Jammers Minde* and transformed it into one or more of his poems, the final result had by all means taken on a completely different shape so as to render a definite determination of his source impossible. As stated by Judith Ryan (albeit pertaining to Malte's memory of himself and his mother contemplating samples of lace together): »[W]ie so oft ist der Gegenstand selbst nur insofern von Bedeutung, als er die Einbildungskraft anregt und von ihr verwandelt wird«.[1375] More than a decade after the publication of *Malte Laurids Brigge* and two decades after his journey to Copenhagen, Rilke applied the same defamiliarising procedure – i.e. what Judith Ryan calls Rilke's »[h]ypothetisches Erzählen«[1376] – to a scene from *Jammers Minde*.

On 21 October 1924 Rilke wrote:

1371 We read, for example, about Hans Ulrik Gyldenløve's extravagantly colourful face and about Henrik Holck's fateful dream. That the story of a King's daughter imprisoned in a tower should not have made a better anecdote than her half-brother's rosy cheeks is rather difficult to believe.

1372 Letter addressed to Anton Klippenberg and dated 23 October 1911, reproduced in Rilke, Rainer Maria. *Briefe an seinen Verleger 1: 1906 bis 1926*, ed. Ruth Sieber-Rilke. Wiesbaden: Insel, 1949, p. 151 ('And Jammersminde?'). The preceding text suggests that Rilke is asking to have *Jammers Minde* sent to him.

1373 Schoolfield, George C. 'Rilke and Leonora Christina', pp. 429-431.

1374 Steffensen, Steffen. *Rilke und Skandinavien: Zwei Vorträge von Steffen Steffensen*. Copenhagen: Munksgaard, 1958, p. 62 (endnote 5).

1375 Ryan, Judith. '>Hypothetisches Erzählen<: Zur Funktion von Phantasie und Einbildung in Rilkes »Malte Laurids Brigge«'. In *Materialien zu Rainer Maria Rilke >Die Aufzeichnungen des Malte Laurids Brigge<*, ed. Hartmut Engelhardt. Frankfurt: Suhrkamp, 1974 (Suhrkamp Taschenbuch 174), p. 263 ('As is often the case, the object itself is of significance only to the degree to which it stimulates the phantasy and is shaped by it').

1376 Ibid., pp. 244-279 ('hypothetical narrating').

Ich benutze, lieber Herr Dr. Pongs, diese übrige vierzehnte Seite um noch einen Beitrag über das Thema ›Reich und Arm‹ anzuschließen. Die hier berichtete kleine Handlung (deren Größe man im Übrigen selbst beurteilen mag) drückt das, was meine persönliche Einstellung wäre, wenn ich mich auf sie besinnen sollte, so vollkommen und so gültig aus, daß ich nichts hinzuzufügen hätte.[1377]

These introductory remarks are followed by a scene Rilke claims to have taken from Leonora Christina's *Jammers Minde*, which will be discussed below. However, Schoolfield doubts that by 1910 Rilke's mastery of the Danish language would have been sufficient enough to be able to fully read and understand *Jammers Minde*, while Rilke himself implied in a letter dated 21 October 1924 that he had read the book in the original language.[1378] Rilke could, of course, have resorted to the German translation published in Vienna in 1871 by Johannes Ziegler, yet, he does not mention this translation anywhere. Notwithstanding his scepticism, Schoolfield also provides reasons in favour of Rilke's knowledge of *Jammers Minde* by the time he wrote *Malte Laurids Brigge*, all of which are refuted by Brigitte von Witzleben. She dismisses, for example, Schoolfield's reference to Sperling's appearance in *Malte Laurids Brigge* as an indication in favour of Rilke's familiarity with *Jammers Minde*[1379] and attributes it to another source instead (see above). At the same time, Witzleben is puzzled by some other details which would confirm Schoolfield's suspicion, such as the dog Cavalier who joins the family of Malte's mother at the coffee table and then runs off to welcome the recently deceased Ingeborg; a dog of the same name appears twice in *Jammers Minde*.[1380] Witzleben furthermore rejects Schoolfield's doubts regarding Rilke's familiarity with *Jammers Minde*, based on

---

1377 Rilke, Rainer Maria. *Briefe 2: 1919-1926*, ed. Horst Nalewski. Frankfurt: Insel 1991, p. 359 ('I use, dear Dr Pongs, this remaining fourteenth page to add a contribution on the topic of ›Rich und Poor‹. The little narration which I will report here (whose magnitude one can deem for oneself) expresses what would be my personal attitutde, if I had to recollect it, to entirely and validly, that I would have nothing to add').
1378 Ibid., p. 360.
1379 Schoolfield, George C. 'Rilke and Leonora Christina', p. 425.
1380 Witzleben, Brigitte von. 'Zu den historischen Quellen von Rilkes >Die Aufzeichnungen des Malte Laurids Brigge<'. In *Materialien zu Rainer Maria Rilke >Die Aufzeichnungen des Malte Laurids Brigge<*, ed. Hartmut Engelhardt. Frankfurt: Suhrkamp, 1974 (Suhrkamp Taschenbuch 174), p. 285. This dog was sent to Leonora Christina by Queen Charlotte Amalie, after it was badly bitten by a marten, so she could nurse it. Although Leonora Christina was not very happy about this burden (cf. *Jammers Minde*, p. 226), she wrote a poem about this dog: 'En hund wed Nafn Cavaillier Forteller sin Skiæfne'. This poem, which Leonora Christina merely mentions in *Jammers Minde* (p. 238) and which is generally considered to be an allegory of Corfitz Ulfeldt's life (see, for example, Hofman, Tycho de. *Historiske Efterretninger om velfortiente Danske Adelsmænd, med deres Stamme-Tavler og Portraiter 2*, transl. C. Liunge and B. C. Sandvig. Copenhagen: A. H. Godiche, 1778, p. 326), was published separately (see ibid., pp. 326-331).

a letter to the Bohemian noblewoman Sidonie Nádherný of Borutín (1885-1950) dated 4 February 1912, in which he states to have become acquainted with this book seven or eight years prior to said letter, i.e. at the time when he commenced his research in Denmark.[1381]

However, apart from all these arguments, the following story, i.e. Rilke's faulty reproduction of Leonora Christina's interaction with the men guarding her on board the boat traversing her from England directly to Copenhagen provided at the beginning of *Jammers Minde*, prompts Schoolfield to doubt that Rilke had fully read, understood *or* remembered the text.[1382] The countless mistakes in Rilke's rendering of the Ulfeldt couple's story indicate that he was not in the possession of his own (perhaps German) copy of *Jammers Minde*, but rather that he had read the story in Denmark and was thus – years later – not quite able to remember it correctly. Hence he mistakes Leonora Christina's imprisonment to have lasted 26 years and he believes Corfitz Ulfeldt to have escaped to Tyrol. However, all further deviations as regards the content of *Jammers Minde* would rather suggest that it had never been Rilke's intention to render Leonora Christina's text, but to make it his own.

In said letter to Pongs, and in response to a discussion previously initiated by the publisher concerning the definition and nature of the concept »Reich und Arm«, Rilke recounts the incidence on the ferry from Dover to Copenhagen, in which *Capitain* Bendix Alfeldt requests of Leonora Christina to surrender all of her jewellery, gold, silver and letters, as well as her knife. In her own testimony, Leonora Christina obeys with feigned indifference; an hour later she would receive everything except for her letters back by order of another visitor, Maj. Gen. Friderich von Anfeldt. Upon retrieving her goods, Leonora Christina immediately puts her bracelets and rings back into place while leaving the rest to her maid (cf. *Jammers Minde*, pp. 3-7).

Rilke, however, rewrote the incidence. In his account, Leonora Christina's possessions are taken from and returned to her by one and the same person, a young and ambitious officer. He addresses her on his own initiative and demands to receive only her jewellery:

1381 See Rilke, Rainer Maria. *Briefe an Sidonie Nádherný von Borutin*, ed. Bernhard Blume. Frankfurt: Insel, 1973, p. 141.

1382 Schoolfield, George C. 'Rilke and Leonora Christina', p. 427.

Es mag dem jungen Lieutenant nicht eben leicht gewesen sein, den Blick, den sein Begehren ihm eintrug, mit Anstand auszuhalten. Dann aber trat die schöne und stattliche Frau, die nach der Mode der damaligen Zeit mit Juwelen und Ketten reichlich geschmückt war, an den Spiegel ihrer Kajüte heran und nahm langsam, ohne Eile, eines nach dem anderen, die Ringe, die Gehänge, die Spangen, die Armbänder und Ohrringe ab, die sich, warm und schwer, in den erschrocken aufgeschlagenen Händen des Offiziers häuften.[1383]

When the young officer shows the booty to his superior, the latter fears that his prisoner (who is still not informed about her arrest) might get suspicious; so he orders the young man to return the goods:

Bleich, zitternd, immer noch den unerhörten Überfluß auf den überladenen Händen, erschien der vernichtete Offizier wieder vor der hohen Frau. Stand, stammelnd ... Sie ließ ihn, hoheitsvoll, einen angemessenen Augenblick in dem Zustande seiner Verzweiflung, nur aber um (obwohl sie doch alles begriffen haben mag, was folgen würde) wieder an ihren Spiegel zu treten und, langsam, wie aus den Händen eines Dieners, das vielfältige Geschmeid an sich zu nehmen und anzulegen: mit genau der gleichen Gelassenheit, die sie vorher im Hingeben bewiesen hatte, und schon vertieft in ihr, im Spiegel festlich sich wieder ergänzendes Bild.[1384]

As highlighted by Schoolfield, Rilke had changed Leonora Christina's account quite a bit. He had added typical accessories of Rilkean poetry, such as the mirror and the removing and receiving hands. On the other hand, Rilke removed Leonora Christina's gold and silver, her knife, and her letters from the account – only her jewellery matters.[1385] Rilke's amalgamation of the originally three people, through whose hands Leonora Christina's possessions went – Alfeldt, Anfeldt and the servant carrying the silver pot containing said possessions – could quite simply be

---

1383 Rilke, Rainer Maria. *Briefe 2*, p. 360 ('It might have been difficult for the young Lieutenant to withstand the look, which his inquiry had provoked. But then the beautiful, lordly woman, who, in the fashion of her time, was richly adorned with jewels and necklaces, stepped in front of the mirror in her cabin and took off, without haste, one after one, the rings, the pendants, the brooches, the bracelets and earrings, which, warm and heavy, piled up in the frightenedly opened hands of the officer').

1384 Ibid., p. 361 ('Pale, shivering, still holding the unheard-of abundance in the overloaded hands, the devastated officer reappeared in front of the woman. Stood, stammering...She left him, majestically, in this condition of desperation for an appropriate amount of time, but only to (even though she must have understood what would follow) return to her mirror and, slowly, like out of a servant's hands, take the manifold jewelry and put it on: with just the same serenity she had demonstrated before in her giving, and already absorbed by her, festively completing, mirror image').

1385 Schoolfield, George C. 'Rilke and Leonora Christina', p. 428.

attributed to the similarity of the former two's names. The reduction to one person has, however, also the effect of creating a more immediate transaction of goods between the two people involved, especially since there is no pot to carry the goods (unlike in *Jammers Minde*); the possessions never leave the hands of the young officer. This, in turn, promotes a direct comparison of Leonora Christina's inner wealth (i.e. her dignity) and the officer's greedy behaviour. The young man had tried to take the matter of relocating wealth into his own hands, but fate was not on his side.

Rilke's focus on Leonora Christina's lustrous possessions, on the other hand, may partially be inspired by the body search-scene reproduced in *Jammers Minde*, the purpose of which is to demonstrate the prisoner's heroic stoicism in the face of her offender's attempt to bereave her of everything including her dignity. During this scene, both sides' objective is to retrieve jewellery as it would signify a temporary victory (cf. *Jammers Minde*, pp. 18-21). The mirror added by Rilke is his hidden signature, but it also serves the purpose of decelerating the interaction between Leonora Christina and the officer. Twice, she takes the time to walk to her mirror to follow the man's request. When Rilke narrated the same scene in a letter to Sidonie Nádherný of Borutin in 1912, he adjusted Leonora Christina's second walk to the mirror to lend her character even more natural authority; in this version, she tells the man to follow her to the mirror through a mere cue:

> Nach einem Bedenken, nicht länger als jenes erste war, nimmt die Gräfin Ulfeldt die Ringe aus den Händen des verwirrten Offiziers, vertheilt sie wieder an die gewohnten Stellen, winkt ihm mitzugehen, tritt an einen Spiegel und bringt dort, aufmerksam und ruhig, wie sies in ihrem Ankleidezimmer würde gethan haben, an sich Halsschmuck und Ohrgehänge an, eines nach dem anderen.[1386]

As Rilke writes in his letter to Hermann Pongs, he had rendered this scene with the intention of exemplifying his very own idea of the opposition of Rich and Poor. Rilke begins by rejecting Pongs' apparent social understanding of this dichotomy and continues by explaining his own concept further ahead in the letter:

1386 See Rilke, Rainer Maria. *Briefe an Sidonie Nádherný von Borutin*, p. 143 ('After a short moment of reflection, not longer than the former one, the Countess Ulfeldt takes the rings out of the hands of the confused officer, puts them back in their usual spots, beckons him over, moves to a mirror and there, carefully and calmly, like she would have in her dressing room, she puts on neck jewellery and earrings, one after another').

Niemandes Lage in der Welt ist so, daß sie seiner Seele nicht eigentümlich zustatten kommen könnte...Und ich muß gestehen, mir ist, wo ich anderem Schicksal teilzunehmen genötigt war, immer vor Allem dieses wichtig und angelegentlich gewesen: dem Bedrückten die eigentümlichen und besonderen Bedingungen seiner Not erkennen zu helfen, was jedesmal nicht so sehr ein Trost, als eine (zunächst unscheinbare) Bereicherung ist.[1387]

Rilke's renunciation of the idea of changing anybody's fortune reflects Leonora Christina's own stoic attitude upon remembering the scene on the ferry, which also initiates her imprisonment: »Ieg Klædde mig, oc satte mig vdi en aff Bodzmendenis Koyer paa Offuerlaaget med en Stadig *Resolution* friimodeligen att tage imod alt ded mig war forrelagt« (*Jammers Minde*, p. 3). As Leonora Christina would maintain her stoicism throughout most of the subsequent account, Rilke – despite all changes and all doubts concerning his mastery of Danish – had indeed assigned the accurate meaning to this scene, for in his letter to the Baroness of Borutin, Rilke highlights its central significance: »[U]nd, mir schien immer, man kann ihr Verhalten voraussagen, wenn man eine gewisse kleine Szene kennt, die sich bei ihrer Verhaftung in England abgespielt hat«.[1388] As Leonora Christina's resolution to lay her future into the hands of God would remain her guideline throughout her imprisonment, Rilke had chosen this scene to represent the whole of Leonora Christina's story, his idea of »Reich und Arm«, and – in his letter to Sidonie Nádherný of Borutin – a story about man's place in the world:

Sagen Sie, liebe Freundin, wissen Sie irgend einen Vorfall, bei dem großartiger an den Tag käme, wie wir uns vor den Schickungen des Lebens verhalten sollen? [...] Jene Geste des Verzichts ist herrlich, hinreißend, – aber sie ist nicht ohne Hochmut, was wieder nur darin sich aufhebt, daß sie, ihrer Art nach, schon zum Himmel gehört. Dieses stille, gefaßte Behalten und Lassen dagegen ist voller Maaß, ist noch ganz irdisch und doch schon größer als sich irgend begreifen läßt.[1389]

[1387] Rilke, Rainer Maria. *Briefe 2*, p. 357 ('Nobody's situation in the world is such that it would not singularly reflect their soul...and I have to admit, where I have been forced to empathise with other people's destiny, what has always and primarily been important and urgent to me: to help the aggrieved acknowledge the singular and special conditions of their distress, which is never consolation, but rather an (initially inconsiderable) enrichment').

[1388] Rilke, Rainer Maria. *Briefe an Sidonie Nádherný von Borutin*, p. 142 ('And, I have always had the impression, that one could predict her behaviour, only by knowing a certain little scene, which occurred during her apprehension in England').

[1389] Ibid., p. 143 ('Tell me, dear friend, would you know of any incident revealing in a greater manner how to behave in the face of life's fickleness? [...] This gesture of surrender is wonderful, enchanting, – but it does not lack haughtiness, which is only neutralised by the fact that she, in her nature, already belongs to heaven. This quiet, composed keeping and letting, however, is full of moderation, is entirely mundane but already grander than can be conceived').

In Rilke's work, Leonora Christina's literary function has thus undergone a tremendous metamorphosis. Initially, Rilke had been captured by the historical-documental value of *Jammers Minde*, a book he assesses as simply 'hard'.[1390] Despite the lack of relevant traces of Leonora Christina in Rilke's fictive writings, and despite his fading fervour for Denmark, he maintained his admiration for Leonora Christina's, in his eyes, exemplary behaviour, and in a way, he had indeed dedicated an entire short story, or, as Rilke implied on one occasion, a Christmas story, to Leonora Christina: »In diesem Sinn, Sidie, hat Ihnen Ihr alter Freund das Ulfeldt'sche Leidens-Gedächtnis ins weihnachtliche Licht gelegt, da er doch nichts, was ihm völlig zur Einsicht wird, Ihnen vorbehalten will«.[1391]

2.7.3. Karin Johnsson: *Kungligt blod. Leonora Kristina Ulfeldt* (1919) – A Woman Making History?

> Løffuindens Hierte er saa Keckmodig som Løwens: Mangen Quinde haffuer større styrcke end som mangen Mand, Mangen Quinde haffuer oc wel saa Keckt ed mod som Mangen Mand; de suare icke alle til Mands Naffn i Gierningen som bærer Tittel aff Mands Naffn, men offte suare Quinder til Helters Naffn i Gierningen, oc bere dog ickun Quinders Naffn: Huoroffte seer man quindactige Hierter i Mands Legemer, oc der imod igien mandelige Kræffter i suage Karr: Ded er Vbilligt, att man maaler Gierningen effter Persohnen, oc skatter icke Persohnen effter Gierningen.[1392]

Through the publication of her otherwise marginal second novel – *Kungligt blod: Leonora Kristina Ulfeldt* – in 1919, the Swedish historian, writer and translator Karin Johnsson (1889-1968) breathed some fresh air into the production of Leonora Christina-literature, which at the time of Johnsson's publication had virtually come to a lackadaisical as well as aesthetic halt. Notwithstanding my current consideration of her in the context of international Leonora Christina-literature, Johnsson's citizenship has no bearing on the novelty factor provided by *Kungligt blod*. Instead, Johnsson's dual identity as a woman and as a historian affects her novel in an unprecendented manner as it offers some reflection on women's place in historiography.

Despite the novel's overall resemblance to popular historiography, Johnsson's preamble still attempts to convey a sense of tragic fatefulness to agitate the reader,

---

1390 Ibid., p. 141.
1391 Ibid., p. 143 ('In this spirit, your old friend has cast the Ulfeldtian memory of lament in a light worthy of the Christmas period for you, since he wants to keep nothing from you, which absorbs his insight').
1392 Leonora Christina. *Hæltinners Pryd*, p. 21.

who, in this case, will be less familiar with Leonora Christina's story (since there is no tradition of Leonora Christina-literature in Sweden) and hence more impartial. After a baleful enumeration of real life tragedies, Johnsson clarifies why a tragedian would choose to write about their subject matter when life itself provides plenty of this dark lore:[1393] »Det finns nämligen en tragik i livet, som är mörkare än någon annan«.[1394] In Johnsson's eyes, the story of Leonora Christina is one of those outstanding tragedies, characterised by an individual's complete self-abandonment in service to a beloved one:

> Kärlekens tragik, som driver en kvinna eller en man icke att ge sig helt men att ge sig ovärdigt, – om kärleken kan bliva ovärdig. Att döda sig själv, att offra sin börd, offra sitt liv. Att älska så djupt, att även den älskades brott måste älskas, icke i lust men nöd. Få kvinnor hava med heder genomlidt den tragiken. Leonora Kristina Ulfeldt var en bland de få.[1395]

After this introductory junction of Leonora Christina's story to a classic topic of world literature, Johnsson returns to her original métier, i.e. history. Subsequent to a highly suggestive comparison of Leonora Christina with Hamlet, one famous archetype of a tragic hero, Johnsson quickly undoes the readership's expectations by dismissing this disastrously indecisive Prince of Denmark as a product not of Denmark's history, but of fiction from another island. Once again, Leonora Christina as a Danish heroine, true in terms of nationality and historicity, stands out: »Danmarks historia är icke rik på tragiska personligheter. […] Men kanske just därför står hennes höga gestalt så imponerande i relief mot historiens bakgrund«.[1396]

With the end of this short preamble, Johnsson irrevocably returns to her favoured discipline. The first chapter is preceded by a bibliography exclusively containing historical studies and records, a large portion of the former written by Sophus Birket Smith. The following twenty-four chapters depict Leonora Christina's life story with an integrity and a style resembling that of popular historiography. Accordingly, Johnsson cannot resist the urge to switch from omniscient narrator to historiographer at rather frequent intervals:

1393 Cf. Johnsson, Karin. *Kungligt blod: Leonora Kristina Ulfeldt: Ett kvinnoöde ur historien.* Stockholm: Lars Hökerberg, 1919, unpaginated preamble: »Även de höra väl till Melpomenes mörka skara, men gudinnans ögon irra vidare ut över världen, som om hon sökte andra än dem«.
1394 Ibid.
1395 Ibid.
1396 Ibid.

> Man kan emellertid icke undgå att erkänna, att denna äregirighet fullkomligt delades av Leonora Kristina. Det kungliga blod, som flöt i hennes ådror, förnekade sig aldrig, och hennes bördsstolthet förlänade alltifrån hennes tidigaste ungdom något visst kyligt och högdraget åt hennes väsen, ett fel, som följde henne hela livet igenom och som omsider skulle bli till största bitterhet för henne själv. – – –[1397]

Sometimes the switch between these two narratives styles occurs in the middle of a phrase, which demonstrates Johnsson's irresolute fluctuation between historiographic caution and the authority of a writer of fiction: »Huruvida Leonora Kristina anade hela vidden av Ulfeldts förskingringar och oredliga förvaltning av sina ämbeten är ovisst, men då han inför henne framlade sina planer till flykt och motiven därför, gick hon genast villigt med på allt«.[1398]

Following the fashion of historiography, Johnsson's account furthermore lacks dialogue. A sort of direct speech is only provided by some excerpts from historical records, such as private letters and other kinds of correspondence. This occurs, for instance, to a rather high degree in the third chapter, which recounts the events revolving around Frants Rantzau's untimely death, which Johnsson apparently intended to document in great detail. The countless letters written by Christian IV and reproduced by Johnsson serve no narrative purpose, but they certainly produce a lively depiction of the historical Christian IV.[1399]

Johnsson's authorial intention, i.e. to provide a preferably complete depiction of Leonora Christina and her environment, as well as her dependency on Sophus Birket Smith's extensive work, both result in a series of déjà vu-experiences, many traces of which lead to H. F. Ewald's novel *Leonora Kristina* (see Chapter 2.4.2.). Her portrayals of Leonora Christina's elder sister Anna Catharina and her eldest daughter of the same name, for example, resemble very much the depiction provided by Ewald. Again, Leonora Christina's elder sister is presented as a favourite and soulmate to her younger sibling. Since Leonora Christina herself did not mention her sister anywhere, this must be due to Anna Catharina's own tragic love story (see Chapter 2.3.1.), which found its bitter end with her fiancé's death, shortly succeeded by her own. Accordingly, both sisters are portrayed in a corresponding manner, with Anna Katharina (as spelled by Johnsson) being gentle, pale and somewhat lugu-

---

[1397] Ibid., p. 43.
[1398] Ibid., p. 133.
[1399] To a similar effect, Johnsson's novel contains countless contemporary portraits of the people mentioned in the account.

brious, while Leonora Kristina,[1400] who – according to Johnsson's preamble – was destined to suffer, is equally anticipating her development: »I såväl kroppslig som andlig utveckling var hon långt före sina år«.[1401] To this effect, Anna Katharina's sad passing serves as an introductory chapter to her younger sister's own bittersweet love story and as one of the many losses in Leonora Kristina's life. Similarly, Leonora Kristina's daughter, Anna Katharina, mirrors her mother's positive attributes, whereas she surpasses her in terms of rumbling unworthy suitors, i.e. her first fiancé Kay Lykke.[1402] The courage, resoluteness and integrity she demonstrates by defying her parents in this regard casts a somewhat dubious light on her mother's appraised loyalty towards her own unworthy suitor, who will wreak havoc on his family.[1403] Eventually, however, both women are bound to succumb to their fate: »– Ja, moder, jag vet, att du har rätt. Dohna äger alla goda egenskaper, under det att Klas Thott är en spelare och drinkare och kvinnojägare – hon upprepade Dohnas ord, – men jag älskar honom ändå…, det är mitt öde…«.[1404]

A more curious correspondence between Johnsson's text and that of Ewald, though, is the two authors' rendition of the Dina affair. When Ewald's Leonora meets Dina for the first time, their shared experience of pregnancy creates an immediate bond: »Leonora saa en smuk, ung Kvinde, som hilste hende ydmygt, og da hun opdagede, at Dina var i samme Tilstand som hun selv, fik hun straks Medlidenhed med hende«.[1405] In the same scene rendered by Johnsson »gjorde Leo-

---

1400 In the present chapter, »Leonora Kristina« specifically refers to the character in Johnsson's novel, particularly when referring to passages that do not correspond to historical events, whereas »Leonora Christina« refers to the historical person or other literary presentations of this character. Further spelling variations used in the literary source text, and hence in this chapter as well, are »Korfitz«, »Kristina« (Queen of Sweden), and »Anna Katharina«.

1401 Johnsson, Karin. *Kungligt blod*, p. 21.

1402 Cf. ibid., p. 159: »Anna Katharina var en djärv, oförskräckt och självständig natur. Kort efter sin ankomst till Stralsund hade hon underrättat föräldrarna om, att hon före avresan från Danmark brutit sin trolovning med Kay Lykke, och de föreställningar, hennes moder gjorde, voro som en sådd på hälleberget. Hon förklarade endast, att hon icke ville gifta sig med Kay Lykke, därför att hon icke älskade honom – och även om hon älskat honom, skulle hon aldrig kunna bliva hans hustru, emedan han var en tom hycklare och en ynkrygg, som vände kappan efter vinden och höll sig framme, var helst han trodde sig kunna vinna några fördelar«. To a limited degree, Johnsson's text furthermore resembles that of Ewald in its occasionally judgemental tone: »Denna balett skilde sig på intet vis från alla andra vid denna tid. Den var huvudsakligen anlagd på att bereda åskådarna mesta möjliga ögonfägnad och hade en fullkomligt meningslös handling« (ibid., p. 164).

1403 »Både Ulfeldt och Leonora Kristina mottogo honom med största vänlighet, utan att genomskåda hans falskhet – det var endast Anna Katharina, som trots sin unga ålder såg klarare än någon annan och i sitt hjärta avslöjade honom som den skrymtare han var« (ibid., p. 124). See also ibid., p. 187: »Hon [Anna Katharina] skulle nu genomgå den första av de många prövningar, som livet hade i beredskap åt henne för hennes ärelystne och brottslige faders skull. – – –«.

1404 Ibid., p. 169.

1405 Ewald, H[erman] F[rederik]. *Leonora Kristina*, p. 160.

nora Kristina genast samma upptäckt som pagen nyss: att den främmande var en underbart vacker kvinna, och då hon såg, i vilket tillstånd hon befann sig, greps hon av djupt medlidande«.[1406] Furthermore, and in agreement with Ulfeldt's own testimony, both Johnsson and Ewald state that it was the fact that Dina and Ulfeldt had never faced each other before the trial that sounded the death knell for Dina, again with remarkable, even suspicious conformity.[1407]

Due to the historiographic disposition of Johnsson's text on the one hand and her faithfulness to her sources on the other hand, *Kungligt blod* offers hardly any novelty within the corpus of Leonora Christina-literature. Even though Johnsson declares the Ulfeldt couple to have played a considerable part in the development of the North's (and hence also Sweden's) history,[1408] the author lacks national paradigms to transform the material provided by history into an appealing work of fiction. The pivotal years in Korfitz's life dominate the account and contain hardly any relevant appearance of his wife. Johnsson abandons any attempt to understand her protagonists' personalities and dwells on facts and vague conclusions while her literary ambitions only prevail in terms of amplifying insignificant scenes in Leonora Christina and her contemporaries' lives. The result is neither felicitous historiography nor captivating fiction.

This circumstance considered in the context of Johnsson's education would suggest that she simply adhered to paradigms known to her through her studies. In the decades before the emergence of feminist historiography, very few historical works dealing with women and their involvement in world affairs were known. There was, of course, the gynæceum, but this sort of comparative historiography dealing exclusively with women provided no model for a consolidating history of Leonora Christina and her husband. Hence the only antetypes available to Johnsson were male-centered historiography, as well as Birket Smith's comprehensive narratives. Now, while Johnsson's overall approach does not seem to challenge the paradigms of traditional historiography, there are some indicators in the text that seem intent on exciting a discussion about a woman's place in history.

1406 Johnsson, Karin. *Kungligt blod*, p. 110.
1407 Cf. ibid., p. 116 (»Makarna Ulfeldt satte nu all sin lit till Dina Vinhoffvers, som från denna dag städse var väl sedd av Leonora Kristina, under det att Ulfeldt sjläv aldrig nedlät sig till mottaga henne. Hon kom sålunda aldrig att en enda gång stå ansikte mot ansikte med rikshovmästaren, en omständighet, som gjorde sitt till för att fälla henne, när vedergällningens dag omsider randades. –«) and Ewald, H[erman] F[rederik]. *Leonora Kristina*, p. 162 (»Nu satte de deres Lid til Dina, og hun var altid velkommen hos Leonora, hvorimod Ulfeldt aldrig nedlod sig til at modtage hende. Hun kom ikke en eneste Gang til at staa Ansigt til Ansigt med Rigshofmesteren, en Omstændighed, der siden gjorde sit til at fælde hende«).
1408 Johnsson, Karin. *Kungligt blod*, p. 47.

As concluded above, Johnsson's novel exhibits all the classic traits of the early Leonora Christina-literature, including the focus on her father and her husband, up until their respective deaths. Only when Leonora Kristina is left to fend for herself and to develop her own destiny does her character take centre stage, as is the case with Johnsson's post-*Jammers Minde* novel. The historian Johnsson, however, pronounces for the first time what has hitherto only been demonstrated:

> Det är detta äktenskap, som gjort Leonora Kristina namnkunnig, icke blott därför att det band henne vid en man, som kom att spela en stor roll i Nordens [!] historia, utan även därför att genom det hennes egen kraft och rika begåvning satte henne i tillfälle att erövra en självständig plats i det allmänna medvetandet. Det är först under senare delen av äktenskapet, då olyckan tvingar henne ut på obanade vägar, som hennes livsöde bliv av större intresse. Så länge lycka och medgång följa hennes gemål på den ärofulla och vanärande bana, han så snart skulle beträda, står hon själv helt och hållet i skuggan. Och dock äro dessa hennes äktenskaps första år av icke ringa betydelse för henne själv.[1409]

Kungligt blod is thus the first and – to my knowledge – so far only work of Leonora Christina-fiction actively dealing with Leonora Christina's place in Nordic history in relation to that of her husband. Initially, Leonora Kristina remains a mere pretence-heroine, (again) similar to that portrayed by H. F. Ewald, but as the plot proceeds, the novel's eponymous heroine acquires her rightful place in history through a specifically gendered discourse of historiography as *res gestae*, i.e. as a narrative of deeds and hence a male monopoly.[1410] It commences with Johnsson's characterisation of Leonora Kristina as both genuinely feminine and masculine:

1409 Ibid.

1410 Johnsson's novel could thus be termed historiographic metafiction, a postmodern genre which »both install[s] and then blur[s] the line between fiction and history« (Hutcheon, Linda. *A Poetics of Postmodernism: History, Theory, Fiction*. New York and London: Routledge, 1990 (1988), p. 113). Johnsson initially implements the line between fictional and factual narration by juxtaposing them (see above). But then, she continues by traversing this line through her discussion of the gendered restrictions of historiography within the parameter of the novel, hence suggesting »the continuing relevance of such an opposition, even if it be a problematic one« (ibid.).

Men om man undantager denna starka och allt uppoffrande kärlek, voro Leonora Kristinas mest framträdande egenskaper sådana som man eljest blott plägar finna hos män. Hon var stor och kraftig till sin kroppsbyggnad, – hennes anletsdrag påminde i hög grad om faderns, – hon ägde en mans mod, handlingskraft och rådsnarhet, och dock var hon trots alla dessa virila dygder först och sist *en sann kvinna*.[1411]

In this paragraph, Johnsson exhibits the same idea as Leopold Schefer (see Chapter 2.7.1.) of self-abandonment being a female trait, while also ascribing typically heroic and hence male attributes – such as courage and determination, and hence deeds in the historical sense – to this otherwise »sann kvinna«. Which of Leonora Kristina's remaining attributes make her a true woman, however, remains unsaid. The reader is thus left with no other choice but to compare Leonora Kristina to the other virile woman portrayed by Johnsson, i.e. the Queen of Sweden. She, too, is a hermaphrodite by virtue:

Det fanns intet kvinnligt i drottningens sätt eller uppträdande, men då hon tog av sig hatten och lät sitt långa, gula hår falla fritt ned efter ryggen och då hon leende slog upp sina stora, blå ögon, förstod Ulfeldt, att hon som kvinna lätt kunde erövra männen och få dem för sina fötter.[1412]

As illustrated in Joachim Grage's article 'Entblößungen: Das zweifelhafte Geschlecht Christinas von Schweden in der Biographik', the infamous Queen's sex had been under constant scrutiny since the moment of her birth.[1413] Most contemporary and subsequent accounts of Queen Christina demonstrate difficulties to reconcile her sex and her gender to a degree which prompted many writers of these texts to denude the Queen narratively in order to present their readership with eyewitness accounts to testify to the Queen's genital configuration. One significant aspect of contemporary portrayals of Queen Christina is that she herself had readily adopted the precariousness surrounding her sex and utilised it to her advantage. While some contemporary texts had thus demonised the Queen's ambiguous fame and portrayed her as a sort of monstrosity,[1414] Christina herself assumed the di-

---

[1411] Johnsson, Karin. *Kungligt blod*, p. 48. See also ibid., p. 52: »Hennes kraftiga kroppsbyggnad och starka fysik gjorde henne i synnerhet skickad att jaga til häst, och denna idrott blev snart hennes käraste förströelse, – det manliga i hennes karaktär och uppträdande kom här till sin fulla rätt«.

[1412] Ibid., p. 150.

[1413] Grage, Joachim. 'Entblößungen: Das zweifelhafte Geschlecht Christinas von Schweden in der Biographik'. In *Frauenbiographik: Lebensbeschreibungen und Porträts*, ed. Christian von Zimmermann. Tübingen: Narr, 2005 (Mannheimer Beiträge zur Sprach- und Literaturwissenschaft 63), pp. 35-59.

[1414] Ibid., p. 40f.

strust in her femininity in order to gain credibility as a regent. Since the Queen seemed hardly intent on correcting her unfeminine image, but would rather spur it through her own, albeit unfinished, autobiography, she soon gained fame as the 'Minerva of the North' – admittedly a female goddess, but one associated with the typically masculine attributes of wisdom and belligerence, as emphasised by Grage.[1415] Grage further contends that in her autobiography, *La Vie de la Reine Christine faite par Elle-même*, Christina stages herself in the tradition of an »imitatio Alexandri magni«,[1416] with regard to the Queen's mature and dignified behaviour in her earliest years[1417] and to the unusual circumstances surrounding her birth, i.e. the anecdote advertised by Christina herself that at the moment of her birth she was thought to be a boy.[1418]

Adopting this image co-created by Queen Christina herself, Johnsson's Korfitz acknowledges the Queen's masculinity to her full advantage: »Vad han först lade märke till var, att Kristina icke blott i klädsel och uppträdande verkade mera man än kvinna, – även hennes åskådnings- och tänkesätt voro en mans«.[1419] Since, however, Korfitz cannot overlook her greatest handicap, i.e. her biological womanhood, he initially attempts an address to Queen Kristina's father, assuming a self-evident omnipresence of the legendary Gustav II Adolf. To Korfitz's great surprise, however, Kristina does not yield to her father, the male authority addressed by Korfitz. Much unlike Leonora Christina, whose independent life story both in fiction and in history depended on the resignation of the men in her life (and who never learned *not* to define herself through her father), Queen Kristina is not responsive to Korfitz's patriarchal attempt to win her over for his own purposes:

1415 Ibid., p. 39.
1416 Ibid., p. 45 in reference to Hættner Aurelius, Eva. *Inför Lagen*, p. 168.
1417 The same applies to Johnsson's Leonora Kristina and – *ex negativo* – Korfitz. He is described as »begåvad«, »energisk« and »hänsynslös« (Johnsson, Karin. *Kungligt blod*, p. 22), and his impious behaviour upon meeting his prospective wife for the first time does not bode well. Little Leonora Kristina is a very serious child, marked by sorrow and losses while Korfitz struggles with an immature impulse to burst out laughing at the little girl's condign demeanour for much of their first encounter. Eventually, however, Korfitz's sense of ridicule yields to sublimation: »Med sänkt huvud lussnade Ulfeldt till denna rörande kärlekssaga, och det föreföll honom, som vore det icke gammalklokhet och brådmogenhet, som talade ur detta barns mun, utan en ren och vacker själ, som genomlidit sin första stora sorg, och som lovat sig själv att bli trogen sitt minne« (ibid., p. 23).
1418 Grage, Joachim. 'Entblößungen', p. 46.
1419 Johnsson, Karin. *Kungligt blod*, p. 151.

På ett högtravade sätt talade han om hennes avlidne fader, den store Gustaf Adolf, men hennes majestät avbröt honom helt kallt. – Han var en skicklig härförare, sade hon, men någon statsman eller erövrare var han icke...se på Alexander den store och Caesar! De voro både härförare och kloka statsmän... Nej, min fader var för stor fanatiker i sin religion och för småaktigt samvetsgrann.[1420]

Korfitz remains dumbfounded at the face of such blasphemy. Unable to attribute a mind of her own to this shrew, he ascribes Kristina's thoughts to her (of course male) protégés Salmasius and Bourdelot: »Ulfeldt häpnade över dessa ord från den store Gustaf Adolfs dotter, och han drog inom sig den slutsatsen, att detta var cynikern Salmasius' och den lika listige som fräcke Bourdelots verk«.[1421] Ironically, Korfitz is just as sly as Bourdelot, yet to no avail. Hence Kristina is forced to take action and initiate a bold alliance against Denmark (»Det blev slutligen drottningen, som hjälpte Ulfeldt att komma fram med sitt ärende«).[1422] In the course of the following conversation, Kristina manoeuvres Korfitz like a puppet by deploying a male course of action, i.e. candour and determination, while her exaggerated reference to the need of women for harmony and safety may well be disregarded as obvious sarcasm: »– Intresse för eder sak hava vi nog, och det fattas oss sannerligen icke heller lust att pröva ett nappatag med konung Fredrik, – men jag är ju blott en svag kvinna och älskar lugnet och freden... Och så ännu en viktig sak, som ej får glömmas, – ett krig kostar pengar«.[1423] Ultimately, Korfitz succumbs to Kristina, yet without seeing the desired result as he suddenly finds himself financing Kristina's war against Poland. Again, Korfitz deploys a chauvinist explanation[1424] in order to excuse his own failure. Ultimately, however, he is left to watch Kristina wage war while twirling his thumbs *i lugn och fred*.

If we were now to compare these two women – Queen Kristina and Leonora Kristina – the former's triumph over her father and Korfitz ought to be apparent by her freedom of both father and husband. Nevertheless, both women, albeit to differing degrees, had to adopt male attributes in order to gain historical importance of any kind. Despite its otherwise conventional format, *Kungligt blod* could

---

1420 Ibid.
1421 Ibid.
1422 Ibid.
1423 Ibid., p. 152.
1424 Ibid., p. 154: »Alla hans förnuftsskäl studsade obevekligt tillbaka mot en sant kvinnlig envishet, och när audiensen omsider var slut, måste Ulfeldt medgiva för sig själv, att den icke lett till det resultat, som hans önskan drömt. Emellertid var han ingalunda den man, som lät en tillfällig motgång nedslå hoppet, utan han beslöt att lugnt avvakta händelserna och se tiden an«.

thus be considered criticism of historiography, of the contemporary public's understanding of history and perhaps even of its own literary corpus, the Leonora Christina-literature. Johnsson goes through great trouble to assign her female characters their rightful place in her story by equipping them with masculine properties, a performative process that does not always manage to convince, for example when Johnsson ascribes hermaphroditic traits to Leonora Kristina, a process resulting in the creation of an indefinite, yet ideal sex.[1425] Nevertheless this declaration of the protagonist's commendable configuration appears to only justify her name on the book cover since her performance in the novel falls short of that of her temporary rival, Queen Kristina. Like in most of the examples predating the 1970's consulted in this study, Ulfeldt commands the plot. *Kungligt blod*, too, dedicates merely two chapters to Leonora Kristina. In spite of her masculine qualities, she remains »en sann kvinna« and must hence leave the stage to her masculine counterparts, her husband Korfitz and Queen Kristina. Due to the latter's portrayal as predominantly male, she receives a central spot in Johnsson's narrative. Kristina's deeds subdue Korfitz's trivial chatter, hence she earns her rightful place in Johnsson's *res gestae*, alongside other heroes of Scandinavian history. The more feminine and hence more passive Leonora Kristina, who had portrayed herself as equal to (most) men,[1426] but first and foremost as a loving mother and wife, has great trouble keeping up with this paradigm. Queen Kristina claims as many chapters of Johnsson's novel as its eponymous heroine and in these chapters the former successfully demands Korfitz's undivided attention. The answer to the implicit question posed by *Kungligt blod* regarding the requirements for a woman to get the attention of her husband, the public and of history is thus an outright criticism of itself and of its own paradigm. Johnsson's dependency on her literary predecessors (who until this point had been almost exclusively male) ultimately exposes the insufficiency of a literary and historical model that attempts to portray a woman's life story in a biographical pattern and in close interaction with her husband.

As the story proceeds, we observe the same pattern provided by Leonora Christina's French autobiography and by many Leonora Christina-novels. As Korfitz's body, mind and fate collapse, his better half Leonora Kristina compensates by de-

---

1425 Incidentally, Joachim Grage observes the same strategy in Queen Christina's autobiography (cf. Grage, Joachim. 'Entblößungen', p. 48).

1426 Cf. some of the statements contained in *Hæltinners Pryd* and *Jammers Minde*, e.g. Leonora Christina. *Hæltinners Pryd*, p. 21: »Mangen Quinde haffuer større styrcke end som mangen Mand« and *Jammers Minde*, p. 119: »ieg kand quæle den stærckeste Karl med miine bare hænder om ieg v-forwarendis fick fat paa ham«.

monstrating the strength he no longer possesses.[1427] She had shared her husband's fame and fortune, hence she would not shy away from sharing his demise.

While Johnsson exhibits trouble endorsing some of her heroine's morally questionable actions,[1428] her analysis of Leonora Kristina's marital situation at the beginning of the novel hits the mark. In order to share her husband's place in Nordic history, she is bound to share his fall from grace. The actual tragedy addressed by Johnsson is thus *not* Leonora Christina's self-abandonment in favour of her husband – as also indicated by Johnsson's inserted protest »om kärleken *kan* [my italics] bliva ovärdig« (see preamble discussed above) – but her complete submission to the laws of history. The story of Leonora Christina is bound to await the end of her husband's story, before it can commence. Despite having lent her name to several publications preceding that of Johnsson, Leonora Christina still had to wait her turn for her own place in history. *Herstory* replaces history in the penultimate chapter – the only chapter exclusively dealing with Leonora Christina's fate, predominantly through paraphrases and quotations of *Jammers Minde*. While Korfitz resigns in the fashion of a semi-legendary, semi-historical hero,[1429] fully in the style of traditional historiography (only to return and dominate the very last chapter, i.e. Johnsson's concluding analysis), Leonora Kristina is left to tell her own story.

1427 Cf. Johnsson, Karin. *Kungligt blod*, p. 227: »Leonora Kristina var själv själen och den drivande kraften i företaget – Ulfeldt och Peter Pflügge voro endast hennes hantlangare«.

1428 Ibid., p. 210: »Men huru stor hennes överlägsenhet än var, överträffades den likväl av hennes djärvhet. Hon ville till vad pris som helst redda sin make, och då hon ingen vart kunde komma på sanningens väg, tillgrep hon sådana medel som lögn och bedrägeri«.

1429 Ibid., p. 256: »Således vet ingen ännu den dag, som i dag är, var stoftet gömmes av den man, som en gång spelade en så framträdande roll i såväl Sveriges som Danmarks historia«.

3. Leonora Christina in Danish Historiography

3.1. Historiography on Leonora Christina in a Nutshell

> But in general there has been a reluctance to consider historical narratives as what they most manifestly are: verbal fictions, the contents of which are as much *invented* as *found* and the forms of which have more in common with their counterparts in literature than they have with those in the sciences.[1430]

As illustrated by the analyses provided in this study's second main chapter, but especially by the previous subchapter examining Karin Johnsson's semi-literary treatment of the Leonora Christina-subject matter, the evolution of Leonora Christina-literature is littered with questions of truth (often in the sense of historicity) and whatever was considered its opposite, as well as references to a steadily prevailing discourse regarding womanhood and – again – whatever was considered its opposite or counterpart. The combination of said pressing topics becomes, however, problematic whenever they seem to form an opposition, as exemplified by Johnsson's, as well as many other authors', obvious difficulties to produce an enthralling, yet factually obliged account of Leonora Christina's life without surrendering much of the stage-time to her historically (in a traditional sense) more significant husband Corfitz Ulfeldt.

Dwelling on the fact-fiction-dichotomy[1431] which had haunted nearly all aspects of Leonora Christina's life and afterlife, it is quickly revealed that all attempts to uncover the facts about this infamous Countess would sooner or later, implicitly or explicitly, revolve around questions of her gender, i.e. her social sex and its implications, as shall be demonstrated in the following chapters.

One need only take a superficial diachronic look at the past centuries' interest in Leonora Christina in order to understand that a demand for the factuality of her story and any historical, i.e. documental aspects associated with it has always been and remained very much topical. In the 17th century there had, of course, been the – not just royal, but public – demand for an elucidation of her exact involvement in

---

1430 White, Hayden. 'The Historical Text as Literary Artifact'. In White, Hayden. *Tropics of Discourse: Essays in Cultural Criticism*. Baltimore and London: Johns Hopkins University Press, 1978, p. 82.

1431 In this specific instance, I am referring to fiction as both fancy and literariness, since both of these synonyms have been central topics in the history of Leonora Christina-reception.

the Dina affair and Ulfeldt's alleged treason of 1663, especially in light of Leonora Christina's subsequent punishment. These incidents entailed public outcries within Denmark and even beyond its border. French writer Michel Rousseau de la Valette, for example, leveraged a widespread compassion for Leonora Christina by publishing *Le Comte d'Ulfeld, Grand Maistre de Danemarc* in 1678 – a written defence of Ulfeldt in the form of a biographical novel, which was subsequently adapted into English (1695) and German (1790). Even his coeval Samuel de Sorbière hazarded the consequences of publishing his travel account entitled *Relation d'un voyage en Angleterre* (first edition published in 1664),[1432] which condemns the English and their habits, including King Charles' shameless betrayal of his kinswoman, »une heroïne«.[1433] This account led to diplomatic tensions between France, England and Denmark, which were resolved at the expense of its author's freedom.[1434] Samuel de Sorbière – perhaps not quite unaffected by Leonora Christina's own words, which she subsequently adopted in her French autobiography – was also among the first to pronounce the idea of turning his interviewee's story into a novel: »Ce que je viens de vous raconteur, Monsieur, ne pourroit-il pas server, avec quelques episodes, de juste subject à un Roman, & ne respond-il pas exactement à la mine haute de ces deux personnes heroïques?«[1435] Thus, historical and literary reception of Leonora Christina's life story merge at this point already – at least in theory – i.e. *before* the period critical to literary scholars interested in Leonora Christina had even commenced.

This interest in the facts constituting the novel of Leonora Christina's life remained unabated throughout the centuries. When *Jammers Minde* was published in 1869, the debate regarding the trustworthiness of a traitor's loving wife was reopened (and will be discussed in more detail below). Even today, as the research, writing and reading community has virtually stopped caring whether or not Leonora Christina was telling the truth on any known occasion, writers of all kinds cannot forbear referring to *Jammers Minde* as the ultimate warrantor's testimony, since

---

1432 In the 17th century, these two accounts were rather successful in propagating empathy with Leonora Christina and her husband. In the ensuing century, though, scholars began to mistrust the accuracy and impartialty of said narratives (see below) and by the 20th century, Rousseau de la Valette and de Sorbière were hardly mentioned any more in historical studies. The historian Victor Lange, for example, refers to these two texts as former (!) sources of information on Corfitz Ulfeldt, yet »ikke for at anbefale dem, men for at advare mod dem« (Lange, Victor. *Corfitz Ulfeld*, p. 16).

1433 Sorbière, Samuel de. *Relation d'un voyage en Angleterre, Où sont touchées plusieurs choses, qui regardent l'estat des Sciences & de la Religion, & autres matieres curieuses.* Cologne: Pierre Michel, 1666, p. 145.

1434 Sarasohn, Lisa T. 'Who Was Then The Gentleman?: Samuel Sorbière, Thomas Hobbes, and the Royal Society', History of Science 42 (2004), pp. 211f.

1435 Sorbière, Samuel de. *Relation d'un voyage en Angleterre*, p. 153.

unconstrained fiction continues to be regarded as something to be avoided. There is ample proof of this unuttered notion, for example in the countless narratives including paraphrases of *Jammers Minde* and the French autobiography to varying degrees – such as Carsten Overskov's *Leonoras latter*, Inger Bentzon's *Frøken Leonora*, Herta J. Enevoldsen's *Leonora Christina i Blåtårn* and Karin Johnsson's *Kungligt blod*, all of which resorted to an unadulterated rendition of Leonora Christina's own life narratives. To paraphrase them, this was because the unprocessed story could not possibly be outvied. A similar view is verbalised by the Danish writer Suzanne Brøgger (*1944), who approached the topic of Leonora Christina's life in the Blue Tower in an essay collection titled *Den pebrede susen*:

> Det blå tårn oven på slottet, en bulden finger, et ømt punkt... I denne lille gevækst på magtens fundament er en sandhed blevet levet, som kom til at sprænge tremmerne og fylde langt mere, end hvad en enkelt menneske kan rumme. Vi har vist alle en underlig fornemmelse af, at der heri tårnet, dette blå mærke på den offentlige opinion, skete noget sandt.[1436]

Brøgger's (and her precursors') essential claim is that there is an intrinsic truth to be extracted from Leonora Christina's accounts, which has come to exceed categories of documented truth (i.e. facts) and verifiable lies – one recognized as the privilege of literature,[1437] which may be termed »societal reality«:[1438] »Tronen, magten og den almene consensus får sig et blåt øje i det tårn, hvor den subjektive, personlige sandhed voksede sig større end den objektive, historiske«.[1439] Notwithstanding the ever-changing definition of historical truth, the term itself has always been central to Leonora Christina-research. In its initial phase, however, the very same topic of truth in the sense of correct and verifiable documentation was an especially precarious issue, due to the shambolic manuscript dependencies following the collaboration between Leonora Christina and Otto Sperling the Younger.

1436 Brøgger, Suzanne. 'Og hun trevlede sine silkestrømper op'. In Brøgger, Suzanne. *Den pebrede susen: Flydende fragmenter og fixeringer*. Rhodos, 1988 (Rhodos Paperbacks), p. 111.

1437 This might be a critical reason why the literary discourse concerning Leonora Christina has become more prolific with every newly discovered proof of her creative abilities, while – as will be demonstrated below – historical discourses have tended to extract her from her husband's account and deport her to the realm of literature.

1438 This is a term used by German cultural historian Susanne Hauser in order to refer to the merits of literary discourse (see Hauser, Susanne. *Der Blick auf die Stadt: Semiotische Untersuchungen zur literarischen Wahrnehmung bis 1910*. Berlin: Dietrich Reimer, 1990 (Reihe Historische Anthropologie 12), p. 62).

1439 Brøgger, Suzanne. 'Og hun trevlede sine silkestrømper op', p. 112.

The initial phase of historical and literary reception of Leonora Christina basically coincides with the history of the gynæceum in Denmark.[1440] This antique genre gained popularity among Danish scholars in the 17th and 18th century[1441] and as presented in Chapter 1.1.3., Leonora Christina herself was both producer and topic of the gynæceum. As is known, *Hæltinners Pryd* is an unfinished gynæceum while the content of the French autobiography is part of another one, i.e. Otto Sperling the Younger's unpublished *De fœminis omni ævi doctis*. The disappearance of the French autobiography from the Royal Library in Copenhagen sometime in the 18th century left all scholars interested in Corfitz Ulfeldt or Leonora Christina no choice but to work with either copies from a French or a Latin adaptation of the French autobiography (all of unknown origin), or with an excerpt from Sperling's *De fœminis omni ævi doctis*, possibly (!) written by Sperling himself. Other authors used the transcripts of the Latin or French adaptation of the French autobiography, an adaptation of the excerpt mentioned above, and sometimes even in combination with the forged autobiography published by Oluf Bang (see Chapter 1.2.1.).[1442] This means essentially that until 1958, when the original French autobiography was published after being found again in 1952 in the school library of the Gymnasium Christianeum in Hamburg-Altona, all reproductions of Leonora Christina's life[1443]

1440 And since the task of the gynæceum was to present historical, i.e. documented examples of what was considered female virtuousness, the discourses of factuality and of womanhood merge at the very emergence of Leonora Christina-narratives.

1441 In this context, I should like to emphasise that the gynæceum, with its moralistic-didactic objective, is a typically early modern genre. Equivalent 20th and 21st-century productions do not demonstrate such an aim, as their depicted heroines are remarkable, yet not ideal. Palle Lauring, for example, portrays Ellen Marsvin, Kirsten Munk, Sophie Amalie and Leonora Christina, and sooner or later he calls each one of them primitive (see Lauring, Palle. *Dronninger og andre kvinder i Danmarkshistorien*, pp. 53-76). And in Grethe Jensen's *Kvinder i Danmarkshistorien*, Leonora Christina, whose story we find in between that of Sophie Amalie and that of »Danmarks mest berømte heks« is characterised as »hoffærdige kongedatter« and »selvretfærdige diva« (see Jensen, Grethe. *Kvinder i Danmarkshistorien*. Copenhagen: Politiken, 2004 (Politikens håndbøger), respectively pp. 65, 71 and 78).

1442 For a detailed history of early reproductions of Leonora Christina's French autobiography, see Brøndum-Nielsen, Johs. and C.O. Bøggild-Andersen. 'Historiske Oplysninger', pp. 297-305. A compact and slightly extended visualisation of this history – including works mentioned by Brøndum-Nielsen/Bøggild-Andersen and below – is provided in Fig. 3.

1443 This includes notable translations of Leonora Christina's life narratives, such as Johannes Ziegler's *Denkwürdigkeiten der Gräfin zu Schleswig-Holstein Leonora Christina vermählten Gräfin Ulfeldt aus ihrer Gefangenschaft im blauen Thurm des Königschlosses zu Copenhagen 1663-1685*, published in 1871, and the *Memoirs of Leonora Christina*, published in 1872 by F. E. Bunnètt.

were based on adaptations, copies and a forgery.[1444] This in turn resulted in countless corrective remarks and endless speculations regarding correct dating (e.g., regarding Leonora Christina's birthday) in the diverse reproductions, since the respective authors of these reproductions had all used different sources supposedly written by Leonora Christina and Otto Sperling the Younger. Despite the obviously flawed and fragmentary information contained in these early historical works, though, they all claim epistemological value.

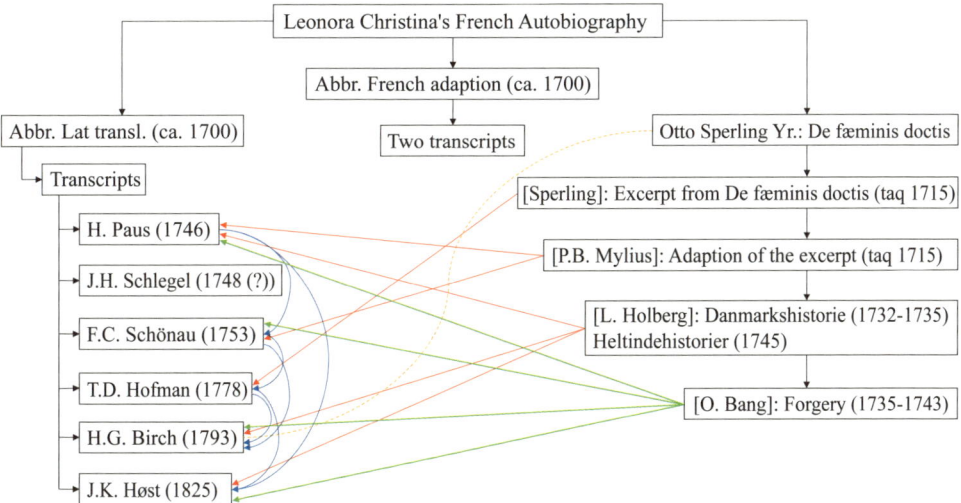

Fig. 3: Birch is not mentioned in the history of the manuscript summarised by Brøndum-Nielsen and Bøggild-Andersen. Which of the preserved versions of *De fæminis doctis* Birch is referring to, is unclear, hence the dashed line. The acronym *taq* indicates the *terminus ante quem*, i.e. the latest time at which the respective texts assumably have been written. The strand on the left-hand side contains only the authors' names due to space constraints, and because the strand on the right-hand side contains the more influential works presented in this stemma, whose authors furthermore are often merely the alleged creators of these texts.

1444 Almost all accounts predating the 19th century also refer to Rousseau de la Valette's *Le Comte d'Ulfeld* as one of their source texts – albeit not always uncritically – which only adds to the problem insofar as it is essentially a romance purporting to be historiography. The author refers to eyewitnesses of Ulfeldt's life (cf. Rousseau de la Valette, Michel. *Le Comte d'Ulfeld, Grand Maistre de Dannemarc. Nouvelle Historique*. Paris: Claude Barbin, 1678, unpaginated preamble), which caused some of his successors to treat his narrative almost as a first-hand-account (see, e.g., Mursinna, Friedrich Samuel. 'Vorerinnerung'. In Rousseau de la Valette, Michel. *Leben des Grafen Corfix Ulfeld, vormaligen Reichshofraths in Dänemark. Ein Pendant zum Leben des Staatsministers Grafen von Struensee*, transl. Friedrich Samuel Mursinna. Breslau and Leipzig: Ernst Gottlieb Meyer, 1790, p. 5).

Among the first writers to adopt Leonora Christina's story in his own writings was Ludvig Holberg, author of *Dannemarks Riges Historie* (1732-1735; see Chapter 3.2.1.) and of the gynæceum *Adskillige Heltinders og navnkundige Damers sammenlignede Historier efter Plutarchi Maade* (1745).[1445] The latter is perhaps Denmark's most influential gynæceum and it certainly takes up a central position in this specific context, as Holberg had gained the fame of an authority – especially in terms of historical research on Leonora Christina – through the publication of his monumental *Dannemarks Riges Historie*, »Denmark's first comprehensive popular history«.[1446]

According to Holberg's 'Fortale til Læseren', the success of the initial volumes of his ethical-historical work *Adskillige store Helte og berømmelige Mænds sammenlignede Historier* (1739-1753) had induced him to compose an equivalent creation about women, i.e. his *Heltindehistorier*. He further clarifies his authorial intent by repudiating the notion of any sex's superiority over the other. Hence, Holberg continues, it would seem only sound that after dedicating a multi-volume book to history's great men, he would complete what he had started by complementing the *Heltehistorier* with *Heltindehistorier*:

> Man seer heraf, at de Domme bestyrkes, som jeg een og anden gang haver fældet over begge Kiøn, nemlig at der findes onde og gode, kloge og daarlige saavel Mænd som Qvinder i Verden, og at jeg smigrer ikke meere for det eene Kiøn end for det andet, men at jeg anfører saavel Qvinders som Mænds Historier og Bedrifter med oprigtig Upartiskhed.[1447]

Holberg explains further that the selection process for his latest project had not given him any trouble at all, since the stories of all women presented in his *Heltindehistorier* »ere alle bekiendte, saa at det haver ikke kostet mig anden Umage end

---

1445 For the sake of efficiency, the latter will henceforth be referred to as *Heltindehistorier*.
1446 Westergaard, Waldemar. 'Danish History and Danish Historians', The Journal of Modern History 24/2 (June 1952), p. 169.
1447 Holberg, Ludvig. *Adskillige Heltinders og navnkundige Damers sammenlignede Historier efter Plutarchi Maade ved L. Holberg I*. Copenhagen, 1745, unpaginated preamble. Holberg's remark is part of a philosophy the author adopted in his young days, when his propagation of highly misogynist ideas backfired and unleashed the anger of many men and women upon the young Holberg: »Da det gik op for mig, at jeg kom i Vanry for den Sags Skyld og blev Gjenstand for Stiklerier, saa at endog en Pige, der gik forb mig, pegede Fingre ad mig og sagde; ‚Der gaar han, som vil lukke Portene til Paradis for os', opgav jeg ikke blot at udbrede dette Kætteri videre, men for des bedre at vise, hvor meget jeg fortrød min tidligere Vildfarelse, holdt jeg siden bestandig Lovtaler over det andet Kjøn« (Holberg, Ludvig. *Holbergs Levned fortalt af ham selv i tre latinske Breve til en fornem Herre*, transl. Fr. Winkel Horn. Copenhagen: A. Christiansen 1897, p. 28).

at giøre Udtog af de mest tilforladelige Skribentere«.[1448] In combination with this not so insignificant statement declaring all of the following narratives part of public, accepted and hence universal knowledge, the ensuing lengthy affirmation that the present book's purpose was not to moralise, but simply to present historical facts, Holberg's mimetic and epistemological claim to truth[1449] is followed by an introduction of the first pair of ladies, of whom the reader may or may not learn exemplary behaviour: Lady Jane Grey (1536/1537-1554), also known as England's Nine-Day Queen, and Leonora Christina.[1450]

In an effort to dissociate his own work from previous, merely moralising ones, and in order to account for these two women's – both perfect examples of virtue and talent – tragic fate, Holberg first establishes several factors that either make or break one's fortune, i.e. parentage, fatherland, education and upbringing, historical environment, and the spouse. He then proceeds to invoke putative laws – often introduced with the words »saa at man kand sige, at« or »man seer saaledes, at« – through these factors,[1451] which ultimately serve to prove the overarching philosophy that fortune is a fickle mistress.[1452] Holberg's Mechanistic[1453] approach leads to the inevitable conclusion that an unlucky combination of historical environment and spousal relations had spelled Leonora Christina's (and Jane Gray's) doom. The former, »Tidernes Leylighed og Conjuncturer«,[1454] follows the major premise that »mangen lider og styrtes udi Uheld ikke fordi en Gierning skeer, men efterdi den skeer paa en Tiid, naar Verden er ikke udi god Humeur«. In combination with the minor premise that Leonora Christina lived at a time when the world was especially moody, Holberg concludes that Leonora Christina – together with the second determining factor, her husband – was bound to get underfoot in the transitional period

---

1448 Holberg, Ludvig. *Heltindehistorier 1*, unpaginated preamble.

1449 »Den [Holberg's configuration, following Plutarch's comparative mode] er meest opbyggelig, eftersom den grunder sig paa Historier, som ere Dyders og Lasters ubedragelige Speyl« (ibid.).

1450 In this comparison, Leonora Christina is once again (cf. Chapter 2.6.1. on Sven Holm's drama *Leonora Christina*) coequal to one of the many victims of Queen Mary I, who is again equated with Sophie Amalie.

1451 In order to exemplify these laws and factors, Holberg uses metaphors, and especially similes; for example when he explains how the factor of education can either perfect or spoil even the most virtuous and ingenious creature: »Thi ligesom et sundt Barn kand forderves ved en usund ammes Melk, saa kand ogsaa et ungt Menneske, som Naturen haver begavet med de herligste Qvaliteter, fordærves, hvis det haver den Uheld at falde udi en ond Informators eller Tugtemesters Hænder« (ibid., p. 11).

1452 Cf. ibid., p. 3: »Verden regieres af sig selv, ja man kand sige, at de fleeste Lykker og Uheld komme af Hendelser, Leyligheder og Conjuncturer, som ikke ere udi et Menneskes Disposition [...]«.

1453 Cf. White, Hayden. *Metahistory: The Historical Imagination in Nineteenth-Century Europe*. Baltimore and London: Johns Hopkins University Press, 1973, p. 17: »The Mechanistic theory of explanation turns upon the search for the causal laws that determine the outcomes of processes discovered in the historical field«. A common tool for employing such causal laws are syllogisms (ibid., p. 11).

1454 Holberg, Ludvig. *Heltindehistorier 1*, p. 13.

between *adelsvælde* and *enevælde*. The latter, however, is presented as the most determinative, albeit fickle factor, as it subjected the two women presented by Holberg to the law that marriage increases every human's risk of becoming collateral damage:

> Endelig grunder Menneskets Skiebne sig meget paa Ægteskab, hvilket er som er [sic!] Lykke-potte: thi den, der tænker at giøre det beste Vall, styrtes ofte i yderste Ulykke. Manden maa følge Qvindens og Qvinden Mandens Skiebne, og de Piile, som treffe een af dem, saare dem begge, saa at man kand sige, at visse Mennesker styrtes i Uheld ikke saa meget ved egen Forseelse som ved Kraft af Sympathie.[1455]

This major premise in combination with the minor premise that at the beginning of their marriage Corfitz Ulfeldt had indeed seemed like the most promising choice at hand and that their »Sympathie« was especially strong, leads to the conclusion already known to readers of Holberg's *Heltindehistorier*: that Leonora Christina had suffered for her husband's sake. Despite Holberg's evident objective to praise Leonora Christina, though, it is by no means his intention to negate any of her original sins.[1456] Accordingly, when it is time for Holberg to pick a winner in this match of heroines, he must admit that Jane Grey was more impeccable. But Leonora Christina triumphs anyway, owing to the principle that imperfection is beautiful:

> Jeg ligner den eene med et skiønt Ansigt uden Lyde, den anden med et langt skiønnere, hvorpaa dog findes nogle Pletter: thi, naar man betragter den sidstes Capacitet, Færdighed, Skarpsindighed og Lærdom, saa kand man regne hende blant de store Heltinder, som Naturen haver produceret.[1457]

Holberg's portrayal of Leonora Christina in *Dannemarks Riges Historie* and in the subsequent *Heltindehistorier* influenced most of the successive bodies of history. It substantially informed Friderich Christian Schönau's *Samling af Danske Lærde Fruentimer* (1753) both in content and in scope, as both authors stress the erudition of Leonora Christina and her equals. Schönau, however, excelled his source in terms of depicting exemplary scholarship through an extensive appropriation of references

---

1455 Ibid., p. 16.
1456 Ibid., p. 54: »Ja man kand sige, at dette Fængsel var for hende Skiærsild, saa at, hvis hun havde Feyl, da hun gik ind, saa kunde man fast ansee hende som en Helgen, da hun gik ud; thi man merkede fra den Tiid, hun kom paa fri Fod, til hendes Dødsdag, intet, uden det som var helligt og opbyggeligt«.
1457 Ibid., p. 55.

and quotations,[1458] all in service of »den Historiske Sandhed og Troværdighed«.[1459] Schönau's explicit intention is to pay tribute to Denmark's educated women, and especially to the writers among them, as the first volume of his *Samling* is dedicated to them. Even though at that time Leonora Christina's French autobiography was missing and *Jammers Minde* was unheard of, she had made it to this exclusive first volume of Schönau's *Samling*, mostly thanks to *Hæltinners Pryd*.

In conformity with his subject matter, Schönau's expressed authorial intention is to advance knowledge in terms of historical truth.[1460] In order to achieve that, he repeatedly addresses »alle Elskere af Fædernelandets Historie«[1461] while opposing his own »jævn og simpel Historisk Stiil«[1462] to the dissimulation of poets:[1463] »Men

---

1458 The interested reader may thus consult Schönau's *Samling*, especially the 'Fortale' and pp. 421-437, for detailed information about any written reference in either historiography or literary history (predating 1753, of course) to Leonora Christina's accomplishments as a writer and about the history of the Danish gynæceum.

1459 Schönau, Friderich Christian. *Samling af Danske Lærde Fruentimer, Som ved deres Lærdom, og Udgivne eller efterladte Skrifter have giort deres Navne i den lærde Verden bekiendte, med adskillige mest Historiske Anmerkninger forøget, og udgivet ved Friderich Christian Schönau 1.* Copenhagen, 1753, unpaginated preamble.

1460 Despite Schönau's honest attempt, however, his text constitutes no reliable historical source. For example, in his *Samling*, Leonora's impressive group of, allegedly, fifteen children (some of whom did not survive their first year), is downsized to six, and most of their births are misdated (or, in the case of Anna Catharina, not mentioned at all).

1461 Schönau, Friderich Christian. *Samling 1*, unpaginated preamble.

1462 Ibid.

1463 Among those poets, Schönau reckons another often-quoted albeit unreliable Leonora Christina-historiographer, i.e. Michel Rousseau de la Valette. With reference to a previous, devastating criticism of some of Rousseau de la Valette's statements by Hans Paus, Schönau, too, deems one of the anecdotes recounted by Rousseau de la Valette a mere »Fabel« (ibid., footnote p. 327) and the author himself a novelist (ibid., footnote p. 331 and Paus, Hans. *Forsøg til navnkundige danske Mænds Livs og Levnets Beskrivelser 2: Indeholdende Anledning til den fra Dannemarks Riges Hofmester og det Romerske Riges Grœve, forvandlede til Dannemarks Riges Forrœder Corfitz Uhlefeld, hans Livs og Levnets Historie.* Copenhagen: Joh. Christ. Groth, 1746-1747, p. 31), a dilettante and, basically, a fraud (ibid., in both sources). Schönau continues to recount Rousseau de la Valette's narrative – i.e. the love story unfolding between Leonora Christina and Corfitz and Hannibal Sehested's jealousy – only for his many female readers (Schönau, Friderich Christian. *Samling 1*, footnote p. 328), while Paus continues with references to the more reliable historian Ludvig Holberg. As unpopular as Rousseau de la Valette's »Romansk« (ibid.) take on history may thus have been in Denmark, it did reverberate beyond its borders. Whether by coincidence or not, German writer Margarete Boie (1880-1946) adopted the same idea as Rousseau de la Valette more than 250 years later in her novel *Eleonora Christine und Corfitz Ulfeldt*. In both accounts, Hannibal Sehested and Corfitz Ulfeldt rival one another for prestigious offices and for Leonora Christina's heart. Boie, however, takes the idea of romantic covetousness as the underlying impetus for parts of the historical plot one step further. She even implies infatuation with Corfitz Ulfeldt as the reason for Sophie Amalie's hatred for Leonora Christina (see Boie, Margarete. *Eleonora Christine und Corfitz Ulfeldt*, pp. 93-101).

Poeter er en slags Frihed frem for andre tilladt nemlig at hykle«.[1464] His quotation style, which could rival that of any 21st-century publication, reflects this intention. Page after page is filled with more footnotes and quotations than actual text.[1465] But even though this tendency of his impedes any reading of Schönau's text, his aim remains clear. Accounts of Leonora Christina's eruditeness[1466] – with Ulfeldt and Sperling figuring as her instructors – as well as episodes that should be of interest to any history aficionado remain in the core text, while anecdotes, bibliographical references and Schönau's own considerations regarding correct dating and the like are dispelled to the – as a result of this separation – often larger footnotes. Schönau managed thusly to resolve »the biographer's dilemma«,[1467] i.e. the balancing act of conveying a sense of complete informedness while not boring the reader too much. However, as a consequence, episodes of no historical consequence (but rather popular with writers of Leonora Christina-novels), such as little Leonora Christina's flirt with Maurits, remain a mere footnote, whereas the Dina affair – something that did not primarily affect Leonora Christina, that she considered to be well known and thus omitted in her own writings[1468] – is narrated in great detail.[1469] Schönau's source material for this particular incident was, however, the fake autobiography published by Oluf Bang, amongst others. The narrator in this account acts as an eyewitness *and* historiographer in this episode, which concerned the King of Denmark and is consequently to be considered an occurrence of historical proportions. Being

---

1464 Schönau, Friderich Christian. *Samling 1*, unpaginated preamble. Through his extensive use of quotations and references as well as through his outspoken attempt to distinguish his own account from that of poets or, alternatively, »galant historie« (cf. Bull, Francis. *Ludvig Holberg som historiker*. Oslo: Aschehoug & Co, 1913, p. 2), Schönau hints at a classification of his Samling as »lærd historisk forskning« (cf. Schönau, Friderich Christian. *Samling 1*, unpaginated preamble), a branch of historiography that emerged in the 17th century, together with its *galant* counterpart.

1465 Schönau himself was well aware of this circumstance, but he insists that they all serve a higher purpose: »Hvad de Historiske Anmerkninger angaaer, da tilstaaer jeg, at de imod min Tanke ere blevne temmelig vidtløftige, dog [...] de fleste af disse Anmerkninger angaae vort eget Fædernelands lærde Historie, have haft Indflydelse deri, og givet Oplysning i adskilligt, og kand følgelig efter mine Tanker ikke være Fædernelandets-Histories Elskere ubehagelige at læse [...]« (Schönau, Friderich Christian. *Samling 1*, unpaginated preamble).

1466 To this end, Schönau simply had to adopt Leonora Christina's French autobiography (which was only known to him through copies and translations), since the narrative of a naturally sophisticated woman attracting the envy of her environment favoured by Schönau was readily available. Schönau also included many of the hymns written by Leonora Christina in his work, as well as other evidence of her intellect (cf. ibid., p. 392-405).

1467 Cf. Zimmermann, Christian von. 'Exemplarische Lebensläufe: Zu den Grundlagen der Biographik'. In *Frauenbiographik: Lebensbeschreibungen und Porträts*, ed. Christian von Zimmermann. Tübingen: Narr, 2005 (Mannheimer Beiträge zur Sprach- und Literaturwissenschaft 63), p. 3.

1468 Cf. *Leonora Christina Grevinde Ulfeldts Franske Levnedsskildring*, p. 5c: »[...] dont je ne ferray point le recit puis que ce passage vous est assez coynnu« (Translation p. 22: »hvorom jeg ikke her vil berette, da alt, hvad der passerede, er eder nok som vitterligt«).

1469 Schönau, Friderich Christian. *Samling 1*, pp. 341-355.

a rather finical researcher, Schönau always makes sure to amply present, compare and scrutinise all of his sources. He did, however, not apply his usual careful enquiry regarding the sources carrying Leonora Christina's name. Schönau refers to his heroine's words as the ultimate guarantee of epistemological value as much as possible. Yet unfortunately, the fabrications and semi-novels circulating in the 17th and 18th century frustrated his otherwise laudable plan to deliver the first comprehensive, critical and hence correct biography of Leonora Christina,[1470] a woman he considered to be a shining example of the intellectual accomplishments of Danish women.

To this effect, though, Schönau's text is a mere exception. Most historians would rather focus on the extraordinariness of Leonora Christina's life, i.e. her novelesque adventures and her fall from Denmark's top position to its very bottom. One particular case in point is Hans Jørgen Birch's *Billedgallerie for Fruentimmer, indeholdende Levnetsbeskrivelser over berømte og lærde, norske og udenlandske Fruentimmere* (1793-1795). This gynæceum contains three main chapters: 1) Om Fruentimmerets Bestemmelse, Opdragelse og Pligter; 2) Mærkværdige og berømte danske og norske Fruentimmere; 3) Særdeles oplyste og lærde danske og norske Fruentimmere og Skribentinder. Judging from Birch's scope and the general outlook of the genre, one would expect to find even just a moderately prolific writer and artist such as Leonora Christina portrayed in the third chapter. She was, however, assigned to the second category – »de for deres Levnet og Handlinger mærkværdige og berømte Fruentimmer«[1471] – which she shares with her nemesis

---

[1470] See for example, Schönau's reference to Ulfeldt's acquittal at the end of the Malmö trial and how this information was deliberately withheld in order to provoke the couple's escape from Sweden: »[…] og at slig en falsk Beretning er blevet dem berettet, bevidner Madame Ulfeld *selv* i sit Liv og Levnet, som hun *med egen Haand* [both my italics] haver skrevet i disse Ord: […]« (ibid., p. 367). I would like to draw the reader's attention to how much Schönau seeks to clarify how his source could not have been any more reliable, for he does not question Leonora Christina's 'own words' even once (I use quotation marks since the subsequent passage quoted by Schönau is actually taken from the fake autobiography published by Bang).

[1471] Birch, Hans Jørgen. *Billedgallerie for Fruentimmer, indeholdende Levnetsbeskrivelser over berømte og lærde danske, norske og udenlandske Fruentimmere I*. Copenhagen: Poulsen, 1793, unpaginated preamble.

Queen Sophie Amalie and her mother Kirsten Munk.[1472] Birch bases his portrayal of »[d]enne af sine ypperlige Egenskaber og haarde Skiebne bekiendte Dame«,[1473] i.e. Leonora Christina, on a transcript of a French adaptation of the French autobiography, Sperling's material,[1474] Rousseau de la Valette's Ulfeldt-biography, as well as the accounts written by the literary historian Albert Thura,[1475] by Holberg, Bang, Schönau and Tycho de Hofman.[1476] Yet, despite this favourable state of source material, Birch's account is rather erratic and at times even inconsistent, which might be the result of Birch's clashing intentions to portray a »viis og kiærlig Moder, en god Huusmoder og en Prydelse for sit Kiøn«[1477] with the many accounts of Leonora Christina's involvement in disputable adventures and evasion.

The crux of the matter is that despite these authors' efforts to advance their audience's knowledge about Danish history and Leonora Christina in particular, one cannot forbear to lament that only faulty and fragmentary information trickled

---

1472 Mostly, but not only due to Birch's introductory statement that a woman's purpose in life was »at være Mændenes Medhielp, at blive Mødre og Opdragersker for dydige og lykkelige Mennesker« (ibid., p. I), his motives for including Kirsten Munk in this book seem cryptic, at best. His intention may, however, have been to simply grant delayed gratification to Leonora Christina's ill-famed mother. One clue is Birch's effort to portray Kirsten Munk as a philanthropist, a patron of hospitals, churches and schools (cf. ibid., p. 65) – a depiction overthrown by most contemporary documents and historical studies (cf. Fussing, Hans H. 'Kirsten Munk som frue paa Boller', pp. 15-60). Another, quite telling indication is Birch's seemingly impartial account of the King's distrust and subsequent renunciation of his formerly beloved wife in 1632, which is followed by an account of Christian IV's relationship with Vibeke Kruse, which bore the first fruit – Ulrik Christian Gyldenløve – in 1630. This annalistic presentation of events would tempt most readers to conclude that this entire affair had been an attack carried out by Christian IV and his mistress, rather than any wrongdoing on the disowned wife's part.

1473 Birch, Hans Jørgen. *Billedgallerie*, p. 66.

1474 Which of the preserved versions of *De fœminis doctis* Birch is referring to, is unclear.

1475 Albert Thura's (1700-1740) writings – *Idea historiæ litterariæ Danorum* (1723) and the *Gynæceum Daniæ litteratum* (1732) – contain not so much accounts of Leonora Christina's life as acknowledgements of her literary activities.

1476 The Danish genealogist Tycho de Hofman's (1714-1754) *Portraits historiques des hommes illustres de Dannemark* (1746) was such a success abroad that an expanded translation into Danish was published in the years 1777-1779 by Christian Liunge and Bertel Christian Sandvig: *Historiske Efterretninger om velfortiente Danske Adelsmænd*. Despite the work's focus on Corfitz Ulfeldt and his lineage, which disposed the author to mention Leonora Christina only occasionally, Ulfeldt's chapter ends with a short recapitulation of his wife's life, as »Leonore Christine er saa berømt ved sin Forstand, forunderlige Hendelser og store Hengivenhed til sin Mand, at jeg med Billighed bør indføre hendes Historie efter Ulfelds« (Hofman, Tycho de. *Historiske Efterretninger*, p. 316). Hofman's account is in many ways a censored version of the Ulfeldts' story, as his work was dedicated to Queen Dowager Juliane Marie, who had ruled Denmark with an iron fist since the execution of Johann Friedrich Struensee and the inofficial removal of King Christian VII in 1772. Accordingly, Sophie Amalie's death is mentioned nowhere near Leonora Christina's release from prison. Instead, her disimprisonment occurs after the solicitation of Ulrik Christian Gyldenløve (ibid., p. 333). This is a classic case of what according to Hayden White may be termed »negative distortion of the factual field« (White, Hayden. 'Historicism, History and the Figurative Imagination', p. 111), since the Queen's death, which in the factual field coincided – if nothing else, temporally – with Leonora Christina's release, was not rearranged but entirely omitted.

1477 Birch, Hans Jørgen. *Billedgallerie*, p. 80.

through to 18th-century historians. However, it is important to note that in these few examples of Danish gynæcea, Leonora Christina took centre stage.[1478] This is not so much the case with the early regular historiography on Leonora Christina, which – much like the early Leonora Christina-literature – uses Leonora Christina as a pretence for an account of her husband's life. This applies, for example, to a German translation of Schönau's chapter on Leonora Christina, published in 1757 by Christian Gottlob Mengel. It seems that Mengel had not taken as much of an interest in Leonora Christina herself, as he had in her husband. Two years earlier, Mengel – using the pen name Philander v. der Weistritz – had published a translation of the Norwegian historian and jurist Hans Paus' *Corfitz Uhlefeld, Hans Livs og Levnets Historie* (1746-1747), i.e. *Merkwürdiges Leben und trauriger Fall des vormaligen weitberühmten dänischen und Reichsgrafens Corfitz von Ulfelds ehemaligen Reichshofmeisters des Reiches Dännemark*. When Mengel subsequently published *Merkwürdige Lebensbeschreibung Eleonoræ Christinæ Gräfinn von Ulfeld einer Tochter Christian des Vierten, Königs in Dännemark und Norwegen hochlöblichen Gedächtnisses*, he stated explicitly that this work was to be considered a sort of sequel or even annex to the Ulfeldt-biography published in 1755.[1479] Accordingly, Mengel's text, which in all other respects is quite true to the Danish original, contains a very lengthy annex consisting of further material on Corfitz Ulfeldt's life, which the author had come across *after* publishing his Ulfeldt-biography.

Another particularly interesting case in point is the text *Eleonore Gräfin von Ulefeld* (1787), which carries the emphatic subtitle *nicht Roman sondern wirkliche Geschichte* ('Not a Novel but a Real Story'). A remark on the book's front page[1480] places its content in the context of Friedrich Freiherr von der Trenck's (1726-1794) multi-volume autobiography *Des Fridrich Freyherrn von der Trenck, merkwürdige Lebensgeschichte* ('The Peculiar Life Story of Fridrich Freyherr von der Trenck'), published in 1786 (1787 in Berlin and Leipzig). This Prussian adventurer could indeed be considered a German counterpart to the Ulfeldt couple, but especially

---

1478 For example in Holberg's *Heltindehistorier*, when Ulfeldt is sent on a diplomatic journey to the Netherlands in 1649. Even though Leonora Christina accompanied her husband on this voyage, Holberg skips this year with the following explanation: »Derom vil jeg intet tale, saasom intet derved forefaldt, som henhører til Eleonoræ Historie« (Holberg, Ludvig. *Heltindehistorier 1*, p. 39).

1479 Mengel, Christian Gottlob. 'Vorrede'. In Schönau, Friderich Christian. *Merkwürdige Lebensbeschreibung Eleonoræ Christinæ Gräfinn von Ulfeld einer Tochter Christian des Vierten, Königs in Dännemark und Norwegen hochlöblichen Gedächtnisses. Aus dem Dänischen übersetzt von Christian Gottlob Mengel*. Copenhagen and Leibzig: Friedrich Christian Pelt, 1757, unpaginated preamble.

1480 G. v. R. *Eleonore Gräfin von Ulefeld: nicht Roman sondern wirkliche Geschichte. Ein würdiger Beitrag zu der merkwürdigen Lebensgeschichte des Freiherrn v. d. Trenck*. Strasburg, 1787. The author of the account is unknown. Due to a handwritten note on one original copy, the Viennese printer Johann Martin Weymar (alternatively spelled Weimar) is sometimes named as potential author of the book, but the preamble is simply signed with the initials »G. v. R.«.

to Leonora Christina. Friedrich von der Trenck was a young nobleman, whose promising career in the Prussian military ended abruptly when he received preferential treatment by his cousin Baron Franz von der Trenck, who fought on the Austrian side. Due to this unfortunate kinship,[1481] King Friedrich II suspected von der Trenck to be an Austrian spy and had him imprisoned in the Polish Kłodzko Fortress, from whence he escaped after one year. After years of wandering he returned to Prussia to attend his mother's funeral, only to be recaptured, reimprisoned in Magdeburg and released after ten years at the request of Empress Maria Theresia of Austria. The following years, he led a quiet, reclusive life, during which he wrote his autobiography, which he dedicated to the spirit of the late Friedrich II. His life ended in France, where he was beheaded in 1794, due to accusations of espionage.

Due to this context – a story deserving of a novel but nevertheless factual – the author's positivist claim to truth pervades the account, but at the same time it is an examination of the reliability of historical narratives. Leonora Christina was chosen as a subject matter for this parallel text not only because of her equally adventurous life, but also because she, too, had documented her life in all of its improbability. The subtitle of von der Trenck's *Merkwürdige Lebensgeschichte – Von ihm selbst als ein Lehrbuch* [!] *für Menschen geschrieben, die wirklich unglücklich sind, oder noch gute Vorbilder für alle Fälle, zur Nachfolge bedürfen*[1482] – correlates thus to the first lines of *Eleonore Gräfin von Ulefeld*, which – in a fashion resembling that of the heroic epic and the gynæceum – present Leonora Christina as the protagonist in a didactic play:

> Ein Weib will ich beschreiben; das beinahe seltenste, größte unter allen den Weibern, die sich bisher auf der Schaubühne der Welt ausgezeichnet, durch Geistesstärke, Heldenmuth und ähnliche Eigenschaften, sich über die Gränzen geschwungen haben, die durch Vorurtheile, Irrthümer und andre Dinge dem weiblichen Geschlechte geszet worden sind.[1483]

1481 Another reason for this punishment may have been von der Trenck's alleged affair with the King's sister.

1482 'Peculiar Life Story – Written by Himself as an Educational Book [!] for People, Who are Indeed Unhappy, or Still in Need of Good Role Models for All Situations, to Imitate'.

1483 G. v. R. *Eleonore Gräfin von Ulefeld*, unpaginated preamble ('A woman I want to describe; the almost rarest, grandest among women, that have distinguished themselves on the world stage, through fortitude of mind, heroic courage and similar characteristics, that have crossed the boundaries set up to women by prejudice, fallacy and other things').

The narrative's poetic and rhetorically suggestive preamble[1484] ends with the assurance of the correspondent that despite all initial doubts, he himself (»Ich selbst«) had taken on the task of investigating the matter (»prüfte jeden Umstand ihres Lebens nach den strengen Regeln der Wahrheit«) and could thus confirm that this story was not fiction (»nicht irgend das Hirngespinst eines schwärmenden Romanschöpfers«), but verifiable truth.[1485] The author subsequently uses Leonora Christina as an example to juxtapose *and* subordinate the epistemological value of fiction to that of his own account, which he claims to be virtually empirical: »und freue mich wirklich, ein Weib öffentlich ausstellen [my italics] zu können, die das mit Thaten *beweiset* [my italics], was Goethe, Wieland, Weiße, Meißner und andere in ihren Schriften schon so oft behauptet haben«.[1486] Incidentally, Rousseau de la Valette's narrative is the only source mentioned by name, albeit with the explicit remark that »die französischen Nouvellen nicht immer historischen Glauben verdienen«.[1487] Both this statement and G. v. R.'s delight at being able to display (»öffentlich ausstellen«) this prime example of a woman – words reminiscent of a cabinet of curiosities – imply a positivist claim to truth.

Corresponding to this claim, the main account begins in annal-style, but soon enough the narrator turns increasingly omniscient. The account exhibits all the traits common to Leonora Christina-literature, including the portrayal of Leonora Christina's first unfortunate love as a prelude to the second and final one as a strategy of

---

1484 See the following terminology: »ihr Leben ein überzeugender Beweis«, »so auffallend seltsam«, »so beispiellos, daß man sich ganz in das dichterische Feenreich versezt zu seyn glaubt, wenn man die Geschichte betrachtet, die eigentlich die Begebenheiten ihres Lebens enthält« (ibid. (all quotations): 'her life convincing proof', 'so strikingly peculiar', 'so unparalleled, one could think to have been transferred to the poetic realm of fairies when considering the story that actually narrates the incidents of her life').

1485 G. v. R. *Eleonore Gräfin von Ulefeld*, unpaginated preamble (all quotations).

1486 Ibid ('and I rejoice in the opportunity to *publically display* [my italics] a woman that *proves* [my italics] through deeds what Goethe, Wieland, Weiße, Meißner and others have often claimed in their writings'. G. v. R.'s mimetic objective – originating from a disdain for the invented – resembles thusly that of Friedrich von der Trenck: »Und ich schreibe nicht, um etwa den leichtgläubigen Pöbel zu hintergehen, um wie Robinson, oder Donquichotte in Abenteuern zu prahlen; sondern für die, welche das Wahre vom Geschminkten, den Kern von der Schale, auch den unglücklichen Mann vom Übelthäter, oder Avanturier zu unterscheiden wissen« (Trenck, Friedrich Freiherr von der. *Des Friedrich Freyherrn von der Trenck, merkwürdige Lebensgeschichte: Von ihm selbst als ein Lehrbuch für Menschen geschrieben, die wirklich unglücklich sind, oder noch gute Vorbilder für alle Fälle, zur Nachfolge bedürfen 1*. 1786, unpaginated preamble: 'And I do not write to deceive the naïve mob, to boast of adventures like Robinson, or Donquichotte; but for those who know to separate truth from made-up, the pip from the shell, even the unfortunate man from the scoundrel, or adventurer').

1487 G. v. R. *Eleonore Gräfin von Ulefeld*, p. 39 ('the French stories are not always deserving of historical credibility').

identity-formation,[1488] the fate-theme (see indented quotation below) and even the subliminally dominant interest in Corfitz Ulfeldt,[1489] whose death might be a fundamental reason for the account's abrupt ending. Due to the author's preference for Ulfeldt as a subject matter, he even feels inclined to excuse occasional digressions on the topic of Leonora Christina (»Doch damit ich auf *seine* [my italics] Schicksale zurückkomme«).[1490] The narrative is, however, regularly interrupted by the author's pondering over the nature of narrative itself. All of the text's self-referential considerations resulting in sporadic meta-emplotment[1491] must, however, eventually bow to the author's mimetic ambitions:

> Warum fällt immer eine Sache, wenn sie einen ungewöhnlichen Grad von Größe oder Höhe erreicht hat? Liegt dieß wirklich so in der Natur der Dinge, oder sind es nur einzelne abstrahirte Vorfälle, aus denen der Mensch sich ein Ganzes gebildet hat? Beinahe bin ich von dem erstern überzeugt. Aber wenn auch dieses ist, warum muß es so seyn?[1492]

The author's evocation of putative laws[1493] serves as an argument for Leonora Christina's alleged refinement through prison: »Auch Eleonore wäre gewiß nie das geworden, was sie ward, wenn sie nicht durch manche Prüfung geläutert, und von den Schlacken gereinigt worden wäre, mit welchen der gemeine Menschenpöbel umgeben ist«.[1494]

1488 »*Schon* [my italics] in diesen jungen ersten Jahren ihres Lebens trübte eine unglückliche Liebe die Tage ihres dortigen Aufenthalts« (ibid., p. 11); »Eleonore, noch zu grössern Schicksalen bestimmt, […]« (ibid., p. 12: '*Already* [my italics] in these early years of her life an unfortunate love cast a shadow over the period of her stay').

1489 Despite Leonora Christina being the account's eponymous heroine, she seems absent from crucial parts of it and the author appears at times more intent on emphasising her husband's qualities. Accordingly, the story of how the little Countess rejected another, wealthier and more powerful suitor after her engagement with Ulfeldt – usually used as an anecdote attesting to Leonora Christina's loyal character – is repurposed as evidence for Ulfeldt's unmatched assets (ibid., p. 17).

1490 Ibid., p. 35 ('but to return to *his* [my italics] lot').

1491 Cf. White, Hayden. *Metahistory*, p. 7: »Providing the 'meaning' of a story by identifying the kind of story that has been told is called explanation by emplotment«. By making his own reflections on the idea of meaning and coherence part of the account, however, the author of *Eleonore Gräfin von Ulefeld* adds another level of emplotment, i.e. the creation of meaning through the formation of a plot, to his own narrative.

1492 G. v. R. *Eleonore Gräfin von Ulefeld*, p. 14 ('Why does something that has reached a certain level of grandness or elevation always fall? Is this really in the nature of things, or is it just single abstract incidents, from which man has made something complete? I am inclined to believe in the former. But even if it is so, why does it have to be?').

1493 See, for example, ibid., p. 15: »Der leidende Mensch ist gewöhnlich allemal besser, als der der im Schimmer und Glüke sizt« ('The suffering human is usually much better than the one that is surrounded by gleam and fortune').

1494 Ibid., p. 17 ('Eleonore, too, would never have become what she was, had she not been purified by many a trial, and cleaned of the cinder surrounding the common human mob').

Another common narrative strategy employed in *Eleonore Gräfin von Ulefeld* is an omission of factual information, i.e. a distortion of the factual field, hence creating a clearly discernible causal chain, which furthermore results in a more pristine portrayal of Leonora Christina. This concerns, for example, her influence on the Malmö trial and, more strikingly, Ulfeldt's sudden disappearance from the account. In the former case, the fact that both spouses *had* been found guilty *after* Leonora Christina's appraised plea (but *before* the verdict was annulled due to the death of Karl X Gustav) remains unmentioned, hence creating the impression that it had been her efforts alone that had saved them.[1495] The latter case concerns the author's absolute secrecy regarding Ulfeldt's fate after his departure to a German health resort, i.e. his final separation from his wife. The author's later reference to the interrogation of Leonora Christina, which included questions regarding her husband's activities,[1496] testify to his own knowledge of the accusations raised against Ulfeldt. The complete absence of any account of Ulfeldt's activities after his departure, however, indicate that the reader is expected to be familiar with Ulfeldt's fate. Nevertheless, the absence of any reference to Ulfeldt's alleged treason[1497] in combination with the subsequently exerted terminology regarding Frederik III – »Sklaverei« and »Despotismus eines souverainen Fürsten«[1498] – necessarily generate the impression of arbitrary, tyrannical exertion of power. Accordingly, the subsequent account of Leonora Christina's imprisonment exhibits all the common traits of classic Leonora Christina-literature, including the theme of refinement through prison, which is rather typical of prison literature from all ages.[1499] Because Leonora Christina was imprisoned by a tyrant, she was to be considered a Robin Hood-figure[1500]

1495 Cf. ibid., p. 46.

1496 »Ich wage es nicht zu entscheiden, ob sie in der That nichts wußte, oder was sie wußte, zu gestehen nicht für gut fand« (ibid., p. 57: 'I do not dare to decide, whether she indeed did not know anything, or did not find it wise to admit what she knew'). There is no explanation in the account as to what exactly there was to know about Ulfeldt's activities.

1497 To that effect, Leonora Christina's apprehension in England is explained by mere suspicions regarding her, which appear completely unrelated to anything Ulfeldt might have done (ibid., p. 53).

1498 Ibid., both quotations p. 56 ('slavery', 'despotism of a souvereign lord').

1499 The reader will, for example, find the same topic in Silvio Pellico's prison narrative *Le mie prigioni* (1832), whose author was a political prisoner for ten years and who implemented his very own refinement through a return to philosophy and – much like Leonora Christina – to religion: »E che altro è il Cristianesimo se non questo perpetuo aspirare a nobilitarsi?« (Pellico, Silvio. *Le mie prigioni: Memorie di Silvio Pellico da Saluzzo con addizioni di Pietro Maroncelli, e notizie preliminary intorno all' autore e l'ode sulla creduta di lui morte. Quarta edizione da Giov. Batta. Ghezzi. Mit vermehrten grammatikalischen Erläuterungen und einem Wörterbuche zum Schul- und Privatgebrauche*. Leipzig: Baumgartner, 1858, p. 5: 'And what else is the Christian faith if not this perpetual aspiration to ennoble oneself?').

1500 Cf. Seiler, Thomas. *Im Leben verschollen*, p. 19. See also Weigel, Sigrid. *Und selbst im Kerker frei...!*, p. 7.

or even a martyr, elevated solely through incarceration (»jene [...] Gefangenschaft von 23 vollen Jahren, die Eleonoren Christinen Gräfin von Ulefeld in die Klasse der größten nicht nur Frauen, sondern selbst Männer versezt«).[1501]

In many regards, G. v. R.'s narrative resembles those of Hans Christian Andersen. There is, most prominently, his interest in Ulfeldt and the consequential utilisation of Leonora Christina as a guarantee of her husband's noble character:

> Auch könnte man ihn durch die Liebe seiner Gattin entschuldigen, wenn auch in der That Ulfeld nach Kronen gestrebet hätte. Sie war aus königlichem Geblüte entsprossen; was war also natürlicher, als ihr den Grad von Hohheit verschaffen zu suchen, in welchem die Natur sie gebohren werden ließ?[1502]

But *Eleonore Gräfin von Ulefeld* also exhibits the same conciliatory structure and conclusion as 'Gudfaders Billedbog' (see Chapter 2.2.3.). The Ulfeldt couple is portrayed as being utterly powerless against an evil, loosely motivated higher force resembling that of Andersen's »Niddets Borre«,[1503] hence one would expect a Tragedy to unfold. The account, however, exhibits the structure of a Romance,[1504] like much of the later Leonora Christina-literature, which depicts a process of overcoming. Due to her separation from Ulfeldt, however, the account also exhibits comedic traits, meaning that the liberation and the overcoming are only partial.[1505]

A similar case with an unexpected twist is the account written by Jens Kragh Høst (1772-1844). Originally educated to be a lawyer, Høst soon gained fame as a translator, historian, publisher and writer. His perhaps most famous work is a largely positive analysis of Johann Friedrich Struensee's[1506] legislation – *Geheimekabinetsminister Grev Johann Friedrich Struensee og hans Ministerium* (1824)

1501 G. v. R. *Eleonore Gräfin von Ulefeld*, p. 54 ('this [...] imprisonment of 23 full years, which placed Eleonore Christine Countess of Ulefeld in the class of not just the grandest of women, but even men').

1502 Ibid., p. 35 ('One could also excuse him through the love of his wife, even if Ulfeld had indeed pursued the crown. She had royal ancestry; what would then have been more natural than to award her the degree of royalty into which nature had born her?').

1503 Andersen, Hans Christian. 'Gudfaders Billedbog', p. 59.

1504 Cf. White, Hayden. *Metahistory*, p. 8: »The Romance is fundamentally a drama of self-identification symbolized by the hero's transcendence of the world of experience, his victory over it, and his final liberation from it – the sort of drama associated with the Grail legend or the story of the resurrection of Christ in Christian mythology«.

1505 White, Hayden. *Metahistory*, p. 9.

1506 Struensee (1737-1772) was a German doctor and reformer, who became the personal physician and adviser of the mentally ill King Christian VII (1749-1808), as well as the Queen's gallant. For nearly two years he was the factual regent of Denmark.

– which was succeeded by an account of Ulfeldt's life.[1507] *Rigshofmester Grev Korfits Ulfelds og Grevinde til Slesvig og Holsten Eleonora Christina Ulfelds Levnet* (1825) begins with the usual reference to their exceptional life stories (»de mærkværdigste Personer«),[1508] and a rather cryptic explanation for his latest undertaking. Besides the correct observation that roughly eight decades have passed since the last comprehensive account of their lives had been published, Høst also reports to have felt coerced to write his latest text »saa meget mere, som ej blot Udlændinger, men hædrede Landsmænd end nu nyligen have højst uværdig behandlet Eleonora Christinas Minde«.[1509] The addressees of this remark remain a mystery, because until 1825, historiography had largely treated Leonora Christina either with the utmost respect, or with indifference, while – apart from very few exceptions – literature had not adopted the topic yet.[1510] Høst himself attempts to undo this mischief by conceding superior historical relevance to Leonora Christina: »Ikke mindre, egentlig endnu langt mere, værd at kjænde er Ulfelds Hustru, Fjerde Christians Datter, Eleonora Christine, en Stolthed for sit Kjøn, for Menneskheden«.[1511] He further delivers on his initially stated intention to provide an updated, comprehensive account of the Ulfeldt couple's life by producing a lengthy, seemingly all-encompassing narrative,[1512] whose integrity he attempts to accentuate through excessive renditions of treaties and legal topics, such as the trial against Dina.[1513] Overall, however, there is little new information provided by Høst. As stated by the historian Johannes Steenstrup, yet pertaining to Høst's publication immediately preceding *Korfits Ulfelds og Eleonora Christina Ulfelds Levnet*: »Her er samlet meget Stof sammen fra ældre periodisk Litteratur og andre Skrifter, ligesom enkelte utrykte Materia-

---

1507 According to A. Jantzen, Høst also wrote the second half of Birch's chronological *Billedgallerie* (Jantzen, A. 'Birch, Hans Jørgen'. In *Dansk Biografisk Leksikon 3: Bille–Brandstrup*. Grundlagt af C. F. Bricka. Red. af Povl Engelstoft. Copenhagen: Schultz 1934, p. 113), whereas Vilhelm Andersen contends that Birch was still very vital in 1795 and »sluttede da Billedgalleriet« (Andersen, Vilhelm. *Illustreret dansk Litteraturhistorie 2: Det attende Aarhundrede*. Copenhagen: Gyldendal, 1934, p. 586).

1508 Høst, Jens Kragh. *Rigshofmester Grev Korfits Ulfelds og Grevinde til Slesvig og Holsten Eleonora Christina Ulfelds Levnet*. Copenhagen: Beekens Forlag, 1825, unpaginated preamble.

1509 Ibid.

1510 The only conclusive cause of Høst's aggravation (cf. ibid., footnote p. 7) is a statement by E. Munthe, who contends that Leonora Christina had been born out of wedlock (Munthe, E[iler]. *De vigtigste indenlandske Tildrag og de merkeligste Personers Levnetsbeskrivelse fra de ældste indtil vore Dage: En Læse- og Lærebog i Fædrelandets Historie for Begyndere og Ustuderede*. Copenhagen: Thoring & Colding, 1806, p. 234).

1511 Høst, Jens Kragh. *Korfits Ulfelds og Eleonora Christina Ulfelds Levnet*, p. 4.

1512 Høst's eclectic ambitions turn particularly salient in his spelling of Leonora Christina's name, which he renders in every version possible, except for the current one. Hence, he writes »Eleonora Christina«, »Eleonora Christine«, »Leonora«, »Christine«, »Eleonore«, »Eleonora« and finally, »Christina Eleonora«.

1513 Høst's excruciatingly detailed account of this affair engrosses a staggering 15% of the entire narrative.

Historiography on Leonora Christina in a Nutshell

lier er benyttede, men dybtgaaende Historieskrivning er det ikke«.[1514] His account is a perfect, albeit very early example of the 19th century's adoration of Leonora Christina.[1515] While most of his predecessors – following Holberg's neutral judgement[1516] – could thus not forbear but to abstain from judging Leonora Christina's intentions regarding Sophie Amalie, particularly in the incident involving the Queen's crown, Høst adopts an authority and a reasoning reminiscent of Sophus Birket Smith: »Hvor skulde man tiltroe hendes høje og ædle Karakter saa lav og gemen en Færd! Slige Usselheder burde man blues ved at paasige en Aand, som, under Skjæbnens Omskiftelser, aldrig viste et Træk, der kunde plettet hendes evig lysende Minde«.[1517]

However, due to Høst's blatant sympathy for Ulfeldt, Leonora Christina – as »Livets bedste Skat, en trofast Veninde, som spredede Fryd over hans [Ulfeldt's] lyse, Trøst over hans mørke Dage«[1518] – is soon reduced to the status of a mere sidekick, a tendency best exemplified by Høst's depiction of the couple's adventures. When Leonora Christina and her husband flee from their arrest in Malmö, to name only one example, Ulfeldt is depicted as the mastermind behind the operation and Leonora Christina as his helper: »Skulde end ikke alle disse Omstændigheder være bogstavelig Sandhed, saa meget er dog vist, at Ulfeld, ved sin snilde Gemalindes Bistand, skuffede den talrige Vagt og undkom i Præstedragt«.[1519] This contempla-

---

1514 Steenstrup, Johannes. 'Høst, Jens Kragh'. In *Dansk Biografisk Leksikon 11: Hultmann-Joachim*. Grundlagt af C. F. Bricka. Red. af Povl Engelstoft. Copenhagen: Schultz 1937, p. 153.

1515 This includes at times nationalistic reasoning. Among 19th-century authors of Leonora Christina-narratives a rationale based on a native-foreigner dichotomy is rather common. The unknown author of the dime novel *Historien om Corfits Ulfeldt, og hans trofaste Hustru, Eleonore Kristine, Kongens Datter, og hvorledes de fra den største Magt og Rigdom sank i dybeste Elendighed*, for example, alludes to the iniquity that »en fjendtlig Udlænding«, i.e. the Elector of Brandenburg, should have been able to spell doom for a Danish nobleman (see Anonymous. *Historien om Corfits Ulfeldt, og hans trofaste Hustru, Eleonore Kristine, Kongens Datter, og hvorledes de fra den største Magt og Rigdom sank i dybeste Elendighed*. Copenhagen: Jul. Strandberg, [1884], p. 34). The term »fjendtlig« may be discarded as a 19th-century annotation, since there are no historical indications of hostilities between the Elector of Brandenburg and the King of Denmark at that time. Incidentally, the author bestows a similar verdict upon the English (cf. ibid., p. 35: »Kong Carl den 2den af England, der, nederdrægtig som de fleste Englændere ere, udlevederede hende til Kongen af Danmark«). The same mindset may account for similar remarks in Høst's account, such as his indignation over degrading statements written not just by foreigners, but even by Danes about Leonora Christina, as well as his disapproval of Ulfeldt's conviction, solely based on the »Forklaring af en Udlænding« (Høst, Jens Kragh. *Korfits Ulfelds og Eleonora Christina Ulfelds Levnet*, p. 317).

1516 See Holberg, Ludvig. *Dannemarks Riges Historie 3*: »Om Madame Ulfeldt giorde dette forsætlig Viis, er noget, som ieg for visse ikke kand sige. Vist nok er det, at hendes forrige Opførsel kunde ikke andet end give Anledning til Mistanke derom«. Many of Holberg's successors adopted this very wording.

1517 Høst, Jens Kragh. *Korfits Ulfelds og Eleonora Christina Ulfelds Levnet*, p. 132.

1518 Ibid., p. 9.

1519 Ibid., p. 276.

tion does not necessarily contradict Leonora Christina's own presentation of events – to which Høst refers frequently – but it is certainly not in keeping with Leonora Christina's self-portrayal as swashbuckling heroine.

Nevertheless, Høst's narrative is not entirely undeserving of reference, as the author performed an unrivalled reversal of a strategy all too common in the 19th century, i.e. the exculpation of Corfitz Ulfeldt through Leonora Christina, known from Count Waldstein-Wartenberg, Hans Christian Andersen and many of their successors. In his own narrative, Høst, too, exploits the involvement of Leonora Christina for the greater good of her husband's reputation. However, he inverts the customary argument, in which Leonora Christina serves as an affirmative background character, by sanctifying Ulfeldt's actions as the impetus that led to the collective recollection of Leonora Christina: »Men havde hans Forvildelser og hans Ulykker ikke været, saa vilde Historien ej heller have kunnet fremstille det store Mynster paa qvindelig Hengivenhed, Bestandighed og Sjælsstyrke i Fjerde Christians evig herlige Datter Christina Eleonora«.[1520]

Besides an unawareness of the existence of *Jammers Minde,* the two common denominators of all of the above-mentioned texts are thus an insistence on the exclusive epistemological value of their individual work and an – implicit or explicit – focus on Corfitz (with the notable exception of the gynæcea). Characteristic of the first feature identified above is a persistent reference to Rousseau de la Valette's text throughout the diverse accounts, which serves, *ex negativo*, as evidence of the authors' diligence and scientific integrity. Common to these authors is thus an equation of literariness with fictionality, which ultimately adds up to untruth. The commonly uttered scruple regarding the French account's creditableness, while sources such as the forgery published by Bang and the diverse transcripts of adaptations of the French autobiography remained unchallenged, however, demonstrate that factuality was considered to be something that meets the eye and that formally should be diametrically opposed to a novel.[1521]

The latter tendency, however, was eliminated in 1869, when the publication of *Jammers Minde* changed the collective memory of Leonora Christina. The extent to which this text has influenced (mostly) Danish literature has been discussed in detail, as required by the topic's complexity. Much unlike the development of Leonora Christina-literature, however, the historical aspect of her reception is marked by a tendency towards extraction and reallocation. For while there has always been an interest in Leonora Christina's literary achievements among historians,

---

1520 Ibid., p. [3]60. The printed page number reads »160«, but this is indubitably a mistake.
1521 Cf. ibid., footnote p. 272: »Hvad Valette fortæller i: le Comte d'Ulfeld […] er øjensynlig [!] en Roman«.

the emergence of *Jammers Minde* in particular has led to an essential regrouping. While virtually all of the historians mentioned above – especially the authors of the gynæcea – refer to Leonora Christina's texts as proof of her erudition, yet always in the context of her historical significance, public awareness of *Jammers Minde* has gradually turned Leonora Christina into a topic exclusively literary, cultural-historical and herstorical. This in turn is a corrective side effect of the research community's prevailing interest in Corfitz Ulfeldt. Women's history as a discipline, alternatively called *herstory*, originated out of the inadequacy of traditional historiography's norms as the conventional term of historical significance would hardly apply to any woman,[1522] unless she could produce masculine traits and accomplishments. However, since the second sex, i.e. women, were defined through their otherness, the gender aspect would in turn become the focal point of the ensuing historical discourse, hence prohibiting a portrayal of women's deeds and accomplishments for the greater good of depicting womanhood itself.[1523] Either way, traditional historiography gradually became an inadequate setting for the staging of Leonora Christina's life.

Prior to the publication of *Jammers Minde*, Denmark furthermore had experienced political losses, which in hindsight might be deemed traumatic. The 19th century had brought about a considerable territorial reduction, starting with the forfeiture of Norway in 1814, and continuing with the loss of roughly a third of Denmark's territory and inhabitants when the country lost the duchies of Schleswig, Holstein and Lauenburg in 1864. Only five years later, the defeat-stricken country was finally presented with a story of Danish success against all odds:

> Her så vore oldeforældre i et billed Danmark slået og lammet, men ikke kuet, den fangne kongedatters rejsning blev et symbol. Hun blev national helgeninde, mens hendes fjende Sofie Amalie [a *German* princess!] i den tids historieskrivning blev skildret som den rene sydende ondskab.[1524]

[1522] Cf. Zimmermann, Nina von. 'Zu den Wegen der Frauenbiographikforschung'. In *Frauenbiographik: Lebensbeschreibungen und Porträts*, ed. Christian von Zimmermann. Tübingen: Narr, 2005 (Mannheimer Beiträge zur Sprach- und Literaturwissenschaft 63), p. 18.

[1523] Cf. ibid., p. 17.

[1524] Lauring, Palle. *Dronninger og andre kvinder i Danmarkshistorien*, p. 70.

The discovery of *Jammers Minde* was thus pivotal in a twofold way. First, it occurred at a highly favourable time, when Denmark was in need of such a text.[1525] Second, it caused a major shift in the collective perception of Leonora Christina, which subsequently resulted in her reallocation in the historical field.

In the century following the emergence of *Jammers Minde*, she became the center of historiographical scrutiny.[1526] At the same time, interest in the veracity of her accounts as well as her position as a woman, was reignited, starting with the work of the foremost Leonora Christina-researcher, Sophus Birket Smith. Despite the honest admiration permeating the librarian's biographies of Leonora Christina, he nevertheless felt obliged to address occasions when her own narratives contained flams, for example when she asserted that she and her husband had been completely uninvolved in the treason against the King of Sweden. Birket Smith excuses Leonora Christina's somewhat lax attitude to truth on the basis of both her age[1527] and her gender. With regard to the latter, he demonstrates his well-known awe at what Leonora Christina could do despite her being a woman[1528] and appreciation of what she did *because* of her womanhood:

1525 Furthermore, in the 1860's the constitutional monarchy of Denmark was only a decade old and the royal couple that had introduced the previous, absolutist system – Frederik III and Sophie Amalie – was understandably unpopular. The subsequent reassessment of Leonora Christina as a dissident occurs only sporadically (and rather late) in literature, but was not uncommon in historiography and critical studies. It is also the most prominent feature of Sigvard Skov's article 'Leonora Christina – helgen eller højforræder'. See, for example, Skov, Sigvard. 'Leonora Christina – helgen eller højforræder', p. 212: »Et diktatur under etablering er efter sagens natur ikke kræsen i valg af midler. [...] En opposition, også en opposition på lovens grund, tvinges uvægerligt ud i lignende suspekte midler«.

1526 The introductory words of Steffen Heiberg's influential Corfitz Ulfeldt-biography, published in 1993, are symptomatic of this tendency: »Mens Leonora Christina er blevet godt og grundigt biograferet, er der gået 168 år siden der udkom en biografi af Corfitz Ulfeldt« (Heiberg, Steffen. *Enhjørningen Corfitz Ulfeldt*, p. 7).

1527 »At Sanddruhed overhovedet for hin Tids Mennesker var et mindre kategorisk Pligtbud end for os, tør vistnok betragtes som en Kjendsgjerning [...]« (Birket Smith, Sophus. *Leonora Christina Grevinde Ulfeldts Historie 1*, p. 409).

1528 »Men også hvad Forsvarets Realitet angår, må det vistnok indrømmes, at hun – især når man betænker hendes Kjøn, hendes Ukjendskab til den Slags Sager og endelig hendes Uformuenhed til på Grund af Mandens Sygdom at skaffe sig bestemte Oplysninger [...] – har løst sin Opgave med ikke ringe Dyktighed [...]« (ibid., p. 408).

> Som hun var stor og kraftig af Legeme – hvad dog ikke udelukkede høj Skjønhed, – havde også hendes Ånd et dristigere Præg og hendes Karakter et større Mål af Styrke, end det selv hos Datidens kraftigere Slægt var almindeligt for hendes Kjøn, og det er ikke noget ringe Vidnesbyrd om den fremtrædende Plads, som hendes inderlige, trofaste og til ethvert Offer redebonne Kjærlighed indtager i hendes Liv og hendes Handlinger, at til Trods for de hist og her uvante og måske lidt hårde Omrids af hendes åndelige Personlighed bliver dog det samlede Indtryk af hendes Skikkelse på os altid Indtrykket af en ægte Kvinde, om end tillige af en Kvinde, der er støbt i en ualmindelig storladen Form.[1529]

This multifunctional topic – Leonora Christina's womanhood and the prerogatives and obligations associated with it – was famously seized by Julius Lange (see Chapter 1.1.1.) and sporadically continued by his successors. In the mid-20th century, research objectives of this kind had reached a climax.[1530] Especially the learned journal *Jyske Samlinger* provided, albeit for a short while, a forum for discussions on Leonora Christina's involvement in her husband's treason. In 1957, Svend Aakjær published an article titled 'Leonora Christinas skyld' in this same journal. Based on some letters written by Leonora Christina's mother regarding Ulfeldt's actions in Sweden, which had not been deciphered and printed until this point, Aakjær – who was not alone in his verdict[1531] – essentially accused Birket Smith of bias (»der sine steder næsten grænser til forelskelse«)[1532] in terms of Leonora Christina's guilt: »Thi om ordet ›forråde‹ og ›forræder‹ nogensinde i Danmark har kunnet bruges med rette om nogen personer og deres handlinger, så er det om Corfitz Ulfeldt og hans nærmeste«.[1533] Aakjær's prosecution was in turn indicted for ignorance and inaccuracy by C. O. Bøggild-Andersen, who in his answer urged his readers to maintain an adequate historical perspective: »Nogen helgeninde blev Leonora Christina aldrig; de som har hævdet andet, fortegner hendes billed. Og set fra en streng fædrelandsstatslig etiks stade falder hun igennem. Men det er urigtigt at forbise, at en saadan etik paa

---

1529 Ibid., p. 83.
1530 By that time, the original manuscript of Leonora Christina's French autobiography had also been rediscovered. This had, however, only a supplementary effect on the course taken by research on Leonora Christina, since the biographical details narrated in this text were known before due to the earlier circulation of diverse transcriptions.
1531 Cf. Lundgaard Simonsen, Vagn. Afterword in Leonora Christina. *Jammers Minde*, ed. Vagn Lundgaard Simonsen. Copenhagen: Gyldendal, 1964 (Gyldendals bibliotek 1), p. 258: »Eftertiden har da også sagt – og ikke helt med urette – at Birket-Smiths skildring af Leonora Christina i indledningen til *Jammers Minde* er en forelsket skildring«.
1532 Aakjær, Svend. 'Leonora Christinas skyld – et aktorat', Jyske Samlinger 4 (Ny række, 1957), p. 233.
1533 Ibid., p. 239.

hendes tid endnu var i støbeskeen«.[1534] Bøggild-Andersen's plea furthermore concerns Leonora Christina's status as a married woman at that time: »Alle andre bånd blev i sammenligning hermed skørere, med al sin senere tale om ›mandelige kræfter i svage kar‹ var hun til roden af sin sjæl kvinde«,[1535] meaning a faithful and loyal supporter of her husband, *not* of her country or King. This latter argument, however, was dismissed in Aakjær's subsequent answer as being too lenient.[1536] More than two decades later, Sigvard Skov reopened the debate and closed it with the words: »Og hermed burde man vel for denne sinde være færdig med Leonora Christina«.[1537] However, the reproduction of Leonora Christina's life was far from being over.

What is most remarkable about the discourse above is that the question of veracity was soon discarded and filed as concluded, for the sake of the more pressing issue of Leonora Christina's status as a wife and how this would determine her relation to truthfulness. This new subject matter is rather typical of the later 20th century, as concluded in a *tilbageblik* by the educationalist Jeanne Bau-Madsen, written in 2001:

> Efter den romantisering som både kunstnere og historikere havde givet udtryk for i 1800-tallet, kom der i 1900-tallet en mere realistisk karakteristik af Eleonora. [...] Eleonoras livshistorie, som den bliver skrevet i slutningen af 1900-tallet, bygger i høj grad på, hvad hun selv har skrevet, men også på en viden om, at en kvinde i 1600-tallet, selv om hun var begavet og veluddannet, kun var noget i kraft af ægtefællens position.[1538]

The last decades have thus demonstrated a gradual dislodgement of Leonora Christina from the historical discourse, which inevitably continued to be dominated by Corfitz Ulfeldt. Ironically, there was hence a tendency to separate Leonora Christina's biography from that of her husband *because* of their inseparability,[1539] which eventually resulted in a reintegration of Leonora Christina in a cultural, and particularly in a herstorical and literary context.

1534 Bøggild-Andersen, C. O. 'Kongedatteren for historiens domstol: Nogle bemærkninger til Svend Aakjærs aktorat mod Leonora Christina', Jyske Samlinger 5 (Ny række, 1959), p. 29.
1535 Ibid., p. 37.
1536 »Der er vel ingen tvivl om, at L. C. stærkt følte sin pligt mod sin ægtefælle til at følge ham i ondt og godt, men hun var dog Christian IV.s datter, og hvorfor følte hun ikke også kongedatterens pligt mod sit fædreland?« (Aakjær, Svend. 'Leonora Christinas dommer', Jyske Samlinger 5 (Ny række, 1959), p. 42).
1537 Skov, Sigvard. 'Leonora Christina – helgen eller højforræder', p. 213. In conformity with Bøggild-Andersen, Skov concludes that Leonora Christina was none of the above.
1538 Bau-Madsen, Jeanne. *Eleonora – en kongedatter*. Holte: Flachs, 2001 (Tilbageblik), p. 44.
1539 See, for example, Bøggild-Andersen's efforts to emphasise how from a legal point of view Leonora Christina was not involved in her husband's actions: »Men hustruen nævnes i domsakten ikke med et ord« (Bøggild-Andersen, C. O. 'Kongedatteren for historiens domstol', p. 30).

3.2 Leonora Christina in Canonical Historiography

In the following chapters, the development of historical research on and reproduction of Leonora Christina's life drafted above will be portrayed in greater detail by means of four case examples; two published before 1869 and two published afterwards. All of the texts chosen – three national (Chapters 3.2.1., 3.2.2. and 3.2.4.) and one anecdotal, biographical history (Chapter 3.2.3.) – are of canonical quality and relevance, as each one represents a critical stage in the development of Leonora Christina-historiography. These four works are analysed using the narratological terminology developed in the American historian Hayden White's influential study *Metahistory: The Historical Imagination in Nineteenth-Century Europe* (1973) for a reading of historiographical texts, which challenges the once uncontested fundamental distinction between historiography and literature and thus constitutes a useful tool for a treatment of historiography as archetypes of literature.

The currently dominant understanding of history and its epistemological potential dates back to, among others, the German historian Leopold von Ranke (1795-1886), who established the use and evaluation of written sources as a core method of historical research. The methodology introduced by Ranke encouraged a separation of literature and history as two distinct disciplines, whereas prior to Ranke – but also prior to the Enlightenment's understanding of fiction as antithetic to reason and fact[1540] – they have been regarded as closely related cognitive instruments. Postmodern theory, in turn, refutes this distinction again[1541] and calls for a focus on the common features of history and literature:

1540 Hamnett, Brian R. *The Historical Novel in Nineteenth-Century Europe: Representations of Reality in History and Fiction.* Oxford University Press, 2011, p. 27.

1541 Cf. Mink, Louis O. 'Narrative Form as a Cognitive Instrument'. In *The Writing of History: Literary Form and Historical Understanding*, eds. Robert H. Canary and Henry Kozicki. University of Wisconsin Press, 1978, p. 131: »Even though narrative form may be, for most people, associated with fairy tales, myths, and the entertainments of the novel, it remains true that narrative is a primary cognitive instrument – in instrument rivaled, in fact, only by theory and by metaphor as irreducible ways of making the flux of experience comprehensible«. Hugo Aust, who militates against a rigid separation of narrative from 'history proper', argues similarly; see Aust, Hugo. *Der historische Roman.* Stuttgart: Metzler, 1994 (Sammlung Metzler 278: Realien zur Literatur), p. 10.

They have both been seen to derive their force more from verisimilitude than from any objective truth; they are both identified as linguistic constructs, highly conventionalized in their narrative forms, and not at all transparent either in terms of language or structure; and they appear to be equally intertextual, deploying the texts of the past within their own complex textuality.[1542]

In the course of the linguistic turn of the 20th century, which – in the context of the scholarly discipline of history – rejected Ranke's positivist understanding of history[1543] and the idea of historiography portraying a past reality which existed as an invariable truth independent of the written word, a scientific understanding of history was replaced by a semiological theory viewing language itself (including historiography) as a »self-contained«[1544] system, instead of a mere medium used for the description of the outside world. Based on this new perception of language, Hayden White contributed significantly[1545] to the development of historiographical narratology through the publication of his influential study *Metahistory: The Hi-*

1542 Hutcheon, Linda. *A Poetics of Postmodernism*, p. 105. This recollection of the relatedness of literature and history has led to the emergence of the genre of historiographic metafiction in the 1960's and 1970's – a type of novel that conveys its awareness of the difficulties of distinguishing between fact/history and fiction/literature to the reader (see ibid., pp. 105-123).

1543 The various biographies of Leonora Christina and Ulfeldt written in the late 18th and 19th century reflect this faith in the reliability of historical sources and historiography. And since the scholarly discussion on Leonora Christina had always been affected by questions of truth, these earlier biographies would often use her life story as a case study on their own epistemological value. In this regard, these early texts are highly self-referential.

1544 Iggers, Georg G. 'Zur »Linguistischen Wende« im Geschichtsdenken und in der Geschichtsschreibung', Geschichte und Gesellschaft 21 (1995), p. 557.

1545 Hayden White's work and terminology are based on earlier works by Aristotle, Giambattista Vico, Northrop Frye, Stephen C. Pepper, and Karl Mannheim, among others. White's work itself has been criticized for its apparent renouncement of any differences between fiction and historiography. For example, the German narratological scholar Ansgar Nünning, though not fundamentally disavowing the validity of White's studies, has called for a theoretical framework establishing the *divergence* in the ways historiography and literature construct their depicted worlds (Nünning, Ansgar. '»Verbal Fictions?« Kritische Überlegungen und narratologische Alternativen zu Hayden Whites Einebnung des Gegensatzes zwischen Historiographie und Literatur', Literaturwissenschaftliches Jahrbuch 40 (1999), p. 355). Nünning argues, for instance, for a more nuanced use of the terms of 'narrative configuration', 'literarisation' and 'fictionalisation' (ibid., p. 366): »Aus diesem Zwischenfazit ergibt sich die Konsequenz, zwischen narrativer Konfiguration, Literarisierung und Fiktionalisierung zu unterscheiden«) and for the establishment of a model using 'fictionality indicators' (»Fiktionalitätsindikatoren«, ibid., p. 368) and 'reality signals' (»Wirklichkeitssignale«, ibid., p. 369) in order to identify the elements which signalise to readers that they are engaging in a project of fiction, instead of one of history. These are valid points of criticism, but since it is not the objective of the present study to argue for or conduct a distinction between 'factual' and 'fictive' Leonora Christina-texts (even though said distinction is implicit through the use of separate main chapters for literary and historiographical texts), but rather to highlight their common topics and strategies in order to depict the interdiscursivity of the Leonora Christina-subject, White's levelling terminology lends itself to the attainment of this objective.

storical Imagination of Nineteenth-Century Europe. In this and other works, White argues for a recollection of the common roots and methods of history and literature:

> In this theory I treat the historical work as what it most manifestly is: a verbal structure in the form of a narrative prose discourse. [...] [T]hey [historical works] contain a deep structural content which is generally poetic, and specifically linguistic, in nature, and which serves as the precritically accepted paradigm of what a distinctively »historical« explanation should be. This paradigm functions as the »metahistorical« element in all historical works that are more comprehensive in scope than the monograph or archival report.[1546]

In order to account for the events of history, historians must choose among the elements of the »historical field«[1547] (i.e. documented events, people, objects, dates, etc.) those which they deem central to their construction of a narrative of the past, and subsequently employ different kinds of explanations for these historical events, in the course of which they utilize elements of poetic language. White distinguishes three explanatory strategies: explanation by emplotment, by formal argument and by ideological implication. The explanation by emplotment (»providing the 'meaning' of a story by identifying the *kind of story* that has been told«)[1548] is of the most interest to the literary-historical scope of the present study since it classifies historical narratives as archetypes of stories. White distinguishes four archetypes:[1549] the Romance, the Tragedy, the Comedy and the Satire.[1550] It is not the objective of the present study to assign one of these story patterns to each Leonora Christina-narrative that has been written to date, nor was it the objective of Chapter 3 to provide a complete list of historical works written about Leonora Christina. Thus, the

---

1546 White, Hayden. *Metahistory*, p. ix. In other words, »history is no less a form of fiction than the novel is a form of historical representation« (White, Hayden. 'The Fictions of Factual Representation'. In White, Hayden. *Tropics of Discourse: Essays in Cultural Criticism*. Baltimore and London: Johns Hopkins University Press, 1978, p. 122).

1547 White, Hayden. *Metahistory*, p. x: »On this level, I believe, the historian performs an essentially *poetic* act, in which he *pre*figures the historical field and constitutes it as a domain upon which to bring to bear the specific theories he will use to explain 'what was *really* happening' in it«.

1548 Ibid., p. 7.

1549 White's categories are, of course, specifically Western archetypes of a story (cf. Engler, Bernd. 'The Dismemberment of Clio', p. 24). The Tragedy, for example, is an archetypal story explaining the concept of Fate: »It is, for example, through the plots of Greek tragedy that we can best understand an idea of Fate that was never explicitly formulated as a philosophical theory and that is far removed from our own presuppositions about causality, responsibility, and the natural order« (Mink, Louis O. 'Narrative Form as a Cognitive Instrument', p. 133).

1550 In this study, White's capitalisation of these four archetypal narrative forms (and of the other types of historical explanation) are adopted when specifically referring to White's terminology, whereas the same genre denominations commonly used for literary works remain lower-case.

objective of the present study is not to determine the exact frequency of the respective archetypes used for Leonora Christina-narratives. However, as the following chapters will demonstrate, I would like to argue that the Romance and the Tragedy – respectively stories of overcoming and resignation at the face of the inevitable – are the most common story patterns used in 19th and early 20th-century Leonora Christina-narratives, whereas the conciliatory Comedy is an archetypal story employed mostly in the late 20th century and 21st century. Satire, however, does not lend itself to the emplotment of Leonora Christina's life story – notwithstanding that the earliest preserved literary work depicting Leonora Christina *is* a satire (see Chapter 2.1.1.). Even though White contends that »there are no apodictically certain theoretical grounds on which one can legitimately claim an authority for any one of the modes over the others as being more 'realistic'«,[1551] the Satirical story form refutes the kind of formation of identity and meaning that has been central to the creation and reception of the Leonora Christina-narrative (in all its interdiscursivity)[1552] and would thus contradict the story, or rather stories, written by Leonora Christina[1553] and reproduced subsequently in all kinds of variations:

1551 White, Hayden. *Metahistory*, p. xii. For example, a simple change of perspective can drastically alter the type of narrative that is being told about one and the same event. The story of Leonora Christina's imprisonment, without the knowledge of her subsequent release from prison, is a Tragedy or even a Satire from the point of view of Leonora Christina, but rather a Romance from that of Sophie Amalie, since it sealed her victory over the haughty Countess Ulfeldt, who had repeatedly challenged and humiliated her in the previous years.

1552 Inspired by the notion pronounced by the New Historicism movement of »einer antimimetischen Konzeption des Verhältnisses zwischen literarischen Texten und historischer Wirklichkeit« (Nünning, Ansgar. *Von historischer Fiktion zu historiographischer Metafiktion I: Theorie, Typologie und Poetik des historischen Romans*. Trier: Wissenschaftlicher Verlag Trier, 1995 (Literatur, Imagination, Realität 11), p. 54: 'an anti-mimetic conception of the relationship between literary texts and historical reality'), out of which follows that literature does not merely reflect historical reality, but contributes to constituting and shaping it (ibid.), it is the objective of the present study to depict the fundamental influence of literature presenting Leonora Christina (including her autobiographical writings) on historiographical texts about the same or related subjects.

1553 As demonstrated in Chapter 1.2., Leonora Christina's autobiographical writings, and most of all *Jammers Minde*, are – though stylistically highly heterogeneous – thematically coherent narratives of their author's overcomings which, through the instrumentalisation of the narrator's faith in a higher plan directing her life, are firmly imbedded in a present that succeeds the author's trials, while conveying the impression of a 'live broadcast' of a past situation. And as argued in Chapter 1.1., this is a common enterprise of autobiography since, as stated by the anthropologists Maria G. Cattell and Jacob J. Climo, »[c]oherence and meaning are what matter [in autobiography]« (Cattell, Maria G. and Jacob J. Climo. 'Introduction: Meaning in Social Memory and History: Anthropological Perspectives'. In *Social Memory and History*, eds. Maria G. Cattell and Jacob J. Climo. Walnut Creek: AltaMira Press, 2002, p. 16).

But Satire represents a different kind of qualification of the hopes, possibilities, and truths of human existence revealed in Romance, Comedy, and Tragedy respectively. It views these hopes, possibilities, and truths Ironically, in the atmosphere generated by the apprehension of the ultimate inadequacy of consciousness to live in the world happily or to comprehend it fully. Satire presupposes the ultimate inadequacy of the visions of the world dramatically represented in the genres of Romance, Comedy, and Tragedy alike.[1554]

The second type of historical explanation identified by White is that by formal argument, through which the historian attempts to depict the implications and meaning of the narrated event:

On this level of conceptualization, the historian explains the events in the story (or the form of the events which he has imposed upon them through his emplotment of them in a particular mode) by construction of a nomological-deductive argument. This argument can be analyzed into a syllogism, the major premise of which consists of some putatively universal laws of causal relationships, the minor premise of the boundary conditions within which the law is applied, and a conclusion in which the events that actually occurred are deduced from the premises by logical necessity.[1555]

There are four types of formal argument: Formist, Organicist, Mechanistic and Contextualist. A Formist historian's objective is to depict the historical field as vividly and as true to original as possible, and to convey the characteristics of his work's subject to the reader. An Organicist historian would rather explain historical events as parts of and contributions to their context, i.e. a greater cause or process. This teleological understanding of historical progression is similar to that of the Mechanist historian, but the latter focuses more on the causal laws that lead to the conclusion of historical processes than on the conclusion, or goal, itself. Finally, Contextualists also view historical events within the context of their occurrence, but they see them as being determined by their mere relation to other events.[1556] Thus, if the historical field depicted by historians employing a formal argument was a cobweb, the Formist historian would highlight the irregularities of the web and the diverse creatures trapped in it, the Organicist would foreground how the web serves to feed the spider (and perhaps how instrumental spider webs are in maintaining a

---

1554 White, Hayden. *Metahistory*, p. 10.
1555 Ibid., p. 11.
1556 Ibid., pp. 14-19.

Leonora Christina in Danish Historiography

healthy spider population), the Mechanist would explain the biological process by which the spider creates and weaves the thread and how this thread traps prey, and the Contextualist would depict the position of the cobweb in an ecosystem and in relation to other organic matters within this ecosystem.

Any of these modes of explanation is connected to an underlying ideology.[1557] Hence, the third type of historical explanation is that by ideological implication, among which White distinguishes Anarchism, Conservatism, Liberalism and Radicalism. In opining that humans should revert to a prehistoric, 'natural' state of coexistence which preceded the corrupt societal conditions of their age, Anarchist historians generally refute the idea of temporal, or historical, progress. Conservatives, on the other hand, believe in progress, yet unlike Liberals, who hold the view that change is effected by cautious action, they are convinced that this progress occurs naturally and should not be tampered with. Radicals, on the other hand, believe in the necessity of fundamental, actively induced change in the interest of altering society, not abolishing it, as an Anarchist would have it.[1558]

Independent of these three types of explanation employed to account for historical events, there are four modes – likened to the tropes of poetic language – in which to prefigure the historical field:[1559] Metaphor, Metonymy, Synecdoche and Irony.[1560]

3.2.1. Ludvig Holberg: *Dannemarks Riges Historie* (1732-1735) – The Tragic Heroine

> Elle se rioit, et disoit, vous pouuez faire de moy ce que vous ne voulez au mettre, mais vous me pouuez jamais humillier de sorte, qu'il ne me souuienne, que vous auez esté le serviteur d'un serviteur du Roy mon Pere.[1561]

Notwithstanding Danish historian Sigvard Skov's statement that Ludvig Holberg had essentially fathered the myth of Leonora Christina »som den store tragiske

---

1557 Cf. White, Hayden. 'Historicism, History, and the Figurative Imagination', p. 105.
1558 White, Hayden. *Metahistory*, pp. 24-26.
1559 Ibid., p. 34: »They are especially useful for understanding the operations by which the contents of experience which resist description in unambiguous prose representations can be prefiguratively grasped and prepared for conscious apprehension«.
1560 Ibid., pp. 34-37.
1561 *Leonora Christina Grevinde Ulfeldts Franske Levnedsskildring*, p. 11c (Translation p. 47: »Hun lo og sagde: ‚I kan gøre med mig, hvad eder lyster, men I kan aldrig gøre mig saa ringe, at jeg ikke kommer ihu, at I har været tjener hos en af min faders kongens tjenere'«).

heltinde i Danmarks historie«,[1562] Holberg did in no way anticipate Kristian Zahrtmann's romanticisation of the great King Christian IV's daughter. As far as Holberg's judgement of Leonora Christina's character and actions is concerned, he follows the rules of conduct among historians, i.e. *upartiskhed*,[1563] as much as his age allowed him to. This alleged impartiality[1564] was in turn criticised by later scholars, such as C. Paludan-Müller, who questioned Holberg's ability, or willingness, to assess past events correctly:

> Hans naturlige Sky for alt overdrevent, alt extremt, viser sig helt igjennem. Hans Dom over Begivenheder og Personer er fri og forstandig, rolig og moderat. Han har alvorlig stræbt efter Upartiskhed, – mere endog end efter Retfærdighed. Derfor er hans Dom ikke altid træffende, men altid billig. Men man kan jo være saa billig, at man bliver uretfærdig.[1565]

Holberg's supposedly misguided detachment from the events narrated concerns in particular the touchier chapters of Denmark's history – such as the allegations raised against Ulfeldt by Dina[1566] or the quarrel between Leonora Christina and Sophie Amalie[1567] – which Holberg resolves always in favour of the winning side. Naturally, this may at least partially be attributed to the prevalent absolutist regime and its enforcement of censorship. As a consequence, Queen Sophie Amalie's de-

---

1562 Skov, Sigvard. 'Leonora Christina – helgen eller højforræder', p. 201.

1563 Cf. Holberg, Ludvig. *Dannemarks Riges Historie 3*, unpaginated preamble ('Betænkning over Historier').

1564 Despite his honest attempt at objectivity, Holberg remained sceptical whether he or other writers of historical accounts could achieve this goal. Cf. Holberg, Ludvig. *Epistler 2*, ed. Chr. Bruun. Copenhagen: Samfundet til den danske Literaturs Fremme, 1868, p. 109: »De fleeste sette dog meest Priis paa min Danmarks Historie, og det saa vel i Henseende til Materien som Formen[.] [...] Hvad Materien angaaer, da dømme de, at Historien er saa upartisk, som mueligt være kand paa de Steder, hvor Skrive-Frihed er underkasted public Censure«. See also Holberg, Ludvig. *Epistler 4*, ed. Chr. Bruun. Copenhagen: Samfundet til den danske Literaturs Fremme, 1873, p. 74: »Adskillige holde for, at min Dannemarks Historie er skreven med Upartiskhed. Jeg drister mig ikke til at sige det samme: Dette alleene siger jeg dog frit, at den er meere u-partiisk end nogen af vore andre Nordiske Historier«.

1565 Paludan-Müller, C[aspar]. 'Dansk Historiografi i det 18de Aarhundrede', Historisk Tidsskrift 5/4 (1883), p. 42.

1566 »Om udi denne Angivelse var nogen Realitet, eller, om det var et opspundet Verk af hans Fiender for at giøre ham end sortere til Hove, er noget hvorudi jeg ikke deciderer. Vist nok er det, at saadant kunde ikke andet end sætte Kong Friderik udi Bekymring, [...] ogsaa efterdi Hans Majestet havde haft adskillige Prøver paa Hoffmesterens slette Affection mod det Kongelige Huus, saa at, om Historien end var ilde digted, saa kunde den dog ikke andet end have Virkning i slige slibrige Conjuncturer« (Holberg, Ludvig. *Dannemarks Riges Historie 3*, p. 56).

1567 »Om Madame Ulfeldt giorde dette forsætlig Viis [dropping the Queen's crown at Kunst-Caspar's smithy], er noget, som jeg for visse ikke kand sige. Vist nok er det, at hendes forrige Opførsel kunde ikke andet end give Anledning til Mistanke derom« (ibid., p. 593).

ath, which coincided with Leonora Christina's release from the Blue Tower in 1685, is not part of Holberg's narrative.

Notwithstanding Holberg's ideological predisposition and the constraints he was subject to, he did provide the core topics subsequent writers and researchers were all engaging in as well as one of the most common paradigms used to discuss these very same topics, i.e. the archetypal story form of Tragedy.[1568] This becomes all the more remarkable if we consider that Holberg had had no access to national archives or any Swedish documents,[1569] which could have illuminated some of the obscurities in Leonora Christina's life, and that he was nevertheless a fundamental source for succeeding scholars. The centrality of Holberg's work to the reception of Leonora Christina becomes particularly manifest if we look at F. C. Schönau's text, which is mostly copied from *Heltindehistorier* and *Dannemarks Riges Historie*. Holberg fathered thus not only the myth of Leonora Christina, but also most of the information and misinformation prevailing about her life until 1869 and beyond. This concerns, for example, the well-known anecdote about Leonora Christina's visit at Kunst-Caspar's smithy, which was penned for the first time by Holberg.[1570]

Ludvig Holberg was well aware of Leonora Christina's historical significance. She appears in several of his historical works as either cause and proof of her husband's importance to Denmark and its allies,[1571] as a fundamental reason why Ul-

---

1568 Cf. White, Hayden. *Metahistory*, p. x. This story form was especially popular in one of the core periods of literary reception of Leonora Christina, i.e. the 19th century *before* 1869, with authors such as Oehlenschläger, Andersen and Hegermann Lindencrone depicting Leonora Christina as a tragic heroine. In the 20th century, however, the Romance story form became more popular (see, for example, the works of Enevoldsen, Holm and Helleberg). This is most likely an effect of the emergence of *Jammers Minde*, which fundamentally repealed Leonora Christina's image as a victim. Rather uncommon within Leonora Christina-literature is the Comedy story form, whereas the paradigm of Satire is almost inconceivable for Leonora Christina-literature.

1569 Paludan-Müller, C[aspar]. 'Dansk Historiografi i det 18de Aarhundrede', p. 50.

1570 See Holberg, Ludvig. *Dannemarks Riges Historie 3*, p. 592: »en curieuse, og hidindtil ubekiendt Historie, som mig derom er communicered«.

1571 See, for example, Holberg's comment on Ulfeldt's first diplomatic visit to the Netherlands (1646-1647): »Faa Ambassader havde været af større anseelse, efftersom den person, som der til blev brugt, var Rigets Hoffmester, havde Kongens ligitimerede Dotter til ægte, og derforuden var over heele Europa bekiendt for sin skarpsindighed, lærdom og veltalenhed« (Holberg, Ludvig. *Dannemarks og Norges Beskrivelse ved Ludvig Holberg, Assessor udi Consistorio og Prof. ved det Kongl. Universitet i Kiøbenhavn*. Copenhagen: Høpffner, 1729, p. 316).

feldt posed a threat to Frederik III,[1572] as a prime example of female excellence,[1573] and as the heroine of her own short account, namely in the third volume of *Dannemarks Riges Historie*.[1574] He introduces and justifies the latter – Leonora Christina's short biography appended at the end of that of her husband – with a reference to his subject's notoriety:

> Hvad Madame Ulfeld angaaer, da, saasom hun er ikke mindre bekiendt i Historien end hendes Herre, saa vill jeg her i sær anføre hendes Historie, hvortil mig ere communicerede nogle materialier saavel af Doct. Otto Sperlings den yngres Manuscript, som af adskillige andre skrevne Documenter, item hvad denne navnkundige Dame selv om sin Skiæbne har antegnet.[1575]

Holberg felt obliged to inform his readers about one of Denmark's most famous women. The peculiar position of Leonora Christina's short biography, however, as well as Holberg's somewhat apologetic remark that he needed to give this information in a separate account, implies that he saw no way to integrate it into the historical core narrative. The prefixed indication of sources (see above), as well as the meticulousness of the ensuing biography allude to an attempt on the author's part to convey scientific substantiality, despite the unorthodox topic, i.e. the content of Leonora Christina's French autobiography, including her pastimes as a young woman. Among other things, Holberg provides an exact chronology of Leonora Christina's activities. The reader learns that Leonora Christina got engaged at the age of seven (sic!), rejected another suitor at the age of twelve, got married at the age of fifteen, started to learn Latin at the age of twenty-one, and travelled in 1646 and then again

---

1572 »Det første af vigtighed, som tildrog sig under Kong Frideriks regiering, vare de 2 største Mænds fald, nemlig Hannibal Sehesteds og Corfitz Ulfeld. Den første var Statholder udi Norge, og den anden Rigets Hoffmester, og havde begge til ægte Christiani 4 døttre avlede med Frue Kirsten Munk« (ibid., p. 340). In this instance, Ulfeldt is not a menace because his wife is the King's half-sister, but because they both belonged to the Munk fraction of the court, whose ambitious members were politically opposed to Christian IV's royal children. See also Holberg, Ludvig. *Dannemarks Riges Historie 2*. Copenhagen: Hans Kongl. Majests. og Universitets Bogtrykkerie, 1733, p. 899, which portrays Leonora Christina as a more active driving force of her husband's aspiration: »Naar man der til lægger [...] hans Gemahls Ambition og store Qualiteter, kand man see hvad som har forført ham at aspirere til højere Ting, end en Undersaatt egner og anstaar«. Later on in the narrative, Ulfeldt is even rumoured to have had royal ambitions himself, because of his wife (»at Rigets Hoffmester Corfitz Ulfeld intet got Hjerte bar til de Kongelige Børn, som Christianus 4 havde avlet med Dronning Anna Catharina, saasom han havde een af Fru Kirstines Døttre til ægte, og derfor efter manges Gisning gik selv frugtsommelig med Konge Tanker« (Holberg, Ludvig. *Dannemarks Riges Historie 3*, p. 26).
1573 Holberg, Ludvig. *Heltindehistorier 1*, pp. 3-16 and 34-55.
1574 Holberg, Ludvig. *Dannemarks Riges Historie 3*, pp. 572-593.
1575 Ibid., p. 572.

in 1649.¹⁵⁷⁶ Obviously, this information is not historically relevant – in the context of a general history as that written by Holberg – but it serves to testify to the seriousness of Holberg's historical studies. It also functions as a means to place this evidentially adept woman alongside her equally competent husband, which ultimately serves to highlight the tragedy of their fall from grace. Holberg's introductory listing of everything Leonora Christina had ever done and that could be deemed intellectual¹⁵⁷⁷ is immediately followed by an opposing report of sorrows: »Hvad hendes Liv og Levnet angaaer, da er det en Kiede af idel Elendighed«.¹⁵⁷⁸ While the initial account of her excellence would thus suggest an equally distinguished life, the ensuing report of her calamities – commencing with her marriage to Ulfeldt, which Holberg summarises as »Begyndelsen til hendes Tragœdie«¹⁵⁷⁹ – only accentuate the depth of her ruin and thus the tragic outline of her life.

Thus, Leonora Christina's erudition and Holberg's academic merit depend upon each other, as the source text referred to by Holberg – the French autobiography – receives its validity as a historical document only through the narrative reproduced by himself, which portrays Leonora Christina as a scholar herself.¹⁵⁸⁰ To the same effect, *Dannemarks Riges Historie* contains lengthy reproductions of hymns and other texts written by Leonora Christina.

In summary, Holberg's historiographical bibliography demonstrates an increasing interest in Leonora Christina, as well as her skills and legacy, since the author went from barely mentioning her (*Dannemarks og Norges Beskrivelse*, 1729), via providing a short biography of Ulfeldt's wife by way of an annex (*Dannemarks Riges Historie 3*, 1735), to dedicating a two-volume publication to Leonora Christina and the likes of her (*Heltindehistorier 1*, 1745). Yet, at the same time, it also demonstrates a trend towards outsourcing the story of Leonora Christina to different academic contexts by annexing them to traditional historiography. This tendency is in all likelihood simply a result of Holberg's patriarchal understanding of history: throughout his general histories, he consistently engages with men first, then with

---

1576 Ibid., p. 572f. The text also reports on Leonora Christina's knowledge of Italian, Spanish, French and German and concludes with the following phrase: »Dette maa være nok talt om hendes naturlige Forstand og Videnskab« (ibid., p. 573).

1577 Holberg's introductory remark at the beginning of the narrative of Leonora Christina's education, which states that she was taught languages, music and mathematics »foruden Fruentimmer-Sager« (ibid., p. 572), additionally affirms her rightful place in the traditionally male-dominated discourse of history.

1578 Ibid., p. 573.

1579 Ibid.

1580 Like all of his successors, Holberg also makes sure to distinguish his own work and sources from »digtet« (ibid., p. 555) texts, such as that published by Rousseau de la Valette, which he deems to be »hans egen Fabriqve« (ibid., p. 558).

women. If there is a list of children to provide, Holberg will proceed not chronologically, but starting with the sons and continuing with the daughters. This prioritisation seems particularly arbitrary in Holberg's depiction of Kirsten Munk's children, of which he mentions the only son, Leonora Christina's insignificant younger brother Valdemar Christian, first. To that effect, the *Heltindehistorier* also originated from the success of the *Heltehistorier*, and Leonora Christina's short biography, provided in the last volume of *Dannemarks Riges Historie*, complements the much longer narrative of Corfitz Ulfeldt (in spite of Holberg's insistence on Leonora Christina's equal notoriety),[1581] whose illustrious career is in turn depicted as an annex to that of Frederik III.

The context of Holberg's engagement with Leonora Christina is furthermore consistent with the author's intention of justifying and promoting the then current state of the Kingdom of Denmark,[1582] which was an absolute monarchy from 1660 until 1849. In accordance with this objective, approximately half of *Dannemarks Riges Historie* consists of the extended biographies of Christian IV and Frederik III (whose death marks the end of the third and last volume), both of which share responsibility for what Holberg presents as the rightful and necessary (re)introduction of absolutism.[1583] C. Paludan-Müller emphasises that Holberg supported the Danish *enevælde* to the point of negating the country's past as an elective monarchy.[1584] According to this ideology, *enevælde* is the kingdom's original and hence

---

1581 Holberg, Ludvig. *Dannemarks Riges Historie 2*, p. 890: »Af Døtterne er den Navnkundigste Eleonora Christina, som blev given til Corfitz Uhlfeld; thi om han var den skarpsindigste Herre paa de Tider, saa blev hun holden for det skarpsindigste Fruentimmer, og er hun i den Henseende lige saa bekiendt i Historien som hendes Herre«.

1582 Cf. Paludan-Müller, C[aspar]. 'Dansk Historiografi i det 18de Aarhundrede', p. 45: »Han har indset, at skulde der henstilles et Billede af det svundne Liv, maatte der vælges blandt dets Efterladenskab, noget forbigaaes, andet fremhæves, ellers vilde der aldrig komme nogen Tegning i Stand«. Besides this educationally motivated reason for primarily depicting the emergence of absolutism, Holberg was of course also subject to censorship – an obstruction of which he made no secret. Cf., e.g., Holberg, Ludvig. *Dannemarks og Norges Beskrivelse*, p. 325: »Der fortælles ellers utallige lystige historier om denne Konge [Christian IV], hvilke jeg ikke tør anføre, saasom de ikke ere autoriserede«.

1583 Holberg's King Christian IV had already attempted to establish the law of succession in his country (ibid., p. 653), but his efforts were frustrated by his younger and hence more dynamic sons-in-law led by Corfitz Ulfeldt, as well as his untimely death in 1648. Frederik III is thus finishing what his father had started.

1584 Paludan-Müller, C[aspar]. 'Dansk Historiografi i det 18de Aarhundrede', p. 43. Cf. Holberg, Ludvig. *Dannemarks Riges Historie 3*, pp. 1-7, but in particular p. 5: »Udi denne Højlovlige Konges [Frederik III's] Tid toge Stænderne den Resolution, som siden skall omtales, og restituerede hans Majestet udi den Rett [the right of succession], som de gamle Danske Konger tilforn havde«.

legitimate state,[1585] degraded only by naturally occurring fluctuations of the King's authority, which Holberg likens to the tides:[1586] the King's authority being at a state of low tide at the end of Christian IV's reign, but quickly approaching high tide with Frederik III. The *adelsvælde* led by Ulfeldt represents thus a necessarily perishable disruption.

With absolute monarchy being thusly presented as a natural, just status, the Ulfeldts' downfall is inevitable. To use both Hayden White's and Ludvig Holberg's terminology, the story of the Ulfeldts is thus a tragedy,[1587] i.e. the exemplification of »resignations of men to the conditions under which they must labor in the world. These conditions, in turn, are asserted to be inalterable and eternal, and the implication is that man cannot change them, but must work within them«.[1588] Ulfeldt, and with him Leonora Christina, was hence bound to fail like a classic tragic hero because he would not accept the parameters of his agency:

> Ja man seer endeligen udi hvad Tilstand Corfitz Ulfeld var, og hvad som kunde forlede ham til at misbruge de store Naturens Gaver, som han besad, til at gaae *uden for en Undersaatts Grændser* [my italics], og at machinere de Ting, som styrtede ham fra den højeste Æres Spidse til den yderste Ulykke og Fordervelse, saa at det Navn, som var den største Prydelse og Zirat for Dannemark, er bleven forhadet, foragteligt og til et Spotte-Navn og Ordsprog blant den gemeene Almue.[1589]

Despite her minor appearance in Holberg's narrative, however, Leonora Christina figures as more than collateral damage to her husband's failure. Instead of simply tagging along, suffering in silence, as many 19th-century depictions would have it, Leonora Christina participates actively in her husband's machinations: »Hun participerede siden i alle de Fortredeligheder, som Corfitz Ulfeld styrtede sig udi [...]«.[1590] She is a tragic heroine on her own account, albeit with the same fatal flaw as Corfitz:

1585 The Norwegian literary historian Francis Bull furthermore points at Holberg's Norwegian roots as another reason for his defence of Danish absolutism in that Norway and Denmark became coequal territories in the new regime, while Holberg's home country had only suffered neglect and exploitation in the preceding decades, when Norway was merely a Danish province and hence governed by Danish noblemen (cf. Bull, Francis. *Ludvig Holberg som historiker*, pp. 88-92).

1586 Cf. Holberg, Ludvig. *Dannemarks Riges Historie 2*, p. 753: »[...] saa at den Kongelige Myndighed har haft sin Flod og Ebbe, og ofte drejet sig efter Tidernes Conjuncturer«.

1587 Cf. Holberg, Ludvig. *Dannemarks Riges Historie 3*, pp. 54, 86, 573, and 596.

1588 White, Hayden. *Metahistory*, p. 9.

1589 Holberg, Ludvig. *Dannemarks Riges Historie 2*, p. 896.

1590 Holberg, Ludvig. *Dannemarks Riges Historie 3*, p. 580.

> [...] Kongen havde ladet dem begge invitere til adskillige Forsamlinger, og tilstaaer Ulfeld selv udi hans saa kalte højtrængende Æres Forsvar, [...] at han formedelst sin Svagheds skyld ikke kunde lade sig indfinde, og at hans Frue ingen Lyst havde dertil, eendel efterdi hun saavel som hendes andre Sødskende vare forbudne at age lige ind paa Slottet, hvilket havde været dem som Kongelige Børn accordered udi Christiani 4 Tid, eendel ogsaa, efterdi dem blev nægted den Titel af Hertuger og Hertuginder af Slesvig Holsten: [...] da Aarsagen dertil gives tilkiende, nemlig at de ingen rett Adkomst havde der til, og at de uden præjudice til det Kongelige og Førstelige Huus ikke kunde føre Titel af begge Førstendommer[.][1591]

As it always happens with tragic heroes, Leonora Christina atones for her sins through repeated and exceptionally harsh punishment: »[H]vis hun i sin Velstand lod sig af Ambition forleede, saa expierede hun den Synd ved trende Fængsler, hvoraf det sidste og haardeste varede udi 23 Aar«.[1592] Holberg's Leonora Christina is thus not an innocent saint – hence the author's positive depiction of Sophie Amalie (see below) – but a human with tragic flaws, for which she is being penalised by a greater power – that greater power being Frederik III as well as the course of history. Since Holberg was unaware of the existence of *Jammers Minde*, he could not transform this narrative into a story of overcoming.

Holberg also ascribes extraordinary agency to Leonora Christina's antagonist Sophie Amalie, whose operations are key to enforce the necessary victory of absolutism:

> Hertil maae man lægge dette, at Dannemark aldrig havde haft en mere heroisk Dronning, og mindre skabt til at leve i Dependence end Sophia Amalia. Man havde forhen seet store Prøver af hendes Fermetet og høje Hierte mod den Uhlfeldske Faction, og man saae end større deraf udi paafølgende Forandring, hvorudi hun spillede den største Rulle.[1593]

Despite their low-key appearance in the narrative, Holberg's women are thus unusually active characters.

A synchronic, or static, narrative[1594] is a common way to construct a Tragedy; but in Holberg's case, this form of emplotment also serves to substantiate his denial

---

1591 Ibid., p. 54.
1592 Ibid., p. 592.
1593 Ibid., p. 436.
1594 White, Hayden. *Metahistory*, p. 10.

of any previous, different forms of regime, i.e. the prevalence of an elected monarchy prior to 1660: »Tragedy and Satire are modes of emplotment« which are consonant with the interest of those historians who perceive behind or within the welter of events contained in the chronicle an ongoing structure of relationships or an eternal return of the Same in the Different«.[1595] By claiming that Denmark had always been a hereditary monarchy, Holberg thus enhances the tragic conformation of the Ulfeldts' story, since it confirms the inescapability of their fate. Tragedy is also an intrinsically educational archetype of a story form, as the fall of the tragic hero is meant to provide its audience with insights into the boundaries of human existence.[1596] This, in turn, coincides with Holberg's didactic intent,[1597] which informed all of his writing but which – with regard to Leonora Christina-literature – had become most evident with the publication of the gynæceum *Heltindehistorier*. In the same text, Holberg employs a Mechanistic paradigm of a historical explanation, which he continues in *Dannemarks Riges Historie*.[1598] Hayden White further contends that the modes of historical explanation mentioned above – the emplotment as Tragedy and the Mechanistic formal argument – generally coincide with a Radical

---

1595 Ibid., p. 11.
1596 Ibid., p. 9.
1597 Cf. Waldemar Westergaard's analysis of 18th-century historiography in Denmark: »The second idea, which had had many adherents but few successes, was to provide readable general accounts of the country's history, representing sound scholarship and serving the practical purpose of providing the country's leaders with histories that would give the needed background and perspective for intelligent performance of duty« (Westergaard, Waldemar. 'Danish History and Danish Historians', p. 169). See also Holberg, Ludvig. *Dannemarks Riges Historie 3*, unpaginated preamble ('Betænkning over Historier'): »[...] gode Historier fornemmeligen skrives [...] for at underviise og at være et Speil, hvorudi man af forbigangne Ting kand see og dømme om tilkommende, lære at kiende sig selv tillige med andre, og erhverve sig den solideste Kundskab udi Morale, Jure publico og Stats-Sager [...]«. An alternative classification of Holberg's didactic historiography has been suggested by Danish historian Sebastian Olden-Jørgensen, who, following a contemporary definition of pragmatic historiography provided in Zedler's *Universallexikon* (1731-1754) in comparison with Holberg's 'Betænkning over Historier', concludes that Holberg's historiographical ideology concurs with the definition of pragmatic historiography: »Den gode historiker er altså kendetegnet ved litterær kvalitet, moralske og politiske vurderinger af historiens aktører, en sammenhængende fortælling og et blik for, hvordan nutiden og fremtiden er resultat af historiske processer, samt ved personlig erfaring og upartiskhed« (Olden-Jørgensen, Sebastian. *Ludvig Holberg som pragmatisk historiker: En historiografisk-kritisk undersøgelse*. Copenhagen: Museum Tusculanum, 2015 (UJDS-Studier), p. 19).
1598 »[A] Mechanist [...] *studies* history in order to divine the laws that actually govern its operations and *writes* history in order to display in a narrative form the effects of those laws« (White, Hayden. *Metahistory*, p. 17). To this effect, Holberg seizes many of the putative laws established in *Heltindehistorier* and exemplifies them in *Dannemarks Riges Historie*. See, for example, Holberg, Ludvig. *Dannemarks Riges Historie 2*, p. 756: »Det er dog merkeligt, at, uanseet all den Habilité, som fandtes hos denne Konge, og den Ævne, som et saa langvarigt Regimente havde givet ham til at extendere den Kongelige Myndighed, og at arbeide paa en Lighed blant Undersaatterne, han dog ikke kunde trænge igiennem med det, som hans sagtmodige Successor bragte til Veje. Den rette Guds Time var endnu ikke kommen: Det heder Accidit in Puncto quod non speratur in Anno. En Leilighed og favorable Conjuncture kand ofte meer udrette end mange Aars Konst og Arbeide«.

ideology,[1599] i.e. the »belie[f] in the necessity of structural transformation [...] in the interest of reconstituting society on new bases«.[1600] While Holberg's advocacy of the tradition of the absolutist regime would thus suggest a Conservative ideology, i.e. the belief that social change occurs naturally and should not be tampered with or even affect the basic structure, i.e. the fundament of the system,[1601] the terminology he applies to the events of 1660 clearly depicts a deep structural change that needed the firm execution of a monarch in order to take place, for the better of society. In particular, Holberg signifies,[1602] and at times literally states,[1603] that the occurrence of a revolution was conducted under the command of Frederik III, which denotes a Radical ideology. Holberg also emphasises repeatedly that the extension of the King's authority occurred only at the high nobility's (*rigsrådet*'s) expense, but for the benefit of everybody else. *Adelsvælde*, unlike *enevælde*, is thus equal to tyranny:

> Kong Frederik I. havde fast lige saa lidet at sige, som en Venetiansk Doga; thi, saasom han ved Adelens Faveur var kommen til Regieringen, saa maatte han stedse leve udi Adelens Dependence, og maatte underskrive alt hvad som sigtede til Adelens Højhed og Almuens Undertrykkelse.[1604]

Finally, Hayden White distinguishes four tropes, which historians may employ for the prefiguration of the historical field. Among these tropes – Metaphor, Metonymy, Synecdoche and Irony – only two apply to an inclusion of Leonora Christina's short biography as a separate narrative in the much broader general history of Denmark. Metonymy and Synecdoche are commonly used to designate parts of an entity: Metonymy in a reductionist, Synecdoche in an integrative manner.[1605] Holberg's general history can hardly be considered to be reduced to the story of Leonora Christina, as Holberg made sure to exclude it from the core narrative. Such a rea-

---

1599 White, Hayden. *Metahistory*, p. 29.
1600 Ibid., p. 24.
1601 Cf. ibid.
1602 Cf. Holberg, Ludvig. *Dannemarks Riges Historie 3*, respectively pp. 9 and 21: »Men, fordi Strengen blev spendt for højt, brast den, og, da man ventede at see Riget forvandlet til en Republiqve, fik det Kongelige Huus med heele Verdens Forundring en Eenevolds Magt og Myndighed«; »Men ved Souverainetets Indførsel ophørte den Tvang tillige med alle andre, da den heele Regierings Machine blev forandret under Kong Friderik, til hvis Historie jeg nu træder«.
1603 Cf. ibid., respectively pp. 434, 435 and 436: »Men just disse mange Uleiligheder gave Aarsag til den paafølgende forunderlige Revolution, hvorved det Kongelige Huus blev bragt udi en florisant Tilstand, og hvorved Riget er kommen udi større Anseelse end tilforn«; »denne store Revolution, som giør en nye Epocha i den Danske Historie«; »den Revolution, som Tidernes Tilstand banede Vei til«.
1604 Ibid., p. 17.
1605 White, Hayden. *Metahistory*, p. 34.

ding of *Dannemarks Riges Historie* would also ignore Holberg's enlightened endeavour to complement his narrative with the diverse positions and viewpoints of the other classes – the clergy, the bourgeoisie and the peasants.[1606] Holberg's Leonora Christina-narrative must thus be considered synecdochal, due to which »a phenomenon can be characterized by using the part to symbolize some *quality* presumed to inhere in the totality«.[1607]

Symptomatic for this type of prefiguration, as well as being typical of the early Leonora Christina-literature, is Holberg's characterisation of Ulfeldt on the private, as opposed to the professional, level. While Ulfeldt's behaviour against his King may be condemned by all accounts, Holberg demonstrates his signature *billighed* by complementing the picture of the unyielding subject with that of the devoted husband and father:

> Han var ellers, som gemeenligen høihiertede Folk ere, complaisant og venlig mod sine Under-Mænd, [...] og elskede og æstimerede sin Gemahl indtil Adoration. Hans Politesse var saa stor, at han derved indtog alles Hierter. Blant andre Exempler paa samme Qvalitet allegeres dette, at da han var bleven forloved med Eleonora Christina, og paa samme Tid havde faaet en Byld paa sit eene Been, tog han i Betænkning at gaae i Sæng med en Frøiken af Kongelig Blod førend han var bleven curered; hvorfor han giorde en Reise til Frankrige, for at give sig udi en habil Chirurgi Hænder, som den Franske Ambassadeur Conte d'Avaux recommenderede ham.[1608]

By constructing a component of Ulfeldt's character out of a relatively unknown anecdote, Holberg adheres to his general prefiguration of the historical field, which essentially consists of an integration of smaller, complementary stories into the main account, whose main predication is generally a different one than those of the micronarratives. Furthermore, though, the example reproduced above is also typical of early writers' attempts to exculpate Ulfeldt through Leonora Christina. Only in this case, the crucial argument is not Leonora Christina's sacrifice – for it is none in this particular narrative – but her husband's love. Holberg *does* in fact allude to the

---

1606 To that effect, Holberg's comment that »det er ikke af Fødselen, men af egen Dyd og Meriter man maa sætte Priis paa Folk«, which was provoked by Ulfeldt's published reproach of Jørgen Walter, stating that he was nothing but »en Hjulmagers Søn« (Holberg, Ludvig. *Dannemarks Riges Historie 3*, both quotations p. 57), is evidence of the author's solidarity with the lower classes and his distaste for the nobility's elitism – a vice Leonora Christina was no stranger to, as evidenced by the present chapter's introductory quotation.

1607 White, Hayden. *Metahistory*, p. 34. See also ibid., p. 35: »By the trope of Synecdoche, however, it is possible to construe the two parts in the manner of an *integration* within a whole that is *qualitatively* different from the sum of the parts and of which the parts are but *microcosmic* replications«.

1608 Holberg, Ludvig. *Dannemarks Riges Historie 3*, p. 571.

detriment Leonora Christina accepted for her husband's sake and he does so by linking what was identified above as the two main topics revolving around her through centuries: her alleged cognisance – and hence the question of truth or factuality – as well as her womanhood:

> Ingen kand vel nægte, at jo den Pligt og Kiærlighed, man er sin Konge og sit Fædreneland skyldig, er større end den som en Hustrue er sin Mand skyldig; men man maa derhos ogsaa bekiende, at den heroiske Dyd, nemlig at røbe sin egen Hosbond af Affection til sit Fædreneland, er rar og fast ubekiendt i vore Tider.[1609]

This notion, repeated by Schönau[1610] and Paus[1611] (see Chapter 3.1.), basically denies any married woman, any culpability in matters concerning her domestic sphere. But it also relativises Holberg's usual approach of *billighed*, according to which – based on the material provided – it was impossible to tell whether Ulfeldt's wife had been guilty or not (and hence, whether she had sacrificed herself or not): »Om hun var Medvider udi det sidste farlige Anslag, som Corfitz Ulfeld havde mod Kongen og Riget, kand ingen for visse sige. Det samme synes dog at have graveret hende mest«.[1612] Holberg's subsequent, concluding reproduction of some of the instances reporting Leonora Christina to have offended Sophie Amalie, which »vise, at det var ikke uden Grund Dronning Sophia Amalia havde fattet saadan Bitterhed mod Frøiken Eleonora«[1613] indicates though, despite all *upartiskhed*, that he considered Leonora Christina guilty to a certain degree.

3.2.2. Ove Malling: *Store og gode Handlinger af Danske, Norske og Holstenere* (1777) – The Romance of the Faithful Wife

> Ej noget synes tungt for Ægte-Kærlighed, Trofasthed er den Dyd, man ej tør blues ved.

In 1775, with the so-called *Guldbergske skoleforordning* named after the Danish theologian and historian Ove Høegh-Guldberg well under way, the Danish language became an essential school subject. Guldberg's decree also stipulated the publica-

---

1609 Ibid., p. 592.
1610 Schönau, Friderich Christian. *Samling 1*, p. 420.
1611 Paus, Hans. *Forsøg til navnkundige danske Mænds Livs og Levnets Beskrivelser 2*, p. 288.
1612 Holberg, Ludvig. *Dannemarks Riges Historie 3*, p. 592.
1613 Ibid., p. 593.

tion of »En Samling af berømmelige og gode Danskes, Norskes, og Holsteiners Handlinger«,[1614] which occurred in 1777. This publication – *Store og gode Handlinger af Danske, Norske og Holstenere* by the historian Ove Malling (1748-1829) – circulated through schools across Denmark and it had two objectives: to establish and teach one correct Danish orthography, and to infuse the country's younger generations with patriotism.[1615] In order to achieve these two goals, Malling's book had to be easy and enjoyable to read, it had to provide short text samples, and its topics had to be carefully selected. Hence, Malling's work is not a general history of Denmark as a country, but a collection of unconnected short stories and anecdotes of great deeds. It consists of eighteen chapters, each dedicated to one particular virtue of which Malling narrates examples from the past.

Leonora Christina is one of the few women to have committed a great deed Malling deemed worth narrating and imitating. Parts of her life's story[1616] are reproduced in the chapter 'Trofasthed', alongside narratives of the great deeds of the Icelander Auðun (known from the Old Norse *Auðunar þáttr vestfirska*) and the Norwegian-Danish missionary Hans Egede, among others, which, like most of Malling's chapters, follows a chronological order. The chronology is only interrupted with the last narrative, the story of the legendary hero Sterkodder, which particularly exemplifies Malling's original statement – that loyalty is a typically *Northern* habit and not to be corrupted by foreign influence:

> Ogsaa har denne National-Tænkemaade længe vedligeholdt sig i Norden; og det var at ønske, at den aldrig maatte tabe sig i dette konstlede Sprog og dette forstilte Væsen, vore fremmede Moder alt for ofte give Navn af fiin Levemaade. Svig bliver dog Svig, om den end forstikkes under nok saa smuk en Maske.[1617]

What Malling addresses here is the Englightenment idea of the noble savage, the idea of a primitive people uncorrupted by the decadence of modern society and culture. This notion is best illustrated by the story of Sterkodder, who, after leaving

---

1614 Hansen, Erik. 'Efterskrift'. In Malling, Ove. *Store og gode Handlinger af Danske, Norske og Holstenere, samlede ved Ove Malling. 1777*, ed. Erik Hansen. Copenhagen: Gyldendal, 1992, p. 567.

1615 Cf. ibid., p. 568.

1616 Malling's sources were the forgery published by Oluf Bang, Tycho de Hofman's *Portraits historiques*, Holberg's *Dannemarks Riges Historie* and Schönau's *Samling* (Malling, Ove. *Store og gode Handlinger af Danske, Norske og Holstenere, samlede ved Ove Malling. 1777*, ed. Erik Hansen. Copenhagen: Gyldendal, 1992, p. 359).

1617 Ibid., p. 347. See also ibid.: »Trofasthed var et af de stærkeste og værdigste Træk i de gamle nordiske Folkes Hoved-Caracteer. [...] Fremmede kiendte vore Forfædre som saadanne trofaste Folk, og ærede dem«.

the Danish court and spending a few years in Sweden, is repulsed to find his former King's son, Ingild, corrupted by foreign manners: »Gamle og gode danske Skikke bleve foragtede, og fremmede Moder bragte ind. Overdaadighed tog Overhaand, Tarvelighed blev forjaget, og det danske Navn, som saa nylig havde været en Skræk for Naboer, begyndte nu at blive til Spot«.[1618] He then urges Ingild to desist from his new ways and return to his native, more natural values:

> [H]an foreholdt ham end videre hvor lidet de nye indbragte sære Skikke passede sig for ham og Landet, og opmuntrede ham med al den Oprigtighed, en gammel troe Tiener kan føle, til at træde i Fædres Fodspor og giøre sit Navn saa agtet som Frodes havde været. [...] Vel viisde han og talede med en Friihed, som i de efterfølgende finere Tider ikke vilde have passet sig; men de Tiders Simpelhed undskyldte den; og Virkningen blev den, han ønskede.[1619]

The message is clear: the simplicity of the Danes exceeds the sophistication of the foreigners in ethical terms and the only way for the Danes to maintain their good values is to keep outsiders aloof. The narrative of Sterkodder is thus that of a people staying true to themselves and that of a loyal servant, who would not abandon his former King's deviated son. This valorisation of the Danish language and the concurrent return to Danish values may be regarded as a backlash of Johann Friedrich Struensee's reign and its end in 1772, which Malling merely discards as collective confusion.[1620] Thus, the story of Sterkodder, who ends all foreign influence on the King, is a centrepiece of his chapter on 'Trofasthed' and hence longer than most of the other narratives.

Leonora Christina's story is also longer than the average. Her long-lasting imprisonment is, of course, the main evidence of her *trofasthed*. Through this punishment, her loyalty becomes exemplary as it is entirely voluntary and unquestioned. It is not a deserved penalty, since Malling rejects the idea that Leonora Christina had been an active participant in Ulfeldt's schemes: »Det kunde ikke nogensinde bevi-

---

1618 Ibid., p. 361.
1619 Ibid., p. 362.
1620 »Atter her kiendte vi da et Beviis paa den Hengivenhed for Landet og Folket, vi have seet og see saa virksom baade hos Ham og hos vores Juliane [King Christian VII's stepmother and mother of the subsequent King]. For at vise den i sin Værd, behøves ikke her at forfriske Erindringen af det forvirrede i de Dage, der endnu ikke ere glemte« (ibid., p. 527). Subsequent scholarship, too, sees Malling's work and its successors mainly as part of a widespread »Reaktion fra nordisk Nationalitets Side [...] imod Tyskeriet« (Paludan-Müller, C[aspar]. 'Dansk Historiografi i det 18de Aarhundrede', p. 144). The Danes' contempt for *Tyskeriet* and its expression in Malling's and subsequent publications may have also been a factor in Sophie Amalie's mostly negative reputation. In this context, *Store og gode Handlinger* serves as no indicator, though, since neither the Queen nor the King play a part in Malling's narrative.

ses at hun havde havt Deel i nogle af de Anslag, Ulfeld var ubesindig og hevngierrig nok til at fatte mod sit Fædreneland. Ikke heller giver Historien nogen grundet Formodning om, at nogen Overeensstemmelse i saadanne Hensigter har været Grunden til hendes Eenighed med ham«. Instead, it is an entirely self-imposed principle to which she sees no alternative:

> Det lader meget meere til at hun stedse lod sig lede af en Trofasthed, som hun havde vant sig til at ansee som Pligt. I det mindste kan man ei slutte andet af en kort Beskrivelse hun i sine sidste Aar har opsat over sit Levnet, hvori hun stedse nævner sin Mand med Høiagtelse, og taler om sin Hengivenhed for ham, som om en Pligt.[1621]

Leonora Christina had cultivated her signature virtue since her childhood, as exemplified by another anecdote narrated by Malling. When the little Countess was twelve years old, she rejected another suitor due to her loyalty towards her fiancé. Malling emphasises that her reaction was self-imposed since others, including her own father, who had arranged the engagement with Ulfeldt (which is also pointed out by Malling),[1622] were willing to renege on his promise to Ulfeldt. Leonora Christina, however, remains steadfast:

> I hendes tolvte Aar blev hun begiert af en Fyrste af Saxen. Denne Forbindelse var vel anseeligere; der menes og at Kongen nu forandrede sin Beslutning, og ønskede at bringe hende til at bryde sit første Løfte; og der skal have været mange andre, der søgde at overtale hende til det samme. Men, endskiønt dette Løfte i saa ung en Alder snarere var giort af andre paa hendes Vegne, end af hende selv, havde hun dog efterhaanden, som Alderen og Skiønsomheden tiltog, meer og meer samtykt det; og dette samtykte Løfte blev hende alt for vigtigt til at hun vilde bryde det.[1623]

Just like the tale of Sterkodder's simple loyalty, this anecdote connects directly to Malling's introductory text, which defines the term *trofasthed*:

1621 Malling, Ove. *Store og gode Handlinger*, p. 358.
1622 »Eleonore Christine, en datter af Christian den Fierde, blev, da hun var syv Aar gammel, efter Kongens hendes Faders Villie, forlovet med Corfitz Ulfeld [...]« (ibid., p. 356). This piece of information could have been omitted, since engagements, at least within the nobility, were usually arranged by the bride's father. It is, however, significant in terms of distinguishing Leonora Christina's *trofasthed* from her father's comparative fickleness.
1623 Ibid., p. 357.

> Foruden de Forbindtligheder, som Lovene paalægge os, ere der endnu andre, som vi selv ved frivilligt Samtykke, ved Løfter og visse Handlinger kan paadrage os: at efterkomme de første er en Lydighed, Lovene fordre: at opfylde de sidste er en Redelighed, en retskaffen Mand, om Love end aldrig bøde det, dog holder sig forpligtet til; og ved at føle, vise og vedligeholde denne Redelighed, kiendes den Trofaste.[1624]

Loyalty is thus only true and just if it is self-determined and not imposed by others. Malling's word choice – *Pligt* and *Lov* – however, refers only to the invariable validity of true loyalty; it is not employed to question the sincere love Leonora Christina experienced, for she and her husband are portrayed as a perfect match:

> Eleonore Christine var ellers et Fruentimmer af usædvanlige Egenskaber. Naturen havde givet hende en ypperlig Forstand: hun selv giorde sig Umage for at dyrke den ved Videnskaber. [...] I de tvende sidste Sprog [Spanish and Italian], som og i andre Videnskaber gav hendes Mand hende Underviisning; thi ogsaa han foreenede mange Indsigter med en fiin Forstand; og denne Lighed i Sinds Kræfter og fælles Agtelse for Kundskab var uden Tvivl det, der meget knyttede det stærke Baand mellem disse Ægtefolk.[1625]

This connection between Leonora Christina and her husband is also the main reason why Leonora Christina overcomes her imprisonment. To be sure, King Christian V releases his relative from the Blue Tower, hence determining her eventual freedom.[1626] However, the process of overcoming her imprisonment occurs much sooner and is initiated by Leonora Christina herself, as she reminds herself of her duties:

> Denne hendes Bestandighed i Ægteskabs Pligter undgieldte hun dyrt, endog efter Ulfelds Død, da hun maatte henbringe 23 Aar i et haardt Fængsel. Hun fortrød den dog ikke, i alt hvad hun endog derfor maatte lide, men ansaae det meget meere som en Trøst i hendes Elendighed, at hun havde iagttaget, hvad hun troede at skylde en Ægtemand.[1627]

A comparison of Leonora Christina's fate with that of the heroine of the preceding narrative, Erik of Pomerania's wife Philippa (1394-1430), suggests that the marital love that strengthened Leonora Christina's belief in her cause is the main reason for

---

1624 Ibid., p. 347.
1625 Ibid., p. 359.
1626 Ibid.
1627 Ibid., p. 358.

her ability to endure and outlive her imprisonment. Philippa is equally loyal to her spouse: she accepts his mistresses and his indifference as a husband, all the while fulfilling his duties as King whenever he is unable to do so.[1628] But when one of her attempts to elevate Erik's renown fails, he castigates her harshly:

> Da Erik fik det at høre, blev han saa forbittret imod Dronningen, at han endog skal have slaget hende. Han bedømde Sagen efter Udfaldet, glemde hendes øvrige store Fortienester, og tænkde ikke paa, at af alt det, han selv hidtil i Regierings Sager havde foretaget, var sielden, end ei det allermindste, lykket. Men Dronningen græmmede dette saa meget, at hun strax gik i et Kloster, og døde der Aaret efter.[1629]

Philippa's story is thus a Tragedy, as she fails to see that the object of her – otherwise admirable – loyalty is unworthy of her virtue. According to the analysis model developed by Hayden White, the narrative of Leonora Christina, however, is a Romance, the classic story of a victory of Good (Leonora Christina) over Evil (her harsh, unjustified punishment)[1630] and of a hero overcoming all obstacles. This is a story archetype that became increasingly popular with 20th-century writers of Leonora Christina-literature, but it can also be found among earlier texts, such as Louise Hegermann Lindencrone's 'Billedet' or G. v. R.'s *Eleonore Gräfin von Ulefeld* (see Chapters 2.4.1. and 3.1., respectively).

Typical of this form of emplotment is a configuration of structural transformation, which results in a diachronic, or processionary, narrative: »Romance and Comedy stress the emergence of new forces or conditions out of processes that appear at first glance either to be changeless in their essence or to be changing only in their phenomenal forms«.[1631] The new forces depicted in Malling's narrative are, on the macro-level, the changing times and the threat posed to Danish identity by intruding, foreign values, and on the micro-level, the drastic changes Leonora Christina experiences, which are also enhanced by the dense, simplified form of the narrative. In this short narrative, high and low points succeed directly: the prosecution

---

[1628] Ibid., p. 355.

[1629] Ibid., p. 356.

[1630] Leonora Christina's imprisonment appears unjustified since Malling questions both her involvement in and approval of Ulfeldt's schemes (ibid., p. 358). The reason for her imprisonment remains unstated, as the account jumps from her successful defence speech in Malmö directly to her sentence in the Blue Tower (ibid.), hence leaving loyalty as the *only* reason for this punishment (while also increasing the dominant image of structural transformation). Finally, Malling emphasises that Leonora Christina's incarceration continued after the actual perpetrator's death (ibid.), which increases the impression that there had been no legal reason at all for her imprisonment.

[1631] White, Hayden. Metahistory, p. 11.

of Ulfeldt begins immediately after the King's death and Leonora Christina's imprisonment follows seemingly immediately after her successful plea in Malmö.[1632]

Malling's emplotment of the Leonora Christina-subject matter in the form of a Romance corresponds with a Formist argument, in that Malling does not tell a *Danmarkshistorie*, but several, unconnected[1633] anecdotes, in which Danes, Norwegians and the people of Holstein have demonstrated virtuousness: »[I]n Formist conceptions of historical explanation, the uniqueness of the different agents, agencies, and acts which make up the 'events' to be explained is central to one's inquiries, not the 'ground' or 'scene' against which these entities arise«.[1634] This authorial intention inured to the benefit of Leonora Christina, whose story has had a traditionally central position in semi-historical, moralistic works, such as the *gynæceum*, while being largely overlooked in general histories. Since Malling's work is far from any attempt to provide a cohesive history of a country or even a dynasty, i.e. what is generally considered to be historiography proper,[1635] Leonora Christina dominates the account as much as any other historical character that commited great and good deeds.

Store og gode Handlinger furthermore promotes nostalgic patriotism, as indicated above. Sometimes this ideology emerges in subtle ways, for example in the opposition of the simple Northman Sterkodder to foreign, Saxon[1636] manners. Quite frequently, though, the notion that everything was better back in the olden days appears as blatant as possible:

1632 Cf. Malling, Ove. *Store og gode Handlinger*, p. 358.

1633 Cf. White, Hayden. Metahistory, p. 15: »To use [Stephen C.] Pepper's terms [as established in *World Hypotheses*], Formism is essentially 'dispersive' in the analytical operations it carries out on the data, rather than 'integrative', as both Formist explanatory strategy tends to be wide in 'scope' – ample in the kinds of particulars it identifies as occupying the historical field – its generalizations about the processes discerned in the field will be inclined to lack conceptual 'precision'«.

1634 Ibid., p. 14.

1635 Accordingly, Malling's work has not been deemed a historical source (Hansen, Erik. 'Efterskrift', p. 569), but a curious example of the late 18th century's ideology: »*Store og gode Handlinger* er ikke historieforskning og slet ikke skønlitteratur, ej heller høj litterær sprogkunst. Derimod ideologi og pædagogik med tykke streger under« (Det Danske Sprog- og Litteraturselskab. 'Forord'. In Malling, Ove. *Store og gode Handlinger af Danske, Norske og Holstenere, samlede ved Ove Malling. 1777*, ed. Erik Hansen. Copenhagen: Gyldendal, 1992, p. 9). Yet despite all current historical criticism of the book, *Store og gode Handlinger* was long regarded a central piece of history by Danish scholars (such as A. D. Jørgensen) and writers (such as Oehlenschläger; see Hansen, Erik. 'Efterskrift', pp. 573 and 579) alike. However, Malling's influence on the Danish playwright hardly concerns Leonora Christina's presentation in the drama *Dina*, as the two writers are concerned with very different periods of Leonora Christina's life, and since Oehlenschläger took considerable liberties with his subject matter.

1636 Malling, Ove. *Store og gode Handlinger*, p. 360.

Ei heller er det ved enhver anmærket i Fortællingen selv, hvad Aar og Tid den har tildraget sig. Aarsagen til det første har været, at jeg ved at følge chronologisk Orden overalt, vilde undertiden have været i Nødvendighed til at sætte de bedste Træk først og de svageste sidst, hvilket jeg under Arbeidet befandt at ville giøre Læsningen mindre behagelig.[1637]

Malling's scorn of societal change involves an insistance on a reversion to the Northerners' original, pristine values and behaviour, partially embodied by Leonora Christina. The ideology is clearly discernible. Among four possible modes of explanation by ideological implication, Hayden White distinguishes the Anarchist ideology as an inclination

> to idealize a *remote past* of natural-human innocence from which men have fallen into the corrupt »social« state in which they currently find themselves. They [Anarchist historians], in turn, project this utopia onto what is effectively a non-temporal plane, viewing it as a possibility of human achievement *at any time*, if men will only seize control of their own essential humanity, either by an act of will or by an act of consciousness which destroys the socially provided belief in the legitimacy of the current social establishment.[1638]

Malling's Anarchist projection of the historical field into an almost ahistorical text – ahistorical due to the lack of a consistent chronology, historical correlation or a critical treatment of his subject – correlates in turn with his Formist, dispersive representation, in that both modes of historical explanation favour anecdotal and moralistic over general history, hence allowing for a dominant portrayal of Leonora Christina instead of Corfitz Ulfeldt.

Finally, all of the modes of historical explanation mentioned above generally correlate to the trope of Synecdoche: »With Synecdoche, which is regarded by some theorists as a form of Metonymy, a phenomenon can be characterized by using the part to symbolize some quality presumed to inhere in the totality, as in the expression 'He is all heart'«.[1639] White's theory of tropes provides the key to understanding the relevance of Malling's text to the contemporary and subsequent reception of Leonora Christina, as it presents *Store og gode Handlinger* as the beginning of the nationalistic utilisation of Leonora Christina, which was so dominant

---

1637 Ibid., p. 23.
1638 White, Hayden. Metahistory, p. 25.
1639 Ibid., p. 34.

in the 19th century. With Synecdoche »using the part to symbolize some quality presumed to inhere in the totality«, the part being Leonora Christina's story, the quality being *trofasthed* and the totality the Northern spirit as it used to and should be, Leonora Christina emerges as a national symbol. Malling even anticipates the romantic period's tendency to disembody (and hence glorify) the once living human[1640] by ascribing narrative preference over the human to the deed: »Men her agte man, at det er Handlingen, der egentlig sees paa, og at den ikke nævnes for Personens, men Personen for Handlingens Skyld«.[1641] Finally, since *Store og gode Handlinger* was widely read in schools across the country as well as by influential writers and historians,[1642] it provided the perfect breeding ground for a continued reception of Leonora Christina as an emblem of Denmark itself.

3.2.3. J. A. Fridericia: *Danmarks Riges Historie 4* (1896-1902) – A Tragedy of Vengeance

> I dette 1684. Aar saae ieg Encke Dronningen falde need aff den Stoel, hun hitzis op med til Kongens Gemack; Stoelen løb paa Tritzerne for hastig need, saa hun falt Neeßkrus need, oc støtte sig paa Knæerne; [...] Ieg begaff mig til ett Gott Taal[.]
>
> (*Jammers Minde*, p. 234f.)

The notion of Leonora Christina as an embodiment of her fatherland continued well into the 19th century (see, for example, Chapters 2.2.1. and 2.2.3. on Hans Christian Andersen). The publication of *Jammers Minde* in 1869, however, changed this idea. Subsequent portrayals of Leonora Christina are not quite as adoring, yet are infinitely more nuanced than the static saint depicted by Hans Christian Andersen or the obedient wife portrayed by Adam Oehlenschläger.

When the historian Julius Albert Fridericia (1849-1912) wrote the fourth volume of *Danmarks Riges Historie*, a monumental, popular national history published in six volumes between 1896 and 1907, he could thus address an audience with

---

1640 This is another fundamental reason for the significant reception shift occasioned by the publication of *Jammers Minde*. Leonora Christina's description of her life in the Blue Tower is highly physical; while reading, one can almost smell the stench of the sullied walls and feel the colony of fleas that inhabited her stockings. This realistic text was hardly compatible with the ethereous image of the martyr in the tower writers of the late 18th and 19th century had created.

1641 Malling, Ove. *Store og gode Handlinger*, p. 22.

1642 On the bearing of *Store og gode Handlinger* »i nationalhistorisk Retning« see Paludan-Müller, C[aspar]. 'Dansk Historiografi i det 18de Aarhundrede', p. 144f.

a different kind of background knowledge[1643] and with a different kind of Leonora Christina in mind. Only two years before starting his work on *Danmarks Riges Historie 4*, Fridericia published *Adelsvældens sidste Dage*, a historical analysis of the years following the death of Christian IV up until 1660. This book constitutes a substantial hypotext to the understanding of Fridericia's depiction of the same period in *Danmarks Riges Historie 4*[1644] as it addresses the same topics, yet in more detail and more bluntly than it was possible in a multi-volume work written by nine authors.[1645]

Both works written by Fridericia generally exhibit an outlook typical of the late 19th century, i.e. one of averseness towards the seemingly more primitive 17th century. This notion is most openly asserted in H. F. Ewald's *Leonora Kristina* (see Chapter 2.4.2.), but the topic of primitivity, of the instinct-driven and at times even brutal Baroque human, was also of essential relevance to J. P. Jacobsen's portrayal of the eponymous heroine of *Fru Marie Grubbe* (see Chapter 2.7.2.), a novel partially inspired by *Jammers Minde*. Fridericia's disesteem for this age, together with the narrative boundaries associated with a division of authorship, resulted in a reserved, almost detached view on the fateful events of the mid-17th century. The agents inhabiting the historical field described in *Danmarks Riges Historie 4* are a different breed than Fridericia's contemporaries. They are more primitive, more vulgar, and hence their age is doomed to remain in its daunting state. Unlike Holberg and Scocozza (see Chapter 3.2.4.), the author of *Danmarks Riges Historie 4* portrays the political revolution of 1660 not as a step in the country's development, but rather as the same old story, only in a different format. Fridericia, however, also

---

1643 In *Danmarks Riges Historie 4* and in *Adelsvældens sidste Dage*, Fridericia refers to many details of Leonora Christina's life without specifying the circumstances, since at this point he could justifiably assume that most readers would be able to fill in the narrative blanks. In *Adelsvældens sidste Dage*, for example, the betrayal and extradition of Leonora Christina at the hands of her relative King Charles II of England is only alluded to (»[e]n anden Tilfredsstillelse for Ulfeldt, der for øvrigt ligeledes senere fik sit triste Efterspil«, see Fridericia, J. A. *Adelsvældens sidste Dage: Danmarks Historie fra Christian IV's Død til Enevældens Indførelse (1648-1660)*. Copenhagen: P. G. Philipsen, 1894, p. 113) while in *Danmarks Riges Historie 4*, the same event is summarised with a point-blank reference to its notoriety: »Det er ikke nødvendigt at dvæle ved Leonora Kristinas Skæbne. Alle veed, hvorledes hun blev udleveret af den engelske Konge Karl II, i Aug. 1663 ført til København, indespærret i Blaataarn og underkastet resultatløse Forhør for at faa udforsket hendes Mands landsforræderske Planer og hendes egen Delagtighed deri« (Fridericia, J. A. *Danmarks Riges Historie 4: 1588-1699. Historisk illustreret*. Copenhagen: Det Nordiske Forlag, [1907], p. 498). Another example is Fridericia's short summary of the Malmö trial, which implies the assumption that the reader will be familiar with details such as those concerning Ulfeldt's illness, which is only briefly mentioned but not explained (see ibid., p. 434).

1644 The fourth volume of *Danmarks Riges Historie* covers the years 1588-1699, i.e. from the beginning of Christian IV's reign until the death of Christian V.

1645 Of the six volumes of *Danmarks Riges Historie*, some were written by more than one author: Volume 3 was written by A. Heise and V. Mollerup, Volume 6 by A. D. Jørgensen (who passed away while working on this volume), N. Neergaard and A. Høyer.

lived in an age beyond this previous phase. Born in 1849, he could not witness the upheaval that ended absolutism and could thus depict the age that preceded his lifetime as if the events narrated in his book belonged to a dim and distant past. The author's narrative is thus emplotted in the structurally continuous way of a Tragedy, an archetypal story of limitation and resignation.[1646] These limitations affect every social stratum ranging from the King to the lower classes, since the incompetence of the former excludes the latter from any real political participation.

Fridericia's narrative of incompetence and greed starts with Christian IV, a ruffian whose ideology and administration are obsolete[1647] and whose private relations are a determining factor in his and his son's reign. The latter circumstance discredits the monarch even further, as the very same relations appear somewhat shady. The King's well-known second marriage to Kirsten Munk occurred privately and could thus be contested,[1648] and it resulted in a fateful series of appointments that can only be termed reversed nepotism – reversed in the sense that he chose his sons-in-law based on their professional potential. Furthermore, the King's liaison with Vibeke Kruse borders on pornocracy, due to the mystical character and extraordinary influence ascribed to her by Fridericia:

> Der hviler et underligt Slør over denne Kvinde; man kjender ikke bestemt hendes Oprindelse, man har ikke noget Billede af hende, man véd ikke, hvilke Egenskaber hos hende der har fængslet Kongen; men sikkert er det, at hun har haft en meget betydelig Magt over ham, en Magt, som hun benyttede paa flere Maader, men især til at berige sig og sine Børn.[1649]

1646 Cf. White, Hayden. *Metahistory*, p. 9.

1647 Fridericia, J. A. *Danmarks Riges Historie 4*, p. 78: »Der var i hans Stemningsliv en ikke ringe Godmodighed, men ved Siden deraf en opfarende Heftighed, en Tilbøjelighed til at anse sig for forurettet, en stærk Sanselighed, higende efter Tilfredsstillelse hos Kvinder og i stærke Drikke, paa Bunden en vis Brutalitet. [...] Ikke alene var der i ham en Rest af Middelalderens Fyrste, for hvem Husholdning var en lige saa magtpaaliggende Gerning som Statskunst, men han manglede i det hele Forstaaelsen af det underordnedes naturlige Plads. [...] Han savnede Selvbeherskelse, Evne til at værdsætte Øjeblikket, dybere politisk Sans, ogsaa mere indgaaende politiske Kundskaber, fremfor alt dog trods sin Naturs rige Anlæg Aandens finere Dannelse«. Incidentally, Fridericia ascribes the blame for the country's financial ruin in the middle of the 17th century to mainly two men (»Den Politik, som førte til Katastrofen 1643, var ikke Raadets Flertals, men Kongens og hans daværende Yndling Korfits Ulfelds« (ibid., p. 327)), both of whom he considers agents of a former, obsolete political system, i.e. the Middle Ages (see above and Fridericia, J. A. *Adelsvældens sidste Dage*, p. 163: »Men ved Siden heraf gik hos ham [Ulfeldt] ogsaa en anden individualistisk, men mere middelalderlig Tankegang, den rent aristokratiske Hævdelse af den forurettede Adelsmands Ret til at opsige sin Herre [...]«).

1648 See Fridericia, J. A. *Danmarks Riges Historie 4*, p. 80.

1649 Fridericia, J. A. *Adelsvældens sidste Dage*, p. 4. See also ibid., p. 9, which provides further evidence of Fridericia's unusual conviction that Vibeke Kruse had any influence at all: »Han [Ulfeldt] havde vel ogsaa en Følelse af, at det ikke kunde vare længe, inden han vilde komme til at staa overfor en Medbejler farligere end Hannibal Sehested, *farligere* [my italics] end Vibeke Kruse og Claus v. Ahlefeldt«.

However, despite Christian IV's flaws and abysmal foreign policy, Fridericia acknowledges that the same flaws lent this monarch the fame of being a King of the people[1650] – another important factor that contributed to Leonora Christina's earlier fame as national heroine – which in turn made his adversaries, i.e. the nobility, the scapegoat of the age: »Ganske vist var Klagerne over Adelens Holdning i Landets onde Dage ikke fuldt berettigede«.[1651]

Frederik III utilised this atmosphere of resentment towards the nobility to his own advantage when he ascended the throne in 1648. Yet this monarch is not beyond reproach either. According to Fridericia, he was less impulsive, and hence more successful, than his father,[1652] but also significantly influenced by his advisers,[1653] his brothers-in-law and his wife, all of German origin:

> Ved det optraadte ogsaa fremmede Gæster med udprægede monarkiske Grundsætninger, især Dronningens Brødre, de brunsvig-lüneburgske Hertuger, hvis hyppige Nærværelse var en Kilde til Ængstelse for Rigsraad og Adel. Og som dette Hofs Midtpunkt stod Dronning Sofie Amalie. [...] Hendes Indflydelse skyldtes det sikkert ogsaa, at Kongen og Hoffet i over et Aar, fra April 1654 til Juni 1655, tog Ophold uden for Kongeriget, mest paa Flensborghus, og, fængslet af Fester paa Fester, ikke lod sig fordrive af Rigsraadernes Opfordringer. Ved hendes Ødselhed steg Udgifterne til Hoffet, men endnu vigtigere var det, at hun var en Hovedkraft til at drive sin Ægtefælle frem mod Planer om Enevælden, og efter samtidiges Opfattelse tillige mod Krigen.[1654]

In *Adelsvældens sidste Dage*, the author pronounces his assessment of the Queen's influence even more bluntly:

1650 Fridericia, J. A. *Danmarks Riges Historie 4*, p. 323: »Mere betød, at Følelsen af Kongen som Rettens Indehaver og de svages Beskytter var vokset under Kristian IV. Store Svagheder havde været forbundne med hans Personlighed, men desuagtet havde han i Iver for sin Gerning, i Opofrelse og personligt Magt raget højt op over sin Samtid; det jævne og folkelige ved hans Optræden havde desuden vundet ham mange Hjerter. Intet Under derfor, at de lavere Klasser havde lagt Ansvaret for de begaaede Fejl, skønt Kongen havde en stor Del af Skylden for dem, over paa Rigsraad og Adel og vendt sin Kærlighed mod ham. I hans Alderdoms sørgelige Dage var Kærligheden bleven forbunden med Medlidenhed; Kongen og Landet var smeltet sammen som det fælles, der var forurettet af de fremmede og af de indfødte fornemme«.
1651 Ibid., p. 327.
1652 Ibid., p. 287: »[E]llers var han de lange og tavse Overvejelsers Mand og under dem let paavirkelig af sine Omgivelser, men ikke desto mindre først og fremmest selvbehersket i Gerning og i Tale«.
1653 Cf. ibid., p. 366: »Men ogsaa den Indflydelse, som Kongens nærmeste tyske Raadgivere, især Gabel og Lente, allerede tidligere havde haft, voksede sikkert betydeligt i disse Aar. Ikke faa andre Tyskere optoges i den danske Adelsstand, og adskillige af dem var nøje knyttede til Kongens og Dronningens Hof«.
1654 Ibid., p. 367.

> Men stærkere Magt end nogen af disse Mænd havde dog maaske allerede paa dette Tidspunkt Hertug Frederiks Hustru, Sophie Amalie, Datteren af en af Trediveaarskrigens ejendommeligste og mest energiske Skikkelser, Hertug Georg af Brunsvig-Lyneborg, Søster til Fyrster med bestemt udprægede enevældige Tendenser, selv en forlystelsessyg, ærgjerrig og fremfor alt lidenskabelig Kvinde.[1655]

The words »allerede paa dette Tidspunkt« imply that Sophie Amalie's grip on her spouse would only increase with the years, but to contend that Sophie Amalie had a tremendous influence on her husband is almost as bold as stating that Vibeke Kruse had any influence on Christian IV at all.[1656] The Queen's hold on Frederik III seems rather to have diminished soon after the introduction of absolutism. When the new constitution, *Kongeloven*, was introduced in 1665, it granted the Queen no influence in the case of her husband's death. This attests to a reluctance on the King's behalf to expand Sophie Amalie's authority. A medal found in the King's private collection in 1681,[1657] and presumably coined in or some time around 1664, furthermore indicates a very aggressive domestic strife due to rumours of the Queen's infidelity. The aforementioned nobleman Kaj Lykke, temporary fiancé of Leonora Christina's eldest daughter and originator of these rumours, was sentenced to death as a result of his improvidence. Notwithstanding this verdict, however, Frederik III may have believed these claims since the medal found in his collection depicts a man covering his face with one hand, looking through his splayed fingers. The heading of this image reads »nicht durch brillen« ('not through glasses') – most likely a hint to the alleged adultery. The verso shows a headless woman underneath the heading »Der Rest ist gutt« ('The rest is good'). All sources agree that this must have been a warning directed at an unfaithful wife.[1658]

Fridericia's portrayal of Vibeke Kruse and Sophie Amalie may thus seem arbitrary, but it fits the author's overall evaluation of this age as having been significantly directed by women, albeit mostly through their men and usually in a very impi-

---

1655 Fridericia, J. A. *Adelsvældens sidste Dage*, p. 11.

1656 Besides the hatred the Munk clan nourished for this woman, the only reason for this rare conviction seems to be the circumstance that Christian IV made sure that his and Vibeke's children were taken care of: their son Ulrik Christian Gyldenløve became a general and their daughter Elisabeth Sophie Gyldenløve married a Danish nobleman. This is, however, an insufficient basis for the assumption that a former servant had an unusual amount of influence over a King, since Christian IV supplied all of his children, even all of the *Gyldenløver* (i.e. the illegitimate ones), with promising futures; the only exception being Kirsten Munk's youngest daughter Dorothea Elisabeth, whom Christian IV believed to be a cuckoo's egg.

1657 Today, the medal can be viewed in *Den kongelige Mønt og Medaillesamling* in the National Museum in Copenhagen.

1658 See, for example, Hein, Jørgen and Katia Johansen. *Sophie Amalie*, image no. 16.

ous manner.[1659] Moreover, a key actor in the 17th century's most dramatic strife was Kirsten Munk's circle, for even though this woman was subject to occasional house arrest outside of Copenhagen after her separation from the King, she continued to intervene through her daughters and, through them, her sons-in-law:

> Thi under Krigen og i de følgende Aar blussede Striden mellem Kristine Munks Slægt og Vibeke Kruse for Alvor op; den sidstes Indflydelse hos Kongen var urokket og tilmed støttet ved hendes og Kongens Datter Elisabet Sofies Trolovelse med den holstenske Adelsmand Generalmajor Klaus Ahlefeld. Kvinderne lagde Tønderet til Ilden, og Følgen blev, at Ægtefællerne til Kristine Munks Døtre, hidtil først og fremmest Kongens Svigersønner, fra nu af, tilskyndede af deres Hustruer og trods al anden Uenighed forenede paa eet Punkt, stod sammen som Svogre for at hævde deres Svigermoders Ret.[1660]

Due to their singular capabilities and marital unity,[1661] Leonora Christina and her husband are the undisputed leaders of the Munk clan:

> Det var uden Tvivl disse Kongedøtre, mellem hvilke Leonora Christina ragede højt op i Henseende til Aand og Sjælskraft, som gav det saakaldte »Svogerskab«, den Kreds, der bestod af Christian IV's og Kirstine Munks Børn og Svigersønner, det Fællesskab, som deres Ægtefællers Skindsyge ellers let fuldstændigt vilde have sønderrevet, og det var dem, som gav Spliden den Tilsætning af Kamp af Kvinde mod Kvinde, der blev karakteristisk for den saa vel under Christian IV som under Frederik III.[1662]

Through her hatred for Vibeke Kruse and Sophie Amalie, as well as through her leading position within the Munk clan, Leonora Christina is thus at the center of the predominantly female conflict which in Fridericia's view coined the century. To complete the collage of influential women, Leonora Christina, too, is said to have had a tremendous influence on her husband. Fridericia states this unmistakably in *Adelsvældens sidste Dage*[1663] and her position and agency in *Danmarks Riges Historie 4* are also more autonomous. While earlier histories and many literary works

---

1659 Cf. Fridericia, J. A. *Adelsvældens sidste Dage*, p. 4: »Elskerinde og forstødt morganatisk Hustru, Kongekuld og Kongekuld stod mod hinanden«.
1660 Fridericia, J. A. *Danmarks Riges Historie 4*, p. 279.
1661 See ibid., pp. 164 and 359.
1662 Fridericia, J. A. *Adelsvældens sidste Dage*, p. 4.
1663 Ibid., p. 163: »Hvad Leonora Christina angaar, er Kilderne til Opklaring af hendes Holdning kun fattige, men adskilligt taler for, at en svensk Beretning staar til Troende, naar den fastslaar hendes store Indflydelse paa hendes Mand. Den stærke Kvinde aandede og levede for Hævnen over den Tort, der var tilføjet hende selv, hendes Mand og hendes Børn«.

tend to stress Leonora Christina's marital loyalty, and hence the dependency on her husband, Fridericia highlights her active participation, either by specifically naming her while depicting Corfitz's path to treason instead of concealing her presence on that path,[1664] or by referring to the thirst for revenge that nobody could deny any longer after 1869:

> Men dannede de faldne og landflygtige end intet Parti, saa var dog Korfits Ulfelds og hans Hustrus Holdning langtfra betydningsløs. De begge, og navnlig Leonora Kristina, var i adskillige Henseender langt finere Naturer end deres Slægt og afgiver en betagende Modsætning til denne ved deres gensidige Trofasthed og ved den Udholdenhed, hvormed de i Medgang og Modgang stod sammen med hinanden. Men paa den anden Side har disse og de nærmest følgende Aar sat den største Plet paa deres Historie. Det kan næppe lade sig gøre her at skille dem ad. Trods Manglen af ligefremme Vidnesbyrd maa det antages berettiget at tro om Leonora Kristina, at hun i sin stærke Attraa efter Hævn over den Uret, hun mente sig ramt af, har billiget sin Husbonds Handlemaade, og hvad denne angaar, udviklede den sig stærkere og stærkere til det ligefremme Landsforræderi.[1665]

Jammers Minde has thus coined the post-1869 reception of Leonora Christina in manifold ways. Not only did it derange the conception of the silently suffering saint evoked by Leonora Christina's martyrdom behind the walls of the Blue Tower and replace this conception with one of everlasting vindictiveness, but it also connected Leonora Christina's autobiographical writings in the way of hypertextuality, which enhanced and continued the image introduced by Leonora Christina's French autobiography, i.e. that of an autonomous woman operating independently of her husband. Finally, *Jammers Minde* attested to Leonora Christina's literary talent (through her use of a modern, relatively new genre, i.e. autobiography) and scholarly ambition (through the integration of church hymns and scientific observations), thus adding to her previously acquired fame of having been an unusually educated woman.

Furthermore, Leonora Christina's sophistication is not only exceptional among women, but even among the entire upper class. Fridericia presents the elite's lack of refinement as a major reason for their inability to further their country or even their

---

1664 See, for example, Fridericia, J. A. *Danmarks Riges Historie 4*, p. 351 (»Den Mængde af Smiger og Æresbevisninger, som blev ham til Del i Holland, bragte hans og Leonora Kristinas Selvophøjelse endnu langt op over hvad den hidtil havde naaet«) or p. 356 (»Vistnok længe havde Tanken om Flugt ikke været ham og hans Hustru fremmed«).

1665 Ibid., p. 359.

own cause.[1666] Christian IV's enormous appetite for alcohol and women, as well as the political implications of his impulsiveness are a prime example in Fridericia's argument that »[der] herskede selv i de højeste Kredse megen Raahed«.[1667] The author furthermore laments a general incongruity between the expenses that went into educating young noblemen and the results of that education: »Kun lidet havde den Politur, som mange unge Adelige erhvervede paa de Udenlandsrejser, der nu var blevne til fuldstændig Mode, gennemsyret deres Aand med virkelig Finhed; tværtimod kom mange kun hjem med blaserede Vaner og ved Udsvævelser ødelagte Legemer«.[1668] Corfitz Ulfeldt presents one of the few exceptions to this rather negative image of the Danish elite. Fridericia concedes that,

> [v]il man søge enkelte Typer for dette Dannelsesideal, kan man næppe vælge bedre end Korfits Ulfeldt og Leonora Christina, der begge til Dels netop derved indtager en saa fremragende Stilling i deres Samtid, begge literaturkyndige, begge med virkelig Smag, begge med Ævne til at gjøre sig gjældende ved deres fine Anstand selv i Udlandets mest forvænte Kultursteder.[1669]

However, Fridericia's above reference to educational travels yielding only »blaserede Vaner og ved Udsvævelser ødelagte Legemer« is also reminiscent of Ulfeldt's life. In *Adelsvældens sidste Dage*, Fridericia contends that even Ulfeldt's personal success abroad is highly overestimated:

1666 Cf. ibid., p. 326: »Kun paa sig selv kunde Adelen derfor stole i Modgangens Dage. Men til at bære sig selv oppe trods sin Lidenhed savnede den, taget som Helhed, baade aandelige Egenskaber, som kraftigt Almensind, politisk Dygtighed eller et højt Dannelsesstandpunkt, og en sikret økonomisk Stilling«. See also ibid., p. 327: »Men rigt paa Talent, paa Sans for at klare Skær, paa dybere Kenskab til den europæiske Politik var Raadet ikke«.

1667 Ibid., p. 327. This awareness of the crude manners and living conditions of the 17th century is another typical feature of the post-1869 Leonora Christina-literature. H. F. Ewald and J. P. Jacobsen hint at this grievance in their novels, but only in the late 20th century writers began to depict the contrast between the supposedly dignified royal household and its actual behaviour in detail. Eva Hemmer Hansen's *Den lykkelige hustru*, for example, portrays the uncouthly fight between Kirsten Munk's children, which only comes to an end whenever the girls' vulgar behaviour could be exposed to the outside world. Perhaps this novel depiction of the King's daughters is inspired by Leonora Christina's portrayal of her sisters in the French autobiography; however, Hemmer Hansen's Leonora Christina *does* participate in the cruelties against her siblings herself (cf. Hemmer Hansen, Eva. *Den lykkelige hustru*, pp. 16-18). *Spardame* by Helle Stangerup is similarly realistic, but this novel focuses rather on the 17th century's lack of sanitary awareness. While Hegermann Lindencrone's Leonora Christina appears thus to the reader (and to the protagonist Elisabeth) singing and playing the harp in a sea of fragrant flowers (Hegermann Lindencrone, Louise. 'Billedet', p. 173), the same person depicted in Helle Stangerup's *Spardame* uses flower water to camouflage the smell of her winds (Stangerup, Helle. *Spardame*, p. 12) even though her buttocks might not be the only source of bothersome odours: »Vand kom kroppen kun i berøring med, hvis de faldt i åen, eller de blev våde på et skib [...]« (ibid.).

1668 Fridericia, J. A. *Danmarks Riges Historie 4*, p. 327.

1669 Fridericia, J. A. *Adelsvældens sidste Dage*, p. 53.

> Ulfeldts Tildbud var ikke blevne modtagne, og skjønt hans og Leonora Christinas Personligheder ved deres Vid og Fornemhed havde gjort et mærkeligt Indtryk paa det franske Hof, havde den rutinerede Skole af Diplomater ikke været blind for Manglerne ved hans politiske Begavelse, det svigtende koldblodige Omdømme og de ikke tilstrækkeligt overvejede Ytringer, [...].[1670]

Much unlike Ove Malling, to whom foreign influence implied a perversion of the Danes' natural virtues, Fridericia considers thus intellectual refinement through contact with other cultures and acquisition of foreign languages to be an essential means of educating the elite, who could then use their knowledge in service of their country. In the latter's view, the potential benefits of cultural exchange and education were massively hindered by a widespread vulgarity manifesting itself in immoderateness of every kind. While Malling praises the noble savage of former times, Fridericia laments thus the amount of savagery among the nobility:

> Det vil saaledes ikke kunne bestrides, at der indenfor den danske Adel var et aandeligt Aristokrati med en vis Sum af aandelige Interesser, med en vis Modtagelighed for den daværende europæiske Kultur, særligt den franske og delvis den hollandske. Men det Dannelsespræg, som udgik fra disse Kredse, modarbejdedes og begrænsedes paa forskjellig Maade, først og fremmest ved Overmaalet i Drik.[1671]

As indicated above, Corfitz Ulfeldt and particularly Leonora Christina were exceptionally educated people, even though their sophistication often took the form of blatant pomposity, which in turn was facilitated through embezzlement and corruption. This, however, concerns mainly Corfitz while Leonora Christina, despite all her flaws, embodies the new Renaissance ideal of the educated, confident woman, i.e. the century's counterpart to the Reformatory age's puritanical, semi-illiterate woman:

1670 Ibid., p. 108.
1671 Ibid., p. 54.

> Et vigtigt Kendetegn paa en forandret Aandsretning viser sig i den Forskydning af Kvindelighedsbegrebet, som foregaar i denne Tidsalder. Igennem største Delen af det 16. Aarhundrede var Kvinden som Regel den fromme Kvinde og den huslige Kvinde. [...] Anderledes er Idealet blevet i Midten af det 17. Aarhundrede for de finest dannede Klassers Vedkommende. Nu stilles der Krav til Kvinden i Retning af boglig Viden og kunstneriske Færdigheder; den unge Kvinde lærer Tegning og Maling, studerer Latin og moderne Sprog, sendes til Udlandet for at opnaa Belevenhed, og som ældre ynder Kvinden Omgang med lærde. Typisk er i denne Henseende Leonora Kristina [...].[1672]

Despite this positive development, Fridericia also contends that the Renaissance's demand for education goes hand in hand with a proliferation of egocentricity:

> Ogsaa Leonora Christina havde hele Renæssancens Dannelsestrang, dens Glæde ved Fester, Spil og Musik, men særligt dens stærke og hensynsløse personlige Selvhævdelse, dens Lyst til den autobiografiske Fremstilling i Forening med dens Kvinders Attraa efter Ligeagtelse med Mændene og deres Stræben efter fremfor alt at besidde den mandige Aand og den mandige Kraft. Hendes Livsnerve var hendes personlige Værdighed, bestemt ved hendes Stilling som Kongedatter, og Viragoidealet har ikke ligget fjernt for hende, der holdt af at optræde i Mandfolkedragt, selv hvor denne ikke behøvede at tjene til en nyttig Forklædning.[1673]

Fridericia's somewhat chauvinist portrayal of the Renaissance woman – his conception that a demand for autonomy implied an imitation of allegedly male assets (»den mandige Aand og den mandige Kraft«) and his amused astonishment over women in men's clothing – is highly reminiscent of the contemporary discourse concerning gender equality, which was fomented by Mathilde Fibiger's writings (see Chapter 2.2.2.) but continued for decades. When Fibiger published *Clara Raphael* in 1851, her idea of a more balanced relationship between the sexes caused bewilderment and exhilaration. In the wake of these reactions, the satirical magazine *Corsaren* published a series of cartoons ('Anticiperede Skizzer af den danske Kvindes Emancipation') depicting women wearing trousers, acting out all kinds of men's activities, such as playing billiard, performing military duty or working as a barber, all the while smoking in most of these images.[1674] Fridericia's reference to Leonora

---

1672 Fridericia, J. A. *Danmarks Riges Historie 4*, p. 310.
1673 Fridericia, J. A. *Adelsvældens sidste Dage*, p. 162.
1674 Some of these and similar cartoons are reproduced in Busk-Jensen, Lise. *Romantikkens forfatterinder 2*, pp. 993-998.

Christina's desire for recognition and to her prolonged disguise as a man embeds her anew into the author's depiction of the women of this age:

> Udviklingens Retning ses ogsaa af, at Malerierne ikke længere, som i det 16. Aarhundrede, fremstiller Kvinden med foldede Hænder og nedslagne Blikke, men i fri, kokette og selvbevidste Stillinger. Og det er i Samklang hermed, at Kvindernes Rolle i Samfundet stiger. Vi har set Eksempler nok herpaa i det offentlige Liv, hvor Kampen mellem Kvinder spiller en saa mægtig Rolle under Kristian IV, og sikkert er det gaaet ligesaa i det private Liv.[1675]

This notion of an age dominated by female quarrel – which is not a perception unique to Fridericia, but has been adopted by many current authors of Leonora Christina-literature such as Helle Stangerup or Maria Helleberg (see Chapters 2.6.2. and 2.6.3., respectively) – may well be another implication of the publication of *Jammers Minde*, since Leonora Christina's work rebranded its author while at the same time damning her worst enemy forever. This effect – the long-term damage done to Sophie Amalie's reputation – has only been addressed relatively late. In 1986, the Rosenborg Castle in Copenhagen hosted a special exhibition with the objective of providing »et mere nuanceret billed af Frederik IIIs dronning«[1676] by showcasing various objects documenting the life of Sophie Amalie in its variety. Such an exhibition had become necessary because Leonora Christina had monopolised the collective memory of Sophie Amalie for centuries: »Enhver dansker har hørt om Leonora Christina, den fangne kongedatter i Blåtårn, færre husker Sophie Amalie, flere måske den onde dronning, der holdt Leonora Christina indespærret«.[1677] Due to the massive impact *Jammers Minde* has had on the reputation of 'the evil Queen', Fridericia, too, produces something that has become a set phrase to summarise Sophie Amalie's position in Danish history:

> Ved det Gilde paa Københavns Slot, der sluttede Hyldingsakten, fandt der et lille Sammenstød Sted mellem Dronning Sofie Amalie og Leonora Kristina, vel det første mellem de to Kvinder, hvis gensidige Had for *lange Tider skulde kaste sit uhyggelige Skær over Danmarks Historie* [my italics].[1678]

1675 Fridericia, J. A. *Danmarks Riges Historie 4*, p. 311.
1676 Hein, Jørgen and Katia Johansen. *Sophie Amalie*, unpaginated preamble.
1677 Bencard, Mogens and Jørgen Hein. 'Forord'. In *Sophie Amalie: Den onde dronning?* Copenhagen: Rosenborg, 1986, unpaginated preamble.
1678 Fridericia, J. A. *Danmarks Riges Historie 4*, p. 293.

The shadow cast over this part of Denmark's history by the actions of these two women[1679] has thus also overshadowed any other of the Queen's deeds. When Fridericia addresses Sophie Amalie's involvement in the events of 1660, he feels obliged to include a reference to what happened afterwards to Leonora Christina – as if the introduction of absolutism alone was not momentous enough:

> Ogsaa Sofie Amalie havde naaet, hvad hun havde tragtet efter. Man mene om dette hvad man vil; det havde dog været en Ærgerrighed værd, den lüneburgske Fyrstinde havde Grund til at være stolt over at være bleven suveræn Arvedronning over Danmark og Norge. Men hvilken Mangel paa Storhed viser hun ikke i sit følgende Liv![1680]

Yet *Jammers Minde* established two more oppositions, which would come to label these two women in a way that would indefinitely favour Leonora Christina. Beyond the antagonism 'evil Queen vs. innocent Princess', her work also depicts her relative powerlessness against omnipotent monocrats and, although Leonora Christina shows no signs of any resentment towards anything German (or anything international, for that matter), *Jammers Minde* helped to implant the idea of a German-Danish antagonism into posterity through the use of Danish for its author's own thoughts and memories, while rendering the speech of the Queen's minions in their original language, which was mostly German.[1681] The former, Leonora Christina's depiction of Sophie Amalie as a despotic hag, hit a nerve when *Jammers Minde* was published not too long after the reversal of her and her husband's lifework in 1848. The latter, a latent and probably unintended portrayal of the Danish capital being dictated by German intruders, was even more in the spirit of the time when Denmark had suffered a devastating loss of people and territory to Prussia and Austria in 1864. The German-Danish opposition theme was hardly seized by Danish Leonora Christina-literature; only in the German writer Margarete Boie's novel *Eleonora Christine und Corfitz Ulfeldt,* published in 1944, Leonora Christina is

---

1679 What is more, the female quarrels depicted in Fridericia's works are particularly *uhyggelig* in their pettiness: »Disse Krænkelser, i hvilke Smaaligheden stikker frem […]« (Fridericia, J. A. *Adelsvældens sidste Dage*, p. 125). Leonora Christina's answer to the Queen's attacks – i.e. the annulment of Leonora Christina's title of Countess and of their previous entitlement to drive their carriages into the royal courtyard – is to not attend her niece's christening. This and other instances of petty, vulgar female quarrels in an age dominated by female strife – as contended by Fridericia – enhances the impression that the 17th century had been raffish *because* of the amount of female involvement in it.

1680 Fridericia, J. A. *Danmarks Riges Historie 4*, p. 462.

1681 Cf. Hein, Jørgen and Katia Johansen. *Sophie Amalie*, unpaginated preamble, on the impact of *Jammers Minde* in the nationalistic context of its publication: »Hun var dansk, tilmed landsfaderen Christian IVs datter, og som hans, havde hendes modersmål marv og kraft. Her over for havde Sophie Amalie som tyskfødt og tysktalende kun gæstearbejderens chance«.

stereotypically Scandinavian while Sophie Amalie has a more southern appeal.[1682] Historians, however, such as J. A. Fridericia, detected the German tendencies in this period and depicted it more keenly in their work.[1683]

Danmarks Riges Historie, which was published only a few decades after the abolition of absolutism in Denmark and the ruinous defeat in the Second Schleswig War of 1864, contains numerous traces of Leonora Christina's self-portrayal in opposition to her environment. There is a clearly discernible tendency to depict the age that was defined through the introduction of a sole ruler as being controlled and corrupted by the personal desires of a handful of individuals.[1684] Depicted in this way are Christian IV's reign,[1685] Corfitz Ulfeldt[1686] and Frederik III, of which the latter's reaction to the Ulfeldts' attacks, at times, lacks an involvement of the law:

1682 Boie's Leonora Christina is »eine echte Dänin: blond und schön, klug und heiter, zum Herrschen fähig – und zur größten Liebe« (Boie, Margarete. *Eleonora Christine und Corfitz Ulfeldt*, p. 168: 'a true Dane: blond and beautiful, intelligent and cheerful, capable of ruling – and of loving to the greatest extent'), and when she expresses this typically Danish love for Corfitz Ulfeldt her eyes glow »wie blauer Stahl« (ibid., p. 37: 'like blue steel'). Meanwhile, Sophie Amalie is »brünett und temperamentvoll« (ibid., p. 93: 'brunette and sultry') and her infatuation with Corfitz Ulfeldt reflects her desire for the possession of Denmark since he – like his wife – embodies the coveted country (ibid.).

1683 »The Danes were fully aware of this 'invasion' from the south, and some of their historians made plans to correct the situation« (Westergaard, Waldemar. 'Danish History and Danish Historians', p. 173. Cf. Fridericia, J. A. *Adelsvældens sidste Dage*, p. 151: »Ulfeldt havde rimeligvis kunnet regne paa Gjenklang hos sine Tilhørere, naar han under en af de med de store Sager forbundne Bisøgsmaal for Herredagen havde udbrudt om sine Fjender: 'Se, de er alle Tyskere'«. Adolf Ditlev Jørgensen, to name another example, who also started the sixth volume of *Danmarks Riges Historie* but died before finishing it, published *Fyrretyve Fortællinger af Fædrelandets Historie* in 1882 in order to come to terms with the events of 1864 (Westergaard, Waldemar. 'Danish History and Danish Historians', p. 175). Even though this book was inspired by Ove Malling's *Store og gode Handlinger* (see Det Danske Sprog- og Litteraturselskab. 'Forord', p. 9 and Hansen, Erik. 'Efterskrift', p. 577f.), Leonora Christina plays no part in Jørgensen's history other than fueling her husband's sense of entitlement: »Allerede faa Aar efter hans [Frederik III's] Tronbestigelse faldt Rigets Hovmester (Formanden i Rigsraadet), Korfits Ulfeld, over sine egne Fejl. Han var gift med Kongens Halvsøster Eleonore Kristine og opfyldt af et ubegrænset Hovmod« (Jørgensen, A. D. *Fyrretyve Fortællinger af Fædrelandets Historie*. Copenhagen: De unges forlag, 1946 (1882), p. 170).

1684 Cf. Fridericia, J. A. *Danmarks Riges Historie 4*, p. 432: »[...] en ny Periode i Danmarks Historie. Det skabtes af viljestærke Personligheder [...]«.

1685 Cf. Fridericia's portrayal of absolutist attempts in Christian IV's reign which, however, do not constitute an implicit argument for the legitimacy of absolutism (as was the case with Holberg's history, see Chapter 3.2.1.), but are rather an example of how his character and personal interests guided his political considerations: »Det ligger nær at formode, at hans selvherskerske Tankegang ikke har kunnet forsone sig med at skulle søge nye Baand for sin Virken. Han stræbte efter saa vidt muligt at frigøre sig for Rigsraadet, men han ønskede ikke at erstatte det med en mere folkelig Repræsentation« (ibid., p. 127).

1686 Cf. ibid., p. 286, which highlights the personalisation of power by means of an anticlimax: »*Aristokratiet, Rigsraadet, Svogrenes Kreds* [my italics] havde sejret. Men som Leder for det sejrende Parti stod Korfits Ulfeld. De nærmest følgende Maaneder blev hans mægtigste Tid. Han nyttede denne Magt, ikke til heldbringende Reformer, men paa forskellig Maade til sin egen og sine Venners, deriblandt de store Leverandørers, personlige Fordel«.

Den samme uværdige Forbindelse af Hævnlyst, Attraa efter at ramme og skræmme Adelen, Pengebegær og Hensynsløshed, som præger Kaj Lykkes Sag, træder ogsaa frem i Regeringens Adfærd mod Korfits Ulfeld og Leonora Kristina. Det vil erindres, at de i Sommeren 1660 var førte som Fanger til Hammershus. Fangenskabet her blev haardt, deres Behandling fra Guvernøren General Adolf Fuchs's Side brutal, især efter et mislykket Flugtforsøg. Imidlertid overvejede man i København, hvilken Fremgangsmaade man skulde anvende imod dem. Efter nogen Tids Vaklen besluttede man sig til ikke at anlægge Proces, men at tilstaa Frihed mod aftvungne Penge, Ydmygelse og bastede Hænder. I Septbr. 1661 sendtes Kristian Rantzau til Bornholm, bl. a. med det Hverv at nøde Ulfeld og hans Hustru til et Forlig. Forpinte som de var, bøjede de sig og maatte endda efter Tilbagekomsten til København ved Juletid gaa ind paa en ny Erklæring, for at det skulde se ud, som om den var afgivet i Frihed.[1687]

It goes without also saying that Sophie Amalie's absolutist aspirations are a result of her personal dreams and desires. However, in the case of her and her husband, these ambitions also correlate with their German background. Sophie Amalie seems to have inherited her conniving character, and hence perhaps her drive for power, from her father.[1688] She and the other German influences[1689] in Frederik III's life are portrayed to have had a tremendous impact on the King's later actions.

The formal argument through which Fridericia explains how and why the 17th century took its course into absolutism is thus a mix of Formism and Mechanism. The author combines a Formist explanation of the historical field with a Mechanistic analysis of events by »identifying [...] the unique characteristics of objects inhabiting the historical field«[1690] – these characteristics being vulgarity, alcoholism, egotism and female quarrels – in order to demonstrate how individuals exhibiting those characteristics shaped the course of history, in the way of the »pessimistic

---

1687 Ibid., p. 496. This, however, does not imply a condemnation of this King's elimination of Corfitz Ulfeldt and the rest of the *rigsråd*. Although, in Fridericia's eyes, one of the greatest crimes against Denmark committed by this King was his introduction of absolutism, one of his greatest achievements in the service of Denmark was his simultaneous victory over Ulfeldt, »da han kastede Rigsraads- og Adelsvælden i Grus som en berettiget Straf for dens Vanrøgt af Rigets Interesser« (see Fridericia, J. A. *Adelsvældens sidste Dage*, p. 549).

1688 Fridericia, J. A. *Danmarks Riges Historie 4*, p. 288: »[...] Sofie Amalie, Datteren af en af Trediveaarskrigens mest energiske og mest intrigante Skikkelser, Hertug Georg af Brunsvig-Lüneburg, selv ung, forlystelsessyg, ærgerrig, lidenskabelig, *tragtende maaske end mere end sin Ægtefælle* [my italics], ikke alene efter Tronen, men ogsaa efter dens Besiddelse med langt større Magt end de hidtidige danske Kongers«.

1689 »Hans Liv var gaaet hen mere som tysk Fyrste end som dansk Prins, hans Erfaringer i Regeringsanliggender var hentede fra det tyske Rige, hans Hof, hans Raadgivere overvejende tyske« (Fridericia, J. A. *Adelsvældens sidste Dage*, p. 10).

1690 White, Hayden. *Metahistory*, p. 13.

conclusions that the strict Mechanist is inclined to draw from his reflections on the nomological nature of historical being«.[1691] The actions of those individuals provoke a particular reaction just as the combined actions of many individuals provoke a mass reaction. Instead of ascribing the nuisances of the 17th century to a tendency or to the dominance of one particular political class, Fridericia thus argues that a few, but powerful, corrupted individuals determined the past and hindered any positive development. This in turn is a very Radical ideology, in that it reflects a belief »in the necessity of structural transformations [...] in the interest of reconstituting society on new bases«[1692] with a high awareness »of the power needed to effect such transformations«[1693] and of »the inertial pull of inherited institutions«.[1694] Fridericia's tendency to portray individuals figuring as agents of history runs counter to the integrative trope of Synecdoche used by Holberg, Malling and Scocozza (see Chapter 3.2.4.), who depict Leonora Christina as a representative of a bigger entity (i.e. the nobility, Danishness and aristocratic women, respectively). Fridericia's narrative asserts that Leonora Christina and her contemporaries represented nobody but themselves. The typicality of Leonora Christina for her age, as well as her similarity and simultaneous difference to the other powerful agents inhabiting the historical field depicted in *Danmarks Riges Historie 4*, including even her opponents, suggest rather a use of Metaphor as a characterisation device,[1695] since Metaphor asserts that a fundamental similarity exists between two objects despite their obvious difference, such as the similarities between Ulfeldt and Frederik III, or between Leonora Christina and Sophie Amalie, i.e. their individualism and lust for power.

Many of these tendencies can and should be viewed in the context of the discovery of *Jammers Minde* and the two incisively historical events that preceded its publication, since *Danmarks Riges Historie 4* addresses many topics contained, explicitly or implicitly, in *Jammers Minde* as well. In this regard, *Jammers Minde* has had a profound and largely positive impact on the ensuing historiography, as Fridericia together with his contemporaries and successors channeled and reworked the documentary content of Leonora Christina's work into their own narratives. One pivotal downside of this effect, however, is the ensuing relocation of its author in historical narratives. As implied by Fridericia's last words, the fame Leonora Chri-

---

1691 Ibid., p. 16.
1692 Ibid., p. 24.
1693 Ibid.
1694 Ibid., p. 25.
1695 Ibid., p. 34: »In Metaphor [...] phenomena can be characterized in terms of their similarity to, and difference from, one another, in the manner of analogy or simile [...]«.

stina acquired through the posthumous publication of her masterpiece was eventually her undoing in the context of national histories. As indicated throughout *Adelsvældens sidste Dage* and *Danmarks Riges Historie 4*, Fridericia assumed that most of his readers would be familiar with the autobiographical writings of the famous Countess Ulfeldt, hence rendering a repetition of her biography dispensable for a non-specialised historical text:

> Det er ikke nødvendigt at dvæle ved Leonora Kristinas Skæbne. Alle veed, hvorledes hun blev udleveret af den engelske Konge Karl II, i Aug. 1663 ført til København, indespærret i Blaataarn og underkastet resultatløse Forhør for at faa udforsket hendes Mands landsforræderske Planer og hendes egen Delagtighed deri. Ingen kan afgøre, hvor vidt hun har talt Sandhed, da hun nægtede ethvert Medviderskab dengang som senere i sit »Jammersminde«. Men sikkert er det, at ingen Beviser fremkom imod hende, og naar Regeringen desuagtet uden nogen Sinde at stævne hende for nogen Ret, endsige faa Dom over hende, i lange Aar holdt hende indesluttet i et haardt Fængsel, da er dette en Brøde, for hvilken Ansvaret hviler tungt paa Frederik III's Minde, endnu tyngere dog paa Sofie Amalies, thi der kan ikke herske Tvivl om, at i hendes Hadefuldhed og Hævnsyge laa den dybeste Grund til den despotiske Adfærd. Og lige saa sikkert er, at Leonora Kristina bar sine Lidelser med den beundringsværdigste Sjælsstyrke.[1696]

Fridericia's performative proclamation of a disciplinary relocation of Leonora Christina could hardly have been stated more bluntly. Under the not entirely unwarranted assumption of *Jammers Minde* having already permeated the realm of general knowledge, Fridericia refers to Leonora Christina's literary works throughout his own writings while refusing to provide his readers with the missing details himself. In some cases, this does not get in the way of understanding his narrative – for example, when Ulfeldt fails to see how the situation in Denmark had changed after his return from his second visit in the Netherlands and »lyttede end ikke til sin Hustrus Advarsler«[1697] (a clear reference to the French autobiography) – but in some other cases, it does (as in the examples provided above). By repeatedly referring readers who might be interested in further information on Leonora Christina's life to consult her own writings, Fridericia pushes her life's story out of the realm of history – a trend continued in the historical work discussed in Chapter 3.2.4.

1696 Fridericia, J. A. *Danmarks Riges Historie 4*, p. 498.
1697 Fridericia, J. A. *Adelsvældens sidste Dage*, p. 123.

3.2.4. Benito Scocozza: *Ved afgrundens rand* (1989) – A Comedy of Historical Materialism

> Løffuindens Hierte er saa Keckmodig som Løwens: Mangen Quinde haffuer større styrcke end som mangen Mand, Mangen Quinde haffuer oc wel saa Keckt ed mod som Mangen Mand; de suare icke alle til Mands Naffn i Gierningen som bærer Tittel aff Mands Naffn men offte suare Quinder til Helters Naffn i Gierningen, oc bere dog ickun Quinders Naffn: Huoroffte seer man quindactige Hierter i Mands Legemer, oc der imod igien mandelige Kræffter i suage Karr: Ded er Vbilligt, att man maaler Gierningen effter Persohnen, oc skatter icke Persohnen effter Gierningen.[1698]

The perspective on and presentation of the 17th century in Denmark by the historian and politician Benito Scocozza is in many regards different from those exhibited in other national histories. Unlike the texts discussed in the previous chapters, Scocozza's volume follows the inclusive fashion of current national histories by providing an eclectic account of the 17th century from the point of view of all actors involved.[1699] *Ved afgrundens rand* – Volume 8 of *Gyldendal og Politikens Danmarkshistorie* – is thus not merely the history of a dynasty, but of a country. Yet despite its complex outline, Scocozza's history produces a clearly discernible story, tightly summarised in the ominous title *Ved afgrundens rand*.

Considering that Scocozza's profession as a historian resulted mostly in publications engaging in the history of the Danish royals[1700] one might be induced to assume that *Ved afgrundens rand* is the story of how the royal house only scantily averted its irreversible decline. However, since Scocozza is also known for his vocation to the cause of Communism and Maoism – he was a founding member of the *Kommunistisk Forbund Marxister-Leninister* (1968) and of the *Kommunistisk Arbejderparti* (1976) – the protagonist, whose near-downfall is narrated in *Ved afgrundens rand*, is not one or several individuals. The principal story unfolding in this volume is that of a country afflicted with the suffocating mismanagement of an old ruling class, i.e. the high nobility, and eventually liberated from this nuisance at the hands of a new ruling class, the bourgeoisie.

1698 Leonora Christina. *Hæltinners Pryd*, p. 21.
1699 Steffen Heiberg, on the other hand, finds fault with Scocozza's modern partisanship against the nobility – an approach he deems unfit and obsolete for an appropriate analysis of a historical subject (see Heiberg, Steffen. Review of *Ved afgrundens rand* by Benito Scocozza, Historisk Tidsskrift 16/1 (1992), p. 169).
1700 See, for example, Scocozza. Benito. *Christian 4*. Copenhagen: Politikens Forlag, 1988 (1987).

Scocozza's egalitarian disposition affects Leonora Christina in two opposing ways. On the one hand, she is the wife and accomplice of the main perpetrator Corfitz Ulfeldt, a fiercely elitarian representative of the ruling high nobility. Through his comprehensive use of graphical material (including extensive captions), which in Scocozza's case does not only serve to supplement (as is the case with the images provided in J. A. Fridericia's *Danmarkshistorie*) but also to comment on the main text, he characterises Leonora Christina early on in the account as aristocratic to the core. The painting chosen to introduce her is a concoction of elitist props:

> Leonora Christina Ulfeldt, malet 1643 af Karel van Mander. Hun bærer den lille hat, hun selv opfattede som tegnet på sin prinsesseværdighed. Hendes venstre hånd hviler på en ulv – symbolet på Ul(v)feldt. Viften, som hun holder med sin højre hånd, var en udbredt renæssancekvindemode, der går igen på mange malerier af samtidens kvinder. Leonora Christina synes nærmest at hæve den som et advarende tegn. Ligesom det faste udtryk i ansigtet understreger den hendes utilnærmelighed. I modsætning til andre hunde på tidens billeder er køteren bidsk og udfordrer ulven, men ulfeldterne lader sig ikke skræmme.[1701]

On the other hand, Leonora Christina is a woman and hence part of a social minority, a topic Scocozza is concerned with to a great extent. Due to this duality of Leonora Christina's identity, she is, on the one hand, a minor component of the core account, i.e. that of Denmark's transition from *adelsvælde* to *enevælde*.[1702] On the other hand, she stands out as a key agent in Danish women's history, namely in a chapter titled 'Heltinders pryd', since »[...] Leonora Christina dristede sig endda til at fremhæve kvinders mod og legemlige styrke som ligeværdige med

---

1701 Scocozza, Benito. *Gyldendal og Politikens Danmarkshistorie 8: Ved afgrundens rand: 1600-1700*. Copenhagen: Gyldendals Bogklubber, 1992 (1989), p. 175. Scocozza gives another example of this mindset attributed to Leonora Christina in the biography *Christian 4.*, in which he refers to Leonora Christina's use of the third person in her French autobiography on more than one occasion. See, for example, Scocozza, Benito. *Christian 4.*, p. 266: »[›]År 1648 forlod lykken vor dame‹ – hun omtaler altid sig selv i tredjeperson [...]«. Scocozza's use of the word *altid* is slightly misleading, since it is not clear whether this refers to the French autobiography or to all of her writings. A few pages earlier, the reader already learns that »[i] selvbiografien omtaler Leonora Christina altid sig selv i tredjeperson« (ibid., p. 263 (caption)). The only partial repetition of this information shortly afterwards is rather deceptive, as it presents Leonora Christina's use of the third person not as a stylistic device employed in one particular text, but as a megalomaniac quirk in the tradition of Caesar himself.

1702 Like in Otto Sperling's autobiography, the occasional appearance of Ulfeldt's wife – as opposed to Leonora Christina as an indivual later on in the account – serves only to affirm her husband's actions, e.g. his scuffle with Christian IV (Scocozza, Benito. *Ved afgrundens rand*, p. 174: »Det gavnede naturligvis heller ikke forholdet mellem kongen og Ulfeldt, at Leonora Christina havde besøgt sin moder«) and his royal ambitions (ibid., p. 183: »Ville han gøre sin hustru til regerende dronning med sig selv som den dominerende førsteminister?«).

mændenes«,[1703] as evidenced by this chapter's introductory citation. She is thus portrayed in her own, independent context but alas, it is outsourced from traditional, i.e. political history and reallocated to an excursus on women's living conditions in the Baroque age, i.e. the two subchapters 'Eva' and 'Heltinders pryd':

> De fleste kvinder opfattede uden tvivl denne arbejdsdeling [the public as a male, the domestic sphere as a female domain] som indstiftet af Herren. Alligevel støder man på enkelte, der ikke veg tilbage for at hævde deres køns lighed med mændene. Kongedatteren Leonora Christina, Corfitz Ulfeldts hustru, der fra 1663 til 1685 uden dom var spærret inde i Blåtårn, skrev foruden sit »Jammersminde«, hvori hun skildrede sin fængselstid, en ufuldendt bog om kvindelige helte, »Heltinders pryd«.[1704]

Scocozza's main narrative, however, is dominated by kings, their allies and their antagonists. The course of history of Denmark's 17th century was essentially operated by Christian IV and Frederik III. The story of the former is that of the climaxing power of the high nobility or, to be more precise, the *rigsråd*, while that of the latter depicts the reversal of the damage done by the former. The introduction of absolutism in 1660 constitutes the critical turning point for this core narrative. Nevertheless, Holberg's simplistic ebb-and-flow-model cannot be applied to Scocozza's narrative, since his interest is not directed at the royal power alone, but concerns all the estates and forces present in the 17th century, whose influence is in a state of fluctuation. In order to depict this century of drastic and complex political change in a compact and comprehensible manner, yet without reducing the entire narrative of this change to merely two agents, Scocozza creates consecutive duels from which a winner arises only to enter the next duel.[1705]

1703 Ibid., p. 337.

1704 Ibid.

1705 In order to highlight the dichotomous nature of these consecutive smaller conflicts, Scocozza simplifies the amount and nature of the forces determining the resolution of these oppositions. For example, in order to make the point that eventually all privileged entities dig their own grave, Scocozza must present the overruling of Christian IV by his sons-in-law as self-inflicted. And in order to convey this impression, Scocozza implies that the death of this King's heir apparent, *den udvalgte prins* Christian, which made the King highly susceptible to blackmail by Ulfeldt and his peers, was not merely an unfortunate incident caused by the – back then – all too common habit of feasting and drinking excessively. Instead, Scocozza turns this event into something that might yet again be King Christian IV's fault: »Den udvalgte prins voksede op i faderens altdominerende skygge. Kongen sørgede naturligvis for, at han fik en passende og nøje tilrettelagt opdragelse og uddannelse, sådan som han selv havde fået det. Men selv da den udvalgte prins nåede voksenalderen, kunne faderen ikke dy sig for at bestemme over hans livsførelse. Kongen var evig og altid på nakken af sønnen, der tog sig de forkerte elskerinder, brugte for mange penge og ikke duede til at regere, da han blev sat til det i faderens fravær under den tyske krig« (Scocozza, Benito. *Ved afgrundens rand*, p. 171).

One major casualty of this never-ending struggle is Christian IV. His life's story ends with a detailed depiction of his undignified marital strife, which exemplifies the ageing King's defeat at the hands of the much stronger nobility, since his wife is a representative of this aspiring estate: »I kongens øjne repræsenterede Kirsten Munk den fejhed, svigefuldhed og selviskhed, som åbenbart var karakteristisk for den danske højadel, der bandt hans hand«.[1706] The main chapter 'Vi mistede slaget' is followed by the subchapter 'Christian 4.s ægteskabelige nederlag'. His professional defeat in the Thirty Years' War is thus supplemented and accentuated by his private degradation, especially since both are self-induced. Both noblemen and his wife desert the ever more difficult King when his catastrophic foreign policy goes awry:

> Selv om Rosenkrantz' udtræden af rigsrådet forblev en enlig svale, var hans hele optræden symptomatisk for de højadeliges reaktion på krigsulykkerne. De følte sig ikke solidariske med den krig, de så kraftigt havde advaret imod, og hvis udbrud de ikke havde haft nogen indflydelse på.[1707]

Scocozza's presentation of Christian IV's marital quarrel is particularly unsympathetic with the cuckolded husband. The accusations raised against Kirsten Munk remain uncommented and hence questionable. Yet in case of doubt, the author roots for the wife:

> I en skilsmissesag er det altid betænkeligt at dømme parterne imellem, når kun den enes udsagn foreligger. Christian 4.s opgør med Kirsten Munk var lige så uligevægtigt, som sager af den art ofte er. Det er umuligt at sige, om fru Kirsten vitterligt gik i seng med rhingreven. Men gjorde hun det, er det næppe uforståeligt.[1708]

1706 Ibid., p. 148.
1707 Ibid., p. 149.
1708 Ibid., p. 148. In the biography of Christian IV written by Scocozza, the author abstains from any decided belief in Kirsten Munk's infidelity as well (»og i den følgende tid sås de to stadig oftere og blev – i hvert fald ifølge kongen – kærester« (Scocozza, Benito. *Christian 4.*, p. 226)) and he questions whether the King's repudiation of the alleged cuckoo's egg Dorotea Elisabeth – Kirsten Munk's last child – was justified: »Spillet omkring Dorotea Elisabeths dåbsnavn skyldtes således, at kongen var begyndt at tælle på fingrene og var nået frem til, at Kirsten måtte være gået langt over tiden, hvis den nyfødte skulle være hans – i hvert fald mindst 14 dage, som han senere hævdede. At dette ikke er så usædvanligt endda, faldt ikke kongen ind, der nok interesserede sig for at sætte svangerskaber i gang, men næppe for deres videre forløb« (ibid.).

Towards the end of his life's story, Christian IV is portrayed in an increasingly pathetic manner,[1709] which serves as an explanation for his declining support among peers and family. In the case of Kirsten Munk, however, the author furthermore introduces feminist considerations – a topic that substantially informed the portrayal of her daughter Leonora Christina as well – to account for her alleged adultery: »Dertil kom, at fru Kirsten sandsynligvis var led ved at gå fra det ene svangerskab til det andet. Det var ikke en selvfølge, at tidens kvinder uden at blinke fandt sig i at være fødemaskiner«.[1710]

Eventually, the imminent replacement of Christian IV by a new, stronger ruling class, the high nobility, becomes increasingly urgent since the latter is a monster created by the King himself, as exemplified by Ulfeldt's meteoric career:

> I 1636, samme år som Corfitz Ulfeldt og Leonora Christina blev gift, blev svigersønnen optaget i rigsrådet, hvis medlemmer i gennemsnit var mere end 20 år ældre end han selv. Året efter blev han Københavns statholder. Om statholderens bestilling hed det i kongens udkast til instruks, at »udi Vores absens [fravær] [comment by Scocozza] skal han repræsentere Vores person« – så det er forståeligt, at Leonora Christina i sine erindringer tillod sig at skrive, at hendes mand blev udnævnt til »viceroi«, vicekonge.[1711]

The consequences of this power shift soon become apparent,[1712] but the time (as well as the King) is not the right one for a reversal. In the meantime, vanity (*for-*

1709 The icing on the cake of the King's professional, emotional and seemingly mental decline is his monument to a sexless night, a stone he commissioned to commemorate the one night Kirsten denied him coitus: »I et anklageskrift fra 1641 mod Kirsten Munk skildrede kongen, hvorledes han, morgenen efter fru Kirsten havde spærret sovekammerdøren for ham, til evig ihukommelse i Frederiksborg Slotshave lod lægge en temmelig stor kampesten med sæde gjort deri og årstallet indhugget. Med stenen ville kongen vise den forhånelse, han havde været udsat for på samme måde som Kristus over for Pontius Pilatus. Kongen har sikkert ment, at stenen havde magisk kraft, eftersom han på et tidspunkt befalede, at hans og fru Kirstens søn, Valdemar Christian, der var ved at tage moderens parti, skulle have stenen forevist, dog uden at få baggrunden for den fortalt. Stenen skulle virke af sig selv og bringe sønnen på bedre tanker« (Scocozza, Benito. *Ved afgrundens rand*, p. 180). The absence of any mention to his potential rival – *rhingreven* – as a reason for the closed bedroom door, as well as the provided photography of said stone, which documents that the stone is still in Frederiksborg and has thus indeed become a monument, enhance the ridiculousness of the entire situation. The placement of this kind of information within the chapter 'Den tornekronede konge' adds the finishing touches: »Når Christian 4. så tilbage på sit liv, så han sikkert sig selv som et spejlbillede af Jesus, hvis himmelske krone blev forvandlet til en tornekrone« (ibid., p. 179).

1710 Ibid., p. 148.

1711 Ibid., p. 166.

1712 Cf. ibid.: »1643 drog kongen konsekvensen af, at Corfitz Ulfeldts magtbeføjelser efterhånden var blevet kraftigt forøgede, og udnævnte ham til rigshofmester. Eller havde svigersønnen, der samtidig var blevet en formuende mand, efterhånden sat sig så centralt i magtmaskinen, at kongen nærmest var tvunget til at give ham det fornemme embede? Noget kunne tyde på det, for allerede før udnævnelsen var han begyndt at skumle over svigersønnens opførsel«.

fængelighed), greed and corruption govern, together with the Ulfeldt couple. Scocozza illustrates this trend, depicted in a chapter titled 'Adelens overmod', which also introduces Leonora Christina to the narrative, by means of graphical material. Besides the portrait of Leonora Christina adorned with her famous hat, a fan and a wolf, this chapter is illustrated and hence subtly commented with a picture of a little balm tin featuring a monkey's face, the symbol of vanity and foolishness,[1713] that had been in the possession of the Ulfeldt couple and a portrait of Leonora Christina's grandmother Ellen Marsvin dressed in mourning and ornamented with a chain ending in a skull filled with perfume. The author's comment on the latter – »forgængeligheden [the skull] over for forfængeligheden [the perfume]«[1714] blatantly decries the elite's extravagance. While the King is forced to pawn his crown due to financial trouble, the high nobility wallows in the lap of luxury, as shown in the accompanying illustrations and told in the text.[1715]

The long decline of the King's autonomy leading to aristocracy at the considerable expense of all other estates ends abruptly with the death of Christian IV and Frederik III's ascension to the throne. Despite some initial setbacks, such as *håndfæstningen*, a contract prepared by the *rigsråd* and signed by the King which would dramatically limit the ruler's (but particularly Frederik III's) authority, this new ruler appears like a *deus ex machina* and dispatches the work of the *adelsvælde*, including the privileged status of the Ulfeldt couple, within a short period of time.[1716] The appearance of King Frederik III as a faceless and nameless saviour of his people is enhanced by the deferral of any characterisation of this hitherto unknown prince and his wife. Only later, once Ulfeldt has left the country and waged war against his fatherland, the reader learns more about Christian IV's quiet

---

1713 The caption reads as follows: »Balsambøsse i form af et abehoved, sandsynligvis indkøbt af Ulfeldt- parret under deres frankrigsophold i 1647. Bøssen er indfattet i forgyldt sølv. En fransk indskrift inde i bøssen lyder på dansk: ‚Menneskenes børn er spejlbilleder for hinanden i deres beundring for fornuften, men de fleste spejler sig selv med abernes forfængelighed'« (ibid., p. 176).

1714 Ibid., p. 177.

1715 Cf. ibid., p. 176: »Tre måneder efter denne nye sejr over den gamle konge [mind the antithesis!] rejste Ulfeldt og Leonora Christina med et større følge på ambassade til Nederlandene og Frankrig«. See also ibid., p. 176: »Og det største udbytte af frankrigsopholdet blev, at den franske enkedronning forærede Leonora Christina et ur med diamanter påsat«.

1716 See ibid., p. 191.

son, who soon gained the image of »en tænksom og noget sky person«.[1717] With the help of a new, quickly emerging class, i.e. the bourgeoisie and among them merchants in particular, Frederik III introduces absolutism, hence marking the definite end of the nobility's rule. The completion of the King's lifework, i.e. the consolidation of absolutism in Denmark, heralds a new age and the breakthrough of a new ruling estate, which had already started to emerge during the reign of Christian IV.[1718] The country is purified for now. Images of artlessly dressed merchant families and of hard-working public servants[1719] replace the portraits of extravagantly garnished noblemen and women that littered the first half of the volume. This crucial step towards becoming a more modern European power is portrayed as a necessary and natural part of the country's development,[1720] notwithstanding the problems arising from the introduction of absolutism. Scocozza implicitly contends that the end of the previous situation had been inevitable, since no one estate could remain in power for a prolonged period of time. It was thus not the King and the bourgeoisie alone that felled Ulfeldt and his peers.[1721] Latently, the process that was made public by Frederik III was already initiated before his emergence as King: »Hertug

---

1717 Ibid., p. 238. Scocozza suggests a connection of this reputation to a portrait of Frederik III of unknown origin but painted approximately in 1650, which shows the puritanically clad King looking through a window, absorbed in thought (ibid.). In this and similar instances, Scocozza highlights how a person's fame is constructed in such depictions. For another example, see ibid. pp. 158 and 159, which confront a painting by the Dutch painter Adrian van de Venne from the year 1643, depicting Christian IV as Europe's peacemaker, with a Dutch chalcography from 1644 illustrating the King and Axel Oxenstierna playing backgammon – a common allegory in the Baroque age for the potentates' careless gamble with their subjects' lives and livelihood – for the Sound Dues, while the tradesmen surrounding them store away unimaginable riches.

1718 Merchants had already played a considerable role in enabling the high nobility's and thus Ulfeldt's financial dominance (cf. ibid., p. 167) and at times, they had compensated the government's monetary ineptitude; cf. ibid., p. 172: »Og så var det, regeringen sendte ilbud til Marselis & Berns, der atter en gang klarede en dansk statsopgave«. Marselis & Berns, a Dutch-German trade and banking company, plays a central role in another depiction of this age by a Communist-Maoist writer, i.e. Ebbe Kløvedal-Reichs trilogy *Rejsen til Messias* (see Chapter 2.4.3.).

1719 See ibid., respectively pp. 235 and 248.

1720 Cf. ibid., p. 259: »Enevældens indførelse og skabelsen af det kollegiale bureaukrati pegede i retning af den danske statsmagts forvandling fra at være en udvidet form for godsdrift til at blive en moderne centralmagt. Ulfeldt evnede som rigshofmester også denne side af sagen. Men han knækkede halsen på modsætningen mellem statsmandsgerningens krav om den private adelsmands stadige ønske om at behandle riget, som om det var hans eget gods. Det kunne Christian 4. gøre, for han var konge. Men det blev til svindel, når statens tjener gjorde det«. See also ibid., p. 199: »Den skarpsindige Dureel [Magnus, the Swedish legate] konstaterede da også, at tilstanden i Danmark efter opgøret med svigersønnerne ville blive væsentlig forbedret, og at lensmændene nu måtte aflægge nøje regnskab, hvilket ville gavne rigets økonomi og gøre det stærkere. Der kunne ikke herske tvivl om, at Danmark atter ‚ville komme på fødderne'«.

1721 See, for example, ibid., p. 186: »Til den særlige modsætning mellem svigersønnernes kreds og den øvrige rigsrådsadel kom stridigheder mellem højadelen og den efterhånden økonomisk og politisk stærkt trængte menige adel, der ikke brød sig om, at de store adelsslægter monopoliserede lenembederne, og at tyske og holstenske adelsfolk sivede ind i landet«.

Frederik kunne fra kulisserne med sindsro overvære, hvordan Ulfeldt overspillede sin rolle i den magtkamp, der fandt sted«.[1722]

Scocozza's portrayal of this historic regime change is thus an intrinsically optimistic one.[1723] His narrative does not conclude that all challenges of the preceding centuries had been overcome, but that the country, and the monarchy to a certain degree, was and still is in a constant state of transformation,[1724] regularly resulting in major and minor improvements. To use a key term employed by Hayden White, *Ved afgrundens rand* depicts a series of reconciliations (i.e. »partial liberation from the condition of the Fall and provisional release from the divided state in which men find themselves in this world«)[1725] and is hence emplotted in the style of a Comedy:

> The reconciliations which occur at the end of Comedy are reconciliations of men with men, of men with their world and their society; the condition of society is represented as being purer, saner, and healthier as a result of the conflict among seemingly inalterably opposed elements in the world; these elements are revealed to be, in the long run, harmonizable with one another, unified, at one with themselves and the others.[1726]

The notion that the events of 1660 were no final solution and that *enevælde* is no ideal regime but rather the best of all possible reactions to the preceding *adelsvælde*, is, not least, conveyed in Scocozza's concluding words on the biographies of Ulfeldt and Leonora Christina. The latter's fate does not go uncriticised: »Efter aftale mellem den danske og den engelske regering blev hun kidnappet i Dover og sendt til København, hvor hun den 8. august blev sat i Blåtårn. Hun blev aldrig stillet for retten, men alligevel holdt i fangenskab i 22 år«.[1727] In the late 17th cen-

---

[1722] Ibid., p. 185.

[1723] To that effect, the ideology communicated through Scocozza's account could be termed Conservative, in spite of the author's involvement in modern-day far-left politics. Cf. White, Hayden. *Metahistory*, p. 28: »The tone of voice is accomodationist, the mood is optimistic, and the ideological implications are Conservative, inasmuch as one can legitimately conclude from a history thus construed that one inhabits the best of possible historical worlds, or at least the best one can 'realistically' hope for«.

[1724] Accordingly, *Ved afgrundens rand* is a diachronic, or processional narrative: »Romance and Comedy [the form of emplotment applied to *Ved afgrundens rand*] stress the emergence of new forces or conditons out of processes that appear at first glance either to be changeless in their essence or to be changing only in their phenomenal forms« (ibid., p. 11). Scocozza implements the hypothetical new forces delineated by White through his introduction of constantly new, stronger and better forces which oust the old, eventually disused ones. Thus, the Ulfeldt couple and their peers practically dethrone the old, weakened King Christian IV only to be replaced themselves by a new King.

[1725] Ibid., p. 9.

[1726] Ibid.

[1727] Scocozza, Benito. *Ved afgrundens rand*, p. 258. Scocozza's word choice – *kidnappet* and *aldrig stillet for retten* – blatantly denunciates the lack of a fair jurisdiction and transparent executive measures.

tury, Denmark is still far from obtaining a rule of law, yet a worse time, the age of Ulfeldt, has passed:

> Mere end nogen anden samtidig politiker kom Corfitz Ulfeldt til at sande sit eget valgsprog, at tilværelsen er en farce, der styres af øjeblikkets luner. Og han bidrog selv til farcen, men det ville være urimeligt at tilskrive hans skæbne et sygt sind. Han blev blot det yderste udtryk for den magtens omskiftelighed, der prægede midten af 1600-tallet. I sine velmagtsdage, da han kunne hundse med Christian 4., skrabe en million daler til sig ved hjælp af korruption og bestikkelse og ydmyge Frederik 3. med en benhård håndfæstning, var han mere end nogen anden legemliggørelsen af rigsrådsadelens yderste overmod i en tid, hvor den af al magt prøvede at bevare sin gamle indflydelse på trods af behovet for, at grundlaget for statsstyret blev bredere end en halv snes storgodsejere.[1728]

The Organicist Scocozza portrays thus a country on the move in the right direction: »The Organicist is inclined to talk about the 'principles' or 'ideas' that inform the individual processes discerned in the field and all the processes taken as a whole. These principles or ideas are seen as imaging or prefiguring the end toward which the process as a whole tends«.[1729] The survival of the fittest informs the 17th century depicted by Scocozza.[1730] It is the principle that configures the dominant mode of presenting the constant replacement of a ruling class, the conciliatory message of the narrative being the assurance that cleptocracy and other misuses of power tend to annihilate themselves as they fail to adept to their developing environment. As reproduced above, Scocozza considers Ulfeldt an embodiment of a major challenge of his time, i.e. the high nobility's unrestrained greed and arrogance. His fate

---

1728 Ibid., p. 258.
1729 White, Hayden. *Metahistory*, p. 16.
1730 Scocozza's somehow Darwinist outlook is most likely the result of his political ideology; Charles Darwin's *On the Origin of species* (1859) was, after all, a major source of inspiration to Karl Marx' *Das Kapital* ('The Capital', first volume published in 1867), in which Marx refers to Darwin's work as 'epoch-making' (Marx, Karl. *Das Kapital: Kritik der politischen Ökonomie*, Cologne: Anaconda, 2009, footnote p. 328). In a letter to Friedrich Engels, Marx furthermore refers to *On the Origin of Species* as »das Buch, das die naturhistorische Grundlage für unsere Ansicht enthält« (Letter addressed to Friedrich Engels and dated 19 December 1860, reproduced in *Karl Marx. Friedrich Engels. Historisch-kritische Gesamtausgabe: Werke, Schriften, Briefe 2: Der Briefwechsel zwischen Marx und Engels 1854-1860*. Berlin: Marx-Engels-Verlag, 1930, p. 533: 'the book which contains the scientific basis for our view'), which Engels confirms a few years later in a review of *Das Kapitel* (Engels, Friedrich. Review of *Das Kapital* published in *Der Beobachter* no. 303, 27 December 1867. In *Karl Marx. Friedrich Engels. Gesamtausgabe (MEGA) I: Werke, Artikel, Entwürfe 21: September 1867 bis März 1871. Text*, ed. Jürgen Herres. Berlin: Akademie Verlag, 2009, p. 39). Marx' ideas on the historical class struggle would later come to be termed 'Historical Materialism' – hence the title of the present chapter.

is thus depicted in more detail and as representative of the fall of an entire social stratum. Alternatively, Scocozza could have characterised Hannibal Sehested in greater detail. This influential statesman met a similar fate as Ulfeldt. He was, however, savvier, more reasonable, more submissive, more adaptable and hence more successful.[1731] His story would thus have been unfit to typify the ideology favoured by Scocozza, according to which the high nobility as a ruling class could not prevail. This use of the historic personnel is metonymic-reductionist on the one hand, in that the fate and vices of one entire class are exemplified by one person's life's story. On the other hand, it is also synecdochal-integrative through its incorporation of Leonora Christina's story, not so much as the minor part of the 'Ulfeldt-package',[1732] but rather as the side glance she provides into Denmark's women's history.

As stated above, for much of the Ulfeldt-narrative Leonora Christina is reduced to a mere side-kick while being eliminated from the account altogether on other occasions. She is, for example, seemingly not with her husband (and hence not part of the account) from the Treaty of Roskilde in 1658, until Ulfeldt's flight from Sweden in 1660. They seem to only meet again in Copenhagen.[1733] Only much later, after her husband's disappearance from the core account, Scocozza provides a different perspective on Leonora Christina by reintroducing her as a precursor to the feminist movement, even though Scocozza suspects that she had other motives as well to write *Hæltinners Pryd*: »[...] Leonora Christinas heltindeepos skulle styrke kongedatterens selvfølelse over for enevældens regerende mænd, der misbrugte deres magt til at holde hende i fængsel«.[1734] In this regard, as well as concerning outline, ideology and authorial intent, Scocozza's narrative resembles the Leonora Christina Fragment written by Eva Hemmer Hansen (see Chapter 2.5.2.), published only a few years earlier than *Ved afgrundens rand*. Both authors establish a central sociocritical perspective in their accounts, which has persisted ever since and which has led to the current, ambivalent reception of Leonora Christina as a historical character. This ambivalence manifests itself in a tendentially negative portrayal

---

1731 Cf. Sehested's characterisation in Bøggild-Andersen, C. O. 'Hannibal Sehested': 1609-1666'. In *Store danske personligheder 1: Fra Knud den Store til Christian X*, ed. Aage Bertelsen. Copenhagen: Berling, 1949, pp. 87-106.

1732 See, for example, Scocozza, Benito. *Ved afgrundens rand*, p. 218: »Corfitz Ulfeldt gjorde sin indflydelse kraftigt gældende ved det svenske hof. Det var hans, Leonora Christinas og den øvrige detroniserede Munkfamilies store drøm, at de ved svensk hjælp kunne genvinde deres tabte positioner«. See ibid., p. 256: »Herfra havde *de* [my italics] søgt at hidse den svenske regering til krig mod Danmark«.

1733 Cf. ibid., p. 257.

1734 Ibid., p. 338.

of Leonora Christina as artistocratic[1735] and an overwhelmingly positive notion of Leonora Christina's significance to the feminist cause.

Ved afgrundens rand constitutes no considerable exception to this modern tendency to separate Leonora Christina's rank from her sex. It rather represents an attempt at charting this separation by apportioning the noble (captured in the French autobiography and in *Jammers Minde*) and the woman (manifested in *Hæltinners Pryd*) among two separate chapters. However, one part of this split characterisation prevails:

> Leonora Christina var sig også bevidst, at hun ikke var en hvilken som helst kvinde. Selv i fængslet bevarede hun sin standsbevidsthed, og selv om hun, i hvert fald ifølge »Jammersminde«, gerne støttede de kvinder, der var sat til at tage vare på hende i fængslet, i at tilegne sig lærdom og gudfrygtighed, veg hun ikke tilbage for at stikke nogle af dem et par ørefigner, hvis hun ikke brød sig om deres opførsel, på samme måde som hun havde gjort det, da hun i sine velmagtsdage herskede i den ulfeldtske rigmandsgård på Gråbrødre Torv.[1736]

As stated above, Scocozza attributes no political or social (i.e. historical in the narrower sense) relevance to Leonora Christina, since in the historical field delineated in the core narrative she plays no active role. Whenever she appears, though, she does so mostly through epitomes of aristocracy. Besides introducing Leonora Christina through a painting in which she flashes several symbols of her peerage, Scocozza furthermore exhibits a conspicuous interest in the legitimacy of her nobility. One of the first official strikes against the Ulfeldt couple is Frederik III's annulment of Leonora Christina's title,[1737] which is countermanded in the Treaty of Roskilde,[1738]

1735 This negative notion of Leonora Christina's social status and the privileges associated with it is relatively new and while it is usually conditioned by accounts of Ulfeldt's corruption and greed – as opposed to Leonora Christina's royal birthright to a life in luxury – Scocozza's account challenges this prerogative at a higher degree. While his empathetic presentation of the Dina affair and its unjust consequences for Dina – a woman that used to be dismissed as a strumpet – is thus not new per se, his social perspective on the outcome of the trial *is* (see ibid., p. 196). The *løse kvinde* Dina could not stand a chance against *velbårne frøken* Leonora Christina and according to Scocozza's sources, this was also the public opinion following the execution of Dina: »Hvis man skal tro den spanske gesandt, Rebolledo, var det også den opfattelse, der var udbredt blandt menig almue. Han berettede, at folk hver dag i store skarer strømmede til det sted, hvor bøddelen havde spiddet Dinas hoved på en stage. De råbte, at hun var omkommet uskyldig, og det sagdes, at om natten lod Gud et forunderligt lys skinne over det sted, hvor hun så nådesløst var stedt til hvile« (ibid., p. 199).

1736 Ibid., p. 338.

1737 Ibid., p. 191.

1738 Ibid., p. 256: »[...] og Leonora Christina fik grevindetitel igen, som Frederik 3. havde frataget hende«.

and reinstated after her arrest in Hammershus, as gleefully noted by Scocozza: »Og Leonora Christina måtte for anden gang slippe sin grevindetitel«.[1739]

Apart from these side notes documenting the volatility of Leonora Christina's rank, Scocozza also involves her in the historical account whenever her autobiographical texts could shed some light on the events. Unlike his predecessors, however, Scocozza refrains from accrediting the French autobiography or *Jammers Minde* as reproductions of reality. Instead they are considered to be just as calculated and conventionalized as the paintings analysed above:

> Leonora Christina, der betegnede sig selv som kongens yndlingsdatter, beretter i *sine* erindringer, at »hun havde endnu den trøst at betjene ham til hans sidste suk«, og at kongen, da hun havde grædt ved hans sygeleje, havde kysset og klappet hende og bedt hende stille sine tårer, idet han sagde: »Jeg har sat dig så fast, at ingen kan rokke dig«.[1740]

Leonora Christina's version of her father's death coincides with that of Otto Sperling the Elder but clearly both texts have forfeited their status as historical documents:

> Begge erindringer er skrevet årtier efter kongens død, på et tidspunkt, hvor det var gået ilde for Leonora Christina og doktor Sperling, der var Ulfeldtfamiliens trofaste ven. Sandsynligvis er det eneste sandfærdige ved de to beretninger, at Corfitz Ulfeldt og Leonora Christina hele tiden var om kongen under hans sidste sygdom. De agtede at sikre sig rigets nøgler ved at beslaglægge kongens aktstykker, forhindre hertug Frederik i at komme til stede og holde Vibeke Kruse fra kongen.[1741]

Despite Leonora Christina's literary and proto-feminist merits, she remains thus a member of the aristocracy, the doomed stratum of society. Accordingly, Scocozza finishes his excursus on Leonora Christina and *Hæltinners Pryd* with the conclusion that a noblewoman's talk is cheap:

1739 Ibid., p. 257.
1740 Ibid., p. 181.
1741 Ibid.

> De lærde kvinder, Anders Bording hyldede, kom fra adelsstanden. De alene havde det overskud af tid, der gav dem muligheder for at beskæftige sig med kunst og litteratur. Men videnskab i alleregentligste forstand lå dog uden for deres horisont. Trods al tale om mænds og kvinders ligeværd koncentrerede adelskvinderne sig om moralske skrifter, historiske emner, visesamlinger og slægtstudier.[1742]

Through this reminder that Leonora Christina's literary and cultural merits were inevitably dependent on her privileged social situation (»[f]or der var også forskel på kvinder, mellem høj og lav«)[1743] Scocozza re-merges the sociohistorical and the literary-feminist discourse and relativises the contemporary impact of *Hæltinners Pryd* altogether: »Den forskel var nok så betydningsfuld for kvindernes livsbane som afstanden mellem kønnene«. In a society on the brink of disaster, social rank outweighs sex.

1742 Ibid., p. 339.
1743 Ibid., p. 338.

Résumé

The versatility and ambiguity of *Jammers Minde* and the Leonora Christina-subject matter is central to its subsequent reception. As demonstrated in Chapter 1, a distinct classification of *Jammers Minde* seems unaccomplishable. Thomas Seiler alone, to name only one example, classifies the text as »Mischform« (in terms of prison literature), »primär [...] Gefängnisliteratur«, »Dokument einer religiösen Krise«, »Rechtfertigungsschrift«, and »Heiligenbiografie«.[1744] As regards the zeitgeist informing Leonora Christina's literary style, scholarly opinion on this matter could not have been more divergent either. While some have concluded that *Jammers Minde* is quintessentially Baroque,[1745] Finn Stein Larsen's assessment, which evaluated the text to be a text, which truly belonged to the late 19th century,[1746] is shared by many other scholars as well. While it is futile to call the text anything but essentially Baroque, it was still somehow ahead of its time.[1747] After all, the mediator of the Modern Breakthrough in Scandinavia, the Danish critic Georg Brandes, acclaimed *Jammers Minde* for its exemplary potential[1748] only two years before commencing his famous series of lectures subsequently published under the title *Hovedstrømninger i det 19de Aarhundredes Litteratur*. *Jammers Minde* was indubitably a great success in the 19th century, yet I would not go as far as Katrin Lunde and Luise F. Pusch, who assume that the manuscript would have been met with no interest, had it been published immediately, because the author's 'female style' deviated too much from the contemporary public's taste.[1749] Aside from the fact that Leonora Christina would not have been the only successful female Scandi-

---

1744 Seiler, Thomas. *Im Leben verschollen*, respectively pp. 11, 51, 60, 64, and 65 ('hybrid', 'primarily [...] prison literature', 'document of a religious crisis', 'apologia' and 'Vita').

1745 See, for example, ibid., p. 51: »Sie [Leonora Christina] macht ihren individuellen Fall zu einem allgemeinen, beispielhaften. Und mit dieser Allegorisierung ist ihr Text tief im barocken Weltbild verhaftet und keinesfalls so revolutionär, wie immer behauptet wird«.

1746 Larsen, Finn Stein. 'En impressionist fra baroktiden?', p. 28.

1747 Cf. Lyngstad, Sverre. 'The Danish Princess Leonora Christina', p. 384. In his analysis of 17th-century literature, Claus Pico Stæhr comes to a similar conclusion. However, he also argues for a clearer separation between Leonora Christina's historical activities and her literary products: »Og HVOR passer så Leonora Christina og *Jammersminde* ind i alt dette. Ret beset: Ikke noget sted. Hun er med sit efter dansk målestok høje dannelsesgrundlag, sin karakter og skæbne et unikt eksempel i 1600-tallets litteratur. Ideologisk kan hun placeres som en renaissancepersonlighed, litterært-stilmæssigt som en relativt fri skribent, der fortæller uden at være bundet eller indfanget af de omtalte stiltendenser og litterære tendenser, som hun udmærket kendte gennem bl.a. oversættelsesarbejde og læsning af europæiske forfattere« (see Stæhr, Claus Pico. 'Leonora Christina og 1600-tallets europæiske litteratur – en oversigt'. In *Leonora Christina: Historien om en heltinde*. Århus: Arkona, 1983 (Acta Jutlandica 58, Humanistisk serie 57), p. 96).

1748 Cf. Brandes, Georg. 'Leonora Christina', p. 70.

1749 Lunde, Katrin and Luise F. Pusch. 'Leonora Christina', p. 89.

navian writer of her age, it is highly doubtful that a person as infamous as Leonora Christina should have been unable to find an interested party for her life story (even though Lunde and Pusch's notion is partially backed by Wilhelm Friese's study on Nordic Baroque literature).[1750] The late 19th century may well have provided the best possible breeding grounds for a national heroine of Leonora Christina's calibre, but recent developments (such as the ferry controversy of 2011) suggest that interest in this notorious noblewoman is not bound to a certain age.

The history of research on *Jammers Minde* mirrors the course of academic interest in and evaluation of the autobiographical genre.[1751] While the 19th century tended to eulogise Leonora Christina based on her self-portrayal in *Jammers Minde*,[1752] literary analysis of the text itself had not commenced yet. By the middle of the 20th century, academic notions of *Jammers Minde* and its author experienced a shift. Scholars were no longer calling the work a mere testimony, but regarded it as autobiography. This change of perception was followed by a dwindling interest in the text. Whether it was the disappointing realisation that *Jammers Minde* was not a trustworthy historical testimony, or a general perplexity in the face of the introduction of a relatively novel literary genre,[1753] the few academic contributions from this period are both uncritical and hazy, thus forming a blatant contrast to the lively discussion provided by the 19th century. Gustav Albeck, for example, comments on *Jammers Minde* as follows: »Leonora Christinas Jammersminde, er det betydeligste prosaværk, som den danske litteratur kan opvise i 1600-tallet. Det er præget af sin forfatters stærke personlighed«.[1754] However, while Albeck commends the »benå-

---

1750 Friese, Wilhelm. *Nordische Barockdichtung: Eine Darstellung und Deutung skandinavischer Dichtung zwischen Reformation und Aufklärung*. Munich: Francke, 1968, p. 141.

1751 Cf. Heitmann, Annegret. 'Zwischen Macht und Marginalität', p. 205: »Wie so oft bei Autobiographien konzentriert sich das Interesse zunächst auf den historischen Informationsgehalt, dann schließt sich eine philologische Aufarbeitung an, bis Genre und Stilfragen den Text literaturwissenschaftlich erschließen« ('As is often the case with autobiographies, the interest [in these texts] concerns first their historical-informative content, then a philological processing follows, until genre and questions of literary style explore the text from a philological perspective').

1752 This romanticisation of Leonora Christina's life and character might have been primarily motivated by the type of narrative provided by *Jammers Minde*. In her study on prison literature, Sigrid Weigel concludes that the mere circumstances resulting in a prison narrative appear to be perceived as something guaranteeing a type of quality of both character and the product (Weigel, Sigrid. *Und selbst im Kerker frei...!*, p. 7).

1753 Cf. Petersen, Carl S. *Illustreret dansk Litteraturhistorie 1*, p. 825: »Med selvbiografisk Litteratur har der ikke før været Anledning til at beskæftige sig; den er i Danmark som overalt i Europa en forholdsvis sen litterær Foreteelse«.

1754 Albeck, Gustav. *Dansk litteraturhistorie 1: Fra Runerne til Johannes Ewald*, ed. P. H. Traustedt. Copenhagen: Politiken, 1967 (1964), p. 203. Many literary histories agree that *Jammers Minde* is the Danish Baroque age's most distinguished prose work (cf., for example, 'Rejsen til Jeg'ets indre: Leonora Christina 1621-1698'. In *Nordiske Forfatterinder: Fra Leonora Christina til Elsa Gress: En Antologi*, ed. Lise Busk-Jensen. Copenhagen: Gyldendal, 1990, p. 12).

dede fortællerske«[1755] of *Jammers Minde* for her literary talent, he fails to explicate what exactly comprises this talent. Literary criticism of this age eventually turns into an appraisal of Leonora Christina's character:

> Hun har mestret den kunst at gå til angreb ved at stille modspørgsmål og bevare hovedet koldt, selv når hendes modparter udfoldede deres taktik ved en hastig skiften mellem venlige henstillinger om at bekende (ledsaget af uforbindende løfter om eventuel frigivelse) og forblommede trusler om den straf, der kunne vente hende, dersom hun fortsat nægtede at vide noget om Corfitz Ulfeldts forræderiplaner.[1756]

In the late 20th century, one can sense the effects of a new kind of literary research. Whereas most scholars began to highlight and appreciate the literary quality of texts like *Jammers Minde*, others could not help but (also) criticize Leonora Christina for not presenting her life in an accurately historical manner. Jens Aage Doctor heralded this new kind of criticism with his now classic essay 'Sandhedens rolle', published in 1970, which reprehends previous scholarship's negligence in terms of treating *Jammers Minde* as proper literature,[1757] while at the same time reminding his audience of what this means for the text: that it is fiction, i.e. a (more or less) conscious deviation of the truth.[1758] Bodil Wamberg's criticism of Leonora Christina's autobiographical writings poses a climax of this development,[1759] but it also offers a fresh way of interpreting some of Leonora Christina's statements, especially regarding Corfitz Ulfeldt (see Chapter 1.2.1.).

The 21st century has brought about less passionate, yet all the more fertile research on Leonora Christina's life and, especially, her work. Due to the late preceding century's insight that autobiography necessarily (and ideally) centres on self-portrayal rather than being a mimetic depiction of the past, more recent academic contributions have focussed on Leonora Christina's way of creating her self-image; for example Lutz Rühling, who analysed the different sides to Leonora Christina's self-perception: »Dabei strukturiert sie ihre Umgebung nach dem schlichten Grund-

---

1755 Albeck, Gustav. *Dansk litteraturhistorie 1*, p. 200.
1756 Ibid.
1757 Doctor, Jens Aage. 'Sandhedens rolle', p. 5: »Det er som om bogen trods alle lovord ikke har kunnet læses som ›rigtig‹ litteratur, for tolkningen ender gerne i den kildekritik der rettelig burde være dens udgangspunkt«.
1758 However, Doctor is inclined to condone this deviation due to its psychological background: »Hun véd de har ret i alt hvad de siger – men hun ved også noget mere om Corfits, og derfor kan hun alligevel ikke tro på deres påstande om ham« (ibid., p. 22).
1759 See, for example, Wamberg's comments on Leonora Christina's plea in the course of the Malmö trial: »Løgnen er ikke blot noget, hun griber til af nød. Man træffer på løgnen i alt, hvad hun skriver« (Wamberg, Bodil. *Leonora Christina*, p. 159).

satz: Wer nicht für mich ist, der ist wider mich«.[1760] Rühling's exposure of Leonora Christina's »narzisstische, um nicht zu sagen egozentrische Wahrnehmung und Darstellung ihrer Umgebung«[1761] may well hit the mark, but such digressions from an initially literary subject leads to a vast field different from, yet also intricately connected with literature and autobiography in particular, i.e. psychology. However, Rühling was not the first scholar to combine literary analysis with a historical-psychological approach. In an essay from 1971, Finn Stein Larsen attributes Leonora Christina's documentary style to her distant, aristocratic mindset:

> Intrigerne mod Ulfeldt og hende selv gjorde, at hun bestandig følte sig en garde, fordømte sine omgivelser hensynsløst over alle bredder, gravede kløfterne mellem sig selv og omverdenen dybere. [...] Alt dette giver betingelserne for at forstå stykkets stilholdning. Forfatteren distancerer sig aristokratisk og mistænksomt fra sine omgivelser.[1762]

At present, publications of the 19th century with their romantic conceptions of the princess in the tower are mostly being dismissed on the grounds of not distinguishing between a narrating and narrated 'I'. Yet, to date, no academic contribution on Leonora Christina and/or *Jammers Minde* comes to mind which was truly able to either focus on the historical Leonora Christina without consulting her autobiographical works at all, or to analyse *Jammers Minde* or the French autobiography without integrating comments and conclusions on its author's character. This circumstance was already pointed out three decades ago by Anne-Marie Mai and Stig Dalager.[1763] The autobiographical genre does not seem to allow a separation of history and literature, nor does such a division seem constructive, as exemplified by the texts presented and discussed in Chapter 2, which readily drew upon the multitude of images of Leonora Christina created by semi-historical records and other fictionalised accounts of her life.

The mid-17th-century texts presented in Chapter 2.1. 'Contemporary Literary Portrayals' attest to a perception of Leonora Christina not as an acting individual, but as a representative of either the Munk clan ('Fru Kirsten Munks Ballet') or the Ulfeldt family (Sperling's *Selbstbiographie*). Furthermore, these contemporary

---

1760 Rühling, Lutz. *Opfergänge der Vernunft*, p. 71 ('She structures her surroundings on the basis of the simple principle: either you are for me, or against me').
1761 Ibid ('narcissistic, even egocentric perception and portrayal of her environment').
1762 Larsen, Finn Stein. *Prosaens mønstre*, p. 26f.
1763 Mai, Anne-Marie and Stig Dalager. '»... et eventyr, som er værdigt en roman«', p. 58: »Leonora Christinas skæbne rører ved noget personligt i mennesker, en fortolkning af den synes uværgerligt at blive subjektiv, og det gælder ikke blot for forfattere og kritikere, men også for flere historikere, der har beskæftiget sig med hende«.

depictions of Leonora Christina indicate contemporary attitudes ranging from reticence to outward resentment towards the wife of Corfitz Ulfeldt.

However, once Leonora Christina had served her time, the public disposition towards her turned, to a large extent, into admiration of her self-sacrifice. The 19th-century romantic nationalism and the concurrent marriage and proto-feminist discourse informed the classic works of Leonora Christina-literature, i.e. the writings of Hans Christian Andersen, Louise Hegermann Lindencrone and Adam Oehlenschläger, but also of Mathilde Fibiger. Both Andersen and Fibiger utilised the story of Leonora Christina to reflect on the concept of Danishness and to assert their own love for their home country in Chapter 2.2. 'Leonora Christina as Subject of Patriotic Debate'. Besides the overarching topic of their texts, however, these two writers have very little in common. In 'Holger Danske' and 'Gudfaders Billedbog', Andersen depicts Leonora Christina as a static image, as the legacy of her father and her country and hence as tantamount to Danishness and representative of Danish history. Fibiger, on the other hand, focuses on Leonora Christina's choices and obligations as an individual, and particularly on her colliding obligations towards husband and country. Notwithstanding the dubiety of Leonora Christina's suitability as a female role model, her function in Fibiger's novel is primarily that of a catalyst of female participation in public debate and hence a seminal one. The publication of *Jammers Minde* in 1869 constitutes a turning point for the work of both authors. While Andersen had evidently been fascinated by Leonora Christina before reading her autobiography, his seemingly decreasing interest in the subject after 1869 confirms a suspicion evoked by most of his works depicting Leonora Christina, i.e. that his admiration was actually aimed at Corfitz Ulfeldt. Fibiger, however, was turned into a fan of Leonora Christina's after reading *Jammers Minde*, since the independence, integrity and conviction exhibited in the text correspond to Fibiger's appeal in *En Skizze*.

The texts discussed in Chapter 2.3. '*Kvinde er kvinde værst*: Leonora Christina and Dina' also testify to the drastic change in the perception and reception of Leonora Christina caused by the publication of her works, yet most of all of *Jammers Minde*. The presentations of the Dina affair written by Louise Hegermann Lindencrone and Adam Oehlenschläger exhibit an idealised and still rather passive, almost static image of Leonora Christina, as well as a hidden (Hegermann Lindencrone) or blatant (Oehlenschläger) focus on Corfitz Ulfeldt. By highlighting the consistency of the love and support Leonora Christina demonstrated for her husband, Hegermann Lindencrone's and Oehlenschläger's Eleonora furthermore emerges as a Madonna, i.e. as an archetypal mother. Overall, 19th-century depictions represent Leonora Christina as an abiding, loyal, sweet-tempered wife. Later literary adaptations, on the other hand, such as Rolf Gjedsted's *Fordærvede kvinder*, react to the rather feisty Leonora Christina depicted in her own texts and also consider the relevance of Leonora Christina to her husband, i.e. that »[æ]gteskabet med Leonora var omdrejnings-punktet i Ulfeldts karriere«.[1764] Gjedsted's novel attests to a fascination with Leonora Christina's age, with the depravity and decadence that distinguished the 17th century in Denmark, and with Leonora Christina's hybrid position as a representative of both offenders (nobility) and victims (women) of this time. Most conspicuous about the three texts discussed in Chapter 2.3., though, is the clearly discernible and chronologically rising tendency to approximate the two women to each other, either by elevating the social and intellectual level of Dina (most evidently in Oehlenschläger's *Dina*), or by lowering the moral level of Leonora Christina to that of her rival (as undertaken in *Fordærvede kvinder*). Out of these three texts, Hegermann Lindencrone's drama exhibits the largest discrepancy between the two women. The trend of aligning the two women is attended by one of increased sympathy with Dina, as she and Leonora Christina have gradually come to be considered kindred: neither was entirely innocent, both fell prey to their beloved's ambitions and in the public's eyes, both women were eventually absolved through their excessively harsh punishment.

The three texts presented in Chapter 2.4. 'Leonora Christina's Via Dolorosa: Stages of a *Christi Kaarßdragerske*'s Life' deal with the spiritual and religious aspects of Leonora Christina's life and writings, i.e. with her (self-)portrayal as spiritually converted and, eventually, as martyr in the tradition of Christ in very diverging ways. While Louise Hegermann Lindencrone and H. F. Ewald present Leonora Christina's life from entirely different angles, their overall approach is the same, as they both depict Leonora Christina in a consistent manner. In Hegermann Lindencrone's tale 'Billedet', as well as in the drama *Eleonora Christina Uhlfeldt*, Eleonora is primarily a mother figure and a saint; but 'Billedet' intensifies the idealisation of Leonora Christina typical of the 19th century by turning her into an idol. This text presents the life of Leonora Christina as a model of rewarding female self-sacrifice, hence also suggesting a new, more inclusive understanding of (historical) significance.

Since the iconisation of Leonora Christina was conditioned by the ideological, cultural and political tenor of the 19th century and by the reading public's ignorance of *Jammers Minde*, texts written towards the end of the century depicted a less idealised, but also less static Leonora Christina. This new tendency is heralded by H. F. Ewald's novel *Leonora Kristina: Billeder af en Kongedatters Liv*, which bears the

---

1764 Scocozza, Benito. *Christian 4.*, p. 257.

mark of Leonora Christina's realistic, ambivalent self-portrayal in *Jammers Minde* and of Julius Lange's subsequent relativising criticism of the text's author. Despite Ewald's focus on Leonora Christina's ordeal, his protagonist is a more profane version of the same person presented in earlier 19th-century texts. Unlike many other authors of Leonora Christina-literature written after 1869 (such as Ebbe Kløvedal Reich), Ewald does not consider his protagonist a representative of her – in his view – vulgar and inferior age. At the same time, he depicts her in a manner more demystified than his predecessors did. Ewald's Leonora is an unconditionally compliant and loyal wife, which, unlike most writers of Leonora Christina-literature, Ewald considers a flaw, albeit also a token of archetypal femininity.

Ebbe Kløvedal Reich, on the other hand, challenges the ideal of female subordination altogether in the trilogy *Rejsen til Messias*. Through her interactions with the protagonist Josef, Leonora constitutes a manifested alternative ideology celebrating female values and universal autonomy. Leonora epitomises female emancipation, independence and equality. However, she is also representative of the 17th century's political, confessional and spiritual struggle. Through its depiction of Leonora Christina's spiritual metamorphosis, as well as through Leonora's functional transformation from a not all too congenial, tertiary character to a central figure and guidepost in the protagonist's life, *Rejsen til Messias* exhibits a contrastive disposition.

Leonora Christina's portrayal in Reich's trilogy thus constitutes a step in the development initiated by H. F. Ewald, but which culminated in Birgithe Kosovic's novel *Leonora Christina* discussed in Chapter 2.5. 'By Order of Education: Leonora Christina's Admittance into Denmark's Literary Canon', which engages in the question of the everlasting educational or even didactic value of Leonora Christina's life story and of *Jammers Minde*. The 21st century turned the former Danish Madonna into a captivating, albeit entirely un-exemplary vamp. Accordingly, Kosovic's Leonora does not shy away from embezzlement, sabotage, treason, and even incitement to murder (in this case, the murder of Fuchs in Bruges by the hands of Leonora's son Christian).[1765] The didactic value of Birgithe Kosovic's *Leonora Christina*, or rather the didactic value of Leonora Christina's life story as rendered

---

[1765] When Christian informs his parents that their former prison guard, Adolph Fuchs, is in Bruges, Corfitz expresses the wish to strike him dead, but Leonora has other plans: »'Nej, du gør ej,' sagde Leonora og rejste sig. 'Du bliver her.' I stedet vendte hun sig mod Christian og så på ham med et unaturligt smil« (see Kosovic, Birgithe. *Leonora Christina*, p. 46). This interpretation of the events resulting in Fuchs' death is not entirely unfounded. Leonora Christina did indirectly incite one of her sons – Leo Ulfeldt – to retaliation. In a letter dated 27 April 1663 and addressed to Otto Sperling, in whose care young Leo had been at that time, she writes the following: »Kan jeg ikke hævne mig, saa kan han maaske gøre det en Dag; var jeg endda vis paa det, vilde jeg dø med et tilfreds Hjerte, naar det skal være« (*Uforbeholdne Breve fra Leonora Christinas Tid*, ed. Ingeborg Buhl. Copenhagen: Hasselbalch, 1956 (Hasselbalchs Kulturbibliotek 156), p. 42).

Résumé

by Birgithe Kosovic, does not derive from its historically educational potential. The account, directed at untrained readers of Danish literature, is barely sixty pages long and erratic, hence leaving little room for historical or any other type of elaboration.[1766] Furthermore, the novel exhibits no traces of ethical didactisation, as the protagonist's character is plainly disagreeable. In this instance, the everlasting value of Leonora Christina's life story is its potential to maintain a modern audience's interest in an otherwise dry subject, i.e. history, but also to demonstrate the value of writing – »hvordan et menneske selv kan skabe sin identitet«[1767] – to an audience increasingly turning towards other media than literature.

Eva Hemmer Hansen's portrayal of Leonora Christina, on the other hand, is highly realistic, in no way idealised, but also more moderate than Kosovic's depiction. Hemmer Hansen's account depicts the lives of all kinds of people in 17th-century Denmark, hence educating its readership on a historical, social and feminist level. However, since Hemmer Hansen's Leonora is the centre of narrative and receptive attention, the depiction of the living conditions and prospects of 17th-century women (as opposed to Leonora's singular fate) remains rudimental. Her portrayal of Ellen Marsvin's loveless youth and of Kirsten Munk's desperation is restricted to a few pages, but the authoress' feminist criticism is – to use the words of Hemmer Hansen's Corfitz Ulfeldt on his future wife – »ufærdig«, but with »interessante muligheder«.[1768] One of the »muligheder« is to consider Hemmer Hansen's portrayal of the women surrounding Leonora Christina in the context of Chapter 2.6. on texts portraying Denmark's 17th-century *femmes fatales*, of which Hemmer Hansen's Leonora Christina-novels can be regarded as a forerunner. In particular, *Den trofaste hustru* offers a – for Hemmer Hansen's contemporaries – novel insight into the potential psyche of Leonora Christina by reconciling her 19th-century image of a saintly wife and mother with her 21st-century reputation as status-conscious *grande dame*. In the background of the public discussion concerning Leonora Christina's accession to the Danish *Kulturkanon*, Hemmer Hansen's novels – especially the sequel *Den trofaste hustru* – illustrates the importance of Leonora Christina's legacy for Danish readers today as well as future generations. The literary master-

---

1766 The novel *Leonora Christina* (1960) by Agnete Elkjær Laursen, on the other hand, exhibits a very evident historically informational intent, since its target group are children. The account offers a broad presentation of its subject matter (including information gathered from historical records, Leonora Christina's own writings and modern research on her), but also background information which serves to help the young readers understand the plot (for example, why Leonora Christina already had a fiancé at the age of nine, see Elkjær Laursen, Agnete. *Leonora Christina*. Copenhagen: Gyldendal, 1968 (1960; Gyldendals lette læseserie 12), p. 8)).

1767 Kosovic, Birgithe. *Leonora Christina*, p. 64.

1768 Hemmer Hansen, Eva. *Den lykkelige hustru*, both quotations p. 20.

piece *Jammers Minde* is the final product of its author's transformation from a 17th-century wife and mother to a modern, emancipated, but also headstrong woman, as depicted by Hammer Hansen (even though a third part that may have reproduced the content of *Jammers Minde* was never written). As such, it provides a valuable lesson and a potential role model to female readers even today.

Finally, Herta J. Enevoldsen's *kulisseromaner* are an adaptation to the interests of a teenage, primarily female readership, yet this adaptation occurs mainly in terms of style and on the thematic level. As far as didactisation is concerned, the account exhibits hardly any trace of such an intention. The protagonist's behaviour is – with only few exceptions – exemplary, but due to the topic of predetermination introduced at the beginning of the novel, her behaviour cannot be attributed to any sort of learning process. In its portrayal of Leonora Christina, Enevoldsen's work resembles the summary of her life in the children's book *Danmark, lidt om Folk og Fædreland, fortalt de kæreste af mine Landsmænd, Børnene* (1943) by the Danish pastor and writer Kaj Munk's (1898-1944). Yet, compared to the latter, Enevoldsen's representation seems much more outmoded. Perhaps as a reaction to the German occupation of Denmark from 1940 onwards,[1769] Munk's portrayal and contextualisation of Leonora Christina is deeply national romanticist, including its focus on the men in Leonora Christina's life. She enters the account as the daughter of Christian IV, a national hero (»[e]lsket højt«), among whose flock of children Leonora Christina stands out like a celestial Queen: »Men i næsten hellig Glans / straaler *Leonor' Christine*. / Som til Dronning var hun kald't. / Hustru, der er tro trods *alt*, / der er mer end Dronning«.[1770]

Other authors of children's books have approached the same topic in an entirely different manner and have thus managed to turn Leonora Christina's life story into a modern account suitable for children: Mette Winge, for example, who published *Da de store var små: 24 historier fra berømte danskeres barndom* in 2009. Her short-story 'Den storsnudede kongedatter' negates any elevation other than at the social level by presenting Leonora Christina's self-elevation in an ironically twisted man-

---

[1769] Cf. Torben Weinreich, who attributes the increase in historical literature (including children's books) in the two decades following the end of World War II to the »netop overståede tyske besættelse af Danmark. Der er brug for at understøtte forestillingen om en særlig dansk identitet, som har rødder langt tilbage i tiden« (Weinreich, Torben. *Historien om børnelitteratur*, p. 443). According to Weinreich, the historical periods of highest interest to Danish writers and readers of historical topics in the post-war years were the ages ranging from the Stone Age up until the time of the Vikings (ibid.). This observation coincides with my own of a decline in Leonora Christina-literature in the post-war years up until the revival of historical literature in the 1980's (cf. Weinreich, Torben. 'I statens tjeneste', p. 182).

[1770] Munk, Kaj. *Danmark, lidt om Folk og Fædreland, fortalt de kæreste af mine Landsmænd, Børnene*. Copenhagen: Arnold Busck, 1943, both quotations p. 18.

ner.[1771] One scene in particular, which is a departure from Leonora Christina's own narration, depicts her looking out of the window while observing two boys working down in the garden and then hurrying down to meet the boys. She approaches them, first running, then at a consciously royal pace, she straightens up and informs the prettier one of the boys that he is dirty. However, she does not receive a satisfying answer as the boy is too intimidated to talk. Her superiority, which she intended to demonstrate in this meeting with the gardener boys hinders any communication – for the same reason, why Enevoldsen's *Kongedatteren Leonora Christina* does not provide a role model the reader can identify with, as the gap between the two worlds is simply too wide. Mette Winge's protagonist, however, is pushed off her high horse, which allows for an approach between the King's daughter and the gardener boys. While attempting to leave in a royal manner,[1772] Leonora Christina stumbles, falls and cannot lift herself off the ground without the help of the – still dumbstruck – gardener boys. The boys refuse to give her a hand unless she begs them to do so. With Leonora Christina on the ground, the boys are at ease and can begin to communicate with her. She now talks at the same, colloquial level as the gardener boys –»»Ska' jeg be' jer om det! I er nogle lømler.«««[1773] – and the two boys agree to carry her back home. In exchange, Leonora Christina must promise to be nicer to them. Both parties abide by their agreement: the boys carry the King's daughter to the castle and are rewarded with kindness and even some coins. However, the ending represents yet another ironic twist. As soon as Leonora Christina disappears into the castle, nothing seems to have changed. The boys get chased away by one of Leonora Christina's maids – »Næ, slotsgården er ikke noget for dem«.[1774]

In a playful manner, 'Den storsnudede kongedatter' reveals some major difficulties concerning Leonora Christina's portrayal in 20th-century fiction. The character's self-portrayal implies a self-elevation, which has been implicitly or explicitly addressed by an increasing number of 20th and 21st-century writers. In line with Winge's scrutiny of Leonora Christina's self-portrayal, most contemporary depictions of Leonora Christina present an extremely ambivalent character. Contemporary authors bridge the problematic gap between 17th-century pride and post-*jantelov* humility by no longer attempting to continue Leonora Christina's outmoded self-

---

1771 Furthermore, the account presents Leonora Christina as a haughty princess – a character, whose fate is already known to most children through the fairy tales of Hans Christian Andersen.

1772 Winge, Mette and Claus Seidel. 'Den storsnudede kongedatter: Leonora Christina Ulfeldt 1621-1698'. In *Da de store var små: 24 historier fra berømte danskeres barndom*. Copenhagen: Gyldendals Bogklubber, 2009, p. 13: »Han er dum i nakken, tænker Leonora Christina og går videre med rank ryg og hævet hoved som en rigtig kongedatter«.

1773 Ibid., p. 14.

1774 Ibid., p. 16.

glorification. Instead, authors like Maria Helleberg lend their accounts an appropriate historical perspective. The result is, perhaps, a negative one for Leonora Christina, as she forfeited her status as national saint, but the outcome for the reader is all the more positive, as the character is now comprehensible, accessible and most of all interesting again.

The texts presented in Chapter 2.6. 'A Chip off the Old Block: Denmark's Century of *Femmes Fatales*' are representative of this current portrayal of Leonora Christina. The works of 19th-century writers, such as Adam Oehlenschläger, H. F. Ewald and Hans Christian Andersen in particular, still exhibited a focus on the two most important men in Leonora Christina's life – Christian IV and Corfitz Ulfeldt. The late 20th century, on the other hand, abandoned the former glorification of Christian IV as an epitomisation of Denmark (which had also led to an equation of his legacy – Leonora Christina – with her home country). Instead, the works of 20th and 21st-century, largely female writers such as Eva Hemmer Hansen, Birgithe Kosovic and even Herta J. Enevoldsen thematise their protagonist's problematic childhood in a broken home. By thusly tainting the formerly immaculate reputation of Christian IV, these writers also scrutinise the image of a perfect unity between Leonora Christina and the man chosen for her by Christian IV, which was cultivated in the 17th and 18th century and excessively staged in the 19th century. The texts written by Sven Holm, Helle Stangerup and Maria Helleberg continue this trend by portraying Leonora Christina largely alongside her female contemporaries. Furthermore, and much like Birgithe Kosovic, all three writers are concerned with Leonora Christina's own legacy – *Jammers Minde* – and with her status as a writer.

Sven Holm's drama *Leonora Christina. Tre scener for en heltinde* depicts Leonora Christina struggling with the diverse images (*billeder*) created by the dissonances in her life's story, or rather, stories. The drama's focus on its protagonist's fibre crafting and writing activities as a metaphor for memory and identity (cf. *text/ile*) highlights the mnemonic and creative function of autobiography, as Holm's Leonora retroactively takes charge of her life and fame, i.e. her own effigy.

The novels written by Helle Stangerup and Maria Helleberg, on the other hand, focus on those aspects of Leonora Christina's life that had been deemed too impious by 19th-century publications, i.e. her descent from two scandalously headstrong women – Ellen Marsvin and Kirsten Munk – and her rivalry with Sophie Amalie. The novels' disposition, i.e. the parallelisation of Leonora Christina with her female contemporaries, renunciates any former moral opposition between these women (as portrayed, for example, by Herta J. Enevoldsen). In addition, all women depicted in Stangerup's novel *Spardame* exhibit, for the Baroque age typical, an obsession with materiality, perishability and deterioration. This period's worldview also included a firm belief in the effective, performative aspects of language and writing. Thus, literature and autobiography in particular are again presented as highly operative means of constructing identity and deconstructing enemies.

Similarly, Maria Helleberg's novel *Leonora Christine* portrays its eponymous heroine's deconstruction in the Blue Tower and her subsequent reconstruction and emancipation through writing. In addition to this contemporary, recurring topic, the precursor novel *Kongens kvinder* engages in excessive descriptions of luxury and clothing as well. Few female writers of Leonora Christina-literature managed to elude the allurement of the Ulfeldts' wealth, but Helleberg's utilisation of the poetics of clothing, i.e. the effective function of costume, results in a portrayal of garments and jewellery as armour, but also as constituting identity and gender. The latter aspect of clothing has been of especial interest to writers of Leonora Christina-literature. Leonora Christina's account of herself travelling in men's attire during her flight from Denmark in combination with her husband's portrayal in the French autobiography as increasingly weak, i.e. as a man bereft of his breeches, has fascinated writers such as Eva Hemmer Hansen, Birgithe Kosovic, Maria Helleberg and Karin Johnsson, even though there are countless historical examples of women travelling dressed as men, largely for safety and practical reasons.[1775] A use of »dress [as] the primary means for playing with or even 'switching' gender identities«[1776] is, accordingly, absent from Leonora Christina's writings, but very much present in 20th-century depictions of her travels in male disguise.

As a historical example of a woman, who has challenged and revised her image as a female, Leonora Christina has been particularly productive, since her story evolves around her position in relation to her country, her father, her husband and her society. She embodies the strained connection between these constants that have been suggested as identification axes to women in earlier centuries. The inherent dichotomies of the Leonora Christina-subject matter have nurtured the contemporary portrayal of Leonora Christina and her coevals as *femmes fatales*.[1777] The texts written by Holm, Stangerup and Helleberg depict their heroine either as a bloodthirsty fibre-craftswoman (Holm) or as an enchanting temptress, who is either the object (Stangerup) or the victim (Helleberg) of fatal insecurity. However, all of these texts depict a »völlige Ästhetisierung der Frau, ihre Stilisierung zum wertvollen Kunst-

---

1775 Cf. Dekker, Rudolf and Lotte van de Pol. *Weibliche Transvestiten und ihre Geschichte*. Berlin: Wagenbach, 1990.

1776 Bauer, Heike. 'General Introduction'. In *Women and Cross-Dressing 1800-1939 1: Theories: Sexology and the Taxonomies of Gender*, ed. Heike Bauer. London and New York: Routledge and Edition Synapse, 2006, p. xiv.

1777 The current, ambivalent depiction of Leonora Christina is, among other things, determined by her self-portrayal, the inconsistencies of which were not highlighted strategically before the late 20th century.

produkt, [...] die Auslöschung ihrer Körperlichkeit, [die] Negation weiblicher Existenz«[1778] either through the protagonists' impotence in the face of the image/s of Leonora Christina (Holm and Stangerup), or through the protagonists' attempt to attain power through an armour of luxury, which coincides with a negation of the human body and its limitations (Stangerup and Helleberg). The literary portrayal of Leonora Christina has thus not abandoned its former strategy of mythologising and iconifying its object; in fact, the end result has merely changed its shape. The disembodiment of Leonora Christina is implemented first through a glorification of Leonora Christina as Madonna and then through her vilification as vixen. Either way, her legendary value and her (positive) symbolic function prevail.[1779] Based on this conclusion, a parallel study of literary portrayals of Corfitz Ulfeldt would be of great interest, as it might reveal a development of his character running counter to that of his wife and culminating in his currently predominant depiction as *homme fragil*.

Chapter 2.7. on 'International Leonora Christina-literature' presents three very diverse approaches to the Leonora Christina-subject matter, yet each with familiar features. *Die Gräfin Ulfeld oder die vierundzwanzig Königskinder* by Leopold Schefer is another mystery by this cryptic writer. Schefer's novel praises a rather abstract idea of women – the ideal of female subservience and self-abandonment (as criticised by Mathilde Fibiger) – while at the same time challenging this ideal by depicting its destructive effects on the object of his admiration. Most interesting, though, is Schefer's use of manuscript fiction – which creates a sense of reliability and immediacy – more than three decades before the discovery of *Jammers Minde*, in which Leonora Christina uses a similar gimmick by purporting a simultaneousness of writing and prison experience.

Despite his equivocal text, Schefer insists on the laudability of allegedly female values such as compliance and consistency; much like Hans Christian Andersen, who cherished the image of Leonora Christina in the Blue Tower as a memorial to Corfitz Ulfeldt. Andersen's work might have also figured as a source of inspiration to Jens Peter Jacobsen's novel *Marie Grubbe*, the eponymous heroine of which has repeatedly been compared to Leonora Christina, particularly in the 19th century. In Jacobsen's opinion, Marie Grubbe, Leonora Christina and *Jammers Minde* are

---

1778 Hilmes, Carola. *Die Femme fatale*, p. 20 ('complete aesthetisation of women, their stylisation to the level of a previous object of art, [...] the annihilation of her physicalness, [the] negation of female existence').

1779 Cf. Binias, Silke. *Symbol and Symptom*, p. 39: »Thus, she is a stereotyped expression of all that is or can be considered negative because subversive in women, and characterising her as an 'erotic icon' does not suffice. She is also an icon of feminine power«.

Résumé

representative of their morally and culturally inferior age and of the social class depicted in these women's literary monuments. However, unlike H. F. Ewald, who considered Leonora Christina to still have been somewhat elevated from her mean-spirited surroundings, Jacobsen's understanding of this woman was that of a human entirely subjected to her physical desires. Nevertheless, Jacobsen drew the attention of Rainer Maria Rilke – whose love for the anecdotal, and for anything aristocratic,[1780] was nourished by the curious story of Leonora Christina and her royal kin – to this woman. In a letter to his publisher, Rilke converted a scene in *Jammers Minde* into a moral tale about stoicism and dignity, i.e. about inner wealth. However, ultimately, Rilke's interest in Leonora Christina was almost as shortlived and unfocussed as that of Hans Christian Andersen – neither man's admiration could be maintained through *Jammers Minde*.

The novel *Kungligt blod* by Karin Johnsson, on the other hand, attests to an early critical presentation of Leonora Christina's biography. Perhaps inspired by H. F. Ewald's novel *Leonora Kristina*, Johnsson's text focuses on the predetermination-aspect of Leonora Christina's narrative. The critical element in Johnsson's novel, however, concerns this very same sense of predetermination, since Leonora Christina's destiny is presented as having been defined by her sex. The only possibility for a *true* woman to attain historical significance seems to be through suffering; otherwise, she is forced to adopt masculine attributes, such as Queen Christina of Sweden. Johnsson's historiographic metafiction thus negotiates Leonora Christina's position within Scandinavian history, which has indeed been re-evaluated lately, as evidenced by Chapter 3.

Thus, Chapters 1 and 2 attest to an early and consistent occupation of literature and research concerned with Leonora Christina with questions of historicity and factuality, but also with womanhood. The confused manuscript situation in the 18th and most of the 19th century – the (original) manuscripts of the French autobiography and *Jammers Minde* being lost for centuries and much of the manuscript of *Hæltinners Pryd* still being missing – as well as the obscurities surrounding multiple events in the Ulfeldts' life (such as the Dina affair) have substantially contributed to maintaining the interest of writers and scholars in uncovering the 'true' story of Leonora Christina. Chapter 3.1. 'Historiography on Leonora Christina in a Nutshell' demonstrates that although the historical and the (semi-)literary reception of the Leonora Christina-subject matter merge rather soon (sometimes in the form of meta-emplotment), early historiographical texts such as those written by F. C. Schönau and Ludvig Holberg also exhibit a positivist claim to truth by referring

---

1780 Cf. Brittnacher, Hans Richard. 'Gespenster aus Dänemark', p. 55.

to Leonora Christina as an illustration of the values allegedly being communicated through these early works and hence of their own epistemological value. Thus, these early works of historiography are highly self-referential. Much like in the texts discussed in Chapter 2, a latent *or* blatant interest in Corfitz Ulfeldt prevails in Danish historiography written before 1869, a prime example of this interest being the works written by Christian Gottlob Mengel. From the late 19th century onwards, however, womanhood, its obligations and prerogatives in combination with historical-ideological considerations became a pressing topic in historiography (and literature) concerned with presenting Leonora Christina.

This more gendered discourse eventually replaced the earlier veracity debate, but it also effected an extraction of the Leonora Christina-subject matter from traditional historiography and its reallocation in other contexts, as illustrated in Chapter 3.2. 'Leonora Christina in Canonical Historiography'. Ludvig Holberg's *Dannemarks Riges Historie* provides many of the core topics subsequently adopted by writers and scholars concerned with the story of Leonora Christina, including the tragic format of the very same story, which presents her as a cognisant participant in her husband's machinations, particularly popular in the 19th century. As one of said core topics, Holberg established Leonora Christina's erudition (for example by presenting her in a gynæceum, i.e. his *Heltindehistorier*), which in turn became vital to the credulity of her historiographers, including Holberg himself. The juxtaposition of Leonora Christina's story to traditional, i.e. tendentially patriarchally inclined historiography in the form of a gynæceum furthermore places her in the midst of an alternative historiographical discourse concerned with questions of womanhood. Ove Malling, on the other hand, introduced the nationalist utilisation of Leonora Christina known from the works of Hans Christian Andersen and Mathilde Fibiger as another dominant feature of the narrative, as well as the story of overcoming that has – especially in the 20th century – become synonymous with Leonora Christina.[1781] Much like Rainer Maria Rilke, Malling considers Leonora Christina an epitome of typically Northern, i.e. Danish values, in Malling's case of loyalty. The hostility towards anything German present in Malling's *Store og gode handlinger*, which has hardly been adopted by literary works depicting Leonora Christina, is also detectable in the fourth volume of *Danmarks Riges Historie* written by J. A. Fridericia. Yet, much unlike Malling, Fridericia – and with him many of his contemporaries such as H. F. Ewald and J. P. Jacobsen – equated Leonora Christina rather with her age than with her country. Fridericia's narrative of incompetence and greed

---

1781 See, for example, the Danish writer Johannes V. Jensen's portrait poem 'Leonora Christina' published in 1906, which includes the following lines: »Ak, kunde vi os væbne / i Danmark med din Skæbne, / vi som har Haabet tabt!« (Jensen, Johannes V. 'Leonora Christina', p. 54).

is, however, also motivated by a contemplation of the dominant female element of the 17th century in Denmark, hence resulting in a portrayal of Leonora Christina as a proactive, but also spiteful, agent in the history of her country. This new depiction of Leonora Christina is evidently elicited by the publication of *Jammers Minde* in 1869. The inclusion of this text as source material complementary to historical records and historiographical writings advanced the treatment of Leonora Christina in contexts alternative to the dominant traditional historical discourse. *Ved afgrundens rand* by Benito Scocozza is one case in point. Although Scocozza, like Fridericia, is highly critical of the Danish upper aristocracy, of which the Ulfeldts were the last representatives, in a different context Leonora Christina as an individual is presented as deserving particular attention due to her position as an early female writer and women's historiographer.

Scocozza's ambivalent presentation of Leonora Christina is an implication, but also characteristic of the past centuries' perspective on this woman and her life's work. Leonora Christina's portrayal as an icon of Danishness, or even as a personification of Denmark, has been opposed by denunciations of her involvement in her husband's treason. While for many writers and scholars she has embodied womanhood through her historically conditioned primary position as wife and mother, her written works have occasioned others to regard her as an early, proto-feminist female role model. The publication of *Jammers Minde* in 1869 has considerably influenced and advanced this conflicting image.

As evidenced by the latest literary *and* historiographical publications, the emergence of *Jammers Minde* has first and foremost occasioned an identification of Leonora Christina as a writer and, more specifically, as an autobiographer. This occupation has, in turn, been identified by several of the writers and historians presented in this study as a key tool for people, but particularly for women, to, albeit retroactively, take charge of their life and to attain fame, significance and hence immortality. The most crucial aspect of *Jammers Minde*, however, which has maintained the work topical and captivating throughout 150 years, is its appeal as a testimony of an astounding life and personality.

Bibliography

Supporting Sources

Albeck, Gustav. *Dansk litteraturhistorie 1: Fra Runerne til Johannes Ewald*, ed. P. H. Traustedt. Copenhagen: Politiken, 1967 (1964).

Andersen, Vilhelm:
– *Illustreret dansk Litteraturhistorie 2: Det attende Aarhundrede*. Copenhagen: Gyldendal, 1934.
– *Illustreret dansk Litteraturhistorie 4: Det nittende Aarhundredes anden Halvdel*. Copenhagen: Gyldendal, 1925.

Auring, Steffen, Søren Baggesen, Finn Hauberg Mortensen, Søren Petersen, Marie-Louise Svane, Erik Svendsen, Poul Aaby Sørensen, Jørgen Vogelius and Martin Zerlang. 'Den romantiske kvindemyte. Louise Hegermann-Lindencrone'. In Auring, Steffen, Søren Baggesen, Finn Hauberg Mortensen, Søren Petersen, Marie-Louise Svane, Erik Svendsen, Poul Aaby Sørensen, Jørgen Vogelius and Martin Zerlang. *Dansk litteraturhistorie 5: Borgerlig enhedskultur 1807-48*. Copenhagen: Gyldendal, 1990 (1984), pp. 444-449.

Bauditz, Sophus. 'H. F. Ewald'. In *Dansk Biografisk Leksikon 6: Devegge–Ferdinandsen*. Grundlagt af C. F. Bricka. Red. af Povl Engelstoft. Copenhagen: Schultz 1935, pp. 478-479.

Brix, Hans. *Danmarks Digtere: Fyrretyve Kapitler af dansk Digtekunsts Historie*. Copenhagen: Aschehoug, 1951 (1925).

Bøggild-Andersen, C. O. 'Hannibal Sehested': 1609-1666'. In *Store danske personligheder 1: Fra Knud den Store til Christian X*, ed. Aage Bertelsen. Copenhagen: Berling, 1949, pp. 87-106.

Damen Conversations Lexikon 9: Rubens bis Tabernakel, ed. C. Herlosssohn. Adorf: Verlags-Bureau, 1837.

Heitmann, Annegret. 'Leonora, Gräfin Christina Ulfeldt'. In *Metzler-Autorinnen-Lexikon*, ed. Ute Hechtfischer. Stuttgart: Metzler, 1998, pp. 297-298.

Hougaard, Jens, Toni Nielsen, Erik Vestergaard Rasmussen, Arne Rindom and Peer E. Sørensen. *Dansk litteraturhistorie 3: Stænderkultur og enevælde 1620-1746*. Copenhagen: Gyldendal, 1983.

Jantzen, A. 'Birch, Hans Jørgen'. In *Dansk Biografisk Leksikon 3: Bille–Brandstrup*. Grundlagt af C. F. Bricka. Red. af Povl Engelstoft. Copenhagen: Schultz 1934, pp. 112-113.

Lexikon der Frau in zwei Bänden 2: I-Z. Zürich: Encyclios, 1954.

Litteraturhåndbogen, ed. Ib Fischer Hansen et al. Copenhagen: Gyldendal, 1987 (1985).

Pedersen, Vibeke A. *Dansk litteraturs historie 1: 1100-1800*, ed. Klaus P. Mortensen. Copenhagen: Gyldendal, 2007.

Petersen, Carl S. *Illustreret dansk Litteraturhistorie 1: Fra Folkevandringstiden indtil Holberg*. Copenhagen: Gyldendal, 1929.

Steenstrup, Johannes. 'Høst, Jens Kragh'. In *Dansk Biografisk Leksikon 11: Hultmann-Joachim*. Grundlagt af C. F. Bricka. Red. af Povl Engelstoft. Copenhagen: Schultz 1937, pp. 152-154.

Primary Literary and Historiographical Sources

Andersen, Hans Christian:
- *At være eller ikke være*. In *H. C. Andersen. Romaner og Rejseskildringer 5: At være eller ikke være. Lykke Per*, ed. H. Topsøe-Jensen. Copenhagen: Gyldendal, 1944, pp. 1-239.
- *Fodreise fra Holmens Canal til Østpynten af Amager i Aarene 1828 og 1829*, ed. Johan de Mylius. Valby: Borgen, 1986 (1829; Danske Klassikere).
- 'Gudfaders Billedbog'. In *H. C. Andersens Nye Eventyr og Historier: 3. Række 1872 og andre sene eventyr*, ed. Erik Dal. Copenhagen: Reitzel, 1967 (H. C. Andersens Eventyr 5), pp. 46-67.
- *H. C. Andersens breve til Therese og Martin R. Henriques 1860-75*, ed. H. Topsøe-Jensen. Copenhagen: H. Hagerup, 1932.
- *H. C. Andersens Dagbøger 1825-1875 I: 1825-1834*, ed. Helga Vang Lauridsen. Copenhagen: Gads Forlag, 1995 (1971).
- 'Holger Danske'. In *H. C. Andersens Nye Eventyr 1844-48, eventyr optagne i* Eventyr 1850 *samt Historier 1852-55*, ed. Erik Dal. Copenhagen: Reitzel, 1964 (H. C. Andersens Eventyr 2), pp. 98-102.
- *Das Märchen meines Lebens ohne Dichtung*. Leipzig: Lorck, 1847.
- *Mit Livs Eventyr 1*, ed. H. Topsøe-Jensen. Copenhagen: Gyldendal, 1975.

Andersen, Hans Christian, Edvard Collin and Henriette Collin. *H. C. Andersens brevveksling med Edvard og Henriette Collin 4: 1867-75*, eds. C. Behrend and H. Topsøe-Jensen. Copenhagen: Levin & Munksgaard, 1936.

Andersen, Hans Christian and Henriette Hanck. *H. C. Andersens brevveksling med Henriette Hanck*, ed. Svend Larsen. Copenhagen: Ejnar Munksgaard, 1941 (Anderseniana 9).

Andersen, Hans Christian and Henriette Wulff. *H.C. Andersen og Henriette Wulff. En Brevveksling*, ed. H. Topsøe-Jensen. Odense: Flensteds Forlag, 1959.

Anonymous. *Eleonore Gräfin von Ulefeld: nicht Roman sondern wirkliche Geschichte. Ein würdiger Beitrag zu der merkwürdigen Lebensgeschichte des Freiherrn v. d. Trenck*. Strasburg, 1787.

Anonymous. 'Eyrbyggja saga'. In *Eyrbyggja saga. Brands þáttr ǫrva. Eiríks saga rauða. Grænlendinga saga. Grænlendinga þáttr*, eds. Einar Ól Sveinsson and Matthías Þórðarson. Reykjavík: Íslenzka fornritafélag, 1957 (Íslenzk fornrit 4), pp. 1-184.

Anonymous. 'Fru Kirsten Munks Ballet', ed. Sophus Birket Smith, Danske Samlinger for Historie, Topographi, Personal- og Literaturhistorie 1/6 (1870-71), pp. 348-360.

Anonymous. 'Frue Eleonoræ Christinæ Sal. Corf. Ulfelds hendes Levnet af hende selv beskreven den 4. Maji 1697 paa Maribo. Rigtig Copie efter det egenhændige Manuscript, som fandtes i Major Becks Giemme i Skaane'. In *Samling af adskillige nyttige og opbyggelige Materier saa vel gamle som nye II*, ed. Oluf Bang. Copenhagen: 1743, pp. 125-159.

Anonymous. *Historien om Corfits Ulfeldt, og hans trofaste Hustru, Eleonore Kristine, Kongens Datter, og hvorledes de fra den største Magt og Rigdom sank i dybeste Elendighed*. Copenhagen: Jul. Strandberg, [1884].

Bau-Madsen, Jeanne. *Eleonora – en kongedatter*. Holte: Flachs, 2001 (Tilbageblik).

Bentzon, Inger. *Frøken Leonora: Udgivet i Forbindelse med Forfatterindens 25 Aars Jubilæum*. Odense: Skandinavistik Bogforlag, 1946.

Birch, Hans Jørgen. *Billedgallerie for Fruentimmer, indeholdende Levnetsbeskrivelser over berømte og lærde danske, norske og udenlandske Fruentimmere 1*. Copenhagen: Poulsen, 1793.

Boie, Margarete. *Eleonora Christine und Corfitz Ulfeldt: Der Lebensroman einer Königstochter*. Oldenburg and Berlin: Stalling, 1944.

Brøgger, Suzanne. 'Og hun trevlede sine silkestrømper op'. In Brøgger, Suzanne. *Den pebrede susen: Flydende fragmenter og fixeringer*. Rhodos: Copenhagen, 1988 (Rhodos Paperbacks), pp. 111-128.

Christian IV. af Danmark. *End lever jeg: Et Udvalg af Christian IVs Breve*, ed. Godfred Hartmann. Copenhagen: Reitzel, 1987.

Corneille, Pierre. *Cinna: Tragédie 1643*, ed. Alain Riffaud. Geneva: Droz, 2011 (Textes littéraires français 614).

Eckermann, Johann Peter. *Gespräche mit Goethe in den letzten Jahren seines Lebens*, ed. Otto Schönberger. Stuttgart: Reclam, 1998 (Reihe Reclam).

Elkjær Laursen, Agnete. *Leonora Christina*. Copenhagen: Gyldendal, 1968 (1960; Gyldendals lette læseserie 12).

Enevoldsen, Herta J.:
– *Kongedatteren Leonora Christina*. Copenhagen: Gyldendal, 2013 (1979).
– *Leonora Christina i Blåtårn*. Copenhagen: Gyldendal, 2013 (1979).

Engels, Friedrich. Review of *Das Kapital* published in *Der Beobachter* no. 303, 27 December 1867. In *Karl Marx. Friedrich Engels. Gesamtausgabe (MEGA) 1: Werke, Artikel, Entwürfe 21: September 1867 bis März 1871. Text*, ed. Jürgen Herres. Berlin: Akademie Verlag, 2009, pp. 38-40.

Ewald, H[erman] F[rederik]. *Leonora Kristina: Billeder af en Kongedatters Liv*. Copenhagen: Jacob Erslevs Forlag 1903 (1895).

Ewald, Johannes. 'Lykkens Tempel: En Drøm'. In *Johannes Ewalds Samlede Skrifter: Efter Tryk og Håndskrifter 1*, ed. Det danske Sprog- og Litteraturselskab. Copenhagen: Gyldendal, 1969 (1914), pp. 62-81.

Fibiger, Mathilde:
– *Clara Raphael*. In Fibiger, Mathilde. *Clara Raphael. Minona*, ed. Lise Busk-Jensen. Valby: Borgen, 1994 (Danske klassikere), pp. 5-87.
– *En Skizze efter det virkelige Liv*. Copenhagen: Reitzel, 1853.
– Letter reproduced in E. K. 'Nordiska Qvinnor. Leonora Christina Ulfeldt', Tidskrift för hemmet 12/2 (1870), pp. 94-111.

Fridericia, J. A.:
– *Adelsvældens sidste Dage: Danmarks Historie fra Christian IV's Død til Enevældens Indførelse (1648-1660)*. Copenhagen: P. G. Philipsen, 1894.
– *Danmarks Riges Historie 4: 1588-1699. Historisk illustreret*. Copenhagen: Det Nordiske Forlag, [1907].

Gjedsted, Rolf. *Fordærvede kvinder: En fortælling omkring året 1650*. Copenhagen: Gyldendal, 1991.

Hegermann Lindencrone, Louise:
- 'Billedet'. In Hegermann Lindencrone, Louise. *Danske Fortællinger*. Copenhagen: C. A. Reitzels Forlag, 1862 (1825), pp. 141-354.
- *Eleonora Christina Uhlfeldt: Historisk Drama*. Copenhagen: Boas Brünnich, 1817.
- 'Faster Dorothea'. In Hegermann Lindencrone, Louise. *Danske Fortællinger*. Copenhagen: C. A. Reitzels Forlag, 1862 (1825), pp. 91-139.
- 'Gjæstekammeret i Præstegaarden'. In Hegermann Lindencrone, Louise. *Danske Fortællinger*. Copenhagen: C. A. Reitzels Forlag, 1862 (1825), pp. 37-89.
- Letter addressed to Peder Hjort and dated 13 November 1824, reproduced in *Udvalg af Breve fra Mænd og Qvinder skrevne gjennem en lang Række År til P. Hjort og nu udgivne med biografiske og literærhistoriske Anmærkninger af Modtageren*. Copenhagen: Gyldendal, 1867, pp. 325-327.

Heiberg, Johan Ludvig. 'Kronborg'. In Heiberg, Johan Ludvig. *Poetiske Skrifter 8: Blandede Digte. Første Afdeling*. Copenhagen: Reitzel, 1862, pp. 223-227.

Helleberg, Maria:
- 'Ellen Marsvin'. In Helleberg, Maria. *Kvinder der forandrede Danmark: Ildhu, vilje og engagement*. Rødovre: Sohn, 2013, pp. 35-41.
- *Kongens kvinder*. Copenhagen: Samleren, 2013.
- *Leonora*. Copenhagen: Gyldendal, 1997.
- 'Leonora Christine'. In Helleberg, Maria. *Danmarkshistorier for børn*. Illustreret af Christian Würgler Hansen. Copenhagen: Sesam, 2005, pp. 164-169.
- *Leonora Christine*. Copenhagen: Samleren, 2014.
- 'Leonora Christine Ulfeldt'. In Helleberg, Maria. *Kvinder der forandrede Danmark: Ildhu, vilje og engagement*. Rødovre: Sohn, 2013, pp. 43-50.

Hemmer Hansen, Eva:
- *Den lykkelige hustru: Leonora Christine I*. Copenhagen: Hernov, 1982.
- *Den trofaste hustru: Leonora Christine II*. Copenhagen: Hernov, 1983.

Hofman, Tycho de. *Historiske Efterretninger om velfortiente Danske Adelsmænd, med deres Stamme-Tavler og Portraiter 2*, transl. C. Liunge and B. C. Sandvig. Copenhagen: A. H. Godiche, 1778.

Holberg, Ludvig:
- *Adskillige Heltinders og navnkundige Damers sammenlignede Historier efter Plutarchi Maade ved L. Holberg 1*. Copenhagen, 1745.
- *Dannemarks og Norges Beskrivelse ved Ludvig Holberg, Assessor udi Consistorio og Prof. ved det Kongl. Universitet i Kiøbenhavn*. Copenhagen: Høpffner, 1729.
- *Dannemarks Riges Historie 2*. Copenhagen: Hans Kongl. Majests. og Universitets Bogtrykkerie, 1733.
- *Dannemarks Riges Historie 3. Med et tilstrækkeligt Register over alle III. Tomer*. Copenhagen: Hans Kongl. Majests. og Universitets Bogtrykkerie, 1735.
- *Epistler 2*, ed. Chr. Bruun. Copenhagen: Samfundet til den danske Literaturs Fremme, 1868.
- *Epistler 4*, ed. Chr. Bruun. Copenhagen: Samfundet til den danske Literaturs Fremme, 1873.
- *Holbergs Levned fortalt af ham selv i tre latinske Breve til en fornem Herre*, transl. Fr. Winkel Horn. Copenhagen: A. Christiansen 1897.

Holm, Sven. *Leonora. Tre scener for en heltinde*. Copenhagen: Rhodos, 1982.

Høst, Jens Kragh. *Rigshofmester Grev Korfits Ulfelds og Grevinde til Slesvig og Holsten Eleonora Christina Ulfelds Levnet*. Copenhagen: Beekens Forlag, 1825.

Jacobsen, Jens Peter:
- *Fru Marie Grubbe*. Copenhagen: Gyldendal, 2006.
- *Samlede Værker 5: Breve: 1863-1877*, ed. Frederik Nielsen. [Copenhagen:] Rosenkilde og Bagger, 1973.

Jensen, Johannes V. 'Leonora Christine'. In Jensen, Johannes V. *Digte*. Copenhagen: Gyldendal, 1954 (Gyldendals nyklassiske lyrikerserie), pp. 53-54.

Johnsson, Karin. *Kungligt blod: Leonora Kristina Ulfeldt: Ett kvinnoöde ur historien*. Stockholm: Lars Hökerberg, 1919.

Jørgensen, A. D. *Fyrretyve Fortællinger af Fædrelandets Historie*. Copenhagen: De unges forlag, 1946 (1882).

Kosovic, Birgithe. *Leonora Christina*. Copenhagen: Alfabeta, 2012.

Lang, Ingrid. *Prinsessen i fengsel: Leonora Christina*. Oslo: Lutherstiftelsen, 1956.

Leonora Christina (editions and translations quoted and mentioned):
- 'Confrontationen i Malmø 1659'. In *Jammers Minde og andre selvbiografiske Skildringer*, eds. Johs. Brøndum-Nielsen and C.O. Bøggild-Andersen. Copenhagen: Rosenkilde og Bagger, 1949, pp. 69-92.
- *Denkwürdigkeiten der Gräfin zu Schleswig-Holstein Leonora Christina vermählten Gräfin Ulfeldt aus ihrer Gefangenschaft im Blauen Thurm des Königsschlosses zu Copenhagen 1663-1685: Nach der Dænischen Original-Handschrift im Besitze Sr. Excell. des Herrn Johan Grafen Waldstein*, ed. Johannes Ziegler. Vienna: Gerold, 1879 (1871).
- *Hæltinners Pryd*, ed. Christopher Maaløe. Copenhagen: Reitzel, 1977.
- *Jammers Minde: Diplomatarisk udgave ved Poul Lindegård Hjorth og Marita Akhøj Nielsen under medvirkning af Ingelise Nielsen*, ed. Det Danske Sprog- og Litteraturselskab. Copenhagen: Reitzel, 1998.
- 'Kong Karl X Gustavs Bryllup 1654'. In *Jammers Minde og andre selvbiografiske Skildringer*, eds. Johs. Brøndum-Nielsen and C.O. Bøggild-Andersen. Copenhagen: Rosenkilde og Bagger, 1949, pp. 51-54.
- *Leonora Christina Grevinde Ulfeldts Franske Levnedsskildring 1673. Trykt i Faksimile*, ed. C. O. Bøggild-Andersen, Copenhagen: Forening for Boghaandværk, 1958.
- *Leonora Christina (Ulfeldt)s Selvbiografi. Udgivet efter et Håndskrift i det store Kgl. Bibliothek*, ed. Sophus Birket Smith, Danske Samlinger for Historie, Topografi, Personal- og Litteraturhistorie 1/2 (1871-72), pp. 129-231.
- *Memoirs of Leonora Christina. Daughter of Christian IV. of Denmark. Written during her Imprisonment in the Blue Tower at Copenhagen 1663-1685*, transl. F. E. Bunnètt. London: King, 1872.
- 'Rejsen til Korsør 1656'. In *Jammers Minde og andre selvbiografiske Skildringer*, eds. Johs. Brøndum-Nielsen and C.O. Bøggild-Andersen. Copenhagen: Rosenkilde og Bagger, 1949, pp. 55-68.

Luther, Martin:
- *Werke: Kritische Gesamtausgabe: Tischreden 1: Tischreden aus der ersten Hälfte der dreißiger Jahre*. Weimar: Hermann Böhlaus Nachfolger, 1912.
- *Werke: Kritische Gesamtausgabe: Tischreden 4: Tischreden aus den Jahren 1538-1540*. Weimar: Hermann Böhlaus Nachfolger, 1916.

Malling, Ove. *Store og gode Handlinger af Danske, Norske og Holstenere, samlede ved Ove Malling. 1777*, ed. Erik Hansen. Copenhagen: Gyldendal, 1992.

Marx, Karl:
- *Das Kapital: Kritik der politischen Ökonomie*. Cologne: Anaconda, 2009.
- *Karl Marx. Friedrich Engels. Historisch-kritische Gesamtausgabe: Werke, Schriften, Briefe 2: Der Briefwechsel zwischen Marx und Engels 1854-1860*. Berlin: Marx-Engels-Verlag, 1930.

Motteville, Madame de. 'Madame de Mottevilles Skildring af Leonora Christinas Optræden ved det franske Hof 1647'. In *Leonora Christina (Ulfeldt)s Selvbiografi. Udgivet efter et Håndskrift i det store Kgl. Bibliothek*, ed. Sophus Birket Smith, Danske Samlinger for Historie, Topografi, Personal- og Litteraturhistorie 1/2 (1871-72), pp. 218-220.

Munk, Kaj. *Danmark, lidt om Folk og Fædreland, fortalt de kæreste af mine Landsmænd, Børnene*. Copenhagen: Arnold Busck, 1943.

Munthe, E[iler]. *De vigtigste indenlandske Tildrag og de merkeligste Personers Levnetsbeskrivelse fra de ældste indtil vore Dage: En Læse- og Lærebog i Fædrelandets Historie for Begyndere og Ustuderede*. Copenhagen: Thoring & Colding, 1806.

Oehlenschläger, Adam:
- *Dina*. In *Oehlenschläger. Poetiske Skrifter 9: Dramatiske Digtninger*, ed. F. L. Liebenberg. Copenhagen: Det Nordiske Forlag, 1898, pp. 1-130.
- *Oehlenschlägers Erindringer 4*. Copenhagen: Andr. Fred. Holts Forlag, 1851.
- *Poetiske Skrifter 3: Nordiske Digte*, ed. H. Topsøe-Jensen. Copenhagen: Jørgensen & Co, 1928 (Danmarks Nationallitteratur).

Overskov, Carsten. *Leonoras latter*. Copenhagen: Branner og Korch, 2004.

Paus, Hans. *Forsøg til navnkundige danske Mænds Livs og Levnets Beskrivelser 2: Indeholdende Anledning til den fra Dannemarks Riges Hofmester og det Romerske Riges Græve, forvandlede til Dannemarks Riges Forræder Corfitz Uhlefeld, hans Livs og Levnets Historie*. Copenhagen: Joh. Christ. Groth, 1746-1747.

Pellico, Silvio. *Le mie prigioni: Memorie di Silvio Pellico da Saluzzo con addizioni di Pietro Maroncelli, e notizie preliminary intorno all' autore e l'ode sulla creduta di lui morte. Quarta edizione da Giov. Batta. Ghezzi. Mit vermehrten grammatikalischen Erläuterungen und einem Wörterbuche zum Schul- und Privatgebrauche*. Leipzig: Baumgartner, 1858.

Rahbek, Ove. *Ad tornede Veje. Historisk Fortælling*. Odense: Søndergaard, 1912 (Søndagsbladets Bogsamling 4).

Reich, Ebbe Kløvedal:
- *Frederik. En folkebog om N. F. S. Grundtvigs tid og liv*. Copenhagen: Gyldendal, 1978 (1972).
- *Rejsen til Messias: Tre bøger fra enevældens tid*. [Copenhagen:] Gyldendal, 1974.

Rilke, Rainer Maria:
- *Die Aufzeichnungen des Malte Laurids Brigge*. Herausgegeben und kommentiert von Manfred Engel. Stuttgart: Reclam, 1997.
- *Briefe 2: 1919-1926*, ed. Horst Nalewski. Frankfurt: Insel, 1991.
- *Briefe an seinen Verleger 1: 1906 bis 1926*, ed. Ruth Sieber-Rilke. Wiesbaden: Insel, 1949.

- *Briefe an Sidonie Nádherný von Borutin*, ed. Bernhard Blume. Frankfurt: Insel, 1973.
- *Briefe aus den Jahren 1902 bis 1906*, ed. Ruth Sieber-Rilke. Leipzig: Insel, 1929.
- *Gesammelte Briefe in sechs Bänden 5: Briefe aus Muzot 1921 bis 1926*, eds. Ruth Sieber-Rilke and Carl Sieber. Leipzig: Insel, 1937.
- *Materialien zu Rainer Maria Rilke >Die Aufzeichnungen des Malte Laurids Brigge<*, ed. Hartmut Engelhardt. Frankfurt: Suhrkamp, 1974 (Suhrkamp Taschenbuch 174).
- *Prosa und Dramen*, ed. August Stahl. Frankfurt and Leipzig: Insel, 1996 (Rainer Maria Rilke. Werke 3).

Rosén, Jerker. 'Kristinas hovliv'. In *Den svenska historien 6: Drottning Kristina. Vetenskap och kultur blomstrar*, ed. Jan Cornell et al. Stockholm: Bonnier, 1983 (1967), pp. 142-147.

Rousseau, Jean-Jacques. *Oeuvres completes 1: Les Confessions. Autres texts autobiographiques*, ed. Bernard Gagnebin and Marcel Raymond. Paris: Gallimard, 1959 (Bibliothèque de la Pléiade 11).

Rousseau de la Valette, Michel:
- *Le Comte d'Ulfeld, Grand Maistre de Dannemarc. Nouvelle Historique*. Paris: Claude Barbin, 1678.
- *Leben des Grafen Corfix Ulfeld, vormaligen Reichshofraths in Dänemark. Ein Pendant zum Leben des Staatsministers Grafen von Struensee*, transl. Friedrich Samuel Mursinna. Breslau and Leipzig: Ernst Gottlieb Meyer, 1790.

Schefer, Leopold:
- 'Die Düvecke, oder die Leiden einer Königin'. In *Leopold Schefer's ausgewählte Werke 4*. Berlin: Veit & Comp, 1845, pp. 139-233.
- *Die Gräfin Ulfeld oder die vierundzwanzig Königskinder. Historischer Roman von Leopold Schefer*. Berlin: Veit & Comp, 1834.
- Letter addressed to Hermann von Pückler-Muskau and dated 9 February 1832, reproduced in *Briefwechsel und Tagebücher des Fürsten Hermann von Pückler-Muskau 7: Briefwechsel des Fürsten Hermann von Pückler-Muskau*, ed. Ludmilla Assing-Grimelli. Berlin: Wedekind & Schwieger, 1875, pp. 401-403.

Schönau, Friderich Christian:
- *Merkwürdige Lebensbeschreibung Eleonoræ Christinæ Gräfinn von Ulfeld einer Tochter Christian des Vierten, Königs in Dännemark und Norwegen hochlöblichen Gedächtnisses. Aus dem Dänischen übersetzt von Christian Gottlob Mengel*. Copenhagen and Leibzig: Friedrich Christian Pelt, 1757.
- *Samling af Danske Lærde Fruentimer, Som ved deres Lærdom, og Udgivne eller efterladte Skrifter have giort deres Navne i den lærde Verden bekiendte, med adskillige mest Historiske Anmerkninger forøget, og udgivet ved Friderich Christian Schönau 1*. Copenhagen, 1753.

Scocozza, Benito:
- *Christian 4*. Copenhagen: Politikens Forlag, 1988 (1987).
- *Gyldendal og Politikens Danmarkshistorie 8: Ved afgrundens rand: 1600-1700*. Copenhagen: Gyldendals Bogklubber, 1992 (1989).

Sorbière, Samuel de. *Relation d'un voyage en Angleterre, Où sont touchées plusieurs choses, qui regardent l'estat des Sciences & de la Religion, & autres matieres curieuses*. Cologne: Pierre Michel, 1666 (Paris: 1664).

Sperling, Otto. *Dr. Med. Otto Sperlings Selvbiografi (1602-1673), oversat i Uddrag efter Originalhaandskriftet med særligt Hensyn til Forfatterens Ophold i Danmark og Norge samt Fangenskab i Blaataarn*, ed. Sophus Birket Smith. Copenhagen: Selskabet for Udgivelse af Kilder til Dansk Historie, 1974 (1885).

Stangerup, Helle. *Spardame*. Copenhagen: Gyldendal, 1991 (1989, Gyldendals Paperbacks).

Stein, Gertrude. *Everybody's Autobiography*. New York: Cooper Square Publishers, Inc., 1971.

Trenck, Friedrich Freiherr von der. *Des Friedrich Freyherrn von der Trenck, merkwürdige Lebensgeschichte: Von ihm selbst als ein Lehrbuch für Menschen geschrieben, die wirklich unglücklich sind, oder noch gute Vorbilder für alle Fälle, zur Nachfolge bedürfen 1*. 1786.

Waldstein-Wartenberg, Johann Nepomuk. Introduction in Leonora Christina. *»Jammers-Minde«. En egenhændig Skildring af hendes Fangenskab i Blaataarn i Aarene 1663-1685 udgivet efter det originale Haandskrift i Grev J. Waldstein Wartembergs Eje. Med et Forord af Hs. Excellence Grev Johan Waldstein Wartemberg*, ed. Sophus Birket Smith. Copenhagen: Gyldendal, 1869, pp. III-VI.

Weitemeyer, Lisbeth. *Leonora Christina – Fra kongedatter til jammer*. Aarhus: Siesta, 2006.

Wilster, Christian. 'Leonora Kristina Ulfeldt'. In Matzen, M. *Dansk Læsebog 3 (For de højere Klasser)*. Copenhagen: Gyldendal, 1875 (1865), pp. 89-90.

Winge, Mette and Claus Seidel. 'Den storsnudede kongedatter: Leonora Christina Ulfeldt 1621-1698'. In *Da de store var små: 24 historier fra berømte danskeres barndom*. Copenhagen: Gyldendals Bogklubber, 2009, pp. 9-16.

Critical Studies

Aakjær, Svend:
- 'Leonora Christinas dommer', Jyske Samlinger 5 (Ny række, 1959), pp. 40-44.
- 'Leonora Christinas skyld – et aktorat', Jyske Samlinger 4 (Ny række, 1957), pp. 233-248.

Aasen, Elisabeth:
- *Fra Gamle Dage: Memoarer, Dagbøker, Salmer og Dikt av Kvinner ca. 1660-1880*, ed. Elisabeth Aasen. Oslo: Universitetsforlaget, 1983.
- 'Grevinnen i fangetårnet: Leonora Christina (1621-1698)'. In *Den skjulte tradisjon: skapende kvinner i kulturhistorien*, ed. Kari Vogt. Bergen: Sigma, 1982, pp. 132-149.

Akhøj Nielsen, Marita:
- 'The conservator's work and literary history: the example of a 17th-century Danish autobiography'. In *Care and conservation of manuscripts 5: Proceedings of the fifth international seminar held at the University of Copenhagen 19th-20th April 1999*, eds. Gillian Fellows-Jensen and Peter Springborg. Copenhagen: The Royal Library, 2000, pp. 38-47.
- 'Leonora Christina: An Imprisoned Princess'. In *Female Voices of the North: An Anthology*, ed. Inger M. Olsen. Vienna: Praesens, 2002 (Wiener Texte zur Skandinavistik 1), pp. 89-116.

- 'Leonora Christina *Jammers Minde* i ny udgave – hvorfor? hvordan?' In *Studier i Nordisk 1998-1999: Selskab for Nordisk Filologi: Foredrag og årsberetning*, ed. Selskab for Nordisk Filologi. Copenhagen, 2000, pp. 64-65.
- 'Manuskriptbeskrivelse: Manuskriptets ydre'. In Leonora Christina. *Jammers Minde: Diplomatarisk udgave ved Poul Lindegård Hjorth og Marita Akhøj Nielsen under medvirkning af Ingelise Nielsen*, ed. Det Danske Sprog- og Litteraturselskab. Copenhagen: Reitzel, 1998, pp. xxxiii-xxxv.
- 'Papirets vidnesbyrd om håndskriftets tilblivelseshistorie'. In Leonora Christina. *Jammers Minde: Diplomatarisk udgave ved Poul Lindegård Hjorth og Marita Akhøj Nielsen under medvirkning af Ingelise Nielsen*, ed. Det Danske Sprog- og Litteraturselskab. Copenhagen: Reitzel, 1998, pp. lii-lv.
- 'Skrifttræk og blæk'. In Leonora Christina. *Jammers Minde: Diplomatarisk udgave ved Poul Lindegård Hjorth og Marita Akhøj Nielsen under medvirkning af Ingelise Nielsen*, ed. Det Danske Sprog- og Litteraturselskab. Copenhagen: Reitzel, 1998, pp. lv-lxvii.

Alenius, Marianne. 'Om alleslags Roosværdige Quindis Personer: Gynæceum – en kvindelitteraturhistorie'. In *Nordisk kvindelitteraturhistorie 1: I Guds navn: 1000-1800*, ed. Elisabeth Møller Jensen. Copenhagen: Rosinante/Munksgaard, 1993, pp. 217-232.

Anders, Bjørn. *Ugift eller lykkelig: Kvinden i 1500 og 1600 tallet*. Copenhagen, 1973.

Andersen, Vilhelm:
- *Adam Oehlenschläger: Et Livs Poesi 2: Manddom og Alderdom*. Copenhagen: Det Nordiske Forlag, 1899.
- 'Marie Grubbe'. In *Omkring Fru Marie Grubbe*, ed. Jørgen Ottosen. Copenhagen: Hans Reitzel, 1972, pp. 238-244.

Anderson, Linda R. *Autobiography*. London: Routledge, 2001 (The New Critical Idiom).

Andreasen, Uffe. 'Ebbe Kløvedal Reich'. In *Danske digtere i det 20. århundrede 5: Fra Anders Bodelsen til Dan Turèll*, eds. Torben Brostrøm and Mette Winge. Copenhagen: Gad 1982, pp. 286-300.

Andrup, Otto. 'Noter'. In Leonora Christina. *Grevinde Leonora Christinas Jammers Minde*, ed. Otto Andrup. Copenhagen: Gyldendal, 1926, pp. 242-273.

Anonymous. Review of *Die Gräfin Ulfeld, oder die vierundzwanzig Königskinder* by Leopold Schefer, Blätter für literarische Unterhaltung 1/21 (21 January 1835), pp. 81-82.

Aust, Hugo. *Der historische Roman*. Stuttgart: Metzler, 1994 (Sammlung Metzler 278: Realien zur Literatur).

Baldwin, Birgit. 'Jammersminde Remembered: A New Look at the Status of History and Literature', Scandinavian Studies 62/3 (1990), pp. 266-279.

Baer, Lydia. 'Rilke and Jens Peter Jacobsen', Publications of the Modern Language Association 54/4 (December 1939), pp. 1133-1180.

Bänsch, Alexandra. *»Katholisch im Kopf«: Die protestantische Romantik in Skandinavien und ihre Prätexte zwischen Mündlichkeit und Schriftlichkeit*. Baden-Baden: Nomos, 2011 (Die kulturelle Konstruktion von Gemeinschaften im Modernisierungsprozeß 11).

Barner, Wilfried. *Barockrhetorik: Untersuchungen zu ihren geschichtlichen Grundlagen*. 2., unveränderte Auflage. Tübingen: Max Niemeyer, 2002 (1970).

Barthes, Roland. *Système de la Mode*. Paris: Éditions du Seuil, 1967.

Bauer, Heike. 'General Introduction'. In *Women and Cross-Dressing 1800-1939 1: Theories: Sexology and the Taxonomies of Gender*, ed. Heike Bauer. London and New York: Routledge and Edition Synapse, 2006, pp. xiii-xxxiv.

Bencard, Mogens and Jørgen Hein. 'Forord'. In *Sophie Amalie: Den onde dronning?* Copenhagen: Rosenborg, 1986, unpaginated preamble.

Billeskov Jansen, F. J. 'Passion og Skæbne: Studier i Oehlenschlägers Æstetik og dens Kilder'. In *Nordisk litteraturhistorie – en bog til Brøndsted: 12. november 1978*, ed. Hans Bekker-Nielsen et al. Odense Universitetsforlag, 1978, pp. 118-137.

Binias, Silke. *Symbol and Symptom: The Femme Fatale in English Poetry of the 19th Century and Feminist Criticism*. Heidelberg: Universitätsverlag Winter 2007 (Anglistische Forschungen 379).

Birket Smith, Sophus:
- 'Indledning'. In Leonora Christina. *Leonora Christina Grevinde Ulfeldt's »Jammers Minde«: En egenhændig Skildring af hendes Fangenskab i Blaataarn i Aarene 1663-85*, ed. Sophus Birket Smith. Copenhagen: Gyldendal, 1900, pp. 1-12.
- Introduction in Anonymous. 'Fru Kirsten Munks Ballet', ed. Sophus Birket Smith, Danske Samlinger for Historie, Topographi, Personal- og Literaturhistorie 1/6 (1870-71), pp. 348-349.
- Introduction in Sperling, Otto. *Dr. med. Otto Sperlings Selvbiografi (1602-1673), oversat i Uddrag efter Originalhaandskriftet med særligt Hensyn til Forfatterens Ophold i Danmark og Norge samt Fangenskab i Blaataarn*, ed. Sophus Birket Smith. Copenhagen: Selskabet for Udgivelse af Kilder til dansk Historie, 1974 (1885), pp. III-VIII.
- *Leonora Christina Grevinde Ulfeldts Historie: Med Bidrag til hendes Ægtefælles og hendes nærmeste Slægts Historie*. Copenhagen: Gyldendal, 1879-81.
- *Leonora Christina (Ulfeldt) på Maribo Kloster: Et Bidrag til Oplysning om hendes sidste Leveår*. Copenhagen: Gyldendal, 1872.

Bjerg, Svend. 'Leonora Christinas Jammers Minde'. In *Selvbiografien*, ed. Lise Bek et al. Viby J.: Centrum, 1983, pp. 45-56.

Bjørn, Hans. 'Leonora Christina – Christian IV's datter'. In *Leonora Christina: Historien om en heltinde*. Århus: Arkona, 1983 (Acta Jutlandica 58, Humanistisk serie 57), pp. 9-57.

Blanchard, Marc Eli. 'The Critique of Autobiography', Comparative Literature 34/2 (Spring 1982), pp. 97-115.

Brandes, Georg:
- 'H. C. Andersen som Eventyrdigter'. In Brandes, Georg. *Kritiker og Portraiter*. Copenhagen: Gyldendal, 1870, pp. 301-371.
- 'Kvindesagen'. In *Georg Brandes – den mangfoldige*, ed. Jørgen Knudsen. Copenhagen: Gyldendal, 2005, pp. 189-194.
- 'Leonora Christina'. In *Georg Brandes – den mangfoldige*, ed. Jørgen Knudsen. Copenhagen: Gyldendal, 2005, pp. 67-70.

Bredsdorff, Thomas. *Sære Fortællere. Hovedtræk af den ny danske prosakunst i tiåret omkring 1960*. Copenhagen: Gyldendal, 1967.

Brittnacher, Hans Richard. 'Gespenster aus Dänemark. Okkultismus und Spiritismus in Rainer Maria Rilkes *Die Aufzeichnungen des Malte Laurids Brigge*'. In *Strahlen sehen: Zu einer Ästhetik des Emanativen*, eds. Roland Innerhofer und Rebecca Schönsee. Vienna: New Academic Press, 2015, pp. 52-71.

Brix, Hans. 'Marie Grubbe'. In *Omkring Fru Marie Grubbe*, ed. Jørgen Ottosen. Copenhagen: Hans Reitzel, 1972, pp. 203-215.

Brøndsted, Mogens. 'En dansk virago'. In *Kvinnor och Skapande: En Antologi om Litteratur och Konst tilägnad Karin Westman Berg*, ed. Birgitta Paget et al. Malmö: Författerförlaget, 1983, pp. 109-120.

Brøndum-Nielsen, Johs. and C.O. Bøggild-Andersen. 'Historiske Oplysninger'. In Leonora Christina. *Jammers Minde og andre selvbiografiske Skildringer*, eds. Johs. Brøndum-Nielsen and C.O. Bøggild-Andersen. Copenhagen: Rosenkilde og Bagger, 1949, pp. 295-400.

Bull, Francis. *Ludvig Holberg som historiker*. Oslo: Aschehoug & Co, 1913.

Busk-Jensen, Lise:
– Heiberg, Johan Ludvig. 'Udgiveren til Læserne'. In Fibiger, Mathilde. *Clara Raphael. Minona*, ed. Lise Busk-Jensen. Valby: Borgen, 1994 (Danske klassikere), pp. 249-302.
– 'Kvindebevægelsens første manifest': Om Mathilde Fibigers Clara Raphael'. In *Nordisk kvindelitteraturhistorie 2: Faderhuset: 1800-tallet*, ed. Elisabeth Møller Jensen. Copenhagen: Rosinante/Munksgaard, 1993, pp. 313-318.
– 'Rejsen til Jeg'ets indre: Leonora Christina 1621-1698'. In *Nordiske Forfatterinder: Fra Leonora Christina til Elsa Gress: En Antologi*, ed. Lise Busk-Jensen. Copenhagen: Gyldendal, 1990, pp. 9-19.
– 'Romantikbegrebet og feministisk litteraturhistorieskrivning'. In *Nordische Romantik: Akten der XVII. Studienkonferenz der International Association for Scandinavian Studies 7.-12. August 1988 in Zürich und Basel*, ed. Oskar Bandle et al. Basel and Frankfurt: Helbing & Lichtenhahn, 1991 (Beiträge zur nordischen Philologie 19), pp. 312-317.
– *Romantikkens forfatterinder*. Copenhagen: Gyldendal, 2009.

Bøggild-Andersen, C. O. 'Kongedatteren for historiens domstol: Nogle bemærkninger til Svend Aakjærs aktorat mod Leonora Christina', Jyske Samlinger 5 (Ny række, 1959), pp. 24-39.

Cadman Seelig, Sharon. *Autobiography and Gender in Early Modern Literature: Reading Women's Lives, 1600-1800*. Cambridge University Press, 2006.

Christow, Swantje. *Der Lilith-Mythos in der Literatur: Der Wandel des Frauenbildes im literarischen Schaffen des 19. und 20. Jahrhunderts*. Aachen: Shaker, 1998 (Sprache und Kultur).

Clausen, Bettina and Lars Clausen. *Zu allem fähig: Versuch einer Sozio-Biographie zum Verständnis des Dichters Leopold Schefer.* Frankfurt: Bangert & Metzler, 1985.

Condren, Conal. 'Specifying the Subject in Early Modern Autobiography'. In *Early Modern Autobiography: Theories, Genres, Practices*, ed. Ronald Bedford et al. Ann Arbor, Michigan: University of Michigan Press, 2006, pp. 35-48.

Dalager, Stig and Anne-Marie Mai: *Danske kvindelige Forfattere 1: Fra Sophie Brahe til Mathilde Fibiger*. Copenhagen: Gyldendal, 1982.

Det Danske Sprog- og Litteraturselskab. 'Forord'. In Malling, Ove. *Store og gode Handlinger af Danske, Norske og Holstenere, samlede ved Ove Malling. 1777*, ed. Erik Hansen. Copenhagen: Gyldendal, 1992, pp. 9-10.

Davis, Lloyd. 'Critical Debates and Early Modern Autobiography'. In *Early Modern Autobiography: Theories, Genres, Practices*, ed. Ronald Bedford et al. Ann Arbor, Michigan: University of Michigan Press, 2006, pp. 19-34.

De Groot, Jerome. *The Historical Novel*. London and New York: Routledge, 2010 (The New Critical Idiom).

De Man, Paul. 'Autobiography as De-facement', Modern Language Notes 94/5 (Dec. 1979), pp. 919-930.

Dekker, Rudolf and Lotte van de Pol. *Weibliche Transvestiten und ihre Geschichte*. Berlin: Wagenbach, 1990.

Delany, Paul. *British Autobiography in the Seventeenth Century*. London: Routledge, 1969.

Dissing Paulsen, Trine and Jan Gorm Madsen. 'Zahrtmanns Leonora Christina motiver'. In Ære være Leonora: Kristian Zahrtmann og Leonora Christina, ed. Den Hirschsprungske Samling. Copenhagen: 2006, pp. 37-73.

Doctor, Jens Aage. 'Sandhedens rolle', Kritik 16 (1970), pp. 5-36.

Dömling, Anna Katharina:
- '»Billigen kand ieg med Iob sige.« Selbstbilder und Selbstinszenierung in den autobiographischen Texten von Leonora Christina Ulfeldt (1693), Agneta Horn (1657) und Christina Regina von Birchenbaum (1651)', Skandinavistik 31 (2001), pp. 24-40.
- '»Klog i Raad; Keck i Striid«: Leonora Christina Ulfeldts Hæltinners Pryd als Weiblichkeitsentwurf und Diskurskonglomerat'. In *Skandinavische Literaturen der frühen Neuzeit*, ed. Jürg Glauser. Tübingen: Francke, 2002 (Beiträge zur nordischen Philologie 32), pp. 307-318.

Dvergsdal, Alvhild. *Adam Oehlenschlägers tragediekunst*. Copenhagen: Museum Tusculanums Forlag, 1997.

Eakin, Paul John. *Fictions in Autobiography: Studies in the Art of Self-invention*. Princeton University Press, 1985.

Elbrønd-Bek, Bo. *Indfald og udfald: Ti nye studier*. [Copenhagen:] Underskoven, 2012.

Elkington, Trevor G. 'Holger Danske as Literary Danish Identity in the Work of H. C. Andersen and B. S. Ingemann'. In *Hans Christian Andersen: A Poet in Time. Papers from the Second International Hans Christian Andersen Conference. 29 July to 2 August 1996*, ed. Johan de Mylius et al. Odense University Press, 1999, pp. 241-253.

Engler, Bernd. 'The Dismemberment of Clio: Fictionality, Narrativity, and the Construction of Historical Reality in Historiographic Metafiction'. In *Historiographic Metafiction in Modern American and Canadian Literature*, eds. Bernd Engler and Kurt Müller. Paderborn: Ferdinand Schöningh, 1994 (Beiträge zur englischen und amerikanischen Literatur 13), pp. 13-33.

Fabricius, Knud. 'Enevældens Dæmring og den ældre Enevælde'. In *Schultz Danmarkshistorie. Vort Folks Historie gennem Tiderne, skrevet af danske Historikere 3*, ed. Aage Friis et al. Copenhagen: J. H. Schultz, 1942, pp. 233-524.

Fatum, Lone. 'Kongedatteren og Gudsfrygten'. In *Gulnares Hus: En Gave til Hendes Majestæt Dronning Margrethe den Anden på Fødselsdagen, den 16. April 1990*, ed. Annelise Bistrup et al. Copenhagen: Samleren, 1990, pp. 193-204.

Feldbæk, Ole. *Danmarks historie*. Copenhagen: Gyldendal, 2010 (2004).

Foucault, Michel. 'Ariane s'est pendue'. In Foucault, Michel. *Dits et Écrits 1954-1988 1: 1954-1969*, eds. Daniel Defert and François Ewald. Paris: Gallimard, 1994, pp. 767-771.

Freiß, Lisbeth. 'Handarbeitsanleitungen als Massenmedien. D.I.Y und Weiblichkeit im 19. Jahrhundert'. In *Craftista! Handarbeit als Aktivismus*, ed. Critical Crafting Circle. Mainz: Ventil, 2011, pp. 29-42.

Friese, Wilhelm. *Nordische Barockdichtung: Eine Darstellung und Deutung skandinavischer Dichtung zwischen Reformation und Aufklärung*. Munich: Francke, 1968.

Fuhrmann, Manfred. 'Rechtfertigung durch Identität: Über eine Wurzel des Autobiographischen'. In *Identität*, eds. Odo Marquard and Karlheinz Stierle. Munich: Fink, 1979 (Poetik und Hermeneutik 8), pp. 685-690.

Fussing, Hans H. 'Kirsten Munk som frue paa Boller og fange paa Stjernholm 1630-35', Jyske Samlinger 5/5 (1939), pp. 15-60.

Gaugele, Elke. 'Revolutionäre Strickerinnen, Textilaktivist_innen und die Militarisierung der Wolle. Handarbeit und Feminismus in der Moderne'. In *Craftista! Handarbeit als Aktivismus*, ed. Critical Crafting Circle. Mainz: Ventil, 2011, pp. 15-28.

Gilmore, Leigh. 'Limit-cases: Trauma, Self-representation, and the Jurisdictions of Identity'. In *Autobiography: Critical Concepts in Literary and Cultural Studies*. Volume IV, ed. Trev Lynn Broughton. London: Routledge, 2007, pp. 229-240.

Glismann, Otto:
– *Om at »handle mis« med en klassiker: Sprog og stil i »Jammers Minde« – En tekstkristisk undersøgelse af udgaverne*. Birkerød: 1997.
– 'Om Tilblivelsen af Leonora Christinas Jammers-Minde', Acta Philologica Scandinavica 28 (1966), pp. 75-102.

Goldsmith, Elizabeth C. *Publishing Women's Life Stories in France, 1647-1720: From Voice to Print*. Aldershot: Ashgate, 2001 (Women and Gender in the Early Modern World).

Goodall, Peter. 'The Author in the Study: Self-Representation as Reader & Writer in the Medieval and Early Modern Periods'. In *Early Modern Autobiography: Theories, Genres, Practices*, ed. Ronald Bedford et al. Ann Arbor, Michigan: University of Michigan Press, 2006, pp. 104-114.

Gotfredsen, Lise. 'Maleren som øjenvidne og digter'. In *Leonora Christina: Historien om en heltinde*. Århus: Arkona, 1983 (Acta Jutlandica 58, Humanistisk serie 57), pp. 97-129.

Gottschall, Rudolph. *Die deutsche Nationalliteratur in der ersten Hälfte des neunzehnten Jahrhunderts: Literarhistorisch und kritisch dargestellt 2*. Breslau: Trewendt & Granier, 1855.

Grage, Joachim. 'Entblößungen: Das zweifelhafte Geschlecht Christinas von Schweden in der Biographik'. In *Frauenbiographik: Lebensbeschreibungen und Porträts*, ed. Christian von Zimmermann. Tübingen: Narr, 2005 (Mannheimer Beiträge zur Sprach- und Literaturwissenschaft 63), pp. 35-59.

Gusdorf, Georges. 'Conditions and Limits of Autobiography'. In *Autobiography: Essays Theoretical and Critical*, ed. James Olney. Princeton University Press, 1980, pp. 28-48.

Gutzkow, Karl. *Beiträge zur Geschichte der neuesten Literatur 1*. Stuttgart: Balz, 1839.
Hamnett, Brian R. *The Historical Novel in Nineteenth-Century Europe: Representations of Reality in History and Fiction*. Oxford University Press, 2011.
Hansen, Erik. 'Efterskrift'. In Malling, Ove. *Store og gode Handlinger af Danske, Norske og Holstenere, samlede ved Ove Malling. 1777*, ed. Erik Hansen. Copenhagen: Gyldendal, 1992, pp. 567-592.
Hansson, Stina. 'Repertoire und Tradition: Über Schreibformen, Denkformen und Literaturgeschichte im 17. Jahrhundert'. In *Skandinavische Literaturen der frühen Neuzeit*, ed. Jürg Glauser. Tübingen: Francke, 2002 (Beiträge zur nordischen Philologie 32), pp. 41-54.
Hartmann, Godfred. *Kongens Børn*. Copenhagen: Gyldendal, 1988 (1981, Gyldendals paperbacks).
Haupt, Hans. 'Das Leonora-Christina-Manuskript des Christianeums in Hamburg-Altona', Zeitschrift der Gesellschaft für Schleswig-Holsteinische Geschichte 80 (1956), pp. 73-92.
Hauser, Susanne. *Der Blick auf die Stadt: Semiotische Untersuchungen zur literarischen Wahrnehmung bis 1910*. Berlin: Dietrich Reimer, 1990 (Reihe Historische Anthropologie 12).
Heiberg, Johan Ludvig:
– 'Oehlenschlägers »Dina«'. In Heiberg, Johan Ludvig. *Prosaiske Skrifter 3*. Copenhagen: Reitzel, 1861, pp. 365-394.
– 'Udgiveren til Læserne'. In Fibiger, Mathilde. *Clara Raphael. Minona*, ed. Lise Busk-Jensen. Valby: Borgen, 1994 (Danske klassikere), pp. 9-13.
Heiberg, Steffen:
– *Enhjørningen Corfitz Ulfeldt*. Copenhagen: Gyldendal, 1993.
– Review of *Ved afgrundens rand* by Benito Scocozza, Historisk Tidsskrift 16/1 (1992), pp. 169-171.
Hein, Jørgen and Katia Johansen. *Sophie Amalie: Den onde dronning?* Copenhagen: Rosenborg, 1986.
Heitmann, Annegret:
– 'Feministischer Umgang mit Literatur'. In *Auf-Brüche: Uppbrott och Uppbrytningar i Skandinavistisk Metoddiskussion*, ed. Julia Zernack. Leverkusen: Literaturverlag Norden, Reinhardt, 1989 (Artes et litterae septentrionales 4), pp. 27-71.
– 'Formen der Selbstdarstellung in dänischen Texten des 17. Jahrhunderts'. In *Skandinavische Literaturen der frühen Neuzeit*, ed. Jürg Glauser. Tübingen: Francke, 2002 (Beiträge zur nordischen Philologie 32), pp. 291-306.
– *Selbst schreiben: Eine Untersuchung der dänischen Frauenautobiographik*. Frankfurt: Lang, 1994 (Beiträge zur Skandinavistik 12).
– 'Zwischen Macht und Marginalität: Leonora Christines Autobiographie »Jammersminde« als Zeugnis eines gesellschaftlichen Umsturzes'. In *Frauen – Literatur – Revolution*, ed. Helga Grubitzsch et al. Pfaffenweiler: Centaurus, 1992 (Thetis 3), pp. 203-215.
Helk, Vello. 'Rigshofmester Corfitz Ulfeldts katolske forbindelser', Kirkehistoriske Samlinger 1987, pp. 121-139.

Helweg, Johannes. 'Var Corfitz Ulfeldt sindssyg?', Tilskueren (1913), pp. 1020-1037.
Hilmes, Carola. *Die Femme fatale: Ein Weiblichkeitstypus in der nachromantischen Literatur*. Stuttgart: Metzler, 1990.
Hodgkin, Katharine. *Madness in Seventeenth-Century Autobiography*. Basingstoke: Palgrave Macmillan, 2007 (Early Modern History: Society and Culture).
Holm-Hansen, Henrik. 'Dina i 1842'. In *Skitser til Romantikkens Teater: Tilegnet Torben Krogh*, ed. Svend Christiansen et al. Copenhagen: G. E. C. Gad, 1967, pp. 100-120.
Hovmann, Flemming:
– 'Gudfaders Billedbog'. In *H. C. Andersens Eventyr 7: Kommentar*, ed. Flemming Hovmann. Copenhagen: Reitzel, 1990, pp. 321-333.
– 'Holger Danske'. In *H. C. Andersens Eventyr 7: Kommentar*, ed. Flemming Hovmann. Copenhagen: Reitzel, 1990, pp. 106-109.
Hutcheon, Linda. *A Poetics of Postmodernism: History, Theory, Fiction*. New York and London: Routledge, 1990 (1988).
Hættner Aurelius, Eva:
– *Inför Lagen: Kvinnliga Svenska Självbiografier från Agneta Horn till Fredrika Bremer*. Lund University Press, 1996 (Litteratur, Teater, Film 13).
– 'Under faderens lov: Om Agneta Horn'. In *Nordisk kvindelitteraturhistorie 1: I Guds navn: 1000-1800*, ed. Elisabeth Møller Jensen. Copenhagen: Rosinante/Munksgaard, 1993, pp. 267-276.
Iggers, Georg G. 'Zur »Linguistischen Wende« im Geschichtsdenken und in der Geschichtsschreibung', Geschichte und Gesellschaft 21 (1995), pp. 557-570.
Jelinek, Estelle C.:
– 'Introduction: Women's Autobiography and the Male Tradition'. In *Women's Autobiography: Essays in Criticism*, ed. Estelle C. Jelinek. Bloomington: Indiana University Press, 1980, pp. 1-20.
– *The Tradition of Women's Autobiography: From Antiquity to the Present*. Boston, Mass.: Twayne, 1986.
Jensen, Grethe. *Kvinder i Danmarkshistorien*. Copenhagen: Politiken, 2004 (Politikens håndbøger).
Jones, Ann Rosalind and Peter Stallybrass. *Renaissance Clothing and the Materials of Memory*. Cambridge University Press, 2000 (Cambridge Studies in Renaissance Literature and Culture 38).
Jørgensen, Aage. 'Mathilde Fibiger og damernes emancipation'. In Jørgensen, Aage. *Kundskaben på ondt og godt: En Studiebog*. Aarhus: Akademisk Boghandel, 1968, pp. 102-108.
Jørgensen, Ellen and Johanne Skovgaard. *Danske Dronninger: Fortællinger og Karakteristikker*. Copenhagen: Hagerup, 1910.
Kelly, Philippa. 'Dialogues of Self Reflection: Early Modern Mirrors'. In *Early Modern Autobiography: Theories, Genres, Practices*, ed. Ronald Bedford et al. Ann Arbor, Michigan: University of Michigan Press, 2006, pp. 62-84.
Kelly, Philippa, Lloyd David and Ronald Bedford. 'Introduction'. In *Early Modern Autobiography: Theories, Genres, Practices*, ed. Ronald Bedford et al. Ann Arbor, Michigan: University of Michigan Press, 2006, pp. 1-16.

Klingberg, Göte. 'Begrebet adaptation', transl. Hans Christian Fink. In *Lyst og lærdom – debat og forskning om børnelitteratur*, ed. Torben Weinreich. Copenhagen: Høst & Søn, 1996, pp. 142-161.

Kondrup, Johnny:
- *Levned og tolkninger: Studier i nordisk selvbiografi*. Odense: Odense Universitetsforlag, 1982 (Odense University Studies in Scandinavian Languages and Literatures 10).
- *Livsværker: Studier i dansk litterær biografi*. Valby: Amadeus, 1986.

Kopp-Sievers, Susanne. *Die Wiederentdeckung des Nationalen in Dänemark: Eine Analyse von Ebbe Kløvedal Reichs* Frederik. En folkebog om N. F. S. Grundtvigs tid og liv <*1972*>. Frankfurt: Lang, 1985 (Beiträge zur Skandinavistik 5).

Kraß, Andreas. *Geschriebene Kleider: Höfische Identität als literarisches Spiel*. Tübingen and Basel: Francke, 2006 (Bibliotheca Germanica 50).

Kühne, F[riedrich] G[ustav]:
- 'Leopold Schefer'. In Kühne, F[riedrich] Gustav. *Portraits und Silhouetten 1*. Hannover: C. F. Kius, 1843, pp. 163-173.
- Review of *Die Gräfin Ulfeld, oder die vierundzwanzig Königskinder* by Leopold Schefer, Jahrbücher für wissenschaftliche Kritik 1835/1, pp. 494-496.

Lange, Julius. 'Contra Leonora Christina', Tilskueren 5 (1888), pp. 721-739.

Lange, Victor. *Corfitz Ulfeld: Fra Rigshovmester til Landsforræder*. Copenhagen: Jacob Lund, 1931.

Larsen, Finn Stein:
- 'En impressionist fra baroktiden? En tekstlæsning i Leonora Christinas Jammersminde', Kritik 25 (1973), pp. 17-33.
- *Prosaens mønstre: Nærlæsninger af danske litterære prosatekster*. Odense: Syddansk Universitetsforlag, 2006 (1971).

Larsson, Lisbeth. 'Kvinnors självbiografier och dagböcker'. In *Lysthuse: Kvindelitteraturhistorier*, ed. Lis Palmvig. Charlottenlund: Rosinante, 1985, pp. 156-168.

Laube, Heinrich:
- *Geschichte der deutschen Literatur 4*. Stuttgart: Hallberg, 1840.
- *Moderne Charakteristiken 2*. Mannheim: Löwenthal, 1835.

Lauring, Palle. *Dronninger og andre kvinder i Danmarkshistorien*. Copenhagen: Høst & Søn, 1990 (1981).

Lejeune, Philippe. *Le Pacte Autobiographique*. Paris: Éditions du Seuil, 1975.

Lenhard, Albin. *Zur Erzählprosa Leopold Schefers*. Cologne and Vienna: Böhlau, 1975 (böhlau forum litterarum 4).

Lervik, Åse Hiorth. 'Leonora Christina som kvinnehistoriker', Edda 78/1 (1978), pp. 11-22.

Lindegård Hjorth, Poul:
- '*Jammers Minde's* udgivelseshistorie'. In Leonora Christina. *Jammers Minde: Diplomatarisk udgave ved Poul Lindegård Hjorth og Marita Akhøj Nielsen under medvirkning af Ingelise Nielsen*, ed. Det Danske Sprog- og Litteraturselskab. Copenhagen: Reitzel, 1998, pp. xiii-xxxii.
- 'Nærværende udgave'. In Leonora Christina. *Jammers Minde: Diplomatarisk udgave ved Poul Lindegård Hjorth og Marita Akhøj Nielsen under medvirkning af Ingelise*

Nielsen, ed. Det Danske Sprog- og Litteraturselskab. Copenhagen: Reitzel, 1998, pp. lxviii-lxxvi.

Lindgärde, Valborg. 'Nu skal også Herren optage mig: To selvbiografiske tekster fra 1600-tallet'. In *Nordisk kvindelitteraturhistorie 1: I Guds navn: 1000-1800*, ed. Elisabeth Møller Jensen. Copenhagen: Rosinante/Munksgaard, 1993, pp. 277-285.

Lindschouw, Jan and Lene Schøsler. 'Leonora Christinas franske ordforråd: En didaktisk og diakron analyse af hendes *Franske selvbiografi* (1673)', Danske Studier (2016), pp. 5-24.

Lionarons, Joyce Tally. 'Women's Work and Women's Magic as Literary Motifs in Icelandic Sagas'. In *Constructing Nations, Reconstructing Myth: Essays in Honour of T. A. Shippey*, ed. Andrew Wawn, with Graham Johnson and John Walter. Turnhout: Brepols, 2007 (Making the Middle Ages 9), pp. 301-317.

Lönnroth, Lars. *Den dubbla scenen: Muntlig diktning från Eddan til ABBA*. Stockholm: Bokförlaget Prisma, 1978.

Lukács, Georg. *The Historical Novel*, transl. Hannah and Stanley Mitchell. Harmondsworth: Penguin Books, 1976 (1969).

Lunde, Katrin and Luise F. Pusch. 'Leonora Christina (1621-1698): Die Tochter von König Christian IV. von Dänemark und Norwegen: Dänemarks erste Feministin?'. In *Töchter berühmter Männer: 9 biographische Porträts*, ed. Luise F. Pusch. Frankfurt: Insel, 1988 (Insel-Taschenbuch 979), pp. 47-115.

Lundgaard Simonsen, Vagn. Afterword in Leonora Christina. *Jammers Minde*, ed. Vagn Lundgaard Simonsen. Copenhagen: Gyldendal, 1964 (Gyldendals bibliotek 1), pp. 255-273.

Lyngstad, Sverre. 'The Danish Princess Leonora Christina'. In *Women Writers of the Seventeenth Century*, eds. Katharina M. Wilson and Frank J. Warnke. Athens and London: The University of Georgia Press, 1989, pp. 377-404.

Maaløe, Christopher. 'Udgiverens indledning'. In Leonora Christina. *Hæltinners Pryd,* ed. Christopher Maaløe. Copenhagen: Reitzel, 1977, pp. 8-15.

Mai, Anne-Marie:
– 'Det danske sprogs inderlige elskerinde: Om Anna Margrethe Lasson'. In *Nordisk kvindelitteraturhistorie 1: I Guds navn: 1000-1800*, ed. Elisabeth Møller Jensen. Copenhagen: Rosinante/Munksgaard, 1993, pp. 341-347.
– 'Troskab, lidelse og lidenskab: Om Leonora Christina'. In *Nordisk kvindelitteraturhistorie 1: I Guds navn: 1000-1800*, ed. Elisabeth Møller Jensen. Copenhagen: Rosinante/ Munksgaard, 1993, pp. 286-298.

Mai, Anne-Marie and Stig Dalager: '»... et eventyr, som er værdigt en roman«'. In *Leonora Christina: Historien om en heltinde*. Århus: Arkona, 1983 (Acta Jutlandica 58, Humanistisk serie 57), pp. 58-88.

Mandel, Barrett J. 'Full of Life Now'. In *Autobiography: Essays Theoretical and Critical*, ed. James Olney. Princeton University Press, 1980, pp. 49-72.

Marcus, Jane. 'Invincible Mediocrity: The Private Selves of Public Women'. In *The Private Self: Theory and Practice of Women's Autobiographical Writings*, ed. Shari Benstock. Chapel Hill and London: The University of North Carolina Press, 1989 (1988), pp. 114-146.

Marcus, Laura. *Auto/biographical Discourses: Theory, Criticism, Practice*. Manchester University Press, 1994.

Mason, Mary G. 'The Other Voice: Autobiographies of Women Writers'. In *Autobiography: Essays Theoretical and Critical*, ed. James Olney. Princeton University Press, 1980, pp. 207-235.

Meyer Spacks, Patricia:
- 'Selves in Hiding'. In *Women's Autobiography: Essays in Criticism*, ed. Estelle C. Jelinek. Bloomington: Indiana University Press, 1980, pp. 112-132.
- 'The Soul's Imaginings: Daniel Defoe, William Cowper', Publications of the Modern Language Association 91 (1976), pp. 420-435.
- 'Stages of Self: Notes on Autobiography and the Life Cycle'. In *The American Autobiography: A Collection of Critical Essays*, ed. Albert E. Stone. Englewood Cliffs, NJ: Prentice Hall, 1981 (A Spectrum Book: Twentieth Century Views), pp. 44-60.

Misch, Georg:
- *Geschichte der Autobiographie 1/1: Das Altertum*. Frankfurt: Schulte, 1976 (1907).
- *Geschichte der Autobiographie 4/2: Von der Renaissance bis zu den autobiographischen Hauptwerken des 18. und 19. Jahrhunderts*. Bern: Francke, 1969.

Mitchell, Stephen A. 'Women's Autobiographical Literature in the Swedish Baroque'. In *Skandinavische Literaturen der frühen Neuzeit*, ed. Jürg Glauser. Tübingen: Francke, 2002 (Beiträge zur nordischen Philologie 32), pp. 269-290.

Müller, Silvia. '»Herren sargar och läker, han slår och hans hand helar«: Konfliktbewältigung in den autobiographischen Texten von Marta Hagman (1765), Sophia Elisabet Brenner (1722) und Christina Regina vom Birchenbaum (1651)', Skandinavistik 30/1 (2000), pp. 1-20.

Mundt, Theodor. *Geschichte der Literatur der Gegenwart: Vorlesungen über deutsche, französische, englische, spanische, italienische, schwedische, dänische, holländische, vlämische, russische, polnische, böhmische und ungarische Literatur. Von dem Jahre 1789 bis zur neuesten Zeit*. Leipzig: Simion, 1853 (1842).

Munslow, Alun. 'Rethinking *Metahistory*: The Historical imagination in nineteenth century Europe', Rethinking History 19/3 (2015), pp. 324-336.

Møller, P. L. 'Dina, tragisk Drama i 5 Acter'. In Møller, P. L. *Kritiske Skizzer fra Aarene 1840-47*. Copenhagen, 1847, pp. 15-22.

Nielsen, Frederik. 'Om at læse Marie Grubbe'. In *J. P. Jacobsen: Samlede værker*, ed. Frederik Nielsen. Copenhagen: Roselkinde og Bagger, 1972, pp. 9-22.

Nielsen, Ingelise. 'Papir og lægopbygning'. In Leonora Christina. *Jammers Minde: Diplomatarisk udgave ved Poul Lindegård Hjorth og Marita Akhøj Nielsen under medvirkning af Ingelise Nielsen,* ed. Det Danske Sprog- og Litteraturselskab. Copenhagen: Reitzel, 1998, pp. xxxv-lii.

Nielsen, Niels Åge. 'Dansk og fremmed tale i Jammersmindet'. In *Runer og rids: Festskrift til Lis Jacobsen, 29. Januar 1952*, ed. Jørgen Glahder. Copenhagen: Rosenkilde og Bagger, 1952, pp. 73-82.

Nin, Anaïs. 'The Personal Life Deeply Lived'. In *The American Autobiography: A Collection of Critical Essays*, ed. Albert E. Stone. Englewood Cliffs, NJ: Prentice Hall, 1981 (A Spectrum Book: Twentieth Century Views), pp. 157-165.

Nünning, Ansgar:
- '»Verbal Fictions?« Kritische Überlegungen und narratologische Alternativen zu Hayden Whites Einebnung des Gegensatzes zwischen Historiographie und Literatur', Literaturwissenschaftliches Jahrbuch 40 (1999), pp. 351-380.
- *Von historischer Fiktion zu historiographischer Metafiktion 1: Theorie, Typologie und Poetik des historischen Romans*. Trier: Wissenschaftlicher Verlag Trier, 1995 (Literatur, Imagination, Realität 11).

Nygaard, Bertel. 'Anti-Politics: Modern politics and its critics in Denmark, 1830-1848', Scandinavian Journal of History 36/4 (2011), pp. 419-442.

Olden-Jørgensen, Sebastian. *Ludvig Holberg som pragmatisk historiker: En historiografisk-kritisk undersøgelse*. Copenhagen: Museum Tusculanum, 2015 (UJDS-Studier).

Olney, James:
- 'Autobiography and the Cultural Moment: A Thematic, Historical, and Bibliographical Introduction'. In *Autobiography: Essays Theoretical and Critical*, ed. James Olney. Princeton University Press, 1980, pp. 3-27.
- *Metaphors of Self: The Meaning of Autobiography*. Princeton University Press, 1972.

Paludan, Hans Aage. 'Corneille i Danmark: En tiljøjelse', Danske Studier (1926), pp. 174-176.

Paludan-Müller, C[aspar]. 'Dansk Historiografi i det 18de Aarhundrede', Historisk Tidsskrift 5/4 (1883), pp. 1-188.

Pascal, Roy. *Design and Truth in Autobiography*. London: Routledge & Kegan Paul, 1960.

Petersen, Margrethe. *Kongedatteren Leonora Christina Ulfeldt og hendes Husbond. Med Kr. Zahrtmanns Leonora Christina Billeder*. Copenhagen: Reitzel, 1928.

Pfister, Manfred:
- *Das Drama: Theorie und Analyse*. Munich: Wilhelm Fink, 1984 (1982).
- *The Theory and Analysis of Drama*, transl. John Halliday. Cambridge University Press, 1991 (European Studies in English Literature).

Pihl, Luise. 'Efterskrift'. In Hemmer Hansen, Eva. *Den trofaste hustru: Leonora Christine II*. Copenhagen: Hernov, 1983, pp. 216-217.

Præstgaard Andersen, Lise. *Sorte damer: Studier i femme fatale-motivet i dansk digtning fra romantik til århundredskifte*. Copenhagen: Gyldendal, 1990.

Reichardt, Dosia. 'The Constitution of Narrative Identity in Seventeenth-Century Prison Writing'. In *Early Modern Autobiography: Theories, Genres, Practices*, ed. Ronald Bedford et al. Ann Arbor, Michigan: University of Michigan Press, 2006, pp. 115-129.

Restrup, Ole. *Leonora Christina: Ein Frauenschicksal des 17. Jahrhunderts*. Bonn: Bonner Univ. Buchdr., 1943 (Friedrich-Wilhelms-Universität Bonn am Rhein 120).

Reynolds, Kimberley. 'Genres and generations – the case of the family story'. In Reynolds, Kimberley. *Children's Literature: A Very Short Introduction*. Oxford University Press, 2011 (Very Short Introductions 288), pp. 77-95.

Rossel, Sven Hakon. »Do You Know the Land, Where the Lemon Trees Bloom?« Hans Christian Andersen and Italy. Rome: Edizioni Nuova Cultura, 2009 (Intersezioni. Testi, Culture, Religioni: Pubblicazioni del Dipartimento di Studi Storico-Religiosi 1).

Rostrup, Egill. *Leonora Christina's Skuespil*. Copenhagen: Krohn, 1918.

Rühling, Lutz. *Opfergänge der Vernunft. Zur Konstruktion von metaphysischem Sinn in Texten der skandinavischen Literaturen vom Barock bis zur Postmoderne*. Göttingen: Vandenhoeck & Ruprecht, 2002 (Palaestra 316).

Ryan, Judith. '>Hypothetisches Erzählen<: Zur Funktion von Phantasie und Einbildung in Rilkes »Malte Laurids Brigge«'. In *Materialien zu Rainer Maria Rilke >Die Aufzeichnungen des Malte Laurids Brigge<*, ed. Hartmut Engelhardt. Frankfurt: Suhrkamp, 1974 (Suhrkamp Taschenbuch 174), pp. 244-279.

Sarasohn, Lisa T. 'Who Was Then The Gentleman?: Samuel Sorbière, Thomas Hobbes, and the Royal Society', History of Science 42 (2004), pp. 211-232.

Schmalensee, Lisa and Lene Torp. 'Leonora Christina Ulfeldt: Jammersminde 1663-1685', Litteratur & samfund 30-32 (1979-81), pp. 6-29.

Schmidt, Julian. *Geschichte der deutschen Literatur im neunzehnten Jahrhundert 2: Das Zeitalter der Restauration*. Leipzig: Herbig, 1856 (1853).

Schoolfield, George C.:
- 'Rilke and Leonora Christina', Modern Language Quarterly 14/4 (1953), pp. 425-431.
- 'Rilke und Skandinavien'. In *Rilke – ein europäischer Dichter aus Prag*, ed. Peter Demetz et al. Würzburg: Königshausen & Neumann, 1998, pp. 115-125.

Schou, Søren. 'En folkelig esoteriker: Ebbe Kløvedal Reich's *En engels vinger* og *Morgendagens mand*', Spring 7 (1994), pp. 120-127.

Seiler, Thomas. *Im Leben verschollen: Zur Rekontextualisierung skandinavischer Gefängnis- und Holocaustliteratur*. Heidelberg: Winter, 2006 (Skandinavische Arbeiten 21).

Sejersted, Jørgen. '»Naar jeg mig fra Top til Fod Betragter«. Barokk Framstilling af Selvet', Edda 97 (1997), pp. 241-259.

Shuger, Debora. 'The »I« of the Beholder: Renaissance Mirrors and the Reflexive Mind'. In *Renaissance Culture and the Everyday*, ed. Patricia Fumerton and Simon Hunt. Philadelphia: University of Pennsylvania Press, 1999 (New Cultural Studies), pp. 21-41.

Skautrup, Peter. *Det danske sprogs historie 2: Fra unionsbrevet til danske lov*. Copenhagen. Gyldendal, 1947.

Skov, Sigvard. 'Leonora Christina – helgen eller højforræder', Jyske Samlinger 14 (Ny række, 1981), pp. 201-215.

Smith, Sidonie and Julia Watson. *Reading Autobiography: A Guide for Interpreting Life Narratives*. Minneapolis and London: University of Minnesota Press, 2003 (2001).

Smyth, Adam. *Autobiography in Early Modern England*. Cambridge University Press, 2010.

Spender, Stephen. *The Making of a Poem*. London: Hamilton, 1955.

Stanley, Liz. *The Auto/biographical I: The Theory and Practice of Feminist Auto/biography*. Manchester and New York: Manchester University Press, 1995.

Starobinski, Jean. 'The Style of Autobiography'. In *Autobiography: Essays Theoretical and Critical*, ed. James Olney. Princeton University Press, 1980, pp. 73-83.

Steffensen, Steffen. *Rilke und Skandinavien: Zwei Vorträge von Steffen Steffensen*. Copenhagen: Munksgaard, 1958.

Sturrock, John. *The Language of Autobiography: Studies in the First Person Singular*. Cambridge University Press, 1993.

Stæhr, Claus Pico. 'Leonora Christina og 1600-tallets europæiske litteratur – en oversigt'. In *Leonora Christina: Historien om en heltinde*. Århus: Arkona, 1983 (Acta Jutlandica 58, Humanistisk serie 57), pp. 89-96.

Tobiesen, Frits. *»En steenig Materie«: Oplysninger om Leonora Christina Ulfeldts Helbred*. Copenhagen: 1922 (Særtryk af Ugeskrift for Læger 19).

Topsøe-Jensen, H. 'Efterskrift'. In *Gudfaders Billedbog. Med Efterskrift af H. Topsøe-Jensen, illustreret af Alex Secher*. Copenhagen: Nordlyndes Bogtrykkeri, 1966 (Udsendelse fra Nordlundes Bogtrykkeri 35), pp. 45-69.

Urne, Dorthea Sophie. 'Frøken Urnes Meddelelser om Leonora Christinas Liv på Maribo Kloster'. In Birket Smith, Sophus. *Leonora Christina (Ulfeldt) på Maribo Kloster: Et Bidrag til Oplysning om hendes sidste Leveår*. Copenhagen: Gyldendal, 1872, pp. 77-86.

Wagner-Edelhaaf, Martina. *Autobiographie*. Stuttgart and Weimar: Verlag J. B. Metzler, 2000 (Sammlung Metzler 323).

Wamberg, Bodil:
- *Leonora Christina: Dronning af Blåtårn*. Copenhagen: Gyldendals Bogklubber, 1992.
- 'Det Ydre og det Indre Fangenskab'. In *Gulnares Hus: En Gave til Hendes Majestæt Dronning Margrethe den Anden på Fødselsdagen, den 16. April 1990*, ed. Annelise Bistrup et al. Copenhagen: Samleren, 1990, pp. 76-81.

Weigel, Sigrid. *Und selbst im Kerker frei...! Schreiben im Gefängnis: Zur Theorie und Gattungsgeschichte der Gefängnisliteratur (1750-1933)*. Marburg/Lahn: Guttandin und Hoppe, 1982.

Weinreich, Torben:
- *Historien om børnelitteratur: Dansk børnelitteratur gennem 400 år*. Copenhagen: Branner og Korch, 2006.
- 'I statens tjeneste: Prosaen i dansk børnelitteratur 1945-1990'. In *Dansk Børnelitteratur Historie*, eds. Kari Sønsthagen and Lena Eilstrup. Copenhagen: Høst & Søns Forlag 1992, pp. 137-189.

Westergaard, Waldemar. 'Danish History and Danish Historians', The Journal of Modern History 24/2 (June 1952), pp. 167-180.

Wethered, Herbert Newton. *The Curious Art of Autobiography: From Benvenuto Cellini to Rudyard Kipling*. London: Johnson, 1946.

White, Hayden:
- *The Content of the Form: Narrative Discourse and Historical Representation*. Baltimore and London: Johns Hopkins University Press, 1987.
- 'The Fictions of Factual Representation'. In White, Hayden. *Tropics of Discourse: Essays in Cultural Criticism*. Baltimore and London: Johns Hopkins University Press, 1978, pp. 121-134.
- 'The Historical Text as Literary Artifact'. In White, Hayden. *Tropics of Discourse: Essays in Cultural Criticism*. Baltimore and London: Johns Hopkins University Press, 1978, pp. 81-100.
- 'Historicism, History and the Figurative Imagination'. In White, Hayden. *Tropics of Discourse: Essays in Cultural Criticism*. Baltimore and London: Johns Hopkins University Press, 1978, pp. 101-120.

– *Metahistory: The Historical Imagination in Nineteenth-Century Europe*. Baltimore and London: Johns Hopkins University Press, 1973.

Willumsen, Dorrit. 'En terrorists mod og en engels tålmodighed: Leonora Christina: Jammers Minde'. In *Læsninger i dansk litteratur 1: 1200-1820*, eds. Ulrik Lehrmann and Lise Præstgaard Andersen. Odense Uni. Forlag, 1998, pp. 128-142.

Winge, Vibeke. 'Hochdeutsch und Niederdeutsch im Blauen Turm'. In *Festschrift für Karl Hyldgaard-Jensen: Zum 70. Geburtstag am 3. Februar 1987*, eds. Mogens Dyhr and Joergen Olsen. Copenhagen: Reitzel, 1987 (Kopenhagener Beiträge zur germanistischen Linguistik: Sonderband 3), pp. 334-343.

Winston, Elizabeth. 'The Autobiographer and Her Readers: From Apology to Affirmation'. In *Women's Autobiography: Essays in Criticism*, ed. Estelle C. Jelinek. Bloomington: Indiana University Press, 1980, pp. 93-111.

Wischmann, Antje. 'Collage City – City Collage: On the Relation Between Aesthetic and Political Mobilisation in Sven Holm's *Min Elskede – En Skabelonroman*', Forum for World Literature Studies 4/1 (2012), pp. 125-133.

Witzleben, Brigitte von. 'Zu den historischen Quellen von Rilkes >Die Aufzeichnungen des Malte Laurids Brigge<'. In *Materialien zu Rainer Maria Rilke >Die Aufzeichnungen des Malte Laurids Brigge<*, ed. Hartmut Engelhardt. Frankfurt: Suhrkamp, 1974 (Suhrkamp Taschenbuch 174), pp. 280-303.

Wåghäll Nivre, Elisabeth and Maren Eckart. 'Narrating Life: Early Modern Accounts of the Life of Queen Christina of Sweden (1626-1689)'. In *Cultural Ways of Worldmaking: Media and Narratives*, ed. Vera Nünning et al. Berlin and New York: De Gruyter, 2010 (Concepts for the Study of Culture 1), pp. 307-327.

Zeller, Rosmarie. *Spiel und Konversation im Barock: Untersuchungen zu Harsdörffers »Gesprächsspielen«*. Berlin and New York: Walter de Gruyter, 1974 (Quellen und Forschungen zur Sprach- und Kulturgeschichte der germanischen Völker 58 (177)).

Zimmermann, Christian von. 'Exemplarische Lebensläufe: Zu den Grundlagen der Biographik'. In *Frauenbiographik: Lebensbeschreibungen und Porträts*, ed. Christian von Zimmermann. Tübingen: Narr, 2005 (Mannheimer Beiträge zur Sprach- und Literaturwissenschaft 63), pp. 3-16.

Zimmermann, Nina von. 'Zu den Wegen der Frauenbiographikforschung'. In *Frauenbiographik: Lebensbeschreibungen und Porträts*, ed. Christian von Zimmermann. Tübingen: Narr, 2005 (Mannheimer Beiträge zur Sprach- und Literaturwissenschaft 63), pp. 17-32.

Contemporary Records

'Greve Christian (Corfiz Søn) Ulfelds Missive dateret Calais d. 3die Fbr. 1662, til En i Bryssel i Flandern angaaende det Mord, han giorde paa General-Major Fuchs, hvorudi han opregner Aarsagerne, som tildrev ham, sligt at bedrive', Journal for Politik, Natur- og Menneske-Kundskab 1816/2, pp. 90-96.

'Noget om Grevinde Eleonore Ulfelds Arrest i Blaataarn', Journal for Politik, Natur- og Menneske-Kundskab October 1815, pp. 282-284.

'Till Corfitz Ulfelds historia', Samlingar utgifna för De skånska landskapens historiska och arkeologiska förening 6 (1877), pp. 26-70.

'Tre Breve, skrevne af den, hos os noksom erindrede, Corfiz Ulfeld, i det sidste Aar af hans Levetid, til Dr. Sperling', Journal for Politik, Natur- og Menneske-Kundskab 1816/1, pp. 121-134.

Uforbeholdne Breve fra Leonora Christinas Tid, ed. Ingeborg Buhl. Copenhagen: Hasselbalch, 1956 (Hasselbalchs Kulturbibliotek 156.

'Underdanigst Relation om Hr. Greve Corfiz Ulfelds Echappade fra Slottet Hammershus paa Bornholm, som skete Torsdag Nat d. 13de Martii 1661. Hvorledes det gik ham paa hans Reise, og den store Ildebrandsfare, som han udentvivl forsætligviis har efterladt sig paa sit Kammer', Journal for Politik, Natur- og Menneske-Kundskab 1816/1, pp. 71-78.

'Vidnernes Udsagn i Forhøret over Corfiz Ulfelds Flugt fra Hammershuus Fæstning', Journal for Politik, Natur- og Menneske-Kundskab 1816/2, pp. 42-47.

'Vidners Udsagn i Forhøret over Corfiz Ulfelds Flugt udaf Hammershuus Fæstning', Journal for Politik, Natur- og Menneske-Kundskab 1816/1, pp. 198-214.

Internet Sources

Akhøj Nielsen, Marita:
- 'Leonora Christina Ulfeldt: Forfatterportræt': http://adl.dk/adl_pub/fportraet/cv/ShowFpItem.xsql?nnoc=adl_pub&ff_id=36&p_fpkat_id=fskab, lastly accessed on 23 November 2016.
- 'Med sod og øl på sukkerpapir: Om Leonora Christina – Årets klassiker 2003', Bogens verden (2003/04): http://wayback.kb.dk:8080/wayback-1.4.2/wayback/20100107153228/http://www2.kb.dk/guests/natl/db/bv/03/4/index1.htm, lastly accessed on 3 September 2013.

Alfabeta:
- http://www.alfabetaforlag.dk/butik?c=Catalog&category=5279, lastly accessed on 7 April 2015.
- http://www.alfabetaforlag.dk/butik?c=Item&category=5279&item=29147, lastly accessed on 7 April 2015.

Christensen, Jan. 'Burgundia igen…': http://tidende.dk/?Id=22819, originally published on 11 January 2011, lastly accessed on 8 September 2019.

Danske Færger A/S. 'Redegørelse vedrørende afstemning om navnet på den nye hurtigfærge til BornholmerFærgens rute Rønne-Ystad': http://www.ft.dk/samling/20101/almdel/tru/bilag/225/970075.pdf, lastly accessed on 15 September 2016.

Ejsing, Jens:
- 'Historisk ballede om færgenavn': http://www.b.dk/danmark/historisk-ballede-om-faergenavn, originally published on 24 November 2010, lastly accessed on 8 September 2019.
- 'Skal Oslo-færgen så hedde Vidkun Quisling?': http://www.b.dk/danmark/skal-oslo-faergen-saa-hedde-vidkun-quisling, originally published on 19 December 2010, lastly accessed on 8 September 2019.

Heiberg, Steffen. 'En magtsyg kvinde': http://www.b.dk/kommentarer/en-magtsyg-kvinde, originally published on 15 December 2015, lastly accessed on 8 September 2019.

Kanonudvalget [2004]. 'Dansk litteraturs kanon – Rapport fra kanonudvalget': http://pub.uvm.dk/2004/kanon/, lastly accessed on 07 April 2015.

Kanonudvalget [2006]. 'Jammers Minde: Udvalgets begrundelse', p. 110: http://kum.dk/uploads/tx_templavoila/KUM_kulturkanonen_OK2.pdf, lastly accessed on 8 September 2019.

Kanonudvalget [2006]. 'Om kanon for litteratur', pp. 108-109: http://kum.dk/uploads/tx_templavoila/KUM_kulturkanonen_OK2.pdf, lastly accessed on 8 September 2019.

Lenler, Jens. 'Glem kulturkanonen – lav en demokratikanon': http://politiken.dk/kultur/ECE315799/glem-kulturkanonen---lav-en-demokratikanon/, originally published on 30 March 2007, lastly accessed on 8 September 2019.

Mai, Anne-Marie. 'Kvindefattig kanon': http://www.folkeskolen.dk/31590/kvindefattig-kanon, originally published on 8 October 2004, lastly accessed on 8 September 2019.

Nielsen, Vilhelm. 'Leonora Christines psyke'. Kronik i Kristeligt Dagblad, mandag den 29. juli 1991: http://www.vilhelmnielsen.dk/LeonoraChristinesPsyke.html, lastly accessed on 9 September 2019.

Qvitzau, Dan:
– 'Helt ny version: Afstemning om navn': http://tidende.dk/?Id=23608, originally published on 8 February 2011, lastly accessed on 8 September 2019.
– 'Så enkelt er det: Klare stemmeregler': http://tidende.dk/?Id=23708, originally published on 11 February 2011, lastly accessed on 8 September 2019.

Sondrup Andersen, Dorthe. 'London, sommeren 1663', pp. 110-111: http://kum.dk/uploads/tx_templavoila/KUM_kulturkanonen_OK2.pdf, lastly accessed on 8 September 2019.

Sterling, Nichole L. 'Authority and Autobiography: The Case for Leonora Christina': http://www.academia.edu/2368850/Authority_and_Autobiography_Leonora_Christina, lastly accessed on 8 September 2019.

Thorsen, Lotte. 'Kvinderne mangler i den litterære kanon': http://politiken.dk/kultur/boger/ECE100109/kvinderne-mangler-i-den-litteraere-kanon/, originally published on 23 November 2004, lastly accessed on 8 September 2019.